STUDY GUIDE

STUDY GUIDE

Richard O. Straub

University of Michigan, Dearborn

to accompany

Exploring
PSYCHOLOGY
NINTH EDITION

David G. Myers

Special Contributor,
C. Nathan DeWall

SPECIAL UPDATE FOR DSM-5

WORTH PUBLISHERS
A Macmillan Higher Education Company

Study Guide
by Richard O. Straub
to accompany
Myers: **Exploring Psychology**, Ninth Edition
Special Update for DSM-5

© 2014, 2011, 2008, 2005 by Worth Publishers

Printed in the United States of America

ISBN 13: 978-1-4641-7949-5
ISBN 10: 1-4641-7949-2

First printing

Worth Publishers
41 Madison Avenue
New York, New York 10010
www.worthpublishers.com

Contents

Preface

This Study Guide is designed for use with the special DSM-5 update of *Exploring Psychology*, Ninth Edition, by David G. Myers. It is intended to help you learn material in the textbook, to evaluate your understanding of that material, and then to review any problem areas. You may also want to read the text student preface that tells you "How to Be a Great Student and Still Have a Life" This preface provides study suggestions based on principles of time management, effective notetaking, evaluation of exam performance, and an effective program for improving your comprehension while studying from textbooks.

The ninth edition of this Study Guide offers many useful features. Each chapter begins with a Chapter Review that is organized by major text section and one or more learning objectives. The Chapter Review includes fill-in and essay-type questions, art to be labeled, art from the text as reminders of important concepts, and summary tables to be completed or that are already completed for you. Also included are practical study tips and applications. These tips and applications are designed to help you evaluate your understanding of the text chapter's broader concepts and make the text material more meaningful by relating it to your own life. Following the Chapter Review are two Progress Tests consisting of multiple-choice, matching, true–false, and essay questions that focus on facts and definitions. For all questions, the correct answers and explanations of why the answer is correct as well as why the other choices are incorrect are given. All chapters also include a Cross-Check, which provides an engaging crossword puzzle review of chapter terms and concepts.

General Internet Resources

To obtain general information about psychology-related topics, you might want to consult some of the following websites. Russ Dewey's Psych Web is an effort to compile a great deal of information for psychology students and teachers, including self-quizzes, lists of psychology journals on the web, self-help resources, tip sheets for psychology majors, and psychology departments on the Internet. Psych Web is available at the following site: www.psychwww.com.

Deborah Kelley-Milburn and Michael A. Milburn's "Cyberspace: Resources for Psychologists on the Internet" (*Psychological Science* [1995, July], Volume 6, 203–211) is another excellent resource. This review provides helpful information on Listservs, Usenet groups, electronic journals and newsletters, databases, grant and job information, and library catalogues.

Both the American Psychological Association (APA) and the American Psychological Society (APS) have Internet services. These services provide not only information about their organizations but also selected articles from their main journals, information about current research in the discipline, and links to other science-related sites on the Internet. Their locations are as follows:

APA: www.apa.org/ and APS: www.psychologicalscience.org

Finally, and perhaps most important, is Psychtalk, a list for students interested in discussion topics and controversies related to psychology. Topics that have been discussed over the past few years include child abuse, the nature–nurture issue, homosexuality, and pornography. To subscribe, send a message to:

psychtalk-request@fre.fsu.umd.edu

The message should read "subscribe psychtalk (your name)."

Acknowledgments

I would like to thank all the students and instructors who used this Study Guide in its previous editions and provided such insightful and useful suggestions. Special thanks are also due to Betty Shapiro Probert for her extraordinary editorial contributions and to Don Probert for his skill and efficiency in the composition of this guide. I would also like to thank Nadina Persaud, Edgar Bonilla, and Stacey Alexander of Worth Publishers for their dedication and energy in skillfully coordinating various aspects of production. Most important, I want to thank Jeremy, Rebecca, Melissa, and Pam for their enduring love and patience.

Richard O. Straub

STUDY GUIDE

Thinking Critically With Psychological Science

Chapter Overview

Psychology's historical development and current activities lead us to define the field as the science of behavior and mental processes. Chapter 1 discusses the development of psychology from ancient times until today and the range of behaviors and mental processes being investigated by psychologists in each of the various specialty areas. In addition, it introduces the biopsychosocial approach that integrates the three main levels of analysis followed by psychologists working from the seven major perspectives. Next is an overview of the diverse subfields in which psychologists conduct research and provide professional services.

The chapter also explains the limits of intuition and common sense in reasoning about behavior and mental processes. To counteract our human tendency toward faulty reasoning, psychologists adopt a scientific attitude that is based on curiosity, skepticism, humility, and critical thinking. The chapter also discusses how psychologists, using the scientific method, employ the research strategies of description, correlation, and experimentation in order to objectively describe, predict, and explain behavior.

The next section presents a discussion of several questions people often ask about psychology, including whether laboratory experiments are relevant, whether animal research is ethical, whether behavior varies with culture and gender, and whether psychology's principles have the potential for misuse.

Chapter 1 introduces a number of concepts and issues that will play an important role in later chapters. Pay particular attention to the strengths and weaknesses of descriptive and correlational research. In addition, make sure that you understand the method of experimentation, especially the importance of control conditions and the difference between independent and dependent variables.

The chapter concludes with a section explaining how to get your study of psychology off on the right foot by learning (and pledging to follow!) the SQ3R study method. This study method is also discussed in the essay at the beginning of the text.

NOTE: Answer guidelines for all Chapter 1 questions begin on page 20.

Chapter Review

First, skim each section, noting headings and boldface items. After you have read the section, review each objective by answering the fill-in and essay-type questions that follow it. In some cases, Study Tips explain how best to learn a difficult concept and Applications help you to know how well you understand the material. As you proceed, evaluate your performance by consulting the answers beginning on page 20. Do not continue with the next section until you understand each answer. If you need to, review or reread the section in the textbook before continuing.

What Is Psychology?

Objective 1-1: Describe some important milestones in psychology's development.

1. The Greek naturalist and philosopher
   _____ developed early theories
   about _____ , _____
   _____ , _____ ,
   _____ , and _____ .

2. The first psychological laboratory
   was founded in 1879 by _____ . His
   student _____ introduced the school of
   _____ , which explored the basic elements of mind using the method of
   _____ . This method proved
   _____ (reliable/unreliable).

3. Under the influence of evolutionary theorist Charles Darwin, philosopher-psychologist _____ assumed that thinking developed because it was _____ . As a _____ , he focused on how mental and behavioral processes enable the organism to adapt and survive. In 1890, he published the first psychology textbook.

4. The first female president of the American Psychological Association was _____ . The first woman to receive a Ph.D. in psychology was _____ , who was the second female APA president and author of *The Animal Mind*.

5. In its earliest years, psychology was defined as the science of _____ life. From the 1920s into the 1960s, psychology in America was redefined by _____ . and _____ as the science of _____ behavior.

6. The other major force was Freudian psychology, which emphasized the ways our _____ thought processes and our _____ responses to childhood experiences affect our behavior.

7. As a response to Freudian psychology and to _____ , which they considered too limiting, pioneers _____ and _____ forged _____ psychology. This new perspective emphasized the ways that current environmental influences can nurture or limit our _____ potential and the importance of having our needs for _____ and _____ satisfied.

8. During the 1960s, psychology underwent a _____ revolution as it began to recapture interest in how our _____ processes and retains information. The study of brain activity linked with mental activity is called _____ _____ .

9. The text author defines *psychology* as the scientific study of _____ and _____ processes. In this definition, "behavior" refers to any action that we can _____ and _____ , and "mental processes" refers to the internal, _____ _____ we _____ from behavior.

10. As a science, psychology is less a set of findings than a way of _____ _____ .

APPLICATIONS:

11. *Psychology* is defined as the "science of behavior and mental processes." Wilhelm Wundt would have omitted which of the following words from this definition?
    a. science
    b. behavior and
    c. and mental processes
    d. Wundt would have agreed with the definition as stated.

12. Jawan believes that psychologists should go back to using introspection as a research tool. This technique is based on
    a. survey methodology.
    b. experimentation.
    c. self-examination of mental processes.
    d. the study of observable behavior.

13. Dharma's term paper on the history of American psychology notes that
    a. psychology began as the science of mental life.
    b. from the 1920s into the 1960s, psychology was defined as the scientific study of observable behavior.
    c. contemporary psychologists study both overt behavior and covert thoughts.
    d. all of these statements are true.

14. During his presentation on the history of psychology, Sanjay notes that Darwin's theory led most directly to the development of the school of
    a. structuralism.
    b. behaviorism.
    c. functionalism.
    d. humanism.

15. The psychological views of William James are to those of Edward Titchener as _____ is to _____ .

    a. nature; nurture
    b. nurture; nature
    c. structuralism; functionalism
    d. functionalism; structuralism

Contemporary Psychology

16. The historical roots of psychology include the fields of _____ and _____ . Some early psychologists included Ivan Pavlov, who pioneered the study of _____ ; the personality theorist _____ ; Jean Piaget, who studied _____ , and William James, an American _____ .

17. Worldwide, the number of psychologists is _____ (increasing/decreasing). Thanks to international publications and meetings, psychological science is also _____ .

Objective 1-2: Summarize the nature–nurture issue in psychology.

18. The nature–nurture issue is the controversy over the relative contributions of _____ and _____ .

19. The Greek philosopher who assumed that character and intelligence are inherited is _____ . The Greek philosopher who argued that all knowledge comes from sensory experience is _____ .

20. In 1859, naturalist _____ explained species variation by proposing the process of _____ , which works through the principle of _____ .

21. Although the debate continues, we will see that _____ works on what _____ endows and that every _____ event is simultaneously a _____ event.

STUDY TIP: The nature–nurture issue is psychology's biggest and most persistent debate. Psychologists explore the issue by asking, for example, how differences in intelligence, personality, and psychological disorders are influenced by heredity and by environment. Today, contemporary science recognizes that *nurture works on what nature endows.* Our species is biologically endowed with an enormous capacity to learn and to adapt. Moreover, every *psychological event is simultaneously a biological event.*

APPLICATION:

22. The philosophical views of Aristotle are to those of Plato as _____ s to _____

    a. nature; nurture
    b. nurture; nature
    c. rationality; irrationality
    d. irrationality; rationality

Objective 1-3: Describe psychology's levels of analysis and related perspectives.

23. Each person is a complex _____ that is part of a larger _____ _____ and at the same time composed of smaller systems. For this reason, psychologists work from three main _____ of _____ — biological , _____ , and _____ - _____ — which together form an integrated _____ approach to the study of behavior and mental processes.

24. Psychologists who study how the body and brain enable emotions, memories, and sensory experiences are working from the _____ perspective.

25. Psychologists who study how natural selection influences behavior tendencies are working from the _____ perspective, whereas those concerned with the relative influences of genes and environment on individual differences are working from the _____ _____ perspective.

26. Psychologists who believe that behavior springs from unconscious drives and conflicts are working from the _____ perspective.

27. Psychologists who study how we learn observable responses are working from the _____ perspective.

28. The _____ perspective explores how we encode, process, store, and retrieve information.

29. Psychologists who study how thinking and behavior vary in different situations are working from the _____-_____ perspective.

30. The different perspectives on the big issues _____ (contradict/complement) one another.

STUDY TIP: This section describes a number of perspectives in psychology. Keep in mind that each perspective is nothing more than how certain psychologists feel behavior and mental processes should be investigated. For example, a clinical psychologist could approach the study of abnormal behavior from any of the perspectives discussed. Typically, however, psychologists work from a combination of perspectives rather than exclusively from only one. To deepen your understanding of the various perspectives, review the chart below. In the first column are listed psychology's contemporary perspectives. In the second column are listed historical roots and the pioneers who contributed to each modern-day perspective and the subfield that derives from it. As you work through the chapters, you might want to annotate this chart to include what you know about these psychologists.

Perspective	Historical Roots and Pioneers
Neuroscience	Aristotle (perception, emotion), Wundt
Evolutionary	Darwin, Freud
Behavior Genetics	Darwin
Psychodynamic	Aristotle (personality), Freud
Behavioral	Aristotle (learning), Pavlov, Watson, Skinner
Cognitive	Aristotle (memory), Wundt (quantifying mental processes), Piaget
Social-Cultural	Piaget, Rogers, Maslow

APPLICATIONS:

31. Professor Gutierrez, who believes that human emotions are best understood as being jointly determined by heredity, learning, and the individual's social and cultural contexts, is evidently a proponent of the
    a. psychodynamic perspective.
    b. biopsychosocial approach.
    c. evolutionary perspective.
    d. neuroscience perspective.

32. In concluding her report on the "nature–nurture issue in contemporary psychology," Karen notes that
    a. most psychologists believe that nature is a more important influence on the development of most human traits.
    b. most psychologists believe that nurture is more influential.
    c. the issue is more heatedly debated than ever before.
    d. nurture works on what nature endows.

33. Dr. Waung investigates how a person's interpretation of a situation affects his or her reaction. Evidently, Dr. Waung is working from the _____ perspective.
    a. neuroscience   c. cognitive
    b. behavioral   d. social-cultural

34. The psychological perspective that places the MOST emphasis on how observable responses are learned is the _____ perspective.
    a. behavioral   c. behavior genetics
    b. cognitive   d. evolutionary

35. During a dinner conversation, a friend says that the cognitive and behavioral perspectives are quite similar. You disagree and point out that the cognitive perspective emphasizes _____, whereas the behavioral perspective emphasizes

_____ .

   a. conscious processes; observable responses
   b. unconscious processes; conscious processes
   c. overt behaviors; covert behaviors
   d. experience; biology

36. Concerning the major psychological perspectives on behavior, the text author suggests that
   a. researchers should work within the framework of only one of the perspectives.
   b. only those perspectives that emphasize objective measurement of behavior are useful.
   c. the different perspectives often complement one another; together, they provide a fuller understanding of behavior than provided by any single perspective.
   d. psychologists should avoid all of these traditional perspectives.

Objective 1-4: Identify psychology's main subfields.

37. Psychologists may be involved in conducting

   _____,

   which builds psychology's knowledge base, or

   _____,

   which seeks solutions to practical problems.

38. Psychologists who help people cope with problems in living are called _____ psychologists.

39. Psychologists who study, assess, and treat troubled people are called _____ psychologists.

40. Medical doctors who provide psychotherapy and treat physical causes of psychological disorders are called _____ .

41. The subfield of _____

   _____ scientifically explores human strengths and human flourishing.

APPLICATIONS:

42. Terrence wants to talk to a professional to help him cope with some academic challenges he's facing. You recommend that he contact a(n)
   a. industrial-organizational psychologist.
   b. developmental psychologist.
   c. counseling psychologist.
   d. psychiatrist.

43. Dr. Aswad is studying people's enduring inner traits. Dr. Aswad is most likely a(n)
   a. clinical psychologist.
   b. psychiatrist.
   c. personality psychologist.
   d. industrial-organizational psychologist.

The Need for Psychological Science

Objective 1-5: Explain how hindsight bias, overconfidence, and the tendency to perceive order in random events illustrate why science-based answers are more valid than those based on intuition and common sense.

44. The tendency to perceive an outcome that has occurred as being obvious and predictable is called the _____

   _____ .

45. Our everyday thinking is also limited by _____ in what we think we know. Most people are _____ (better/worse/equally wrong) in predicting their social behavior.

46. Another common tendency is to perceive order in

   _____ _____ .

   Patterns and streaks in random sequences occur _____ (more/less) often than people expect, and they _____ (do/do not) appear random.

Objective 1-6: Explain how the three main components of the scientific attitude relate to critical thinking.

47. The scientific approach is characterized by the attitudes of _____ , _____ , and _____ .

48. Scientific inquiry thus encourages reasoning that examines assumptions, discerns hidden values, evaluates evidence, and assesses conclusions, which is called _____ _____ .

STUDY TIP: Try applying a scientific attitude toward how you evaluate your knowledge of psychology in preparation for an upcoming quiz or exam. As is true of researchers, many students develop a false sense of overconfidence in their mastery of course material. Be skeptical! Remain humble! You'll likely do better.

APPLICATIONS:

49. The scientific attitude in psychology refers to the fact that
    a. psychologists study only observable behaviors.
    b. psychologists study thoughts and actions with an attitude of skepticism and derive their conclusions from direct observations.
    c. psychological research should be free of value judgments.
    d. all of these statements are true.

50. The scientific attitude of humility is based on the idea that
    a. researchers must evaluate new ideas and theories objectively rather than accept them blindly.
    b. scientific theories must be testable.
    c. simple explanations of behavior make better theories than do complex explanations.
    d. researchers must be prepared to reject their own ideas in the face of conflicting evidence.

How Do Psychologists Ask and Answer Questions?

Objective 1-7: Describe how theories advance psychological science.

51. Psychological science uses the _____ _____ to evaluate competing ideas. They make careful _____ and form _____ , which may be _____ based on new _____ .

52. An explanation using an integrated set of principles that organizes and predicts behaviors or events is a _____ . Testable predictions that allow a scientist to evaluate a theory are called _____ . These predictions give direction to _____ .

53. To prevent theoretical biases from influencing scientific observations, research must be reported precisely—using clear _____ _____ of all concepts and procedures—so that others can _____ the findings.

54. The test of a useful theory is the extent to which it effectively _____ a range of self-reports and observations and implies clear _____ .

55. Psychologists conduct research using _____ , _____ , and _____ methods.

Objective 1-8: Describe how psychologists use case studies, surveys, and naturalistic observation to observe and describe behavior, and explain why random sampling is important.

56. The research strategy in which one or more individuals is studied in depth in order to reveal universal principles of behavior is the

    _____ _____ .

    Although case studies can suggest _____ for further study, a potential problem with this method is that any given individual may be _____ .

57. The research method in which people or animals are directly observed in their natural environments is called _____

    _____ .

58. Using naturalistic observation, researchers have found that people are more likely to laugh in _____ situations than in _____ situations. Also, using observations of walking speed and the accuracy of public clocks, researchers have concluded that the pace of life _____ (varies/does not vary) from one culture to another.

59. The method in which a group of people is questioned about their attitudes or behavior is the _____ . An important factor in the validity of survey research is the _____ of questions.

60. We are more likely to overgeneralize from samples we observe, especially _____ ones.

61. Surveys try to obtain a _____ sample, one that will be representative of the _____ being studied. In such a sample, every person _____ (does/does not) have a chance of being included.

62. Large, representative samples _____ (are/are not) better than small ones.

63. Case studies, surveys, and naturalistic observation do not explain behavior; they simply _____ it.

APPLICATIONS:

64. Your roommate is conducting a survey to learn how many hours the typical student studies each day. She plans to pass out her questionnaire to the members of her sorority. You point out that her findings will be flawed because
    a. she has not surveyed them in their natural settings.
    b. she has not specified a hypothesis.
    c. the sample will probably not be representative of the population of interest.
    d. of all of these reasons.

65. A professor constructs a questionnaire to determine how students at the university feel about nuclear disarmament. Which of the following techniques should be used to survey a random sample of the student body?
    a. Every student should be sent the questionnaire.
    b. Only students majoring in psychology should be asked to complete the questionnaire.
    c. Only students living on campus should be asked to complete the questionnaire.
    d. From an alphabetical listing of all students, every tenth (or fifteenth, e.g.) student should be asked to complete the questionnaire.

Objective 1-9: Describe positive and negative correlations, and explain why they enable prediction but not cause-effect explanation.

66. When changes in one factor are accompanied by changes in another, the two factors are said to be _____ , and one is thus able to _____ the other. The statistical expression of this relationship is called a
    _____ _____ .

67. If two factors increase or decrease together, they are _____ _____ .
    If, however, one decreases as the other increases, they are _____ _____ .
    Another way to state the latter is that the two variables relate _____ .

68. Correlation does not prove _____ ;
    rather, it merely indicates the possibility of a
    _____ - _____
    relationship.

If your level of test anxiety goes down as your time spent studying for the exam goes up, would you say these events are positively or negatively correlated? Explain your reasoning.

69. A correlation between two events or behaviors means only that one event can be
    _____ from the other.

70. Because two events may both be caused by some other _____ , a correlation does not mean that one _____ the other. For this reason, correlation thus does not enable _____ .

STUDY TIP: Many students find the concept of correlation confusing. A common mistake is the belief that a negative correlation indicates a weak or absent relationship between two variables. Remember that correlation does not prove causation; rather, it indicates the degree to which you can predict changes in one variable from another. The strength of a correlation, indicated by a numerical value, is independent of the direction (positive [+] or negative [–]) of the relationship. A negative correlation simply means that two variables change in opposite directions, such as when sales of hot chocolate decrease as the average daily temperature increases.

APPLICATIONS:

71. A researcher was interested in determining whether her students' test performance could be predicted from their proximity to the front of the classroom. So she matched her students' scores on a math test with their seating position. This study is an example of
    a. experimentation.
    b. correlational research.
    c. a survey.
    d. naturalistic observation.

72. If eating saturated fat and the likelihood of contracting cancer are positively correlated, which of the following is true?
    a. Saturated fat causes cancer.
    b. People who are prone to develop cancer prefer foods containing saturated fat.
    c. A separate factor links the consumption of saturated fat to cancer.
    d. None of these statements are necessarily true.

73. If height and body weight are positively correlated, which of the following is true?
    a. There is a cause-effect relationship between height and weight.
    b. As height increases, weight decreases.
    c. Knowing a person's height, one can predict his or her weight.
    d. All of these statements are true.

Objective 1-10: Describe the characteristics of experimentation that make it possible to isolate cause and effect.

74. To isolate _____ and _____ , researchers control for other _____ .

75. Research studies have found that breast-fed infants _____ (do/do not) grow up with somewhat higher intelligence scores than those of infants who are bottle-fed with cow's milk. To study cause-effect relationships, psychologists conduct _____ . Using this method and _____ assigning participants to groups, a researcher _____ the factor of interest while _____ _____ (controlling) other factors.

76. If a _____ changes when an _____ factor is varied, the researcher knows the factor is having an _____ .

77. An experiment must involve at least two groups: the _____ group, in which the experimental treatment is present, and the _____ group, in which it is absent.

78. To ensure that the two groups are identical, experimenters rely on the _____

_____ of individuals to the experimental conditions.

79. When neither the participants nor the person collecting the data knows which condition a participant is in, the researcher is making use of the _____-_____ procedure.

80. Researchers sometimes give certain participants a pseudotreatment, called a _____ , and compare their behavior with that of participants who receive the actual treatment. When merely thinking that one is receiving a treatment produces results, a _____ _____ is said to occur.

81. The factor that is being manipulated in an experiment is called the _____ variable. The measurable factor that may change as a result of these manipulations is called the _____ variable. Other factors that can potentially influence the results of an experiment are called _____ _____ .

STUDY TIP: Students often confuse independent variables and dependent variables. Remember that independent variables are manipulated (controlled) directly by the researcher to determine how they affect dependent variables. Dependent variables are the behaviors and mental processes that psychologists are trying to understand. In a sense, dependent variables *depend* on the actions of independent variables. When you are struggling to distinguish two variables, ask yourself, "Which of these two variables can affect the other?" Consider, for example, a researcher investigating caffeine and reaction time. After randomly assigning different students to groups that drink a highly caffeinated drink and a weakly caffeinated drink, she measures each student's speed in pushing a button in response to a signal light. Which variable is the independent variable, and which is the dependent variable? If the answer is not obvious, try the test question, "Which variable can affect the other?" Clearly, reaction time cannot affect caffeine. So, in this example, the dose of caffeine is the independent variable and reaction time is the dependent variable.

82. The aim of an experiment is to _____

a(n) _____ variable, measure the

_____ variable, and

_____ all other variables.

Explain at least one advantage of the experiment as a research method.

STUDY TIP/APPLICATIONS: The concepts of control and operational definition are important in experimental research. In an experiment, researchers strive to hold constant (control) the possible effects of all variables on the dependent variable, except the one that is being manipulated (independent variable). Operational definitions, which were explained earlier, are like recipes for measuring a variable so that other researchers can replicate your results. They are much more precise than dictionary definitions. For example, the dictionary might define intelligence as "the capacity to reason." Because this definition is too vague for research purposes, a psychologist might create the operational definition of intelligence as "a person's answers to a specific set of IQ test questions." Test your understanding of these important concepts by completing the following exercises.

83. You decide to test your belief that men drink more soft drinks than women by finding out whether more soft drinks are consumed per day in the men's dorm than in the women's dorm. Your belief is a(n) _____ , and your research prediction is a(n) _____ .

   a. hypothesis; theory
   b. theory; hypothesis
   c. independent variable; dependent variable
   d. dependent variable; independent variable

84. The concept of control is important in psychological research because

   a. without control over independent and dependent variables, researchers cannot describe, predict, or explain behavior.

   b. experimental control allows researchers to study the influence of one or two independent variables on a dependent variable while holding other potential influences constant.
   c. without experimental control, results cannot be generalized from a sample to a population.
   d. of all of these reasons.

85. Martina believes that high doses of caffeine slow a person's reaction time. To test this belief, she has five friends each drink three 8-ounce cups of coffee and then measures their reaction time on a learning task. What is wrong with Martina's research strategy?

   a. No independent variable is specified.
   b. No dependent variable is specified.
   c. There is no control condition.
   d. There is no provision for replication of the findings.

86. Rashad, who is participating in a psychology experiment on the effects of alcohol on perception, is truthfully told by the experimenter that he has been assigned to the "high-dose condition." What is wrong with this experiment?

   a. There is no control condition.
   b. Rashad's expectations concerning the effects of "high doses" of alcohol on perception may influence his performance.
   c. Rashad was given a placebo, so the results may be tainted.
   d. All of these statements are correct.

87. Which of the following procedures is an example of the use of a placebo?

   a. In a test of the effects of a drug on memory, a participant is led to believe that a harmless pill actually contains an active drug.
   b. A participant in an experiment is led to believe that a pill, which actually contains an active drug, is harmless.
   c. Participants in an experiment are not told which treatment condition is in effect.
   d. Neither the participants nor the experimenter knows which treatment condition is in effect.

SUMMARY STUDY TIP: As we will note through this Study Guide, preparing a table to summarize what you have learned about a topic is a good way to promote understanding. Table 1.2 in the text compares the three research methods. Without looking at the text, try to complete the table on the next page on your own. We've partially filled in a couple of column entries for you.

Research Method	Basic Purpose	How Conducted	What Is Manipulated	Weaknesses
Descriptive		Do case studies, surveys, or naturalistic observations	Nothing	
Correlational	To detect naturally			
Experimental	To explore			

Frequently Asked Questions About Psychology

Objective 1-11: Explain whether laboratory conditions can illuminate everyday life.

88. In laboratory experiments, psychologists' concern is not with specific behaviors but with the underlying theoretical _____ .

89. Psychologists conduct experiments on simplified behaviors in a laboratory environment to gain _____ over the many variables present in the "real world." In doing so, they are able to test _____ _____ of behavior that also operate in the real world.

Objective 1-12: Discuss whether behavior depends on one's culture and gender.

90. Culture refers to the enduring _____ , _____ , _____ , _____ , and _____ shared by a group of people and passed on from one generation to the next.

91. Although specific attitudes and behaviors vary across cultures, the underlying _____ are the same. For instance, throughout the world people diagnosed with _____

(a reading problem) exhibit the same _____ malfunction. Likewise, similarities between the _____ far outweigh differences.

Objective 1-13: Explain why psychologists study animals, and describe the ethical guidelines that safeguard human and animal research participants.

92. Many psychologists study animals because they are fascinating. More important, they study animals because of the _____ (similarities/differences) between humans and other animals. These studies have led to treatments for human _____ and to a better understanding of human functioning.

93. Some people question whether experiments with animals are _____ . They wonder whether it is right to place the _____ of humans over that of animals.

94. Opposition to animal experimentation also raises the question of what _____ should protect the well-being of animals.

95. The ethics code of the _____ _____ _____ urges researchers to obtain participants' _____ _____ and fully _____ people after the research.

Describe two other ethical guidelines for psychological research.

Objective 1-14: Discuss whether psychology is free of value judgments.

96. Psychologists' values _____ (do/do not) influence their theories, observations, and professional advice.

97. Although psychology _____ (can/cannot) be used to manipulate people, its purpose is to _____ .

APPLICATIONS:

98. Your best friend criticizes psychological research for being artificial and having no relevance to behavior in real life. In defense of psychology's use of laboratory experiments you point out that
    a. psychologists make every attempt to avoid artificiality by setting up experiments that closely simulate real-world environments.
    b. psychologists who conduct basic research are not concerned with the applicability of their findings to the real world.
    c. most psychological research is not conducted in a laboratory environment.
    d. psychologists intentionally study behavior in simplified environments in order to gain greater control over variables and to test general principles that help to explain many behaviors.

99. A friend majoring in anthropology is critical of psychological research because it often ignores the influence of culture on thoughts and actions. You point out that
    a. there is very little evidence that cultural diversity has a significant effect on specific behaviors and attitudes.
    b. most researchers assign participants to experimental and control conditions in such a way as to fairly represent the cultural diversity of the population under study.
    c. it is impossible for psychologists to control for every possible variable that might influence research participants.

d. even when specific thoughts and actions vary across cultures, as they often do, the underlying processes are much the same.

Improve Your Retention—and Your Grades

Objective 1-15: Explain how psychological principles can help you learn and remember.

100. Repeated _____ and _____ of previously studied material improves retention of information. This phenomenon is called the _____ _____ .

101. To master any subject, you must _____ process it.

102. The _____ study method incorporates five steps: a. _____ ,
    b. _____ , c. _____ ,
    d. _____ , and
    e. _____ .

List four additional study tips identified in the text.

a. _____

b. _____

c. _____

d. _____

APPLICATIONS:

103. Your roommate announces that her schedule permits her to devote three hours to studying for an upcoming quiz. You advise her to
    a. spend most of her time reading and rereading the text material.
    b. focus primarily on her lecture notes.
    c. space study time over several short sessions.
    d. cram for three hours just before the quiz.

104. A fraternity brother rationalizes the fact that he spends very little time studying by saying that he "doesn't want to peak too soon and have the test material become stale." You tell him that
    a. he is probably overestimating his knowledge of the material.
    b. if he devotes extra time to studying, his retention of the material will be improved.
    c. the more often students test themselves on the material, the better their exam scores.
    d. all of these statements are true.

105. Brad, who prepares for exams simply by reading the textbook assignment several times, evidently has not heard about

    a. replication.
    b. positive psychology.
    c. the testing effect.
    d. the nature–nurture issue.

Progress Test 1

Multiple-Choice Questions

Circle your answers to the following questions and check them with the answers beginning on page 23. If your answer is incorrect, read the explanation for why it is incorrect and then consult the text.

1. In its earliest days, *psychology* was defined as the
    a. science of mental life.
    b. study of conscious and unconscious activity.
    c. science of observable behavior.
    d. science of behavior and mental processes.

2. Who would be most likely to agree with the statement, "Psychology should investigate only behaviors that can be observed"?
    a. Wilhelm Wundt
    b. Sigmund Freud
    c. John B. Watson
    d. William James

3. Today, *psychology* is defined as the
    a. science of mental phenomena.
    b. science of conscious and unconscious activity.
    c. science of behavior.
    d. science of behavior and mental processes.

4. After detailed study of a gunshot wound victim, a psychologist concludes that the brain region destroyed is likely to be important for memory functions. Which type of research did the psychologist use to deduce this?
    a. the case study
    b. a survey
    c. correlation
    d. experimentation

5. Who wrote an important early psychology textbook?
    a. Wilhelm Wundt   **c.** Jean Piaget
    b. Ivan Pavlov   **d.** William James

6. Psychologists who study the degree to which genes influence our personality are working from the _____ perspective.
    a. behavioral   **c.** behavior genetics
    b. evolutionary   **d.** neuroscience

7. Which of the following exemplifies the issue of the relative importance of nature and nurture on our behavior?
    a. the issue of the relative influence of biology and experience on behavior
    b. the issue of the relative influence of rewards and punishments on behavior
    c. the debate as to the relative importance of heredity and instinct in determining behavior
    d. the debate as to whether mental processes are a legitimate area of scientific study

8. To study the effects of lighting on mood, Dr. Cooper had students fill out questionnaires in brightly lit or dimly lit rooms. In this study, the independent variable consisted of
    a. the number of students assigned to each group.
    b. the students' responses to the questionnaire.
    c. the room lighting.
    d. the subject matter of the questions asked.

9. Which psychological perspective emphasizes the interaction of the brain and body in behavior?
    a. neuroscience
    b. cognitive
    c. behavioral
    d. behavior genetics

10. A psychologist who explores how Asian and North American definitions of attractiveness differ is working from the _____ perspective.
    a. behavioral   **c.** cognitive
    b. evolutionary   **d.** social-cultural

11. A psychologist who conducts experiments solely intended to build psychology's knowledge base is engaged in
    a. basic research.
    b. applied research.
    c. industrial-organizational research.
    d. clinical research.

12. Psychologists who study, assess, and treat troubled people are called
    a. basic researchers.
    b. applied psychologists.
    c. clinical psychologists.
    d. psychiatrists.

13. Today, psychology is a discipline that
    a. connects with a diversity of other fields.
    b. is largely independent of other disciplines.
    c. is focused primarily on basic research.
    d. is focused primarily on applied research.

14. In order, the sequence of steps in the SQ3R method is
    a. survey, review, retrieve, question, read.
    b. review, question, survey, read, retrieve.
    c. question, review, survey, read, retrieve.
    d. survey, question, read, retrieve, review.

15. Psychologists who study how brain activity is linked to memory, perception, and other thought processes are called
    a. humanistic psychologists.
    b. psychiatrists.
    c. clinical psychologists.
    d. cognitive neuroscientists.

16. In an experiment to determine the effects of exercise on motivation, exercise is the
    a. control condition.
    b. confounding variable.
    c. independent variable.
    d. dependent variable.

17. To determine the effects of a new drug on memory, one group of people is given a pill that contains the drug. A second group is given a sugar pill that does not contain the drug. This second group constitutes the
    a. random sample.   c. control group.
    b. experimental group.   d. test group.

18. *Theories* are defined as
    a. testable propositions.
    b. factors that may change in response to manipulation.
    c. statistical indexes.
    d. principles that help to organize observations and predict behaviors or events.

19. A psychologist studies the play behavior of young children by watching groups during recess at school. Which type of research is being used?
    a. correlation
    b. case study
    c. experimentation
    d. naturalistic observation

20. To ensure that other researchers can repeat their work, psychologists use
    a. control groups.
    b. random assignment.
    c. double-blind procedures.
    d. operational definitions.

21. The scientific attitude of skepticism is based on the belief that
    a. people are rarely candid in revealing their thoughts.
    b. mental processes can't be studied objectively.
    c. the scientist's intuition about behavior is usually correct.
    d. ideas need to be tested against observable evidence.

22. Which of the following is NOT a basic research technique used by psychologists?
    a. description
    b. replication
    c. experimentation
    d. correlation

23. Psychologists' personal values
    a. have little influence on how their experiments are conducted.
    b. do not influence the interpretation of experimental results because of the use of statistical techniques that guard against subjective bias.
    c. can bias both scientific observation and interpretation of data.
    d. have little influence on investigative methods but a significant effect on interpretation.

24. If shoe size and IQ are negatively correlated, which of the following is true?
    a. People with large feet tend to have high IQs.
    b. People with small feet tend to have high IQs.
    c. People with small feet tend to have low IQs.
    d. IQ is unpredictable based on a person's shoe size.

25. Which of the following would be best for determining whether alcohol impairs memory?
    a. case study   c. survey
    b. naturalistic observation d. experiment

26. Well-done surveys measure attitudes in a representative subset, or _____ , of an entire group, or _____ .
    a. population; random sample
    b. control group; experimental group
    c. experimental group; control group
    d. random sample; population

27. Juwan eagerly opened an online trading account, believing that his market savvy would allow him to pick stocks that would make him a rich day trader. This belief best illustrates

   a. a placebo effect.

   b. a double blind.

   c. hindsight bias.

   d. overconfidence.

28. Who introduced the early school of structuralism?

   a. Edward Titchener

   b. Wilhelm Wundt

   c. William James

   d. Mary Whiton Calkins

Matching Items

Match each psychological perspective, school, and subfield with its definition or description.

Terms

_____ **1.** neuroscience perspective

_____ **2.** social-cultural perspective

_____ **3.** psychiatry

_____ **4.** clinical psychology

_____ **5.** behavior genetics perspective

_____ **6.** behavioral perspective

_____ **7.** industrial-organizational psychology

_____ **8.** cognitive perspective

_____ **9.** basic research

_____ **10.** applied research

_____ **11.** evolutionary perspective

_____ **12.** psychodynamic perspective

_____ **13.** positive psychology

_____ **14.** behaviorism

_____ **15.** cognitive neuroscience

_____ **16.** culture

_____ **17.** placebo effect

_____ **18.** hindsight bias

_____ **19.** critical thinking

_____ **20.** functionalism

Definitions or Descriptions

a. behavior in the workplace

b. how people differ as products of different environments

c. the study of practical problems

d. the scientific study of the strengths and virtues of human functioning

e. how we learn observable responses

f. how the body and brain create emotions, memories, and sensations

g. school of psychology that explored how mental and behavioral processes function—how they enable the organism to adapt, survive, and flourish

h. the view that psychology should be an objective science that avoids reference to mental processes

i. how natural selection favors traits that promote the perpetuation of one's genes

j. the study, assessment, and treatment of troubled people

k. brain activity linked with perception, thinking, memory, and language

l. the disguised effects of unfulfilled wishes and childhood traumas

m. adds to psychology's knowledge base

n. how much genes and environment contribute to individual differences

o. the medical treatment of psychological disorders

p. shared ideas and behaviors passed from one generation to the next

q. "I-knew-it-all-along" phenomenon

r. reasoning that does not blindly accept arguments

s. experimental results caused by expectations alone

t. how we encode, process, store, and retrieve information

Progress Test 2

Progress Test 2 should be completed during a final chapter review. Answer the following questions after you thoroughly understand the correct answers for the section reviews and Progress Test 1.

Multiple-Choice Questions

1. The first psychology laboratory was established by _____ in the year _____ .
   a. Wundt; 1879   c. Freud; 1900
   b. James; 1890   d. Watson; 1913

2. Who would be most likely to agree with the statement, "Psychology is the science of mental life"?
   a. Wilhelm Wundt
   b. John Watson
   c. Ivan Pavlov
   d. virtually any American psychologist during the 1960s

3. In psychology, *behavior* is best defined as
   a. anything a person says, does, or feels.
   b. any action we can observe and record.
   c. any action, whether observable or not.
   d. anything we can infer from a person's actions.

4. Carl Rogers and Abraham Maslow are most closely associated with
   a. cognitive psychology.
   b. behaviorism.
   c. psychodynamic theory.
   d. humanistic psychology.

5. In defining *psychology,* the text notes that psychology is most accurately described as a
   a. way of asking and answering questions.
   b. field engaged in solving applied problems.
   c. set of findings related to behavior and mental processes.
   d. nonscientific approach to the study of mental disorders.

6. Two historical roots of psychology are the disciplines of
   a. philosophy and chemistry.
   b. physiology and chemistry.
   c. philosophy and biology.
   d. philosophy and physics.

7. The Greek philosopher who believed that intelligence was inherited was
   a. Aristotle.   c. Descartes.
   b. Plato.   d. Simonides.

8. The way we encode, process, store, and retrieve information is the primary concern of the _____ perspective.
   a. neuroscience   c. social-cultural
   b. evolutionary   d. cognitive

9. Which of the following individuals is also a physician?
   a. clinical psychologist
   b. experimental psychologist
   c. psychiatrist
   d. biological psychologist

10. Dr. Jones' research centers on the relationship between changes in our thinking over the life span and changes in moral reasoning. Dr. Jones is most likely a
    a. clinical psychologist.
    b. personality psychologist.
    c. psychiatrist.
    d. developmental psychologist.

11. Which subfield is most directly concerned with studying human behavior in the workplace?
    a. clinical psychology
    b. personality psychology
    c. industrial-organizational psychology
    d. psychiatry

12. Dr. Ernst explains behavior in terms of different situations. Dr. Ernst is working from the _____ perspective.
    a. behavioral   c. social-cultural
    b. evolutionary   d. cognitive

13. Which perspective emphasizes the learning of observable responses?
    a. behavioral   c. neuroscience
    b. social-cultural d. cognitive

14. A psychologist who studies how worker productivity might be increased by changing office layout is engaged in _____ research.
    a. applied   c. clinical
    b. basic   d. developmental

15. A major principle underlying the SQ3R study method is that
    a. people learn and remember material best when they actively process it.
    b. many students overestimate their mastery of text and lecture material.
    c. study time should be spaced over time rather than crammed into one session.
    d. overlearning disrupts efficient retention.

16. The biopsychosocial approach emphasizes the importance of
    a. different levels of analysis in exploring behavior and mental processes.
    b. basic research over pure research.
    c. pure research over basic research.
    d. having a single academic perspective to guide research.

17. Which of the following research methods does NOT belong with the others?
    a. case study   c. naturalistic observation
    b. survey   d. experiment

18. To prevent the possibility that a placebo effect or researchers' expectations will influence a study's results, scientists employ
    a. control groups.
    b. experimental groups.
    c. random assignment.
    d. the double-blind procedure.

19. Which statement about the ethics of experimentation with people and animals is FALSE?
    a. The same processes by which humans learn are present in rats, monkeys, and other animals.
    b. Views on whether it is right to place the well-being of humans above that of animals are the same in every culture.
    c. The American Psychological Association and the British Psychological Society have set strict guidelines for the care and treatment of human and animal subjects.
    d. Most psychological studies are free of such stress as the delivery of electric shock.

20. In an experiment to determine the effects of attention on memory, memory is the
    a. control condition.
    b. intervening variable.
    c. independent variable.
    d. dependent variable.

21. Which of the following BEST describes the hindsight bias?
    a. Events seem more predictable before they have occurred.
    b. Events seem more predictable after they have occurred.
    c. A person's intuition is usually correct.
    d. A person's intuition is usually not correct.

22. The procedure designed to ensure that the experimental and control groups do not differ in any way that might affect the experiment's results is called
    a. variable controlling.
    b. random assignment.
    c. representative sampling.
    d. stratification.

23. Debriefing refers to
    a. the perception that two negatively correlated variables are positively correlated.
    b. explaining the purpose of a research study after its conclusion.
    c. an insignificant correlation.
    d. a correlation that equals −1.0.

24. In generalizing from a sample to the population, it is important that
    a. the sample be representative.
    b. the sample be nonrandom.
    c. the sample not be too large.
    d. all of these conditions exist.

25. The strength of the relationship between two vivid events will most likely be
    a. significant.
    b. positive.
    c. negative.
    d. overestimated.

26. Which of the following is true, according to the text?
    a. Because laboratory experiments are artificial, any principles discovered cannot be applied to everyday behaviors.
    b. Psychological science demonstrates why we cannot rely on intuition and common sense.
    c. Psychology's theories reflect common sense.
    d. Psychology has few ties to other disciplines.

27. Which type of research would allow you to determine whether students' grades accurately predict later income?
    a. case study   c. experimentation
    b. naturalistic observation   d. correlation

28. In a test of the effects of air pollution, groups of students performed a reaction-time task in a polluted or an unpolluted room. To what condition were students in the unpolluted room exposed?
    a. experimental   c. randomly assigned
    b. control   d. dependent

True–False Items

Place a T or an F in the blank next to each statement.

_____   1. Psychology's three main levels of analysis often contradict one another.

_____   2. The primary research tool of the first psychologists was the experiment.

_____   3. The subject matter of psychology has changed over the history of the field.

_____   4. Every psychological event is simultaneously a biological event.

_____   5. Today, most psychologists work within the behavioral perspective.

_____   6. The major perspectives in psychology contradict one another.

_____   7. Repeated self-testing and rehearsal promote better retention than rereading.

_____   8. Overlearning hinders retention.

_____   9. A major goal of psychology is to teach us how to ask important questions and to think critically as we evaluate competing ideas.

Matching Items

Match each term with its definition or description.

Terms

_____   1. hypothesis
_____   2. theory
_____   3. independent variable
_____   4. dependent variable
_____   5. experimental group
_____   6. control group
_____   7. case study
_____   8. survey
_____   9. replication
_____   10. random assignment
_____   11. experiment
_____   12. double-blind
_____   13. debriefing
_____   14. informed consent

Definitions or Descriptions

a. an in-depth observational study of one person

b. the variable being manipulated in an experiment

c. the variable being measured in an experiment

d. giving research participants information that enables them to choose whether to participate

e. testable proposition

f. repeating an experiment to see whether the same results are obtained

g. the process in which research participants are selected by chance for different groups in an experiment

h. an explanation using an integrated set of principles that organizes observations and predicts behaviors or events

i. the research strategy in which the effects of one or more variables on behavior are tested

j. the "treatment-present" group in an experiment

k. the research strategy in which a representative sample of individuals is questioned

l. experimental procedure in which neither the research participant nor the experimenter knows which condition the participant is in

m. the "treatment-absent" group in an experiment

n. explaining the purpose of a research study after its conclusion

Essay Questions

1. Explain how researchers working from each of psychology's major perspectives might investigate an emotion such as love. (Use the space below to list the points you want to make, and organize them. Then write the essay on a separate piece of paper.)

2. Elio has a theory that regular exercise for one month can improve thinking. Help him design an experiment evaluating this theory. (Use the space below to list the points you want to make, and organize them. Then write the essay on a separate piece of paper.)

Terms and Concepts to Remember

Using your own words, on a separate piece of paper write a brief definition or explanation of each of the following.

1. structuralism
2. functionalism
3. behaviorism
4. humanistic psychology

5. cognitive neuroscience
6. psychology
7. nature–nurture issue
8. natural selection
9. levels of analysis
10. biopsychosocial approach
11. basic research
12. applied research
13. counseling psychology
14. clinical psychology
15. psychiatry
16. positive psychology
17. hindsight bias
18. critical thinking
19. theory
20. hypothesis
21. operational definition
22. replication
23. case study
24. naturalistic observation
25. survey
26. population
27. random sample
28. correlation
29. correlation coefficient
30. experiment
31. experimental group
32. control group
33. random assignment
34. double-blind procedure
35. placebo effect
36. independent variable
37. confounding variable
38. dependent variable
39. culture
40. informed consent
41. debriefing
42. testing effect
43. SQ3R

Cross-Check

As you learned in this chapter, reviewing and overlearning of material are important to the learning process. After you have written the definitions of the key terms in this chapter, you should complete the crossword puzzle to ensure that you can reverse the process—recognize the term, given the definition.

ACROSS

1. Process of repeating the essence of a research study, often with different participants and in different situations
7. Explanation using an integrated set of principles that organizes and predicts behaviors or events.
11. Descriptive research strategy in which one person is studied in great depth.
12. When a research participant's expectations produce the results of an experiment, it is called a _____ effect.
14. Descriptive research technique in which a representative, random sample of people is questioned about their attitudes or behaviors.
15. Measure that indicates the extent to which one factor predicts another factor.

DOWN

2. Condition in which research participants are exposed to the independent variable being studied.
3. In an experiment, the variable being manipulated and tested by the investigator.
4. Research method in which behavior is observed and recorded in naturally occurring situations without any manipulation or control.
5. A precise definition of the procedures used to identify a variable.
6. Careful reasoning that examines assumptions, discerns hidden values, evaluates evidence, and assesses conclusions.
8. The bias in which we believe, after learning an outcome, that we could have foreseen it.
9. Control procedure in which neither the experimenter nor the research participants are aware of which condition is in effect.
10. Testable prediction, often implied by a theory.
13. Experimental condition in which the treatment of interest is withheld.
16. Sample in which every member of the population has an equal chance of being included.

ANSWERS

Chapter Review

What Is Psychology?

1. Aristotle; learning; memory; motivation; emotion; perception; personality

2. Wundt; Edward Titchener; structuralism; introspection; unreliable

3. William James; adaptive; functionalist

4. Mary Whiton Calkins; Margaret Floy Washburn

5. mental; John B. Watson; B. F. Skinner; observable

6. unconscious; emotional

7. behaviorism; Carl Rogers; Abraham Maslow; humanistic; growth; love; acceptance

8. cognitive; mind; cognitive neuroscience

9. behavior; mental; observe; record; subjective experiences; infer

10. asking and answering questions

11. **b.** is the answer.
    a. As the founder of the first psychology laboratory, Wundt certainly based his research on the scientific method.
    c. The earliest psychologists, including Wilhelm Wundt, were concerned with the fastest and simplest mental processes.

12. **c.** is the answer.

13. **d.** is the answer.

14. **c.** is the answer. Like Darwin, James assumed that thinking, like smelling, developed because it was adaptive.

15. **d.** is the answer. James emphasized the adaptive value of our thoughts and behaviors (functionalism). Titchener used the method of introspection to examine the basic contents of the mind (structuralism).
    a. & b. The text does not discuss the views of these psychologists regarding the nature–nurture issue.

Contemporary Psychology

16. biology; philosophy; learning; Sigmund Freud; children; philosopher

17. increasing; globalizing

18. biology; experience

19. Plato; Aristotle

20. Charles Darwin; evolution; natural selection

21. nurture; nature; psychological; biological

22. **b.** is the answer. Aristotle believed that all knowledge comes from experience (nurture). Plato believed that some ideas are innate (nature).
    c. & d. The text does not discuss the views of these philosophers regarding this issue.

23. system; social system; levels; analysis; psychological; social-cultural; biopsychosocial

24. neuroscience

25. evolutionary; behavior genetics

26. psychodynamic

27. behavioral

28. cognitive

29. social-cultural

30. complement

31. **b.** is the answer.
    a., c., & d. Each of these perspectives is too narrow to apply to Professor Gutierrez's belief. Moreover, the psychodynamic perspective (a.) emphasizes unconscious processes, in which Professor Gutierrez has not expressed a belief.

32. **d.** is the answer. Because both nature and nurture influence most traits and behaviors, the tension surrounding this issue has dissolved.

33. **c.** is the answer.
    a. This perspective emphasizes the influences of physiology on behavior.
    b. This perspective emphasizes environmental influences on observable behavior.
    d. This perspective emphasizes how behavior and thinking vary across situations and cultures.

34. **a.** is the answer.

35. **a.** is the answer.
    b. Neither perspective places any special emphasis on unconscious processes.
    c. Neither perspective emphasizes covert behaviors.
    d. Experience and biology refer to the nature–nurture issue.

36. **c.** is the answer.
    a. The text suggests just the opposite: By studying behavior from several perspectives, psychologists gain a fuller understanding.
    b. & d. Each perspective is useful in that it calls researchers' attention to different aspects of behavior. This is equally true of those perspectives that do not emphasize objective measurement.

37. basic research; applied research

38. counseling

39. clinical

40. psychiatrists

41. positive psychology

42. **c.** is the answer.
    a. Industrial-organizational psychologists study and advise on behavior in the workplace.
    b. Developmental psychologists investigate behavior and mental processes over the life span.
    d. Psychiatrists are medical doctors who treat medical disorders. There is no indication that Terrence is suffering from a medical disorder.

43. **c.** is the answer.
    a. Clinical psychology is concerned with the study and treatment of psychological disorders.
    b. Psychiatry is the branch of medicine concerned with the physical diagnosis and treatment of psychological disorders.
    d. Industrial-organizational psychologists study behavior in the workplace.

The Need for Psychological Science

44. hindsight bias

45. overconfidence; equally wrong

46. random events; more; do not

47. curiosity; skepticism; humility

48. critical thinking

49. **b.** is the answer. Psychologists approach their studies of behavior and mental processes with attitudes of curiosity, skepticism, and humility.
    a. Psychologists study both overt (observable) behaviors and covert thoughts and feelings.
    c. Psychologists' values definitely do influence their research.

50. **d.** is the answer.
    a. This follows from the attitude of skepticism, rather than humility.
    b. & c. Although both of these are true of the scientific method, neither has anything to do with humility.

How Do Psychologists Ask and Answer Questions?

51. scientific method; observations; theories; revised; observations

52. theory; hypotheses; research

53. operational definitions; replicate

54. organizes; predictions

55. descriptive; correlational; experimental

56. case study; directions; atypical

57. naturalistic observation

58. social; solitary; varies

59. survey; wording

60. vivid

61. random; population; does

62. are

63. describe

64. **c.** is the answer. The members of one sorority are likely to share more interests, traits, and attitudes than will the members of a random sample of college students.
    a. & b. Surveys do not involve observing respondents, and they do not predict an outcome.

65. **d.** is the answer. Selecting every tenth person would probably result in a representative sample of the entire population of students at the university.
    a. It would be difficult, if not impossible, to survey every student on campus.
    b. Psychology students are not representative of the entire student population.
    c. This answer is incorrect for the same reason as b. This would constitute a biased sample.

66. correlated; predict; correlation coefficient

67. positively correlated; negatively correlated; inversely

68. causation; cause-effect

This is an example of a negative correlation. As one factor (time spent studying) increases, the other factor (anxiety level) decreases.

69. predicted

70. event; caused; explanation

71. **b.** is the answer.
    a. This is not an experiment because the researcher is not manipulating a variable (seating position); she is merely measuring whether variation in this factor predicts test performance.
    c. If the study were based entirely on students' self-reported responses, this would be a survey.
    d. This study goes beyond naturalistic observation, which merely describes behavior as it occurs, to determine if test scores can be predicted from students' seating position.

72. **d.** is the answer.
    a. Correlation does not imply causality.
    b. Again, a positive correlation simply means that two factors tend to increase or decrease together; further relationships are not implied.
    c. A separate factor may or may not be involved. That the two factors are correlated does not imply a separate factor. There may, for example, be a direct causal relationship between the two factors themselves.

73. **c.** is the answer. If height and weight are positively correlated, increased height is associated with increased weight. Thus, one can predict a person's weight from his or her height.

a. Correlation does not imply causality.
b. This situation depicts a negative correlation between height and weight.

74. cause; effect; factors

75. do; experiments; randomly; manipulates; holding constant

76. behavior; experimental; effect

77. experimental; control

78. random assignment

79. double-blind

80. placebo; placebo effect

81. independent; dependent; confounding variables

82. manipulate; independent; dependent; control

Experimentation has the advantage of increasing the investigator's control of both relevant and irrelevant variables that might influence behavior. Experiments also permit the investigator to go beyond observation and description to uncover cause-effect relationships in behavior.

83. **b.** is the answer. A general belief such as this one is a theory; it helps organize, explain, and generate testable predictions (called hypotheses) such as "men drink more soft drinks than women."
c. & d. Independent and dependent variables are experimental treatments and behaviors, respectively. Beliefs and predictions may involve such variables, but are not themselves those variables.

84. **b.** is the answer.

a. Although the descriptive methods of case studies, surveys, naturalistic observation, and correlational research do not involve control of variables, they nevertheless enable researchers to describe and predict behavior.
c. Whether a sample is representative of a population, rather than control over variables, determines whether results can be generalized from a sample to a population.

85. **c.** is the answer. To determine the effects of caffeine on reaction time, Martina needs to measure reaction time in a control, or comparison, group that does not receive caffeine.
a. Caffeine is the independent variable.
b. Reaction time is the dependent variable.
d. Whether Martina's experiment can be replicated is determined by the precision with which she reports her procedures, which is not an aspect of research strategy.

86. **b.** is the answer.
a. The low-dose comparison group is the control group.
c. Rashad was not given a placebo.

87. **a.** is the answer.
b. Use of a placebo tests whether the behavior of a research participant, who mistakenly believes that a treatment (such as a drug) is in effect, is the same as it would be if the treatment were actually present.
c. & d. These are examples of *blind* and *double-blind* control procedures.

STUDY TIP: COMPARING RESEARCH METHODS (For your convenience the text table is repeated here.)

Research Method	Basic Purpose	How Conducted	What Is Manipulated	Weaknesses
Descriptive	To observe and record behavior	Do case studies, naturalistic observations, or surveys	Nothing	No control of variables; single cases may be misleading
Correlational	To detect naturally occurring relationships; to assess how well one variable predicts another	Collect data on two or more variables; no manipulation	Nothing	Does not specify cause and effect
Experimental	To explore cause and effect	Manipulate one or more factors; use random assignment	The independent variable(s)	Sometimes not feasible; results may not generalize to other contexts; not ethical to manipulate certain variables

Frequently Asked Questions About Psychology

88. principles

89. control; theoretical principles

90. ideas; behaviors; attitudes; values; traditions

91. processes; specific learning disorder; brain; genders

92. similarities; diseases

93. ethical; well-being

94. safeguards

95. American Psychological Association; informed consent; debrief

Ethical guidelines require investigators to protect research participants from harm and discomfort and treat information obtained from participants confidentially.

96. do

97. can; enlighten

98. **d.** is the answer.

99. **d.** is the answer.
    a. In fact, just the opposite is true.
    b. Actually, psychological experiments tend to use the most readily available people, often white North American college students.
    c. Although this may be true, psychological experiments remain important because they help explain underlying processes of human behavior everywhere. Therefore, d. is a much better response than c.

Improve Your Retention—and Your Grades

100. self-testing; rehearsal; testing effect

101. actively

102. SQ3R; a. survey; b. question; c. read; d. retrieve; e. review
    a. Distribute study time.
    b. Process class information actively.
    c. Overlearn material.
    d. Learn to think critically.

103. **c.** is the answer.
    a. To be effective, study must be active rather than passive in nature.
    b. Most exams are based on lecture and textbook material.
    d. Cramming hinders retention.

104. **d.** is the answer.

105. **c.** is the answer.

Progress Test 1

Multiple-Choice Questions

1. **a.** is the answer.
    b. Psychology has never been defined in terms of conscious and unconscious activity.
    c. From the 1920s into the 1960s, psychology was defined as the scientific study of observable behavior.
    d. Psychology today is defined as the scientific study of behavior and mental processes. In its earliest days, however, psychology focused exclusively on mental phenomena.

2. **c.** is the answer.
    a. Wilhelm Wundt, the founder of the first psychology laboratory, was seeking to measure the simplest mental processes.
    b. Sigmund Freud developed an influential theory of personality that focused on unconscious processes.
    d. William James, author of an 1890 psychology textbook, was a philosopher and was more interested in mental phenomena than observable behavior.

3. **d.** is the answer.
    a. In its earliest days psychology was defined as the science of mental phenomena.
    b. Psychology has never been defined in terms of conscious and unconscious activity.
    c. From the 1920s into the 1960s, psychology was defined as the scientific study of behavior.

4. **a.** is the answer. In a case study, one person is studied in depth.
    b. In survey research, a group of people is interviewed.
    c. Correlations identify whether two factors are related.
    d. In an experiment, an investigator manipulates one variable to observe its effect on another.

5. **d.** is the answer
    a. Wilhelm Wundt founded the first psychology laboratory.
    b. Ivan Pavlov pioneered the study of learning.
    c. Jean Piaget was the twentieth century's most influential observer of children.

6. **c.** is the answer.

7. **a.** is the answer. Biology and experience are internal and external influences, respectively.
    b. Rewards and punishments are both external influences on behavior.
    c. Heredity and instinct are both internal influences on behavior.
    d. The legitimacy of the study of mental processes does not relate to the internal/external issue.

8. **c.** is the answer. The lighting is the factor being manipulated.
    a. & d. These answers are incorrect because they involve aspects of the experiment other than the variables.
    b. This answer is the dependent, not the independent, variable.

9. **a.** is the answer.
    b. The cognitive perspective is concerned with how we encode, process, store, and retrieve information.

c. The behavioral perspective studies the mechanisms by which observable responses are acquired and changed.

d. The behavior genetics perspective focuses on the relative contributions of genes and environment to individual differences.

10. **d.** is the answer.
a. Behavioral psychologists investigate how learned behaviors are acquired. They generally do not focus on subjective opinions, such as attractiveness.
b. The evolutionary perspective studies how natural selection favors traits that promote the perpetuation of one's genes.
c. Cognitive psychologists study the mechanisms of thinking and memory, and generally do not investigate attitudes. Also, because the question specifies that the psychologist is interested in comparing two cultures, d. is the best answer.

11. **a.** is the answer.
b. & c. Applied and industrial-organizational psychologists tackle practical problems.
d. Clinical psychologists (and researchers) focus on treating troubled people.

12. **c.** is the answer.
d. Psychiatrists are medical doctors rather than psychologists.

13. **a.** is the answer.
c. & d. Psychologists are widely involved in *both* basic and applied research.

14. **d.** is the answer.

15. **d.** is the answer.

16. **c.** is the answer. Exercise is the variable being manipulated in the experiment.
a. A control condition for this experiment would be a group of people not permitted to exercise.
b. A confounding variable is a variable other than those being manipulated that may influence behavior.
d. The dependent variable is the behavior measured by the experimenter—in this case, the effects of exercise.

17. **c.** is the answer. The control condition is that for which the experimental treatment (the new drug) is absent.
a. A random sample is a subset of a population in which every person has an equal chance of being selected.
b. In the experimental condition, the experimental treatment (the new drug) is present.
d. "Test group" is an ambiguous term; both the experimental and control group are tested.

18. **d.** is the answer.
a. Hypotheses are testable propositions.
b. Dependent variables are factors that may change in response to manipulated independent variables.
c. Statistical indexes may be used to test specific hypotheses (and therefore as indirect tests of theories), but they are merely mathematical tools, not general principles, as are theories.

19. **d.** is the answer. In this case, the children are being observed in their normal environment rather than in a laboratory.
a. Correlational research measures relationships between two factors. The psychologist may later want to determine whether there are correlations between the variables studied under natural conditions.
b. In a case study, one subject is studied in depth.
c. This is not an experiment because the psychologist is not directly controlling the variables being studied.

20. **d.** is the answer.

21. **d.** is the answer.

22. **b.** is the answer. Replication is the repetition of an experiment to determine whether its findings are reliable. It is not a research method.

23. **c.** is the answer.
a., b., & d. Psychologists' personal values can influence all of these.

24. **b.** is the answer.
a. & c. These answers would have been correct had the question stated that there is a *positive* correlation between shoe size and IQ. Actually, there is probably no correlation at all!

25. **d.** is the answer. In an experiment, it would be possible to manipulate alcohol consumption and observe the effects, if any, on memory.
a., b., & c. These answers are incorrect because only by directly controlling the variables of interest can a researcher uncover cause-effect relationships.

26. **d.** is the answer.
a. A sample is a subset of a population.
b. & c. Control and experimental groups are used in experimentation, not in survey research.

27. **d.** is the answer.
a. In an experiment, a placebo effect means that results were achieved by expectation alone.
b. In a double-blind procedure, neither the experimenter nor the participants know who has received the treatment of interest.
c. This is the tendency to believe, after learning an outcome, that one could have foreseen it.

28. a. is the answer.
b. Wilhelm Wundt established the first psychology laboratory in 1879.
c. William James established the school of functionalism.
d. Mary Whiton Calkins was a student of James and the first woman president of APA.

Matching Items

1. f	7. a	13. d	19. r
2. b	8. t	14. h	20. g
3. o	9. m	15. k	
4. j	10. c	16. p	
5. n	11. i	17. s	
6. e	12. l	18. q	

Progress Test 2

Multiple-Choice Questions

1. **a.** is the answer.

2. **a.** is the answer.
b. & d. John Watson, like many American psychologists during this time, believed that psychology should focus on the study of observable behavior.
c. Because he pioneered the study of learning, Pavlov focused on observable behavior and would certainly have *disagreed* with this statement.

3. **b.** is the answer.

4. **d.** is the answer.

5. **a.** is the answer.
b. Psychology is equally involved in basic research.
c. Psychology's knowledge base is constantly expanding.
d. Psychology is the *scientific study* of behavior and mental processes.

6. **c.** is the answer.

7. **b.** is the answer.
a. Aristotle believed that all knowledge originates with sensory experience.
c. René Descartes was a 17th century philosopher.
d. Simonides was a well-known Greek orator.

8. **d.** is the answer.
a. The neuroscience perspective studies the biological bases for a range of psychological phenomena.
b. The evolutionary perspective studies how natural selection favors traits that promote the perpetuation of one's genes.

c. The social-cultural perspective is concerned with variations in behavior across situations and cultures.

9. **c.** is the answer. After earning their MD degrees, psychiatrists specialize in the diagnosis and treatment of mental health disorders.
a., b., & d. These psychologists generally earn a Ph.D. rather than an MD.

10. **d.** is the answer. The emphasis on change during the life span indicates that Dr. Jones is most likely a developmental psychologist.
a. Clinical psychologists study, assess, and treat people who are psychologically troubled.
b. Personality psychologists study our inner traits.
c. Psychiatrists are medical doctors.

11. **c.** is the answer.
a. Clinical psychologists study, assess, and treat people with psychological disorders.
b. & d. Personality psychologists and psychiatrists do not usually study people in work situations.

12. **c.** is the answer.
a. Psychologists who follow the behavioral perspective emphasize observable, external influences on behavior.
b. The evolutionary perspective focuses on how natural selection favors traits that promote the perpetuation of one's genes.
d. The cognitive perspective places emphasis on conscious, rather than unconscious, processes.

13. **a.** is the answer.

14. **a.** is the answer. The research is addressing a practical issue.
b. Basic research is aimed at contributing to the base of knowledge in a given field, not at resolving particular practical problems.
c. & d. Clinical and developmental research would focus on issues relating to psychological disorders and life-span changes, respectively.

15. **a.** is the answer.
b. & c. Although each of these is true, SQ3R is based on the more *general* principle of active learning.
d. In fact, just the opposite is true.

16. **a.** is the answer.
b. & c. The biopsychosocial approach has nothing to do with the relative importance of basic research and applied research and is equally applicable to both.
d. On the contrary, the biopsychosocial approach is based on the idea that single academic perspectives are often limited.

17. **d.** is the answer. Only experiments can reveal cause-effect relationships; the other methods can only *describe* relationships.

18. **d.** is the answer.
a. & b. The double-blind procedure is one way to create experimental and control groups.
c. Research participants are randomly assigned to either an experimental or a control group.

19. **b.** is the answer. Just the opposite is true. Cultures differ in their views about valuing human well-being over animal well-being.

20. **d.** is the answer.
a. In the control condition, which involves the comparison group, the experimental treatment (the treatment of interest) is absent.
b. Memory is a directly observed and measured dependent variable in this experiment.
c. Attention is the independent variable, which is being manipulated.

21. **b.** is the answer.
a. The phenomenon is related to hindsight rather than foresight.
c. & d. The phenomenon doesn't involve whether the intuitions are correct but rather people's attitude that they had the correct intuition.

22. **b.** is the answer. If enough participants are used in an experiment and they are randomly assigned to the two groups, any differences that emerge between the groups should stem from the experiment itself.
a., c., & d. None of these terms describes precautions taken in setting up groups for experiments.

23. **b.** is the answer.

24. **a.** is the answer.
b. & c. Large, random samples are more likely to be representative of the populations from which they are drawn.

25. **d.** is the answer. Because we are sensitive to dramatic or unusual events, we are especially likely to perceive a relationship between them.
a., b., & c. The relationship between vivid events is no more likely to be significant, positive, or negative than that between less dramatic events.

26. **b.** is the answer.
a. In fact, the artificiality of experiments is part of an intentional attempt to create a controlled environment in which to test theoretical principles that are applicable to all behaviors.
c. Some psychological theories go against what we consider common sense; furthermore, on many issues that psychology addresses, it's far from clear what the "common sense" position is.

d. Psychology has always had ties to other disciplines, and in recent times, these ties have been increasing.

27. **d.** is the answer. Correlations show how well one factor can be predicted from another.
a. Because a case study focuses in great detail on the behavior of an individual, it's probably not useful in showing whether predictions are possible.
b. Naturalistic observation is a method of describing, rather than predicting, behavior.
c. In experimental research the effects of manipulated independent variables on dependent variables are measured. It is not clear how an experiment could help determine whether students' grades predict later income.

28. **b.** is the answer. The control condition is the one in which the treatment—in this case, pollution—is absent.
a. Students in the polluted room would be in the experimental condition.
c. Presumably, all students in both conditions were randomly assigned to their groups. Random assignment is a method for establishing groups, rather than a condition.
d. The word *dependent* refers to a kind of variable in experiments; conditions are either experimental or control.

True–False Items

1. F	5. F	9. T
2. F	6. F	
3. T	7. T	
4. T	8. F	

Matching Items

1. e	5. j	9. f	13. n
2. h	6. m	10. g	14. d
3. b	7. a	11. i	
4. c	8. k	12. l	

Essay Questions

1. A psychologist working from the neuroscience perspective might study the brain circuits and body chemistry that trigger attraction and sexual arousal. A psychologist working from the evolutionary perspective might analyze how love has facilitated the survival of our species. A psychologist working from the behavior genetics perspective might attempt to compare the extent to which the emotion is attributable to our genes and the extent to which it is attributable to our environment. A psychologist working from the psycho-

dynamic perspective might search for evidence that a person's particular emotional feelings are disguised effects of unfulfilled wishes. A psychologist working from the behavioral perspective might study the external stimuli, such as body language, that elicit and reward approach behaviors toward another person. A psychologist working from the cognitive perspective might study how our thought processes, attitudes, and beliefs foster attachment to loved ones, and a psychologist working from the social-cultural perspective might explore situational influences on attraction and how the development and expression of love vary across cultural groups.

2. Elio's hypothesis is that daily aerobic exercise for one month will improve memory. Exercise is the independent variable. The dependent variable is memory. Exercise could be manipulated by having people in an experimental group jog for 30 minutes each day. Memory could be measured by comparing the number of words they recall from a test list studied before the exercise experiment begins, and again afterward. A control group that does not exercise *is* needed so that any improvement in the experimental group's memory can be attributed to exercise, and not to some other factor, such as the passage of one month's time or familiarity with the memory test. The control group should engage in some nonexercise activity for the same amount of time each day that the experimental group exercises. The participants should be randomly selected from the population at large, and then randomly assigned to the experimental and control groups.

Terms and Concepts to Remember

1. **Structuralism** was an early school of thought promoted by Wilhelm Wundt and Edward Titchener; used introspection to reveal the structure of the human mind.

2. **Functionalism** was an early school of thought promoted by William James and influenced by Charles Darwin; explored how mental and behavioral processes function—how they enable the organism to adapt, survive, and flourish.

3. **Behaviorism** is the view that psychology should focus only on the scientific study of observable behaviors without reference to mental processes.

4. **Humanistic psychology** is a historically significant perspective that emphasized the growth potential of healthy people.

5. **Cognitive neuroscience** is the interdisciplinary study of how brain activity is linked with cognition (including thinking, language, memory, and perception).

6. **Psychology** is the science of behavior and mental processes.

7. The **nature–nurture issue** is the longstanding controversy over the relative contributions that genes (nature) and experience (nurture) make to the development of psychological traits and behaviors.

8. **Natural selection** is the principles that those traits of a species that contribute to reproduction and survival are most likely to be passed on to succeeding generations.

9. Psychologists analyze behavior and mental processes from differing complementary views, or **levels of analysis,** from biological to psychological to social-cultural.

10. The **biopsychosocial approach** is an integrated approach that focuses on biological, psychological, and social-cultural levels of analysis for a given behavior or mental process.

11. **Basic research** is pure science that aims to increase psychology's scientific knowledge base rather than to solve practical problems.

12. **Applied research** is scientific study that aims to solve practical problems.

13. **Counseling psychology** is the branch of psychology that helps people with challenges in their daily lives and in achieving greater well-being.

14. **Clinical psychology** is the branch of psychology concerned with the study, assessment, and treatment of people with psychological disorders.

15. **Psychiatry** is the branch of medicine concerned with the physical diagnosis and treatment of psychological disorders.

16. **Positive psychology** is the scientific study of the strengths and virtues of human functioning that help people and communities thrive.

17. **Hindsight bias** refers to the tendency to believe, after learning an outcome, that one would have foreseen it; also called the *I-knew-it-all-along phenomenon.*

18. **Critical thinking** is careful reasoning that examines assumptions, discerns hidden values, evaluates evidence, and assesses conclusions.

19. A **theory** is an explanation using an integrated set of principles that organizes observations and predicts behaviors or events.

20. A **hypothesis** is a testable prediction, often implied by a theory. Testing the hypothesis helps scientists to test the theory.

    Example: To test his theory of why people conform, Solomon Asch formulated the testable **hypothesis** that an individual would be more likely to go along with the majority opinion of a large group than with that of a smaller group.

21. An **operational definition** is a precise statement of the procedures (operations) used to define research variables.

22. **Replication** is the process of repeating the essence of a research study, often with different participants and in different situations, to see whether the basic finding generalizes to other people and circumstances.

23. The **case study** is an observation technique in which one person is studied in great depth in the hope of revealing universal principles.

24. **Naturalistic observation** involves observing and recording behavior in naturally occurring situations without trying to manipulate and control the situation.

25. The **survey** is a technique for ascertaining the self-reported attitudes or behaviors of a representative, random sample of people.

26. A **population** consists of all the members of a group being studied.

27. A **random sample** is one that is representative because every member of the population has an equal chance of being included.

28. **Correlation** is a measure of the extent to which two factors vary together, and thus of how well either factor predicts the other.

29. The **correlation coefficient** is a statistical measure of the relationship between two things. It can be positive or negative (from –1 to +1).

    Example: If there is a positive correlation between air temperature and ice cream sales, the warmer (higher) it is, the more ice cream is sold. If there is a negative correlation between air temperature and sales of cocoa, the cooler (lower) it is, the more cocoa is sold.

30. An **experiment** is a research method in which a researcher directly manipulates one or more factors (independent variables) to observe the effect on some behavior or mental process (the dependent variable); experiments therefore make it possible to establish cause-effect relationships.

31. The **experimental group** in an experiment is one in which participants are exposed to the independent variable being studied.

    Example: In the study of the effects of a new drug on reaction time, participants in the **experimental group** would actually receive the drug being tested.

32. The **control group** in an experiment is one in which the treatment of interest, or independent variable, is withheld so that comparison to the experimental group can be made.

    Example: The **control group** in an experiment testing the effects of a new drug on reaction time would be a group of participants given a placebo (inactive drug or sugar pill) instead of the drug being tested.

33. **Random assignment** is the procedure of assigning participants to the experimental and control groups by chance, thus minimizing preexisting differences between those assigned to the different groups.

34. A **double-blind procedure** is an experimental procedure in which both the experimenter and the research participants are ignorant (blind) about whether the research participants have received the treatment or a placebo. It is used to prevent experimenters' and participants' expectations from influencing the results of an experiment.

35. The **placebo effect** occurs when the results of an experiment are caused by expectations alone.

36. The **independent variable** of an experiment is the factor being manipulated and tested by the investigator.

    Example: In the study of the effects of a new drug on reaction time, the drug is the **independent variable**.

37. In an experiment, a **confounding variable** is a factor other than the independent variable that might influence the results.

38. The **dependent variable** of an experiment is the factor being measured by the investigator, that is, the factor that may change in response to manipulations of the independent variable.

    Example: In the study of the effects of a new drug on reaction time, the participants' reaction time is the **dependent variable.**

39. **Culture** is the enduring behaviors, ideas, attitudes, values, and traditions shared by a group of people and transmitted from one generation to the next.

40. **Informed consent** is the ethical practice of giving research participants enough information to enable them to choose whether they wish to take part in a study.

41. **Debriefing** is the ethical practice of explaining a study, including its purpose and any deceptions, to participants after they have finished.

42. The **testing effect** (also called the *retrieval practice effect* or *test-enhanced learning*) refers to the beneficial effects on memory of actively retrieving, rather than simply reading, information.

43. **SQ3R** is a study method consisting of five steps: *s*urvey, *q*uestion, *r*ead, *r*etrieve, and *r*eview.

Cross-Check

ACROSS
1. replication
7. theory
11. case study
12. placebo
14. survey
15. correlation

DOWN
2. experimental
3. independent
4. naturalistic
5. operational
6. critical thinking
8. hindsight
9. double-blind
10. hypothesis
13. control
16. random

The Biology of Behavior

Chapter Overview

Chapter 2 is concerned with the functions of the brain and its component neural systems, which provide the basis for all human behavior. Under the direction of the brain, the nervous and endocrine systems coordinate a variety of voluntary and involuntary behaviors and serve as the body's mechanisms for communication with the external environment.

The brain consists of the brainstem, the thalamus, the cerebellum, the limbic system, and the cerebral cortex. Knowledge of the workings of the brain has increased with advances in neuroscientific methods. Studies of split-brain patients have also given researchers a great deal of information about the specialized functions of the brain's right and left hemispheres.

Chapter 2 also explores the field of behavior genetics, which studies twins and adopted children to weigh genetic and environmental influences on behaviors. The next section discusses psychology's use of evolutionary principles to answer universal questions about human behavior.

NOTE: Answer guidelines for all Chapter 2 questions begin on page 49.

Chapter Review

First, skim each section, noting headings and bold-face items. After you have read the section, review each objective by answering the fill-in and essay-type questions that follow it. In some cases, Study Tips explain how best to learn a difficult concept and Applications help you to know how well you understand the material. As you proceed, evaluate your performance by consulting the answers beginning on page 49. Do not continue with the next section until you understand each answer. If you need to, review the section in the textbook before continuing.

Biology and Behavior

Objective 2-1: Explain why psychologists are concerned with human biology.

1. In the most basic sense, every idea, mood, memory, and behavior that an individual has ever experienced is a _____ phenomenon.

2. Researchers who study the links between biology and behavior are referred to as

   _____ _____ .

STUDY TIP: Many students find the technical material in this chapter difficult to master. Not only are there many terms for you to remember, but you must also know the organization and function of the various divisions of the nervous system. Learning this material will require a great deal of active processing, testing yourself frequently to be sure you know and understand the many structures and their functions. Working the chapter review several times, drawing and labeling brain diagrams, making flash cards, and mentally defining the terms are all useful techniques for learning this type of material.

APPLICATION:

3. A biological psychologist would be more likely to study
   a. how you learn to express emotions.
   b. how to help people overcome emotional disorders.
   c. life-span changes in the expression of emotion.
   d. the chemical changes that accompany emotions.

Neural Communication

Objective 2-2: Describe the parts of a neuron, and explain how neurons transmit information.

4. Our body's neural system is built from billions of nerve cells, or _____ .

5. The extensions of a neuron that receive messages from other neurons are the _____ . The extension of a neuron that transmits information to other neurons is the _____ . Some of these extensions are insulated by a fatty tissue called the _____ _____ , which helps speed the neuron's impulses.

6. Identify the major parts of the neuron diagrammed below.

a. _____   c. _____
b. _____   d. _____

7. The cells that support, protect, and nourish neurons are called _____ _____ . These cells may also play a role in _____ and _____ .

8. The neural impulse, or _____ _____ , is a brief electrical charge that travels down a(n) _____ .

9. The fluid interior of a resting axon carries mostly _____ (positively/negatively) charged ions, while the fluid outside has mostly _____ (positively/negatively) charged ions.

10. An action potential occurs when the first part of the axon opens its gates and _____ (positively/negatively) charged sodium ions rush in, causing that part of the neuron to become _____ . During the resting pause following an action potential, the neuron pumps _____ (positively/negatively) charged potassium ions back outside the cell.

11. To trigger a neural impulse, _____ signals minus _____ signals must exceed a certain intensity, called the _____ . Increasing a stimulus above this level _____ (will/will not) increase the neural impulse's intensity. This phenomenon is called an _____-_____-_____ response.

12. The strength of a stimulus _____ (does/does not) affect the intensity of a neural impulse. A strong stimulus _____ (can/cannot) trigger more neurons to fire and to fire more often.

Objective 2-3: Describe how nerve cells communicate with other nerve cells.

13. The junction between two neurons is called a _____ , and the gap is called the _____ _____ . This discovery was made by _____ .

14. The chemical messengers that convey information across the gaps between neurons are called _____ . These chemicals bind to receptor sites and unlock tiny channels, allowing electrically charged _____ to enter the neuron.

15. Neurotransmitters influence neurons either by _____ or _____ their readiness to fire. Excess neurotransmitters are reabsorbed by the sending neuron in a process called _____ .

Outline the sequence of reactions that occur when a neural impulse is generated and transmitted from one neuron to another.

Objective 2-4: Describe how neurotransmitters influence behavior.

16. A neurotransmitter that is important in muscle contraction is _____ ; it is also important in learning and _____ .

17. Naturally occurring opiate-like neurotransmitters that are present in the brain are called _____ . When the brain is flooded with drugs such as _____ or _____ , it may stop producing these neurotransmitters.

STUDY TIP: To understand the relationships among excitatory and inhibitory synapses, threshold, and the all-or-none response, you should think of the neuron as a simple switch that is always either "on" or "off." This "all-or-none" response is in contrast to the graded, "partially on" response of the more complex dimmer switch. Whether the all-or-none response occurs depends on whether the input to the neuron is sufficient to allow it to reach its threshold—much as a simple light switch requires a certain amount of force to operate. In the neuron's case, the "force" refers to the combination of excitatory inputs (which promote a response) and inhibitory inputs (which promote the neuron's remaining in its resting state).

APPLICATIONS:

18. Several shy neurons send an inhibitory message to neighboring neuron Joni. At the same time, a larger group of party-going neurons sends Joni excitatory messages. What will Joni do?
    a. fire, assuming that her threshold has been reached
    b. not fire, even if her threshold has been reached
    c. pause to rest
    d. become hyperpolarized

19. I am a relatively fast-acting chemical messenger that influences muscle action, learning, and memory. What am I?
    a. dopamine   c. acetylcholine
    b. a hormone   d. glutamate

20. Since Malcolm has been taking a drug prescribed by his doctor, he no longer enjoys the little pleasures of life, such as eating and drinking. His doctor explains that this is because the drug
    a. triggers release of serotonin.
    b. inhibits release of serotonin.
    c. triggers release of ACh.
    d. inhibits release of ACh.

21. Lolita is feeling depressed for no particular reason. It is possible that she has an undersupply of _____ .

22. Punjab had lunch at the local Chinese restaurant. Afterward, he suffered a migraine, most likely caused by an _____ of _____ .

The Nervous System

Objective 2-5: Describe the functions of the nervous system's main divisions, and identify the three main types of neurons.

23. Taken altogether, the neurons of the body form the _____ _____ .

24. The brain and spinal cord form the _____ nervous system. The neurons that link the brain and spinal cord to the rest of the body form the _____ nervous system.

25. Axons are bundled into electrical cables called _____ , which link the CNS with muscles, glands, and sense organs. Information arriving in the brain and spinal cord from the body's tissues and sensory receptors travels in _____ neurons. Instructions from the brain and spinal cord are sent to the body's tissues via _____ neurons. The neurons that enable internal communication within the brain and spinal cord are called _____ .

26. The division of the peripheral nervous system that enables voluntary control of the skeletal muscles is the _____ nervous system.

27. Involuntary, self-regulating responses—those of the glands and muscles of internal organs—are controlled by the _____ nervous system.

28. The body is made ready for action by the _____ division of the autonomic nervous system.

29. The _____ division of the autonomic nervous system produces relaxation. The two divisions of the peripheral nervous system work together to maintain the steady internal state called _____ .

Describe and explain the sequence of physical reactions that occur in the body as an emergency is confronted and then passes.

30. The brain's neurons cluster into work groups called _____ _____ .

31. Automatic responses to stimuli, called _____ , illustrate the work of the _____ _____ . Simple pathways such as these are involved in the _____-_____ response and in the _____ reflex.

Beginning with the sensory receptors in the skin, trace the course of a spinal reflex as a person reflexively jerks his or her hand away from an unexpectedly hot burner on a stove.

STUDY TIP: To keep the various functions of the peripheral nervous system (PNS) straight, remember that the PNS consists of two main divisions: somatic and autonomic. The somatic ("S") division primarily regulates "S functions," such as the *senses* and *skeletal* muscles. The autonomic ("A") division regulates *automatic* ("A") physical systems that do not require conscious attention. These include breathing, heart rate, and digestion, to name a few.

APPLICATIONS:

32. You are sitting at your desk at home, studying for an exam. No one else is home, but you hear creaking floorboards. You sneak downstairs, only to discover your parents have returned home early. Describe and explain the sequence of phys-

ical reactions that occurred in your body as you felt fear and then relief.

33. You are able to pull your hand quickly away from hot water before pain is felt because
    a. movement of the hand is a reflex that involves intervention of the spinal cord only.
    b. movement of the hand does not require intervention by the central nervous system.
    c. the brain reacts quickly to prevent severe injury.
    d. the autonomic division of the peripheral nervous system intervenes to speed contraction of the muscles of the hand.

34. Following Jayshree's near-fatal car accident, her physician noticed that the pupillary reflex of her eyes was abnormal. This MAY indicate that Jayshree's _____ _____ _____ was damaged in the accident.

35. Your brother has been taking prescription medicine and experiencing a number of unpleasant side effects, including unusually rapid heartbeat and excessive perspiration. It is likely that the medicine is exaggerating activity in the
    a. central nervous system.
    b. sympathetic nervous system.
    c. parasympathetic nervous system.
    d. somatic nervous system.

The Endocrine System

Objective 2-6: Describe how the endocrine system transmits information and how it interacts with the nervous system.

36. The body's chemical communication network is called the _____ _____ . This system transmits information through chemical messengers called _____ at a much _____ (faster/slower) rate than the nervous system, and its effects last _____ (a longer time/a shorter time).

37. In a moment of danger, the autonomic nervous system orders the _____ glands to release _____ and _____ . These hormones increase _____ _____ , _____ _____ , and _____ _____ .

38. The most influential gland is the

_____ , which, under the control of an adjacent brain area called the

_____ , helps regulate

_____ and the release of hormones by other endocrine glands. The hormone

_____ enables contractions associated with birthing, milk flow during nursing, and orgasm. It also promotes _____

_____ .

Write a paragraph describing the feedback system that links the nervous and endocrine systems.

APPLICATIONS:

39. I am a relatively slow-acting (but long-lasting) chemical messenger carried throughout the body by the bloodstream. What am I?

a. a hormone   c. acetylcholine
b. a neurotransmitter   d. dopamine

40. A bodybuilder friend suddenly seems to have grown several inches in height. You suspect that your friend's growth spurt has occurred because he has been using drugs that affect the

a. pituitary gland.   c. adrenal glands.
b. pancreas.   d. parathyroids.

The Brain

Objective 2-7: Describe how neuroscientists study the brain's connections to behavior and mind.

41. Researchers sometimes study brain function by producing _____ or by selectively destroying brain cells. The oldest technique for studying the brain involves _____

_____ of patients with brain injuries or diseases.

42. (Close-Up) The _____ is an amplified recording of the waves of electrical activity that sweep across the brain's surface.

43. (Close-Up) The technique depicting the level of activity of brain areas by measuring the brain's consumption of glucose is called the

_____ _____ .

Briefly explain the purpose of the PET scan.

44. (Close-Up) A technique that produces clearer images of the brain (and other body parts) by using magnetic fields and radio waves is known as _____ .

45. (Close-Up) By comparing scans taken less than a second apart, the _____ _____ detects oxygen-laden bloodflow to the part of the brain thought to control the bodily activity being studied. Using this technique, researchers found that bloodflow to the back of the brain _____ (increases/decreases) when people view a scene because that is where _____ information is processed.

STUDY TIP/APPLICATIONS: To help keep the various research methods for studying the brain straight, think of the methods as falling into two categories: (1) those that measure ongoing electrical or metabolic brain activity in real time (EEG, PET scan, fMRI) and (2) those that merely provide a momentary picture of the brain's anatomical structure (MRI).

46. a. Which method would be most useful to a neurologist attempting to locate a tumor in a patient's brain?

_____

b. Which method would be most useful to a researcher attempting to pinpoint the area of the brain that is most critical to speaking aloud?

_____

c. What are some other instances when a researcher would be best advised to use methods that give a picture of the brain's structure?

d. What are some other instances when a researcher would be best advised to use methods that measure brain activity?

Objective 2-8: Identify the components of the brainstem, and describe the functions of the brainstem, thalamus, and cerebellum.

47. The oldest and innermost region of the brain is the _____ .

48. At the base of the brainstem, where the spinal cord enters the skull, lies the _____ , which controls _____ and _____ . Just above this part is the _____ , which helps coordinate movements.

49. Nerves from each side of the brain cross over to connect with the body's opposite side in the _____ .

50. At the top of the brainstem sits the _____ , which serves as the brain's sensory router, receiving information from all the senses except _____ and routing it to the regions dealing with those senses. These egg-shaped structures also receive replies from the higher regions, which they direct to the _____ and to the _____ .

51. The finger-shaped network of neurons, the _____ _____ , is contained inside the brainstem and plays an important role in controlling _____ . Electrically stimulating this area will produce an _____ animal. Lesioning this area will cause an animal to lapse into a _____ .

52. At the rear of the brainstem lies the _____ . It influences one type of _____ _____ and memory. It also helps us judge time, modulate our _____ , and discriminate

sounds and textures; and it coordinates voluntary movement and _____ control.

53. The lower brain functions occur without _____ effort, indicating that our brains process most information _____ (inside/outside) of our awareness.

Objective 2-9: Describe the structures and functions of the limbic system.

54. Between the brainstem and cerebral hemispheres is the _____ system. One component of this system that processes conscious memories is the _____ (see a in drawing).

55. Aggression or fear will result from stimulation of different regions of the lima-bean-sized neural clusters, the _____ (see b).

56. We must remember, however, that the brain _____ (is/is not) neatly organized into structures that correspond to our categories of behavior. For example, aggressive behavior _____ (does/does not) involve neural activity in many brain levels.

57. Below the thalamus is the _____ (c), which regulates bodily maintenance behaviors such as _____ , _____ , _____ _____ , and _____ behavior, thus helping to maintain a steady (_____) internal state. This area also regulates behavior by secreting _____ that enable it to control the _____ gland. Olds and Milner discovered that this region also contains _____ centers, which animals will work hard to have stimulated. More recently, researchers have discovered other

such centers in the _____

_____ .

58. Some researchers believe that substance use disorders, binge eating, and other _____ disorders may stem from a genetic _____

_____ _____

in the natural brain systems for pleasure and well-being.

Objective 2-10: Describe the functions of the various regions of the cerebral cortex.

59. The most complex functions of human behavior are linked to the most developed part of the brain, the _____ _____ .
This thin layer of interconnected neural cells is the body's ultimate control and

_____-_____

center.

60. Compared with the cortexes of lower mammals, the human cortex has a _____ (smoother/more wrinkled) surface. This _____ (increases/decreases) the overall surface area of our brains.

61. Each hemisphere's cortex is subdivided into four lobes, separated by prominent _____ , or folds. List the four lobes of the brain.

   a. _____   c. _____

   b. _____   d. _____

62. Electrical stimulation of one side of the _____ cortex, an arch-shaped region at the back of the _____ lobe, will produce movement on the opposite side of the body. The more precise the control needed, the _____ (smaller/greater) amount of cortical space occupied.

63. Researchers believe that one day mind-reading computers may enable paralyzed people to control machines directly with their _____ . For example, recording electrodes implanted in the _____ _____ of a 25-year-old man's brain have enabled him to mentally control a TV, draw shapes on a screen, and play video games.

64. At the front of the parietal lobes lies the _____ cortex, which, when stimulated, elicits a sensation of _____ . The more sensitive a body region, the greater the area of _____ _____ devoted to it.

65. Visual information is received in the _____ lobes, whereas auditory information is received in the _____ lobes.

66. Areas of the brain that don't receive sensory information or direct movement but, rather, integrate and interpret information received by other regions are known as _____ _____ . Approximately _____ of the human cortex is of this type. Such areas in the _____ lobe are involved in judging, planning, and processing of new memories and in some aspects of personality. In the _____ lobe, these areas enable mathematical and spatial reasoning, and an area of the _____ lobe enables us to recognize faces.

67. Although the mind's subsystems are localized in particular brain regions, the brain _____ (does/does not) act as a unified whole.

APPLICATION:

68. In the diagrams to the right, the numbers refer to brain locations that have been damaged. Match each location with its probable effect on behavior.

Location		*Behavioral Effect*
_____ 1.		**a.** vision disorder
_____ 2.		**b.** insensitivity to touch
_____ 3.		**c.** motor paralysis
_____ 4.		**d.** hearing problem
_____ 5.		**e.** lack of coordination
_____ 6.		**f.** abnormal hunger
_____ 7.		**g.** split brain
_____ 8.		**h.** sleep/arousal
_____ 9.		disorder
		i. altered personality

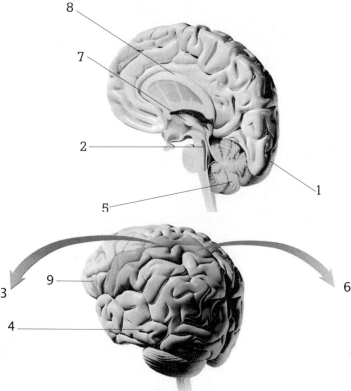

Objective 2-11: Discuss the brain's ability to reorganize itself, and define *neurogenesis*.

69. The quality of the brain that makes it possible for undamaged brain areas to take over the functions of damaged regions is known as _____ . This quality is especially apparent in the brains of _____ (young children/adolescents/adults).

70. Although severed neurons usually _____ (will/will not) regenerate, some neural tissue can _____ in response to damage. New evidence suggests that adult mice, birds, monkeys, and humans _____ (can/cannot) generate new brain cells through a process called _____ . Research also reveals the existence of master _____ cells in the human embryo that can develop into any type of brain cell.

Objective 2-12: Explain how split-brain research helps us understand the functions of our two brain hemispheres.

71. The brain's two sides serve differing functions, which is referred to as hemispheric specialization, or _____ . Because damage to the _____ hemisphere will impair such important functions as reading, writing, speaking, arithmetic reasoning, and understanding, the _____ hemisphere was thought to be a subordinate or minor hemisphere.

72. In treating several patients with severe epilepsy, Philip Vogel and Joseph Bogen separated the two hemispheres of the brain by cutting the _____ _____ . When this structure is severed, the result is referred to as a _____ _____ .

73. In a split-brain patient, only the _____ hemisphere will be aware of an unseen object held in the left hand. In this case, the person would not be able to

_____ the object. When different words are shown in the left and right visual fields, if the patient fixates on a point on the center line between the fields, the patient will be able to say only the word shown on the

_____ .

Explain why a split-brain patient would be able to read aloud the word _pencil_ flashed to his or her right visual field, but would be unable to identify a _pencil_ by touch using only the left hand.

74. When the "two minds" of a split brain are at odds, the _____ hemisphere tries to rationalize what it doesn't understand. The _____ hemisphere often acts on autopilot. This phenomenon demonstrates that the _____ mind _____ (can/cannot) control our behavior.

75. Deaf people use the _____ hemisphere to process sign language.

76. Although the _____ hemisphere is better at making literal interpretations of language, the _____ hemisphere excels in making inferences, modulating our _____ , orchestrating our sense of _____ , and perceiving objects.

APPLICATIONS:

77. The part of the human brain that is most like that of a fish is the
   a. cortex.
   b. limbic system.
   c. brainstem.
   d. right hemisphere.

78. To pinpoint the location of a tumor, a neurosurgeon electrically stimulated parts of the patient's sensory cortex. If the patient was conscious during the procedure, which of the following was probably experienced?
   a. "hearing" faint sounds
   b. "seeing" random visual patterns
   c. movement of the arms or legs
   d. a sense of having the skin touched

79. If Dr. Rogers wishes to conduct an experiment on the effects of stimulating the reward centers of a rat's brain, he should insert an electrode into the
   a. thalamus.
   b. sensory cortex.
   c. hypothalamus.
   d. corpus callosum.

80. A split-brain patient has a picture of a knife flashed to her left hemisphere and that of a fork to her right hemisphere. She will be able to
   a. identify the fork using her left hand.
   b. identify a knife using her left hand.
   c. identify a knife using either hand.
   d. identify a fork using either hand.

81. Anton is applying for a technician's job with a neurosurgeon. In trying to impress his potential employer with his knowledge of the brain, he says, "After my father's stroke I knew immediately that the blood clot had affected his left cerebral hemisphere because he no longer recognized his friend." Should Anton be hired?
   a. Yes. Anton obviously understands brain structure and function.
   b. No. The right hemisphere, not the left, specializes in facial recognition.
   c. Yes. Although blood clots never form in the left hemisphere, Anton should be rewarded for recognizing the left hemisphere's role in facial recognition.
   d. No. Blood clots never form in the left hemisphere, and the right hemisphere is more involved than the left in recognizing faces.

82. Dr. Johnson briefly flashed a picture of a key in the right visual field of a split-brain patient. The patient could probably
   a. verbally report that a key was seen.
   b. write the word key using the left hand.
   c. draw a picture of a key using the left hand.
   d. do none of these things.

83. In primitive vertebrate animals, the brain primarily regulates _____ ; in lower mammals, the brain enables _____ .
   a. emotion; memory
   b. memory; emotion
   c. survival functions; emotion
   d. reproduction; emotion

84. A scientist from another planet wishes to study the simplest brain mechanisms underlying emotion and memory. You recommend that the scientist study the
   a. brainstem of a frog.
   b. limbic system of a dog.
   c. cortex of a monkey.
   d. cortex of a human.

85. Dr. Frankenstein made a mistake during neuro-surgery on his monster. After the operation, the monster "saw" with his ears and "heard" with his eyes. It is likely that Dr. Frankenstein "rewired" neural connections in the monster's

   a. hypothalamus.   **c.** amygdala.
   b. cerebellum.   **d.** thalamus.

86. Raccoons have much more precise control of their paws than dogs. You would expect that raccoons have more cortical space dedicated to "paw control" in the _____ of their brains.

   a. frontal lobes   **c.** temporal lobes
   b. parietal lobes   **d.** occipital lobes

Behavior Genetics: Predicting Individual Differences

Objective 2-13: Define *genes*, and describe how behavior geneticists explain our individual differences.

87. The term environment refers to every _____ influence.

88. Researchers who specifically study genetic and environmental influences on behavior are called

   _____ _____ .

89. The master plans for development are stored in the _____ . In number, each person inherits _____ of these structures, _____ from each parent. Each is composed of a coiled chain of the molecule

   _____ .

90. If chromosomes are the chapters of heredity, the words that make each of us a distinctive human being are called _____ .

91. Genes can either be _____ (active) or inactive. Genes are "turned on" by

   _____ _____ . When turned on, genes provide the code for creating

   _____ _____ , our body's building blocks.

STUDY TIP/APPLICATION: To keep the relationship among genes, DNA, and chromosomes straight, try thinking about them visually. Chromosomes are the largest of the units. They are made up of genes, which are in turn made up of DNA. Test your understanding by identifying the elements of heredity in the drawing in the next column. Note that c. is the unit that contains the code for proteins, and d. is the spiraling, complex molecule.

92. a. _____   c. _____
    b. _____   d. _____

93. To study the power and limits of genetic influences on behavior, researchers use _____ and _____ studies.

94. Twins who developed from a single (monozygotic) fertilized egg are genetically

   _____ . Twins who developed from different (dizygotic) fertilized eggs are no more genetically alike than siblings and are called _____ twins.

95. In terms of the personality traits of extraversion and neuroticism, identical twins are

   _____ (more/no more) alike than are fraternal twins.

96. Twin pairs reported _____ (being treated alike/being treated differently). However, their similarities _____ (could/could not) be attributed to how they were treated.

97. Through research on identical twins raised apart, psychologists are able to study the influence of the _____ .

98. Studies tend to show that the personalities of adopted children _____ (do/do not) closely resemble those of their adoptive parents. However, adoption studies show that parenting _____ (does/does not) matter. For example, many adopted children score _____ (higher/lower) than their biological parents on intelligence tests.

APPLICATIONS:

99. Despite growing up in the same home environment, Karen and her brother John have personalities as different from each other as two people selected randomly from the population.

    a. Personality is inherited. Because Karen and John are not identical twins, it is not surprising they have very different personalities.
    b. Gender is the most important factor in personality. If Karen had a sister, the two of them would probably be much more alike.
    c. The interaction of their individual genes and nonshared experiences accounts for the common finding that children in the same family are usually very different.
    d. Their case is unusual; children in the same family usually have similar personalities.

100. Dr. Gonzalez is conducting research on whether people who do well in school can thank their genes or their environment for their success. To distinguish how much genetic and environmental factors affect school success, Dr. Gonzalez should compare children with _____ (the same/different) genes and _____ (the same/different) environments.

101. My sibling and I developed from a single fertilized egg. Who are we?

    a. opposite-sex identical twins
    b. same-sex identical twins
    c. opposite-sex fraternal twins
    d. same-sex fraternal twins

Objective 2-14: Discuss the interaction of heredity and environment.

102. Many human traits are the result of both _____ and _____ influences.

103. Throughout life, we are the product of the _____ of our _____ predispositions and our _____ .

104. Environments trigger activity in _____ , and our genetically influenced traits evoke _____ in other people. This may explain why _____ twins recall greater variations in their early family life than do _____ twins.

105. The new field of _____ studies the _____ mechanisms by which

_____ trigger _____ expression.

Evolutionary Psychology: Understanding Human Nature

Objective 2-15: Describe evolutionary psychologists' use of natural selection to explain behavior tendencies.

106. Researchers who study natural selection and the adaptive nature of human behavior are called _____ _____ .

107. Researchers in this field focus mostly on what makes people so _____ (much alike/different from one another).

108. According to the principle of _____ _____ , traits that lead to increased reproduction and survival will be most likely to be passed on to succeeding generations.

109. Genetic _____ are random errors in genetic replication that lead to _____ .

110. Genetic constraints on human behavior are generally _____ (tighter/looser) than those on animal behavior. The human species' ability to _____ to different _____ contributes to our _____ , defined as our ability to _____ and _____ .

111. Because of our genetic legacy, we love the tastes of sweets and _____ , which we tend to _____ , even though famine is unlikely in industrialized societies.

Progress Test 1

Multiple-Choice Questions

Circle your answers to the following questions and check them with the answers beginning on page 52. If your answer is incorrect, read the explanation for why it is incorrect and then consult the text.

1. The axons of certain neurons are covered by a layer of fatty tissue that helps speed neural transmission. This tissue is

    a. dopamine.
    b. the myelin sheath.
    c. acetylcholine.
    d. an endorphin.

2. Heartbeat, digestion, and other self-regulating bodily functions are governed by the
   a. voluntary nervous system.
   b. autonomic nervous system.
   c. sympathetic division of the autonomic nervous system.
   d. somatic nervous system.

3. A strong stimulus can increase the
   a. speed of the impulse the neuron fires.
   b. intensity of the impulse the neuron fires.
   c. number of times the neuron fires.
   d. threshold that must be reached before the neuron fires.

4. The pain of heroin withdrawal may be attributable to the fact that
   a. under the influence of heroin the brain ceases production of endorphins.
   b. under the influence of heroin the brain ceases production of all neurotransmitters.
   c. during heroin withdrawal the brain's production of all neurotransmitters is greatly increased.
   d. heroin destroys endorphin receptors in the brain.

5. The brain research technique that involves monitoring the brain's usage of glucose is called (in abbreviated form) the
   a. PET scan.   c. EEG.
   b. fMRI.   d. MRI.

6. An evolutionary psychologist would be most interested in studying
   a. why most parents are so passionately devoted to their children.
   b. hereditary influences on skin color.
   c. why certain diseases are more common among certain age groups.
   d. genetic differences in personality.

7. Though there is no single "control center" for emotions, their regulation is primarily attributed to the brain region known as the
   a. limbic system.   c. brainstem.
   b. reticular formation. d. cerebellum.

8. Which is the correct sequence in the transmission of a simple reflex?
   a. sensory neuron, interneuron, sensory neuron
   b. interneuron, motor neuron, sensory neuron
   c. sensory neuron, interneuron, motor neuron

   d. interneuron, sensory neuron, motor neuron

9. In a resting state, the axon is
   a. depolarized, with mostly negatively charged ions outside and positively charged ions inside.
   b. depolarized, with mostly positively charged ions outside and negatively charged ions inside.
   c. polarized, with mostly negatively charged ions outside and positively charged ions inside.
   d. polarized, with mostly positively charged ions outside and negatively charged ions inside.

10. Which of the following is typically controlled by the right hemisphere?
    a. language
    b. learned voluntary movements
    c. arithmetic reasoning
    d. perceptual tasks

11. Dr. Hernandez is studying neurotransmitter abnormalities in depressed patients. She would most likely consider herself to be a _____ psychologist.
    a. personality   c. psychoanalytic
    b. psychodynamic   d. biological

12. The increasing complexity of animals' behavior is accompanied by an
    a. increase in the size of the brainstem.
    b. increase in the depth of the corpus callosum.
    c. increase in the size of the frontal lobes.
    d. increase in the amount of association area.

13. Voluntary movements, such as writing with a pencil, are directed by the
    a. sympathetic nervous system.
    b. somatic nervous system.
    c. parasympathetic nervous system.
    d. autonomic nervous system.

14. A neuron will generate action potentials when it
    a. remains below its threshold.
    b. receives an excitatory input.
    c. receives more excitatory than inhibitory inputs.
    d. is stimulated by a neurotransmitter.

15. Which is the correct sequence in the transmission of a neural impulse?
    a. axon, dendrite, cell body, synapse
    b. dendrite, axon, cell body, synapse

    c. synapse, axon, dendrite, cell body
    d. dendrite, cell body, axon, synapse

16. Chemical messengers produced by endocrine glands are called
    a. glia.
    b. neurotransmitters.
    c. hormones.
    d. enzymes.

17. Following a head injury, a person has ongoing difficulties staying awake. Most likely, the damage occurred to the
    a. thalamus.
    b. corpus callosum.
    c. reticular formation.
    d. cerebellum.

18. An experimenter flashes the word FLYTRAP onto a screen facing a split-brain patient so that FLY projects to her right hemisphere and TRAP to her left hemisphere. When asked what she saw, the patient will
    a. say she saw FLY.
    b. say she saw TRAP.
    c. point to FLY using her right hand.
    d. point to TRAP using her left hand.

19. Cortical areas that are not primarily concerned with sensory, motor, or language functions are
    a. called projection areas.
    b. called association areas.
    c. located mostly in the parietal lobe.
    d. located mostly in the temporal lobe.

20. In the brain, learning occurs as experience strengthens certain connections in cell work groups called
    a. action potentials.
    b. neural networks.
    c. endocrine systems.
    d. dendrites.

21. Unlike _____ twins, who develop from a single fertilized egg, _____ twins develop from separate fertilized eggs.
    a. fraternal; identical
    b. identical; fraternal
    c. placental; nonplacental
    d. nonplacental; placental

22. Several studies of long-separated identical twins have found that these twins
    a. have little in common because of the different environments in which they were raised.
    b. have many similarities, in everything from medical histories to personalities.
    c. have similar personalities, but very different likes, dislikes, and lifestyles.
    d. are no more similar than are fraternal twins reared apart.

23. Chromosomes are composed of a coiled chain of
    a. DNA molecules that contain genes.
    b. DNA molecules that contain neurotransmitters.
    c. DNA molecules that contain endorphins.
    d. DNA molecules that contain enzymes.

24. When the effect of one factor (such as environment) depends on another (such as heredity), we say there is a(n)_____ between the two factors.
    a. norm
    b. positive correlation
    c. negative correlation
    d. interaction

25. Most human traits are
    a. learned.
    b. determined by a single gene.
    c. influenced by many genes acting together.
    d. unpredictable.

Matching Items

Match each structure or technique with its corresponding function or description.

Structures

_____ **1.** hypothalamus
_____ **2.** lesion
_____ **3.** EEG
_____ **4.** fMRI
_____ **5.** reticular formation
_____ **6.** MRI
_____ **7.** thalamus
_____ **8.** corpus callosum
_____ **9.** cerebellum
_____ **10.** amygdala
_____ **11.** medulla
_____ **12.** DNA

Functions or Descriptions

a. amplified recording of brain waves
b. technique that uses radio waves and magnetic fields to image brain anatomy
c. serves as sensory switchboard
d. contains reward centers
e. tissue destruction
f. a complex molecule containing the genetic information that makes up the chromosomes
g. helps control arousal
h. links the cerebral hemispheres
i. influences rage and fear
j. regulates breathing and heartbeat
k. enables coordinated movement
l. technique that uses radio waves and magnetic fields to show brain function

Progress Test 2

Progress Test 2 should be completed during a final chapter review. Answer the following questions after you thoroughly understand the correct answers for the section reviews and Progress Test 1.

Multiple-Choice Questions

1. A researcher stimulates the area of the brain that receives visual information. She is stimulating the
  a. occipital lobe.   **c.** frontal lobe.
  b. temporal lobe.   **d.** parietal lobe.

2. Which of the following is typically controlled by the left hemisphere?
  a. making inferences
  b. word recognition
  c. the left side of the body
  d. perceptual skills

3. When Sandy scalded her toe in a tub of hot water, the pain message was carried to her spinal cord by the _____ nervous system.
  a. somatic   **c.** parasympathetic
  b. sympathetic   **d.** central

4. Which of the following are governed by the simplest neural pathways?
  a. emotions
  b. physiological drives, such as hunger
  c. reflexes
  d. movements, such as walking

5. Melissa has just completed running a marathon. She is so elated that she feels little fatigue or discomfort. Her lack of pain is probably the result of the release of
  a. ACh.   **c.** dopamine.
  b. endorphins.   **d.** norepinephrine.

6. If a fraternal twin develops schizophrenia, the likelihood of the other twin developing serious mental illness is much lower than with identical twins. This suggests that
  a. schizophrenia is caused by genes.
  b. schizophrenia is influenced by genes.
  c. environment is unimportant in the development of schizophrenia.
  d. identical twins are especially vulnerable to mental disorders.

7. The technique that uses magnetic fields and radio waves to produce computer images of structures within the brain is called
  a. the EEG.   **c.** a PET scan.
  b. a lesion.   **d.** MRI.

8. The myelin sheath that is on some neurons
  a. increases the speed of neural transmission.
  b. slows neural transmission.
  c. regulates the release of neurotransmitters.
  d. prevents positive ions from passing through the membrane.

9. I am a relatively fast-acting chemical messenger that affects mood, hunger, sleep, and arousal. What am I?
   a. acetylcholine
   b. dopamine
   c. norepinephrine
   d. serotonin

10. The neurotransmitter acetylcholine (ACh) is most likely to be found
    a. at the junction between sensory neurons and muscle fibers.
    b. at the junction between motor neurons and muscle fibers.
    c. at junctions between interneurons.
    d. in all of these locations.

11. The gland that regulates body growth is the
    a. adrenal.
    b. thyroid.
    c. hypothalamus.
    d. pituitary.

12. Epinephrine and norepinephrine are _____ that are released by the _____ gland.
    a. neurotransmitters; pituitary
    b. hormones; pituitary
    c. neurotransmitters; thyroid
    d. hormones; adrenal

13. Jessica experienced difficulty keeping her balance after receiving a blow to the back of her head. It is likely that she injured her
    a. medulla.
    b. thalamus.
    c. hypothalamus.
    d. cerebellum.

14. Moruzzi and Magoun caused a cat to lapse into a coma by severing neural connections between the cortex and the
    a. reticular formation.
    b. hypothalamus.
    c. thalamus.
    d. cerebellum.

15. Research has found that the amount of representation in the motor cortex reflects the
    a. size of the body parts.
    b. degree of precise control required by each of the parts.
    c. sensitivity of the body region.
    d. area of the occipital lobe being stimulated by the environment.

16. The best way to separate the effects of genes and environment in research is to study
    a. fraternal twins.
    b. identical twins.
    c. adopted children and their adoptive parents.
    d. identical twins raised in different environments.

17. The nerve fibers that enable communication between the right and left cerebral hemispheres and that have been severed in split-brain patients form a structure called the
    a. reticular formation.
    b. association areas.
    c. corpus callosum.
    d. parietal lobes.

18. Beginning at the front of the brain and moving toward the back of the head, then down the skull and back around to the front, which of the following is the correct order of the cortical regions?
    a. occipital lobe; temporal lobe; parietal lobe; frontal lobe
    b. temporal lobe; frontal lobe; parietal lobe; occipital lobe
    c. frontal lobe; occipital lobe; temporal lobe; parietal lobe
    d. frontal lobe; parietal lobe; occipital lobe; temporal lobe

19. Following a nail gun wound to his head, Jack became more uninhibited, irritable, dishonest, and profane. It is likely that his personality change was the result of injury to his
    a. parietal lobe.
    b. temporal lobe.
    c. occipital lobe.
    d. frontal lobe.

20. In the nervous system, I outnumber neurons. I also provide nutrients to the neurons and help remove excess neurotransmitters. I am a
    a. hormone.
    b. myelin sheath.
    c. glial cell.
    d. gland.

21. Three-year-old Marco suffered damage to the speech area of the brain's left hemisphere when he fell from a swing. Research suggests that
    a. he may never speak again.
    b. his motor abilities may improve so that he can easily use sign language.
    c. his right hemisphere may take over much of the language function.
    d. his earlier experience with speech may enable him to continue speaking.

22. When evolutionary psychologists use the word *fitness*, they are specifically referring to
    a. an animal's ability to adapt to changing environments.
    b. the diversity of a species' gene pool.
    c. the total number of members of the species currently alive.
    d. our ability to survive and reproduce.

23. Each cell of the human body has a total of
  a. 23 chromosomes.
  b. 23 genes.
  c. 46 chromosomes.
  d. 46 genes.

24. Genes direct our physical development by synthesizing
  a. hormones.
  b. proteins.
  c. DNA.
  d. chromosomes.

Matching Items

Match each structure or term with its corresponding function or description.

Structures or Terms

_____ **1.** right hemisphere
_____ **2.** brainstem
_____ **3.** temporal lobes
_____ **4.** occipital lobes
_____ **5.** plasticity
_____ **6.** neurogenesis
_____ **7.** reuptake
_____ **8.** limbic system
_____ **9.** association areas
_____ **10.** left hemisphere
_____ **11.** epigenetics
_____ **12.** environment

Essay Question

Discuss how the endocrine and nervous systems become involved when a student feels stress—such as that associated with an upcoming final exam. (Use the space below to list the points you want to make, and organize them. Then write the essay on a separate sheet of paper.)

25. Mutations are random errors in _____ replication.
  a. gene
  b. chromosome
  c. DNA
  d. protein

Functions or Descriptions

  a. the formation of new neurons
  b. specializes in rationalizing reactions
  c. the study of influences on gene expression that occur without a change in DNA
  d. specializes in spatial relations
  e. brain areas containing the auditory cortex
  f. brain areas containing the visual cortex
  g. oldest part of the brain
  h. regulates emotion
  i. the brain's capacity for modification
  j. absorption of excess neurotransmitters
  k. brain areas involved in higher mental functions
  l. nongenetic influences

Terms and Concepts to Remember

Writing Definitions

Using your own words, on a piece of paper write a brief definition or explanation of each of the following terms.

  1. biological perspective
  2. neuron
  3. dendrites
  4. axon
  5. myelin sheath
  6. glial cells (glia)
  7. action potential
  8. threshold
  9. synapse

10. neurotransmitters
11. endorphins
12. nervous system
13. central nervous system (CNS)
14. peripheral nervous system (PNS)
15. nerves
16. sensory neurons
17. motor neurons
18. interneurons
19. somatic nervous system
20. autonomic nervous system
21. sympathetic nervous system
22. parasympathetic nervous system
23. reflex
24. endocrine system
25. hormones
26. adrenal glands
27. pituitary gland
28. lesion
29. electroencephalogram (EEG)
30. PET (positron emission tomography) scan
31. MRI (magnetic resonance imaging)
32. fMRI (functional magnetic resonance imaging)
33. brainstem
34. medulla
35. thalamus
36. reticular formation
37. cerebellum

38. limbic system
39. amygdala
40. hypothalamus
41. cerebral cortex
42. frontal lobes
43. parietal lobes
44. occipital lobes
45. temporal lobes
46. motor cortex
47. sensory cortex
48. association areas
49. plasticity
50. neurogenesis
51. corpus callosum
52. split brain
53. environment
54. behavior genetics
55. chromosomes
56. DNA (deoxyribonucleic acid)
57. genes
58. identical twins
59. fraternal twins
60. interaction
61. epigenetics
62. evolutionary psychology
63. natural selection
64. mutation

Cross-Check

As you learned in Chapter 1, reviewing and overlearning of material are important to the learning process. After you have written the definitions of the key terms in this chapter, you should complete the crossword puzzle to ensure that you can reverse the process— recognize the term, given the definition.

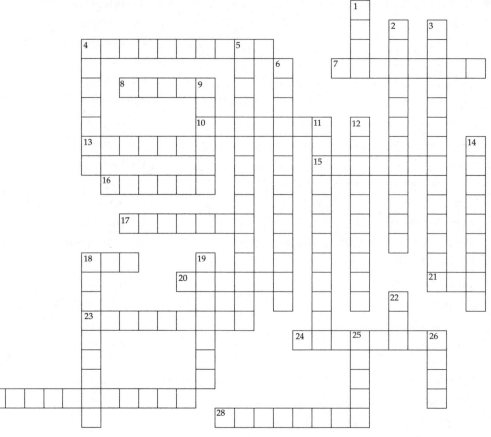

ACROSS

4. The division of the nervous system that connects the brain and spinal cord to the body's sense receptors, muscles, and glands.
7. Located on the sides of the brain, these lobes contain the auditory areas, which receive information from the ears.
8. Located at the back of the frontal lobe, the part of the cortex that controls voluntary movement.
10. Located just behind the forehead, these lobes are involved in speaking and muscle movements and in making plans and judgments.
13. Glands that produce the hormones epinephrine and norepinephrine.
15. Located in the brainstem, this structure controls breathing and heartbeat.
16. The thin outer covering of the cerebral hemispheres.
17. Junction between the axon tip of the sending neuron and the dendrite or cell body of the receiving neuron.
18. Amplified recording of the waves of electrical activity of the brain.
20. Destruction of tissue.
21. Technique that uses magnetic fields and radio waves to produce computer-generated images of brain structures.
23. Located at the back and base of the brain, these lobes contain the visual cortex, which receives information from the eyes.

24. The part of the limbic system involved in regulation of the emotions of fear and rage.
27. The study of environmental influences on gene expression.
28. Situated between the frontal and occipital lobes, these lobes contain the sensory cortex.

DOWN

1. The biochemical units of heredity that make up the chromosomes.
2. Limbic system structure that regulates hunger, thirst, and body temperature and contains the so-called reward centers of the brain.
3. Large band of neural fibers that links the right and left hemispheres.
4. Technique that measures the levels of activity of different areas of the brain by tracing their consumption of a radioactive form of glucose.
5. Neural impulse generated by the movement of positively charged atoms in and out of channels in the axon's membrane.
6. Neurotransmitter that triggers muscle contractions.
9. Simple, automatic, inborn response to a sensory stimulus.

11. Doughnut-shaped neural system that plays an important role in the regulation of emotions and basic physiological drives.
12. Natural opiate-like neurotransmitters linked to pain control and to pleasure.
14. Division of the peripheral nervous system that controls the glands and the muscles of internal organs.
18. The body's slower chemical communication system, consisting of glands that secrete hormones into the bloodstream.
19. The brain and spinal cord, collectively, are the _____ nervous system.
22. A complex molecule containing the genetic information that makes up the chromosomes.
25. Cells that guide neural connections and provide nutrients and insulating myelin.
26. Extension of a neuron that sends impulses to other nerve cells or to muscles or glands.

Answers

Chapter Review

Biology and Behavior

1. biological
2. biological psychologists
3. **d.** is the answer. Someone working from the biological perspective studies the links between biology (chemical changes in this example) and behavior (emotions in this example).
   a., b., & c. Experimental, clinical, and developmental psychologists would be more concerned with the learning of emotional expressions, the treatment of emotional disorders, and life-span changes in emotions, respectively.

Neural Communication

4. neurons
5. dendrites; axon; myelin sheath
6. **a.** dendrites
   b. cell body
   c. axon
   d. myelin sheath
7. glial cells; learning; thinking
8. action potential; axon
9. negatively; positively
10. positively; depolarized; positively
11. excitatory; inhibitory; threshold; will not; all-or-none
12. does not; can

13. synapse; synaptic cleft (gap); Sir Charles Sherrington
14. neurotransmitters; atoms
15. exciting; inhibiting; reuptake

A neural impulse is generated by excitatory signals minus inhibitory signals exceeding a certain threshold. The stimuli are received through the dendrites, combined in the cell body, and electrically transmitted in an all-or-none fashion down the length of the axon. When the combined signal reaches the end of the axon, chemical messengers called neurotransmitters are released into the synaptic cleft, or gap, between two neurons. Neurotransmitter molecules bind to receptor sites on the dendrites of neighboring neurons and have either an excitatory or inhibitory influence on that neuron's tendency to generate its own neural impulse.

16. acetylcholine (ACh); memory
17. endorphins; heroin; morphine
18. **a.** is the answer.
   b. Because she has reached her threshold, she will probably fire.
   c. Because Joni has received a large number of excitatory messages, she will not be at rest.
   d. *Hyperpolarization* is not a term.
19. **c.** is the answer.
20. **b.** is the answer.
   a. By triggering release of dopamine, such a drug would probably enhance Malcolm's enjoyment of the pleasures of life.
   c. & d. ACh is the neurotransmitter at synapses between motor neurons and muscle fibers.
21. norepinephrine. An undersupply can cause depression.
22. oversupply; glutamate. Glutamate is in MSG, which is sometimes used in Chinese cooking. Glutamate can cause migraines because an oversupply can overstimulate the brain.

The Nervous System

23. nervous system
24. central; peripheral
25. nerves; sensory; motor; interneurons
26. somatic
27. autonomic
28. sympathetic
29. parasympathetic; homeostasis

The sympathetic division of the autonomic nervous system becomes aroused in response to an emergency. The physiological changes that occur include accelerated heartbeat, raised blood pressure, elevated blood sugar, slowing of digestion, and increased perspiration to cool the body. When the emergency is over, the parasympathetic nervous system produces the opposite physical reactions.

30. neural networks

31. reflexes; spinal cord; knee-jerk; pain

From sensory receptors in the skin the message travels via sensory neurons to an interneuron in the spinal cord, which in turn activates a motor neuron. This motor neuron causes the muscles in the hand to contract, and the person jerks his or her hand away from the heat.

32. When you hear the creaking, you become afraid. The sympathetic division of your autonomic nervous system becomes aroused, causing these physiological changes: accelerated heartbeat, elevated blood sugar, increase in blood pressure, slowing of digestion, and increased perspiration to cool the body. When you realize it's only your parents, your parasympathetic nervous system produces the opposite physical reactions, calming your body.

33. **a.** is the answer. Because this reflex is an automatic response and involves only the spinal cord, the hand is jerked away before the brain has even received the information that causes the sensation of pain.

b. The spinal cord, which organizes simple reflexes such as this one, is part of the central nervous system.

c. The brain is not involved in directing spinal reflexes.

d. The autonomic nervous system controls the glands and the muscles of the internal organs; it does not influence the skeletal muscles controlling the hand.

34. autonomic nervous system

35. **b.** is the answer. Sympathetic arousal produces several effects, including accelerated heartbeat and excessive perspiration.

a. & d. Activation of the central nervous system and the somatic nervous system does not have these effects.

c. Arousal of the parasympathetic nervous system would have effects opposite to those stated.

The Endocrine System

36. endocrine system; hormones; slower; a longer time

37. adrenal; epinephrine; norepinephrine; heart rate; blood pressure; blood sugar

38. pituitary; hypothalamus; growth; oxytocin; pair bonding, group cohesion, and social trust

The hypothalamus in the brain influences secretions by the pituitary. The pituitary regulates other endocrine glands, which release hormones that influence the brain, which directs behavior.

39. **a.** is the answer.

b., c., & d. Acetylcholine and dopamine are fast-acting neurotransmitters released at synapses, not in the bloodstream.

40. **a.** is the answer. Hormones of the pituitary gland regulate body growth.

b. The pancreas regulates the level of sugar in the blood.

c. The adrenal glands produce hormones that provide energy during emergencies; they are not involved in regulating body growth.

d. The parathyroids help regulate the level of calcium in the blood.

The Brain

41. lesions; clinical observation

42. electroencephalogram (EEG)

43. PET (positron emission tomography) scan

By depicting the brain's consumption of temporarily radioactive glucose, the PET scan allows researchers to see which brain areas are most active as a person performs various tasks by tracking the gamma rays released. This provides additional information on the specialized functions of various regions of the brain.

44. MRI (magnetic resonance imaging)

45. functional MRI; increases; visual

46. **a.** MRI
   b. PET scan
   c. to study developmental changes in brain structure, to compare brain anatomy in women and men
   d. to learn which areas of the brain become active during strong emotions, to determine whether brain activity is abnormal in people suffering from dementia (memory and language problems)

47. brainstem

48. medulla; breathing; heartbeat; pons

49. brainstem

50. thalamus; smell; medulla; cerebellum

51. reticular formation; arousal; alert (awake); coma

52. cerebellum; nonverbal learning; emotions; balance

53. conscious; outside

54. limbic; hippocampus

55. amygdala

56. is not; does

57. hypothalamus; hunger; thirst; body temperature; sexual; homeostatic; hormones; pituitary; reward; nucleus accumbens

58. addictive; reward deficiency syndrome

59. cerebral cortex; information-processing

60. more wrinkled; increases

61. fissures
    a. frontal lobe
    b. parietal lobe
    c. occipital lobe
    d. temporal lobe

62. motor; frontal; greater

63. thoughts; motor cortex

64. sensory; touch; sensory cortex

65. occipital; temporal

66. association areas; three-fourths; frontal; parietal; temporal

67. does

68. Brain Damage Diagram
1. a	4. d	7. f
2. h	5. e	8. g
3. c	6. b	9. i

69. plasticity; young children

70. will not; reorganize; can; neurogenesis; stem

71. lateralization; left; right

72. corpus callosum; split brain

73. right; name; right

The word *pencil* when flashed to a split-brain patient's right visual field would project only to the opposite, or left, hemisphere of the patient's brain. Because the left hemisphere contains the language control centers of the brain, the patient would be able to read the word aloud. The left hand is controlled by the right hemisphere of the brain. Because the right hemisphere would not be aware of the word, it would not be able to guide the left hand in identifying a pencil by touch.

74. left; right; unconscious; can

75. left

76. left; right; speech; self

77. **c.** is the answer. The brainstem is the oldest and most primitive region of the brain. It is found in lower vertebrates, such as fish, as well as in humans and other mammals. The structures mentioned in the other choices are associated with stages of brain evolution beyond that seen in the fish.

78. **d.** is the answer. Stimulation of the sensory cortex elicits a sense of touch, as the experiments of Penfield demonstrated.
    a., b., & c. Hearing, seeing, or movement might be expected if the temporal, occipital, and motor regions of the cortex, respectively, were stimulated.

79. **c.** is the answer. As Olds and Milner discovered, electrical stimulation of the hypothalamus is a highly reinforcing event because it is the location of the animal's reward centers. The other brain regions mentioned are not associated with reward centers.

80. **a.** is the answer. The left hand, controlled by the right hemisphere, would be able to identify the fork, the picture of which is flashed to the right hemisphere.

81. **b.** is the answer.
    a., c., & d. The left hemisphere does not specialize in picture recognition. And blood clots can form anywhere in the brain.

82. **a.** is the answer. The right visual field projects directly to the verbal left hemisphere.
    b. & c. The left hand is controlled by the right hemisphere, which, in this situation, would be unaware of the word since the picture has been flashed to the left hemisphere.

83. **c.** is the answer.
    d. Reproduction is only one of the basic survival functions the brain regulates.

84. **b.** is the answer. The hippocampus of the limbic system is involved in processing memory. The amygdala of the limbic system influences fear and anger.
    a. The brainstem controls vital functions such as breathing and heartbeat; it is not directly involved in either emotion or memory.
    c. & d. These answers are incorrect because the limbic system is an older brain structure than the cortex. Its involvement in emotions and memory is therefore more basic than that of the cortex.

85. **d.** is the answer. The thalamus relays sensory messages from the eyes, ears, and other receptors to the appropriate projection areas of the cortex. "Rewiring" the thalamus, theoretically, could have the effects stated in this question.
    a., b., & c. These brain structures are not directly involved in brain processes related to sensation or perception.

86. **a.** is the answer. The motor cortex, which determines the precision with which various parts of the body can be moved, is located in the frontal lobes.

b. The parietal lobes contain the sensory cortex, which controls sensitivity to touch.

c. The temporal lobes contain the primary projection areas for hearing and, on the left side, are also involved in language use.

d. The occipital lobes contain the primary projection areas for vision.

Behavior Genetics: Predicting Individual Differences

87. nongenetic

88. behavior geneticists

89. chromosomes; 46; 23; DNA

90. genes

91. expressed; environmental events; protein molecules

92. **a.** cell nucleus   **b.** chromosome
   c. gene   **d.** DNA

93. twin; adoption

94. identical; fraternal

95. more

96. being treated alike; could not

97. environment

98. do not; does; higher

99. **c.** is the answer.

   a. Although heredity does influence certain traits, such as outgoingness and emotional instability, it is the interaction of heredity and experience that ultimately molds personality

   b. There is no single "most important factor" in personality. Moreover, for the same reason two sisters or brothers often have dissimilar personalities, a sister and brother may be very much alike.

   d. Karen and John's case is not at all unusual.

100. the same; different

101. **b.** is the answer.

   a. Because they are genetically the same, identical twins are always of the same sex.

   c. & d. Fraternal twins develop from two fertilized eggs.

102. genetic; environmental

103. interaction; genetic; environment

104. genes; responses; fraternal; identical

105. epigenetics; molecular; environments; genetic

Evolutionary Psychology: Understanding Human Nature

106. evolutionary psychologists

107. much alike

108. natural selection

109. mutations; change

110. looser; adapt; environments; fitness; survive; reproduce

111. fats; store

Progress Test 1

Multiple-Choice Questions

1. **b.** is the answer.
   a. Dopamine is a neurotransmitter that influences movement, learning, attention, and emotion.
   c. Acetylcholine is a neurotransmitter that triggers muscle contraction.
   d. Endorphins are opiate-like neurotransmitters linked to pain control and to pleasure.

2. **b.** is the answer. The autonomic nervous system controls internal functioning, including heartbeat, digestion, and glandular activity.
   a. The functions mentioned are all automatic, not voluntary, so this answer cannot be correct.
   c. This answer is incorrect because most organs are affected by both divisions of the autonomic nervous system.
   d. The somatic nervous system transmits sensory input to the central nervous system and enables voluntary control of skeletal muscles.

3. **c.** is the answer. Stimulus strength can affect only the number of times a neuron fires or the number of neurons that fire.
   a., b., & d. These answers are incorrect because firing is an all-or-none response, so intensity remains the same regardless of stimulus strength. Nor can stimulus strength change the neuronal threshold or the impulse speed.

4. **a.** is the answer. Endorphins are neurotransmitters that function as natural painkillers. When the body has a supply of artificial painkillers such as heroin, endorphin production stops.
   b. The production of neurotransmitters other than endorphins does not cease.
   c. Neurotransmitter production does not increase during withdrawal.
   d. Heroin makes use of the same receptor sites as endorphins.

5. **a.** is the answer. The PET scan measures glucose consumption in different areas of the brain to determine their levels of activity.
   b. The fMRI compares MRI scans taken less than a second apart to reveal brain structure and function.

c. The EEG is a measure of electrical activity in the brain.

d. MRI uses magnetic fields and radio waves to produce computer-generated images of soft tissues of the body.

6. **a.** is the answer. This is an example of a trait that contributes to survival of the human species and the perpetuation of one's genes.

b., c., & d. These traits and issues would likely be of greater interest to a behavior geneticist because they concern the influence of specific genes on behavior.

7. **a.** is the answer.

b. The reticular formation is linked to arousal.

c. The brainstem governs the mechanisms of basic survival—heartbeat and breathing, for example—and has many other roles.

d. The cerebellum coordinates movement output and balance.

8. **c.** is the answer. In a simple reflex, a sensory neuron carries the message that a sensory receptor has been stimulated to an interneuron in the spinal cord. The interneuron responds by activating motor neurons that will enable the appropriate response.

9. **d.** is the answer.

10. **d.** is the answer.

a. In most persons, language is primarily a left hemisphere function.

b. Learned movements are unrelated to hemispheric specialization.

c. Arithmetic reasoning is generally a left hemisphere function.

11. **d.** is the answer. Biological psychologists study the links between biology (in this case, neurotransmitters) and psychology (depression, in this example).

12. **d.** is the answer. As animals increase in complexity, there is an increase in the amount of association areas.

a. The brainstem controls basic survival functions and is not related to the complexity of an animal's behavior.

b. The corpus callosum connects the brain's two hemispheres; it's not necessarily related to more complex behaviors.

c. The frontal lobe is concerned with personality, planning, and other mental functions, but its size is unrelated to intelligence or the complexity of behavior.

13. **b.** is the answer.

a., c., & d. The autonomic nervous system, which is divided into the sympathetic and parasym-

pathetic divisions, is concerned with regulating basic bodily maintenance functions.

14. **c.** is the answer.

a. An action potential will occur only when the neuron's threshold is *exceeded.*

b. An excitatory input that does not reach the neuron's threshold will not trigger an action potential.

d. This answer is incorrect because some neurotransmitters inhibit a neuron's readiness to fire.

15. **d.** is the answer. A neuron receives incoming stimuli on its dendrites and cell body. These electrochemical signals are combined in the cell body, generating an impulse that travels down the axon, causing the release of neurotransmitter substances into the synaptic cleft or gap.

16. **c.** is the answer.

a. Glia are cells that support and nourish nerve cells.

b. Neurotransmitters are the chemicals involved in synaptic transmission in the nervous system.

d. Enzymes are chemicals that facilitate various chemical reactions throughout the body but are not involved in communication within the endocrine system.

17. **c.** is the answer. The reticular formation plays an important role in arousal.

a. The thalamus relays sensory input.

b. The corpus callosum links the two cerebral hemispheres.

d. The cerebellum is involved in coordination of movement output and balance.

18. **b.** is the answer.

19. **b.** is the answer. Association areas interpret, integrate, and act on information from other areas of the cortex.

20. **b.** is the answer.

a. Action potentials are neural impulses that occur in all forms of communication in the nervous system.

c. The endocrine system is the body's glandular system of chemical communication.

d. Dendrites are the branching extensions of neurons that receive messages from other nerve cells.

21. **b.** is the answer.

c. & d. There are no such things as "placental" or "nonplacental" twins. All twins have a placenta during prenatal development.

22. **b.** is the answer.

a., c., & d. Despite being raised in different environments, long-separated identical twins often have much in common, including likes, dislikes, and lifestyles.

23. **a.** is the answer.

b. Neurotransmitters are the chemicals involved in synaptic transmission in the nervous system.
d. Enzymes are chemicals that facilitate various chemical reactions throughout the body but are not involved in heredity.

24. **d.** is the answer.
a. A norm is a culturally determined set of expected behaviors for a particular role, such as a gender role.
b. & c. When two factors are correlated, it means either that increases in one factor are accompanied by increases in the other (positive correlation) or that increases in one factor are accompanied by decreases in the other (negative correlation).

25. **c.** is the answer.

Matching Items

1. d	5. g	9. k
2. e	6. b	10. i
3. a	7. c	11. j
4. l	8. h	12. f

Progress Test 2

Multiple-Choice Questions

1. **a.** is the answer. The visual cortex is located at the very back of the brain.

2. **b.** is the answer.
a., c., & d. making inferences, perceptual skills, and the left side of the body are primarily influenced by the right hemisphere.

3. **a.** is the answer. Sensory neurons in the somatic nervous system relay such messages.
b. & c. These divisions of the autonomic nervous system are concerned with the regulation of bodily maintenance functions such as heartbeat, digestion, and glandular activity.
d. The spinal cord itself is part of the central nervous system, but the message is carried to the spinal cord by the somatic division of the peripheral nervous system.

4. **c.** is the answer. As automatic responses to stimuli, reflexes are the simplest complete units of behavior and require only simple neural pathways.
a., b., & d. Emotions, drives, and voluntary movements are all behaviors that are much more complex than reflexes and therefore involve much more complicated neural pathways.

5. **b.** is the answer. Endorphins are neurotransmitters that function as natural painkillers and are evidently involved in the "runner's high" and

other situations in which discomfort or fatigue is expected but not experienced.
a. ACh is a neurotransmitter involved in muscular control.
c. Dopamine is a neurotransmitter involved in, among other things, movement.
d. Norepinephrine is an adrenal hormone released to help us respond in moments of danger.

6. **b.** is the answer.
a. & c. Although an identical twin is at increased risk, the relationship is far from perfect. Mental disorders, like all psychological traits, are influenced by both nature and nurture.
d. This is not at all implied by the evidence from twin studies.

7. **d.** is the answer.
a. The EEG is an amplified recording of the brain's electrical activity.
b. A lesion is destruction of tissue.
c. The PET scan is a visual display of brain activity that detects the movement of a radioactive form of glucose as the brain performs a task.

8. **a.** is the answer.
c. & d. Myelin sheaths are not involved in regulating the release of neurotransmitters.

9. **d.** is the answer.

10. **b.** is the answer. ACh is a neurotransmitter that causes the contraction of muscle fibers when stimulated by motor neurons. This function explains its location.
a. & c. Sensory neurons and interneurons do not directly stimulate muscle fibers.

11. **d.** is the answer. The pituitary regulates body growth, and some of its secretions regulate the release of hormones from other glands.
a. The adrenal glands are stimulated by the autonomic nervous system to release epinephrine and norepinephrine.
b. The thyroid gland affects metabolism, among other things.
c. The hypothalamus, which is not a gland, regulates the pituitary but does not itself directly regulate growth.

12. **d.** is the answer. Also known as adrenaline and noradrenaline, epinephrine and norepinephrine are hormones released by the adrenal glands.

13. **d.** is the answer. The cerebellum is involved in the coordination of voluntary muscular movements.
a. The medulla regulates breathing and heartbeat.

b. The thalamus relays sensory inputs to the appropriate higher centers of the brain.

c. The hypothalamus is concerned with the regulation of basic drives and emotions.

14. **a.** is the answer. The reticular formation controls arousal via its connections to the cortex. Thus, separating the two produces a coma.

b., c., & d. None of these structures controls arousal. The hypothalamus regulates hunger, thirst, sexual behavior, and other basic drives; the thalamus is a sensory relay station; and the cerebellum is involved in the coordination of voluntary movement.

15. **b.** is the answer.

c. & d. These refer to the sensory cortex.

16. **d.** is the answer.

a., b., & c. In order to pinpoint the influence of one of the two factors (genes and environment), it is necessary to hold one of the factors constant.

17. **c.** is the answer. The corpus callosum is a large band of neural fibers linking the right and left cerebral hemispheres. To sever the corpus callosum is in effect to split the brain.

18. **d.** is the answer. The frontal lobe is in the front of the brain. Just behind is the parietal lobe. The occipital lobe is located at the very back of the head and just below the parietal lobe. Next to the occipital lobe and toward the front of the head is the temporal lobe.

19. **d.** is the answer. As demonstrated in the case of Phineas Gage, injury to the frontal lobe may produce such changes in personality.

a. Damage to the parietal lobe might disrupt functions involving the sensory cortex.

b. Damage to the temporal lobe might impair hearing.

c. Occipital damage might impair vision.

20. **c.** is the answer.

a. Hormones are secreted by endocrine glands directly into the bloodstream.

b. Myelin sheath is the fatty tissues that intermittently surrounds the axons of neurons.

d. Glands are part of the endocrine system.

21. **c.** is the answer.

22. **d.** is the answer.

a. Survival ability is only one aspect of fitness.

b. & c. Neither of these is related to fitness.

23. **c.** is the answer.

b. & d. Each cell of the human body contains hundreds of genes.

24. **b.** is the answer.

a. Hormones are chemical messengers produced by the endocrine glands.

c. & d. Genes are segments of DNA, which are the makeup of chromosomes.

25. **a.** is the answer.

Matching Items

1.	d	**5.**	i	**9.**	k
2.	g	**6.**	a	**10.**	b
3.	e	**7.**	j	**11.**	c
4.	f	**8.**	h	**12.**	l

Essay Question

The body's response to stress is regulated by the nervous system. As the date of the exam approaches, the stressed student's cerebral cortex activates the hypothalamus, triggering the release of hormones that in turn activate the sympathetic branch of the autonomic nervous system and the endocrine system. The autonomic nervous system controls involuntary bodily responses such as breathing, heartbeat, and digestion. The endocrine system contains glands that secrete hormones into the bloodstream that regulate the functions of body organs.

In response to activation by the hypothalamus, the student's pituitary gland would secrete a hormone which in turn triggers the release of epinephrine, norepinephrine, and other stress hormones from the adrenal glands. These hormones would help the student's body manage stress by making nutrients available to meet the increased demands for energy stores the body often faces in coping with stress. These hormones activate the sympathetic division of the autonomic system, causing increased heart rate, breathing, and blood pressure and the suppression of digestion. After the exam date has passed, the student's body would attempt to restore its normal, pre-stress state. The parasympathetic branch of the autonomic system would slow the student's heartbeat and breathing and digestive processes would no longer be suppressed, perhaps causing the student to feel hungry.

Terms and Concepts to Remember

Writing Definitions

1. The **biological perspective** is concerned with the links between biological and psychological processes.

2. The **neuron**, or nerve cell, is the basic building block of the nervous system.

3. The **dendrites** of a neuron are the bushy, branching extensions that receive messages from other

nerve cells and conduct impulses toward the cell body.

4. The **axon** of a neuron is the extension that sends impulses to other nerve cells or to muscles or glands.

5. The **myelin sheath** is a layer of fatty tissue that segmentally covers many axons and helps speed neural impulses.

6. More numerous than neurons, the **glial cells (glia)** of the nervous system guide neural connections, provide nutrients and insulating myelin, and clean up after neurons send messages to one another.

7. An **action potential** is a neural impulse; a brief electrical charge that travels down an axon.

8. A neuron's **threshold** is the level of stimulation required to trigger a neural impulse.

9. A **synapse** is the junction between the axon tip of the sending neuron and the dendrite or cell body of the receiving neuron. The tiny gap at this junction is called the *synaptic gap* or *cleft*.

10. **Neurotransmitters** are chemicals that are released into synaptic gaps and so transmit neural messages from neuron to neuron.

11. **Endorphins** are natural, opiate-like neurotransmitters linked to pain control and to pleasure.

    Memory aid: Endorphins *end* pain.

12. The **nervous system** is the speedy, electrochemical communication system, consisting of all the nerve cells of the peripheral and central nervous systems.

13. The **central nervous system (CNS)** consists of the brain and spinal cord; it is located at the *center*, or internal core, of the body.

14. The **peripheral nervous system (PNS)** includes the sensory and motor neurons that connect the central nervous system to the body's sense receptors, muscles, and glands; it is at the *periphery* of the body relative to the brain and spinal cord.

15. **Nerves** are bundles of neural axons, which are part of the PNS, that form "cables" connecting the central nervous system with muscles, glands, and sense organs.

16. **Sensory (afferent) neurons** carry information from the sensory receptors to the central nervous system for processing.

17. **Motor (efferent) neurons** carry information and instructions for action from the central nervous system to muscles and glands.

18. **Interneurons** are the neurons of the central nervous system that link the sensory and motor neurons in the transmission of sensory inputs and motor outputs.

19. The **somatic nervous system** is the division of the peripheral nervous system that enables voluntary control of the skeletal muscles; also called the *skeletal nervous system.*

20. The **autonomic nervous system (ANS)** is the division of the peripheral nervous system that controls the glands and the muscles of internal organs and thereby controls internal functioning; it regulates the *automatic* behaviors necessary for survival.

21. The **sympathetic nervous system** is the division of the autonomic nervous system that arouses the body, mobilizing its energy in stressful situations.

22. The **parasympathetic nervous system** is the division of the autonomic nervous system that calms the body, conserving its energy.

23. A **reflex** is a simple, automatic response to a sensory stimulus; it is governed by a very simple neural pathway.

24. The **endocrine system**, the body's "slow" chemical communication system, consists of glands that secrete hormones into the bloodstream.

25. **Hormones** are chemical messengers, manufactured by the endocrine glands, that circulate through the bloodstream and affect other tissues, including the brain.

26. The **adrenal glands** are a pair of endocrine glands that produce epinephrine and norepinephrine, hormones that prepare the body to deal with emergencies or stress.

27. The **pituitary gland**, under the influence of the hypothalamus, regulates growth and controls other endocrine glands; it is a sort of master gland.

28. A **lesion** is destruction of tissue; studying the consequences of lesions in different regions of the brain—both surgically produced in animals and naturally occurring—helps researchers to determine the normal functions of these regions.

29. An **electroencephalogram (EEG)** is an amplified recording of the waves of electrical activity sweeping across the brain's surface. *Encephalo* comes from a Greek word meaning "related to the brain."

30. The **PET (positron emission tomography) scan** measures the levels of activity of different areas of the brain by tracing their consumption of a radioactive form of glucose, the brain's fuel.

31. **MRI (magnetic resonance imaging)** uses magnetic fields and radio waves to produce computer-generated images that show brain structures more clearly.

32. In a **fMRI (functional magnetic resonance imaging),** MRI scans taken less than a second apart are compared to reveal bloodflow and, therefore, brain function.

33. The **brainstem**, the oldest and innermost region of the brain, is an extension of the spinal cord and is the central core of the brain; its structures direct automatic survival functions.

34. Located in the brainstem, the **medulla** controls breathing and heartbeat.

35. Located atop the brainstem, the **thalamus** routes incoming messages to the sensory receiving areas in the cortex and transmits replies to the medulla and cerebellum.

36. The **reticular formation** is a nerve network that travels through the brainstem and plays an important role in controlling arousal.

37. The **cerebellum** processes sensory input, coordinates movement output and balance, and enables nonverbal learning and memory.

38. The **limbic system** is a neural system associated with emotions such as fear and aggression and basic physiological drives.

    Memory aid: Its name comes from the Latin word *limbus,* meaning "border"; the **limbic system** is at the border of the brainstem and cerebral hemispheres.

39. The **amygdala** is two lima-bean-sized neural clusters in the limbic system; it influences the emotions of fear and aggression.

40. Also part of the limbic system, the **hypothalamus** regulates hunger, thirst, body temperature, and sexual behavior; helps govern the endocrine system via the pituitary gland; and contains the so-called reward centers of the brain.

41. The **cerebral cortex** is a thin intricate covering of interconnected neural cells atop the cerebral hemispheres. The seat of information processing, the cortex is responsible for those complex functions that make us distinctively human.

    Memory aid: Cortex in Latin means "bark." As bark covers a tree, the **cerebral cortex** is the "bark of the brain."

42. Located at the front of the brain, just behind the forehead, the **frontal lobes** are involved in speaking and muscle movements and in making plans and judgments.

43. Situated between the frontal and occipital lobes, the **parietal lobes** contain the sensory cortex, which receives sensory input for touch and body position.

44. Located at the back and base of the brain, the **occipital lobes** contain the visual cortex, which receives information from the visual fields.

45. Located on the sides of the brain, the **temporal lobes** contain the auditory areas, each receiving information from the opposite ear.

    Memory aid: The **temporal lobes** are located near the *temples.*

46. Located at the back of the frontal lobe, the **motor cortex** controls voluntary movement.

47. The **sensory cortex** is located at the front of the parietal lobes, just behind the motor cortex. It registers and processes body touch and movement sensations.

48. Located throughout the cortex, **association areas** of the brain are involved in higher mental functions, such as learning, remembering, thinking, and speaking.

    Memory aid: Among their other functions, **association areas** of the cortex are involved in integrating, or *associating*, information from different areas of the brain.

49. **Plasticity** is the brain's capacity for modification, as evidenced by brain reorganization following damage (especially in children).

50. **Neurogenesis** is the formation of new neurons.

51. The **corpus callosum** is the large band of neural fibers that links the right and left cerebral hemispheres. Without this band of nerve fibers, the two hemispheres could not interact.

52. **Split brain** is a condition in which the major connections between the two cerebral hemispheres (the corpus callosum) are severed, literally resulting in a split brain.

53. In behavior genetics, **environment** refers to every nongenetic, or external, influence on our traits and behaviors.

54. **Behavior genetics** is the study of the relative power and limits of genetic and environmental influences on behavior.

55. **Chromosomes** are thread-like structures made of DNA molecules that contain the genes. In conception, the 23 chromosomes in the egg are paired with the 23 chromosomes in the sperm.

56. **DNA** *(deoxyribonucleic acid)* is a complex molecule containing the genetic information that makes up the chromosomes.

57. **Genes** are the biochemical units of heredity that make up the chromosomes; they are segments of the DNA molecules capable of synthesizing a protein.

58. **Identical twins** develop from a single (monozygotic) fertilized egg that splits in two and therefore are genetically identical.

59. **Fraternal twins** develop from two separate (dizygotic) eggs fertilized by different sperm and therefore are no more genetically similar than ordinary siblings.

60. An **interaction** occurs when the effects of one factor (such as environment) depend on another factor (such as heredity).

    Example: Because the way people react to us (an environmental factor) depends on our genetically influenced temperament (a genetic factor), there is an interaction between environment and heredity.

61. **Epigenetics** is the study of environmental influences on gene expression that occur without a change in DNA.

62. **Evolutionary psychology** is the study of the evolution of behavior and the mind, using principles of natural selection.

63. **Natural selection** is the evolutionary principle that traits that lead to increased reproduction and survival are the most likely to be passed on to succeeding generations.

64. **Mutations** are random errors in gene replication that lead to change

Cross-Check

ACROSS	DOWN
4. peripheral	1. gene
7. temporal	2. hypothalamus
8. motor	3. corpus callosum
10. frontal	4. PET scan
13. adrenal	5. action potential
15. medulla	6. acetylcholine
16. cortex	9. reflex
17. synapse	11. limbic system
18. EEG	12. endorphins
20. lesion	14. autonomic
21. MRI	18. endocrine
23. occipital	19. central
24. amygdala	22. DNA
27. epigenetics	25. glial
28. parietal	26. axon

Consciousness and the Two-Track Mind

Chapter Overview

Consciousness—our awareness of ourselves and our environment—can be experienced in various states. Chapter 3 examines not only normal consciousness but also sleep and dreaming, hypnotic states, and drug-altered states.

Most of the terminology in this chapter is introduced in the sections on Sleep and Dreams and on Drugs and Consciousness. Among the issues discussed are why we sleep and dream, whether hypnosis is a unique state of consciousness, and possible psychological and social-cultural roots of drug use.

NOTE: Answer guidelines for all Chapter 3 questions begin on page 75.

Chapter Review

First, skim each section, noting headings and bold-face items. After you have read the section, review each objective by answering the fill-in and essay-type questions that follow it. In some cases, Study Tips explain how best to learn a difficult concept and Applications help you to know how well you understand the material. As you proceed, evaluate your performance by consulting the answers beginning on page 75. Do not continue with the next section until you understand each answer. If you need to, review the section in the textbook before continuing.

The Brain and Consciousness

Objective 3-1: Describe the place of consciousness in psychology's history.

1. The study of _____ was central in the early years of psychology and in recent decades, but for quite some time it was displaced by the study of observable _____ .

2. Advances in neuroscience made it possible to relate _____ _____ to various mental states; as a result, psychologists once again affirmed the importance of _____ .

Define consciousness in a sentence.

3. The interdisciplinary study of how brain activity is linked with mental processes is called _____ _____ .

Objective 3-2: Explain what is meant by "dual processing," as revealed by today's cognitive neuroscience.

4. Much of our everyday thinking, feeling, and acting operates outside of our _____ awareness.

5. Unconscious information processing occurs _____ on _____ (sequential/parallel) tracks.

6. The principle that information is often processed on separate _____ and _____ tracks is called _____ _____ .

7. The condition in which a person responds to a visual stimulus without consciously experiencing it is called _____ .

8. Our vision is actually a _____-_____ system with a visual _____ track enabling us to recognize things and plan future actions and a visual _____ track guiding our moment-to-moment movements.

9. Solving new problems _____ (requires/does not require) conscious attention.

Objective 3-3: Discuss how much information we can consciously attend to at once.

10. When we focus our conscious awareness on a particular stimulus, we are using _____ _____ .

11. Your ability to attend to only one voice among many is called the _____ _____ _____ .

12. When researchers distracted participants with a counting task, the participants failed to notice a gorilla-suited assistant who passed among people tossing a basketball, thus displaying _____ _____ .

    One form of this phenomenon is _____ _____ .

13. Some stimuli are so powerful they demand our attention, causing us to experience _____-_____ .

APPLICATIONS:

14. Concluding his presentation on levels of information processing, Miguel states that
    a. humans process both conscious and unconscious information in parallel.
    b. conscious processing occurs in parallel, while unconscious processing is sequential.
    c. conscious processing is sequential, while unconscious processing is parallel.
    d. all information processing is sequential in nature.

15. When we become absorbed in reading a book, we do not hear the people talking around us. This *selective attention* is most accurately defined as
    a. the focusing of conscious awareness on a particular stimulus.
    b. our awareness of ourselves and our environment.
    c. failing to see visible objects when our attention is directed elsewhere.
    d. separating our conscious awareness to focus on two tasks at the same time.

Sleep and Dreams

Objective 3-4: Describe how our biological rhythms influence our daily functioning.

16. Our bodies' internal "clocks" control several _____ _____ .

17. The sleep-waking cycle follows a 24-hour clock called the _____ _____ .

18. Body temperature _____ (rises/falls) as morning approaches and begins to _____ (rise/fall) again before we go to sleep.

19. When people are at their daily peak in circadian arousal, _____ is sharpest and _____ is most accurate.

20. Our circadian rhythm is altered by _____ and _____ . Morning types tend to do better in school, to take more _____ , and to be less vulnerable to _____ .

Objective 3-5: Describe the biological rhythm of our sleeping and dreaming stages.

21. The sleep cycle consists of _____ distinct stages.

22. The rhythm of sleep cycles was discovered when Aserinsky noticed that, at periodic intervals during the night, the _____ of a sleeping child moved rapidly. This stage of sleep, during which _____ occur, is called _____ _____ .

23. The relatively slow brain waves of the awake but relaxed state are known as _____ waves. As you grow tired, you slip into _____ .

24. During non-REM stage 1 sleep, people often experience _____ sensations similar to _____ . These sensations may later be incorporated into _____ .

25. The bursts of brain-wave activity that occur during NREM-2 sleep are called _____ .

26. Large, slow brain waves are called
_____ waves. They occur in
non-REM stage _____ , which is
therefore called _____-
_____ sleep. A person in this stage
of sleep generally will be _____
(easy/difficult) to awaken. It is during this stage
that children may wet the bed or begin
_____ .

Describe the bodily changes that accompany REM
sleep.

27. During REM sleep, the motor cortex is
_____ (active/relaxed), while
the muscles are _____ (active/
relaxed), so much so that you are essentially
_____ . For this reason, REM is
often referred to as _____ sleep.

28. The sleep cycle repeats itself about every
_____ minutes. As the night progresses, deep NREM-3 sleep becomes
_____ (longer/briefer), and REM
and NREM-2 periods become _____
(longer/briefer). Approximately _____
percent of a night's sleep is spent in REM sleep.

APPLICATIONS:

29. Match the sleep stage with a description of that
stage or an activity that occurs then.

Sleep Stage

_____ 1. NREM-1 sleep
_____ 2. NREM-2 sleep
_____ 3. NREM-3 sleep
_____ 4. REM sleep

Description or Example

a. Bonita dreams that she's dancing with Orlando
Bloom at a grand ball.
b. Manfred feels like he's floating above the bed.
c. Rapid, rhythmic brain-wave activity indicates you
are clearly asleep.
d. You are in slow-wave sleep and you do not
awaken easily.

30. Given that REM is referred to as *paradoxical
sleep*, which of the following is true about what
happens when Nicholas dreams that he is running
around the school track?

a. Studies of people deprived of REM sleep indicate that REM sleep is unnecessary.
b. The body's muscles remain relaxed while other
body systems are active.
c. It is very easy to awaken a person from REM
sleep.
d. The body's muscles are very tense while the
brain is in a nearly meditative state.

31. Although her eyes are closed, Adele's brain is
generating bursts of electrical activity. It is likely
that Adele is

a. having hypnagogic sensations.
b. in NREM-3 sleep.
c. in REM sleep.
d. hallucinating.

Objective 3-6: Explain how biology and environment
interact in our sleep patterns.

32. Newborns spend nearly _____
(how much?) of their day asleep, while adults
spend no more than _____ .

33. Sleep patterns are influenced by
_____ , as indicated by the fact that
sleep patterns among _____
(identical/fraternal) twins are very similar. Sleep
is also influenced by _____ , as
indicated by the fact that people now sleep
_____ (more/less) than a century ago.

34. Bright light activates light-sensitive retinal proteins that signal the brain's _____
_____ to suppress the
_____ gland's production of
_____ , a sleep-inducing hormone.

Objective 3-7: Describe sleep's functions.

35. Two possible reasons for sleep are to
    _____ us and to help us
    _____ by restoring and repairing
    _____ tissue. Animals with high
    waking _____ produce an abun-
    dance of chemical _____
    _____ that are toxic to
    _____ . Sleep also facilitates our
    _____ of the day's experiences and
    stimulates _____ thinking.

36. During deep sleep, a growth hormone is released
    by the _____ gland. Adults spend
    _____ (more/less) time in deep
    sleep than children and so release
    _____ (more/less) growth hor-
    mone.

37. Sleep _____ (improves/disrupts)
    athletic performance.

APPLICATION:

38. Concluding her presentation on contemporary
    theories of why sleep is necessary, Marilynn
    makes all of the following points except that
    a. sleep may have evolved because it kept our
       ancestors safe during potentially dangerous
       periods.
    b. sleep gives the brain time to heal, as it restores
       and repairs damaged neurons.
    c. sleep encourages growth through a hormone
       secreted during NREM-3.
    d. slow-wave sleep provides a "psychic safety
       valve" for stressful waking experiences.

Objective 3-8: Describe the effects of sleep loss, and
identify the major sleep disorders.

39. Allowed to sleep unhindered, most people will
    sleep _____ (how many?) hours a
    night.

40. Young people who sleep _____
    (how many?) or fewer hours each night have a
    higher risk of _____ than those
    who sleep _____ hours or more.

41. Another effect of sleep deprivation is to promote
    weight gain by increasing the hormone
    _____ and decreasing the hormone
    _____ ; it also increases

_____ , a stress hormone that stimulates the body to make fat. Another is that sleep
deprivation may suppress the functioning of the
body's _____ system, which battles
_____ _____ and
_____ . Another indication of the
hazards of this state is that the rate of
_____ tends to increase immediately
after the spring time change in Canada and the
United States.

42. A persistent difficulty in falling or staying asleep
    is characteristic of _____ . Sleeping
    pills and alcohol may make the problem worse
    because they tend to _____
    (increase/reduce) REM sleep.

(Table 3.1) State several tips for those suffering from
insomnia.

43. The sleep disorder in which a person experiences
    uncontrollable sleep attacks is _____ .
    People with severe cases of this disorder may col-
    lapse directly into _____ sleep and
    experience a loss of _____
    _____ .

44. Individuals suffering from _____
    _____ stop breathing while
    sleeping. This disorder is especially prevalent
    among _____ _____ .

45. The sleep disorder characterized by extreme
    fright and doubled heart and breathing rates is
    called _____ _____ .
    Unlike nightmares, these episodes usually hap-
    pen early in the night, during NREM-_____
    sleep. The same is true of episodes of
    _____ and _____ ,
    problems that _____ (run/do not
    run) in families. These sleep episodes are most
    likely to be experienced by _____
    (young children/adolescents/older adults), in

whom this stage tends to be the

_____ and _____ .

APPLICATIONS:

46. Norbert's wife complains that she has to stay up all night to be sure he starts breathing again each time he stops breathing for a minute or so. So, Norbert consults his doctor and learns that he is suffering from

    a. sleep apnea.   c. night terrors.
    b. narcolepsy.   d. insomnia.

47. A person who falls asleep in the midst of a heated argument probably suffers from

    a. sleep apnea.   c. night terrors.
    b. narcolepsy.   d. insomnia.

Objective 3-9: Describe the most common content of dreams.

48. Dreams experienced during _____ sleep are vivid, emotional, and bizarre.

49. On average, people spend _____ (how many?) years of life in dreams.

50. For both men and women, 8 in 10 dreams are marked by _____ (positive/negative) emotions, such as fears of being

    _____

    _____ .

51. Most dreams _____ (incorporate/do not incorporate) traces of previous days' nonsexual experiences and preoccupations.

52. While we sleep, our mind _____ (monitors/does not monitor) stimuli in the environment.

Objective 3-10: Describe the functions of dreams.

53. Freud referred to the actual content of a dream as its _____ content. Freud believed that this is a censored, symbolic version of the true meaning, or _____ content, of the dream.

54. According to Freud, most of the dreams of adults reflect _____ wishes and are the key to understanding inner _____ . To Freud, dreams serve as a psychic

_____ _____ that discharges otherwise unacceptable feelings.

55. Researchers who believe that dreams serve an _____-processing function receive support from the fact that REM sleep facilitates _____ .

56. Brain scans confirm the link between _____ sleep and _____ .

57. Other theories propose that dreaming serves some _____ function, for example, that REM sleep provides the brain with needed _____ .

58. Still other theories propose that dreams are elicited by random bursts of _____ activity originating in lower regions of the brain, such as the _____ . According to one version, dreams are the brain's attempt to make sense of this activity. The bursts have been shown by PET scans to be given their emotional tone by the brain's _____ system, especially the _____ . Other theorists see dreams as a natural part of brain _____ and _____ development.

59. Researchers agree that we _____ (need/do not need) REM sleep. After being deprived of REM sleep, a person spends more time in REM sleep; this is the _____ _____ effect.

60. REM sleep _____ (does/does not) occur in other mammals. Animals such as fish, whose behavior is less influenced by learning, _____ (do/do not) experience REM sleep. This finding supports the _____-_____ theory of dreaming.

APPLICATIONS:

61. Arsenio is participating in a sleep experiment. While he sleeps, a PET scan of his brain reveals increased activity in the amygdala of the limbic system. This most likely indicates that Arsenio is in _____ sleep.

62. Barry has participated in a sleep study for the last four nights. He was awakened each time he entered REM sleep. Now that the experiment is over, Barry will most likely show a(n) _____ (increase/ decrease) in REM sleep, a phenomenon known as

   _____ _____ .

63. Bahara dreams that she trips and falls as she walks up the steps to the stage to receive her college diploma. Her psychoanalyst suggests that the dream might symbolize her fear of moving on to the next stage of her life—a career. The analyst is evidently attempting to interpret the _____ content of Bahara's dream.

64. Six-month-old Piper spend two-thirds of the day sleeping and most of that time in REM sleep. Her 25-year-old mother sleeps only 8 hours with fewer hours in REM sleep than her daughter. According to a physiological theory of dreaming, this makes sense because the brain activity associated with REM sleep
   a. fixes the day's activities in memory.
   b. gives meaning to random neural activity.
   c. provides the brain with periodic stimulation.
   d. keeps the infant in deep sleep.

Hypnosis

Objective 3-11: Define *hypnosis*, and describe how a hypnotist can influence a hypnotized subject.

65. Hypnosis is a _____ _____ in which a hypnotist suggests that a subject will experience certain feelings, thoughts, or behaviors.

66. Most people are _____ (somewhat/ not at all) hypnotically suggestible.

Describe people who are the most susceptible to hypnosis.

67. Research studies show that "hypnotically refreshed" memories combine _____ with _____ .

68. To find out if hypnosis can get people to act against their will, Orne and Evans introduced a _____ group of people who pretended to be hypnotized.

69. Hypnotherapists have helped some people alleviate headaches, asthma, and stress-related skin disorders through the use of _____ suggestions. Hypnosis _____ (is/ is not) especially helpful for the treatment of obesity. It _____ (is/is not) useful in treating smoking, drug, and alcohol addictions.

70. Hypnosis _____ (can/cannot) relieve pain.

Objective 3-12: Discuss whether hypnosis is an extension of normal consciousness or an altered state.

71. Skeptics believe that hypnosis may reflect the workings of _____ _____ . These findings provide support for the _____ _____ theory of hypnosis.

72. An _____ person in a legitimate _____ can induce people— hypnotized or not—to perform some unlikely acts.

Summarize the argument that hypnosis is not an altered state of consciousness.

73. Hilgard has advanced the idea that during hypnosis there is a special _____- _____ state of _____ , or split, between different levels of consciousness. For example, he believes that there is a split between the _____ and _____ aspects of pain. Hypnotic pain relief may also be due to selective _____ , that is, to the person's focusing on stimuli other than pain.

APPLICATIONS:

74. An attorney wants to know if the details and accuracy of an eyewitness's memory for a crime would be improved under hypnosis. Given the results of relevant research, what should you tell the attorney?

    a. Most hypnotically retrieved memories are either false or contaminated.
    b. Hypnotically retrieved memories are usually more accurate than conscious memories.
    c. Hypnotically retrieved memories are purely the product of the subject's imagination.
    d. Hypnosis only improves memory of anxiety-provoking childhood events.

75. Of the following individuals, who is likely to be the most hypnotically suggestible?

    a. Bill, a reality-oriented stockbroker
    b. Janice, an actress with a rich imagination
    c. Megan, a sixth-grader who has trouble focusing her attention on a task
    d. Darren, who has never been able to really "get involved" in movies or novels

76. Research studies of the effectiveness of hypnosis as a form of therapy have demonstrated that

    a. for problems of addiction, such as smoking, hypnosis has not been especially effective.
    b. posthypnotic suggestions have helped alleviate headaches, asthma, and stress-related skin disorders.
    c. as a form of therapy, hypnosis is no more effective than positive suggestions given without hypnosis.
    d. all of these statements are true.

77. Those who consider hypnosis a social phenomenon contend that

    a. hypnosis is an altered state of consciousness.
    b. hypnotic phenomena are unique to hypnosis.
    c. hypnotized subjects become unresponsive when they are no longer motivated to act as instructed.
    d. all of these statements are true.

Drugs and Consciousness

Objective 3-13: Describe tolerance, withdrawal, and addiction, and identify the substance use disorders.

78. Drugs that alter moods and perceptions are called _____ drugs. Continued craving and use of a drug despite significant life disruption indicates a _____

    _____ _____ .

79. Drug users who require larger and larger doses to experience a drug's effects have developed

_____ for the drug. With continued use, the user's brain counteracts the disruption to its normal functioning; thus, the user experiences _____ .

80. If a person abruptly stops taking a drug, he or she may experience the undesirable side effects of _____ . A person who has a compulsive craving for drugs or certain behaviors despite adverse consequences is _____ to that substance.

(Thinking Critically) Briefly state three reasons addictions may not be as irresistible as commonly believed.

81. The three broad categories of drugs discussed in the text include _____ , which tend to slow body functions; _____ , which speed body functions; and _____ , which alter perception. These drugs all work by mimicking, stimulating, or inhibiting the activity of the brain's _____ .

APPLICATION:

82. Dan has recently begun using an addictive, euphoria-producing drug. Which of the following will probably occur if he repeatedly uses this drug?

    a. As tolerance to the drug develops, Dan will experience increasingly pleasurable "highs."
    b. The dosage needed to produce the desired effect will increase.
    c. After each use, he will become more and more elated.
    d. Addiction will become less of a problem.

Objective 3-14: Identify the depressants, and describe their effects.

83. Depressants _____ nervous system activity and _____ body function. Low doses of alcohol, which is classified as a _____ , slow the activity of the _____ nervous system.

84. Alcohol is a _____ ; it may make a person more _____ or more _____ aggressive. Alcohol also disrupts _____ formation. Heavy drinking may lead to blackouts, which result partly from alcohol's suppression of _____ _____ .

85. Excessive use of alcohol can also affect cognition by _____ the brain, especially in _____ (men/women). Alcohol use marked by tolerance and withdrawal and a drive to continue problematic use indicates _____ _____ _____ . Alcohol also reduces _____ and focuses one's attention on an _____ situation and away from _____ _____ and _____ consequences.

Describe how a person's expectations can influence the behavioral effects of alcohol.

86. Tranquilizers, which are also known as _____ , have effects similar to those of alcohol. They are sometimes prescribed to induce _____ or reduce _____ .

87. Opium, morphine, and heroin all _____ (excite/depress) neural functioning. Together, these drugs are called the _____ . When they are present, the brain eventually stops producing _____ .

Objective 3-15: Identify the stimulants, and describe their effects.

88. The most widely used stimulants are _____ , _____ , the _____ , _____ , _____ , and _____ . Stimulants _____ (are/are not) addictive.

89. Eliminating _____ would increase life expectancy more than any other preventive measure. Smokers _____ (do/do not) develop tolerance to the drug. Quitting causes _____ symptoms that include _____ .

90. Nicotine quickly triggers the release of _____ and _____ , two neurotransmitters that diminish _____ and boost _____ and _____ _____ . Nicotine also stimulates the _____ _____ system to release _____ and _____ , neurotransmitters that calm _____ and reduce sensitivity to _____ .

91. Cocaine and crack deplete the brain's supply of the neurotransmitters _____ , _____ , and _____ and result in depression as the drugs' effects wear off. They do this by blocking the _____ of the neurotransmitters, which remain in the nerve cell's _____ .

92. Cocaine's psychological effects depend not only on dosage and form but also on the user's _____ and _____ and the _____ .

93. Methamphetamine triggers the release of the neurotransmitter _____ , which stimulates brain cells that enhance _____ and _____ .

94. The drug _____ , or MDMA, is both a _____ and a _____ _____ . This drug triggers the release of the neurotransmitters _____ and _____ and blocks the reabsorption of _____ . Among the adverse effects of this drug are disruption of the body's _____ clock, suppression of the _____ _____ , impaired _____ , and slow _____ .

Objective 3-16: Identify the hallucinogens, and describe their effects.

95. Hallucinogens are also referred to as _____ . Two common synthetic hallucinogens are _____ and _____ .

96. The reports of people who have had _____-_____ _____ are very similar to the _____ reported by drug users. These experiences may be the result of a deficient supply of _____ or other insults to the brain.

97. The active ingredient in marijuana is abbreviated _____ .

Describe some of the physical and psychological effects of marijuana.

98. All psychoactive drugs trigger _____ _____ , which helps explain both _____ and _____ .

APPLICATIONS:

99. Roberto is moderately intoxicated by alcohol. Which of the following changes in his behavior is likely to occur?
    a. If angered, he is more likely to become aggressive than when he is sober.
    b. He will be less self-conscious about his behavior.
    c. If sexually aroused, he will be less inhibited about engaging in sexual activity.
    d. All of these changes are likely.

100. Which of the following statements concerning marijuana is true?
    a. The by-products of marijuana are cleared from the body more slowly than are the by-products of alcohol.
    b. Regular users may need a larger dose of the drug to achieve a high than occasional users would need to get the same effect.
    c. Marijuana is as addictive as nicotine or cocaine.
    d. Even small doses of marijuana hasten the loss of brain cells.

101. I am a synthetic stimulant and mild hallucinogen that produces euphoria and social intimacy by triggering the release of dopamine and serotonin. What am I? _____

102. Lyndall was in a car accident and required critical surgery to repair her damaged internal organs. During surgery, she had a sense of being outside her body, floating above the operating room. These _____-_____ experiences are similar to sensations of an LSD "trip."

103. Which of the following statements concerning near-death experiences is true?
    a. Fewer than 1 percent of patients who come close to dying report having them.
    b. They typically consist of fantastic, mystical imagery.
    c. They are more commonly experienced by women than by men.
    d. They are more commonly experienced by men than by women.

Objective 3-17: Explain why some people become regular users of consciousness-altering drugs.

104. Drug use by North American youth _____ (increased/declined) during the 1970s, then declined until the early 1990s because of increased _____ _____ and efforts by the media to deglamorize drug use.

105. Having a(n) _____ (identical/fraternal) twin rather than a(n) _____ (identical/fraternal) twin with alcohol use disorder puts one at risk for alcohol problems. Boys who at age 6 are _____ (more/less) excitable are more likely as teens to smoke, drink, and use other drugs. Genes that are more common among people predisposed to alcohol use disorder may cause deficiencies in the brain's _____ _____ system.

Identify some of the psychological and social-cultural roots of drug use.

106. Among teenagers, drug use _____ (varies/is about the same) across _____ and _____ groups.

107. Studies reveal that African-American teens have the _____ (highest/lowest) rates of drug use. A major social influence on drug use is the _____ culture.

108. State three possible channels of influence for drug prevention and treatment programs.

a. _____

b. _____

c. _____

APPLICATIONS:

109. Which of the following statements concerning alcohol use disorder is NOT true?
   a. Adopted individuals are more susceptible to alcohol use disorder if they had an adoptive parent with alcohol use disorder.
   b. Having an identical twin with alcohol use disorder puts a person at increased risk for alcohol problems.
   c. Geneticists have identified genes that are more common among people predisposed to alcohol use disorder.
   d. Researchers have bred rats that prefer alcohol to water.

110. Which of the following was NOT suggested by the text as an important aspect of drug prevention and treatment programs?
   a. education about the long-term costs of a drug's temporary pleasures
   b. efforts to boost people's self-esteem and purpose in life
   c. attempts to modify peer associations
   d. "scare tactics" that frighten prepubescent children into avoiding drug experimentation

111. Which of the following statements concerning the roots of drug use is true?
   a. Heavy users of alcohol, marijuana, and cocaine often are always on a high.
   b. If an adolescent's friends use drugs, odds are that he or she will, too.
   c. Teenagers who are academically average students seldom use drugs.
   d. It is nearly impossible to predict whether a particular adolescent will experiment with drugs.

STUDY TIP: This chapter discusses three major categories of psychoactive drugs, drugs that when abused may lead to clinically significant impairment or distress. Information about their psychological effects and their actions on the nervous system is best organized in the form of a chart. To help you review this material, complete the missing information in the chart below. To get you started, the first drug category has already been filled in. In combination with text Table 3.3, you should have a useful summary of substance-related disorders.

112. Psychoactive Drug Category	Specific Drugs in This Category	Psychological Effects of These Drugs	How These Drugs Affect the Nervous System
Depressants	alcohol, barbiturates, opiates	disrupt judgment and inhibition, induce sleep, reduce anxiety	decrease neural activity, slow body functions
Stimulants			
Hallucinogens			

Progress Test 1

Multiple-Choice Questions

Circle your answers to the following questions and check them with the answers on page 78. If your answer is incorrect, read the explanation for why it is incorrect and then consult the text.

1. As defined by the text, *consciousness* includes which of the following?
   a. focused attention
   b. sleeping
   c. hypnosis
   d. all of these conditions

2. Which of the following is NOT true regarding our circadian rhythm?
   a. Our circadian rhythm can be altered by age.
   b. Our circadian rhythm can be altered by experience.
   c. People who are "morning types" are more vulnerable to depression.
   d. People who are "morning types" tend to do better in school.

3. Which of the following best illustrates dual processing?
   a. Jack experiences uncontrollable sleep attacks in which he falls directly into REM sleep.
   b. Despite the loud conversations around her, Karen is able to concentrate on what her friend is saying.
   c. At the soccer game, Gavin misses seeing a goal kick when his cell phone rings.
   d. While listening to the symphony, Marisol concentrates on what the pianist plays while automatically responding to the tempo and theme of the overall performance.

4. Sleep spindles predominate during which stage of sleep?
   a. NREM-1
   b. NREM-3
   c. NREM-2
   d. REM sleep

5. During which stage of sleep does the body experience increased heart rate, rapid breathing, and genital arousal?
   a. NREM-2
   b. NREM-3
   c. NREM-1
   d. REM sleep

6. The sleep cycle is approximately _____ minutes.
   a. 30
   b. 50
   c. 75
   d. 90

7. The effects of chronic sleep deprivation include
   a. suppression of the immune system.
   b. diminished productivity.
   c. depression.
   d. all of these effects.

8. One effect of sleeping pills is to
   a. decrease REM sleep.
   b. increase REM sleep.
   c. decrease NREM-2 sleep.
   d. increase NREM-2 sleep.

9. Cocaine and crack produce a euphoric rush by
   a. blocking the actions of serotonin.
   b. depressing neural activity in the brain.
   c. blocking the reuptake of dopamine in brain cells.
   d. stimulating the brain's production of endorphins.

10. Which of the following is classified as a depressant?
    a. methamphetamine
    c. marijuana
    b. LSD
    d. alcohol

11. Which of the following preventive measures would have the greatest impact on average life expectancy?
    a. eliminating obesity
    b. eliminating smoking
    c. eliminating sleep deprivation
    d. eliminating binge drinking

12. Which of the following statements concerning hypnosis is true?
    a. People will do anything under hypnosis.
    b. Hypnosis is the same as sleeping.
    c. Hypnosis is in part an extension of the division between conscious awareness and automatic behavior.
    d. Hypnosis improves memory recall.

13. People who heard unusual phrases prior to sleep were awakened each time they began REM sleep. The fact that they remembered less the next morning provides support for the _____ theory of dreaming.
    a. manifest content
    b. physiological
    c. information-processing
    d. cognitive development

14. According to Freud, dreams are
    a. a symbolic fulfillment of erotic wishes.
    b. the result of random neural activity in the brainstem.
    c. the brain's mechanism for self-stimulation.
    d. the transparent expressions of inner conflicts.

15. Psychoactive drugs affect behavior and perception through
    a. the power of suggestion.
    b. the placebo effect.
    c. alteration of neural activity in the brain.
    d. psychological, not physiological, influences.

16. (Thinking Critically) All of the following are common misconceptions about addiction, EXCEPT the statement that
    a. to overcome an addiction a person almost always needs professional therapy.
    b. psychoactive and medicinal drugs very quickly lead to addiction.
    c. biological factors place some individuals at increased risk for addiction.
    d. many other repetitive, pleasure-seeking behaviors fit the drug-addiction-as-disease-needing-treatment model.

17. At its beginning, psychology focused on the study of
    a. observable behavior.
    b. consciousness.
    c. abnormal behavior.
    d. all of these behaviors.

18. Which of the following is NOT a theory of dreaming mentioned in the text?
    a. Dreams facilitate information processing.
    b. Dreaming stimulates the developing brain.
    c. Dreams result from random neural activity originating in the brainstem.
    d. Dreaming is an attempt to escape from social stimulation.

19. The sleep-waking cycles of young people who stay up too late typically are _____ hours in duration.
    a. 23
    c. 25
    b. 24
    d. 26

20. The lowest rates of drug use among high school seniors is reported by
    a. Asian-Americans.
    b. Hispanic-Americans.
    c. African-Americans.
    d. Native Americans.

Matching Items

Match each term with its appropriate definition or description.

Definitions or Descriptions

_____ 1. surface meaning of dreams
_____ 2. deeper meaning of dreams
_____ 3. stage of sleep associated with delta waves
_____ 4. stage of sleep associated with muscular relaxation
_____ 5. sleep disorder in which breathing stops
_____ 6. sleep disorder occurring in NREM-3 sleep
_____ 7. depressant
_____ 8. hallucinogen
_____ 9. stimulant
_____ 10. simultaneous unconscious and conscious tracks
_____ 11. disorder in which sleep attacks occur
_____ 12. study of how brain activity is linked to mental activity
_____ 13. twilight stage of sleep associated with imagery resembling hallucinations

Terms

a. marijuana
b. alcohol
c. NREM-1 sleep
d. cognitive neuroscience
e. manifest content
f. cocaine
g. narcolepsy
h. sleep apnea
i. NREM-3 sleep
j. REM sleep
k. latent content
l. night terrors
m. dual processing

Progress Test 2

Progress Test 2 should be completed during a final chapter review. Answer the following questions after you thoroughly understand the correct answers for the section reviews and Progress Test 1.

Multiple-Choice Questions

1. Which of the following statements regarding REM sleep is true?
   a. Adults spend more time than infants in REM sleep.
   b. REM sleep deprivation results in a REM rebound.
   c. People deprived of REM sleep adapt easily.
   d. Sleeping medications tend to increase REM sleep.

2. The perceptual error in which we fail to see an object when our attention is directed elsewhere is
   a. dissociation.
   b. inattentional blindness.
   c. perceptual adaptation.
   d. divided consciousness.

3. Because they have less of a stomach enzyme that digests alcohol _____ can become addicted to alcohol more readily than _____ do.
   a. boys and young men; girls and young women do
   b. girls and young women; boys and young men
   c. older adults; younger adults
   d. younger adults; older adults

4. A person whose EEG shows a high proportion of alpha waves is most likely
   a. dreaming.   **c.** in NREM-3 sleep.
   b. in NREM-2 sleep.   **d.** awake and relaxed.

5. Circadian rhythms are the
   a. brain waves that occur during deep sleep.
   b. muscular tremors that occur during opiate withdrawal.
   c. regular body cycles that occur on a 24-hour schedule.
   d. brain waves that are indicative of NREM-2 sleep.

6. A person who requires increasing amounts of a drug in order to feel its effect is said to have developed
   a. tolerance.
   b. REM rebound.
   c. withdrawal symptoms.
   d. resistance.

7. Which of the following is NOT an example of a biological rhythm?
   a. the circadian rhythm
   b. the 90-minute sleep cycle
   c. the four sleep stages
   d. sudden sleep attacks during the day

8. Which of the following is characteristic of REM sleep?
   a. genital arousal
   b. increased muscular tension
   c. night terrors
   d. alpha waves

9. Which of the following is NOT a stimulant?
   a. amphetamines
   b. caffeine
   c. nicotine
   d. alcohol

10. Hypnotic responsiveness is
    a. the same in all people.
    b. generally greater in women than men.
    c. generally greater in men than women.
    d. greater when people are led to expect it.

11. According to Hilgard, hypnosis is
    a. no different from a state of heightened motivation.
    b. the same as dreaming.
    c. a dissociation between different levels of consciousness.
    d. a form of deep sleep.

12. Which of the following was NOT cited in the text as evidence that heredity influences alcohol use?
    a. Children whose parents abuse alcohol have a lower tolerance for multiple alcoholic drinks taken over a short period of time.
    b. Boys who are impulsive and fearless at age 6 are more likely to drink as teenagers.
    c. Having an identical twin with alcohol use disorder puts one at increased risk for alcohol problems.
    d. Researchers have found certain genes to be more common among people predisposed to alcohol use disorder.

13. As a form of therapy for relieving problems such as drug addiction, hypnosis is
    a. ineffective.
    b. no more effective than positive suggestions given without hypnosis.
    c. highly effective.
    d. more effective with adults than children.

14. Which of the following is usually the most powerful determinant of whether teenagers begin using drugs?
    a. family strength
    b. religiosity
    c. school adjustment
    d. peer influence

15. THC is the major active ingredient in
    a. nicotine.
    b. MDMA.
    c. marijuana.
    d. cocaine.

16. Those who believe that hypnosis is a social phenomenon argue that "hypnotized" individuals are
    a. consciously faking their behavior.
    b. merely acting out a role.
    c. underachievers striving to please the hypnotist.
    d. doing all of these things.

17. *Consciousness* is defined in the text as
    a. mental life.
    b. selective attention to ongoing perceptions, thoughts, and feelings.
    c. information processing.
    d. our awareness of ourselves and our environment.

18. I am a synthetic stimulant and mild hallucinogen that produces euphoria and social intimacy by triggering the release of dopamine and serotonin. What am I?
    a. LSD
    b. MDMA
    c. THC
    d. cocaine

19. According to one physiological theory, dreaming represents
    a. the brain's efforts to integrate unrelated bursts of activity in visual brain areas with the emotional tone provided by limbic system activity.
    b. a mechanism for coping with the stresses of daily life.
    c. a symbolic depiction of a person's unfulfilled wishes.
    d. an information-processing mechanism for converting the day's experiences into long-term memory.

20. How a particular psychoactive drug affects a person depends on
    a. the dosage and form in which the drug is taken.
    b. the user's expectations and personality.
    c. the situation in which the drug is taken.
    d. all of these conditions.

Matching Items

Match each term with its appropriate definition or description.

Definitions or Descriptions

_____ **1.** drug that is both a stimulant and mild hallucinogen

_____ **2.** drugs that increase energy and stimulate neural activity

_____ **3.** brain wave of awake, relaxed person

_____ **4.** unconscious response to a visual stimulus

_____ **5.** sleep stage associated with dreaming

_____ **6.** drugs that reduce anxiety and depress central nervous system activity

_____ **7.** natural painkillers produced by the brain

_____ **8.** focusing conscious awareness on a particular stimulus

_____ **9.** our awareness of ourselves and our environment

_____ **10.** theory that dreaming reflects our erotic drives

_____ **11.** a split between different levels of consciousness

_____ **12.** neurotransmitter that LSD resembles

_____ **13.** brain-wave activity during NREM-2 sleep

Terms

a. Freud's theory
b. serotonin
c. Ecstasy
d. alpha
e. dissociation
f. amphetamines
g. consciousness
h. sleep spindle
i. endorphins
j. REM
k. barbiturates
l. selective attention
m. blindsight

Essay Question

You have just been assigned the task of writing an article tentatively titled "Alcohol and Alcohol use disorder: Roots, Effects, and Prevention." What information should you include in your article? (Use the space provided to list the points you want to make, and organize them. Then write the essay on a separate piece of paper.)

Terms and Concepts to Remember

Writing Definitions

Using your own words, on a separate piece of paper write a brief definition or explanation of each of the following terms.

1. consciousness

2. cognitive neuroscience

3. dual processing

4. blindsight

5. selective attention

6. inattentional blindness

7. change blindness

8. circadian rhythm

9. REM sleep

10. alpha waves

11. sleep

12. hallucinations

13. delta waves

14. suprachiasmatic nucleus

15. insomnia

16. narcolepsy

17. sleep apnea

18. night terrors

19. dream

20. manifest content

21. latent content

22. REM rebound

23. hypnosis

24. posthypnotic suggestion

25. dissociation

26. substance use disorder

27. psychoactive drugs

28. tolerance

29. addiction

30. withdrawal

31. depressants

32. alcohol use disorder

33. barbiturates

34. opiates

35. stimulants

36. amphetamines

37. nicotine

38. methamphetamine

39. Ecstasy (MDMA)

40. hallucinogens

41. LSD

42. near-death experience

43. THC

Cross-Check

As you learned in Chapter 1, reviewing and overlearning of material are important to the learning process. After you have written the definitions of the key terms in this chapter, you should complete the crossword puzzle to ensure that you can reverse the process—recognize the term, given the definition.

ACROSS

2. Term for REM sleep reflecting that the body is aroused but the muscles are relaxed.
8. Widely used stimulant that is inhaled.
9. Brain wave that predominates in Stage 4 sleep.
10. Powerful hallucinogen first used by Albert Hofmann.
11. Type of brain wave that occurs during NREM-2 sleep.
13. NREM-1 dream sensation similar to a hallucination.
14. Also known as tranquilizers.
16. Drug category that includes alcohol.

DOWN

1. Relatively slow brain waves of a relaxed, awake state.
3. Drugs that "speed up" neural activity.
4. Drugs that depress neural activity, temporarily lessening pain.
5. Theory suggesting that dreams help fix daily experiences in our memories.

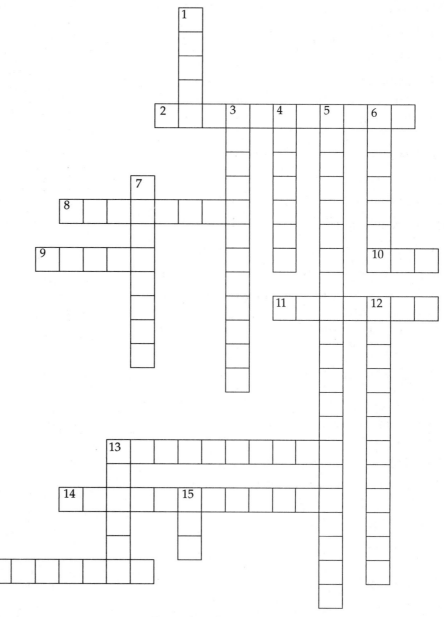

6. Drug that disrupts the processing of recent experiences into long-term memories.
7. Neurotransmitter whose reuptake is blocked by cocaine.
12. Divided consciousness (as during hypnosis).
13. Depressant that causes a rush of euphoria.
15. Active ingredient in marijuana.

Answers
Chapter Review

The Brain and Consciousness

1. consciousness; behavior
2. brain activity; cognition

Consciousness is our awareness of ourselves and our environment.

3. cognitive neuroscience
4. conscious
5. simultaneously; parallel
6. conscious; unconscious; dual processing
7. blindsight
8. dual-processing; perception; action
9. requires
10. selective attention
11. cocktail party effect
12. inattentional blindness; change blindness
13. pop-out
14. c. is the answer.
15. a. is the answer.
   b. This is the definition of consciousness.
   c. This defines inattentional blindness.
   d. In selective attention, awareness is focused on one stimulus.

Sleep and Dreams

16. biological rhythms
17. circadian rhythm
18. rises; fall
19. thinking; memory
20. age; experience; initiative; depression
21. four
22. eyes; dreams; REM sleep
23. alpha; sleep
24. hypnagogic; hallucinations; memories
25. sleep spindles
26. delta; 3; slow-wave; difficult; sleepwalking

During REM sleep, brain waves become as rapid as those of NREM-1 sleep, heart rate rises and breathing becomes more rapid and irregular, and genital arousal (except during very scary dreams) and rapid eye movements occur. Even men with erectile disorder experience "morning erections."

27. active; relaxed; paralyzed; paradoxical
28. 90; briefer; longer; 20 to 25
29. 1. b   3. d
    2. c   4. a
30. b. is the answer. Although the body is aroused internally, the messages of the activated motor cortex do not reach the muscles.
   a. Studies of REM-deprived people indicate just the opposite.

c. It is difficult to awaken a person from REM sleep.
   d. Just the opposite occurs in REM sleep: the muscles are relaxed, yet the brain is aroused.
31. c. is the answer. The rapid eye movements of REM sleep coincide with bursts of activity in brain areas that process visual images.
32. two-thirds; one-third
33. genes; identical; environment; less
34. suprachiasmatic nucleus; pineal; melatonin
35. protect; recuperate; brain; metabolism; free radicals; neurons; memory; creative
36. pituitary; less; less
37. improves
38. d. is the answer. Freud's theory proposed that dreams, which occur during fast-wave REM sleep, serve as a psychic safety valve.
39. 9
40. 5; depression; 8
41. ghrelin; leptin; cortisol; immune; viral infections; cancer; accidents
42. insomnia; reduce

Tips for promoting healthy sleep include exercising regularly (especially during late afternoon), avoiding caffeine after early afternoon and food and drink before bedtime, sleeping on a regular schedule, and relaxing before bedtime.

43. narcolepsy; REM; muscular tension
44. sleep apnea; overweight men
45. night terrors; 3; sleepwalking; sleeptalking; run; young children; lengthiest; deepest
46. a. is the answer. With sleep apnea, the person stops breathing for a minute or so, then is awakened by decreased blood oxygen and snorts in the air. This happens hundreds of times each night.
47. b. is the answer. Narcolepsy is characterized by uncontrollable sleep attacks.
   a. Sleep apnea is characterized by the temporary cessation of breathing while asleep.
   c. Night terrors are characterized by high arousal and terrified behavior, occurring during NREM-3 sleep.
   d. Insomnia refers to chronic difficulty in falling or staying asleep.
48. REM
49. six
50. negative; failing in an attempt to do something, attacked, pursued, or rejected, or experiencing misfortune

51. incorporate

52. monitors

53. manifest; latent

54. erotic; conflicts; safety valve

55. information; memory

56. REM; memory

57. physiological; stimulation

58. neural; brainstem; limbic; amygdala; maturation; cognitive

59. need; REM rebound

60. does; do not; information-processing

61. REM. The amygdala is involved in emotion, and dreams during REM sleep often tend to be emotional.

62. increase; REM rebound

63. latent. The analyst is evidently trying to go beyond the events in the dream and understand the dream's hidden meaning, or the dream's latent content.

64. c. is the answer.

Hypnosis

65. social interaction

66. somewhat

Those who are most susceptible frequently become deeply absorbed in imaginative activities. Many researchers refer to this as hypnotic ability.

67. fact; fiction

68. control

69. posthypnotic; is; is not

70. can

71. normal consciousness; social influence

72. authoritative; context

The behavior of hypnotized subjects is not fundamentally different from that of other people. Therefore, hypnosis may be mainly a social phenomenon, with hypnotized subjects acting out the role of a "good hypnotic subject."

73. dual-processing; dissociation; sensory; emotional; attention

74. a. is the answer. Although people recall more under hypnosis, they "recall" a lot of fiction along with fact and appear unable to distinguish between the two.
b. Hypnotically refreshed memories are usually no more accurate than conscious memories.
c. Although the hypnotized subject's imagination may influence the memories retrieved, some actual memory retrieval also occurs.

d. Hypnotically retrieved memories don't normally focus on anxiety-provoking events.

75. b. is the answer. People with the ability to become imaginatively absorbed have essentially the characteristics associated with hypnotic suggestibility. The fact that Janice is an actress also suggests she possesses such traits.
a. Bill's reality orientation makes him an unlikely candidate for hypnosis.
c. The hypnotically suggestible are generally able to focus on tasks or on imaginative activities.
d. People who are hypnotically suggestible tend to become deeply engrossed in novels and movies.

76. d. is the answer.

77. c. is the answer.

Drugs and Consciousness

78. psychoactive; substance use disorder

79. tolerance; neuroadaptation

80. withdrawal; addicted

The following are reasons that addictions may not be as irresistible as commonly believed:
a. Taking a psychoactive drug automatically leads to addiction.
b. A person cannot overcome an addiction without professional help.
c. The addiction-as-disease-needing-treatment model is applicable to a broad spectrum of repetitive, pleasure-seeking behaviors.

81. depressants; stimulants; hallucinogens; neurotransmitters

82. b. is the answer. Continued use of a drug produces a tolerance; to experience the same "high," Dan will have to use larger and larger doses.

83. calm; slow; depressant; sympathetic

84. disinhibitor; helpful; sexually; memory; REM sleep

85. shrinking; women; alcohol use disorder; self-awareness; arousing; normal inhibitions; future

Studies have found that if people believe that alcohol affects social behavior in certain ways, then, when they drink alcohol (or even mistakenly think that they have been drinking alcohol), they will behave according to their expectations, which vary by culture. For example, if people believe alcohol promotes sexual feeling, on drinking they are likely to behave in a sexually aroused way.

86. barbiturates; sleep; anxiety

87. depress; opiates; endorphins

88. caffeine; nicotine; amphetamines; cocaine; Ecstasy; methamphetamine; are

89. smoking; do; nicotine; do; nicotine-withdrawal; craving, insomnia, anxiety, irritability, and distractibility

90. epinephrine; norepinephrine; appetite; alertness; mental efficiency; central nervous; dopamine; opioids; anxiety; pain

91. dopamine; serotonin; norepinephrine; reuptake (reabsorption); synapses

92. expectations; personality; situation

93. dopamine; energy; mood

94. Ecstasy; stimulant; mild hallucinogen; dopamine; serotonin; serotonin; circadian; immune system; memory; thinking

95. psychedelics; Ecstasy (MDMA); LSD

96. near-death experiences; hallucinations; oxygen

97. THC
Like alcohol, marijuana relaxes, disinhibits, and may produce a euphoric high. Also like alcohol, marijuana impairs perceptual and motor skills. Marijuana is a mild hallucinogen; it can amplify sensitivity to colors, sounds, tastes, and smells. Marijuana also interrupts memory formation. Unlike alcohol, THC remains in the body for a week or more. Also, the users' experience can vary with the situation.

98. negative aftereffects; tolerance; withdrawal

99. d. is the answer. Alcohol loosens inhibitions and reduces self-consciousness, making people more likely to act on their feelings of anger or sexual arousal. It also disrupts memory formation.

100. a. is the answer. THC, the active ingredient in marijuana, and its by-products linger in the body for a week or more.

101. Ecstasy (MDMA)

102. near-death

103. b. is the answer.
a. Approximately 15 percent of patients revived from cardiac arrest report a near-death experience.
c. & d. There is no gender difference in the prevalence of near-death experiences.

104. increased; drug education

105. identical; fraternal; more; dopamine reward
A psychological factor in drug use is the feeling that one's life is meaningless and lacks direction. Regular users of psychoactive drugs often have experienced stress or failure and are somewhat depressed. Drug use often begins as a temporary way to relieve depression, anger, anxiety, or insomnia. A powerful social factor in drug use, especially among adolescents, is peer influence. For example, smoking usually begins during early adolescence. Peers shape attitudes about drugs, provide drugs, and establish the social context for their use.

106. varies; cultural; ethnic

107. lowest; peer

108. a. education about the long-term costs of a drug's temporary pleasures
b. efforts to boost people's self-esteem and purpose in life
c. attempts to "inoculate" youths against peer pressures

109. a. is the answer. Adopted individuals are more susceptible to alcohol use disorder if they had a *biological* parent with alcohol use disorder.
b., c., & d. Each of these is true, which indicates that susceptibility to alcohol use disorder is at least partially determined by heredity.

110. d. is the answer.

111. b. is the answer.

112. Stimulants include caffeine, nicotine, amphetamines, cocaine, Ecstasy, and methamphetamines. They enhance energy and mood and can be addictive. They excite neural activity and speed up body functions.
Hallucinogens include Ecstasy, LSD, and marijuana. They distort perceptions and evoke sensory images in the absence of sensory input. They produce their effects by interfering with the serotonin neurotransmitter system.

Progress Test 1

Multiple-Choice Questions

1. d. is the answer.

2. c. is the answer. Morning types are less vulnerable to depression.

3. d. is the answer.
a. Jack apparently suffers from narcolepsy.
b. Karen is demonstrating selective attention.
c. Gavin's experience is an example of inattentional blindness.

4. c. is the answer.
b. Delta waves predominate during NREM-3.
a. NREM-1 sleep is characterized by slowed breathing and irregular brain waves.
d. Faster, nearly waking brain waves occur during REM sleep.

5. d. is the answer.

a., b., & c. During non-REM stages 1–3 heart rate and breathing are slow and regular and the genitals are not aroused.

6. **d.** is the answer.

7. **d.** is the answer.

8. **a.** is the answer. Like alcohol, sleeping pills carry the undesirable consequence of reducing REM sleep and may make insomnia worse in the long run.
b., c., & d. Sleeping pills do not produce these effects.

9. **c.** is the answer. They also block the reuptake of serotonin and norepinephrine.
a. This answer describes the effect of LSD.
b. Depressants such as alcohol have this effect. Cocaine and crack are classified as stimulants.
d. None of the psychoactive drugs has this effect. Opiates, however, *suppress* the brain's production of endorphins.

10. **d.** is the answer. Alcohol, which slows body functions and neural activity, is a depressant.
a. Methamphetamine is a stimulant.
b. & c. LSD and marijuana are hallucinogens.

11. **b.** is the answer.

12. **c.** is the answer.
a. Hypnotized subjects usually perform only acts they might perform normally.
b. The text does not suggest that sleeping and hypnosis are the same states. In fact, the brain waves of hypnotized subjects are not like those associated with sleeping.
d. Hypnosis typically *disrupts*, or contaminates, memory.

13. **c.** is the answer. They remembered less than if they were awakened during other stages.

14. **a.** is the answer. Freud saw dreams as psychic safety valves that discharge unacceptable feelings that are often related to erotic wishes.
b. & c. These physiological theories of dreaming are not associated with Freud.
d. According to Freud, dreams represent the individual's conflicts and wishes but in disguised, rather than transparent, form.

15. **c.** is the answer. Such drugs work primarily at synapses, altering neural transmission.
a. What people believe will happen after taking a drug will likely have some effect on their individual reactions, but psychoactive drugs actually work by altering neural transmission.
b. Because a placebo is a substance without active properties, this answer is incorrect.

d. This answer is incorrect because the effects of psychoactive drugs on behavior, perception, and so forth have a physiological basis.

16. **c.** is the answer. This is true. Heredity, for example, influences tendencies toward alcoholism.

17. **b.** is the answer.
a. The behaviorists' emphasis on observable behavior occurred much later in the history of psychology.
c. Psychology has never been primarily concerned with abnormal behavior.

18. **d.** is the answer.
a., b., & c. Each of these describes a valid theory of dreaming that was mentioned in the text.

19. **c.** is the answer. We can reset our biological clocks by adjusting our sleep schedules. Thus, young adults adopt something closer to a 25-hour day by staying up too late to get 8 hours of sleep.

20. **c.** is the answer.

Matching Items

1. e	6. l	11. g
2. k	7. b	12. d
3. i	8. a	13. c
4. j	9. f	
5. h	10. m	

Progress Test 2

Multiple-Choice Questions

1. **b.** is the answer. Following REM deprivation, people temporarily increase their amount of REM sleep, in a phenomenon known as REM rebound.
a. Just the opposite is true: the amount of REM sleep is greatest in infancy.
c. Deprived of REM sleep by repeated awakenings, people return more and more quickly to the REM stages after falling back to sleep. They by no means adapt easily to the deprivations.
d. Just the opposite occurs: they tend to suppress REM sleep.

2. **b.** is the answer.

3. **b.** is the answer.

4. **d.** is the answer.
a. The brain waves of REM sleep (dream sleep) are more like those of NREM-1 sleepers.
b. NREM-2 is characterized by sleep spindles.
c. NREM-3 characterized by slow delta waves.

5. **c.** is the answer.

6. **a.** is the answer.

b. PREM rebound refers to the increase in REM following REM sleep deprivation.

c. Withdrawal refers to the discomfort and distress that follow discontinuing use of an addictive drug.

d. There is no such thing as drug "resistance."

7. **d.** is the answer.

8. **a.** is the answer.
    b. During REM sleep, muscular tension is low.
    c. Night terrors are associated with NREM-3 sleep.
    d. Alpha waves are characteristic of the relaxed, awake state.

9. **d.** is the answer. Alcohol is a depressant.

10. **d.** is the answer.
    a. Hypnotic responsiveness varies greatly from person to person.
    b. & c. There is no evidence of a gender difference in hypnotic responsiveness.

11. **c.** is the answer. Hilgard believes that hypnosis reflects a dissociation, or split, in consciousness, as occurs normally, only to a much greater extent.

12. **a.** is the answer. Compared with other children, children whose parents misuse alcohol have a *higher* tolerance for multiple drinks, making it more likely that they will, in fact, consume more alcohol.

13. **a.** is the answer.

14. **d.** is the answer. If adolescents' friends use drugs, the odds are that they will, too.
    a., b., & c. These are also predictors of drug use but seem to operate mainly through their effects on peer association.

15. **c.** is the answer.

16. **b.** is the answer.
    a. & c. There is no evidence that hypnotically responsive individuals fake their behaviors or that they are underachievers.

17. **d.** is the answer.

18. **b.** is the answer.
    a. & c. Unlike stimulants, LSD and THC do not speed up body functions.
    d. Unlike hallucinogens, cocaine is a stimulant and does not generally distort perceptions.

19. **a.** is the answer.
    b. & c. These essentially Freudian explanations of the purpose of dreaming are based on the idea that a dream is a psychic safety valve that harmlessly discharges otherwise inexpressible feelings.

d. This explanation of the function of dreaming is associated with the information-processing viewpoint.

20. **d.** is the answer.

Matching Items

1.	c	5.	j	9.	g	13.	h
2.	f	6.	k	10.	a		
3.	d	7.	i	11.	e		
4.	m	8.	l	12.	b		

Essay Question

As a depressant, alcohol slows neural activity and body functions. Although low doses of alcohol may produce relaxation, with larger doses reactions slow, speech slurs, skilled performance deteriorates, and memory formation is disrupted. Alcohol also reduces self-awareness and may facilitate sexual and aggressive urges the individual might otherwise resist.

Some people may be biologically vulnerable to alcohol use disorder. This is indicated by the fact that individuals who have a biological parent with alcohol use disorder, or people who have an identical twin with alcohol use disorder, are more susceptible to alcohol use disorder.

Stress, depression, and the feeling that life is meaningless and without direction are common feelings among heavy users of alcohol and may create a psychological vulnerability to alcohol use disorder.

Especially for teenagers, peer group influence is strong. If an adolescent's friends use alcohol, odds are that he or she will too.

Research suggests three important channels of influence for drug prevention and treatment programs: (1) education about the long-term consequences of alcohol use; (2) efforts to boost people's self-esteem and purpose in life; and (3) attempts to counteract peer pressure that leads to experimentation with drugs.

Terms and Concepts to Remember

Writing Definitions

1. For most psychologists, **consciousness** is our awareness of ourselves and our environment.

2. **Cognitive neuroscience** is the interdisciplinary study of the links between brain activity and cognition.

3. **Dual processing** is the principle that information is often simultaneously processed on separate conscious and unconscious tracks.

4. **Blindsight** is a condition in which a person responds to a visual experience without consciously experiencing it.

5. **Selective attention** is the focusing of conscious awareness on a particular stimulus.

6. **Inattentional blindness** is a perceptual error in which we fail to see visible objects when our attention is directed elsewhere.

7. **Change blindness** occurs when we fail to notice changes in the environment.

8. A **circadian rhythm** is any regular bodily rhythm, such as body temperature and sleep-wakefulness, that follows a 24-hour cycle.

   Memory aid: In Latin, *circa* means "about" and *dies* means "day." A **circadian rhythm** is one that is about a day, or 24 hours, in duration.

9. **REM sleep** (rapid eye movement sleep) is the sleep stage in which the muscles are relaxed but other body systems are active, and vivid dreaming occurs; also known as *paradoxical sleep*.

   Memory aid: **REM** is an acronym for rapid eye movement, the distinguishing feature of this sleep stage that led to its discovery.

10. **Alpha waves** are the relatively slow brain waves characteristic of an awake, relaxed state.

11. **Sleep** is the natural, periodic loss of consciousness, on which the body and mind depend for healthy functioning.

12. **Hallucinations** are false sensory experiences that occur without any sensory stimulus.

13. **Delta waves** are the large, slow brain waves associated with deep sleep.

14. The **suprachiasmatic nucleus** is a a pair of cell clusters in the hypothalamus that responds to light-sensitive retinal proteins. It causes pineal gland to increase or decrease production of melatonin, thus modifying our feelings of sleepiness.

15. **Insomnia** is a sleep disorder in which the person regularly has difficulty in falling or staying asleep.

16. **Narcolepsy** is a sleep disorder in which the victim suffers sudden, uncontrollable sleep attacks, often characterized by entry directly into REM.

17. **Sleep apnea** is a sleep disorder in which the person ceases breathing while asleep, briefly arouses to gasp for air, falls back asleep, and repeats this cycle throughout the night.

    Example: One theory of the sudden infant death syndrome is that it is caused by **sleep apnea**.

18. A person suffering from **night terrors** experiences episodes of high arousal with apparent terror. Night terrors usually occur during NREM-3 sleep.

19. **Dreams** are sequences of images, emotions, and thoughts, the most vivid of which occur during REM sleep.

20. In Freud's theory of dreaming, the **manifest content** is the remembered story line.

21. In Freud's theory of dreaming, the **latent content** is the underlying but censored meaning of a dream.

    Memory aids for 19 and 20: *Manifest* means "clearly apparent, obvious"; *latent* means "hidden, concealed." A dream's **manifest content** is that which is obvious; its **latent content** remains hidden until its symbolism is interpreted.

22. **REM rebound** is the tendency for REM sleep to increase following REM sleep deprivation.

23. **Hypnosis** is a social interaction in which one person (the hypnotist) suggests to another (the subject) that certain perceptions, feelings, thoughts, or behaviors will spontaneously occur.

24. A **posthypnotic suggestion** is a suggestion made during a hypnosis session that is to be carried out after the subject is no longer hypnotized.

25. **Dissociation** is a split between different levels of consciousness, allowing a person to divide attention between two or more thoughts or behaviors.

26. **Substance use disorder** involves continued substance craving and use despite significant life disruption and/or physical risk.

27. **Psychoactive drugs**—which include stimulants, depressants, and hallucinogens—are chemical substances that alter moods and perceptions. They work by affecting or mimicking the activity of neurotransmitters.

28. **Tolerance** is the diminishing of a psychoactive drug's effect that occurs with repeated use, requiring progressively larger doses to produce the same effect.

29. An **addiction** is a compulsive craving of drugs or certain behaviors despite known harmful consequences.

30. **Withdrawal** refers to the discomfort and distress that follow the discontinued use of an addictive drug or behavior.

31. **Depressants** are psychoactive drugs, such as alcohol, opiates, and barbiturates, that reduce neural activity and slow body functions.

32. **Alcohol use disorder** (popularly known as alcoholism) is alcohol use that is marked by tolerance, withdrawal if use is suspended, and a drive to continue use.

33. **Barbiturates** are depressants, sometimes used to induce sleep or reduce anxiety. In larger doses, they impair memory and judgment.

34. **Opiates** are depressants derived from the opium poppy, such as opium, morphine, and heroin; they reduce neural activity and temporarily lessen pain and anxiety.

35. **Stimulants** are psychoactive drugs, such as caffeine, nicotine, amphetamines, Ecstasy, methamphetamine, and cocaine, that excite neural activity and speed up body functions.

36. **Amphetamines** are a type of stimulant and, as such, speed up body functions and neural activity.

37. **Nicotine** is the stimulating and highly addictive psychoactive drug found in tobacco.

38. **Methamphetamine** is a powerfully addictive stimulant that speeds up body functions and is associated with energy and mood changes.

39. Classified as both a synthetic stimulant and a mild hallucinogen, **Ecstasy (MDMA)** produces short-term euphoria and social intimacy by increasing serotonin levels in the brain. Repeated use may permanently damage serotonin neurons, suppress immunity, and impair memory and other cognitive functions.

40. **Hallucinogens** are psychedelic drugs, such as LSD and marijuana, that distort perceptions and evoke sensory images in the absence of sensory input.

41. **LSD** (*lysergic acid diethylamide*) is a powerful hallucinogen capable of producing vivid false perceptions and disorganization of thought processes.

42. The **near-death experience** is an altered state of consciousness that has been reported by some people who have had a close brush with death.

43. The major active ingredient in marijuana, **THC** is classified as a mild hallucinogen.

Cross-Check

ACROSS	DOWN
2. paradoxical	1. alpha
8. nicotine	3. amphetamines
9. delta	4. opiates
10. LSD	5. information processing
11. spindle	6. alcohol
13. hypnagogic	7. dopamine
14. barbiturates	12. dissociation
16. depressant	13. heroin
	15. THC

Developing Through the Life Span

Chapter Overview

Developmental psychologists study the life cycle, from conception to death. Chapter 4 covers physical, cognitive, and social development over the life span and introduces three major issues in developmental psychology: (1) the relative impact of genes and experience on behavior, (2) whether development is best described as gradual and continuous or as a discontinuous sequence of stages, and (3) whether the individual's personality remains stable or changes over the life span.

Although there are not too many terms to learn in this chapter, there are a number of important research findings to remember. Pay particular attention to the stage theories of Piaget, Kohlberg, and Erikson, as well as to the discussion regarding intellectual stability during adulthood.

NOTE: Answer guidelines for all Chapter 4 questions begin on page 99.

Chapter Review

First, skim this section, noting headings and boldface items. After you have read the section, review each objective by completing the sentences and answering the questions that follow it. In some cases, Study Tips explain how best to learn a difficult concept and Think About It and Applications help you to know how well you understand the material. As you proceed, evaluate your performance by consulting the answers beginning on page 99. Do not continue with the next section until you understand each answer. If you need to, review or reread the section in the textbook before continuing.

Developmental Psychology's Major Issues

Objective 4-1: Identify three issues that have engaged developmental psychologists.

1. Scientists who study physical, cognitive, and social changes throughout the life cycle are called

   _____ _____ .

2. One of the major issues in developmental psychology concerns the relative importance of genetic inheritance and experience in determining behavior; this is called the issue of

   _____ and_____ .

3. A second developmental issue concerns whether developmental changes are gradual or abrupt; this is called the issue of _____ and

   _____ .

4. A third controversial issue concerns the consistency of personality and whether development is characterized more by _____

   over time or by change.

Prenatal Development and the Newborn

Objective 4-2: Discuss the course of prenatal development, and explain how teratogens affect that development.

5. Conception begins when a woman's

   _____ releases a mature

   _____ .

6. The few _____ from the man that reach the egg release digestive _____ that eat away the egg's protective covering. As soon as one sperm penetrates the egg, the egg's surface _____ all other sperm.

7. The egg and sperm _____ fuse and become one.

8. Fertilized human eggs are called _____ . During the first week, the cells in this cluster begin to specialize in structure and function, that is, they begin to _____ . About 10 days after conception, the fertilized egg attaches to the mother's _____ wall.

9. From about 2 until 8 weeks of age the developing human, formed from the inner cells of the fertilized egg, is called a(n) _____ . The outer cells become the _____ , which transfers _____ and _____ from mother to fetus. Along with nutrients, a range of harmful substances (such as toxins and viruses), known as _____ , can pass through the placenta.

10. During the final stage of prenatal development, the developing human is called a(n) _____ .

11. Moderate consumption of alcohol during pregnancy _____ (usually does not affect/can affect) the fetal brain. If a mother drinks heavily, her baby is at risk for the birth defects and intellectual disability that accompany _____ _____ _____ .

APPLICATION:

12. Marissa has just learned that she is two months pregnant. She is concerned about her baby's health because in the last few months she has been drinking heavily. Marissa is afraid that her unborn child may be at risk for birth defects and for future behavior problems, _____ , and lower _____ .

Objective 4-3: Describe some abilities of the newborn, noting how researchers explore their mental abilities.

13. When an infant's cheek is touched, it will vigorously _____ for a nipple. Finding one, it will automatically close on it and begin _____ , which requires _____ , _____ , and _____ .

14. American psychologist _____ believed that the newborn experiences a "blooming, buzzing confusion." This belief is _____ (correct/incorrect).

Give some evidence supporting the claim that a newborn's sensory equipment is biologically prewired to facilitate social responsiveness.

15. To study infants' thinking, developmental researchers have used _____ , which involves a _____ in responding with repeated stimulation.

APPLICATION:

16. Leonardo is only 6 months old, so he can't tell his Mom what he likes. However, by looking away from a mobile that now seems to bore him, he is saying that he sees and remembers the mobile. His behavior indicates that he has _____ to the mobile.

Infancy and Childhood

Objective 4-4: Describe some developmental changes in brain and motor abilities during infancy and childhood.

17. Biological growth processes that enable orderly changes in behavior are called _____ .

18. The developing brain _____ (over/under)produces neurons. At birth, the human nervous system _____ (is/is not) fully mature. Between 3 and 6 years of age, the brain is developing most rapidly in the _____ lobes, which enable _____ _____ . The last areas of the brain to develop are the _____ _____ linked with _____ , _____ , and _____ .

19. After puberty, a process of _____ shuts down unused neural connections and strengthens others. Young rats raised in an enriched environ-ment develop a thicker _____ than do rats raised in an impover-ished enviornment.

20. Grammar and accent are most easily mastered during _____ _____ , when there seems to be a _____ _____ for the development of such skills.

21. Infants pass the milestones of _____ development at different rates, but the basic _____ of stages is fixed. Infants sit before they _____ and walk before they _____ .

22. Genes play a _____ (major/minor) role in motor development.

23. Until the necessary muscular and neural matura-tion is complete, including the rapid develop-ment of the brain's _____ , experience has a _____ (large/small) effect on learning to walk, for example.

24. Our earliest memories generally do not occur before age _____ . This phenom-enon has been called _____ _____ .

25. Research has shown that babies _____ (are/are not) capable of learning.

APPLICATION:

26. Calvin, who is trying to impress his psychology professor with his knowledge of infant motor development, asks why some infants learn to roll over before they lift their heads from a prone position, while others develop these skills in the opposite order. What should Calvin's professor conclude from this question?
   a. Calvin clearly understands that the sequence of motor development is not the same for all infants.
   b. Calvin doesn't know what he's talking about. Although some infants reach these develop-mental milestones ahead of others, the order is the same for all infants.
   c. Calvin needs to be reminded that rolling over is an inherited reflex, not a learned skill.
   d. Calvin understands an important principle: Motor development is unpredictable.

Objective 4-5: Describe how a child's mind devel-ops from the perspectives of Piaget, Vygotsky, and today's researchers.

27. *Cognition* refers to all the mental activities associ-ated with _____ , _____ , _____ , and _____ .

28. The first researcher to show that the thought processes of adults and children are very differ-ent was _____ .

29. To organize and interpret his or her experiences, the developing child constructs cognitive con-cepts called _____ .

30. The interpretation of new experiences in terms of existing ideas is called _____ . The adaptation of existing ideas to fit new experiences is called _____ .

31. In Piaget's first stage of development, the _____ stage, children experience the world through their motor and sensory inter-actions with objects. This stage occurs between birth and nearly age _____ .

32. The awareness that things continue to exist even when they are removed from view is called _____ _____ . This awareness begins to develop at about _____ months of age.

33. Developmental researchers have found that Piaget and his followers _____ (overestimated/underestimated) young children's competence. For instance, babies have an intuitive grasp of simple laws of _____ , as seen in their reaction to a ball stopping in midair, and an understanding of _____ , as Karen Wynn demonstrated.

34. According to Piaget, during the preschool years and up to age _____ , children are in the _____ stage.

35. The principle that the quantity of a substance remains the same even when the shape of its container changes is called _____ . Piaget believed that preschoolers _____ (have/have not) developed this concept.

36. When children can perform mental operations and think in symbols, they begin to enjoy

    _____ _____ .

    Preschoolers have difficulty perceiving things from another person's point of view. Piaget called this inability _____ . Even adults may overestimate the extent to which others share their opinions and perspectives, a trait known as the _____ _____

    _____ .

37. The child's growing ability to take another's perspective is evidence that the child is acquiring a

    _____ _____

    _____ . Between the ages of about 3½ and 4½, children come to realize that others may hold _____ _____ .

38. (Close-Up) The disorder characterized by significant deficiencies in _____ and _____ interaction and an impaired

    _____ _____

    _____ , as well as rigidly fixated interests and _____ behaviors, is referred to as _____ _____

    _____ .

39. (Close-Up) This disorder is related to poor communication among brain areas that normally

work together to enable taking another's

_____ .

40. (Close-Up) Baron-Cohen's theory proposes that autism spectrum disorder represents an "extreme _____ brain." According to this theory, girls tend to be _____ , who are better than boys at reading facial expressions and gestures. Boys tend to be _____ , who understand things in terms of rules or laws.

41. Piaget believed that children acquire the mental abilities needed to comprehend mathematical transformations and conservation by about _____ years of age. At this time, they enter the _____

    _____ stage.

42. In Piaget's final stage, the _____ _____ stage, reasoning expands from the purely concrete to encompass _____ thinking. Piaget believed most children begin to enter this stage by about age _____ .

43. Russian psychologist _____ noted that by age _____ children stop thinking aloud and instead rely on

    _____ _____ . Talking to themselves helps children control their _____ and _____ and master new skills.

44. Complementing Piaget's emphasis on interaction with the _____ environment is Vygotsky's emphasis on interaction with the _____ environment. To Vygotsky, children were young _____ mentored by parents and others who give them new words. Thus, they provide a _____ upon which the child can build higher-level thinking.

Explain briefly how contemporary researchers view Piaget's theory.

STUDY TIP: Jean Piaget was the first major theorist to realize that each stage of life has its own characteristic way of thinking. To deepen your understanding of Jean Piaget's stages of cognitive development, fill in the blanks in the chart below. Do as much as you can without reviewing the text. To get you started, the first stage has been completed.

45. Typical Age Range	Stage	New Developments	Test to Determine If Someone Is in This Stage
Birth to nearly 2 years	Sensorimotor	Stranger anxiety Object permanence	Have the child's mother leave the room Hide a toy under a blanket
2 to _____	_____		
	Concrete _____		
About 12 through _____	_____		

APPLICATIONS:

46. Compared with when he was younger, 4-year-old Antonio is better able to empathize with his friend's feelings. This growing ability to take another's perspective indicates that Antonio is acquiring a _____ _____ _____ .

47. As 8-year-old Gabriella observes, liquid is transferred from a tall, thin tube into a short, wide jar. She is asked if there is now less liquid in order to determine if she has mastered the concept of _____ .

48. Caleb is 14 months old and he behaves as though "out of sight is out of existence." He is in Piaget's _____ stage of cognitive development.

49. Makayla is 3 years old, can use language, and has trouble taking another person's perspective. She is in Piaget's _____ stage of cognitive development.

50. Four-year-old Jamail has a younger sister. When asked if he has a sister, he is likely to answer _____ (yes/no); when asked if his sister has a brother, Jamail is likely to answer _____ (yes/no).

51. In Piaget's theory, conservation is to egocentrism as the _____ stage is to the _____ stage.
a. sensorimotor; formal operational
b. formal operational; sensorimotor
c. preoperational; sensorimotor
d. concrete operational; preoperational

Objective 4-6: Describe how parent-infant attachment bonds form.

52. Soon after _____ _____ emerges and children become mobile, a new fear, called _____ _____ , emerges. This fear emerges at about age _____ .

53. The development of a strong emotional bond between infant and parent is called _____ .

54. The Harlows' studies of monkeys have shown that mother-infant attachment does not depend on the mother providing nourishment as much as it does on her providing the comfort of body _____ . Another key to attachment is _____ .

55. Human attachment involves one person providing another with a safe haven when distressed and a _____ _____ from which to explore.

56. In some animals, attachment will occur only during a restricted time called a _____
_____ . Konrad Lorenz discovered
that young birds would follow almost any object
if it were the first moving thing they observed.
This phenomenon is called _____ .

57. Human infants _____ (do/do
not) have a precise critical period for becoming
attached. However, because of _____
_____ , they attach to what they
know.

APPLICATION:

58. In a 1998 movie, a young girl finds that a flock
of geese follows her wherever she goes because
she was the first "object" they saw after they
were born. This is an example of

   a. conservation.   **c.** egocentrism.

   b. imprinting.   **d.** basic trust.

Objective 4-7: Describe how psychologists study
attachment differences, and discuss their findings.

59. Placed in a research setting called the
_____ _____ , children
show one of two patterns of attachment:
_____ attachment or
_____ attachment.

60. A person's characteristic emotional reactivity and
intensity, called _____ , is
_____ influenced. One form of a
gene that regulates the neurotransmitter
_____ predisposes a fearful infant
and, in combination with unsupportive caregiving, an inhibited child.

Contrast the responses of securely and insecurely
attached infants to strange situations.

Discuss the impact of responsive parenting on infant
attachment.

61. A father's love and acceptance for his children are
_____ (comparable to/less impor-
tant than) a mother's love in predicting their
children's health and well-being.

62. Separation anxiety peaks in infants around
_____ months, then
_____ (gradually declines/remains
constant for about a year). This is true of children
_____ (in North America/through-
out the world).

63. According to Erik and Joan Erikson, securely
attached infants approach life with a sense of
_____ _____ .

64. Most researchers now believe that early attachments _____ (do/do not) form the
basis of adult attachments.

APPLICATION:

65. Layla and Christian Bishop have a 13-month-old
boy. According to Erikson, the Bishops' sensitive,
loving care of their child contributes to the
child's _____ _____ .

Objective 4-8: Describe how parental neglect or abuse
affects children's attachment.

66. The Harlows found that when monkeys reared in
social isolation were placed with other monkeys,
they reacted with either fear or _____ .

67. Most abused children _____
(do/do not) later become abusive parents.

68. Although most children who grow up under
adversity are _____ and become
normal adults, early abuse and excessive exposure to _____ _____
may alter the development of the brain chemical
_____ .

Objective 4-9: Describe the effect of day care on children.

69. Experts agree that child care per se _____ (does/does not) constitute a risk factor in children's development.

70. High-quality child care consists of warm, supportive interactions with adults in an environment that is _____ , _____ , and _____ .

71. More important than time spent in day care in influencing a child's aggression are _____ _____ .

Objective 4-10: Describe three parenting styles, and explain how children's traits relate to them.

72. Parents who impose rules and expect obedience are exhibiting a(n) _____ style of parenting.

73. Parents who make few demands of their children and tend to submit to their children's desires are identified as _____ parents.

74. Setting and enforcing standards after discussion with their children is the approach taken by _____ parents.

75. Studies have shown that children with the highest self-esteem, self-reliance, and social competence usually have _____ parents. However, the association between parenting style and childhood outcome is _____ and does not indicate _____ .

76. Child-rearing practices reflect individual values and _____ values, which vary across _____ and _____ . Western families promote _____ in children, whereas many _____ and _____ cultures place more value on a strong sense of _____ _____ .

Adolescence

Objective 4-11: Define *adolescence,* and explain how physical changes affect developing teens.

77. Although many psychologists once believed that our traits were set during _____ ,

psychologists today see development as _____ . This is called the _____ perspective.

78. *Adolescence* is defined as the transition period between _____ and _____ .

79. The "storm and stress" view of adolescence is credited to _____ , one of the first American psychologists to describe adolescence.

80. Adolescence begins with the time of developing sexual maturity known as _____ .

81. The _____ (timing/sequence) of pubertal changes is more predictable than their _____ (timing/sequence)—for example, breast buds and visible pubic hair before the first menstrual period, called _____ .

82. Boys who mature _____ (early/late) tend to be more popular, self-assured, and independent; they also are at increased risk for _____ _____ .

83. For girls, _____ (early/late) maturation can be stressful, especially when their bodies are out of sync with their _____ _____ . This reminds us that _____ and _____ interact.

84. The adolescent brain undergoes a selective _____ of unused neurons and connections. The growth of _____ around axons speeds _____ and promotes better _____ between brain regions. Also, teens' occasional impulsiveness and risky behaviors may be due, in part, to the fact that development in the brain's _____ _____ lags behind that of the _____ _____ .

APPLICATION:

85. Based on the text discussion of maturation and popularity, who among the following is probably the most popular sixth grader?
    a. Jessica, the most physically mature girl in the class
    b. Roger, the most intellectually mature boy in the class
    c. Rob, the tallest, most physically mature boy in the class
    d. Cindy, who is average in physical development and is on the school debating team

Objective 4-12: Describe adolescent cognitive and moral development, according to Piaget, Kohlberg, and later researchers.

86. Adolescents' developing cognitive ability enables them to think about what is _____ possible and _____ that with imperfect reality.

87. During the early teen years, reasoning is often _____ , as adolescents often feel their experiences are unique.

88. Piaget's final stage of cognitive development is the stage of _____ _____ . Adolescents in this stage are capable of thinking logically about _____ as well as concrete propositions. This enables them to detect _____ in others' reasoning and to spot hypocrisy.

89. The theorist who proposed that moral thought progresses through stages is _____ . These stages are divided into three basic levels: _____ , _____ , and _____ .

90. In the preconventional stages of morality, characteristic of children, the emphasis is on obeying rules to avoid _____ or gain concrete _____ .

91. Conventional morality usually emerges by early _____ . The emphasis is on gaining social _____ or maintaining the social _____ .

92. Individuals who base moral judgments on their own perceptions of basic ethical principles are said by Kohlberg to employ _____ morality.

Explain why critics fault Kohlberg's theory of moral development.

93. The idea that moral feelings precede moral reasoning is expressed in the moral _____ view of morality. Research studies using _____ _____ support the idea that moral judgment involves more than merely thinking; it is also gut-level feeling.

94. Morality involves doing the right thing, and what we do depends on _____ influences. Today's _____ _____ _____ focus on moral issues and doing the right thing. They teach children _____ for others' feelings.

95. Children who learn to delay _____ become more socially responsible. They also become more _____ successful and more productive.

96. Moral ideas grow _____ (stronger/ weaker) when acted on.

APPLICATIONS:

97. Thirteen-year-old Irene has no trouble defeating her 11-year-old brother at a detective game that requires following clues in order to deduce the perpetrator of a crime. How might Piaget explain Irene's superiority at the game?
    a. Being older, Irene has had more years of schooling.
    b. Girls develop intellectually at a faster rate than boys.
    c. Being an adolescent, Irene is beginning to develop abstract reasoning skills.
    d. Girls typically have more experience than boys at playing games.

98. Jake, a junior in high school, regularly attends church because his family and friends think he should. Jake is in Kohlberg's _____ stage of moral reasoning.

99. In Jada's country, people believe in family togetherness above all else. Because her culture does not give priority to _____ , Kohlberg would say that she is not at his highest level of moral reasoning, the _____ level.

Objective 4-13: Describe the social tasks and challenges of adolescence.

Complete the missing information in the following table of Erikson's stages of psychosocial development.

Group Age	Psychosocial Stage
Infancy	_____
_____	Autonomy vs. shame and doubt
Preschooler	_____
_____	Competence vs. inferiority
Adolescence	_____
_____	Intimacy vs. isolation
Middle adulthood	_____
_____	Integrity vs. despair

100. To refine their sense of identity, adolescents in individualistic cultures experiment with different "_____" in different situations. The result may be role _____ , which is resolved by forming a self-definition, or _____ . The aspect of peoples self-concept that forms around their group membership is their _____ _____ .

101. Some adolescents forge their identity early, simply by _____ their parents' values and expectations. Others may adopt the identity of a particular _____ _____ .

102. During the early to mid-teen years, self-esteem generally _____ (rises/falls/remains stable). During the late teens and twenties, self-esteem generally _____ (rises/falls/remains stable) and agreeableness and emotional stability scores _____ (increase/decrease).

103. Erikson saw the formation of identity as a prerequisite for the development of _____ in young adulthood.

Objective 4-14: Contrast parental and peer influences during adolescence.

104. Adolescence is typically a time of increasing influence from one's _____ and decreasing influence from _____ .

105. Most adolescents report that they _____ (do/do not) get along with their parents. They see their parents as having the most influence in shaping their _____ _____ , for example.

106. Research on social relationships between parents and their adolescent children shows that high school girls who have the most _____ relationships with their mothers tend to enjoy the most _____ friendships with girlfriends.

107. When rejected adolescents withdraw, they are vulnerable to _____ , low _____ , and _____ .

108. (Thinking Critically) In personality measures, shared environmental influences account for less than _____ percent of children's differences.

APPLICATION:

109. Fourteen-year-old Cassandra feels freer and more open with her friends than with her family. Knowing this is the case, Cassandra's parents should
    a. be concerned, because deteriorating parent-teen relationships, such as this one, are often followed by a range of problem behaviors.
    b. encourage Cassandra to find new friends.
    c. seek family counseling.
    d. not worry, since adolescence is typically a time of growing peer influence and diminishing parental influence.

Objective 4-15: Discuss the characteristics of emerging adulthood.

110. Adolescents today are taking _____ (more/less) time to establish their independence as adults. At the same time, sexual maturity is beginning _____ (earlier/later) than in the past.

111. Because the time from 18 to the mid-twenties is increasingly a not-yet-settled phase of life, some psychologists refer to this period as a time of _____ _____ .

Objective 4-1: Identify three issues that have engaged developmental psychologists.

112. Although research casts doubt on the idea that life proceeds through age-linked _____ , there are spurts of _____ growth during childhood and puberty that correspond roughly to the stages proposed by _____ .

Adulthood

Objective 4-16: Identify the physical changes that occur during middle and late adulthood.

113. During adulthood, age _____ (is/is not) a very good predictor of people's traits.

114. The mid-twenties are the peak years for

    _____ _____ ,
    _____ _____ ,
    _____ _____ , and
    _____ _____ .

    Because they mature earlier, _____ (women/men) also peak earlier.

115. During early and middle adulthood, physical vigor has less to do with _____ than with a person's _____ and _____ habits.

116. The cessation of the menstrual cycle, known as _____ , occurs within a few years of age _____ . A woman's experience during this time depends largely on her _____ and _____ .

117. With age, the eye's pupil _____ (shrinks/enlarges) and its lens becomes _____ (more/less) transparent. As a result, the amount of light that reaches the retina is _____ (increased/reduced).

118. Although older adults are _____ (more/less) susceptible to life-threatening ailments, they suffer from short-term ailments such as flu _____ (more/less) often than younger adults.

119. Aging _____ (slows/speeds/has no effect on) neural processing and causes a gradual loss of _____ .

120. Late in life, atrophy of the inhibition-controlling _____ _____ seemingly explains older people's occasional blunt questions and comments.

121. Physical exercise stimulates the development of _____ connections and promotes _____ , the birth of new nerve cells, in the hippocampus.

122. With age, the tips of our chromosomes, called _____ , shorten. However, they can be maintained by _____ .

Objective 4-17: Assess the impact of aging on memory.

123. Studies of developmental changes in learning and memory show that during adulthood there is a decline in the ability to _____ (recall/recognize) new information but not in the ability to _____ (recall/recognize) such information. One factor that

influences memory in older people is the

_____ of material.

124. Cognitive abilities among 70-year-olds are

_____ (less/more) varied than

among 20-year-olds.

125. A research study in which people of various

ages are compared with one another is called a

_____-_____ study.

126. A research study in which the same people are

retested over a period of years is called a

_____ study.

127. Especially in the last three or four years of

life, cognitive decline typically accelerates.

Researchers call this near-death drop

_____ _____ .

APPLICATION:

128. Which statement illustrates cognitive development during the course of adult life?
   a. Forty-three-year-old Sophia has better recognition memory than 72-year-old Kylie.
   b. Both Sophia and Kylie have strong recall and
recognition memory.
   c. Kylie's recognition memory decreased sharply
at age 50.
   d. Forty-three-year-old Sophia has better recall
memory than 72-year-old Kylie.

Objective 4-18: Discuss the themes and influences
that mark the social journey from early adulthood to
death.

129. Contrary to popular opinion, job and marital

dissatisfaction do not surge during the forties,

thus suggesting that a midlife _____

need not occur.

130. The term used to refer to the culturally pre-

ferred timing for leaving home, getting a job,

marrying, and so on is the _____

_____ . Today, the timing of such

life events is becoming _____

(more/less) predictable. More important than

age are _____ _____

and chance encounters.

131. According to Erikson, the two basic

tasks of adulthood are achieving _____

and _____ . According to Freud,

the healthy adult is one who can

_____ and _____ .

132. Marriage bonds are usually lasting when cou-

ples marry after age _____ and are

_____ _____ .

133. Marriages today are _____

(half/twice) as likely to end in divorce as they

were in the 1960s. Couples who live together

before marrying have a _____

(higher/lower) divorce and marital dysfunction

rate than those who do not.

134. Marriage is a predictor of _____ ,

_____ _____ ,

_____ , and physical and mental

_____ . Lesbian couples report

_____ (greater/less) well-being

than those who are alone.

135. As children begin to absorb time and energy,

satisfaction with the marriage itself

_____ (increases/decreases). This

is particularly true among _____

women, who shoulder most of the burden.

136. For most couples, the children's leaving home

produces a(n) _____ (increase/

decrease) in marital satisfaction.

137. During the first two years of college or univer-

sity, most students _____ (can/

cannot) predict their later careers. Happiness is

finding work that provides a sense of

_____ and _____ .

APPLICATION:

138. After a series of unfulfilling relationships,
30-year-old Carlos tells a friend that he doesn't
want to marry because he is afraid of losing his
freedom and independence. Erikson would say
that Carlos is having difficulty with the psychosocial task of

   a. trust versus mistrust.
   b. autonomy versus doubt.
   c. intimacy versus isolation.
   d. identity versus role confusion.

Objective 4-19: Describe trends in people's self-confidence and life satisfaction across the life span.

139. From the teens to midlife, people typically experience a strengthening sense of

_____ , _____ , and

_____ .

140. According to studies, older people
_____ (do/do not) report as much happiness and satisfaction with life as younger people do. In addition, their feelings
_____ (do/do not) mellow.

141. As we age, the brain area called the
_____ shows _____
(increased/decreased) activity in response to negative events.

142. More and more people flourish into later life, thanks to _____ influences.

APPLICATION:

143. The text discusses well-being across the life span. Which of the following people is likely to report the greatest life satisfaction?
    a. Billy, a 7-year-old second-grader
    b. Kathy, a 17-year-old high-school senior
    c. Mildred, a 70-year-old retired teacher
    d. too little information to tell

Objective 4-20: Describe the range of reactions to the death of a loved one.

144. Grief over a loved one's death is especially severe when it comes _____
_____ .

145. Reactions to a loved one's death
_____ (do/do not) vary according to cultural norms. Those who express the strongest grief immediately _____
(do/do not) purge their grief more quickly.

146. Terminally ill and bereaved people
_____ (do/do not) go through predictable stages.

147. According to Erikson, the final task of adulthood is to achieve a sense of
_____ .

Objective 4-1: Identify three issues that have engaged developmental psychologists.

148. The early years of life _____
(do/do not) provide a good basis for predicting a person's eventual traits.

149. Research on the consistency of personality shows that some traits, such as those related to
_____ , are more stable than others, such as social attitudes.

APPLICATION:

150. In thinking about stability and change over the life span, most developmental psychologists believe that
    a. Development occurs in a series of sharply defined stages.
    b. The first two years are the most crucial in determining the individual's personality.
    c. The consistency of personality in most people tends to increase over the life span.
    d. Social and emotional style are among the characteristics that show the least stability over the life span.

Progress Test 1

Multiple-Choice Questions

Circle your answers to the following questions and check them with the answers beginning on page 103. If your answer is incorrect, read the explanation for why it is incorrect and then consult the text.

1. Dr. Joan Goodman is studying how memory changes as people get older. She is most likely a(n) _____ psychologist.
    a. social   c. developmental
    b. cognitive   d. experimental

2. In Piaget's stage of concrete operational intelligence, the child acquires an understanding of the principle of
    a. conservation.   c. attachment.
    b. abstract reasoning. d. object permanence.

3. Piaget held that egocentrism is characteristic of the
    a. sensorimotor stage.
    b. preoperational stage.
    c. concrete operational stage.
    d. formal operational stage.

4. During which stage of cognitive development do children acquire object permanence?
   a. sensorimotor
   b. preoperational
   c. concrete operational
   d. formal operational

5. Newborns vigorously root for a nipple when
   a. their foot is tickled.
   b. their cheek is touched.
   c. they hear a loud noise.
   d. they make eye contact with their caregiver.

6. The Harlows' studies of attachment in monkeys showed that
   a. provision of nourishment was the single most important factor motivating attachment.
   b. a cloth mother produced the greatest attachment response.
   c. whether a cloth or wire mother was present mattered less than the presence or absence of other infants.
   d. attachment in monkeys is based on imprinting.

7. When psychologists discuss maturation, they are referring to stages of growth that are NOT influenced by
   a. conservation.
   b. nature.
   c. nurture.
   d. continuity.

8. The developmental theorist who suggested that securely attached children develop an attitude of basic trust is
   a. Piaget.
   b. Harlow.
   c. Vygotsky.
   d. Erikson.

9. Research findings on infant motor development are consistent with the idea that
   a. cognitive development lags significantly behind motor skills development.
   b. maturation of physical skills is relatively unaffected by experience.
   c. in the absence of relevant earlier learning experiences, the emergence of motor skills will be slowed.
   d. in humans, the process of maturation may be significantly altered by cultural factors.

10. According to Erikson, the central psychological challenges pertaining to adolescence, young adulthood, and middle age, respectively, are
    a. identity formation; intimacy; generativity.
    b. intimacy; identity formation; generativity.
    c. generativity; intimacy; identity formation.
    d. intimacy; generativity; identity formation.

11. In preconventional morality, the person
    a. obeys out of a sense of social duty.
    b. conforms to gain social approval.
    c. obeys to avoid punishment or to gain concrete rewards.
    d. follows the dictates of his or her conscience.

12. Which of the following is correct?
    a. Early maturation places both boys and girls at a distinct social advantage.
    b. Early maturing girls are more popular and self-assured than girls who mature late.
    c. Early maturation places both boys and girls at a distinct social disadvantage.
    d. Early maturing boys are more popular and self-assured than boys who mature late.

13. The decrease in cognitive function that occurs near death in some people is called
    a. habituation.
    b. egocentrism.
    c. terminal decline.
    d. assimilation.

14. An older person who can look back on life with satisfaction and reminisce with a sense of completion has attained Erikson's stage of
    a. generativity.
    b. intimacy.
    c. isolation.
    d. integrity.

15. According to Piaget, the ability to think logically about abstract propositions is indicative of the stage of
    a. preoperational thought.
    b. concrete operations.
    c. formal operations.
    d. postconventional thought.

16. The cognitive ability that has been shown to decline during adulthood is the ability to
    a. recall new information.
    b. recognize new information.
    c. learn meaningful new material.
    d. use judgment in dealing with daily life problems.

17. Which of the following statements concerning the effects of aging is true?
    a. Aging almost inevitably leads to total memory failure if the individual lives long enough.
    b. Aging increases susceptibility to short-term ailments such as the flu.
    c. Significant increases in life satisfaction are associated with aging.
    d. The aging process can be significantly affected by the individual's activity patterns.

18. Longitudinal research
    a. compares people of different ages.
    b. studies the same people at different times.
    c. usually involves a larger sample than does cross-sectional research.
    d. usually involves a smaller sample than does cross-sectional research.

19. Telomeres are
    a. clusters of cells formed by the union of sperm and egg at conception.
    b. chemicals, viruses, and other toxins that can harm a developing embryo.
    c. mental concepts that organize and interpret information.
    d. the tips of chromosomes that shorten with age.

20. Adolescence is marked by the onset of
    a. an identity crisis.
    b. parent-child conflict.
    c. the concrete operational stage.
    d. puberty.

21. The end of menstruation is called
    a. menarche.   c. the midlife crisis.
    b. menopause.   d. generativity.

True–False Items

Indicate whether each statement is true or false by placing *T* or *F* in the blank next to the item.

_____   1. Most abused children later become abusive parents.
_____   2. At birth, the brain and nervous system of a healthy child are fully developed.
_____   3. The sequence in which children develop motor skills varies by culture.
_____   4. Current research shows that young children are more capable and development is more continuous than Piaget believed.
_____   5. The process of grieving is much the same throughout the world.
_____   6. The impact of day care on child development, even if it is high quality, remains controversial.
_____   7. During adulthood, age only moderately correlates with people's traits.
_____   8. By the age of 50, most adults have experienced a "midlife crisis."
_____   9. Compared with those who are younger, older people are more susceptible to short-term ailments such as the flu.
_____   10. Shared environmental influences account for about 50 percent of children's differences in personality.

Progress Test 2

Progress Test 2 should be completed during a final chapter review. Answer the following questions after you thoroughly understand the correct answers for the section reviews and Progress Test 1.

1. Stranger anxiety develops soon after
    a. the concept of conservation.
    b. egocentrism.
    c. a theory of mind.
    d. the concept of object permanence.

2. Before Piaget, people were more likely to believe that
    a. the child's mind is a miniature model of the adult's.
    b. children think about the world in radically different ways from adults.
    c. the child's mind develops through a series of stages.
    d. children interpret their experiences in terms of their current understandings.

3. Which is the correct sequence of stages in Piaget's theory of cognitive development?
    a. sensorimotor, preoperational, concrete operational, formal operational
    b. sensorimotor, preoperational, formal operational, concrete operational
    c. preoperational, sensorimotor, concrete operational, formal operational
    d. preoperational, sensorimotor, formal operational, concrete operational

4. A child can be born a drug addict because
    a. drugs used by the mother will pass into the child's bloodstream.
    b. addiction is an inherited personality trait.
    c. drugs used by the mother create genetic defects in her chromosomes.
    d. the fetus' blood has not yet developed a resistance to drugs.

5. A child whose mother drank heavily when she was pregnant is at heightened risk of
    a. being emotionally excitable during childhood.
    b. becoming insecurely attached.
    c. being born with the physical and cognitive abnormalities of fetal alcohol syndrome.
    d. addiction to a range of drugs throughout life.

6. Which is the correct order of stages of prenatal development?
    a. zygote, fetus, embryo

b. zygote, embryo, fetus
c. embryo, zygote, fetus
d. embryo, fetus, zygote

7. The term *critical period* refers to
   a. prenatal development.
   b. the initial 2 hours after a child's birth.
   c. the preoperational stage.
   d. a restricted time for learning.

8. Which of the following was NOT found by the Harlows in socially deprived monkeys?
   a. They had difficulty mating.
   b. They showed extreme fear or aggression when first seeing other monkeys.
   c. They showed abnormal physical development.
   d. The females were abusive mothers.

9. Most people's earliest memories do not predate _____ of age.
   a. 6 months   c. 2 years
   b. 1 year   d. 3 years

10. Insecurely attached infants who are left by their mothers in an unfamiliar setting often will
    a. hold fast to their mothers on their return.
    b. explore the new surroundings confidently.
    c. be indifferent toward their mothers on their return.
    d. display little emotion at any time.

11. Whose stage theory of moral development was based on how people reasoned about ethical dilemmas?
    a. Erikson   c. Harlow
    b. Piaget   d. Kohlberg

12. Cross-sectional research
    a. compares people of different ages with one another.
    b. studies the same group of people at different times.
    c. is used for studying cognitive development during infancy.
    d. is used for studying social development during infancy.

13. The social clock refers to
    a. an individual or society's distribution of work and leisure time.
    b. adulthood responsibilities.
    c. typical ages for starting a career, marrying, and so on.
    d. age-related changes in one's circle of friends.

14. To which of Kohlberg's levels would moral reasoning based on the existence of fundamental human rights pertain?
    a. preconventional morality
    b. conventional morality
    c. postconventional morality
    d. generative morality

15. In Erikson's theory, individuals generally focus on developing _____ during adolescence and then _____ during young adulthood.
    a. identity; intimacy
    b. intimacy; identity
    c. basic trust; identity
    d. identity; basic trust

16. Teratogens are
    a. physical abnormalities in the developing fetus.
    b. cognitive abnormalities in the developing fetus.
    c. chemicals and viruses that cross the placenta and may harm the developing fetus.
    d. fertilized eggs.

17. After their grown children have left home, most couples experience
    a. the distress of the empty nest syndrome.
    b. increased strain in their marital relationship.
    c. the need to have their children visit often.
    d. greater happiness and enjoyment in their relationship.

18. In terms of incidence, susceptibility to short-term illnesses _____ with age and susceptibility to long-term ailments _____ with age.
    a. decreases; increases
    b. increases; decreases
    c. increases; increases
    d. decreases; decreases

19. Research on the American family indicates that
    a. fewer than 23 percent of unmarried adults, but nearly 40 percent of married adults, report being "very happy" with life.
    b. the divorce rate is now one-half the marriage rate.
    c. children born to cohabiting parents are five times more likely to experience their parents' separation.
    d. all of these statements are true.

20. The idea that terminally ill and bereaved people go through predictable stages, such as denial, anger, and so forth
    a. is widely supported by research.
    b. more accurately describes grieving in some cultures than others.
    c. is true of women but not men.
    d. is not supported by research studies.

21. The idea that morality is rooted in moral intu-itions rather than moral reasoning is the basis for
    a. Lawrence Kohlberg's theory.
    b. Jean Piaget's theory.
    c. Jonathan Haidt's theory.
    d. Erik Erikson's theory.

Essay

Sheryl is a 12-year-old living in the United States. She is in the sixth grade. Describe the developmental changes she is likely to be experiencing according to Piaget, Kohlberg, and Erikson. (Use the space below to list the points you want to make, and organize them. Then write the essay on a separate sheet of paper.)

Terms and Concepts to Remember

Writing Definitions

Using your own words, on a piece of paper write a brief definition or explanation of each of the following terms.

1. developmental psychology

2. zygote

3. embryo

4. fetus

5. teratogens

6. fetal alcohol syndrome (FAS)

7. habituation

8. maturation

9. critical period

10. cognition

11. schema

12. assimilation

13. accommodation

14. sensorimotor stage

15. object permanence

16. preoperational stage

17. conservation

18. egocentrism

19. theory of mind

20. concrete operational stage

21. autism spectrum disorder

22. formal operational stage

23. stranger anxiety

24. attachment

25. imprinting

26. temperament

27. basic trust

28. adolescence

29. puberty

30. identity

31. social identity

32. intimacy

33. emerging adulthood

34. menopause

35. cross-sectional study

36. longitudinal study

37. social clock

Cross-Check

As you learned in Chapter 1, reviewing and overlearning of material are important to the learning process. After you have written the definitions of the key terms in this chapter, you should complete the crossword puzzle to ensure that you can reverse the process—recognize the term, given the definition.

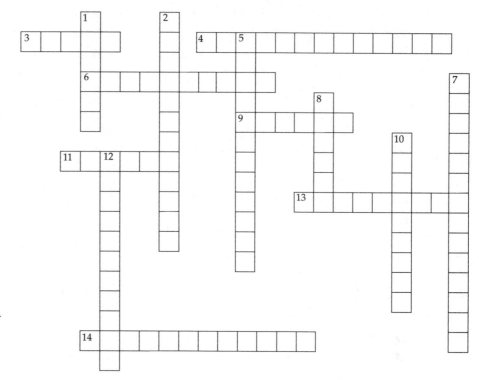

ACROSS

3. The developing person from 9 weeks after conception until birth.
4. In Piaget's theory, changing an existing schema to incorporate new information.
6. Process by which certain animals form attachments during a critical period.
9. The developing person from 2 weeks through 2 months after conception.
11. Mental concepts or frameworks that organize information.
13. Cessation of menstruation.
14. A study in which the same people are retested over a period of years.

Down

1. A childhood disorder marked by deficiencies in communication and social interaction is referred to as _____ spectrum disorder.
2. In Piaget's theory, interpreting a new experience in terms of an existing schema.
5. Principle that properties such as number or volume remain constant despite changes in appearance.
7. A study in which people of different ages are compared with one another.
8. Fertilized human egg.
10. Any drug, virus, or other toxic substance that crosses the mother's placenta.
12. Decreasing responsiveness to a stimulus that is repeatedly presented.

Answers

Chapter Review

Developmental Psychology's Major Issues

1. developmental psychologists
2. nature; nurture
3. continuity; stages
4. stability

Prenatal Development and the Newborn

5. ovary; egg
6. sperm; enzymes; blocks
7. nuclei
8. zygotes; differentiate; uterine
9. embryo; placenta; nutrients; oxygen; teratogens
10. fetus
11. can affect; fetal alcohol syndrome
12. hyperactivity; intelligence
13. root; sucking; swallowing; tonguing; breathing
14. William James; incorrect

Newborns reflexively turn their heads in the direction of human voices. They gaze longer at a drawing of a face-like image. They focus best on objects about 8 to 12 inches away, which is about the distance between a nursing infant's eyes and the mother's. Within days, they recognize their mother's smell and voice.

15. habituation; decrease
16. habituated

Infancy and Childhood

17. maturation
18. over; is not; frontal; rational planning; association areas; thinking; memory; language
19. pruning; cortex

20. early childhood; critical period
21. motor; sequence; crawl; run
22. major
23. cerebellum; small
24. 3; infantile amnesia
25. are
26. **b.** is the answer.
    a. & d. Although the rate of motor development varies from child to child, the basic sequence is universal and, therefore, predictable.
    c. Rolling over and head lifting are both learned.
27. thinking; knowing; remembering; communicating
28. Jean Piaget
29. schemas
30. assimilation; accommodation
31. sensorimotor; 2
32. object permanence; 8
33. underestimated; physics; numbers
34. 6 or 7; preoperational

35. conservation; have not
36. pretend play; egocentrism; curse of knowledge
37. theory of mind; false beliefs
38. communication; social; theory of mind; repetitive; autism spectrum disorder
39. viewpoint (perspective)
40. male; empathizers; systemizers
41. 6 or 7; concrete operational
42. formal operational; abstract; 12
43. Lev Vygotsky; 7; inner speech; behavior; emotions
44. physical; social; apprentices; scaffold

Contemporary researchers see development as more continuous than did Piaget. By detecting the beginnings of each type of thinking at earlier ages, they have revealed conceptual abilities that Piaget missed. They also see formal logic as a smaller part of cognition than Piaget did. Despite these revisions to Piaget's theory, studies support the basic idea that cognitive development unfolds in the sequence Piaget described.

45.

Typical Age Range	Stage	New Developments	Test to Determine If Someone Is in This Stage
Birth to nearly 2 years	Sensorimotor	Stranger anxiety Object permanence	Have the child's mother leave the room Hide a toy under a blanket
2 to 6 or 7 years	Preoperational	Egocentrism Not yet logical	Ask questions to determine child's ability to take another's perspective
6 or 7 to 11 years	Concrete operational	Conservation Simple math	Transfer liquid from a tall, thin glass into a short, wide glass
About 12 through adulthood	Formal operational	Abstract logic	Give child a hypothetical reasoning problem

46. theory of mind
47. conservation. This test is designed to determine if the child understands that the quantity of liquid is conserved, despite the shift to a container that is different in shape.
48. sensorimotor. The sensorimotor period is Piaget's first stage. Object permanence develops some time during this period.
49. preoperational. This child's age, ability to use language, and egocentrism clearly place her within Piaget's preoperational stage.
50. yes; no. Being 4 years old, Jamail would be in Piaget's preoperational stage. Preoperational thinking is egocentric, which means Jamail would find it difficult to "put himself in his sister's shoes" and perceive that she has a brother.
51. **d.** is the answer. Conservation is a hallmark of the concrete operational stage; egocentrism is a hallmark of the preoperational stage.
52. object permanence; stranger anxiety; 8 months
53. attachment
54. contact; familiarity
55. secure base
56. critical period; imprinting
57. do not; mere exposure
58. **b.** is the answer.
    a. Conservation is the ability to realize that the

amount of an object does not change even if its shape changes.

c. Egocentrism is having difficulty perceiving things from another's perspective.

d. According to Erikson, basic trust is feeling that the world is safe as a result of sensitive, loving caregivers.

59. strange situation; secure; insecure

60. temperament; genetically; serotonin

Placed in a strange situation, securely attached infants play comfortably, happily exploring their new environment. In contrast, insecurely attached infants are less likely to explore their surroundings and may even cling to their mothers. When separated from their mothers, insecurely attached infants are much more distressed than securely attached infants. When reunited with their mothers, insecurely attached infants may be indifferent.

Research studies conducted by Mary Ainsworth have revealed that sensitive, responsive mothers tend to have securely attached infants, whereas insensitive, unresponsive mothers often have insecurely attached infants. Other studies have found that temperamentally difficult infants whose mothers receive training in responsive parenting are more likely to become securely attached than are control infants. This points to the importance of considering the infant's temperament in studying attachment.

61. comparable to

62. 13; gradually declines; throughout the world

63. basic trust

64. do

65. basic trust. Although loving parents will also produce securely attached children, Erikson's theory deals with trust or mistrust.

66. aggression

67. do not

68. resilient; stress hormones; serotonin

69. does not

70. safe; healthy; stimulating

71. the parents' sensitivity, the child's temperament, and the family's economic and educational level

72. authoritarian

73. permissive

74. authoritative

75. authoritative; correlational; causation

76. cultural; time; place; independence; Asian; African; family self

Adolescence

77. childhood; lifelong; life-span

78. childhood; adulthood

79. G. Stanley Hall

80. puberty

81. sequence; timing; menarche

82. early; alcohol use, delinquency, and premature sexual activity

83. early; emotional maturity; heredity; environment

84. pruning; myelin; neurotransmission; communication; frontal lobe; limbic system

85. **c.** is the answer. Early maturing boys tend to be more popular.

    a. Early maturing girls may suffer teasing or sexual harassment.

    b. & d. The social benefits of early or late maturation are based on physical development, not on cognitive skills.

86. ideally; compare

87. self-focused

88. formal operations; abstract; inconsistencies

89. Lawrence Kohlberg; preconventional; conventional; postconventional

90. punishment; rewards

91. adolescence; approval; order

92. postconventional

Kohlberg's critics note that his postconventional stage is culturally limited, appearing mostly among people who prize individualism.

93. intuitionist; moral paradoxes

94. social; character education programs; empathy

95. gratification; academically

96. stronger

97. **c.** is the answer.

    a., b., & d. Piaget did not link cognitive ability to amount of schooling, gender, or differences in how boys and girls are socialized.

98. conventional. Conventional morality is based in part on a desire to gain others' approval.

99. individualism; postconventional

Erikson's stages of psychosocial development

Group Age	Psychosocial Stage
Infancy	Trust vs. mistrust
Toddlerhood	Autonomy vs. shame and doubt
Preschooler	Initiative vs. guilt
Elementary school	Competence vs. inferiority
Adolescence	Identity vs. role confusion

Group Age	Psychosocial Stage
Young adulthood	Intimacy vs. isolation
Middle adulthood	Generativity vs. stagnation
Late adulthood	Integrity vs. despair

100. selves; confusion; identity; social identity
101. adopting; peer group
102. falls; rises; increase
103. intimacy
104. peers; parents
105. do; religious faith
106. affectionate; intimate
107. loneliness; self-esteem; depression
108. 10
109. **d.** is the answer.
     a. This description of Cassandra's feelings does not suggest that her relationship with her parents is deteriorating. Cassandra's social development, like that of most adolescents, is coming under increasing peer influence and diminishing parental influence.
     b. & c. Because Cassandra's feelings are normal, there is no reason for her to change her circle of friends or for her parents to seek counseling.
110. more; earlier
111. emerging adulthood
112. stages; brain; Piaget

Adulthood

113. is not
114. muscular strength, reaction time, sensory keenness, cardiac output; women
115. age; health; exercise
116. menopause; 50; expectations; attitude
117. shrinks; less; reduced
118. more; less
119. slows; brain cells
120. frontal lobes
121. neural; neurogenesis
122. telomeres; exercise
123. recall; recognize; meaningfulness
124. more
125. cross-sectional
126. longitudinal
127. terminal decline
128. **d.** is the answer.

a. & c. In tests of recognition memory, the performance of older persons shows little decline.
b. The ability to recall material, especially meaningless material, declines with age.
129. transition (crisis)
130. social clock; less; chance events
131. intimacy; generativity; love; work
132. 20; well educated
133. twice; higher
134. happiness; sexual satisfaction; income; health; greater
135. decreases; employed
136. increase
137. cannot; competence; accomplishment
138. **c.** is the answer. Carlos' age and struggle to form a close relationship place him squarely in this stage.
     a. Trust versus mistrust is the psychosocial task of infancy.
     b. Autonomy versus doubt is the psychosocial task of toddlerhood.
     d. Identity versus role confusion is the psychosocial task of adolescence.
139. identity; confidence; self-esteem
140. do; do
141. amygdala; decreased
142. biopsychosocial
143. **d.** is the answer. Research has not uncovered a tendency for people of any particular age group to report greater feelings of satisfaction or well-being.
144. suddenly and before its expected time on the social clock
145. do; do not
146. do not
147. integrity
148. do not
149. temperament
150. **c.** is the answer. Although some researchers emphasize stability and others emphasize potential for change, they all agree that stability increases over the life span.
     a. One criticism of stage theories is that development does not occur in sharply defined stages.
     b. Research has shown that individuals' adult personalities cannot be predicted from their first two years.
     d. Social and emotional style are two of the most stable traits.

Progress Test 1

Multiple-Choice Questions

1. **c.** is the answer. Developmental psychologists study physical, cognitive (memory, in this example), and social change throughout the life span.
   a. Social psychologists study how people influence and are influenced by others.
   b. Cognitive psychologists *do* study memory; because Dr. Goodman is interested in life-span *changes* in memory, she is more likely a developmental psychologist.
   d. Experimental psychologists study physiology, sensation, perception, learning, and other aspects of behavior. Only developmental psychologists focus on developmental changes in behavior and mental processes.

2. **a.** is the answer.
   b. Abstract reasoning is a formal operational ability.
   c. Piaget's theory is not concerned with attachment.
   d. Attaining object permanence is the hallmark of sensorimotor thought.

3. **b.** is the answer. The preoperational child sees the world from his or her own vantage point.
   a. As immature as egocentrism is, it represents a significant cognitive advance over the sensorimotor child, who knows the world only through senses and actions. Even simple self-awareness takes a while to develop.
   c. & d. As children attain the operational stages, they become more able to see the world through the eyes of others.

4. **a.** is the answer. Before object permanence is attained, "out of sight" is truly "out of mind."
   b., c., & d. Developments during the preoperational, concrete operational, and formal operational stages include the use of language, conservation, and abstract reasoning, respectively.

5. **b.** is the answer. The infant turns its head and begins sucking when its cheek is stroked.
   a., c., & d. These stimuli produce other reflexes in the newborn.

6. **b.** is the answer.
   a. When given the choice between a wire mother with a bottle and a cloth mother without, the monkeys preferred the cloth mother.
   c. The presence of other infants made no difference.
   d. Imprinting plays no role in the attachment of higher primates.

7. **c.** is the answer. Through maturation—an orderly sequence of biological growth processes that are relatively unaffected by experience—all humans develop.
   a. Conservation is the cognitive awareness that objects do not change with changes in shape.
   b. The forces of nature *are* those that direct maturation.
   d. The issue of continuity and stages has to do with whether development is a gradual and continuous process or a discontinuous, stagelike process. Those who emphasize maturation see development as occurring in stages, not continuously.

8. **d.** is the answer. Erikson proposed that development occurs in a series of stages, in the first of which the child develops an attitude of either basic trust or mistrust.
   a. Piaget's theory is concerned with cognitive development.
   b. Harlow conducted research on attachment and deprivation.
   c. Vygotsky focused on the influence of social factors on cognitive development.

9. **b.** is the answer.

10. **a.** is the answer.

11. **c.** is the answer. At the preconventional level, moral reasoning centers on self-interest, whether this means obtaining rewards or avoiding punishment.
    a. & b. Moral reasoning based on a sense of social duty or a desire to gain social approval is associated with the conventional level of moral development.
    d. Reasoning based on ethical principles is characteristic of the postconventional level of moral development.

12. **d.** is the answer. Boys who show early physical maturation are generally stronger and more athletic than boys who mature late; these qualities may lead to greater popularity and self-assurance.
    a. & c. Early maturation tends to be socially advantageous for boys but not for girls.
    b. Early maturing girls often suffer teasing or sexual harrassment.

13. **c.** is the answer.
    a. Habituation is decreasing responsiveness to a stimulus that is repeatedly presented.
    b. In Piaget's theory, egocentrism refers to the difficulty preoperational children have in considering another's viewpoint.

d. In Piaget's theory, assimilation refers to interpreting a new experience in terms of an existing schema.

14. **d.** is the answer.
    a. Generativity is associated with middle adulthood.
    b. & c. Intimacy and isolation are associated with young adulthood.

15. **c.** is the answer. Once formal operational thought has been attained, thinking is no longer limited to concrete propositions.
    a. & b. Preoperational thought and concrete operational thought emerge before, and do not include, the ability to think logically about abstract propositions.
    d. Postconventional thought is Kohlberg's final stage of moral development.

16. **a.** is the answer.
    b., c., & d. These cognitive abilities remain essentially unchanged as the person ages.

17. **d.** is the answer. "Use it or lose it" seems to be the rule: Often, changes in activity patterns contribute significantly to problems regarded as being part of usual aging.
    a. Most older people suffer some memory loss but remember some events very well.
    b. Although older people are more subject to long-term ailments than younger adults, they actually suffer fewer short-term ailments.
    c. People of all ages report equal happiness or satisfaction with life.

18. **b.** is the answer.

19. **d.** is the answer.
    a. This refers to a zygote.
    b. These are teratogens.
    c. These are schemas.

20. **d.** is the answer. The physical changes of puberty mark the onset of adolescence.
    a. & b. An identity crisis or parent-child conflict may or may not occur during adolescence; neither of these formally marks its onset.
    c. Formal operational thought, rather than concrete reasoning, typically develops in adolescence.

21. **b.** is the answer.
    a. Menarche refers to the onset of menstruation.
    c. When it does occur, the midlife crisis is a psychological, rather than biological, phenomenon.
    d. Generativity is Erikson's term for productivity during middle adulthood.

True–False Items

1. F	5. F	9. F
2. F	6. F	10. F
3. F	7. T	
4. T	8. F	

Progress Test 2

1. **d.** is the answer. With object permanence, a child develops schemas for familiar objects, including faces, and may become upset by a stranger who does not fit any of these schemas.
   a. The concept of conservation develops during the concrete operational stage, whereas stranger anxiety develops during the sensorimotor stage.
   b. & c. Egocentrism and a theory of mind both develop during the preoperational stage. This follows the sensorimotor stage, during which stranger anxiety develops.

2. **a.** is the answer.
   b., c., & d. Each of these is an understanding developed by Piaget.

3. **a.** is the answer.

4. **a.** is the answer. Any drug taken by the mother passes through the placenta and enters the child's bloodstream.
   b. Addiction cannot be inherited; it requires exposure to an addictive drug.
   c. Drugs may disrupt the mechanisms of heredity, but there is no evidence that such changes promote addiction.
   d. This answer is incorrect because at no age does the blood "resist" drugs.

5. **c.** is the answer.
   a., b., & d. A child's emotional temperament, attachment, and addiction have not been linked to the mother's drinking while pregnant.

6. **b.** is the answer.

7. **d.** is the answer. A critical period is a restricted time during which an organism must be exposed to certain influences or experiences for a particular kind of learning to occur.
   a. Critical periods refer to developmental periods after birth.
   b. Critical periods vary from behavior to behavior, but they are not confined to the hours following birth.
   c. Critical periods are not specifically associated with the preoperational period.

8. **c.** is the answer. Deprived monkeys were impaired in their social behaviors but not in their physical development.

a., b., & d. Each of these was found in socially deprived monkeys.

9. **d.** is the answer. This is because of a lack of neural connections before that age.

10. **c.** is the answer.
    a. Insecurely attached infants often cling to their mothers when placed in a new situation; yet, when the mother returns after an absence, the infant's reaction tends to be one of indifference.
    b. These behaviors are characteristic of securely attached infants.
    d. Insecurely attached infants in unfamiliar surroundings will often exhibit a range of emotional behaviors.

11. **d.** is the answer.
    a. Erikson is known for his theory of psychosocial development.
    b. Piaget is known for his theory of cognitive development.
    c. Harlow is known for his studies of attachment in infant monkeys.

12. **a.** is the answer.
    b. This answer describes the longitudinal research method.
    c. Cross-sectional studies compare people of different ages throughout the life span, generally beginning after the person is able to verbalize.
    d. Cross-sectional studies do not deal with social development.

13. **c.** is the answer. Different societies and eras have somewhat different ideas about the age at which major life events should ideally occur.

14. **c.** is the answer.
    a. Preconventional morality is based on avoiding punishment and obtaining rewards.
    b. Conventional morality is based on gaining the approval of others and/or on following the law and social convention.
    d. There is no such thing as generative morality.

15. **a.** is the answer.
    b. According to Erikson, identity develops before intimacy.
    c. & d. The formation of basic trust is the task of infancy.

16. **c.** is the answer.
    a. & b. Physical and cognitive abnormalities usually result from teratogens, but that's not a definition of a teratogen.
    d. A fertilized egg is a zygote.

17. **d.** is the answer.
    a., b., & c. Most couples do not feel a loss of purpose or marital strain following the departure of grown children.

18. **a.** is the answer.
19. **d.** is the answer.
20. **d.** is the answer.
21. **c.** is the answer.
    a. Kohlberg focused on moral reasoning.
    b. Piaget studied cognitive development in children.
    d. Erikson proposed eight stages of social development throughout the life span.

Essay Question

Sheryl's age would place her at the threshold of Piaget's stage of formal operations. Although her thinking is probably still somewhat self-focused, Sheryl is becoming capable of abstract, logical thought. This will increasingly allow her to reason hypothetically. Because her logical thinking also enables her to detect inconsistencies in others' reasoning and between their ideals and actions, Sheryl and her parents may be having some heated debates about now.

According to Kohlberg, Sheryl is probably at the threshold of postconventional morality. When she was younger, Sheryl probably abided by rules in order to gain social approval, or simply because "rules are rules" (conventional morality). Now that she is older, Sheryl's moral reasoning will increasingly be based on her own personal code of ethics and an affirmation of people's agreed-upon rights.

According to Erikson, psychosocial development occurs in eight stages, each of which focuses on a particular task. As an adolescent, Sheryl's psychosocial task is to develop a sense of self by testing roles, then integrating them to form a single identity. Erikson called this stage *identity versus role confusion*.

Terms and Concepts to Remember

Writing Definitions

1. **Developmental psychology** is the branch of psychology concerned with physical, cognitive, and social change throughout the life span.

2. The **zygote** (a term derived from the Greek word for "joint") is the fertilized egg, that is, the cluster of cells formed during conception by the union of sperm and egg.

3. The **embryo** is the developing prenatal organism from about 2 weeks through 2 months after conception; formed from the inner cells of the zygote.

4. The **fetus** is the developing prenatal human from 9 weeks after conception to birth.

5. **Teratogens** (literally, "monster makers") are agents, such as toxins, chemicals, and viruses,

that cross the mother's placenta and can harm the developing embryo or fetus.

6. **Fetal alcohol syndrome (FAS)** refers to the physical and cognitive abnormalities that heavy drinking by a pregnant woman may cause in the developing child.

7. **Habituation** is decreasing responsiveness to a stimulus that is repeatedly presented. It is used by researchers to find out what infants see, hear, smell, and think.

8. **Maturation** refers to the biological growth processes that enable orderly changes in behavior, relatively uninfluenced by experience.

   Example: The ability to walk depends on a certain level of neural and muscular **maturation.** For this reason, until the toddler's body is physically ready to walk, practice "walking" has little effect.

9. A **critical period** is an optimal period early in the life of an organism during which the organism must be exposed to certain stimuli or experiences if it is to develop normally.

10. **Cognition** refers to all the mental processes associated with thinking, knowing, remembering, and communicating.

11. In Piaget's theory of cognitive development, **schemas** are mental concepts or frameworks that organize and interpret information.

12. In Piaget's theory, **assimilation** refers to interpreting a new experience in terms of an existing schema.

13. In Piaget's theory, **accommodation** refers to changing an existing schema to incorporate new information that cannot be assimilated.

14. In Piaget's theory of cognitive stages, the **sensorimotor stage** lasts from birth to nearly age 2. During this stage, infants gain knowledge of the world through their senses and their actions.

15. **Object permanence,** which develops during the sensorimotor stage, is the awareness that things do not cease to exist when not perceived.

16. In Piaget's theory, the **preoperational stage** lasts from about 2 to 6 or 7 years of age. During this stage, language development is rapid, but the child is unable to understand the mental operations of concrete logic.

17. **Conservation** is the principle that properties such as number, volume, and mass remain constant despite changes in the forms of objects; according to Piaget, it is acquired during the concrete operational stage.

18. In Piaget's theory, **egocentrism** refers to the difficulty that preoperational children have in considering another's viewpoint. *Ego* means "self," and *centrism* indicates "in the center"; the preoperational child is "self-centered."

19. Our ideas about our own and others' thoughts, feelings, and perceptions and the behaviors these might predict constitute our **theory of mind**.

20. In Piaget's theory, during the **concrete operational stage,** lasting from about ages 6 or 7 to 11, children can think logically about concrete events and objects.

21. **Autism spectrum disorder** is a disorder that appears in childhood and is marked by deficient communication, social interaction, and understanding of others' states of mind.

22. In Piaget's theory, the **formal operational stage** normally begins about age 12. During this stage people begin to think logically about abstract concepts.

   Memory aid: To help differentiate Piaget's stages remember that "operations" are mental transformations. *Pre*operational children, who lack the ability to perform transformations, are "before" this developmental milestone. Concrete operational children can operate on real, or concrete, objects. Formal operational children can perform logical transformations on abstract concepts.

23. **Stranger anxiety** is the fear of strangers that infants begin to display by about 8 months of age.

24. **Attachment** is an emotional tie with another person, shown in young children by their seeking closeness to a caregiver and showing distress on separation.

25. **Imprinting** is the process by which certain animals form attachments during a critical period early in life.

26. **Temperament** refers to a person's characteristic emotional reactivity and intensity.

27. According to Erikson, **basic trust** is a sense that the world is predictable and trustworthy, a concept that infants form if their needs are met by responsive caregiving.

28. **Adolescence** refers to the life stage from puberty to independent adulthood, denoted physically by a growth spurt, cognitively by the onset of formal operational thought, and socially by the formation of identity.

29. **Puberty** is the early adolescent period of sexual maturation, during which a person becomes capable of reproducing.

30. In Erikson's theory, establishing an **identity,** or one's sense of self, is the primary task of adolescence.

31. **Social identity** refers to person's self-concept as defined by the groups to which he or she belongs.

32. In Erikson's theory, **intimacy**, or the ability to establish close, loving relationships, is the primary task of late adolescence and early adulthood.

33. For some people in modern cultures, **emerging adulthood** is the period from the late teens to mid-twenties, bridging the gap between adolescent dependence and full independence and responsible adulthood.

34. **Menopause** is the cessation of menstruation and typically occurs within a few years of age 50. It also refers to the biological changes experienced during a woman's years of declining ability to reproduce.

35. In a **cross-sectional study,** people of different ages are compared with one another.

36. In a **longitudinal study,** the same people are restudied and retested over a long period.

37. The **social clock** refers to the culturally preferred timing of social events, such as leaving home, marrying, having children, and retiring.

Cross-Check

ACROSS	DOWN
3. fetus	1. autism
4. accommodation	2. assimilation
6. imprinting	5. conservation
9. embryo	7. cross-sectional
11. schema	8. zygote
13. menopause	10. teratogen
14. longitudinal	12. habituation

Gender and Sexuality

Chapter Overview

Chapter 5 is concerned with gender and sexuality. The first section explores how genes and environment interact to shape both the biological and social aspects of our gender. In the end, the message is clear: Our genes and our experience together form who we are.

The next section discusses human sexuality, including the sexual response cycle, how hormones influence sexual motivation, and the impact of external and imagined stimuli on sexual arousal. Sexually transmitted infections and adolescents' use of contraceptives are also explored. Sexual motivation in men and women is triggered less by physiological factors and more by external incentives. Even so, research studies demonstrate that sexual orientation is neither willfully chosen nor easily changed.

The third section explores an evolutionary explanation of gender differences and mating preferences. The chapter concludes with reflections on nature–nurture interactions in gender development and sexuality.

NOTE: Answer guidelines for all Chapter 5 questions begin on page 121.

Chapter Review

First, skim each section, noting headings and boldface items. After you have read the section, review each objective by answering the fill-in and essay-type questions that follow it. In some cases, Study Tips will help you to learn difficult concepts and Applications help you to know how well you understand the material. As you proceed, evaluate your performance by consulting the answers beginning on page 121. Do not continue with the next section until you understand each answer. If you need to, review the section in the textbook before continuing.

Gender Development

Objective 5-1: Discuss gender similarities and differences in aggression, social power, and social connectedness.

1. The socially constructed roles by which your culture defines male or female defines your

   _____ .

2. Among your _____ (how many?) chromosomes, _____ (how many?) are unisex.

3. Compared with the average man, an average woman has more _____ , less _____ , and is a few inches _____ . Women are more likely than men to suffer from _____ , _____ , and _____ _____ .

4. Compared with women, men are more likely to commit _____ and to suffer _____ _____ . They are also more likely to be diagnosed with _____ , _____ - _____ , _____ - _____ _____ _____ , and _____ _____ _____ as an adult.

5. *Aggression* is defined as _____ or _____ behavior that is _____ to hurt someone.

6. The aggression gender gap pertains to _____ rather than _____ aggression.

7. Throughout the world, men are more likely than women to engage in _____ , _____ , and _____ .

8. Compared with women, men are perceived as being more _____ , _____ , and _____ . As leaders, they tend to be more _____ , while women are more _____ .

9. Compared with men, women are perceived as being more _____ , _____ , and _____ .

10. These perceived differences occur _____ (throughout the world/only in certain cultures).

11. This difference is noticeable in how children _____ , and it continues throughout the teen and adult years. Girls play in groups that are _____ and less _____ than boys' groups.

12. Because they are more _____ , women are likely to use conversation to _____ _____ , while men are likely to use conversation to _____ _____ .

13. When wanting understanding, both men and women turn to women, and both report their friendships with women to be more _____ , _____ , and _____ .

14. Women tend and befriend—for example, they turn to others for _____ , especially when coping with _____ .

15. Gender differences in power, connectedness, and other traits peak in late _____ and early _____ . By age 50, the differences have _____ (decreased/increased).

APPLICATION:

16. Mackenzie and Zachary live next door to Ella and Michael. They've become good friends, and every Sunday they get together for dinner. Zachary and Michael discuss the best way to clean their roofs, demonstrating the male tendency to _____ _____ . Mackenzie and Ella talk about how to make their new neighbors feel welcome, demonstrating the female tendency to _____ _____ .

Objective 5-2: Explain how biological sex is determined, and describe how sex hormones influence prenatal and adolescent development.

17. Our biology may influence our gender differences in two ways: genetically, by our differing sex _____ , and physiologically, from our differing concentrations of _____ _____ .

18. The twenty-third pair of chromosomes determines the developing person's _____ . The mother always contributes a(n) _____ chromosome. When the father contributes a(n) _____ chromosome, the testes begin producing the hormone _____ . In about the _____ (what week?), this hormone initiates the development of external male sex organs.

19. Adolescence begins with the time of developing sexual maturity known as _____ . A two-year period of rapid physical development begins in girls at about the age of _____ and in boys at about the age of _____ . This growth spurt is marked by the development of the reproductive organs and external genitalia, or _____ _____ characteristics, as well as by the development of traits such as pubic hair and enlarged breasts in females and facial hair in males. These nonreproductive traits are known as _____ characteristics.

20. In some countries, girls are reaching puberty _____ (earlier/later) than in the past. This phenomenon is attributed to increased

_____ _____ ,

_____-_____

_____ , and _____

_____ .

21. The first menstrual period is called _____ . In boys, the first ejaculation is called _____ .

22. Individuals born with intermediate combinations of male and female physical features are said to be _____ .

Objective 5-3: Describe how gender roles and gender typing influence gender development.

23. Everything shared by a group and transmitted across generations defines a _____ . Its shaping power is seen in our expectations about the way men and women behave, or our _____ _____ .

24. Gender roles _____ (are/are not) rigidly fixed, as evidenced by the fact that they vary across _____ and over _____ . For instance, in _____ societies there tends to be minimal division of labor by sex; by contrast, in _____ societies, women remain close to home while men roam freely, herding cattle or sheep.

25. Our individual sense of being male or female is called our _____ _____ . The degree to which we exhibit traditionally male or female traits and interests is called _____ _____ .

26. According to _____ _____ theory, children learn gender-linked behaviors by observing and imitating others and being rewarded or punished. When their families discourage traditional gender typing, children _____ (do/do not) organize themselves into "boy worlds" and "girl worlds."

27. Children also learn from their _____ _____ what it means to be male or female and adjust their behavior accordingly, thereby demonstrating that _____ is important in the formation of gender identity.

28. People who are _____ have a sense of being male or female that differs from their birth sex.

APPLICATIONS:

29. Rod has always felt pressure to be the driver when traveling in a car with Sue because he learned that this was expected of men. Rod's feelings illustrate the influence of _____ _____ .

30. Pat and Alex have been married for about 10 years. During that time, Alex is the one most likely to spend less time at work, more time with household chores, and more time caring for the very young and the very old. Alex is most likely _____ (male/female).

31. When his son cries because another child has taken his favorite toy, Brandon admonishes him by saying, "Big boys don't cry." Evidently, Brandon is an advocate of

_____ _____

in accounting for the development of gender-linked behaviors.

32. Three-year-old Caleb shares a toy chest with his 18-month-old sister Elena. Caleb has put all cars, trucks, and superheros to his side of the chest and all the dolls, stuffed animals, and miniature furniture to Elena's side. Caleb has clearly formed a _____ _____ about gender-linked behaviors.

33. Four-year-old Sarah, who has very specific ideas about what it means to be female and frequently adjusts her behavior accordingly, is demonstrating the importance of _____ _____ in the formation of gender identity.

Human Sexuality

Objective 5-4: Describe how hormones influence human sexual motivation.

34. Unlike hunger, sex is not an actual _____ .

35. In most mammals, females are sexually receptive only during ovulation, when the hormones, called _____ (such as _____), have peaked.

36. The importance of the hormone _____ to male sexual arousal is confirmed by the fact that sexual interest declines in animals if their _____ are removed. In women, low levels of the hormone _____ may cause a waning of sexual interest.

37. Hormonal surges or declines occur at two predictable points in the life span: during _____ when a surge triggers the development of _____ _____ , and in later life, when _____ levels fall and women experience _____ . Hormonal shifts may also be caused by _____ or _____ .

Objective 5-5: Describe the human sexual response cycle, and distinguish between sexual dysfunctions and paraphilias.

38. The two researchers who identified a four-stage sexual response cycle are _____ and _____ . In order, the stages of the cycle are the _____ phase, the _____ phase, _____ , and the _____ phase. During the final stage, males experience a _____ _____ , during which they are incapable of another orgasm.

39. Problems that consistently impair sexual arousal or functioning are called _____ _____ . Examples of such problems include _____ _____ , _____ _____ , and _____ _____ _____ .

40. When a person's sexual arousal is related to socially unacceptable behavior, it is called a _____ , Examples include _____ and _____ .

Objective 5-6. Explain how sexually transmitted infections can be prevented.

41. Teenage girls, because of their not yet fully mature biological development and lower levels of protective _____ , may be especially vulnerable to _____ _____ _____ . Rates of such infections are _____ (rising/falling), especially among people under age _____ .

42. Condoms are about 80 percent effective in preventing transmission of _____ , the virus that causes _____ . The rates of this syndrome are increasing fastest among _____ (women/men), partly because the virus is passed from _____ (man to woman/woman to man) more often than from _____ (man to woman/woman to man).

43. Recent studies show that oral sex _____ (is/is not) linked to transmission of STIs, such as the _____ _____ _____ .

Objective 5-7: Describe how external and imagined stimuli contribute to sexual arousal.

44. With repeated exposure, the emotional response to an erotic stimulus often _____ .

Explain some of the possible harmful consequences of sexually explicit material.

45. Most women and men _____ (have/do not have) sexual fantasies. Compared with women's fantasies, men's sexual fantasies are more _____ _____ .

Sexual fantasies _____ (do/do not) indicate sexual problems or dissatisfaction.

Objective 5-8: Discuss the factors that influence teenagers' sexual behaviors and use of contraceptives.

46. Compared with European teens, American teens have _____ (higher/lower) rates of teen pregnancy.

State four factors that contribute to the high rate of unprotected sex among teenagers.

47. (Close-Up) An APA report points to the increasing _____ of girls, which harms their _____ and leads to unhealthy _____ _____ . This occurs when girls (a) are led to value themselves in terms of their _____ _____ ; (b) compare themselves with narrowly defined _____ _____ ; and (c) see themselves as _____ _____ .

State several predictors of sexual restraint (reduced teen sexuality and pregnancy).

APPLICATIONS:

48. Which of the following was NOT identified as a contributing factor in the high rate of unprotected sex among adolescents?
    a. alcohol use
    b. thrill-seeking
    c. mass media sexual norms
    d. guilt

49. Which of the following teens is most likely to delay the initiation of sex?
    a. Jack, who has below-average intelligence
    b. Jason, who is not religiously active
    c. Ron, who regularly volunteers his time in community service
    d. It is impossible to predict.

Sexual Orientation

Objective 5-9: Summarize what research has taught us about sexual orientation.

50. A person's sexual attraction toward members of a particular gender is referred to as

_____ _____ .

51. Studies in Europe and the United States indicate that approximately _____ percent of men and _____ percent of women are exclusively homosexual. This finding suggests that popular estimates of the rate of homosexuality are _____ (high/low/accurate).

52. Sexual orientation _____ (is/is not) an indicator of mental health.

53. Some homosexuals struggle with their sexual orientation and are at increased risk of _____ attempts.

54. A person's sexual orientation _____ (does/does not) appear to be voluntarily chosen. Several research studies reveal that sexual orientation among _____ (women/men) tends to be less strongly felt and potentially more changeable than among the other gender. This phenomenon has been called the gender difference in _____ _____ .

55. Childhood events and family relationships _____ (are/are not) important factors in determining a person's sexual orientation. Also, homosexuality _____ (does/does not) involve a fear of the other gender that leads people to direct their sexual desires toward members of their own gender.

56. Sex hormone levels _____ (do/do not) predict sexual orientation.

57. As children, most homosexuals _____ (were/were not) sexually victimized.

58. The lack of evidence for _____ causes of homosexuality has led to an exploration of possible _____ influences.

59. Same-sex attraction _____ (does/does not) occur among animals.

60. Researcher Simon LeVay discovered a cluster of cells in the _____that is larger in _____ men than in all others. Gays and lesbians differ from their straight counterparts in their preference for sex-related

    _____ .

61. Studies of twins suggest that genes probably _____ (do/do not) play a role in homosexuality. Research has confirmed that homosexual men have more homosexual relatives on their _____ (mother's/father's) side than on their _____ (mother's/father's) side.

62. In animals and some exceptional human cases, sexual orientation has been altered by abnormal _____ conditions during prenatal development. In humans, prenatal exposure to hormone levels typical of _____ , particularly between _____ and _____ months after conception, may predispose an attraction to males.

63. Men who have older brothers are somewhat _____ (more/less) likely to be gay. This phenomenon, which has been called the _____ _____- _____ _____ , may represent a defensive maternal _____ response to substances produced by _____ (male/female) fetuses.

64. Gays and lesbians may have certain physical traits that fall midway between straight males and females, including _____ _____ counts and greater odds of being _____ (right/left)-handed. Gay men's scores on tests of _____ _____ resemble those of straight women.

65. The consistency of brain, genetic, and prenatal findings suggest that _____ plays the larger role in predisposing sexual orientation, which explains why sexual orientation is _____ (difficult/relatively easy) to change.

APPLICATION:

66. Summarizing his presentation on the origins of homosexuality, Dennis explains that the fraternal birth-order effect refers to the fact that
    a. men who have younger brothers are somewhat more likely to be gay.
    b. men who have older brothers are somewhat more likely to be gay.
    c. women with older sisters are somewhat more likely to be gay.
    d. women with younger sisters are somewhat more likely to be gay.

An Evolutionary Explanation of Human Sexual Behavior

Objective 5-10: Discuss how an evolutionary psychologist might explain gender differences in sexuality and mating preferences.

67. Compared with women, men are _____ (equally/more/less) likely to engage in casual, impulsive sex, and they are _____ (equally/more/less) likely to initiate sexual activity. This is an example of a _____ difference.

68. The _____ explanation of gender differences in attitudes toward sex is based on differences in the optimal strategy by which women and men pass on their _____ . According to this view, men and women _____ (are/are not) selected for different patterns of sexuality.

69. Evolutionary psychologists use _____ _____ to explain why men's approach to sex is more _____ and women's more _____ . According to this explanation, most women incubate and nurse one _____ at a time, while men can spread their genes by mating with _____ (one/many) females. They further suggest that men who were drawn to

_____ women were most likely to perpetuate their genes. Research studies demonstrate that men generally are most attracted to women whose ages in the ancestral past would have been associated with peak

_____ .

70. Cross-cultural research reveals that men judge women as more attractive if they have a _____ appearance, whereas women judge men who appear _____ , _____ , _____ , and _____ as more attractive.

Objective 5-11: List the key criticisms of evolutionary explanations of human sexuality, and describe how evolutionary psychologists respond.

71. Critics of the evolutionary explanation of the gender sexuality difference argue that it often works _____ (forward/backward) to propose a _____ explanation.

72. Another critique is that gender differences in sexuality vary with _____ expectations. Gender differences in mate preferences are largest in cultures characterized by greater gender _____ (equality/inequality).

73. Evolutionary psychologists counter the criticisms by noting that the sexes, having faced similar adaptive problems, are more _____ (alike/different) than they are _____ (alike/different). They also note that evolutionary principles offer testable _____ .

STUDY TIP: A key concept closely related to the principle of natural selection is fitness. We've all heard about "survival of the fittest," but the phrase is often misunderstood. It is not always true that "only the strong survive." From the standpoint of evolutionary psychology, "fitness" most directly refers to reproductive success. Traits and behaviors that have a genetic basis obviously cannot be passed on to succeeding generations if individuals do not have offspring. As you think about gender issues and sexuality, it may be helpful to consider the question, "How might this trait or behavior have promoted reproductive success over evolutionary time?"

Reflections on Gender, Sexuality, and Nature–Nurture Interaction

74. As brute strength becomes _____ (more/less) relevant to power and status, gender roles are _____ (converging/diverging).

75. We are the product of both _____ and _____ , but we are also a system that is _____ . We know this because a _____ approach to development shows that no single factor is all-powerful.

Progress Test 1

Multiple-Choice Questions

Circle your answers to the following questions and check them with the answers on page 122. If your answer is incorrect, read the explanation for why it is incorrect and then consult the text.

1. Which of the following is NOT true regarding gender and sexuality?
   a. Men more often than women attribute a woman's friendliness to sexual interest.
   b. Women are more likely than men to cite affection as a reason for first intercourse.
   c. Men are more likely than women to initiate sexual activity.
   d. Gender differences in sexuality are noticeably absent among gay men and lesbian women.

2. Evolutionary psychologists attribute gender differences in sexuality to the fact that women have
   a. greater reproductive potential than do men.
   b. lower reproductive potential than do men.
   c. weaker sex drives than men.
   d. stronger sex drives than men.

3. According to evolutionary psychology, men are drawn sexually to women who seem _____ , while women are attracted to men who seem _____ .
   a. nurturing; youthful
   b. youthful and fertile; mature and affluent
   c. slender; muscular
   d. exciting; dominant

4. Gender refers to
   a. the biological and social definition of male and female.
   b. the biological definition of male and female.
   c. one's sense of being male or female.
   d. the extent to which one exhibits traditionally male or female traits.

5. The fertilized egg will develop into a boy if, at conception,
   a. the sperm contributes an X chromosome.
   b. the sperm contributes a Y chromosome.
   c. the egg contributes an X chromosome.
   d. the egg contributes a Y chromosome.

6. The hormone testosterone
   a. is found only in females.
   b. determines the sex of the developing person.
   c. stimulates growth of the female sex organs.
   d. stimulates growth of the male sex organs.

7. The correct order of the stages of Masters and Johnson's sexual response cycle is
   a. plateau; excitement; orgasm; resolution.
   b. excitement; plateau; orgasm; resolution.
   c. excitement; orgasm; resolution; refractory.
   d. plateau; excitement; orgasm; refractory.

8. Which of the following is NOT true regarding sexual orientation?
   a. Sexual orientation is neither willfully chosen nor willfully changed.
   b. Some homosexuals struggle with their sexual orientation.
   c. Men's sexual orientation is potentially more fluid and changeable than women's.
   d. Women, regardless of sexual orientation, respond to both female and male erotic stimuli.

9. Surgical removal of the testes of male rats results in
   a. reduced testosterone and sexual interest.
   b. reduced testosterone, but no change in sexual interest.
   c. reduced estradiol and sexual interest.
   d. reduced estradiol, but no change in sexual interest.

10. Some scientific evidence makes a preliminary link between homosexuality and
    a. late sexual maturation.
    b. the age of an individual's first erotic experience.
    c. atypical prenatal hormones.
    d. early problems in relationships with parents.

11. Among the hallmarks of growing up are a boy's first ejaculation and a girl's first menstrual period, which also is called
    a. puberty.   c. menarche.
    b. menopause.   d. spermarche.

12. The average age at which puberty begins is _____ in boys; in girls, it is _____ .
    a. 14; 13   c. 11; 10
    b. 13; 11   d. 10; 9

13. A sex hormone that is secreted in greater amounts by females than by males is
    a. testosterone.   c. spermarche.
    b. Depo-Provera.   d. estradiol.

14. The body structures that allow us to reproduce are the
    a. secondary sex characteristics.
    b. primary sex characteristics.
    c. estrogens.
    d. X and Y chromosomes.

15. Transgender refers to people whose
    a. gender identity doesn't match their birth sex
    b. gender typing is especially strong.
    c. gender role development is incomplete.
    d. sex chromosomes are abnormal.

16. The fraternal birth-order effect refers to the fact that
    a. men who have younger brothers are somewhat more likely to be gay.
    b. men who have older brothers are somewhat more likely to be gay.
    c. women with older sisters are somewhat more likely to be gay.
    d. women with younger sisters are somewhat more likely to be gay.

17. Teenage _____ are especially vulnerable to sexually transmitted infections because they have _____ antibody levels.
    a. boys; higher
    b. girls; higher
    c. boys; lower
    d. girls; lower

18. Men who view explicit material depicting women being sexually coerced
    a. tend to be strongly gender typed.
    b. are more willing to hurt women.
    c. often suffer from one or more sexual dysfunctions.
    d. report greater satisfaction with their own sexual partners.

19. Adolescents who drink alcohol prior to having sex experience

   a. impaired inhibition and are more likely to use condoms.

   b. enhanced inhibition and are less likely to use condoms.

   c. impaired judgment and are less likely to use condoms.

   d. impaired judgment and are more likely to use condoms.

20. Which of the following factors has NOT been found to predict sexual restraint among teens?

   a. high intelligence

   b. religious engagement

   c. father absence

   d. volunteering in service learning programs

Matching Items

Match each term with its corresponding definition or description.

Terms

_____ **1.** X chromosome
_____ **2.** sexual orientation
_____ **3.** gender
_____ **4.** aggression
_____ **5.** testosterone
_____ **6.** estrogen
_____ **7.** Y chromosome
_____ **8.** gender role
_____ **9.** gender identity
_____ **10.** gender typing
_____ **11.** primary sex characteristic
_____ **12.** transgender
_____ **13.** secondary sex characteristic

Functions or Descriptions

a. a person's attraction to members of a particular sex

b. sex hormones secreted in greater amounts by females than by males

c. one's personal sense of being female or male

d. the socially constructed roles and characteristics by which a culture defines *male* or *female*

e. nonreproductive sexual traits

f. behavior intended to hurt someone

g. body structures that enable reproduction

h. a term used to describe people whose gender identity doesn't match their birth sex

i. the acquisition of a traditional gender role

j. the most important male sex hormone

k. the sex chromosome found only in men

l. a set of expected behaviors for males and females

m. the sex chromosome found in both women and men

Progress Test 2

Progress Test 2 should be completed during a final chapter review. Answer the following questions after you thoroughly understand the correct answers for the section reviews and Progress Test 1.

Multiple-Choice Questions

1. Casual, impulsive sex is most frequent among

   a. males with high circulating levels of testosterone.

   b. males with traditional masculine attitudes.

   c. females and males who are weakly gender typed.

   d. females and males who are strongly gender typed.

2. Evolutionary explanations of gender differences in sexuality have been criticized because

   a. they offer "after-the-fact" explanations.

   b. standards of attractiveness vary with time and place.

   c. they underestimate cultural influences on sexuality.

   d. of all of these reasons.

3. Women and men are most likely to be attracted to strongly gender-typed mates in cultures characterized by

   a. gender inequality.

   b. gender equality.

   c. flexible gender roles.

   d. a lack of gender roles.

4. Children who are raised by parents who discourage traditional gender typing
   a. are less likely to display gender-typed behaviors themselves.
   b. often become confused and develop an ambiguous gender identity.
   c. nevertheless organize themselves into "girl worlds" and "boy worlds."
   d. display excessively masculine and feminine traits as adults.

5. Genetically male children who underwent sex-reassignment surgery and were raised as girls later
   a. all described themselves as female.
   b. all described themselves as male.
   c. all had an unclear sexual identity.
   d. described themselves either as female or male, or had an unclear sexual identity.

6. Which of the following statements concerning homosexuality is true?
   a. Homosexuals have abnormal hormone levels.
   b. As children, most homosexuals were molested by an adult homosexual.
   c. Homosexuals had a domineering opposite-sex parent.
   d. Research indicates that sexual orientation may be at least partly physiological.

7. Sexual orientation refers to
   a. a person's tendency to display behaviors typical of males or females.
   b. a person's sense of identity as a male or female.
   c. a person's enduring sexual attraction toward members of a particular gender.
   d. all of these.

8. According to Masters and Johnson, the sexual response of males is most likely to differ from that of females during
   a. the excitement phase.
   b. the plateau phase.
   c. orgasm.
   d. the resolution phase.

9. Exposure of a fetus to the hormones typical of females between _____ and _____ months after conception may predispose the developing human to become attracted to males.
   a. 1; 3   c. 4; 7
   b. 2; 5   d. 6; 9

10. Which of the following was NOT identified as a factor in why girls in some countries are reaching puberty earlier than in the past?
    a. body fat
    b. chemicals that mimic hormones
    c. family stress
    d. gender typing

11. Secondary sex characteristics are to _____ as primary sex characteristics are to

    _____.
    a. deepened male voice; external genitalia
    b. female ovaries; facial hair growth
    c. male testes; underarm hair
    d. adrenal glands; pubic hair growth

12. Sexual maturation occurs during
    a. gender typing.
    b. early childhood.
    c. late adolescence.
    d. puberty.

13. Gender identity refers to
    a. a culture's socially constructed definition of male and female.
    b. the biological definition of male and female.
    c. one's sense of being male or female.
    d. the extent to which one exhibits traditionally male or female traits.

14. A problem that consistently impairs sexual arousal or functioning is called
    a. a refractory period.
    b. a sexually transmitted infection.
    c. a sexual dysfunction.
    d. transgender.

15. Compared with European adolescents, American adolescents have _____ rates of sexually transmitted infections and _____ rates of pregnancy,
    a. higher; higher
    b. lower; lower
    c. higher; lower
    d. lower; higher

16. Which theory states that we form gender identity by observing and imitating others?
    a. social learning theory
    b. sociocultural theory
    c. cognitive theory
    d. gender schema theory

17. Two-thirds of new sexually transmitted infections occur in
   a. girls.
   b. boys.
   c. people under age 25.
   d. people under age 18.

18. With repeated exposure, the emotional response to any erotic stimulus
   a. often becomes stronger.
   b. often habituates.
   c. does not change.
   d. registers in increasing numbers of brain regions.

19. Viewing images of sexually attractive women and men
   a. may lead people to devalue their own partners and relationships.
   b. contributes to the development of sexual dysfunctions.
   c. tends to increase people's satisfaction with their own sexual partners.
   d. weakens gender typing in both women and men.

20. Sexualization occurs when girls
   a. are led to devalue their own sexual appeal.
   b. compare themselves to narrowly defined beauty standards.
   c. see themselves as sexual beings for others' use
   d. experience all of these feelings.

True–False Items

Indicate whether each statement is true or false by placing *T* or *F* in the blank next to the item.

_____ 1. Gender differences in mate preferences vary widely from one culture to another.

_____ 2. According to Masters and Johnson, only males experience a plateau period in the cycle of sexual arousal.

_____ 3. Testosterone affects the sexual arousal of the male only.

_____ 4. Unlike men, women tend not to be aroused by sexually explicit material.

_____ 5. One's sexual orientation is not voluntarily chosen.

_____ 6. Eighty percent of people in the United States think homosexuality is never justified.

_____ 7. Oral sex is not associated with the transmission of STIs.

_____ 8. Risks of HPV and other STIs increase with the number of sexual partners.

_____ 9. As far as we know, all cultures throughout history have been predominantly heterosexual.

_____ 10. Gender differences in social connectedness peak in early adolescence.

_____ 11. In various countries, girls are reaching puberty later than in the past.

Essay Question

Lakia's new boyfriend has been pressuring her to become more sexually intimate than she wants to be at this early stage in their relationship. Strongly gender typed and "macho" in attitude, Jerome is becoming increasingly frustrated with Lakia's hesitation, while Lakia is starting to wonder if a long-term relationship with this type of man is what she really wants. In light of your understanding of the evolutionary explanation of gender differences in sexuality, explain why the tension between Lakia and Jerome would be considered understandable.

Terms and Concepts to Remember

Writing Definitions

Using your own words, on a piece of paper write a brief definition or explanation of each of the following terms.

1. gender
2. aggression
3. X chromosome
4. Y chromosome
5. testosterone

6. puberty
7. primary sex characteristic
8. secondary sex characteristic
9. menarche
10. gender role
11. role
12. gender identity
13. social learning theory
14. gender typing

15. transgender
16. estrogens
17. sexual response cycle
18. refractory period
19. sexual dysfunction
20. paraphilia
21. AIDS (acquired immune deficiency syndrome)
22. sexual orientation

Cross-Check

As you learned in Chapter 1, reviewing and overlearning of material are important to the learning process. After you have written the definitions of the key terms in this chapter, you should complete the crossword puzzle to ensure that you can reverse the process—recognize the term, given the definition.

ACROSS

2. Hormones secreted in greater amounts by females than by males.
4. The body structures that enable reproduction are the _____ characteristics.
8. The sex chromosome found in both men and women.
10. A resting period after orgasm, during which a male cannot be aroused to another orgasm.
11. A life-threatening sexually transmitted infection caused by HIV.
12. People whose gender identity does not match their birth sex.

DOWN

1. The most important male sex hormone.
3. The socially constructed roles and characteristics by which a culture defines *male* or *female*.
4. The early adolescent period of sexual maturation.
5. The first period.
6. Masters and Johnson's four stages of sexual responding are referred to as the _____ cycle.
7. A cluster of prescribed behaviors expected of those who occupy a particular social position.

9. The acquisition of a traditional feminine or masculine is referred to as gender _____ .
13. One sense of being male or female is one's gender _____ .

Answers

Chapter Review

Gender Development

1. gender
2. 46; 45
3. fat; muscle; shorter; depression; anxiety; eating disorders
4. suicide; alcohol use disorder; autism spectrum disorder; color-blindness; attention-deficit/ hyperactivity disorder; antisocial personality disorder
5. physical; verbal; intended
6. physical; verbal
7. hunting; fighting; warring
8. dominant; forceful; independent; directive (or autocratic); democratic
9. submissive; nurturing; socially connected
10. throughout the world
11. play; smaller; competitive
12. interdependent; explore relationships; communicate solutions
13. intimate; enjoyable; nurturing
14. support; stress
15. adolescence; adulthood; decreased
16. communicate solutions; explore relationships
17. chromosomes; sex hormones
18. sex; X; Y; testosterone; seventh
19. puberty; 11; 13; primary sex; secondary sex
20. earlier; body fat; hormone-mimicking chemicals; stress related to family disruption
21. menarche; spermarche
22. intersex
23. culture; gender roles
24. are not; time; place; nomadic; agricultural
25. gender identity; gender typing
26. social learning; do
27. gender schemas; cognition
28. transgender
29. gender roles
30. female
31. gender typing
32. gender schema
33. gender schemas

Human Sexuality

34. need
35. estrogens; estradiol
36. testosterone; testes; testosterone
37. puberty; sex characteristics; estrogen; menopause; surgery; drugs
38. William Masters; Virginia Johnson; excitement; plateau; orgasm; resolution; refractory period
39. sexual dysfunctions; premature ejaculation; erectile disorder; female orgasmic disorder
40. paraphilia; exhibitionism; pedophilia
41. antibodies; sexually transmitted infections (STIs); rising; 25
42. HIV; AIDS; women; man to woman; woman to man
43. is; human papilloma virus (HPV)
44. habituates

Erotic material may increase the viewer's acceptance of the false idea that women enjoy rape, may increase men's willingness to hurt women, may lead people to devalue their partners and relationships, and may diminish people's satisfaction with their own sexual partners.

45. have; frequent, physical, and less romantic; do not
46. higher

Among the factors that contribute to unprotected sex among adolescents are (1) minimal communication about birth control, (2) guilt related to sexual activity, (3) alcohol use that influences judgment, and (4) mass media norms of unprotected promiscuity.

47. sexualization; self-image; sexual development; sexual appeal; beauty standards; sexual beings for others' use

Teens with high intelligence test scores, those who are actively religious, those whose father is present, and those who participate in service learning programs more often delay sex.

48. **b.** is the answer.
49. **c.** is the answer.

    a., b., & d. Teens with high rather than average intelligence (therefore, not a.), and those who are religiously active (therefore, not b.) are most likely to delay sex.

Sexual Orientation

50. sexual orientation
51. 3; 1 or 2; high
52. is not

53. suicide
54. does not; women; erotic plasticity
55. are not; does not
56. do not
57. were not
58. environmental; biological
59. does
60. hypothalamus; heterosexual; odors
61. do; mother's; father's
62. hormone; females; 2; 5
63. more; fraternal birth-order effect; immune; male
64. fingerprint ridge; left; spatial abilities
65. biology; difficult
66. **b.** is the answer.
67. more; more; gender
68. evolutionary; genes; are
69. natural selection; recreational; relational; infant; many; healthy; fertility
70. youthful; mature; dominant; bold; affluent
71. backward; hindsight
72. social; inequality
73. alike; different; predictions

Reflections on Gender, Sexuality, and Nature–Nurture Interaction

74. less; converging
75. nature; nurture; open; biopsychosocial

Progress Test 1

Multiple-Choice Questions

1. **d.** is the answer. Such gender differences characterize both heterosexual and homosexual people.

2. **b.** is the answer. Women usually incubate only one infant at a time.
   c. & d. The text does not suggest that there is a gender difference in the strength of the sex drive.

3. **b.** is the answer.
   a. According to this perspective, women prefer mates with the potential for long-term nurturing investment in their joint offspring.
   c. While men are drawn to women whose waists are roughly a third narrower than their hips, the text does not suggest that women equate muscularity with fertility.
   d. Excitement was not mentioned as a criterion for mating.

4. **a.** is the answer.
   b. This definition is incomplete.

   c. This defines gender identity.
   d. This defines gender typing.

5. **b.** is the answer.
   a. In this case, a female would develop.
   c. & d. The egg can contribute only an X chromosome. Thus, the sex of the child is determined by which chromosome the sperm contributes.

6. **d.** is the answer.
   a. Although testosterone is the principal male hormone, it is present in both females and males.
   b. This is determined by the sex chromosomes.
   c. In the absence of testosterone, female sex organs will develop.

7. **b.** is the answer.

8. **c.** is the answer. Research studies suggest that women's sexual orientation is potentially more fluid and changeable than men's.

9. **a.** is the answer.
   c. & d. Castration of the testes, which produce testosterone, does not alter estrogen levels.

10. **c.** is the answer.
    a., b., & d. None of these is linked to homosexuality.

11. **c.** is the answer.
    a. Puberty refers to the early adolescent period during which accelerated growth and sexual maturation occur, not to the first menstrual period.
    b. Menopause is the cessation of menstruation, which typically occurs in the early fifties.
    d. Spermarche is the boy's first ejaculation.

12. **b.** is the answer.

13. **b.** is the answer
    a. Menarche refers to the onset of menstruation.
    c. Spermarche is the boy's first ejaculation.
    d. Estradiol is a female hormone.

14. **b.** is the answer.
    a. Secondary sex characteristics are nonreproductive traits such as facial hair.
    c. Estrogens are sex hormones, such as estradiol, secreted in greater amounts by females than by males.
    d. X and Y chromosomes contain the genetic material that determines sex.

15. **a.** is the answer.

16. **b.** is the answer.

17. **d.** is the answer.

18. **b.** is the answer.

19. **c.** is the answer.

20. **c.** is the answer. Father absence *predicts* reduced sexual restraint among teens.

Matching Items

1. m	**5.** j	**9.** c	**13.** e
2. a	**6.** b	**10.** i	
3. d	**7.** k	**11.** g	
4. f	**8.** l	**12.** h	

Progress Test 2

Multiple-Choice Questions

1. **b.** is the answer.
   a. Testosterone levels have not been linked to the frequency of casual sex.
   c. & d. Males are far more accepting of casual sex than are females.

2. **d.** is the answer.

3. **a.** is the answer.
   b. In such cultures, gender differences in mate preferences tend to be much smaller.
   c. Although flexibility in gender roles was not discussed per se, it is likely that greater flexibility would equate with greater equality in gender roles.
   d. All cultures have some gender roles.

4. **c.** is the answer.
   b. & d. There is no evidence that being raised in a "gender neutral" home confuses children or fosters a backlash of excessive gender typing.

5. **d.** is the answer. Some later described themselves as female, and some as male.

6. **d.** is the answer. Researchers have not been able to find any clear differences, psychological or otherwise, between homosexuals and heterosexuals. Thus, the basis for sexual orientation remains unknown, although recent evidence points more to a physiological basis.

7. **c.** is the answer.

8. **d.** is the answer. During the resolution phase males experience a refractory period.
   a., b., & c. The male and female responses are very similar in each of these phases.

9. **b.** is the answer. The time between the middle of the second and fifth months after conception may be a critical period for the brain's neurohormonal control system. Exposure to abnormal hormonal conditions at other times has no effect on sexual orientation

10. **d.** is the answer. Gender typing refers to the acquisition of a traditional masculine or feminine role.

11. **a.** is the answer.

12. **d.** is the answer.

13. **c.** is the answer.
    a. This refers to a person's gender.
    b. This refers to an individual's sex.
    d. This refers to gender typing.

14. **c.** is the answer.
    a. The refractory period is the period during resolution when a man is incapable of another orgasm.
    b. STIs are infections passed from one person to another during sexual contact.
    d. Transgender refers to people whose gender identity doesn't match their birth sex.

15. **a.** is the answer.

16. **a.** is the answer.

17. **c.** is the answer.

18. **b.** is the answer.

19. **a.** is the answer.

20. **d.** is the answer.

True–False Items

1. F	**5.** T	**9.** T
2. F	**6.** F	**10.** F
3. F	**7.** F	**11.** F
4. F	**8.** T	

Essay Question

Evolutionary psychologists would not be surprised by the tension between Lakia and Jerome and would see it as a reflection of women's more relational and men's more recreational approach to sex. Since eggs are expensive, compared with sperm, women prefer mates with the potential for long-term investment in their joint offspring. According to this perspective, this may be why Lakia is not in a hurry to become sexually intimate with Jerome. Men, on the other hand, are selected for "pairing widely" but not necessarily wisely in order to maximize the spreading of their genes. This is especially true of men like Jerome, who have traditional masculine attitudes.

Terms and Concepts to Remember

Writing Definitions

1. **Gender** is the socially constructed roles and characteristics by which a culture defines *male* or *female*.

2. **Aggression** is physical or verbal behavior intended to hurt someone.

3. The **X chromosome** is the sex chromosome found in both men and women. Females inherit an X chromosome from each parent.

4. The **Y chromosome** is the sex chromosome found only in men. Males inherit an X chromosome from their mothers and a Y chromosome from their fathers.

5. **Testosterone** is the most important male sex hormone. During prenatal development, testosterone stimulates the development of the external male sex organs. During puberty, it stimulates the development of the male sex characteristics.

6. **Puberty** is the early adolescent period of sexual maturation, during which a person becomes capable of reproducing.

7. The **primary sex characteristics** are the body structures (ovaries, testes, and external genitalia) that enable reproduction.

8. The **secondary sex characteristics** are the nonreproductive sexual characteristics, for example, female breasts, male voice quality, and body hair.

9. **Menarche** is the first menstrual period.

10. A **gender role** is a set of expected behaviors for males or for females.

11. A **role** is a cluster of prescribed behaviors expected of those who occupy a particular social position.

12. **Gender identity** is one's sense of being male or female.

13. According to **social learning theory,** people learn social behavior (such as gender roles) by observing and imitating and by being rewarded or punished.

14. **Gender typing** is the acquisition of a traditional feminine or masculine role.

15. **Transgender** refers to people whose gender identity or expression doesn't match their birth sex.

16. **Estrogens** are sex hormones, such as estradiol, secreted in greater amounts by females than by males and contributing to female sex characteristics. In mammals other than humans, estrogen levels peak during ovulation and trigger sexual receptivity.

17. The **sexual response cycle** described by Masters and Johnson consists of four stages of sexual responding: excitement, plateau, orgasm, and resolution.

18. The **refractory period** is a resting period after orgasm, during which a male cannot be aroused to another orgasm.

19. A **sexual dysfunction** is a problem—such as erectile disorder, premature ejaculation, and female orgasmic disorder—that consistently impairs sexual arousal or functioning.

20. **Paraphilias** involve experiencing sexual arousal from fantasies, behaviors, or urges involving nonhuman objects, the suffering of self or others, and/or nonconsenting persons.

21. **AIDS (acquired immune deficiency syndrome)** is a life-threatening, sexually transmitted infection caused by the human immunodeficiency virus (HIV), which depletes the immune system and leaves the person vulnerable to infections.

22. **Sexual orientation** refers to a person's enduring attraction to members of either the same or the opposite sex or to both sexes.

Cross-Check

ACROSS	DOWN
2. estrogens	1. testosterone
4. primary sex	3. gender
8. X chromosome	4. puberty
10. refractory	5. menarche
11. AIDS	6. sexual response
12. transgender	7. role
	9. typing
	13. identity

Sensation and Perception

Chapter Overview

Chapter 6 explores the processes by which our sense receptors and nervous system represent our external environment (sensation), as well as how we mentally organize and interpret this information (perception). The senses of vision, hearing, taste, touch, smell, and body position and movement are described, along with the ways in which we organize the stimuli reaching these senses to perceive form; depth; motion; and constant shape, size, and brightness. To enhance your understanding of these processes, the chapter also discusses research findings from studies of subliminal stimulation, sensory restriction, recovery from blindness, adaptation to distorted environments, perceptual set, and extrasensory perception.

In this chapter there are many terms to learn and several theories you must understand. Many of the terms are related to the structure of the eye, ear, and other sensory receptors. Doing the chapter review several times, labeling the diagrams, and rehearsing the material frequently will help you to memorize these structures and their functions. The theories discussed include the Young-Helmholtz three-color and opponent-process theories of color vision, the Gestalt theory of form perception. the place and frequency theories of hearing, and the gate-control theory of pain. As you study these theories, concentrate on understanding the strengths and weaknesses (if any) of each.

NOTE: Answer guidelines for all Chapter 6 questions begin on page 145.

Chapter Review

First, skim each section, noting headings and boldface items. After you have read the section, review each objective by answering the fill-in and essay-type questions that follow it. Study Tips explain how best to learn a difficult concept and Applications help you to know how well you understand the material. As you proceed, evaluate your performance by consulting the answers beginning on page 145. Do not continue with the next section until you understand each answer. If you need to, review or reread the section in the textbook before continuing.

Basic Principles of Sensation and Perception

Objective 6-1: Contrast sensation and perception, and explain the difference between bottom-up and top-down processing.

1. The perceptual disorder in which a person has lost the ability to recognize familiar faces is

   _____ .

2. The process by which we detect physical energy from the environment and encode it as neural signals is _____ . The process by which sensations are organized and interpreted is

   _____ .

3. Sensory analysis, which starts at the entry level and works up, is called _____ -

   _____ _____ .

   Perceptual analysis, which works from our experience and expectations, is called

   _____ -_____

   _____ .

STUDY TIP: An excellent way to study all the technical material in this chapter is to organize it into a chart. For each sense you need to know several facts, including the nature of the stimulus input, the type of receptor that transmits the stimulus energy, and how the information is processed in the brain. To help you review your understanding of sensation and perception, refer often to the summary chart on the next page.

Sense	Stimulus Input	Receptors	Notes
Vision	Visible electromagnetic energy	Rods and cones	Wavelength = hue; intensity = brightness; rods = black and white; cones = color
Hearing	Sound waves of moving air molecules	Hair cells in the cochlea	Wavelength = pitch; amplitude = loudness
Touch	Pressure, warmth, cold, pain	Specialized nerve endings	Cold + pressure = wetness; side-by-side pressure = tickle
Pain	No one type of stimulus	No special receptors	Natural endorphins relieve pain; hypnosis used for treating pain
Taste	Chemical molecules corresponding to sweet, salty, sour, bitter, and umami	Hair cells in the taste pores	Sensory interaction: smell influences; taste; smell + texture = taste = flavor
Smell	Airborne chemical molecules	Olfactory receptor cells in the nasal cavity	The brain's circuitry for smell connects with areas involved in memory storage
Position and movement	Changes in body's position (kinesthesis) Changes in head's (and thus body's position (vestibular sense)	Sensors in muscles, tendons, and joints Hair-like receptors in the ear's semicircular canals and vestibular sacs of the inner ear	Millions of position and motion sensors Messages sent to the brain's cerebellum

APPLICATIONS:

4. Sensation is to _____ as perception is to_____ .

   a. recognizing a stimulus; interpreting a stimulus
   b. detecting a stimulus; recognizing a stimulus
   c. interpreting a stimulus; detecting a stimulus
   d. seeing; hearing

5. Superman's eyes used _____ , while his brain used _____ .

   a. perception; sensation
   b. top-down processing; bottom-up processing
   c. bottom-up processing; top-down processing

6. Concluding her presentation on sensation and perception, Kelly notes that

   a. perception is bottom-up processing.
   b. sensation is top-down processing.
   c. without sensation there is no perception.
   d. sensation and perception blend into one continuous process.

Objective 6-2: Identify the three steps that are basic to all our sensory systems.

7. All our senses perform three basic steps; they _____ sensory information, transform (or _____) that stimulation into neural impulses that our brain can use, and _____ that neural information to our brain.

Objective 6-3: Distinguish between *absolute* and *difference thresholds*, and discuss whether we can sense and be affected by stimuli below the absolute threshold.

8. The _____ _____ refers to the minimum stimulation necessary for a stimulus to be detected _____ percent of the time.

9. According to _____ _____ theory, a person's experience, expectations, motivation, and alertness all influence the detection of a stimulus.

10. Some entrepreneurs claim that exposure to "below threshold," or _____ , stimuli can be persuasive, but their claims are probably unwarranted. Some weak stimuli may trigger in our sensory receptors a response that is processed by the brain, even though the response doesn't cross the threshold into _____ awareness.

11. Under certain conditions, an invisible image or word can _____ a person's response to a later question. This illustrates that much of our information processing occurs _____ .

12. The minimum difference required to distinguish two stimuli 50 percent of the time is called the

_____ _____ .

Another term for this value is the

_____ _____

_____ .

13. The principle that the difference threshold is not a constant amount, but a constant proportion, is known as _____

_____ . The proportion depends on the _____ .

STUDY TIP: The concept of threshold can be confusing. Since you can count on at least one exam question on this topic, be sure you understand the concept: "Below threshold" means the stimulus is undetectable; "above threshold" means the stimulus is strong enough to be detected.

APPLICATIONS:

14. In shopping for a new stereo, you discover that you cannot differentiate between the sounds of models X and Y. The difference between X and Y is below your
    a. absolute threshold.
    b. subliminal threshold.
    c. receptor threshold.
    d. difference threshold.

Objective 6-4: Explain the function of sensory adaptation.

15. After constant exposure to an unchanging stimulus, the receptor cells of our senses begin to fire less vigorously; this phenomenon is called

_____ _____ .

16. This phenomenon illustrates that sensation is designed to focus on _____ changes in the environment.

APPLICATION:

17. Calvin usually runs his fingertips over a cloth's surface when trying to decide whether the texture is right for what he wants. By moving his fingers over the cloth, he prevents the occurrence

of _____ _____ to the

feel.

Objective 6-5: Explain how our expectations, contexts, emotions, and motivation influence our perceptions.

18. A mental predisposition that influences perception is called a _____

_____ .

19. How a stimulus is perceived depends on our perceptual _____ and the

_____ in which it is experienced.

20. The context of a stimulus creates a

_____ (top-down/bottom-up) expectation that influences our perception as we match

our _____ (top-down/bottom-up)

signal against it.

21. Through experience we form concepts, or

_____ , that organize and interpret

unfamiliar information.

22. Our perception is also influenced by

_____ about gender and the

_____ context of our experiences.

Our perceptions are also directed by our

_____ , as when a water bottle

appears closer if we are thirsty.

APPLICATION:

23. Although carpenter Smith perceived a briefly viewed object as a screwdriver, police officer Wesson perceived the same object as a knife. This illustrates that perception is guided by
    a. bottom-up processing.
    b. sensory adaptation.
    c. transduction.
    d. perceptual set.

Vision

Objective 6-6: Describe the characteristics of the energy we see as visible light.

24. The visible spectrum of light is a small portion of the larger spectrum of _____

energy.

25. The distance from one light wave peak to the next is called _____ . This value

determines the wave's color, or

_____ .

26. The amount of energy in light waves, or
_____ , determined by a wave's
_____ , or height, influences the
_____ of a light.

STUDY TIP: The stimulus energy for both vision and hearing can be described as a traveling wave that varies in wavelength and amplitude. The wavelength of a visual or auditory stimulus is measured as the distance from the peak of one wave to the next—the shorter the distance, the greater the frequency of the waves. Short, high frequency waves produce "cool" or bluish colors for visual stimuli. They produce high-pitched sounds for auditory stimuli. Long, low frequency waves produce "warm" or reddish colors and low-pitched sounds. (See also the section on Hearing.)

The wave's amplitude is measured as the distance from the top of its peak to the bottom. High amplitude waves produce bright colors and loud sounds, while low amplitude waves produce dull colors and soft sounds.

To test your understanding, take a look at these two waves.

27. **a.** Assuming that these two waves were light energy, would they differ in appearance? How so?

b. Assuming that these two waves were sound energy, would they sound the same? If not, how would they differ?

Objective 6-7: Describe how the eye transforms light energy into neural messages, and how the eye and brain process that information.

28. Light enters the eye through the
_____ , then passes through a
small opening called the _____ ;
the size of this opening is controlled by the
colored _____ .

29. By changing its curvature, the
_____ can focus the image of an
object onto the _____ , the light-
sensitive inner surface of the eye. The process by
which the lens changes shape to focus images is
called _____ .

30. The retina's receptor cells are the
_____ and _____ .

31. The neural signals produced in the rods and
cones activate the neighboring
_____ cells, which then activate a
network of _____ cells.

32. The axons of ganglion cells converge to form the
_____ _____ ,
which carries the visual information to the
_____ , the brain region that dis-
tributes the information.

33. Where this nerve leaves the eye, there are no
receptor cells; thus, the area is called the
_____ .

34. Most cones are clustered around the retina's
point of central focus, called the
_____ , whereas the rods are concentrated in more _____
regions of the retina. Many cones have their own
_____ cells to communicate with
the visual cortex. Rods _____
(do/do not) have direct links.

35. It is the _____ (rods/cones) of the
eye that permit the perception of color, whereas
_____ (rods/cones) enable black-
and-white vision.

36. Unlike cones, in dim light the rods are
_____ (sensitive/insensitive).
Adapting to a darkened room will take the retina
approximately _____ minutes.

37. Visual information percolates through progressively more _____ levels. In the
brain, it is routed by the _____
to higher-level brain areas.

38. Hubel and Wiesel discovered that certain neurons in the _____ _____ of the
brain respond only to specific features of what is
viewed. Because they respond only to particular
_____ , _____ ,
_____ , and _____ ,

they called these neurons _____ _____ . These neurons pass their information to other cortical areas, where teams of cells (_____ _____) respond to complex patterns.

39. The brain achieves its remarkable speed in visual perception by processing several subdivisions of a stimulus _____ (simultaneously/sequentially). This procedure, called _____ _____ , may explain why people who have suffered a stroke may lose just one aspect of vision.

40. Other brain-damaged people may demonstrate _____ by responding to a stimulus that is not consciously perceived.

APPLICATIONS:

41. To maximize your sensitivity to fine visual detail you should
    a. stare off to one side of the object you are attempting to see.
    b. close one eye.
    c. decrease the intensity of the light falling upon the object.
    d. stare directly at the object.

42. In comparing the human eye to a camera, the film would be located in the eye's
    a. pupil.   c. cornea.
    b. lens.   d. retina.

43. Which of the following is true of cones?
    a. Cones enable color vision.
    b. Cones are highly concentrated in the foveal region of the retina.
    c. Cones have a higher absolute threshold for brightness than rods.
    d. All of these statements are true.

44. Assuming that the visual systems of humans and other mammals function similarly, you would expect that the retina of a nocturnal mammal (one active only at night) would contain
    a. mostly cones.
    b. mostly rods.
    c. an equal number of rods and cones.
    d. more bipolar cells than an animal active only during the day.

45. As the football game continued into the night, LeVar noticed that he was having difficulty distinguishing the colors of the players' uniforms. This is because the _____ , which enable color vision, have a _____ absolute threshold for brightness than the available light intensity.
    a. rods; higher
    b. cones; higher
    c. rods; lower
    d. cones; lower

Objective 6-8: Discuss the theories that help us understand color vision.

46. An object appears to be red in color because it _____ the long wavelengths of red and because of our mental _____ of the color.

47. One out of every 50 people is color deficient; this is usually a male because the defect is genetically _____ _____ .

48. According to the _____ - _____ _____ theory, the eyes have three types of color receptors: one reacts most strongly to _____ , one to _____ , and one to _____ .

49. After staring at a green square for a while, you will see the color red, its _____ color, as an _____ .

50. Hering's theory of color vision is called the _____ - _____ theory. According to this theory, after visual information leaves the receptors it is analyzed in terms of pairs of opposing colors: _____ versus _____ , _____ versus _____ , and _____ versus _____ .

Summarize the two stages of color processing.

APPLICATIONS:

51. I am a cell in the thalamus that is excited by red and inhibited by green. I am a(n)

    a. feature detector.
    b. cone.
    c. bipolar cell.
    d. opponent-process cell.

52. After staring at a very intense red stimulus for a few minutes, Carrie shifted her gaze to a beige wall and "saw" the color _____ . Carrie's experience provides support for the _____ theory.

    a. green; trichromatic
    b. blue; opponent-process
    c. green; opponent-process
    d. blue; trichromatic

Objective 6-9: Describe Gestalt psychologists' understanding of perception, and explain how figure-ground and grouping principles contribute to our perceptions.

53. According to the _____ school of psychology, we tend to organize a cluster of sensations into a _____ , or form.

54. When we view a scene, we see the central object, or _____ , as distinct from surrounding stimuli, or the _____ .

55. Proximity, continuity, and closure are examples of Gestalt rules of_____ .

56. The principle that we organize stimuli into smooth, continuous patterns is called _____ . The principle that we fill in gaps to create a complete, whole object is _____ . The grouping of items that are close to each other is the principle of _____ .

APPLICATION:

57. Studying the road map before her trip, Colleen had no trouble following the route of the highway she planned to travel. Colleen's ability illustrates the principle of

    a. closure.
    b. relative size.
    c. continuity.
    d. proximity.

Objective 6-10: Explain how we use binocular and monocular cues to perceive the world in three dimensions.

58. The ability to see objects in three dimensions despite their two-dimensional representations on our retinas is called _____ _____ . It enables us to estimate _____ .

59. Gibson and Walk developed the _____ _____ to test depth perception in infants. They found that each species, by the time it is _____ , has the perceptual abilities it needs.

Summarize the results of Gibson and Walk's studies of depth perception.

For questions 60–68, identify the depth perception cue that is defined.

60. Any cue that requires both eyes: _____ .

61. The greater the difference between the images received by the two eyes, the nearer the object: _____ _____ . 3-D movies simulate this cue by photographing each scene with two cameras.

62. Any cue that requires either eye alone: _____ .

63. If two objects are presumed to be the same size, the one that casts a smaller retinal image is perceived as farther away: _____ _____ .

64. An object partially covered by another is seen as farther away: _____ .

65. Objects lower in the visual field are seen as nearer: _____ _____ .

66. As we move, objects at different distances appear to move at different rates: _____ _____ .

67. Parallel lines appear to converge in the distance: _____ _____ .

68. The dimmer of two objects seems farther away:

_____ _____

_____ .

STUDY TIP: Monocular depth cues are used by either eye alone to determine the distance of objects. They include relative height and size, interposition, linear perspective, and light and shadow.

69. Test your understanding of these cues by drawing a picture (in the box below) of a person on a bus or train, a fence, a house, and trees. Use each cue at least once, and in your drawing place the objects in the following order (closest to most distant): person, fence, house, and trees.

APPLICATIONS:

70. When two familiar objects of equal size cast unequal retinal images, the object that casts the smaller retinal image will be perceived as being

a. closer than the other object.
b. more distant than the other object.
c. larger than the other object.
d. smaller than the other object.

71. As her friend Milo walks toward her, Noriko perceives his size as remaining constant because his perceived distance _____ at the same time that her retinal image of him _____ .

a. increases; decreases
b. increases; increases
c. decreases; decreases
d. decreases; increases

72. How do we perceive a pole that partially covers a wall?

a. as farther away
b. as nearer
c. as larger
d. There is not enough information to determine the object's size or distance.

73. An artist paints a tree orchard so that the parallel rows of trees converge at the top of the canvas. Which cue has the artist used to convey distance?

a. interposition
b. retinal disparity
c. linear perspective
d. figure-ground

74. Objects higher in our field of vision are perceived as _____ due to the principle of _____ .

a. nearer; relative height
b. nearer; linear perspective
c. farther away; relative height
d. farther away; linear perspective

Objective 6-11: Explain how perceptual constancies help us organize our sensations into meaningful perceptions.

75. Our tendency to see objects as unchanging while the stimuli from them change in size, shape, and brightness is a _____ - _____ process called

_____ _____ .

76. The experience of color depends on the surrounding _____ in which an object is seen. In an unvarying context, a familiar object will be perceived as having consistent color, even as the light changes. This phenomenon is called

_____ _____ .

77. We see color as a result of our brains' computations of the light _____ by any object relative to its _____

_____ .

78. The brain computes an object's brightness _____ (relative to/independent of) surrounding objects.

79. The amount of light an object reflects relative to its surroundings is called _____

_____ .

80. Due to shape and size constancy, familiar objects _____ (do/do not) appear to change shape or size despite changes in our _____ images of them.

81. Several illusions, including the _____ illusion, are explained by the interplay between perceived _____ and perceived

_____ . When distance cues are removed, these illusions are _____ (diminished/strengthened).

APPLICATIONS:

82. The fact that a white object under dim illumination appears lighter than a gray object under bright illumination is called
    a. relative luminance.
    b. perceptual adaptation.
    c. color contrast.
    d. brightness constancy.

83. In the absence of perceptual constancy
    a. objects would appear to change size as their distance from us changed.
    b. depth perception would be based exclusively on monocular cues.
    c. depth perception would be based exclusively on binocular cues.
    d. depth perception would be impossible.

84. Your friend tosses you a Frisbee. You know that it is getting closer instead of larger because of
    a. shape constancy.
    b. relative motion.
    c. size constancy.
    d. all of these factors.

Objective 6-12: Describe what research on restored vision, sensory restriction, and perceptual adaptation reveals about the effects of experience on perception.

85. The idea that knowledge comes from inborn ways of organizing sensory experiences was proposed by the philosopher _____ .

86. On the other side were philosophers who maintained that we learn to perceive the world by experiencing it. One philosopher of this school was _____ .

87. Studies of cases in which vision has been restored to a person who was blind from birth show that, upon seeing tactilely familiar objects for the first time, the person _____ (can/cannot) recognize them.

88. Studies of sensory restriction demonstrate that visual experiences during _____ are crucial for perceptual development. Such experiences suggest that there is a _____ _____ for normal sensory and perceptual development.

89. Humans given glasses that shift or invert the visual field _____ (will/will not) adapt to the distorted perception. This is called

_____ _____ .

Animals such as chicks _____ (adapt/do not adapt) to distorting lenses.

Hearing

Objective 6-13: Describe the characteristics of air pressure waves that we hear as sound, and explain the process by which the ear transforms sound energy into neural messages.

90. The stimulus for hearing, or

_____ , is sound waves, created by the compression and expansion of

_____ _____ .

91. The amplitude of a sound wave determines the sound's _____ .

92. The frequency of a sound wave determines the _____ we perceive.

93. Sound energy is measured in units called _____ . The absolute threshold for hearing is arbitrarily defined as _____ such units.

94. The ear is divided into three main parts: the _____ ear, the _____ ear, and the _____ ear.

95. The outer ear channels sound waves toward the _____ , a tight membrane that then vibrates.

96. The middle ear transmits the vibrations through a piston made of three small bones: the

_____ , _____ , and _____ .

97. In the inner ear, a coiled, bony, fluid-filled tube called the _____ contains the receptor cells for hearing. The incoming vibrations cause the _____ _____ to vibrate the fluid that fills the tube, which causes ripples in the

_____ _____ , bending the _____ _____ that line its surface. This movement triggers impulses in the adjacent nerve cells. Axons of those cells converge to form the auditory nerve, which carries the neural messages (via the _____) to the _____ lobe's auditory cortex.

98. Damage to the cochlea's hair cell receptors or their associated auditory nerves can cause _____ hearing loss. It may be caused by disease, but more often it results from the biological changes linked with heredity, _____ , and prolonged exposure to ear-splitting noise or music.

99. Problems in the mechanical system that conducts sound waves to the cochlea may cause

_____ _____

_____ .

100. An electronic device that restores hearing among nerve-deafened people is a

_____ _____ .

101. The brain interprets loudness from the _____ of hair cells a sound activates.

APPLICATIONS:

102. Which of the following correctly lists the order of structures through which sound travels after entering the ear?
    a. auditory canal, eardrum, middle ear, cochlea
    b. eardrum, auditory canal, middle ear, cochlea
    c. eardrum, middle ear, cochlea, auditory canal
    d. cochlea, eardrum, middle ear, auditory canal

103. Dr. Frankenstein has forgotten to give his monster an important part; as a result, the monster cannot transduce sound. Dr. Frankenstein omitted the
    a. eardrum.
    b. middle ear.
    c. semicircular canals.
    d. basilar membrane.

Objective 6-14: Discuss the theories that help us understand pitch perception.

104. One theory of pitch perception proposes that different pitches activate different places on the cochlea's basilar membrane; this is the _____ theory. This theory has difficulty accounting for how we hear _____-pitched sounds, which do not have such localized effects.

105. A second theory proposes that the frequency of neural impulses, sent to the brain at the same frequency as sound waves, allows the perception of different pitches. This is the _____ theory. This theory fails to account for the perception of _____-pitched sounds because individual neurons cannot fire faster than _____ times per second.

106. For the higher pitches, cells may alternate their firing to match the sound's frequency, according to the _____ principle.

Objective 6-15: Describe how we locate sounds.

107. We locate a sound by sensing differences in the _____ and _____ with which it reaches our ears.

108. A sound that comes from directly ahead will be _____ (easier/harder) to locate than a sound that comes from off to one side.

The Other Senses

Objective 6-16: Describe the sense of touch.

109. The sense of touch is a mixture of at least four senses: _____ ,

_____ , _____ ,

and _____ . Other skin sensations, such as tickle, itch, hot, and wetness, are _____ of the basic ones.

Objective 6-17: Discuss how we best understand and control pain.

110. People born without the ability to feel pain may be unaware of experiencing severe _____ . More numerous are those who live with _____ pain in the form of persistent headaches and backaches, for example.

111. Pain is a property of our _____ and _____ as well as our _____ and _____ , and our surrounding _____ .

112. The pain system _____ (is/is not) triggered by one specific type of physical energy. The body has specialized _____ , sensory receptors that detect hurtful stimuli.

113. Melzack and Wall have proposed a theory of pain called the _____- _____ theory, which proposes that there is a neurological _____ in the _____ _____ that blocks pain signals or lets them through. It may be opened by activation of _____ (small/large) nerve fibers and closed by activation of _____ (small/large) fibers or by information from the _____ . When we are distracted from pain or soothed by our naturally painkilling _____ , our experience of pain diminishes.

114. Pain-producing brain activity may be triggered with or without _____ _____ .

115. A sensation of pain in an amputated leg is referred to as a _____ _____ sensation. Another example is _____ , experienced by people who have a ringing-in-the-ears sensation.

116. Because our experience of pain is also influenced by psychological factors as well as our social situation and our _____ traditions, we can say our perception of pain is a _____ phenomenon.

List some pain control techniques used in health care situations.

APPLICATIONS:

117. The phantom limb sensation indicates that
    a. pain is a purely sensory phenomenon.
    b. the central nervous system plays only a minor role in the experience of pain.
    c. pain involves the brain's interpretation of neural activity.
    d. all of these are true.

118. While competing in the Olympic trials, marathoner Kirsten O'Brien suffered a stress fracture in her left leg. That she did not experience significant pain until the race was over is probably attributable to the fact that during the race
    a. the pain gate in her spinal cord was closed by information coming from her brain.
    b. her body's production of endorphins decreased.
    c. an increase in the activity of small pain fibers closed the pain gate.
    d. a decrease in the activity of large pain fibers closed the pain gate.

119. How does pain differ from other senses?
    a. It has no special receptors.
    b. It has no single stimulus.
    c. It is influenced by both physical and psychological phenomena.
    d. All of these statements are true.

Objective 6-18: Describe how we experience taste and smell.

120. The basic taste sensations are _____ , _____ , _____ , _____ , and a meaty taste called _____ .

121. Taste, which is a _____ sense, is enabled by the 200 or more _____ _____ on the top and sides of the tongue. Each contains a _____ that catches food chemicals.

122. Taste receptors reproduce themselves every _____ . As we age, the number of taste buds _____ (increases/decreases/remains unchanged) and our taste sensitivity _____ (increases/decreases/remains unchanged). Taste is also affected by _____ and by _____ use, and by our _____ .

123. Like taste, smell (or _____) is a _____ sense. There _____ (is/is not) a distinct receptor for each detectable odor.

124. Odors are able to evoke memories and feelings because there is a direct link between the brain area that gets information from the nose and the ancient _____ centers associated with memory and emotion.

APPLICATION:

125. Seventy-year-old Mrs. Martinez finds that she must spice her food heavily or she cannot taste it. Unfortunately, her son often finds her cooking inedible because it is so spicy. What is the likely explanation for their taste differences?

    a. Women have higher taste thresholds than men.
    b. Men have higher taste thresholds than women.
    c. Being 70 years old, Mrs. Martinez probably has fewer taste buds than her son.
    d. All of these are likely explanations.

Objective 6-19: Explain how we sense our body's position and movement.

126. The system for sensing the position and movement of body parts is called _____ . The receptors for this sense are located in the _____ , _____ , and _____ .

127. The sense that monitors the position and movement of the head (and thus the body) is the _____ _____ . The receptors for this sense are located in the _____ _____ and _____ _____ of the inner ear.

Sensory Interaction

Objective 6-20: Describe how our senses interact.

128. When the sense of smell is blocked, as when we have a cold, foods do not taste the same; this illustrates the principle of _____ . The _____ effect occurs when we _____ a speaker saying one syllable while _____ another.

129. The influence of bodily sensations, gestures, and other states on our cognitive preferences and judgments is called _____ .

APPLICATIONS:

130. Which of the following is an example of sensory interaction?

    a. finding that despite its delicious aroma, a weird-looking meal tastes awful
    b. finding that food tastes bland when you have a bad cold
    c. finding it difficult to maintain your balance when you have an ear infection
    d. All of these are examples.

131. Tamiko hates the bitter taste of her cough syrup. Which of the following would she find most helpful in minimizing the syrup's bad taste?

    a. tasting something very sweet before taking the cough syrup
    b. keeping the syrup in her mouth for several seconds before swallowing it
    c. holding her nose while taking the cough syrup
    d. gulping the cough syrup so that it misses her tongue

(Thinking Critically) ESP—Perception Without Sensation?

Objective 6-21: List the claims of ESP, and discuss the conclusions of most research psychologists after putting these claims to the test.

132. Perception outside the range of normal sensation is called _____ .

133. Psychologists who study ESP are called _____ .

134. The form of ESP in which people claim to be capable of reading others' minds is called _____ . A person who "senses" that a friend is in danger might claim to have the ESP ability of _____ . An ability to "see" into the future is called _____ . A person who claims to be able to levitate and move objects is claiming the power of _____ .

135. Analyses of psychic visions and premonitions reveal _____ (high/chance-level) accuracy. Nevertheless, some people continue to believe in their accuracy because vague predictions often are later _____ to match events that have already occurred. In

addition, people are more likely to recall or _____ dreams that seem to have come true.

136. Critics point out that a major difficulty for parapsychology is that ESP phenomena are not consistently _____ .

137. Daryl Bem, who has been skeptical of stage psychics, conducted research in which Cornell University participants _____ (did/did not) accurately guess the position of an erotic scene.

APPLICATIONS:

138. Regina claims that she can bend spoons, levitate furniture, and perform many other "mind over matter" feats. Regina apparently believes she has the power of

  a. telepathy.
  b. clairvoyance.
  c. precognition.
  d. psychokinesis.

139. Which of the following is true of the predictions of leading psychics?

  a. They are often ambiguous prophecies later interpreted to match actual events.
  b. They are no more accurate than guesses made by others.
  c. They are nearly always inaccurate.
  d. All of these statements are true.

Progress Test 1

Multiple-Choice Questions

Circle your answers to the following questions and check them with the answers beginning on page 149. If your answer is incorrect, read the explanation for why it is incorrect and then consult the text.

1. Which of the following is true?

  a. The absolute threshold for any stimulus is a constant.
  b. The absolute threshold for any stimulus varies somewhat.
  c. The absolute threshold is defined as the minimum amount of stimulation necessary for a stimulus to be detected 75 percent of the time.
  d. The absolute threshold is defined as the minimum amount of stimulation necessary for a stimulus to be detected 60 percent of the time.

2. If you can just notice the difference between 10- and 11-pound weights, which of the following weights could you differentiate from a 100-pound weight?

  a. 101-pound weight
  b. 105-pound weight
  c. 110-pound weight
  d. There is no basis for prediction.

3. A decrease in sensory responsiveness accompanying an unchanging stimulus is called

  a. sensory fatigue.
  b. accommodation.
  c. sensory adaptation.
  d. sensory interaction.

4. The size of the pupil is controlled by the

  a. lens.   **c.** cornea.
  b. retina.   **d.** iris.

5. The process by which the lens changes its curvature is

  a. accommodation.   **c.** feature detection.
  b. sensory adaptation. **d.** transduction.

6. The receptor of the eye that functions best in dim light is the

  a. fovea.   **c.** bipolar cell.
  b. cone.   **d.** rod.

7. The Young-Helmholtz theory proposes that

  a. there are three different types of color-sensitive cones.
  b. retinal cells are excited by one color and inhibited by its complementary color.
  c. there are four different types of cones.
  d. rod, not cone, vision accounts for our ability to detect fine visual detail.

8. Frequency is to pitch as _____ is to_____ .

  a. wavelength; loudness
  b. amplitude; loudness
  c. wavelength; intensity
  d. amplitude; intensity

9. Our experience of pain when we are injured depends on

  a. our biological makeup and the type of injury we have sustained.
  b. how well medical personnel deal with our injury.
  c. our physiology, experiences and attention, and surrounding culture.
  d. what our culture allows us to express in terms of feelings of pain.

10. According to the gate-control theory, a way to alleviate chronic pain would be to stimulate the _____ nerve fibers that _____ the spinal gate.

    a. small; open   **c.** large; open

    b. small; close   **d.** large; close

11. The transduction of light energy into nerve impulses takes place in the

    a. iris.   **c.** lens.

    b. retina.   **d.** optic nerve.

12. The brain breaks vision into separate dimensions such as color, depth, movement, and form, and works on each aspect simultaneously. This is called

    a. feature detection.

    b. parallel processing.

    c. accommodation.

    d. opponent processing.

13. Kinesthesis involves

    a. the bones of the middle ear.

    b. information from the tendons, joints, and muscles.

    c. membranes within the cochlea.

    d. the body's sense of balance.

14. One light may appear reddish and another greenish if they differ in

    a. wavelength.   **c.** opponent processes.

    b. amplitude.   **d.** brightness.

15. Which of the following explains why a rose appears equally red in bright and dim light?

    a. the Young-Helmholtz theory

    b. the opponent-process theory

    c. feature detection

    d. color constancy

16. Which of the following is an example of sensory adaptation?

    a. finding the cold water of a swimming pool warmer after you have been in it for a while

    b. developing an increased sensitivity to salt the more you use it in foods

    c. becoming very irritated at the continuing sound of a dripping faucet

    d. All of these are examples.

17. Most color-deficient people will probably

    a. lack functioning red- or green-sensitive cones.

    b. see the world in only black and white.

    c. also suffer from poor vision.

    d. have above-average vision to compensate for the deficit.

18. The historical movement associated with the statement "The whole may exceed the sum of its parts" is

    a. parapsychology.

    b. behavioral psychology.

    c. functional psychology.

    d. Gestalt psychology.

19. Figures tend to be perceived as whole, complete objects, even if spaces or gaps exist in the representation, thus demonstrating the principle of

    a. interposition.   **c.** continuity.

    b. linear perspective. **d.** closure.

20. The figure-ground relationship has demonstrated that

    a. perception is largely innate.

    b. perception is simply a point-for-point representation of sensation.

    c. the same stimulus can trigger more than one perception.

    d. different people see different things when viewing a scene.

21. When we stare at an object, each eye receives a slightly different image, providing a depth cue known as

    a. interposition.   **c.** relative motion.

    b. linear perspective. **d.** retinal disparity.

22. As we move, viewed objects cast changing shapes on our retinas, although we do not perceive the objects as changing. This is part of the phenomenon of

    a. perceptual constancy.

    b. relative motion.

    c. linear perspective.

    d. continuity.

23. A person claiming to be able to read another's mind is claiming to have the ESP ability of

    a. psychokinesis.   **c.** clairvoyance.

    b. precognition.   **d.** telepathy.

24. Which philosopher maintained that knowledge comes from inborn ways of organizing our sensory experiences?

    a. Locke   **c.** Gibson

    b. Kant   **d.** Walk

25. Kittens and monkeys reared seeing only diffuse, unpatterned light
    a. later had difficulty distinguishing color and brightness.
    b. later had difficulty perceiving color and brightness, but eventually regained normal sensitivity.
    c. later had difficulty perceiving the shape of objects.
    d. showed no impairment in perception, indicating that neural feature detectors develop even in the absence of normal sensory experiences.

26. Adults who are born blind but later have their vision restored
    a. are almost immediately able to recognize familiar objects.
    b. typically fail to recognize familiar objects.
    c. are unable to follow moving objects with their eyes.
    d. have excellent eye-hand coordination.

27. _____ processing refers to how the physical characteristics of stimuli influence their interpretation.
    a. Top-down
    b. Bottom-up
    c. Parapsychological
    d. Parallel

28. Which of the following is NOT a monocular depth cue?
    a. light and shadow
    b. relative height
    c. retinal disparity
    d. interposition

29. The Moon illusion occurs in part because distance cues at the horizon make the Moon seem
    a. farther away and therefore larger.
    b. closer and therefore larger.
    c. farther away and therefore smaller.
    d. closer and therefore smaller.

30. Figure is to ground as _____ is to _____ .
    a. night; day
    b. top; bottom
    c. cloud; sky
    d. sensation; perception

31. The study of perception is primarily concerned with how we
    a. detect sights, sounds, and other stimuli.
    b. sense environmental stimuli.
    c. develop sensitivity to illusions.
    d. interpret sensory stimuli.

32. Which of the following influences perception?
    a. biological maturation
    b. the context in which stimuli are perceived
    c. expectations
    d. all of these factors

33. Jack claims that he often has dreams that predict future events. He claims to have the power of
    a. telepathy.
    b. clairvoyance.
    c. precognition.
    d. psychokinesis.

34. Which of the following is true regarding scientific investigations of precognition?
    a. A growing body of research demonstrates that some people are truly "psychic."
    b. Studies that seem to provide evidence of precognitive ability have been criticized for being badly flawed.
    c. The search for a valid test of ESP has resulted in only a handful of studies.
    d. All of these statements are true.

35. The frequency theory of hearing is better than place theory at explaining our sensation of
    a. the lowest pitches.
    b. pitches of intermediate range.
    c. the highest pitches.
    d. all of these pitches.

Matching Items

Match each of the structures with its function or description.

Structures or Conditions

_____   **1.** lens
_____   **2.** iris
_____   **3.** pupil
_____   **4.** rods
_____   **5.** cones
_____   **6.** middle ear
_____   **7.** inner ear
_____   **8.** large nerve fiber
_____   **9.** small nerve fiber
_____   **10.** semicircular canals
_____   **11.** sensors in joints

Progress Test 2

Progress Test 2 should be completed during a final chapter review. Answer the following questions after you thoroughly understand the correct answers for the section reviews and Progress Test 1.

Multiple-Choice Questions

1. Which of the following is NOT one of the basic tastes?

   a. sweet   **c.** umami
   b. salty   **d.** bland

2. Bottom-up processing begins with the
   a. feature detectors.   **c.** retina.
   b. cerebral cortex.   **d.** sensory receptors.

3. The process by which sensory information is converted into neural energy is
   a. sensory adaptation.   **c.** sensory interaction.
   b. feature detection.   **d.** transduction.

4. The receptors for taste are located in the
   a. taste buds.   **c.** fovea.
   b. cochlea.   **d.** cortex.

5. The inner ear contains receptors for
   a. audition and kinesthesis.
   b. kinesthesis and the vestibular sense.
   c. audition and the vestibular sense.
   d. audition, kinesthesis, and the vestibular sense.

Functions or Descriptions

a. amplifies sounds
b. closes pain gate
c. vestibular sense
d. controls pupil
e. accommodation
f. opens pain gate
g. admits light
h. vision in dim light
i. transduction of sound
j. kinesthesis
k. color vision

6. According to the opponent-process theory
   a. there are three types of color-sensitive cones.
   b. the process of color vision begins in the cortex.
   c. neurons involved in color vision are stimulated by one color's wavelength and inhibited by another's.
   d. all of these statements are true.

7. What enables you to feel yourself wiggling your toes even with your eyes closed?
   a. vestibular sense
   b. kinesthesis
   c. the skin senses
   d. sensory interaction

8. Hubel and Wiesel discovered feature detectors in the visual
   a. fovea.   **c.** iris.
   b. optic nerve.   **d.** cortex.

9. Weber's law states that
   a. the absolute threshold for any stimulus is a constant.
   b. the jnd for any stimulus is a constant.
   c. the absolute threshold for any stimulus is a constant proportion.
   d. the jnd for any stimulus is a constant proportion.

10. The principle that one sense may influence another is
    a. transduction.   **c.** Weber's law.
    b. sensory adaptation.   **d.** sensory interaction.

11. Which of the following is the correct order of the structures through which light passes after entering the eye?
    a. lens, pupil, cornea, retina
    b. pupil, cornea, lens, retina
    c. pupil, lens, cornea, retina
    d. cornea, pupil, lens, retina

12. In the opponent-process theory, the three pairs of processes are
    a. red-green, blue-yellow, black-white.
    b. red-blue, green-yellow, black-white.
    c. red-yellow, blue-green, black-white.
    d. dependent upon the individual's experience.

13. Wavelength is to _____ as_____ is to brightness.
    a. hue; intensity
    b. intensity; hue
    c. frequency; amplitude
    d. brightness; hue

14. A subliminal stimulus is one that
    a. is too weak to cross the different threshold.
    b. is too weak to cross the absolute threshold.
    c. is too weak to cross either the difference threshold or the absolute threshold.
    d. strikes the blind spot of the eye's retina.

15. Which of the following is the most accurate description of how we process color?
    a. Throughout the visual system, color processing is divided into separate red, green, and blue systems.
    b. Red-green, blue-yellow, and black-white opponent processes operate throughout the visual system.
    c. Color processing occurs in two stages: (1) a three-color system in the retina and (2) opponent-process cells en route to the visual cortex.
    d. Color processing occurs in two stages: (1) an opponent-process system in the retina and (2) a three-color system en route to the visual cortex.

16. One reason that your ability to detect fine visual details is greatest when scenes are focused on the fovea of your retina is that
    a. there are more feature detectors in the fovea than in the peripheral regions of the retina.
    b. cones in the fovea are nearer to the optic nerve than those in peripheral regions of the retina.

    c. many rods, which are clustered in the fovea, have individual bipolar cells to relay their information to the cortex.
    d. many cones, which are clustered in the fovea, have individual bipolar cells to relay their information to the cortex.

17. Given normal sensory ability, a person standing atop a mountain on a dark, clear night can see a candle flame atop a mountain 30 miles away. This is a description of vision's
    a. difference threshold.   c. absolute threshold.
    b. jnd.   d. feature detection.

18. The tendency to organize stimuli into smooth, uninterrupted patterns is called
    a. closure.   c. interposition.
    b. continuity.   d. proximity.

19. Which of the following statements is consistent with the Gestalt theory of perception?
    a. Perception develops largely through learning.
    b. Perception is the product of heredity.
    c. The mind organizes sensations into meaningful perceptions.
    d. Perception results directly from sensation.

20. Experiments with distorted visual environments demonstrate that
    a. adaptation rarely takes place.
    b. animals adapt readily, but humans do not.
    c. humans adapt readily, while lower animals typically do not.
    d. adaptation is possible during a critical period in infancy but not thereafter.

21. The phenomenon that refers to the ways in which an individual's expectations influence perception is called
    a. perceptual set.   c. interposition.
    b. retinal disparity.   d. kinesthesis.

22. According to the philosopher _____ , we learn to perceive the world.
    a. Locke   c. Gibson
    b. Kant   d. Walk

23. The phenomenon of size constancy is based on the close connection between an object's perceived _____ and its perceived _____ .
    a. size; shape   c. size; brightness
    b. size; distance   d. shape; distance

24. Which of the following statements best describes the effects of sensory restriction?

    a. It produces functional blindness when experienced for any length of time at any age.
    b. It has greater effects on humans than on animals.
    c. It has more damaging effects when experienced during infancy.
    d. It has greater effects on adults than on children.

25. Psychologists who study ESP are called

    a. clairvoyants.   c. parapsychologists.
    b. telepaths.   d. levitators.

26. The depth cue that occurs when we watch stable objects at different distances as we are moving is

    a. linear perspective.   c. relative height.
    b. interposition.   d. relative motion.

27. Which of the following statements concerning ESP is true?

    a. Most ESP researchers are quacks.
    b. There have been a large number of reliable demonstrations of ESP.
    c. Most research psychologists are skeptical of the claims of defenders of ESP.
    d. There have been reliable laboratory demonstrations of ESP, but the results are no different from those that would occur by chance.

28. Each time you see your car, it projects a different image on the retinas of your eyes, yet you do not perceive it as changing. This is because of

    a. perceptual set.
    b. retinal disparity.
    c. perceptual constancy.
    d. figure-ground.

29. The term *gestalt* means

    a. grouping.   c. perception.
    b. sensation.   d. whole.

30. Studies of the visual cliff have provided evidence that much of depth perception is

    a. innate.
    b. learned.
    c. innate in lower animals, learned in humans.
    d. innate in humans, learned in lower animals.

31. All of the following are laws of perceptual organization, EXCEPT

    a. proximity.   c. continuity.
    b. closure.   d. retinal disparity.

32. You probably perceive the diagram above as three separate objects due to the principle of

    a. proximity.   c. closure.
    b. continuity.   d. linear perspective.

33. _____ processing refers to how our knowledge and expectations influence perception.

    a. Top-down   c. Parapsychological
    b. Bottom-up   d. Parallel

34. The place theory of pitch perception cannot account for how we hear

    a. low-pitched sounds.
    b. middle-pitched sounds.
    c. high-pitched sounds.
    d. chords (three or more pitches simultaneously).

35. Sensorineural hearing loss is caused by

    a. wax buildup in the outer ear.
    b. damage to the eardrum.
    c. blockage in the middle ear because of infection.
    d. damage to the cochlea.

True–False Items

Indicate whether each statement is true or false by placing *T* or *F* in the blank next to the item.

_____ 1. Once we perceive an item as a figure, it is impossible to see it as ground.

_____ 2. Laboratory experiments have laid to rest all criticisms of ESP.

_____ 3. Six-month-old infants will cross a visual cliff if their mother calls.

_____ 4. Unlike other animals, humans have no critical period for visual stimulation.

_____ 5. Immanuel Kant argued that experience determined how we perceive the world.

_____ 6. It is just as easy to touch two pencil tips together with only one eye open as it is with both eyes open.

_____ 7. After some time, humans are able to adjust to living in a world made upside down by distorting goggles.

_____ 8. As our distance from an object changes, the object's size seems to change.

_____ **9.** Perception is influenced by psychological factors such as set and expectation as well as by physiological events.

_____ **10.** John Locke argued that perception is inborn.

Essay Questions

1. A dancer in a chorus line uses many sensory cues when performing. Discuss three senses that dancers rely on, and explain why each is important. (Use the space below to list the points you want to make, and organize them. Then write the essay on a separate sheet of paper.)

2. In many movies from the 1930s, dancers performed seemingly meaningless movements which, when viewed from above, were transformed into intricate patterns and designs. Similarly, the formations of marching bands often create pictures and spell words. Identify and describe at least four Gestalt principles of grouping that explain the audience's perception of the images created by these types of formations. (Use the space below to list the points you want to make, and organize them. Then write the essay on a separate piece of paper.)

Summing Up

Use the diagrams to identify the parts of the eye and ear, then describe how each contributes to vision or hearing. Also, briefly explain the role of each structure.

The Eye

1. _____

_____

2. _____

_____

3. _____

_____

4. _____

_____

5. _____

_____

6. _____

_____

7. _____

The Ear

1. _____

   _____

2. _____

   _____

3. _____

   _____

4. _____

   _____

5. _____

   _____

6. _____

   _____

7. _____

   _____

8. _____

   _____

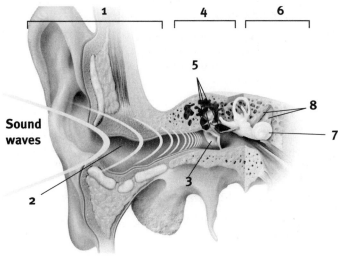

Sound waves

Terms and Concepts to Remember

Writing Definitions

Using your own words, on a piece of paper write a brief definition or explanation of each of the following terms.

1. sensation
2. perception
3. bottom-up processing
4. top-down processing
5. transduction
6. absolute threshold
7. signal detection theory
8. subliminal
9. priming
10. difference threshold
11. Weber's law
12. sensory adaptation
13. perceptual set
14. wavelength and hue

15. intensity
16. retina
17. accommodation
18. rods and cones
19. optic nerve
20. blind spot
21. fovea
22. feature detectors
23. parallel processing
24. Young-Helmholtz trichromatic (three-color) theory
25. opponent-process theory
26. gestalt
27. figure-ground
28. grouping
29. depth perception
30. visual cliff
31. binocular cue
32. retinal disparity
33. monocular cue

34. perceptual constancy

35. color constancy

36. perceptual adaptation

37. audition

38. frequency and pitch

39. middle ear

40. cochlea

41. inner ear

42. sensorineural hearing loss

43. conduction hearing loss

44. cochlear implant

45. place theory

46. frequency theory

47. gate-control theory

48. kinesthesis

49. vestibular sense

50. sensory interaction

51. embodied cognition

52. extrasensory perception (ESP)

53. parapsychology

Cross-Check

As you learned in Chapter 1, reviewing and overlearning of material are important to the learning process. After you have written the definitions of the key terms in this chapter, you should complete the crossword puzzle to ensure that you can reverse the process—recognize the term, given the definition.

ACROSS

1. The retina's point of central focus.
5. Part of the ear in which sounds are converted to nerve impulses.
6. The ear's membrane that is lined with hair cells.
8. English physicist who contributed to the theory of color vision that proposed three different color receptors in the retina.
10. Grouping principle that we fill in gaps in visual stimuli to create a complete, whole image.
11. Receptors that enable color vision.
12. The study of ESP.
14. Information processing in which several aspects of a problem are processed simultaneously.
15. Another term for the difference threshold (abbreviation).
16. Minimum stimulation needed to detect a stimulus 50 percent of the time is the _____ threshold.
17. The sense of the position and movement of the parts of the body.
19. Snail-like structure of the inner ear that contains the receptors for hearing.
20. A binocular cue for perceiving depth is retinal _____ .

DOWN

1. Number of complete wavelengths that pass a given point in a given time.
2. Part of the eye that contains the rods and cones.
3. Monocular cue for perceiving distance that involves the convergence of parallel lines.
4. The organization of the visual field into two parts is referred to as the _____ relationship.
7. Psychological characteristic of light that is determined by wavelength.
9. School of psychology that emphasied our tendency to integrate pieces of information into meaningful wholes.
13. Psychological characteristic of a sound that is determined by its frequency.
18. Visual receptors that are concentrated in the periphery of the retina.

Answers

Chapter Review

Basic Principles of Sensation and Perception

1. prosopagnosia
2. sensation; perception
3. bottom-up processing; top-down processing
4. **b.** is the answer.
   a. Both recognition and interpretation are examples of perception.
   c. This answer would have been correct if the question had read, "Perception is to sensation as _____ is to _____ ."
   d. Sensation and perception are important processes in both hearing and seeing.
5. **c.** is the answer.
6. **d.** is the answer.
7. receive; transduce; deliver
8. absolute threshold; 50
9. signal detection
10. subliminal: conscious
11. prime; automatically
12. difference threshold; just noticeable difference (jnd)
13. Weber's law; stimulus
14. **d.** is the answer.
   a. The absolute threshold refers to whether a single stimulus can be detected, not to whether two stimuli can be differentiated.
   b. Subliminal refers to stimuli below the absolute threshold.

c. A receptor threshold is a minimum amount of energy that will elicit a neural impulse in a receptor cell.
15. sensory adaptation
16. informative
17. sensory adaptation. This occurs when we remain fixed on a stimulus. Moving his fingers prevents his sense of touch from adapting.
18. perceptual set
19. set; context
20. top-down; bottom-up
21. schemas
22. stereotypes; emotional; motives
23. **d.** is the answer. The two people interpreted a briefly perceived object in terms of their perceptual sets, or mental predispositions, in this case conditioned by their work experiences.
   a. Their different interpretations reflect top-down processing.
   b. Sensory adaptation refers to the decreased sensitivity that occurs with continued exposure to an unchanging stimulus.
   c. Transduction is the transformation of one form of energy into another.

Vision

24. electromagnetic
25. wavelength; hue
26. intensity; amplitude; brightness
27. **a.** yes. The left-hand wave has lower amplitude and the colors would be duller. The right-hand wave has similar frequency (and therefore hue) but a higher amplitude, making it brighter.

   b. yes. The sounds have similar frequency (and therefore pitch), but the right-hand sound has higher amplitude and would therefore be louder.
28. cornea; pupil; iris
29. lens; retina; accommodation
30. rods; cones
31. bipolar; ganglion
32. optic nerve; thalamus
33. blind spot
34. fovea; peripheral; bipolar; do not
35. cones; rods
36. sensitive; 20
37. abstract; thalamus
38. visual cortex; edges; lines; angles; movements; feature detectors; supercell clusters

39. simultaneously; parallel processing

40. blindsight

41. **d.** is the answer. Greater sensitivity to fine visual detail is associated with the cones, which have their own bipolar cells to relay information to the cortex. The cones are concentrated in the fovea, the retina's point of central focus. For this reason, staring directly at an object maximizes sensitivity to fine detail.
    a. If you stare off to one side, the image falls onto peripheral regions of the retina, where rods are concentrated and sensitivity to fine visual detail is poor.
    b. Sensitivity to detail is not directly influenced by whether one or both eyes are stimulated.
    c. Decreasing the intensity of light would only impair the functioning of the cones, which are sensitive to visual detail but have a high threshold for light intensity.

42. **d.** is the answer. Just as light strikes the film of a camera, visual images entering the eye are projected onto the retina.
    a. The pupil would be analogous to the aperture of a camera, since both control the amount of light permitted to enter.
    b. The lens of the eye performs a focusing function similar to the lens of the camera.
    c. The cornea would be analogous to a camera's lens cap in that both protect delicate inner structures.

43. **d.** is the answer.

44. **b.** is the answer. Rods and cones enable vision in dim and bright light, respectively. If an animal is active only at night, it is likely to have more rods than cones in its retinas.
    d. Bipolar cells link both cones and rods to ganglion cells. There is no reason to expect that a nocturnal mammal would have more bipolar cells than a mammal active both during the day and at night. If anything, because several rods share a single bipolar cell, whereas many cones have their own, a nocturnal animal (with a visual system consisting mostly of rods) might be expected to have fewer bipolar cells than an animal active during the day (with a visual system consisting mostly of cones).

45. **b.** is the answer.
    a. & c. It is the cones, rather than the rods, that enable color vision.
    d. If the cones' threshold were lower than the available light intensity, they would be able to function and therefore detect the colors of the players' uniforms.

46. reflects (rejects); construction

47. sex linked

48. Young-Helmholtz trichromatic; red; green; blue

49. opponent; afterimage

50. opponent-process; red; green; yellow; blue; black; white

In the first stage of color processing, the retina's red, green, and blue cones respond in varying degrees to different color stimuli, as suggested by the three-color theory. The resulting signals are then processed in the retina and in the thalamus by red-green, blue-yellow, and black-white opponent-process cells, which are turned "on" by one wavelength and turned "off" by its opponent.

51. **d.** is the answer.
    a. Feature detectors are located in the visual cortex and respond to features such as movement, shape, and angle.
    b. & c. Cones and bipolar cells are located in the retina. Moreover, neither are excited by some colors and inhibited by others.

52. **c.** is the answer.
    a. The trichromatic theory cannot account for the experience of afterimages.
    b. & d. Afterimages are experienced as the complementary color of a stimulus. Green, not blue, is red's complement.

53. Gestalt; whole

54. figure; ground

55. grouping

56. continuity; closure; proximity

57. **c.** is the answer. She perceives the line for the road as continuous, even though it is interrupted by lines indicating other roads.
    a. Closure refers to the perceptual filling in of gaps in a stimulus to create a complete, whole object.
    d. Proximity is the tendency to group objects near to one another as a single unit.

58. depth perception; distance

59. visual cliff; mobile

Research on the visual cliff suggests that in many species the ability to perceive depth is present at, or very shortly after, birth. Learning is also a factor because crawling seems to increase infants' wariness of heights.

60. binocular

61. retinal disparity

62. monocular

63. relative size

64. interposition
65. relative height
66. relative motion
67. linear perspective
68. light and shadow
69.

70. **b.** is the answer. The phenomenon described is the basis for the monocular cue of relative size.

    a. The object casting the *larger* retinal image would be perceived as closer.

    c. & d. Because of size constancy, the perceived size of familiar objects remains constant, despite changes in their retinal image size.

71. **d.** is the answer.

72. **b.** is the answer. This is an example of the principle of interposition in depth perception.

    a. The partially obscured object is perceived as farther away.

    c. The perceived size of an object is not altered when that object overlaps another.

73. **c.** is the answer.

    a. Interposition is a monocular depth cue in which an object that partially covers another is perceived as closer.

    b. Retinal disparity refers to the difference between the two images received by our eyes that allows us to perceive depth. It has nothing to do with the way the artist placed the trees.

    d. Figure-ground refers to the organization of the field into objects that stand out from their surroundings.

74. **c.** is the answer.

    b. & d. Linear perspective is the apparent convergence of parallel lines as a cue to distance.

75. top-down; perceptual constancy

76. context; color constancy

77. reflected; surrounding objects

78. relative to

79. relative luminance

80. do not; retinal

81. Moon; size; distance; diminished

82. **d.** is the answer. Although the amount of light reflected from a white object is less in dim light than in bright light—and may be less than the amount of light reflected from a brightly lit gray object—the brightness of the white object is perceived as remaining constant. Because a white object reflects a higher percentage of the light falling on it than does a gray object, and the brightness of objects is perceived as constant despite variations in illumination, white is perceived as brighter than gray even under dim illumination.

    a. Relative luminance refers to the relative intensity of light falling on surfaces that are in proximity. Brightness constancy is perceived despite variations in illumination.

    b. Perceptual adaptation refers to the ability to adjust to an artificially modified perceptual environment, such as an inverted visual field.

    c. Color contrast is not discussed in this text.

83. **a.** is the answer. Because we perceive the size of a familiar object as constant even as its retinal image grows smaller, we perceive the object as being farther away.

    b. & c. Perceptual constancy is a cognitive, rather than sensory, phenomenon. Therefore, the absence of perceptual constancy would not alter sensitivity to monocular or binocular cues.

    d. Although the absence of perceptual constancy would impair depth perception based on the size-distance relationship, other cues to depth, such as texture gradient, could still be used.

84. **c.** is the answer.

85. Immanuel Kant

86. John Locke

87. cannot

88. infancy; critical period

89. will; perceptual adaptation; do not adapt

Hearing

90. audition; air molecules

91. loudness

92. pitch

93. decibels; zero

94. outer; middle; inner

95. eardrum

96. hammer; anvil; stirrup

97. cochlea; oval window; basilar membrane; hair cells; thalamus; temporal

98. sensorineural; aging

99. conduction hearing loss

100. cochlear implant

101. number

102. **a.** is the answer.

103. **d.** is the answer. The hair cells, which transduce sound energy, are located on the basilar membrane.
a. & b. The eardrum and bones of the middle ear merely conduct sound waves to the inner ear, where they are transduced.
c. The semicircular canals are involved in the vestibular sense, not hearing.

104. place; low

105. frequency; high; 1000

106. volley

107. speed (timing); intensity

108. harder

The Other Senses

109. pressure; warmth; cold; pain; variations

110. injury; chronic

111. genes; physiology; experience; attention; culture

112. is not; nociceptors

113. gate-control; gate; spinal cord; small; large; brain; endorphins

114. sensory input

115. phantom limb; tinnitus

116. cultural; biopsychosocial

Pain control techniques include drugs, surgery, acupuncture, thought distraction, exercise, hypnosis, relaxation training, electrical stimulation, and massage. Similarly, for burn victims, distraction during painful wound care can be created by immersion in a computer-generated 3-D world.

117. **c.** is the answer. Because pain is felt in the limb that does not exist, the pain is simply the brain's (mis)interpretation of neural activity.
a. If pain were a purely sensory phenomenon, phantom limb pain would not occur because the receptors are no longer present.
b. That pain is experienced when a limb is missing indicates that the central nervous system, especially the brain, is where pain is sensed.

118. **a.** is the answer.
b. Since endorphins relieve pain, a decrease in their production would have made Kirsten more likely to experience pain. Moreover, because endorphins are released in response to pain, their production probably would have increased.
c. Neural activity in small fibers tends to open the pain gate.

d. An increase in large-fiber activity would tend to close the pain gate.

119. **d.** is the answer.

120. sweet; sour; salty; bitter; umami

121. chemical; taste buds; pore

122. week or two; decreases; decreases; smoking; alcohol; expectations

123. olfaction; chemical; is not

124. limbic

125. **c.** is the answer. As people age they lose taste buds and their taste thresholds increase. For this reason, Mrs. Martinez needs more concentrated tastes than her son to find food palatable.
a. & b. There is no evidence that women and men differ in their absolute thresholds for taste.

126. kinesthesis; tendons; joints; muscles

127. vestibular sense; semicircular canals; vestibular sacs

Sensory Interaction

128. sensory interaction; McGurk; see; hearing

129. embodied cognition

130. **d.** is the answer. Each of these is an example of the interaction of two senses—vision and taste in the case of (a.), taste and smell in the case of (b.), and hearing and the vestibular sense in the case of (c.).

131. **c.** is the answer. Because of the powerful sensory interaction between taste and smell, eliminating the odor of the cough syrup should make its taste more pleasant.
a. If anything, the contrasting tastes might make the bitter syrup even less palatable.
b. If Tamiko keeps the syrup in her mouth for several seconds, it will ensure that her taste pores fully "catch" the stimulus, thus intensifying the bitter taste.
d. It's probably impossible to miss the tongue completely.

(Critical Thinking) ESP—Perception Without Sensation?

132. extrasensory perception

133. parapsychologists

134. telepathy; clairvoyance; precognition; psychokinesis

135. chance-level; interpreted (retrofitted); reconstruct

136. reproducible

137. did

138. **d.** is the answer.
a. Telepathy is the claimed ability to "read" minds.
b. Clairvoyance refers to the claimed ability to perceive remote events.
c. Precognition refers to the claimed ability to perceive future events.

139. **d.** is the answer.

Progress Test 1

Multiple-Choice Questions

1. **b.** is the answer. Psychological factors can affect the absolute threshold for a stimulus.
   a. The absolute threshold for detecting a stimulus depends not only on the strength of the stimulus but also on psychological factors such as experience, expectations, motivation, and fatigue. Thus, the threshold cannot be a constant.
   c. & d. The absolute threshold is defined as the minimum stimulus that is detected 50 percent of the time.

2. **c.** is the answer. According to Weber's law, the difference threshold is a constant proportion of the stimulus. There is a 10 percent difference between 10 and 11 pounds; since the difference threshold is a constant proportion, the weight closest to 100 pounds that can nonetheless be differentiated from it is 110 pounds (or 100 pounds plus 10 percent).

3. **c.** is the answer.
   a. "Sensory fatigue" is not a term in psychology.
   b. Accommodation refers to an adaptive change in shape by the lens of the eye.
   d. Sensory interaction is the principle that one sense may influence another.

4. **d.** is the answer.
   a. The lens lies behind the pupil and focuses light on the retina.
   b. The retina is the inner surface of the eyeball and contains the rods and cones.
   c. The cornea lies in front of the pupil and is the first structure that light passes through as it enters the eye.

5. **a.** is the answer.
   b. Sensory adaptation is our diminishing sensitivity to an unchanging stimulus.
   c. Feature detection is the process by which neural cells in the brain respond to specific visual features.

   d. Transduction refers to the conversion of an environmental stimulus, such as light, into a neural impulse by a receptor—a rod or a cone.

6. **d.** is the answer.
   a. The fovea is not a receptor; it is a region of the retina that contains only cones.
   b. Cones have a higher threshold for brightness than rods and therefore do not function as well in dim light.
   c. Bipolar cells are not receptors; they are neurons in the retina that link rods and cones with ganglion cells, which make up the optic nerve.

7. **a.** is the answer. The Young-Helmholtz theory proposes that there are red-, green-, and blue-sensitive cones.
   b. This answer describes Hering's opponent-process theory.
   c. The Young-Helmholtz theory proposes that there are three types of cones, not four.
   d. The Young-Helmholtz theory concerns only color vision, not the detection of visual detail.

8. **b.** is the answer. Just as wave frequency determines pitch, so wave amplitude determines loudness.
   a. Amplitude is the physical basis of loudness; wavelength determines frequency and thereby pitch.
   c. & d. Wavelength, amplitude, and intensity are physical aspects of light and sound. Because the question is based on a relationship between a physical property (frequency) of a stimulus and its psychological attribute (pitch), these answers are incorrect.

9. **c.** is the answer. The biopsychosocial approach tells us that our experience of pain depends on biological, psychological, and social-cultural factors.

10. **d.** is the answer. The small fibers conduct most pain signals; the large fibers conduct most other sensory signals from the skin. The gate either allows pain signals to pass on to the brain or blocks them from passing. When the large fibers are stimulated, the pain gate is closed and other sensations are felt in place of pain.

11. **b.** is the answer.
    a. The iris controls the diameter of the pupil.
    c. The lens accommodates its shape to focus images on the retina.
    d. The optic nerve carries nerve impulses from the retina to the visual cortex.

12. **b.** is the answer.

a. Feature detection is the process by which nerve cells in the brain respond to specific visual features of a stimulus, such as movement or shape.

c. Accommodation is the process by which the lens changes its curvature to focus images on the retina.

d. The opponent-process theory suggests that color vision depends on the response of brain cells to red-green, yellow-blue, and black-white opposing colors.

13. **b.** is the answer. Kinesthesis, or the sense of the position and movement of body parts, is based on information from the tendons, joints, and muscles.

    a. & c. The ear plays no role in kinesthesis.

    d. Equilibrium, or the vestibular sense, is not involved in kinesthesis but is, rather, a companion sense.

14. **a.** is the answer. Wavelength determines hue, or color.

    b. & d. The amplitude of light determines its brightness.

    c. Opponent processes are neural systems involved in color vision, not properties of light.

15. **d.** is the answer. Color constancy is the perception that a familiar object has consistent color, even if changing illumination alters the wavelengths reflected by that object.

    a. & b. These theories explain how the visual system detects color; they do not explain why colors do not seem to change when lighting does.

    c. Feature detection explains how the brain recognizes visual images by analyzing their distinctive features of shape, movement, and angle.

16. **a.** is the answer. Sensory adaptation means a diminishing sensitivity to an unchanging stimulus. Only the adjustment to cold water involves a decrease in sensitivity; the other examples involve an increase.

17. **a.** is the answer. Thus, they have difficulty discriminating these two colors.

    b. Those who are color deficient are usually not "color blind" in a literal sense. Instead, they are unable to distinguish certain hues, such as red from green.

    c. Failure to distinguish red and green is separate from, and does not usually affect, general visual ability.

    d. Color deficiency does not enhance vision. A deficit in one sense often is compensated for by overdevelopment of another sense—for example, hearing in blind people.

18. **d.** is the answer. Gestalt psychology, which developed in Germany early in the twentieth century, was interested in how clusters of sensations are organized into "whole" perceptions.

    a. Parapsychology is the study of ESP and other paranormal phenomena.

    b. & c. Behavioral and functional psychology developed later in the United States.

19. **d.** is the answer.

    a. Interposition is the tendency to perceive objects that partially block our view of another object as closer.

    b. Linear perspective is when parallel lines appear to meet in the distance.

    c. Continuity refers to the tendency to group stimuli into smooth, continuous patterns.

20. **c.** is the answer. Although we always differentiate a stimulus into figure and ground, those elements of the stimulus we perceive as figure and those as ground may change. In this way, the same stimulus can trigger more than one perception.

    a. The idea of a figure-ground relationship has no bearing on the issue of whether perception is innate.

    b. Perception cannot be simply a point-for-point representation of sensation, since in figure-ground relationships a single stimulus can trigger more than one perception.

    d. Figure-ground relationships demonstrate the existence of general, rather than individual, principles of perceptual organization. Significantly, even the same person can see different figure-ground relationships when viewing a scene.

21. **d.** is the answer. The greater the retinal disparity, or difference between the images, the less the distance.

    a. Interposition is the monocular distance cue in which an object that partially blocks another object is seen as closer.

    b. Linear perspective is the monocular distance cue in which parallel lines appear to converge in the distance.

    c. Relative motion is the monocular distance cue in which objects at different distances change their relative positions in our visual image, with those closest moving most.

22. **a.** is the answer. Perception of constant shape, like perception of constant size, is part of the phenomenon of perceptual constancy.

    b. Relative motion is a monocular distance cue in which objects at different distances appear to move at different rates.

    c. Linear perspective is a monocular distance cue in which lines we know to be parallel converge in the distance, thus indicating depth.

d. Continuity is the perceptual tendency to group items into continuous patterns.

23. **d.** is the answer.
a. Psychokinesis refers to the claimed ability to perform acts of "mind over matter."
b. Precognition refers to the claimed ability to perceive future events.
c. Clairvoyance refers to the claimed ability to perceive remote events.

24. **b.** is the answer.
a. Locke argued that knowledge is not inborn but comes through learning.
c. & d. Gibson and Walk studied depth perception using the visual cliff; they made no claims about the source of knowledge.

25. **c.** is the answer.
a. & b. The kittens had difficulty only with lines they had never experienced, and never regained normal sensitivity.
d. Both perceptual and feature-detector impairment resulted from visual restriction.

26. **b.** is the answer. Because they have not had early visual experiences, these adults typically have difficulty learning to perceive objects.
a. Such patients typically could not visually recognize objects with which they were familiar by touch, and in some cases this inability persisted.
c. Being able to perceive figure-ground relationships, patients are able to follow moving objects with their eyes.
d. This answer is incorrect because eye-hand coordination is an acquired skill and requires much practice.

27. **b.** is the answer.
a. Top-down processing refers to how our knowledge and expectations influence perception.
c. Parapsychology is the study of perception outside normal sensory input.
d. Parallel processing is information processing in which several aspects of a stimulus, such as light or sound, are processed simultaneously.

28. **c.** is the answer. Retinal disparity is a *binocular* cue; all the other cues mentioned are monocular.

29. **a.** is the answer. The Moon appears larger at the horizon than overhead in the sky because objects at the horizon provide distance cues that make the Moon seem farther away and therefore larger. In the open sky, of course, there are no such cues.

30. **c.** is the answer. We see a cloud as a figure against the background of sky.
a., b., & d. The figure-ground relationship refers to the organization of the visual field into objects (figures) that stand out from their surroundings (ground).

31. **d.** is the answer.
a. & b. The study of sensation is concerned with these processes.
c. Although studying illusions has helped psychologists understand ordinary perceptual mechanisms, it is not the primary focus of the field of perception.

32. **d.** is the answer.

33. **c.** is the answer.
a. This answer would be correct had Jack claimed to be able to read someone else's mind.
b. This answer would be correct had Jack claimed to be able to sense remote events, such as a friend in distress.
d. This answer would be correct had Jack claimed to be able to levitate objects or bend spoons without applying any physical force.

34. **b.** is the answer.

35. **a.** is the answer. Frequency theory best explains the lowest pitches. Place theory best explains the highest pitches, and some combination of the two theories probably accounts for our sensation of intermediate-range pitches.

Matching Items

1. e	**6.** a	**11.** j
2. d	**7.** i	
3. g	**8.** b	
4. h	**9.** f	
5. k	**10.** c	

Progress Test 2

Multiple-Choice Questions

1. **d.** is the answer.

2. **d.** is the answer.

3. **d.** is the answer.
a. Sensory adaptation refers to the diminished sensitivity that occurs with unchanging stimulation.
b. Feature detection refers to the process by which nerve cells in the brain respond to specific aspects of visual stimuli, such as movement or shape.
c. Sensory interaction is the principle that one sense may influence another.

4. **a.** is the answer.
b. The cochlea contains receptors for hearing.
c. The fovea contains receptors for vision (the cones).

d. The cortex is the outer layer of the brain, where information detected by the receptors is processed.

5. **c.** is the answer. The inner ear contains the receptors for audition (hearing) and the vestibular sense; those for kinesthesis are located in the tendons, joints, and muscles.

6. **c.** is the answer. After leaving the receptor cells, visual information is analyzed in terms of pairs of opponent colors; neurons stimulated by one member of a pair are inhibited by the other.
   a. The idea that there are three types of color-sensitive cones is the basis of the Young-Helmholtz three-color theory.
   b. According to the opponent-process theory, and all other theories of color vision, the process of color vision begins in the retina.

7. **b.** is the answer. Kinesthesis, the sense of movement of body parts, would enable you to feel your toes wiggling.
   a. The vestibular sense is concerned with movement and position, or balance, of the whole body, not of its parts.
   c. The skin, or tactile, senses are pressure, pain, warmth, and cold; they have nothing to do with movement of body parts.
   d. Sensory interaction, the principle that the senses influence each other, does not play a role in this example, which involves only kinesthesis.

8. **d.** is the answer. Feature detectors are cortical neurons and so are located in the visual cortex.
   a. The fovea contains cones.
   b. The optic nerve contains neurons that relay nerve impulses from the retina to higher centers in the visual system.
   c. The iris is simply a ring of muscle tissue, which controls the diameter of the pupil.

9. **d.** is the answer. Weber's law concerns difference thresholds (jnd's), not absolute thresholds, and states that these are constant proportions of the stimuli, not that they remain constant.

10. **d.** is the answer.
    a. Transduction is the process by which stimulus energy is converted into nerve impulses.
    b. Sensory adaptation is diminished sensitivity to unchanging stimulation.
    c. Weber's law states that the jnd is a constant proportion of a stimulus.

11. **d.** is the answer.

12. **a.** is the answer.

13. **a.** is the answer. Wavelength determines hue, and intensity determines brightness.

14. **b.** is the answer.

15. **c.** is the answer.
    a. This answer is incorrect because separate red, green, and blue systems operate only in the retina.
    b. This answer is incorrect because opponent-process systems operate en route to the brain, after visual processing in the receptors is completed.
    d. This answer is incorrect because it reverses the correct order of the two stages of processing.

16. **d.** is the answer.
    a. Feature detectors are nerve cells located in the visual cortex, not in the fovea of the retina.
    b. The proximity of rods and cones to the optic nerve does not influence their ability to resolve fine details.
    c. Rods are concentrated in the peripheral regions of the retina, not in the fovea; moreover, several rods share a single bipolar cell.

17. **c.** is the answer. The absolute threshold is the minimum stimulation needed to detect a stimulus 50 percent of the time.
    a. & b. The difference threshold, which is also known as the jnd, is the minimum difference between two stimuli that a person can detect. In this example, there is only one stimulus—the sight of the flame.
    d. Feature detection refers to nerve cells in the brain responding to specific features of a stimulus.

18. **b.** is the answer.
    a. Closure refers to the tendency to perceptually fill in gaps in recognizable objects in the visual field.
    c. Interposition is the tendency to perceive objects that partially block our view of another object as closer.
    d. Proximity refers to the tendency to group items that are near one another.

19. **c.** is the answer.
    a. & b. The Gestalt psychologists did not deal with the origins of perception; they were more concerned with its form.
    d. In fact, they argued just the opposite: Perception is more than mere sensory experience.

20. **c.** is the answer. Humans are able to adjust to upside-down worlds and other visual distortions, figuring out the relationship between the perceived and the actual reality; lower animals, such as chicks, are typically unable to adapt.
    a. Humans are able to adapt quite well to distorted visual environments (and then to readapt).
    b. This answer is incorrect because humans are the most adaptable of creatures.

d. Humans are able to adapt at any age to distorted visual environments.

21. **a.** is the answer.
b. Retinal disparity is a binocular depth cue based on the fact that each eye receives a slightly different view of the world.
c. Interposition is the monocular distance cue in which an object that partially blocks another object is seen as closer.
d. Kinesthesis is the sense of the position and movement of the parts of the body.

22. **a.** is the answer.
b. Kant claimed that knowledge is inborn.
c. & d. Gibson and Walk make no claims about the origins of perception.

23. **b.** is the answer.

24. **c.** is the answer. There appears to be a critical period for perceptual development, in that sensory restriction has severe, even permanent, disruptive effects when it occurs in infancy but not when it occurs later in life.
a. & d. Sensory restriction does not have the same effects at all ages, and it is more damaging to children than to adults. This is because there is a critical period for perceptual development; whether functional blindness will result depends in part on the nature of the sensory restriction.
b. Research studies have not indicated that sensory restriction is more damaging to humans than to animals.

25. **c.** is the answer.
a., b., & d. These psychics claim to exhibit the phenomena studied by parapsychologists.

26. **d.** is the answer. When we move, stable objects we see also appear to move, and the distance and speed of the apparent motion cue us to the objects' relative distances.
a., b., & c. These depth cues are unrelated to movement and thus work even when we are stationary.

27. **c.** is the answer.
a. Many ESP researchers are sincere, reputable researchers.
b. & d. There have been no reliable demonstrations of ESP.

28. **c.** is the answer. Because of perceptual constancy, we see the car's shape and size as always the same.
a. Perceptual set is a mental predisposition to perceive one thing and not another.
b. Retinal disparity means that our right and left eyes each receive slightly different images.

d. Figure-ground refers to the organization of the visual field into two parts.

29. **d.** is the answer. Gestalt means a "form" or "organized whole."

30. **a.** is the answer. Most infants refused to crawl out over the "cliff" even when coaxed, suggesting that much of depth perception is innate. Studies with the young of "lower" animals show the same thing.

31. **d.** is the answer.

32. **a.** is the answer. Proximity is the tendency to group objects near to one another. The diagram is perceived as three distinct units because we tend to group items closest to each to each other.
b. Continuity is the tendency to group stimuli into smooth, uninterrupted patterns. There is no such continuity in the diagram.
c. Closure is the perceptual tendency to fill in gaps in a form. In the diagram, three disconnected units are perceived rather than a single whole.
d. Linear perspective is when parallel lines appear to meet in the distance.

33. **a.** is the answer.
b. Bottom-up processing refers to the physical characteristics of stimuli rather than their perceptual interpretation.
c. Parapsychology is the study of perception outside normal sensory input.
d. Parallel processing is information processing in which several aspects of a stimulus, such as light or sound, are processed simultaneously.

34. **a.** is the answer.
b. & c. Although the localization of low-pitched sounds along the basilar membrane is poor, that for sounds of middle and, especially, high pitch is good. Therefore, place theory accounts well for high-pitched sounds and, together with frequency theory, can account for middle-pitched sounds.
d. As long as the notes of a chord are within the range of responsiveness of the basilar membrane, place theory can account for chord perception.

35. **d.** is the answer. Sensorineural hearing loss is caused by destruction of neural tissue as a result of problems with the cochlea's receptors or the auditory nerve.
a. & c. Wax buildup and blockage because of infection are temporary states; sensorineural hearing loss is permanent. Moreover, sensorineural hearing loss involves the inner ear rather than the outer or middle ear.

b. Damage to the eardrum impairs the mechanical system that conducts sound waves; it could therefore cause conduction hearing loss, not sensorineural hearing loss.

True–False Items

1. F	5. F	9. T
2. F	6. F	10. F
3. F	7. T	
4. F	8. F	

Essay Question 1

The senses that are most important to dancers are vision, hearing, kinesthesis, and the vestibular sense. Your answer should refer to any three of these senses and include, at minimum, the following information.

Dancers rely on vision to gauge their body position relative to other dancers as they perform specific choreographed movements. Vision also helps dancers assess the audience's reaction to their performance. Whenever dance is set to music, hearing is necessary so that the dancers can detect musical cues for certain parts of their routines. Hearing also helps the dancers keep their movements in time with the music. Kinesthetic receptors in dancers' tendons, joints, and muscles provide their brains with information about the position and movement of body parts to determine if their hands, arms, legs, and heads are in the proper positions. Receptors for the vestibular sense located in the dancers' inner ears send messages to their brains that help them maintain their balance and determine the correctness of the position and movement of their bodies.

Essay Question 2

1. *Proximity.* We tend to perceive items that are near each other as belonging together. Thus, a small section of dancers or members of a marching band may separate themselves from the larger group in order to form part of a particular image.
2. *Similarity.* Because we perceive similar figures as belonging together, choreographers and band directors often create distinct visual groupings within the larger band or dance troupe by having the members of each group wear a distinctive costume or uniform.
3. *Continuity.* Because we perceive smooth, continuous patterns rather than discontinuous ones, dancers or marching musicians moving together (as in a column, for example) are perceived as a separate unit.
4. *Closure.* If a figure has gaps, we complete it, filling in the gaps to create a whole image. Thus, we perceptually fill in the relatively wide spacing between dancers or marching musicians in order to perceive the complete words or forms they are creating.

Summing Up

The Eye

1. Cornea. Light enters the eye through this transparent membrane, which protects the inner structures from the environment.
2. Iris. The colored part of the eye, the iris functions like the aperture of a camera, controlling the size of the pupil to optimize the amount of light that enters the eye.
3. Pupil. The adjustable opening in the iris, the pupil allows light to enter.
4. Lens. This transparent structure behind the pupil changes shape to focus images on the retina.
5. Retina. The light-sensitive inner surface of the eye, the retina contains the rods and cones, which transduce light energy into neural impulses.
6. Blind spot. The region of the retina where the optic nerve leaves the eye, the blind spot contains no rods or cones and so there is no vision here.
7. Optic nerve. This bundle of nerve fibers carries neural impulses from the retina to the brain.

The Ear

1. Outer ear. Hearing begins as sound waves enter the auditory canal of the outer ear.
2. Auditory canal. Sound waves passing through the auditory canal are brought to a point of focus at the eardrum.
3. Eardrum. Lying between the outer and middle ear, this membrane vibrates in response to sound waves.
4. Middle ear. Lying between the outer and inner ear, this air-filled chamber contains the hammer, anvil, and stirrup.
5. Hammer, anvil, and stirrup. These tiny bones of the middle ear concentrate the eardrum's vibrations on the cochlea's oval window.
6. Inner ear. This region of the ear contains the cochlea and the semicircular canals, which play an important role in balance.
7. Cochlea. This fluid-filled multichambered structure contains the hair cell receptors that transduce sound waves into neural impulses.
8. Auditory nerve. This bundle of fibers carries nerve impulses from the inner ear to the brain.

Terms and Concepts to Remember

Writing Definitions

1. **Sensation** is the process by which our sensory receptors and nervous system receive and represent physical energy from the environment.

2. **Perception** is the process by which we organize and interpret sensory information, enabling us to recognize meaningful objects and events.

3. **Bottom-up processing** is analysis that begins with the sensory receptors and works up to the brain's integration of sensory information.

4. **Top-down processing** is information processing guided by higher-level mental processes.

5. **Transduction** refers to the conversion of one form of energy into another. In sensation, it is the process by which receptor cells in the eyes, ears, skin, and nose convert stimulus energies into neural impulses our brain can interpret.

6. The **absolute threshold** is the minimum stimulation needed to detect a stimulus 50 percent of the time.

7. **Signal detection theory** explains precisely how and when we detect the presence of a faint stimulus *(signal)* amid background stimulation *(noise)*. Detection depends partly on experience, expectations, motivation, and alertness.

8. A stimulus that is **subliminal** is one that is below the absolute threshold for conscious awareness.
   Memory aid: Limen is the Latin word for "threshold." A stimulus that is **subliminal** is one that is *sub-* ("below") the *limen*, or threshold.

9. **Priming** is the activation, often unconsciously, of an association by an imperceptible stimulus, the effect of which is to predispose a perception, memory, or response.

10. The **difference threshold** (also called the *just noticeable difference,* or *jnd*), is the minimum difference between two stimuli required for detection 50 percent of the time.

11. **Weber's law** states that, to be perceived as different, the just noticeable difference between two stimuli must differ by a constant minimum percentage.
    Example: If a difference of 10 percent in weight is noticeable, **Weber's law** predicts that a person could discriminate 10- and 11-pound weights or 50- and 55-pound weights.

12. **Sensory adaptation** refers to the diminished sensitivity that occurs with continued exposure to an unchanging stimulus.

13. **Perceptual set** is a mental predisposition to perceive one thing and not another.

14. **Wavelength**, which refers to the distance from the peak of one light or sound wave to the next, gives rise to the perceptual experiences of **hue**, or color, in vision and **pitch** in hearing.

15. The **intensity,** the amount of energy in a light or sound wave, of light and sound is determined by the amplitude of the waves and is experienced as brightness and loudness, respectively.
    Example: Sounds that exceed 85 decibels in amplitude, or **intensity**, will damage the auditory system.

16. The **retina** is the light-sensitive, multilayered inner surface of the eye that contains the rods and cones as well as neurons that form the beginning of the optic nerve.

17. **Accommodation** is the process by which the lens of the eye changes shape to focus near or far objects on the retina.

18. The **rods** and **cones** are visual receptors that convert light energy into neural impulses. The rods are concentrated in the periphery of the retina, the cones in the fovea. The rods have poor sensitivity; detect black, white, and gray; function well in dim light; and are needed for peripheral vision. The cones have excellent sensitivity, enable color vision, and function best in daylight or bright light.

19. Composed of the axons of retinal ganglion cells, the **optic nerve** carries neural impulses from the eye to the brain.

20. The **blind spot** is the region of the retina where the optic nerve leaves the eye. Because there are no rods or cones in this area, there is no vision here.

21. The **fovea** is the retina's point of central focus. It contains only cones; therefore, images focused on the fovea are the clearest.

22. **Feature detectors**, located in the occipital lobe's visual cortex, are nerve cells that selectively respond to specific visual features, such as movement, shape, or angle. Feature detectors are evidently the basis of visual information processing.

23. **Parallel processing** is information processing in which several aspects of a stimulus, such as light or sound, are processed simultaneously.

24. The **Young-Helmholtz trichromatic (three-color) theory** maintains that the retina contains red-, green-, and blue-sensitive color receptors that in combination can produce the perception of any color. This theory explains the first stage of color processing.

25. The **opponent-process theory** maintains that color vision depends on pairs of opposing retinal processes (red-green, yellow-blue, and white-black). This theory explains the second stage of color processing.

26. **Gestalt** means organized whole. The Gestalt psychologists emphasized our tendency to integrate pieces of information into meaningful wholes.

27. **Figure-ground** refers to the organization of the visual field into two parts: the figure, which stands out from its surroundings, and the surroundings, or background.

28. **Grouping** is the perceptual tendency to organize stimuli into coherent groups. Gestalt psychologists identified various principles of grouping.

29. **Depth perception** is the ability to see objects in three dimensions although the images that strike the retina are two-dimensional; it allows us to judge distance.

30. The **visual cliff** is a laboratory device for testing depth perception, especially in infants and young animals. In their experiments with the visual cliff, Gibson and Walk found strong evidence that depth perception is at least in part innate.

31. **Binocular cues** are depth cues that depend on information from both eyes.

    Memory aid: Bi- indicates "two"; *ocular* means something pertaining to the eye. **Binocular cues** are cues for the "two eyes."

32. **Retinal disparity** refers to the differences between the images received by the left eye and the right eye as a result of viewing the world from slightly different angles. It is a binocular depth cue, since the greater the difference between the two images, the nearer the object.

33. **Monocular cues** are depth cues that depend on information from either eye alone.

    Memory aid: Mono- means one; a monocle is an eyeglass for one eye. A **monocular cue** is one that is available to either the left or the right eye.

34. **Perceptual constancy** is the perception that objects have consistent lightness, color, shape, and size, even as illumination and retinal images change.

35. **Color constancy** is the perception that familiar objects have consistent color despite changes in illumination that shift the wavelengths they reflect.

36. In vision, **perceptual adaptation** refers to our ability to adjust to an artificially displaced or even inverted visual field. Given distorting lenses, we perceive things accordingly but soon adjust by learning the relationship between our distorted perceptions and the reality.

37. **Audition** refers to the sense or act of hearing.

38. **Frequency** is directly related to wavelength: longer waves produce lower pitch; shorter waves produce higher pitch. The **pitch** of a sound is determined by its frequency, that is, the number of complete wavelengths that can pass a point in a given time.

39. The **middle ear** is the chamber between the eardrum and cochlea containing the three bones (hammer, anvil, and stirrup) that concentrate the eardrum's vibrations on the cochlea's oval window.

40. The **cochlea** is the coiled, bony, fluid-filled tube of the inner ear through which sound waves trigger neural impulses.

41. The **inner ear** contains the semicircular canals and the cochlea, which includes the receptors that transform sound energy into neural impulses. Because it also contains the vestibular sac, the inner ear plays an important role in balance, as well as in audition.

42. **Sensorineural hearing loss** (nerve deafness) is hearing loss caused by damage to the auditory receptors of the cochlea or to the auditory nerve due to disease, aging, or prolonged exposure to ear-splitting noise.

43. **Conduction hearing loss** refers to the hearing loss that results from damage in the mechanical system of the outer or middle ear, which impairs the conduction of sound waves to the cochlea.

44. A **cochlear implant** is an electronic device that converts sounds into electrical signals that stimulate the auditory nerve.

45. The **place theory** of hearing states that we hear different pitches because sound waves of various frequencies trigger activity at different places on the cochlea's basilar membrane.

    Memory aid: **Place theory** maintains that the *place* of maximum vibration along the cochlea's membrane is the basis of pitch discrimination.

46. The **frequency theory** of hearing presumes that the rate, or frequency, of nerve impulses in the auditory nerve matches the frequency of a tone, thus enabling us to sense its pitch.

47. Melzack and Wall's **gate-control theory** maintains that a "gate" in the spinal cord determines whether pain signals are permitted to reach the brain. Neural activity in small nerve fibers opens the gates; activity in large fibers or information from the brain closes the gate.

Example: The **gate-control theory** gained support with the discovery of endorphins. Production of these opiate-like chemicals may be the brain's mechanism for closing the spinal gate.

48. **Kinesthesis** is the sense of the position and movement of the parts of the body.

49. The sense of your head's (and thus your body's) body movement and position, including the sense of balance, is called the **vestibular sense**.

50. **Sensory interaction** is the principle that one sense may influence another.

51. **Embodied cognition** refers to the influence of bodily sensations, gestures, and other states on cognitive preferences and judgments.

52. **Extrasensory perception (ESP)** refers to the controversial claim that perception can occur without sensory input. Supposed ESP powers include telepathy, clairvoyance, and precognition.

Memory aid: *Extra-* means "beyond" or "in addition to"; **extrasensory perception** is perception outside or beyond the normal senses.

53. **Parapsychology** is the study of paranormal phenomena, including ESP and psychokinesis.

Memory aid: *Para-*, like *extra-*, indicates "beyond"; thus, paranormal is beyond the normal and **parapsychology** is the study of phenomena beyond the realm of psychology and known natural laws.

Cross-Check

ACROSS	DOWN
1. fovea	1. frequency
5. inner ear	2. retina
6. basilar	3. linear perspective
8. Young	4. figure-ground
10. closure	7. hue
11. cones	9. Gestalt
12. parapsychology	13. pitch
14. parallel	18. rods
15. jnd	
16. absolute	
17. kinesthesis	
19. cochlea	
20. disparity	

Learning

Chapter Overview

"No topic is closer to the heart of psychology than learning, a relatively permanent change in an organism's behavior due to experience." Chapter 7 covers the basic principles of three forms of learning: classical, or respondent, conditioning, in which we learn associations between events; operant conditioning, in which we learn to engage in behaviors that are rewarded and to avoid behaviors that are punished; and observational learning, in which we learn by observing and imitating others.

The chapter also covers several important issues, including the generality of principles of learning, the role of cognitive processes in learning, and the ways in which learning is constrained by the biological predispositions of different species.

NOTE: Answer guidelines for all Chapter 7 questions begin on page 174.

Chapter Review

First, skim each section, noting headings and boldface items. After you have read the section, review each objective by answering the fill-in and essay-type questions that follow it. Study Tips explain how best to learn a difficult concept and Applications help you to know how well you understand the material. As you proceed, evaluate your performance by consulting the answers beginning on page 174. Do not continue with the next section until you understand each answer. If you need to, review or reread the section in the textbook before continuing.

How Do We Learn?

Objective 7-1: Define *learning,* and identify some basic forms of learning.

1. The process of acquiring through experience new and relatively enduring information or behaviors is called _____ .

2. An important factor in learning is our tendency to _____ events that occur in sequence. Even simple animals, such as the sea slug *Aplysia,* can learn simple _____ between stimuli. This type of learning is called _____ _____ .

3. The type of learning in which the organism learns to associate two stimuli is _____ conditioning. A situation or event that evokes a response is a _____ .

4. The tendency of organisms to associate a response and its consequence forms the basis of _____ conditioning.

5. We acquire mental information that guides our behavior through _____ _____ . Complex animals often learn behaviors merely by _____ others perform them. This is called _____ _____ .

Classical Conditioning

Objective 7-2: Describe the basic components of classical conditioning, and discuss behaviorism's view of learning.

6. Classical conditioning was first explored by the Russian physiologist _____ . Early in the twentieth century, psychologist _____ urged psychologists to discard references to mental concepts in favor of studying observable behavior. This view, called _____ , influenced American psychology during the first half of that century.

7. In Pavlov's classic experiment, a tone, or

_____ _____ ,

is sounded just before food, the

_____ _____ ,

is placed in the animal's mouth.

8. An animal will salivate when food is placed in its mouth. This salivation is called the

_____ _____ .

9. Eventually, the dogs in Pavlov's experiment would salivate on hearing the tone, now called the _____ _____ .
This salivation is called the _____

_____ .

STUDY TIP: Students often confuse *stimulus* with *response* and *conditioned* with *unconditioned*. The stimulus is the event that causes something else, the response, to happen. Unconditioned means "unlearned"; conditioned means "learned." Thus, an unconditioned response (UR) is an event that occurs naturally in response to some stimulus. An unconditioned stimulus (US) is something that naturally and automatically triggers the unlearned response. A conditioned stimulus (CS) is an originally neutral stimulus (NS) that, through learning, comes to be associated with some unlearned response. A conditioned response (CR) is the learned response to the originally neutral but now conditioned stimulus.

Stimulus (event or other trigger) → Response
Unconditioned = unlearned
Conditioned = learned
So, unconditioned stimulus + conditioned stimulus
↓   ↓
unconditioned response   conditioned response

APPLICATIONS:

Classical conditioning is all around us. It is especially common in the realm of emotional behavior. Test your understanding of the basic elements of classical conditioning in the following example. Then, consider whether there are emotions of your own that might have developed as the product of classical conditioning.

As a child, you were playing in the yard one day when a neighbor's cat wandered over. Your mother

(who has a terrible fear of animals) screamed and snatched you into her arms. Her behavior caused you to cry. You now have a fear of cats.

10. The NS, then CS is _____

11. The US is _____

12. The CR is _____

13. The UR is _____

14. You always rattle the box of dog biscuits before giving your dog a treat. As you do so, your dog salivates. At first, rattling the box is a _____ , which eventually becomes a _____ . Your dog's salivation is a _____ .

   a. NS; CS; CR   **c.** NS; US; CR
   b. CS; NS; UR   **d.** US; NS; UR

Objective 7-3: Summarize the processes of acquisition, extinction, spontaneous recovery, generalization, and discrimination.

Use the following graph as a reference for the answers to 15(a), 18(b), and 19(c).

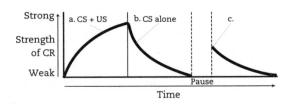

15. The initial learning of a conditioned response is called (a) _____ . For many conditioning situations, the optimal interval between a neutral stimulus and the US is

_____ _____ .

16. When the US is presented prior to a neutral stimulus, conditioning _____ (does/does not) occur.

17. Sexual conditioning studies with quail demonstrate that classical conditioning is highly adaptive because it helps animals

_____ and _____ .

18. If a CS is repeatedly presented without the US, (b) _____ soon occurs; that is, the CR diminishes.

19. Following a pause, however, the CR reappears in response to the CS; this phenomenon is called (c) _____ _____ .

20. Subjects often respond to a similar stimulus as they would to the original CS. This phenomenon is called _____ .

21. Humans and other animals can also be trained not to respond to _____ stimuli. This learned ability is called

_____ .

22. Being able to recognize differences among stimuli has _____ value because it lets us limit our learned responses to appropriate stimuli.

STUDY TIP: Some students find the terms *discrimination* and *generalization* confusing because of their negative social connotations. In the context of classical conditioning, discrimination is a healthy sign that the subject of conditioning has learned the difference between two stimuli, much as a "discriminating coffee lover" can taste subtle variations between two coffee blends. Generalization is apparent when discrimination does not occur.

APPLICATION:

Bill had an American-made car that was in the shop more than it was out. Since then he will not even consider owning an American-made car.

23. Bill's attitude is an example of

_____ . Bill's friend Andy also had an American-made car with similar problems. Deciding that it was just that brand, Andy decided to try another brand. Rather than bunch all American-made cars together, he was a

_____ buyer of cars.

Objective 7-4: Explain why Pavlov's work remains so important, and describe some applications of his work to human health and well-being.

24. Classical conditioning is one way that virtually all organisms learn to _____ to their environment.

25. Another aspect of Pavlov's legacy is that he showed how a process such as learning could be studied _____ .

Explain why the study of classical conditioning is important.

26. Through classical conditioning, former drug users often feel a _____ when they are in the _____ associated with previous highs.

27. Research studies demonstrate that the body's immune system _____ (can/cannot) be classically conditioned.

Describe the Watson and Rayner experiment.

Operant Conditioning

Objective 7-5: Define *operant conditioning,* and describe how operant behavior is reinforced and shaped.

28. B. F. Skinner used Thorndike's _____

_____ _____ as a starting point in developing a behavioral technology. This principle states that _____ behavior is likely to

_____ .

29. In operant conditioning, organisms associate their own actions with _____ . Actions followed by _____ increase; actions followed by _____ decrease.

30. Skinner designed an apparatus, called the

_____ _____ , to investigate learning in animals. This design creates a stage on which organisms act out Skinner's concept of

_____ , any event that increases the frequency of a preceding response.

31. The procedure in which a person teaches an animal to perform an intricate behavior by building up to it in small steps is called _____ . This method involves reinforcing successive _____ of the desired behavior.

32. In experiments to determine what an animal can perceive, researchers have found that animals are capable of forming _____ and _____ between stimuli. Similar experiments have been conducted with babies, who also can't verbalize their responses.

33. A situation, event, or signal that a certain response will be reinforced is a

    _____ _____ .

APPLICATION:

34. Which of the following is an example of shaping?
    a. A dog learns to salivate at the sight of a box of dog biscuits.
    b. A new driver learns to stop at an intersection when the light changes to red.
    c. A parrot is rewarded first for making any sound, then for making a sound similar to "Laura," and then for "speaking" its owner's name.

Objective 7-6: Discuss the differences between positive and negative reinforcement, and identify the basic types of reinforcers.

35. A stimulus that strengthens a response by presenting a typically pleasurable stimulus after a response is a _____

    _____ .

36. A stimulus that strengthens a response by reducing or removing an aversive (unpleasant) stimulus is a _____ _____ .

37. Reinforcers, such as food and shock, that are related to basic needs and therefore do not rely on learning are called _____

    _____ .

38. Reinforcers that must be conditioned and therefore derive their power through learned association are called _____

    _____ .

39. Children who are able to delay gratification tend to become _____ (more/less) socially competent and high achieving as they mature.

40. Immediate reinforcement _____ (is/is not) sometimes more effective than its alternative, _____ reinforcement. This

explains in part the tendency of some teens to engage in risky, _____

_____ .

STUDY TIP: Some students have a problem differentiating positive and negative reinforcers because they naturally think "positive" indicates a "good," or desirable, outcome, while "negative" connotes a "bad," or undesirable, outcome. Remember that from the organism's point of view, reinforcement is always a desirable outcome. You may find it useful to think of a photography analogy. A "negative" is a reverse image in which the "positive" photographic image is not present. So too, negative reinforcement involves taking away an event—in this case, one that is undesirable.

Objective 7-7: Explain how the different reinforcement schedules affect behavior.

41. A _____ _____ is a pattern specifying how often a _____

    _____ is reinforced.

42. The procedure involving reinforcement of each and every response is called

    _____ _____ .

    Under these conditions, learning is _____ (rapid/slow). When this type of reinforcement is discontinued, extinction is _____ (rapid/slow).

43. The procedure in which responses are reinforced only part of the time is called _____ reinforcement. Under these conditions, learning is generally _____ (faster/slower) than it is with continuous reinforcement. Behavior reinforced in this manner is _____ (very/not very) resistant to extinction.

44. When behavior is reinforced after a set number of responses, a _____-

    _____ schedule is in effect.

45. Three-year-old Yusef knows that if he cries when he wants a treat, his mother will sometimes give in. When, as in this case, reinforcement occurs after an unpredictable number of responses, a

    _____-_____

    schedule is being used.

46. Reinforcement of the first response after a set interval of time defines the

_____-_____ schedule. An example of this schedule is

_____ .

47. When the first response after varying amounts of time is reinforced, a _____-

_____ schedule is in effect.

Describe the typical patterns of response under fixed-interval, fixed-ratio, variable-interval, and variable-ratio schedules of reinforcement.

APPLICATIONS:

48. You are expecting an important letter in the mail. As the regular delivery time approaches you glance more and more frequently out the window, searching for the letter carrier. Your behavior in this situation typifies that associated with which schedule of reinforcement?

   a. fixed-ratio   **c.** fixed-interval
   b. variable-ratio   **d.** variable-interval

49. From a casino owner's viewpoint, which of the following jackpot-payout schedules would be the most desirable for reinforcing customer use of a slot machine?

   a. variable-ratio   **c.** variable-interval
   b. fixed-ratio   **d.** fixed-interval

50. Lars, a shoe salesman, is paid every two weeks, whereas Tom receives a commission for each pair of shoes he sells. Evidently, Lars is paid on a _____ schedule of reinforcement, and Tom on a _____ schedule of reinforcement.

   a. fixed-ratio; fixed-interval
   b. continuous; intermittent
   c. fixed-interval; fixed-ratio
   d. variable-interval; variable-ratio

51. Jack finally takes out the garbage in order to get his father to stop pestering him. Jack's behavior is being influenced by _____

_____ .

52. Your instructor invites you to her home as part of a select group of students to discuss possible careers in psychology. The invitation is an example of a _____

_____ .

Objective 7-8: Discuss how punishment and negative reinforcement differ, and explain how punishment affects behavior.

53. Negative reinforcement _____ (increases/decreases) a response by _____ an aversive stimulus after that response. Punishment _____ (increases/decreases) a response by _____ an aversive stimulus after that response.

54. An aversive consequence that decreases the likelihood of the behavior that preceded it is called _____ . If an aversive stimulus is administered, it is called _____ . If a desirable stimulus is withdrawn, it is called _____

_____ .

55. Because punished behavior is merely _____ , it may reappear. Also, punishment teaches _____ , that behavior that is unacceptable in one context may be acceptable in another. Punishment can also lead to _____ and a sense of helplessness, as well as to the association of the aversive event with _____

_____ .

56. Punishment also often increases _____ and does not guide the individual toward more desirable behavior.

STUDY TIP/APPLICATION: To avoid the natural tendency to confuse punishment and negative reinforcement, remember that positive reinforcement and negative reinforcement both lead to an *increase* in behavior, while punishment *decreases* behavior. In punishment, something bad occurs following an undesirable behavior; in negative reinforcement, something bad is removed. Complete the chart below of examples of punishment and negative reinforcement. The first example has been filled in for you.

57.

Behavior	Consequence	Which Is Taken Away, Something Good or Bad?	Is This Punishment or Negative Reinforcement?
Driving while intoxicated	Lose driver's license	Good	Punishment
a. Forgetting to give your roommate a phone message			
b. Putting on your coat so that you are no longer cold			
c. Getting a drink when you are thirsty			
d. Using your laptop until the battery dies			
e. Your brother nagging you until you help him with his homework			

Objective 7-9: Describe the controversy over Skinner's views of human behavior, and identify some ways to apply operant conditioning principles at school, in sports, at work, and at home.

58. Skinner's views were controversial because he insisted that _____ influences, rather than _____ _____ and _____, shape behavior.

59. Skinner also advocated the use of _____ principles to influence people in ways that promote more desirable _____ .

60. Skinner's critics argued that he _____ people by neglecting their personal _____ and by seeking to _____ their actions.

61. The use of teaching machines and programmed textbooks was an early application of the operant conditioning procedure of _____ to education. Online _____ systems, software that is _____ , and _____-based learning are newer examples of this application of operant principles.

62. Reinforcement principles can also be used to enhance _____ abilities by shaping successive approximations of new skills.

63. In boosting productivity in the workplace, positive reinforcement is _____ (more/less) effective when applied to specific behaviors than when given to reward general merit and when the desired performance is well defined and _____ . For such behaviors, immediate reinforcement is _____ (more/no more) effective than delayed reinforcement.

64. In using operant conditioning to change your own behavior, you would follow these four steps
   a. _____
   b. _____
   c. _____
   d. _____

APPLICATIONS:

65. The manager of a manufacturing plant wishes to use positive reinforcement to increase the productivity of workers. Which of the following procedures would probably be the most effective?
   a. Deserving employees are given a general merit bonus at the end of each fiscal year.

b. A productivity goal that seems attainable, yet is unrealistic, is set for each employee.
c. Employees are given immediate bonuses for specific behaviors related to productivity.
d. Employees who fail to meet standards of productivity receive pay cuts.

66. Reggie's mother tells him that he can watch TV after he cleans his room. Evidently, Reggie's mother is attempting to use _____ to increase room cleaning.

a. operant conditioning
b. secondary reinforcement
c. positive reinforcement
d. all of these procedures

Objective 7-10: Explain how operant conditioning differs from classical conditioning.

67. Classical conditioning and operant conditioning are both forms of _____ _____ .

68. Both types of conditioning involve similar processes of _____ , _____ , _____ , _____ , _____ , and _____ .

69. Classical conditioning associates _____ stimuli with stimuli that trigger responses that are _____ . Thus, in this form of conditioning, the organism _____ (does/does not) control the responses.

70. The reflexive responses of classical conditioning involve _____ behavior.

71. In contrast, behavior that is more spontaneous and that is influenced by its consequences is called _____ behavior.

72. Classical and operant conditioning are both subject to the influences of _____ and _____ processes.

STUDY TIP/APPLICATION: If you still find yourself confusing classical conditioning and operant conditioning, try the following. Ask yourself two questions: (1) Is the behavior voluntary (operant conditioning) or involuntary (classical conditioning)? (2) Does the learning involve an association between two stimuli (classical conditioning) or between a response and an outcome (operant conditioning)? Test your understanding with the following examples.

73. Behavior	Is the Behavior Voluntary or Involuntary?	Type of Conditioning
a. After receiving a mild shock from the "invisible fence" surrounding his yard, a dog no longer crosses the boundary.		
b. You flinch when someone yells, "Duck!"		
c. You ask more questions in class after the professor praises you for a good question.		
d. The pupil of your eye dilates (opens wider) after you enter a darkened theater.		

Biology, Cognition, and Learning

Objective 7-11: Explain how biological constraints affect classical and operant conditioning.

74. Some psychologists once believed that any natural _____ could be conditioned to any neutral _____ .

75. Garcia discovered that rats would associate _____ with taste but not with other stimuli. Garcia found that taste-aversion conditioning _____ (would/would not) occur when the delay between the CS and the US was more than an hour.

76. Results such as these demonstrate that the principles of learning are constrained by the _____ predispositions of each animal species and that they help each species _____ to its environment. Thus

they support Darwin's principle that

_____ _____ favors

traits that aid _____ .

77. Operant conditioning _____ (is/is not) constrained by an animal's biological predispositions.

78. For instance, with animals it is difficult to use food as a _____ to _____ behaviors that are not naturally associated with _____ .

79. Biological constraints predispose organisms to learn associations that are naturally _____ . When animals revert to their biologically predisposed patterns, they are exhibiting what is called

_____ _____ .

APPLICATIONS:

80. A pigeon can easily be taught to flap its wings to avoid shock but not for food reinforcement. According to the text, this is most likely so because
    a. pigeons are biologically predisposed to flap their wings to escape aversive events and to use their beaks to obtain food.
    b. shock is a more motivating stimulus for birds than food is.
    c. hungry animals have difficulty delaying their eating long enough to learn any new skill.
    d. of all of these reasons.

81. Last evening May-Ling ate her first cheeseburger and french fries at an American fast-food restaurant. A few hours later she became ill. It can be expected that May-Ling will
    a. develop an aversion to the sight of a cheeseburger and french fries.
    b. develop an aversion to the taste of a cheeseburger and french fries.
    c. not associate her illness with the food she ate.
    d. associate her sickness with something she experienced immediately before she became ill.

Objective 7-12: Explain how cognitive processes affect classical and operant conditioning.

82. The early behaviorists believed that to understand behavior in various organisms, any presumption of _____ was unnecessary.

83. Experiments by Rescorla and Wagner demonstrate that a CS must reliably _____ the US for an association to develop and, more generally, that _____ processes play a role in conditioning. It is as if the animal learns to _____ that the US will occur.

84. The importance of cognitive processes in human conditioning is demonstrated by the failure of classical conditioning as a treatment for

_____ _____

_____ .

85. Skinner and other behaviorists resisted the growing belief that expectations, perceptions, and other _____ processes have a valid place in the science of psychology.

86. When a well-learned route in a maze is blocked, rats sometimes choose an alternative route, acting as if they were consulting a _____

_____ .

87. Animals may learn from experience even when reinforcement is not available. When learning is not apparent until reinforcement has been provided, _____

_____ is said to have occurred.

88. Excessive rewards may undermine

_____ _____ ,

which is the desire to perform a behavior for its own sake. The motivation to seek external rewards and avoid punishment is called

_____ _____ .

APPLICATIONS:

89. After discovering that her usual route home was closed due to road repairs, Sharetta used her knowledge of the city and sense of direction to find an alternative route. This is an example of
    a. latent learning.
    b. observational learning.
    c. shaping.
    d. using a cognitive map.

90. Two rats are independently placed in a maze. One rat is rewarded with food in the goal box. The other receives no food reward. On a later trial, food is placed in the goal box for the "unrewarded" rat. What can you say about the rat's behavior on that trial?
   a. The "unrewarded" rat will run to the goal box just as quickly as the rewarded rat.
   b. The rat will wander around the maze and never find the food reward.
   c. The rat will find the food reward, but it will take much longer than the rewarded rat.
   d. The rat will not even try to find the food reward.

91. Nancy decided to take introductory psychology because she has always been interested in human behavior. Jack enrolled in the same course because he thought it would be easy. Nancy's behavior was motivated by

   _____ ; Jack's by _____ .
   a. extrinsic motivation; intrinsic motivation
   b. intrinsic motivation; extrinsic motivation
   c. drives; incentives
   d. incentives; drives

Learning by Observation

Objective 7-13: Describe the process of observational learning, and explain how some scientists believe it is enabled by mirror neurons.

92. Learning by observing and imitating others is called _____ , or
   _____ _____ . This form of learning _____ (occurs/ does not occur) in species other than our own.

93. The psychologist best known for research on observational learning is _____ .

94. In one experiment, the child who viewed an adult punch an inflatable doll played
   _____ (more/less) aggressively than the child who had not observed the adult.

95. Bandura believes people imitate a model because of _____ and _____ , those received by the model as well as by imitators.

96. Models are most effective when they are perceived as _____ ,
   _____ , or _____ .

97. Neuroscientists have found _____ neurons in the brain's _____ lobe that may provide a neural basis for _____ learning. These neurons have been observed to fire when monkeys perform a simple task and when they _____ . Whether the human ability to _____ and _____ is due to these neurons or to distributed brain _____ is an issue currently being debated.

98. By age _____ , infants will imitate various novel gestures. By age _____ , they will imitate acts modeled on television. Children's brains enable their _____ and their _____ _____ .

APPLICATIONS: Children—and, of course, adults—learn a great deal by watching other people. Depending on the models, the behavior they learn may be good or bad.

99. During holiday breaks Lionel watches wrestling, which _____ his aggressive tendencies. His brother Michael won't watch the wrestling because he feels the pain of the choke hold, for example, as reflected in his brain's _____ _____ . Instead, Michael spends time with Grandma, who cooks for the poor during the holiday season, helping Michael to learn _____ behavior.

100. Mrs. Ramirez often tells her children that it is important to buckle their seat belts while riding in the car, but she rarely does so herself. Her children will probably learn to
   a. use their seat belts and tell others it is important to do so.
   b. use their seat belts but not tell others it is important to do so.
   c. tell others it is important to use seat belts but rarely use them themselves.
   d. neither tell others that seat belts are important nor use them.

101. After watching coverage of the Olympics on television recently, Lynn and Susan have been staging their own "summer games." Which of the following best accounts for their behavior?

    a. classical conditioning

    b. observational learning

    c. latent learning

    d. shaping

Objective 7-14: Discuss the impact of prosocial modeling and of antisocial modeling.

102. Children will model positive, or _____ , behaviors. Models are also most effective when their words and actions are _____ .

103. Children will also model negative, or _____ , behaviors. This may help explain why _____ parents might have _____ children. However, _____ factors may also be involved.

104. Children in developed countries spend more time _____ _____ than they spend in school.

105. Compared with the real world, television depicts a much higher percentage of crimes as being _____ in nature.

106. (Thinking Critically) Correlational studies _____ (link/do not link) watching television violence with violent behavior.

107. (Thinking Critically) Elementary schoolchildren heavily exposed to media violence have tended to get into more _____ and as teens are at greater risk for _____ behavior.

108. (Thinking Critically) Correlation does not prove _____ . Most researchers believe that watching violence on television _____ (does/does not) lead to aggressive behavior.

109. (Thinking Critically) The violence-viewing effect stems from several factors, including _____ of observed aggression and the tendency of prolonged exposure to violence to _____ viewers.

Progress Test 1

Multiple-Choice Questions

Circle your answers to the following questions and check them with the answers beginning on page 177. If your answer is incorrect, read the explanation for why it is incorrect and then consult the text.

1. *Learning* is best defined as

    a. any behavior produced by an organism without being provoked.

    b. a change in the behavior of an organism.

    c. the process of acquiring through experience new and relatively enduring information or behaviors.

    d. behavior based on operant rather than respondent conditioning.

2. The type of learning associated with Skinner is

    a. classical conditioning.

    b. operant conditioning.

    c. respondent conditioning.

    d. observational learning.

3. In Pavlov's original experiment with dogs, the meat served as a

    a. CS.   **c.** US.

    b. CR.   **d.** UR.

4. In Pavlov's original experiment with dogs, the tone was initially a(n) _____ stimulus; after it was paired with meat, it became a(n) _____ stimulus.

    a. conditioned; neutral

    b. neutral; conditioned

    c. conditioned; unconditioned

    d. unconditioned; conditioned

5. To obtain a reward, a monkey learns to press a lever when a 1000-Hz tone is on but not when a 1200-Hz tone is on. What kind of training is this?

    a. extinction

    b. generalization

    c. classical conditioning

    d. discrimination

6. Which of the following statements concerning reinforcement is correct?

    a. Learning is most rapid with intermittent reinforcement, but continuous reinforcement produces the greatest resistance to extinction.

    b. Learning is most rapid with continuous reinforcement, but intermittent reinforcement produces the greatest resistance to extinction.

c. Learning is fastest and resistance to extinction is greatest after continuous reinforcement.

d. Learning is fastest and resistance to extinction is greatest following intermittent reinforcement.

7. Cognitive processes are
   a. unimportant in classical and operant conditioning.
   b. important in both classical and operant conditioning.
   c. more important in classical than in operant conditioning.
   d. more important in operant than in classical conditioning.

8. The highest and most consistent rate of response is produced by a _____ schedule.
   a. fixed-ratio
   b. variable-ratio
   c. fixed-interval
   d. variable-interval

9. A response that leads to the removal of an unpleasant stimulus is one being
   a. positively reinforced.
   b. negatively reinforced.
   c. punished.
   d. extinguished.

10. When a conditioned stimulus is presented without an accompanying unconditioned stimulus, _____ will soon take place.
   a. generalization
   b. discrimination
   c. extinction
   d. aversion

11. One difference between classical and operant conditioning is that
   a. in classical conditioning the responses operate on the environment to produce rewarding or punishing stimuli.
   b. in operant conditioning the responses are triggered by preceding stimuli.
   c. in classical conditioning the responses are automatically triggered by stimuli.
   d. in operant conditioning the responses are reflexive.

12. In Garcia and Koelling's studies of taste-aversion learning, rats learned to associate
   a. taste with electric shock.
   b. sights and sounds with sickness.
   c. taste with sickness.
   d. taste and sounds with electric shock.

13. In Pavlov's original experiment with dogs, salivation to meat was the
   a. CS.
   b. CR.
   c. US.
   d. UR.

14. Learning by imitating others' behaviors is called _____ learning. The researcher best known for studying this type of learning is _____ .
   a. secondary; Skinner
   b. observational; Bandura
   c. secondary; Pavlov
   d. observational; Watson

15. Punishment is a controversial way of controlling behavior because
   a. behavior is not forgotten and may return.
   b. punishing stimuli often create fear.
   c. punishment often increases aggressiveness.
   d. of all of these reasons.

16. Classical conditioning experiments by Rescorla and Wagner demonstrate that an important factor in conditioning is
   a. the research participant's age.
   b. the strength of the stimuli.
   c. the predictability of an association.
   d. the similarity of stimuli.

17. Which of the following is an example of reinforcement?
   a. presenting a positive stimulus after a response
   b. removing an unpleasant stimulus after a response
   c. being told that you have done a good job
   d. All of these are examples.

18. Which of the following is a form of associative learning?
   a. classical conditioning
   b. cognitive learning
   c. observational learning
   d. all of these types of learning

19. For the most rapid conditioning, a CS should be presented
   a. about 1 second after the US.
   b. about one-half second before the US.
   c. about 15 seconds before the US.
   d. at the same time as the US.

20. Mirror neurons are found in the brain's _____ and are believed by some scientists to be the neural basis for _____ .
   a. frontal lobe; observational learning
   b. frontal lobe; classical conditioning
   c. temporal lobe; operant conditioning
   d. temporal lobe; observational learning

Matching Items

Match each definition or description with the appropriate term.

Definitions or Descriptions

_____ 1. presentation of a desired stimulus
_____ 2. tendency for similar stimuli to evoke a CR
_____ 3. removal of an aversive stimulus
_____ 4. an innately reinforcing stimulus
_____ 5. an acquired reinforcer
_____ 6. responses are reinforced after an unpredictable amount of time
_____ 7. the motivation to perform a behavior for its own sake
_____ 8. reinforcing closer and closer approximations of a behavior
_____ 9. the reappearance of a weakened CR
_____ 10. presentation of an aversive stimulus
_____ 11. learning that becomes apparent only after reinforcement is provided
_____ 12. each and every response is reinforced
_____ 13. a desire to perform a behavior because of promised rewards

Terms

a. shaping
b. punishment
c. spontaneous recovery
d. latent learning
e. positive reinforcement
f. negative reinforcement
g. primary reinforcer
h. generalization
i. conditioned reinforcer
j. continuous reinforcement
k. variable-interval schedule
l. extrinsic motivation
m. intrinsic motivation

Progress Test 2

Progress Test 2 should be completed during a final chapter review. Answer the following questions after you thoroughly understand the correct answers for the section reviews and Progress Test 1.

Multiple-Choice Questions

1. During extinction, the _____ is omitted; as a result, the _____ seems to disappear.
   a. US; UR
   b. CS; CR
   c. US; CR
   d. CS; UR

2. In Watson and Rayner's experiment, the loud noise was the _____ and the white rat was the _____ .
   a. CS; CR
   b. US; CS
   c. CS; US
   d. US; CR

3. In which of the following may classical conditioning play a role?
   a. emotional problems
   b. the body's immune response
   c. helping drug addicts
   d. in all of these cases

4. Shaping is a(n) _____ technique for _____ a behavior.
   a. operant; establishing
   b. operant; suppressing
   c. respondent; establishing
   d. respondent; suppressing

5. In Pavlov's studies of classical conditioning of a dog's salivary responses, spontaneous recovery occurred
   a. during acquisition, when the CS was first paired with the US.
   b. during extinction, when the CS was first presented by itself.
   c. when the CS was reintroduced following extinction of the CR and a rest period.
   d. during discrimination training, when several conditioned stimuli were introduced.

6. For operant conditioning to be most effective, when should the reinforcers be presented in relation to the desired response?
   a. immediately before
   b. immediately after
   c. at the same time as
   d. at least a half hour before

7. In distinguishing between negative reinforcers and punishment, we note that
   a. punishment, but not negative reinforcement, involves use of an aversive stimulus.
   b. in contrast to punishment, negative reinforcement decreases the likelihood of a response by the presentation of an aversive stimulus.
   c. in contrast to punishment, negative reinforcement increases the likelihood of a response by the presentation of an aversive stimulus.
   d. in contrast to punishment, negative reinforcement increases the likelihood of a response by the termination of an aversive stimulus.

8. The "piecework," or commission, method of payment is an example of which reinforcement schedule?
   a. fixed-interval
   b. variable-interval
   c. fixed-ratio
   d. variable-ratio

9. Putting on your coat when it is cold outside is a behavior that is maintained by
   a. discrimination learning.
   b. punishment.
   c. negative reinforcement.
   d. classical conditioning.

10. On an intermittent reinforcement schedule, reinforcement is given
    a. in very small amounts.
    b. randomly.
    c. for successive approximations of a desired behavior.
    d. only some of the time.

11. You teach your dog to fetch the paper by giving him a cookie each time he does so. This is an example of
    a. operant conditioning.
    b. classical conditioning.
    c. conditioned reinforcement.
    d. partial reinforcement.

12. In promoting observational learning, the most effective models are those that we perceive as
    a. similar to ourselves.
    b. respected and admired.
    c. successful.
    d. having any of these characteristics.

13. A cognitive map is a
    a. mental representation of one's environment.
    b. sequence of thought processes leading from one idea to another.
    c. set of instructions detailing the most effective means of teaching a particular concept.
    d. biological predisposition to learn a particular skill.

14. After exploring a complicated maze for several days, a rat subsequently ran the maze with very few errors when food was placed in the goal box for the first time. This performance illustrates
    a. classical conditioning.
    b. discrimination learning.
    c. observational learning.
    d. latent learning.

15. Leon's psychology instructor has scheduled an exam every third week of the term. Leon will probably study the most just before an exam and the least just after an exam. This is because the schedule of exams is reinforcing studying according to which schedule?
    a. fixed-ratio
    b. variable-ratio
    c. fixed-interval
    d. variable-interval

16. Operant conditioning is to _____ as classical conditioning is to _____ .
    a. Pavlov; Watson
    b. Skinner; Bandura
    c. Pavlov; Skinner
    d. Skinner; Pavlov

17. Online testing systems and interactive software are applications of the operant conditioning principles of
    a. shaping and immediate reinforcement.
    b. immediate reinforcement and punishment.
    c. shaping and primary reinforcement.
    d. continuous reinforcement and punishment.

18. Which of the following is the best example of a conditioned reinforcer?
    a. putting on a coat on a cold day
    b. relief from pain after the dentist stops drilling your teeth
    c. receiving a cool drink after washing your mother's car on a hot day
    d. receiving an approving nod from the boss for a job well done

19. Experiments on taste-aversion learning demonstrate that
    a. for the conditioning of certain stimuli, the US need not immediately follow the CS.
    b. any perceivable stimulus can become a CS.
    c. all animals are biologically primed to associate illness with the taste of a tainted food.
    d. all of these statements are true.

20. Regarding the impact of watching television violence on children, most researchers believe that

  a. aggressive children simply prefer violent programs.
  b. television simply reflects, rather than contributes to, violent social trends.
  c. watching violence on television leads to aggressive behavior.
  d. there is only a weak correlation between exposure to violence and aggressive behavior.

True–False Items

Indicate whether each statement is true or false by placing *T* or *F* in the blank next to the item.

_____ **1.** Operant conditioning involves behavior that is primarily reflexive.

_____ **2.** The optimal interval between CS and US is about 15 seconds.

_____ **3.** Negative reinforcement decreases the likelihood that a response will recur.

_____ **4.** The learning of a new behavior proceeds most rapidly with continuous reinforcement.

_____ **5.** As a rule, variable schedules of reinforcement produce more consistent rates of responding than fixed schedules.

_____ **6.** Cognitive processes are of relatively little importance in learning.

_____ **7.** Although punishment may be effective in suppressing behavior, it can have several undesirable side effects.

_____ **8.** All animals, including rats and birds, are biologically predisposed to associate taste cues with sickness.

_____ **9.** Whether the CS or US is presented first seems not to matter in terms of the ease of classical conditioning.

_____ **10.** Spontaneous recovery refers to the tendency of extinguished behaviors to reappear suddenly.

_____ **11.** Elementary schoolchildren with heavy exposure to media violence also tend to get into more fights.

Essay Question

Describe the best way for a pet owner to condition her dog to roll over. (Use the space below to list the points you want to make, and organize them. Then write the essay on a separate piece of paper.)

Terms and Concepts to Remember

Writing Definitions

Using your own words, on a piece of paper write a brief definition or explanation of each of the following terms.

  1. learning
  2. associative learning
  3. stimulus
  4. cognitive learning
  5. classical conditioning
  6. behaviorism
  7. neutral stimulus
  8. unconditioned response (UR)
  9. unconditioned stimulus (US)
  10. conditioned response (CR)
  11. conditioned stimulus (CS)
  12. acquisition
  13. extinction
  14. spontaneous recovery
  15. generalization
  16. discrimination
  17. operant conditioning
  18. law of effect
  19. operant chamber (Skinner box)
  20. reinforcement
  21. shaping

22. positive reinforcement
23. negative reinforcement
24. primary reinforcer
25. conditioned reinforcer
26. continuous reinforcement
27. reinforcement schedule
28. partial (intermittent) reinforcement
29. fixed-ratio schedule
30. variable-ratio schedule
31. fixed-interval schedule
32. variable-interval schedule

33. punishment
34. respondent behavior
35. operant behavior
36. cognitive map
37. latent learning
38. intrinsic motivation
39. extrinsic motivation
40. observational learning
41. modeling
42. mirror neurons
43. prosocial behavior

Cross-Check

As you learned in Chapter 1, reviewing and over-learning of material are important to the learning process. After you have written the definitions of the key terms in this chapter, you should complete the crossword puzzle to ensure that you can reverse the process—recognize the term, given the definition.

ACROSS

1. Behavior that occurs as an automatic response to a stimulus.
4. Relatively permanent change in behavior due to experience.
6. Reinforcer that, when removed after a response, strengthens the response.
9. Type of stimulus that naturally triggers an unconditioned response.
12. Unlearned, involuntary response.
14. Type of behavior that is positive and helpful.
17. Behavior that produces reinforcing or punishing stimuli.
20. Procedure that involves reinforcing successive approximations of a behavior.
21. Learned response to a previously neutral stimulus.

22. Learning that occurs in the absence of reinforcement but only becomes apparent when an incentive is introduced.
23. Initial stage of conditioning, in which a new response is established.

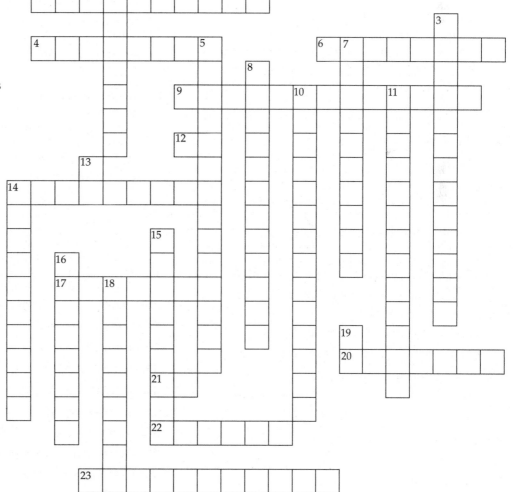

DOWN

2. Type of reinforcement in which responding is intermittently reinforced.
3. Schedule in which the first response following a set period of time is reinforced.
5. Tendency for stimuli similar to the original CS to evoke a CR.
7. This occurs when a response is no longer reinforced.
8. Mental picture of the environment
10. Responding differently to stimuli that signal whether a behavior will be reinforced.
11. Learning that involves watching and imitating others.
13. Stimulus that automatically triggers an unconditioned response.
14. The presentation of an aversive stimulus, which decreases the behavior it follows.
15. Type of learning also called Pavlovian conditioning.
16. The process of watching and then imitating a behavior.
18. Motivation to perform a behavior in order to obtain a reward or avoid a punishment.
19. Originally neutral stimulus that comes to trigger a conditioned response.

Answers

Chapter Review

How Do We Learn?

1. learning
2. associate; associations; associative learning
3. classical; stimulus
4. operant
5. cognitive learning; observing; observational learning

Classical Conditioning

6. Ivan Pavlov; John Watson; behaviorism
7. neutral stimulus; unconditioned stimulus
8. unconditioned response
9. conditioned stimulus; conditioned response
10. the cat
11. your mother's behavior
12. your fear today
13. your crying
14. **a.** is the answer. Your dog had to learn to associate the rattling sound with the food. Rattling is therefore a conditioned, or learned, stimulus, and

salivation in response to this rattling is a learned, or conditioned, response.

15. acquisition; one-half second
16. does not
17. survive; reproduce
18. extinction
19. spontaneous recovery
20. generalization
21. similar; discrimination
22. adaptive
23. generalization; discriminating
24. adapt
25. objectively

Classical conditioning is one way that virtually all organisms learn to adapt to their environment. Classical conditioning also provided an example to the young field of psychology of how complex, internal processes could be studied objectively. In addition, classical conditioning has proven to have many helpful applications to human health and well-being.

26. craving; context
27. can

In Watson and Rayner's experiment, classical conditioning was used to condition fear of a rat in Albert, an 11-month-old infant. When Albert touched the white rat (neutral stimulus), a loud noise (unconditioned stimulus) was sounded. After several pairings of the rat with the noise, Albert began crying at the mere sight of the rat. The rat had become a conditioned stimulus, triggering a conditioned response of fear. This showed that human emotions and behaviors, though biologically influenced, may actually be conditioned responses. Unfortunately, Albert's response may have been influenced by his brain damage. Also, some psychologists have had difficulty repeating Watson and Rayner's findings.

Operant Conditioning

28. law of effect; rewarded; recur
29. consequences; reinforcers; punishers
30. operant chamber (Skinner box); reinforcement
31. shaping; approximations
32. concepts; discriminating
33. discriminative stimulus
34. **c.** is the answer. The parrot is reinforced for making successive approximations of a goal behavior. This defines shaping.

a. Shaping is an operant conditioning procedure; salivation at the sight of dog biscuits is a classically conditioned response.

b. Shaping involves the systematic reinforcement of successive approximations of a more complex behavior. In this example there is no indication that the response of stopping at the intersection involved the gradual acquisition of simpler behaviors.

35. positive reinforcer

36. negative reinforcer

37. primary reinforcers

38. conditioned (secondary) reinforcers

39. more

40. is; delayed; unprotected sex

41. reinforcement schedule; desired response

42. continuous reinforcement; rapid; rapid

43. partial (intermittent); slower; very

44. fixed-ratio

45. variable-ratio

46. fixed-interval; checking the mail as delivery time approaches

47. variable-interval

Following reinforcement on a fixed-interval schedule, there is a pause in responding and then an increasing rate of response as time for the next reinforcement draws near. On a fixed-ratio schedule there also is a postreinforcement pause, followed, however, by a return to a consistent, high rate of response. Both kinds of variable schedules produce steadier rates of response, without the pauses associated with fixed schedules. In general, schedules linked to responses produce higher response rates and variable schedules produce more consistent responding than the related fixed schedules.

48. **c.** is the answer. Reinforcement (the letter) comes after a fixed interval, and as the likely end of the interval approaches, your behavior (glancing out the window) becomes more frequent.

a. & b. These answers are incorrect because with ratio schedules, reinforcement is contingent upon the number of responses rather than on the passage of time.

d. Assuming that the mail is delivered at about the same time each day, the interval is fixed rather than variable. Your behavior reflects this, since you glance out the window more often as the delivery time approaches.

49. **a.** is the answer. Ratio schedules maintain higher rates of responding—gambling in this example—than do interval schedules. Furthermore, variable

schedules are not associated with the pause in responding following reinforcement that is typical of fixed schedules. The slot machine would therefore be used more often, and more consistently, if jackpots were scheduled according to a variable-ratio schedule.

50. **c.** is the answer. Whereas Lars is paid (reinforced) after a fixed period of time (fixed-interval), Tom is reinforced for each sale (fixed-ratio) he makes.

51. negative reinforcement. By taking out the garbage, Jack terminates a negative stimulus—his father's nagging.

52. conditioned reinforcer. Being invited to your instructor's home as part of a select group is a conditioned reinforcer in that it doesn't satisfy an innate need but has become linked with desirable consequences.

53. increases; removing; decreases; presenting

54. punishment; positive punishment; negative punishment

55. suppressed; discrimination; fear; the person who administered it

56. aggressiveness

57. **a.** Punishment. You lose something good— conversation with your roommate.

b. Negative reinforcement. You are no longer cold, which means something bad has been removed.

c. Negative reinforcement. You are no longer thirsty, so something bad has been removed.

d. Punishment. You can't use your laptop; certainly, something good has been taken away.

e. Negative reinforcement. Your brother stops nagging you, so something bad has been removed.

58. external; internal thoughts; feelings

59. operant; behavior

60. dehumanized; freedom; control

61. shaping; testing; interactive; Web

62. athletic

63. more; achievable; more

64. **a.** State your goal in measurable terms.

b. Monitor the behavior (when and where it occurs).

c. Reinforce the desired behavior.

d. Reduce the rewards gradually.

65. **c.** is the answer.

a. Positive reinforcement is most effective in boosting productivity in the workplace when specific behavior, rather than vaguely defined general merit, is rewarded. Also, immediate reinforcement is much more effective than the delayed reinforcement described in a.

b. Positive reinforcement is most effective in boosting productivity when performance goals are achievable, rather than unrealistic.

d. The text does not specifically discuss the use of punishment in the workplace. However, it makes the general point that although punishment may temporarily suppress unwanted behavior, it does not guide one toward more desirable behavior. Therefore, workers who receive pay cuts for poor performance may learn nothing about how to improve their productivity.

66. **d.** is the answer. By making a more preferred activity (watching TV) contingent on a less preferred activity (room cleaning), Reggie's mother is employing the operant conditioning technique of positive reinforcement.

67. associative learning

68. acquisition; extinction; spontaneous recovery; generalization; discrimination

69. neutral; automatic; does not

70. respondent

71. operant

72. cognitive; biological

73. **a.** voluntary; operant conditioning
    b. involuntary; classical conditioning
    c. voluntary; operant conditioning
    d. involuntary; classical conditioning

Biology, Cognition, and Learning

74. response; stimulus

75. sickness; would

76. biological; adapt; natural selection; survival

77. is

78. reinforcer; shape; food

79. adaptive; instinctive drift

80. **a.** is the answer. As in this example, conditioning must be consistent with the particular organism's biological predispositions.

    b. Some behaviors, but certainly not all, are acquired more rapidly than others when shock is used as negative reinforcement.

    c. Pigeons are able to acquire many new behaviors when food is used as reinforcement.

81. **b.** is the answer.

    a., c., & d. Taste-aversion research demonstrates that humans and some other animals, such as rats, are biologically primed to associate ill-

ness with the taste of tainted food, rather than with other cues, such as the food's appearance. Moreover, taste aversions can be acquired even when the interval between the CS and the illness is several hours.

82. cognition

83. predict; cognitive; expect

84. alcohol use disorder

85. cognitive

86. cognitive map

87. latent learning

88. intrinsic motivation; extrinsic motivation

89. **d.** is the answer. Sharetta is guided by her mental representation of the city, or cognitive map.

    a. Latent learning, or learning in the absence of reinforcement that is demonstrated when reinforcement becomes available, has no direct relevance to the example.

    b. Observational learning refers to learning from watching others.

    c. Shaping is the technique of reinforcing successive approximations of a desired behavior.

90. **a.** is the answer. The unrewarded rat is demonstrating latent learning. It has developed a cognitive map of the maze.

91. **b.** is the answer. Wanting to do something for its own sake is intrinsic motivation; wanting to do something for a reward (in this case, presumably, a high grade) is extrinsic motivation.

    a. The opposite is true. Nancy was motivated to take the course for its own sake, whereas Jack was evidently motivated by the likelihood of a reward in the form of a good grade.

    c. & d. A good grade, such as the one Jack is expecting, is an incentive. Drives, however, are aroused states that result from physical deprivation; they are not involved in this example.

92. modeling; observational learning; occurs

93. Albert Bandura

94. more

95. rewards; punishments

96. similar; successful; admirable

97. mirror; frontal; observational; observe other monkeys performing the same task; empathize; imitate; networks

98. 8 to 16 months; 14 months; empathy; theory of mind

99. increases; mirror neurons; prosocial

100. **c.** is the answer. Studies indicate that when a model says one thing but does another, subjects do the same and learn not to practice what they preach.

101. **b.** is the answer. The girls are imitating behavior they have observed and admired.
a. Because these behaviors are clearly willful rather than involuntary, classical conditioning plays no role.
c. Latent learning plays no role in this example.
d. Shaping is a procedure for teaching the acquisition of a new response by reinforcing successive approximations of the behavior.

102. prosocial; consistent

103. antisocial; abusive; aggressive; genetic

104. watching television

105. violent

106. link

107. fights; violent

108. causation; does

109. imitation; desensitize

Progress Test 1

Multiple-Choice Questions

1. **c.** is the answer.
a. This answer is incorrect because it simply describes any behavior that is automatic rather than being triggered by a specific stimulus.
b. This answer is too general, since behaviors can change for reasons other than learning.
d. Respondently conditioned behavior also satisfies the criteria of our definition of learning.

2. **b.** is the answer.
a. & c. Classical conditioning is associated with Pavlov; respondent conditioning is another name for classical conditioning.
d. Observational learning is most closely associated with Bandura.

3. **c.** is the answer. Meat automatically triggers the response of salivation and is therefore an unconditioned stimulus.
a. A conditioned stimulus acquires its response-triggering powers through learning. A dog does not learn to salivate to meat.
b. & d. Responses are behaviors triggered in the organism, in this case the dog's salivation. The meat is a stimulus.

4. **b.** is the answer. Prior to its pairing with meat (the US), the tone did not trigger salivation and was therefore a neutral stimulus. Afterward, the tone triggered salivation (the CR) and was therefore a conditioned stimulus (CS).
c. & d. Unconditioned stimuli, such as meat, innately trigger responding. Pavlov's dogs had to learn to associate the tone with the food.

5. **d.** is the answer. In learning to distinguish between the conditioned stimulus and another, similar stimulus, the monkey has received training in discrimination.
a. In extinction training, a stimulus and/or response is allowed to go unreinforced.
b. Generalization training involves responding to stimuli similar to the conditioned stimulus; here the monkey is being trained not to respond to a similar stimulus.
c. This cannot be classical conditioning since the monkey is acting in order to obtain a reward. Thus, this is an example of operant conditioning.

6. **b.** is the answer. A continuous association will naturally be easier to learn than one that occurs on only some occasions, so learning is most rapid with continuous reinforcement. Yet, once the continuous association is no longer there, as in extinction training, extinction will occur more rapidly than it would have had the organism not always experienced reinforcement.

7. **b.** is the answer.
c. & d. The text does not present evidence regarding the relative importance of cognitive processes in classical and operant conditioning.

8. **b.** is the answer.
a. With fixed-ratio schedules, there is a pause following each reinforcement.
c. & d. Because reinforcement is not contingent on the rate of response, interval schedules, especially fixed-interval schedules, produce lower response rates than ratio schedules.

9. **b.** is the answer.
a. Positive reinforcement involves presenting a favorable stimulus following a response.
c. Punishment involves presenting an unpleasant stimulus following a response.
d. In extinction, a previously reinforced response is no longer followed by reinforcement. In this situation, a response causes a stimulus to be terminated or removed.

10. **c.** is the answer. In this situation, the CR will decline, a phenomenon known as extinction.
a. Generalization occurs when the subject makes a CR to stimuli similar to the original CS.
b. Discrimination is when the subject does not make a CR to stimuli other than the original CS.

d. An aversion is a CR to a CS that has been associated with an unpleasant US, such as shock or a nausea-producing drug.

11. **c.** is the answer.
    a. In *operant* conditioning the responses operate on the environment.
    b. In *classical* conditioning responses are triggered by preceding stimuli.
    d. In *classical* conditioning responses are reflexive.

12. **c.** is the answer.
    a. & d. These studies also indicated that rats are biologically predisposed to associate visual and auditory stimuli, but not taste, with shock.
    b. Rats are biologically predisposed to associate taste with sickness.

13. **d.** is the answer. A dog does not have to learn to salivate to food; therefore, this response is unconditioned.
    a. & c. Salivation is a response, not a stimulus.

14. **b.** is the answer.
    a. Skinner is best known for studies of *operant* learning. Moreover, there is no such thing as secondary learning.
    c. Pavlov is best known for classical conditioning.
    d. Watson is best known as an early proponent of behaviorism.

15. **d.** is the answer.

16. **c.** is the answer.
    a., b., & d. Rescorla and Wagner's research did not address the importance of these factors in classical conditioning.

17. **d.** is the answer. a. is an example of positive reinforcement, b. is an example of negative reinforcement, and c. is an example of conditioned reinforcement.

18. **a.** is the answer.

19. **b.** is the answer.
    a. Backward conditioning, in which the US precedes the CS, is ineffective.
    c. This interval is longer than is optimum for the most rapid acquisition of a CS–US association.
    d. Simultaneous presentation of CS and US is ineffective because it does not permit the subject to anticipate the US.

20. **a.** is the answer.

Matching Items

1. e	6. k	11. d
2. h	7. m	12. j
3. f	8. a	13. l
4. g	9. c	
5. i	10. b	

Progress Test 2

Multiple-Choice Questions

1. **c.** is the answer.

2. **b.** is the answer. The loud noise automatically triggered Albert's fear and therefore functioned as a US. After being associated with the US, the white rat acquired the power to trigger fear and thus became a CS.

3. **d.** is the answer.

4. **a.** is the answer. Shaping works on operant behaviors by reinforcing successive approximations to a desired goal.

5. **c.** is the answer.
   a., b., & d. Spontaneous recovery occurs after a CR has been extinguished, and in the absence of the US. The situations described here all involve the continued presentation of the US and, therefore, the further strengthening of the CR.

6. **b.** is the answer.
   a., c., & d. Reinforcement that is delayed, presented before a response, or at the same time as a response does not always increase the response's frequency of occurrence.

7. **d.** is the answer.
   a. Both involve an aversive stimulus.
   b. All reinforcers, including negative reinforcers, increase the likelihood of a response.
   c. In negative reinforcement, an aversive stimulus is withdrawn following a desirable response.

8. **c.** is the answer. Payment is given after a fixed number of pieces have been completed.
   a. & b. Interval schedules reinforce according to the passage of time, not the amount of work accomplished.
   d. Fortunately for those working on commission, the work ratio is fixed and therefore predictable.

9. **c.** is the answer. By learning to put on your coat before going outside, you have learned to reduce the aversive stimulus of the cold.
   a. Discrimination learning involves learning to make a response in the presence of the appropriate stimulus and not other stimuli.
   b. Punishment is the suppression of an undesirable response by the presentation of an aversive stimulus.
   d. Putting on a coat is a response that operates on the environment. Therefore, this is an example of operant, not classical, conditioning.

10. **d.** is the answer.

a. Intermittent reinforcement refers to the ratio of responses to reinforcers, not the overall quantity of reinforcement delivered.

b. Unlike intermittent reinforcement, in which the delivery of reinforcement is contingent on responding, random reinforcement is delivered independently of the subject's behavior.

c. This defines the technique of shaping, not intermittent reinforcement.

11. **a.** is the answer. You are teaching your dog by rewarding him when he produces the desired behavior.

   b. This is not classical conditioning because the cookie is a primary reinforcer presented after the operant behavior of the dog fetching the paper.

   c. Food is a primary reinforcer; it satisfies an innate need.

   d. Rewarding your dog each time he fetches the paper is continuous reinforcement.

12. **d.** is the answer.

13. **a.** is the answer.

14. **d.** is the answer. The rat had learned the maze but did not display this learning until reinforcement became available.

   a. Negotiating a maze is clearly operant behavior.

   b. This example does not involve learning to distinguish between stimuli.

   c. This is not observational learning because the rat has no one to observe!

15. **c.** is the answer. Because reinforcement (earning a good grade on the exam) is available according to the passage of time, studying is reinforced on an interval schedule. Because the interval between exams is constant, this is an example of a fixed-interval schedule.

16. **d.** is the answer.

   a. Pavlov and Watson are both associated with classical conditioning.

   b. Skinner is associated with operant conditioning, and Bandura is associated with observational learning.

17. **a.** is the answer. Online testing systems apply operant principles such as reinforcement, immediate feedback, and shaping to the teaching of new skills.

   b. & d. Online testing systems provide immediate, and continuous, reinforcement for correct responses, but do not use aversive control procedures such as punishment.

   c. Online testing systems are based on feedback for correct responses; this feedback constitutes conditioned, rather than primary, reinforcement.

18. **d.** is the answer. An approving nod from the boss is a conditioned reinforcer in that it doesn't satisfy an innate need but has become linked with desirable consequences. Cessation of cold, cessation of pain, and a drink are all primary reinforcers, which meet innate needs.

19. **a.** is the answer. Taste-aversion experiments demonstrate conditioning even with CS-US intervals as long as several hours.

   b. Despite being perceivable, a visual or auditory stimulus cannot become a CS for illness in some animals, such as rats.

   c. Some animals, such as birds, are biologically primed to associate the *appearance* of food with illness.

20. **c.** is the answer.

True–False Items

1.	F	5.	T	9.	F
2.	F	6.	F	10.	T
3.	F	7.	T	11.	T
4.	T	8.	F		

Essay Question

The first step in shaping an operant response, such as rolling over, is to find an effective reinforcer. Some sort of biscuit or dog treat is favored by animal trainers. This primary reinforcement should be accompanied by effusive praise (secondary reinforcement) whenever the dog makes a successful response.

Rolling over (the goal response) should be divided into a series of simple approximations, the first of which is a response, such as lying down on command, that is already in the dog's repertoire. This response should be reinforced several times. The next step is to issue a command, such as "Roll over," and withhold reinforcement until the dog (usually out of frustration) makes a closer approximation (such as rotating slightly in one direction). Following this example, the trainer should gradually require closer and closer approximations until the goal response is attained. When the new response has been established, the trainer should switch from continuous to partial reinforcement, in order to strengthen the skill.

Terms and Concepts to Remember

Writing Definitions

1. **Learning** is the process of acquiring through experience new and relatively enduring information or behaviors.

2. In **associative learning**, organisms learn that certain events occur together. Two variations of associative learning are classical conditioning and operant conditioning.

3. A **stimulus** is any situation or event that evokes a response.

4. **Cognitive learning** is the acquisition of mental information that guides our behavior.

5. **Classical conditioning** is a type of learning in which one learns to link two or more stimuli and anticipate events; specifically, a neutral stimulus becomes capable of triggering a conditioned response after having become associated with an unconditioned stimulus.

6. **Behaviorism** is the view that psychology should be an objective science that studies only observable behaviors without reference to mental processes.

   Example: Because he was an early advocate of the study of observable behavior, John Watson is often called the father of **behaviorism.**

7. In classical conditioning, a **neutral stimulus (NS)** is one that elicits no response before conditioning.

8. In classical conditioning, the **unconditioned response (UR)** is an unlearned, naturally occurring response to an unconditioned stimulus.

9. In classical conditioning, the **unconditioned stimulus (US)** is a stimulus that naturally and automatically triggers a reflexive unconditioned response.

10. In classical conditioning, the **conditioned response (CR)** is a learned response to a previously neutral (but now conditioned) stimulus, which results from the acquired association between the CS and US.

11. In classical conditioning, the **conditioned stimulus (CS)** is an originally irrelevant stimulus that comes to trigger a CR after association with an unconditioned stimulus.

12. In a learning experiment, **acquisition** refers to the initial stage of conditioning when one links a neutral stimulus and an unconditioned stimulus, so that the neutral stimulus begins triggering the conditioned response. In operant conditioning, it is the strengthening of a reinforced response.

13. **Extinction** refers to the diminishing of a CR when the CS is no longer followed by the US; in operant conditioning, extinction occurs when a response is no longer reinforced.

14. **Spontaneous recovery** is the reappearance of an extinguished CR after a pause.

15. **Generalization** refers to the tendency, once a response has been conditioned, for stimuli similar to the original CS to elicit similar responses.

16. **Discrimination** in classical conditioning refers to the ability to distinguish the CS from similar stimuli that do not signal a US. In operant conditioning, it refers to responding differently to stimuli that signal a behavior will be reinforced or will not be reinforced.

17. **Operant conditioning** is a type of learning in which behavior is strengthened if followed by a reinforcer or diminished if followed by a punisher.

    Example: Unlike classical conditioning, which works on automatic behaviors, **operant conditioning** works on behaviors that operate on the environment.

18. E. L. Thorndike proposed the **law of effect**, which states that behaviors followed by favorable consequences are likely to recur, and that behaviors followed by unfavorable consequences become less likely.

19. An **operant chamber** (*Skinner box*) is an experimental chamber for the operant conditioning of an animal such as a pigeon or rat. The controlled environment enables the investigator to present visual or auditory stimuli, deliver reinforcement or punishment, and precisely measure simple responses such as bar presses or key pecking.

20. In operant conditioning, **reinforcement** is any event that strengthens the behavior it follows.

21. **Shaping** is the operant conditioning procedure for establishing a new response by reinforcing successive approximations of the desired behavior.

22. In operant conditioning, **positive reinforcement** strengthens a response by *presenting* a typically pleasurable stimulus after that response.

23. In operant conditioning, **negative reinforcement** strengthens a response by *removing* an aversive stimulus after that response.

24. The powers of **primary reinforcers** are inborn and do not depend on learning.

25. **Conditioned reinforcers** are stimuli that acquire their reinforcing power through their association with primary reinforcers; also called *secondary reinforcers*.

26. **Continuous reinforcement** is the operant procedure of reinforcing the desired response every time it occurs. In promoting the acquisition of a new response it is best to use continuous reinforcement.

27. In operant conditioning, a **reinforcement schedule** is a pattern that defines how often a desired response will be reinforced.

28. **Partial (intermittent) reinforcement** is the operant procedure of reinforcing a response intermittently. A response that has been partially reinforced is much more resistant to extinction than one that has been continuously reinforced.

29. In operant conditioning, a **fixed-ratio schedule** is one in which reinforcement is presented after a set number of responses.

    Example: Continuous reinforcement is a special kind of **fixed-ratio schedule**: Reinforcement is presented after *each* response, so the ratio of reinforcements to responses is one to one.

30. In operant conditioning, a **variable-ratio schedule** is one in which reinforcement is presented after a varying number of responses.

31. In operant conditioning, a **fixed-interval schedule** is one in which a response is reinforced after a specified time has elapsed.

32. In operant conditioning, a **variable-interval schedule** is one in which responses are reinforced after varying intervals of time.

33. In operant conditioning, **punishment** is the presentation of an aversive stimulus, such as shock, which decreases the behavior it follows.

    Memory aid: People often confuse negative reinforcement and **punishment**. The former strengthens behavior, while the latter weakens it.

34. **Respondent behavior** is behavior that occurs as an automatic response to some stimulus.

    Example: In classical conditioning, conditioned and unconditioned responses are examples of **respondent behavior** in that they are automatic responses triggered by specific stimuli.

35. **Operant behavior** is behavior that operates on the environment, producing consequences.

36. A **cognitive map** is a mental representation of the layout of one's environment.

37. **Latent learning** is learning that occurs in the absence of reinforcement but only becomes apparent when there is an incentive to demonstrate it.

38. **Intrinsic motivation** is the desire to perform a behavior effectively for its own sake, rather than for some external reason.

    Memory aid: Intrinsic means "internal": A person who is **intrinsically motivated** is motivated from within.

39. **Extrinsic motivation** is the desire to perform a behavior to receive promised rewards or avoid threatened punishment.

    Memory aid: Extrinsic means "external": A person who is **extrinsically motivated** is motivated by some outside factor.

40. **Observational learning** is learning by watching and imitating the behavior of others.

41. **Modeling** is the process of watching and then imitating a specific behavior and is thus an important means through which observational learning occurs.

42. Found in the brain's frontal lobe, **mirror neurons** may be the neural basis for observational learning. These neurons generate impulses that some scientists believe fire when certain actions are performed or when another individual who performs those actions is observed.

43. The opposite of antisocial behavior, **prosocial behavior** is positive, helpful, and constructive and is subject to the same principles of observational learning as is undesirable behavior, such as aggression.

Cross-Check

ACROSS
 1. respondent
 4. learning
 6. negative
 9. unconditioned
12. UR
14. prosocial
17. operant
20. shaping
21. CR
22. latent
23. acquisition

DOWN
 2. partial
 3. fixed interval
 5. generalization
 7. extinction
 8. cognitive map
10. discrimination
11. observational
13. US
14. punishment
15. classical
16. modeling
18. extrinsic
19. CS

CHAPTER 8

Memory

Chapter Overview

Chapter 8 explores human memory as a system that processes information in three steps. Encoding refers to the process of putting information into the memory system. Storage is the mechanism by which information is maintained in memory. Retrieval is the process by which information is accessed from memory through recall or recognition.

Chapter 8 also discusses the important role of meaning, distributed practice, and organization in encoding new memories, how memory is represented physically in the brain, and how forgetting may result from failure to encode or store information or to find appropriate retrieval cues. The final section of the chapter discusses the issue of memory construction. How "true" are our memories of events? A particularly controversial issue in this area involves suspicious claims of long-repressed memories of sexual abuse and other traumas that are "recovered" with the aid of hypnosis and other techniques. As you study this chapter, try applying some of the memory and studying tips discussed in the text.

NOTE: Answer guidelines for all Chapter 8 questions begin on page 196.

Chapter Review

First, skim this section, noting headings and boldface items. After you have read the section, review each objective by completing the sentences and answering the questions that follow it. Study Tips explain how best to learn a difficult concept and Applications help you to know how well you understand the material. As you proceed, evaluate your performance by consulting the answers beginning on page 196. Do not continue with the next section until you understand each answer. If you need to, review or reread the section in the textbook before continuing.

Studying Memory

Objective 8-1: Define *memory*, and describe how it is measured.

1. Learning that persists over time indicates the existence of _____ for that learning.

2. The ability to retrieve information not in conscious awareness but that was learned at an earlier time is called _____ . The ability to identify previously learned items is called _____ .

3. If you have learned something and then forgotten it, you will probably be able to _____ it_____ (more/less) quickly than you did originally.

Objective 8-2: Explain how psychologists describe the human memory system.

4. Both human memory and computer memory can be viewed as _____-_____ systems that perform three tasks: _____ , _____ , and _____ . Unlike the computer, which processes _____ (sequentially/simultaneously), our brain processes many things _____ (sequentially/simultaneously) by means of _____ _____ . The model called _____ views memory as emerging from interconnected _____ _____ .

5. Atkinson and Shiffrin proposed a memory model involving _____ _____ . According to this model, we first record information as a fleeting _____ . _____ , from which it is processed into _____ - _____ memory, where the information is _____ through rehearsal into _____ - _____ memory for later retrieval.

6. The phenomenon of short-term memory has been clarified by the concept of _____ memory, which focuses more on the _____ processing of briefly stored information. Baddeley suggested that a _____ _____ handles the focused processing of _____ and _____ - _____ information as well as of information retrieved from _____ - _____ memory.

Sensory Memory	Working/Short-Term Memory	Long-Term Memory
Encoding: light reflecting from printed words in the poem automatically triggers a response in the eye's receptor cells	*Encoding:* automatic processing of location of words on the page; effortful processing of meaning	*Encoding:* Memorable passage triggers deep processing of material from STM to LTM
Storage: image of each word persists in the visual system for about 1/2 sec.	*Storage:* limited capacity and duration of storing words on the page	*Storage:* relatively permanent and limitless; meaningful passage stays with you
Retrieval: visual image is attended to as it passes into Working/STM memory	*Retrieval:* conscious working memory allows reader to process the meaning of the poem's words	*Retrieval:* recall, recognition, or relearning of memorized passage from the poem

Building Memories: Encoding

Objective 8-3: Distinguish between explicit and implicit memories.

7. Facts and experiences that we can consciously declare make up _____ memory, which is also called _____ memory. Such memories are processed through conscious, _____ processing. Processing that happens without our awareness, called _____ _____ , produces _____ memories, which are also called _____ _____ .

Objective 8-4: Identify the information we process automatically.

8. Implicit memories include _____ memory for skills and associations among stimuli formed by _____ _____ .

Give examples of material that is typically encoded with little or no effort.

APPLICATIONS:

9. The first thing Karen did when she discovered that she had misplaced her keys was to re-create in her mind the day's events. That she had little difficulty in doing so illustrates _____ processing.

10. Elderly Mr. Flanagan, a retired electrician, can easily remember how to wire a light switch, but he cannot remember the name of the president of the United States. Evidently, Mr. Flanagan's _____ memory is better than his _____ memory.
    a. implicit; explicit
    b. explicit; implicit
    c. declarative; nondeclarative
    d. explicit; declarative

Objective 8-5: Explain how sensory memory works.

11. Stimuli from the environment are first recorded in _____ memory.

12. George Sperling found that when people were briefly shown three rows of letters, they could recall _____ (virtually all/about half) of them. When Sperling sounded a tone immediately after a row of letters was flashed to indicate which letters were to be recalled, the participants were much _____ (more/less) accurate. This suggests that people have a brief photographic, or _____, memory lasting about a few tenths of a second.

13. Sensory memory for sounds is called _____ memory. This memory fades _____ (more/less) rapidly than photographic memory, lasting for as long as _____ .

Objective 8-6: Describe the capacity of our short-term and working memory.

14. Our short-term memory capacity is about _____ chunks of information. This capacity was discovered by_____ .

15. Peterson and Peterson found that when _____ was prevented by asking people to count backward, memory for letters was gone after 12 seconds. Without _____ processing, short-term memories have a limited life.

16. Working memory capacity varies, depending on _____ and other factors. We do better and more efficient work when _____ , without _____ , on one task at a time.

APPLICATION:

17. Brenda has trouble remembering her new five-digit ZIP plus four-digit address code. What is the most likely explanation for the difficulty Brenda is having?
    a. Nine digits are at or above the upper limit of most people's short-term memory capacity.
    b. Nine digits are at or above the upper limit of most people's iconic memory capacity.
    c. The extra four digits cannot be organized into easily remembered chunks.
    d. Brenda evidently has an impaired implicit memory.

Objective 8-7: Describe the effortful processing methods that help us remember new information.

18. Memory may be aided by grouping information into meaningful units called _____ .

19. Memory aids are known as _____ devices.

20. Using a jingle, such as the one that begins "one is a bun," is an example of the _____-_____ system.

21. Another memory aid involves forming words from the first letters of to-be-remembered words; the resulting word is called an _____ .

22. When people develop expertise in an area, they process information not only in _____ but also in _____ .

23. A pioneering researcher in verbal memory was _____ . In one experiment, he found that distributed rehearsal is more effective for retention; this is called the _____ _____ .

24. Repeated self-testing is a good way to _____ practice. Henry Roediger and Jeffrey Karpicke called this the _____ _____ .

Objective 8-8: Describe the levels of processing and their effect on encoding.

25. Encoding material on a basic level based on _____ or the _____ of words, for example, is called _____ _____ .

Encoding material _____ , based on the meaning of words, is called _____ _____ . _____ (Shallow/Deep) processing tends to yield the best retention.

26. Material that is not _____ is difficult to process. We have especially good recall for information we can meaningfully relate to ourselves, called the _____- _____ effect.

Memory Storage

Objective 8-9: Describe the capacity and location of our long-term memories.

27. In contrast to short-term memory—and contrary to popular belief—the capacity of permanent memory is essentially_____ .

28. Psychologist _____ attempted to locate memory by cutting out pieces of rats' _____ after they had learned a maze. He found that no matter where he cut, the rats _____ (did/did not) retain at least a partial memory of the maze.

Objective 8-10: Describe the role of the frontal lobes and hippocampus in memory storage.

29. Many brain regions send input to your _____ lobes for working memory processing.

30. Cognitive neuroscientists have found that a temporal-lobe neural center in the limbic system, the _____ , is important in the processing and storage of _____ memories. Damage on the left side of this structure impairs _____ memory; damage on the right side impairs memory for _____ designs and locations. The rear part of this structure processes _____ memory.

31. The hippocampus seems to function as a zone where the brain _____ (temporarily/permanently) stores the elements of a

memory. However, memories _____ (do/do not) migrate for storage elsewhere. The hippocampus is active during _____ sleep, as memories are processed and filed for later retrieval. Areas of the _____ surrounding the hippocampus support the processing and storing of _____ memories.

APPLICATIONS:

32. Brad, who suffered accidental damage to the left side of his hippocampus, has trouble remembering
    a. visual designs.
    b. locations.
    c. all nonverbal information.
    d. verbal information.

33. After suffering damage to the hippocampus, a person would probably
    a. lose memory for skills such as bicycle riding.
    b. be incapable of being classically conditioned.
    c. lose the ability to store new facts.
    d. experience all of these changes.

Objective 8-11: Describe the role of the cerebellum and basal ganglia in our memory processing.

34. The cerebellum is important in the processing of _____ memories. Humans and laboratory animals with a damaged cerebellum are incapable of simple _____ conditioning.

35. Deep brain structures called the _____ _____ , which are also involved in _____ movement, facilitate formation of _____ memories for skills.

36. The dual explicit-implicit memory system helps explain _____ amnesia. We do not have explicit memories of our first three years for two reasons: explicit memory requires the use of words that nonspeaking children _____ (have/have not) learned and the _____ is one of the last brain structures to mature.

Objective 8-12: Discuss how emotions affect our memory processing.

37. Emotions trigger _____ hormones that _____ (influence/do not influence) memory formation by making more _____ available to fuel brain activity.

38. Stress hormones provoke the _____ to initiate a memory trace in the _____ _____ and _____ _____ to boost activity in the brain's memory-forming areas.

39. Memories for surprising, significant moments that are especially clear are called _____ memories. Like other memories, these memories _____ (can/ cannot) err.

APPLICATION:

40. Which of the following is the best example of a flashbulb memory?
    a. suddenly remembering to buy bread while standing in the checkout line at the grocery store
    b. recalling the name of someone from high school while looking at his or her yearbook snapshot
    c. remembering to make an important phone call
    d. remembering what you were doing on September 11, 2001, when terrorists crashed planes into the World Trade Center towers

Objective 8-13: Explain how changes at the synapse level affect our memory processing.

41. Eric Kandel and James Schwartz have found that when learning occurs in the California sea slug, *Aplysia*, the neurotransmitter _____ is released in greater amounts onto certain neurons, making these cells more efficient.

42. After learning has occurred, a sending neuron needs _____ (more/less) prompting to release its neurotransmitter, and the number of _____ _____ it stimulates may increase. This phenomenon, called _____-_____ _____ , may be the neural basis for learning and memory. Blocking this process

with a specific _____ , or by genetic engineering that causes the absence of an _____ , interferes with learning. Rats given a drug that enhances _____ will learn a maze _____ (faster/more slowly).

43. After LTP has occurred, an electric current passed through the brain _____ (will/will not) disrupt old memories and _____ (will/will not) wipe out recent experiences.

44. To enhance memory, one approach focuses on drugs that boost the LTP-enhancing neurotransmitter _____ . Another approach involves developing drugs that boost production of _____ , a protein that also enhances the LTP process.

Retrieval: Getting Information Out

Objective 8-14: Describe how external cues, internal emotions, and order of appearance influence memory retrieval.

45. Researchers found that 25 years after graduation, people were not able to _____ (recall/recognize) the names of their classmates but were able to _____ (recall/recognize) 90 percent of their names and their yearbook pictures.

46. Using _____ _____ , Ebbinghaus found that the more frequently he repeated the list aloud on day 1, the fewer repetitions he required to relearn the list on day 2. Additional rehearsal of learned material, called _____ , _____ (increases/does not increase) retention.

47. The best retrieval cues come from the associations formed at the time we _____ a memory.

48. The process by which associations can lead to retrieval is called _____ .

49. Studies have shown that retention is best when learning and testing are done in _____ (the same/different) contexts.

50. What we learn in one condition is best remembered in that condition, called

_____-_____

memory. For example, we tend to recall experiences that are consistent with our current emotional state, which is called _____-

_____ memory.

Describe the effects of mood on memory.

51. People who are currently depressed may recall their parents as _____

_____ . People who have recovered from depression typically recall their parents about the same as do people who _____

_____ .

52. The tendency to remember the first and last items in a list best is called the _____

_____ _____ .

53. People briefly recall the last items in a list quickly and well, called the _____ effect. Following a delay, first items are remembered _____ (better/less well) than last items, called the _____ effect.

APPLICATIONS:

54. Complete this analogy: Fill-in-the-blank test questions are to multiple-choice questions as

   a. encoding is to storage.
   b. storage is to encoding.
   c. recognition is to recall.
   d. recall is to recognition.

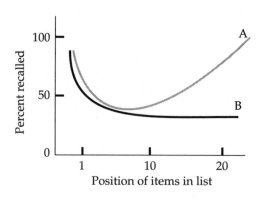

55. The above figure depicts the recall of a list of words under two conditions. Which of the following best describes the difference between the conditions?

   a. In A, the words were studied and retrieved in the same context; in B, the contexts were different.
   b. In B, the words were studied and retrieved in the same context; in A, the contexts were different.
   c. The delay between presentation of the last word and the test of recall was longer for A than for B.
   d. The delay between presentation of the last word and the test of recall was longer for B than for A.

56. Being in a bad mood after a hard day of work, Susan could think of nothing positive in her life. This is best explained as an example of

   a. priming.
   b. the spacing effect.
   c. mood-congruent memory.
   d. shallow processing.

57. In an effort to remember the name of the classmate who sat behind her in fifth grade, Martina mentally recited the names of other classmates who sat near her. Martina's effort to refresh her memory by activating related associations is an example of

   a. priming.   c. encoding.
   b. mnemonics.   d. relearning.

58. Walking through the halls of his high school 10 years after graduation, Tom experienced a flood of old memories. Tom's experience showed the role of

   a. state-dependent memory.
   b. context effects.
   c. implicit memory.
   d. echoic memory.

Forgetting

Objective 8-15: Explain why we forget.

59. Without the ability to _____ , we would constantly be overwhelmed by information.

60. The disorder called _____ _____ involves an inability to form new memories. The disorder called _____ _____ involves an inability to retrieve old memories.

61. People who cannot form new memories can learn _____ _____ and can be _____ _____ . However, they have no _____ memory of having learned these things.

62. The type of forgetting caused by _____ failure occurs because some of the information that we sense never actually _____ .

63. One reason for age-related memory decline is that the brain areas responsible for _____ new information are _____ (more/less) responsive in older adults.

64. Studies by Hermann Ebbinghaus and by Harry Bahrick indicate that most forgetting occurs _____ (soon/a long time) after the material is learned.

65. This type of forgetting is known as _____ _____ , which may be caused by a gradual fading of the physical _____ _____ .

66. When information that is stored in memory temporarily cannot be found, _____ failure has occurred.

67. Research suggests that memories are also lost as a result of _____ , which is especially possible if we simultaneously learn similar, new material.

68. The disruptive effect of previous learning on current learning is called _____ _____ . The disruptive effect of learning new material on efforts to recall material previously learned is called _____ _____ .

69. John Jenkins and Karl Dallenbach found that if people went to sleep after learning, their memory for a list of nonsense syllables was _____ (better/worse) than it was if they stayed awake.

70. In some cases, old information facilitates our learning of new information. This is called _____ _____ .

71. Freud proposed that motivated forgetting, or _____ , may protect a person from painful memories.

72. Increasing numbers of memory researchers think that motivated forgetting is _____ (less/more) common than Freud believed.

When Do We Forget?

Information bits

Sensory memory
The senses momentarily register amazing detail.

Working (short-term) memory
A few items are both noticed and encoded.

Long-term storage
Some items are altered or lost.

Retrieval from long-term memory
Depending on interference, retrieval cues, moods, and motives, some things get retrieved, some don't.

APPLICATIONS:

73. At your high school reunion you cannot remember the last name of your homeroom teacher. Your failure to remember is most likely the result of _____ failure.

74. Which of the following sequences would be best to follow if you wanted to minimize interference-induced forgetting in order to improve your recall on the psychology midterm?
    a. study, eat, test
    b. study, sleep, test
    c. study, listen to music, test
    d. study, exercise, test

75. When Carlos was promoted, he moved into a new office with a new phone extension. Every time he is asked for his phone number, Carlos first thinks of his old extension, illustrating the effects of

   a. proactive interference.
   b. retroactive interference.
   c. encoding failure.
   d. storage failure.

76. Lewis cannot remember the details of the torture he experienced as a prisoner of war. According to Freud, Lewis' failure to remember these painful memories is an example of

   a. repression.
   b. retrieval failure.
   c. state-dependent memory.
   d. flashbulb memory.

77. After finding her old combination lock, Janice can't remember its combination because she keeps confusing it with the combination of her new lock. She is experiencing

   a. proactive interference.
   b. retroactive interference.
   c. encoding failure.
   d. storage failure.

Memory Construction Errors

Objective 8-16: Explain how misinformation, imagination, and source amnesia influence our memory construction, and describe how we decide whether a memory is real or false.

78. As memories are replayed, they are often modified. This process is called _____ .

79. When witnesses to an event receive misleading information about it, they may experience a _____ _____ and misremember the event. A number of experiments have demonstrated that false memories _____ (can/cannot) be created when people are induced to imagine nonexistent events; that is, these people later experience _____ _____ . This occurs in part because visualizing something and actually perceiving it _____ .

Describe what Loftus' studies have shown about the effects of misleading postevent information.

80. At the heart of many false memories is _____ _____ , which occurs when we _____ an event to the wrong source. This phenomenon helps explain _____ _____ , which is the sense that a current situation has already been experienced.

81. Because memory is reconstruction as well as reproduction, we _____ (can/cannot) be sure whether a memory is real by how real it feels.

82. Memory construction explains why memories "refreshed" under _____ are often inaccurate.

APPLICATION:

83. Which of the following illustrates the constructive nature of memory?

   a. Janice keeps calling her new boyfriend by her old boyfriend's name.
   b. After studying all afternoon and then getting drunk in the evening, Don can't remember the material he studied.
   c. After getting some good news, elated Kareem has a flood of good memories from his younger years.
   d. Although Mrs. Harvey, who has Alzheimer's disease, has many gaps in her memory, she invents sensible accounts of her activities so that her family will not worry.

Objective 8-17: Describe the reliability of young children's eyewitness descriptions, and discuss why reports of repressed and recovered memories are so hotly debated.

84. Whether a child produces an accurate eyewitness memory depends heavily on how he or she is _____ . Children are most accurate when it is a first interview with a _____ person who asks _____ questions.

85. Researchers increasingly agree that memories obtained under the influence of hypnosis or using other "memory work" techniques _____ (are/are not) reliable.

86. Memories of events that happened before age _____ are unreliable. As noted earlier, this phenomenon is called _____ _____ .

Improving Memory

Objective 8-18: Describe how you can use memory research findings to do better in this and other courses.

87. The SQ3R study technique identifies five strategies for boosting memory: _____ , _____ , _____ , _____ , and _____ .

Discuss several specific strategies for improving memory.

Progress Test 1

Multiple-Choice Questions

Circle your answers to the following questions and check them with the answers beginning on page 199. If your answer is incorrect, read the explanation for why it is incorrect and then consult the text.

1. The three steps in memory information processing are
   a. input, processing, output.
   b. input, storage, output.
   c. input, storage, retrieval.
   d. encoding, storage, retrieval.

2. Visual sensory memory is referred to as
   a. iconic memory.   c. photomemory.
   b. echoic memory.   d. semantic memory.

3. Echoic memories fade after approximately
   a. 1 hour.   c. 1 second.
   b. 1 minute.   d. 3 to 4 seconds.

4. Which of the following is NOT a measure of retention?
   a. recall   c. relearning
   b. recognition   d. retrieval

5. Our short-term memory span is approximately _____ items.
   a. 2   c. 7
   b. 5   d. 10

6. Memory techniques such as acronyms and the peg-word system are called
   a. consolidation devices.
   b. imagery techniques.
   c. encoding strategies.
   d. mnemonic devices.

7. One way to increase the amount of information in memory is to group it into larger, familiar units. This process is referred to as
   a. consolidating.   c. encoding.
   b. organization.   d. chunking.

8. Kandel and Schwartz have found that when learning occurs, more of the neurotransmitter _____ is released into synapses.
   a. ACh   c. serotonin
   b. dopamine   d. noradrenaline

9. Research on memory construction reveals that memories
   a. are stored as exact copies of experience.
   b. reflect a person's biases and assumptions.
   c. may be chemically transferred from one organism to another.
   d. even if long term, usually decay within about five years.

10. In a study on context cues, people learned words while on land or when they were underwater. In a later test of recall, those with the best retention had
    a. learned the words on land, that is, in the more familiar context.
    b. learned the words underwater, that is, in the more exotic context.
    c. learned the words and been tested on them in different contexts.
    d. learned the words and been tested on them in the same context.

11. The spacing effect means that
    a. distributed study yields better retention than cramming.
    b. retention is improved when encoding and retrieval are separated by no more than 1 hour.
    c. learning causes a reduction in the size of the synaptic gap between certain neurons.
    d. delaying retrieval until memory has consolidated improves recall.

12. Studies demonstrate that learning causes permanent neural changes in the _____ of animals' neurons.
    a. myelin
    b. cell bodies
    c. synapses
    d. all of these parts

13. In Sperling's memory experiment, research participants were shown three rows of three letters, followed immediately by a low, medium, or high tone. The participants were able to report
    a. all three rows with perfect accuracy.
    b. only the top row of letters.
    c. only the middle row of letters.
    d. any one of the three rows of letters.

14. The basal ganglia of the brain play a critical role in the formation of
    a. iconic memory.
    b. echoic memory.
    c. procedural memory.
    d. explicit memory.

15. Memory for skills is called
    a. explicit memory.
    b. declarative memory.
    c. prime memory.
    d. implicit memory.

16. The eerie feeling of having been somewhere before is an example of
    a. state dependency.
    b. encoding failure.
    c. priming.
    d. déjà vu.

17. When Gordon Bower presented words grouped by category or in random order, recall was
    a. the same for all words.
    b. better for the categorized words.
    c. better for the random words.
    d. improved when participants developed their own mnemonic devices.

18. The three-stage processing model of memory was proposed by
    a. Atkinson and Shiffrin.
    b. Hermann Ebbinghaus.
    c. Loftus and Palmer.
    d. George Sperling.

19. Hypnotically "refreshed" memories may prove inaccurate—especially if the hypnotist asks leading questions—because of
    a. encoding failure.
    b. state-dependent memory.
    c. proactive interference.
    d. memory construction.

20. Which area of the brain is most important in the processing of implicit memories?
    a. hippocampus
    b. cerebellum
    c. hypothalamus
    d. amygdala

Matching Items

Match each definition or description with the appropriate term.

Definitions or Descriptions

_____ 1. sensory memory that decays more slowly than visual sensory memory

_____ 2. the process by which information gets into the memory system

_____ 3. the blocking of painful memories

_____ 4. the phenomenon in which one's mood can influence retrieval

_____ 5. memory for a list of words is affected by word order

_____ 6. "one is a bun, two is a shoe" mnemonic device

_____ 7. word that chunks to-be-remembered information into a more familiar form

_____ 8. new learning interferes with previous knowledge

_____ 9. a measure of memory

_____ 10. old knowledge interferes with new learning

_____ 11. misattributing the origin of an event

_____ 12. encoding the meaning of words

_____ 13. inability to form new memories

_____ 14. inability to retrieve old memories

Terms

a. repression
b. relearning
c. serial position effect
d. anterograde amnesia
e. peg-word system
f. acronym
g. proactive interference
h. deep processing
i. retroactive interference
j. source amnesia
k. retrograde amnesia
l. mood-congruent memory
m. echoic memory
n. encoding

Progress Test 2

Progress Test 2 should be completed during a final chapter review. Answer the following questions after you thoroughly understand the correct answers for the section reviews and Progress Test 1.

Multiple-Choice Questions

1. Which of the following best describes the typical forgetting curve?
   a. a steady, slow decline in retention over time
   b. a steady, rapid decline in retention over time
   c. a rapid initial decline in retention becoming stable thereafter
   d. a slow initial decline in retention becoming rapid thereafter

2. Jenkins and Dallenbach found that memory was better in people who were
   a. awake during the retention interval, presumably because decay was reduced.
   b. asleep during the retention interval, presumably because decay was reduced.
   c. awake during the retention interval, presumably because interference was reduced.
   d. asleep during the retention interval, presumably because interference was reduced.

3. Which of the following measures of retention is the least sensitive in triggering retrieval?
   a. recall   c. relearning
   b. recognition   d. They are equally sensitive.

4. Amnesia victims typically have experienced damage to the _____ of the brain.
   a. frontal lobes   c. thalamus
   b. cerebellum   d. hippocampus

5. According to the serial position effect, when recalling a list of words you should have the greatest difficulty with those
   a. at the beginning of the list.
   b. at the end of the list.
   c. at the end and in the middle of the list.
   d. in the middle of the list.

6. Experimenters gave people a list of words to be recalled. When the participants were tested after a delay, the items that were best recalled were those
   a. at the beginning of the list.
   b. in the middle of the list.
   c. at the end of the list.
   d. at the beginning and the end of the list.

7. Which type of word processing results in the greatest retention?
   a. shallow
   b. deep
   c. visual
   d. auditory

8. Lashley's studies, in which rats learned a maze and then had various parts of their brains surgically removed, showed that the memory
   a. was lost when surgery took place within 1 hour of learning.
   b. was lost when surgery took place within 24 hours of learning.
   c. was lost when any region of the brain was removed.
   d. partially remained no matter which area of the brain was tampered with.

9. Anterograde amnesia is the inability to
   a. retrieve old memories.
   b. remember where information came from.
   c. form new memories.
   d. hold more than 7 items in working memory.

10. *Long-term potentiation* refers to
    a. the disruptive influence of old memories on the formation of new memories.
    b. the disruptive influence of recent memories on the retrieval of old memories.
    c. our tendency to recall experiences that are consistent with our current mood.
    d. the increased efficiency of synaptic transmission between certain neurons following learning.

11. Repression is an example of
    a. encoding failure.   c. motivated forgetting.
    b. memory decay.   d. all of these things.

12. Studies by Loftus and Palmer, in which people were quizzed about a film of an accident, indicate that
    a. when quizzed immediately, people can recall very little because of the stress of witnessing an accident.
    b. when questioned as little as one day later, their memory was very inaccurate.
    c. most people had very accurate memories as much as 6 months later.
    d. people's recall may easily be affected by misleading information.

13. Which of the following was NOT recommended as a strategy for improving memory?
    a. active rehearsal
    b. distributed study
    c. speed reading
    d. encoding meaningful associations

14. The process of getting information out of memory storage is called
    a. encoding.   c. rehearsal.
    b. retrieval.   d. storage.

15. Amnesia patients typically experience disruption of
    a. implicit memories.   c. iconic memories.
    b. explicit memories.   d. echoic memories.

16. Information is maintained in short-term memory only briefly unless it is
    a. encoded.   c. iconic or echoic.
    b. rehearsed.   d. retrieved.

17. Textbook chapters are often organized into _____ to facilitate information processing.
    a. mnemonic devices   c. hierarchies
    b. chunks   d. recognizable units

18. Memory researchers are suspicious of long-repressed memories of traumatic events that are "recovered" with the aid of drugs or hypnosis because
    a. such experiences usually are vividly remembered.
    b. such memories are unreliable and easily influenced by misinformation.
    c. memories of events happening before about age 3 are especially unreliable.
    d. of all of these reasons.

19. Semantic encoding is a type of
    a. mnemonic.
    b. shallow processing.
    c. deep processing.
    d. echoic memory.

20. The misinformation effect provides evidence that memory
    a. is constructed during encoding.
    b. is unchanging once established.
    c. may be reconstructed during recall according to how questions are framed.
    d. is highly resistant to misleading information.

True–False Items

Indicate whether each statement is true or false by placing *T* or *F* in the blank next to the item.

_____ 1. Studying that is distributed over time produces better retention than cramming.

_____ 2. Preschool children can be induced to report false events through the use of suggestive interview techniques.

_____ 3. Most people do not have memories of events that occurred before the age of 3.

_____ 4. Studies by Ebbinghaus show that most forgetting takes place soon after learning.

_____ 5. The persistence of a memory is a good clue as to whether it derives from an actual experience.

_____ 6. Recall of newly acquired knowledge is no better after sleeping than after being awake for the same period of time.

_____ 7. Time spent in developing imagery, chunking, and associating material with what you already know is more effective than time spent repeating information again and again.

_____ 8. Although repression has not been confirmed experimentally, most psychologists believe it happens.

_____ 9. Overlearning material by continuing to restudy it beyond mastery often disrupts recall.

Essay Question

Discuss the points of agreement among experts regarding the validity of recovered memories of child abuse. (Use the space below to list the points you want to make, and organize them. Then write the essay on a separate piece of paper.)

Terms and Concepts to Remember

Writing Definitions

Using your own words, on a separate piece of paper write a brief definition or explanation of each of the following terms.

1. memory
2. recall
3. recognition
4. relearning
5. encoding
6. storage
7. retrieval
8. sensory memory
9. short-term memory
10. long-term memory
11. working memory
12. explicit memory
13. effortful processing
14. automatic processing
15. implicit memory
16. iconic memory
17. echoic memory
18. chunking
19. mnemonics
20. spacing effect
21. testing effect
22. shallow processing
23. deep processing
24. hippocampus
25. flashbulb memory
26. long-term potentiation
27. priming
28. mood-congruent memory
29. serial position effect
30. anterograde amnesia
31. retrograde amnesia
32. proactive interference
33. retroactive interference

34. repression

35. misinformation effect

36. source amnesia

37. déjà vu

Cross-Check

As you learned in Chapter 1, reviewing and overlearning of material are important to the learning process. After you have written the definitions of the key terms in this chapter, you should complete the crossword puzzle to ensure that you can reverse the process—recognize the term, given the definition.

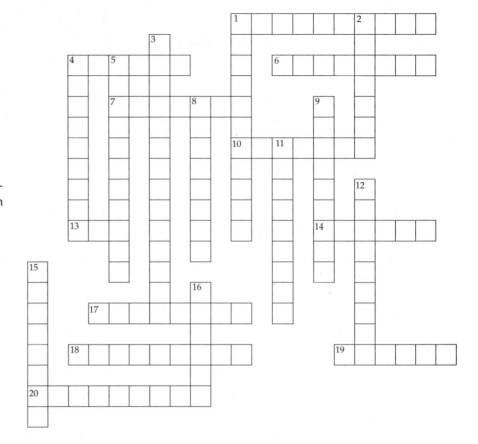

ACROSS

1. Example of motivated forgetting.

4. Sensory memories of auditory stimuli.

6. Encoding of information according to its meaning.

7. Activating associations in order to retrieve a specific memory.

10. Mental pictures.

13. Believed to be the neural basis for learning and memory.

14. Visual sensory memory.

17. Organizing material into familiar, meaningful units.

18. Unusually vivid memory of an emotionally important moment.

19. The false sense of having already experienced a situation.

20. Effortful repetition of information.

DOWN

1. A measure of retention that requires identifying previously learned material.

2. The immediate, initial recording of information in memory.

3. An effect in which eyewitnesses to an event incorporate misleading information in their memories.

4. Type of processing that requires attention and some degree of work.

5. Brain area that processes explicit memories for storage.

8. Type of memory of skills, preferences, and dispositions.

9. Memory aids.

11. Unconscious encoding of incidental information into memory.

12. Type of interference in which old knowledge interferes with new learning.

15. Relatively permanent memory that is unlimited in capacity.

16. Baddeley's model of working memory includes _____ input and auditory rehearsal of new information.

Answers

Chapter Review

Studying Memory

1. memory

2. recall; recognition

3. relearn; more

4. information-processing; encoding; storage; retrieval; sequentially; simultaneously; parallel processing; connectionism; neural networks

5. three stages; sensory memory; short-term; encoded; long-term

6. working; active; central executive; auditory; visual-spatial; long-term

Building Memories: Encoding

7. explicit; declarative; effortful; automatic processing; implicit; nondeclarative memory

8. procedural; classical conditioning

Automatic processing includes the encoding of information about space, time, and frequency. It also includes well-learned information, such as words in your native language.

9. automatic

10. **a.** is the answer.
b., c., & d. Explicit memory, also called declarative memory, is the memory of facts that one can consciously "declare." Nondeclarative memory is what Mr. Flanagan has retained.

11. sensory

12. about half; more; iconic

13. echoic; less; 3 or 4 seconds

14. 7; George Miller

15. rehearsal; active

16. age; focused; distractions

17. **a.** is the answer. Short-term memory capacity is approximately seven digits.
b. Because iconic memory lasts no more than a few tenths of a second, regardless of how much material is experienced, this cannot be the explanation for Brenda's difficulty.
c. The final four digits should be no more difficult to organize into chunks than the first five digits of the address code.
d. Memory for digits is an example of explicit, rather than implicit, memory.

18. chunks

19. mnemonic

20. peg-word

21. acronym

22. chunks; hierarchies

23. Hermann Ebbinghaus; spacing effect

24. distribute; testing effect

25. structure; appearance; shallow processing; semantically; deep processing; Deep

26. meaningful; self-reference

Memory Storage

27. unlimited (limitless)

28. Karl Lashley; cortexes; did

29. frontal

30. hippocampus; explicit; verbal; visual; spatial

31. temporarily; do; deep; cortex; explicit

32. **d.** is the answer.
a., b., & c. Damage to the right side, not the left side, of the hippocampus would cause these types of memory deficits.

33. **c.** is the answer. The hippocampus is involved in processing new facts for storage.
a., b., & d. Brain scans of people recalling words and autopsies of people who had amnesia show that neither classical conditioning nor skill memory are impaired with hippocampus damage, indicating that these aspects of memory are controlled by other regions of the brain.

34. implicit; eyeblink

35. basal ganglia; motor; procedural

36. infantile; have not; hippocampus

37. stress; influence; glucose

38. amygdala; frontal lobes; basal ganglia

39. flashbulb; can

40. **d.** is the answer. Flashbulb memories are unusually clear memories of emotionally significant moments in life.

41. serotonin

42. less; receptor sites; long-term potentiation; drug; enzyme; LTP; faster

43. will not; will

44. glutamate; CREB

Retrieval: Getting Information Out

45. recall; recognize

46. nonsense syllables; overlearning; increases

47. encode

48. priming

49. the same

50. state-dependent; mood-congruent

When happy, for example, we perceive things in a positive light and recall happy events; these perceptions and memories, in turn, prolong our good mood.

51. rejecting, punitive, and guilt promoting; have never suffered depression

52. serial position effect

53. recency; better; primacy

54. **d.** is the answer.

a. & b. To correctly answer either type of question, the knowledge must have been encoded and stored.

c. With fill-in-the-blank questions, the answer must be recalled with no retrieval cues other than the question. With multiple-choice questions, the correct answer merely has to be recognized from among several alternatives.

55. **d.** is the answer.
a. & b. A serial position effect would presumably occur whether the study and retrieval contexts were the same or different.
c. As researchers found, when recall is delayed, only the first items in a list are recalled more accurately than the others. With immediate recall, both the first and last items are recalled more accurately.

56. **c.** is the answer. Susan's memories are affected by her bad mood.
a. Priming refers to the conscious or unconscious activation of particular associations in memory.
b. The spacing effect is the tendency for distributed study to yield better long-term retention than is achieved through massed study.
d. Shallow processing refers only to the idea that words are encoded on a basic level.

57. **a.** is the answer. Priming is the conscious or unconscious activation of particular associations in memory.
b. Mnemonics are are memory aids.
c. That Martina is able to retrieve her former classmates' names implies that they already have been encoded.
d. Relearning is a measure of retention based on how long it takes to relearn something already mastered. Martina is recalling her former classmates' names, not relearning them.

58. **b.** is the answer. Being back in the context in which the original experiences occurred triggered memories of these experiences.
a. The memories were triggered by similarity of place, not mood.
c. Implicit memories are procedural memories for automatic skills and classically conditioned associations.
d. Echoic memory refers to momentary memory of auditory stimuli.

Forgetting

59. forget

60. anterograde amnesia; retrograde amnesia

61. nonverbal tasks; classically conditioned; explicit

62. encoding; enters the memory system

63. encoding; less

64. soon

65. storage decay; memory trace

66. retrieval

67. interference

68. proactive interference; retroactive interference

69. better

70. positive transfer

71. repression

72. less

73. retrieval

74. **b.** is the answer.
a., c., & d. Involvement in other activities, even just eating or listening to music, is more disruptive than sleeping.

75. **a.** is the answer. Proactive interference occurs when old information makes it difficult to recall new information.
b. If Carlos were having trouble remembering the old extension, this answer would be correct.
c. & d. Carlos has successfully encoded and stored the extension; he's just having problems retrieving it.

76. **a.** is the answer.
b. Although Lewis' difficulty in recalling these memories could be considered retrieval failure, it is caused by repression, which is therefore the best explanation.
c. This answer is incorrect because it is clear that Lewis fails to remember these experiences because they are painful memories and not because he is in a different emotional or physiological state.
d. Flashbulb memories are especially vivid memories for emotionally significant events. Lewis has no memory at all.

77. **b.** is the answer. Retroactive interference is the disruption of something you once learned by new information.
a. Proactive interference occurs when old information makes it difficult to correctly remember new information.
c. & d. Interference produces forgetting even when the forgotten material was effectively encoded and stored. Janice's problem is at the level of retrieval.

Memory Construction Errors

78. reconsolidation

79. misinformation effect; can; imagination inflation; activate similar brain areas

When people viewed a film of a traffic accident and were quizzed a week later, phrasing of questions affected answers; the word "smashed," for instance, made viewers mistakenly think they had seen broken glass.

80. source amnesia; misattribute; déjà vu

81. cannot

82. hypnosis

83. **d.** is the answer.
   a. This is an example of proactive interference.
   b. This is an example of the disruptive effects of depressant drugs, such as alcohol, on the formation of new memories.
   c. This is mood-congruent memory.

84. questioned; neutral; nonleading

85. are not

86. 3; infantile amnesia

Improving Memory

87. Survey; Question; Read; Retrieve; Review

Suggestions for improving memory include rehearsing material over many separate and distributed study sessions with the objective of overlearning material. Studying should also involve making the material meaningful rather than mindlessly repeating information. Using mnemonic devices that incorporate vivid imagery is helpful, too. Frequent activation of retrieval cues, such as the context and mood in which the original learning occurred, can also help strengthen memory. Studying should also be arranged to minimize potential sources of interference. And, of course, sleep more, so the brain has a chance to organize and consolidate information. Finally, self-tests in the same format (recall or recognition) that will later be used on the actual test are useful.

Progress Test 1

Multiple-Choice Questions

1. **d.** is the answer. Information must be encoded, or put into appropriate form; stored, or retained over time; and retrieved, or located and gotten out when needed.

2. **a.** is the answer. Iconic memory is our fleeting memory of visual stimuli.
   b. Echoic memory is auditory sensory memory.
   c. There is no such thing as photomemory.
   d. Semantic memory is memory for meaning, not a form of sensory memory.

3. **d.** is the answer. Echoic memories last 3 to 4 seconds.

4. **d.** is the answer. Retrieval refers to the *process* of remembering.

5. **c.** is the answer.

6. **d.** is the answer.
   a. There is no such term as "consolidation techniques."
   b. & c. Imagery and encoding strategies are important in storing new memories, but mnemonic device is the general designation of techniques that facilitate memory, such as acronyms and the peg-word system.

7. **d.** is the answer.
   a. There is no such process of "consolidating."
   b. Organization *does* enhance memory, but it does so through hierarchies, not grouping.
   c. Encoding refers to the processing of information into the memory system.

8. **c.** is the answer. Kandel and Schwartz found that when learning occurred in the sea slug *Aplysia*, serotonin was released at certain synapses, which then became more efficient at signal transmission.

9. **b.** is the answer. In essence, we construct our memories, bringing them into line with our biases and assumptions, as well as with our subsequent experiences.
   a. If this were true, it would mean that memory construction does not occur. Through memory construction, memories may deviate significantly from the original experiences.
   c. There is no evidence that such chemical transfers occur.
   d. Many long-term memories are apparently unlimited in duration.

10. **d.** is the answer. In general, being in a context similar to that in which you experienced something will tend to help you recall the experience.
   a. & b. The learning environment per se—and its familiarity or exoticness—did not affect retention.

11. **a.** is the answer.
   b. & d. The text does not suggest that there is an optimal interval between encoding and retrieval.
   c. Learning increases the efficiency of synaptic transmission in certain neurons, but not by altering the size of the synapse.

12. **c.** is the answer.

13. **d.** is the answer. When asked to recall all the letters, participants could recall only about half; however, if immediately after the presentation they were signaled to recall a particular row, their recall was near perfect. This showed that they had a brief photographic memory—so brief that it faded in less time than it would have taken to say all nine letters.

14. **c.** is the answer.
    a & b. The basal ganglia are involved in motor movement, not visual or auditory sensory memory.
    d. The basal ganglia are involved in the formation of implicit memories, not explicit memories.

15. **d.** is the answer.
    a. & b. Explicit memory (also called declarative memory) is memory of facts and experiences that one can consciously know and declare.
    c. There is no such thing as prime memory.

16. **d.** is the answer.
    a. State-dependent memory is the phenomenon in which information is best retrieved when the person is in the same emotional or physiological state he or she was in when the material was learned.
    b. Encoding failure occurs when a person has not processed information sufficiently for it to enter the memory system.
    c. Priming is the process by which a memory is activated through retrieval of an associated memory.

17. **b.** is the answer. When the words were organized into categories, recall was two to three times better, indicating the benefits of hierarchical organization in memory.
    d. This study did not examine the use of mnemonic devices.

18. **a.** is the answer.
    b. Hermann Ebbinghaus conducted pioneering studies of verbal learning and memory.
    c. Loftus and Palmer conducted influential research studies of eyewitness memory.
    d. George Sperling is known for his research studies of iconic memory.

19. **d.** is the answer. It is in both encoding and retrieval that we construct our memories, and as Loftus' studies showed, leading questions affect people's memory construction.
    a. The memory encoding occurred at the time of the event in question, not during questioning by the hypnotist.
    b. State-dependent memory refers to the influence of one's own emotional or physiological

state on encoding and retrieval, and would not apply here.
    c. Proactive interference is the interfering effect of prior learning on the recall of new information.

20. **b.** is the answer.
    a. The hippocampus is a temporary processing site for *explicit memories.*
    c. & d. These areas of the brain are not directly involved in the memory system.

Matching Items

1. m	**6.** e	**11.** j
2. n	**7.** f	**12.** h
3. a	**8.** i	**13.** d
4. l	**9.** b	**14.** k
5. c	**10.** g	

Progress Test 2

Multiple-Choice Questions

1. **c.** is the answer. As Ebbinghaus and Bahrick both showed, most of the forgetting that is going to occur happens soon after learning.

2. **d.** is the answer.
    a. & b. This study did not find evidence that memories fade (decay) with time.
    c. When one is awake, there are many *more* potential sources of memory interference than when one is asleep.

3. **a.** is the answer. A test of recall presents the fewest retrieval cues and usually produces the most limited retrieval.

4. **d.** is the answer.

5. **d.** is the answer. According to the serial position effect, items at the beginning and end of a list tend to be remembered best.

6. **a.** is the answer.
    b. In the serial position effect, the items in the middle of the list always show the *poorest* retention.
    c. & d. Delayed recall erases the memory facilitation for items at the end of the list.

7. **b.** is the answer.
    a., c., & d. Visual and auditory processing, both of which are examples of shallow processing, are not as effective in enhancing memory formation as deep processing.

8. **d.** is the answer. Surprisingly, Lashley found that no matter where he cut, the rats had at least a partial memory of how to solve the maze.

a. & b. Lashley's studies did not investigate the significance of the interval between learning and cortical lesioning.

9. **c.** is the answer.
   a. This is retrograde amnesia.
   b. This is source amnesia.
   d. The capacity of working memory *averages 7* items.

10. **d.** is the answer.

11. **c.** is the answer. According to Freud, we repress painful memories to preserve our self-concepts.
    a. & b. The fact that repressed memories can sometimes be retrieved suggests that they were encoded and have not decayed with time.

12. **d.** is the answer. When misled by the phrasings of questions, subjects incorrectly recalled details of the film and even "remembered" objects that weren't there.

13. **c.** is the answer. Speed reading, which entails little active rehearsal, yields poor retention.

14. **b.** is the answer.
    a. Encoding is the process of getting information *into* memory.
    c. Rehearsal is the conscious repetition of information in order to maintain it in memory.
    d. Storage is the maintenance of encoded material over time.

15. **b.** is the answer. Amnesia patients typically have suffered damage to the hippocampus, a brain structure involved in processing explicit memories for facts.
    a. Amnesia patients do retain implicit memories for how to do things; these are processed in the cerebellum.
    c. & d. Amnesia patients generally do not experience impairment in their iconic and echoic sensory memories.

16. **b.** is the answer.
    a. Information in short-term memory has *already* been encoded.
    c. Iconic and echoic are types of *sensory* memory.
    d. Retrieval is the process of getting material out of storage and into conscious, short-term memory. Thus, all material in short-term memory has either already been retrieved or is about to be placed in storage.

17. **c.** is the answer. By breaking concepts down into subconcepts and yet smaller divisions and showing the relationships among these, hierarchies facilitate information processing. Use of main heads and subheads is an example of the organization of textbook chapters into hierarchies.

a. Mnemonic devices are the method of loci, acronyms, and other memory *techniques* that facilitate retention.
b. Chunks are organizations of knowledge into familiar, manageable units.
d. Recognition is a measure of retention.

18. **d.** is the answer.

19. **c.** is the answer.
    a. Mnemonics are memory aids such as acronyms and peg-words.
    b. Shallow processing is encoding words on a basic level based on their appearance or some other superficial characteristic.
    d. Echoic memory is the momentary sensory memory of auditory stimuli.

20. **c.** is the answer. Loftus and Palmer found that eyewitness testimony could easily be altered when questions were phrased to imply misleading information.
    a. Although memories *are* constructed during encoding, the misinformation effect is a retrieval, rather than an encoding, phenomenon.
    b. & d. In fact, just the opposite is true.

True–False Items

1.	T	**6.**	F
2.	T	**7.**	T
3.	T	**8.**	F
4.	T	**9.**	F
5.	F		

Essay Question

Experts agree that child abuse is a real problem that can have long-term adverse effects on individuals. They also acknowledge that forgetting of isolated events, both good and bad, is an ordinary part of life. Although experts all accept the fact that recovered memories are commonplace, they warn that memories "recovered" under hypnosis or with the use of drugs are unreliable, as are memories of events before age 3. Finally, they agree that memories can be traumatic, whether real or false.

Terms and Concepts to Remember

Writing Definitions

1. **Memory** is the persistence of learning over time through the storage and retrieval of information.

2. **Recall** is a measure of memory in which the person must retrieve information learned earlier, with few retrieval cues.

3. **Recognition** is a measure of memory in which one need only identify, rather than recall, previously learned information.

4. **Relearning** is a measure of memory that assesses the amount of time saved when learning material again.

5. **Encoding** is the first step in memory; information is translated into some form that enables it to enter our memory system.

6. **Storage** is the process by which encoded information is maintained over time.

7. **Retrieval** is the process of getting information out of memory storage.

8. **Sensory memory** is the immediate, very brief recording of sensory information in the memory system.

9. **Short-term memory** is activated memory, which can hold about seven items for a short time.

10. **Long-term memory** is the relatively permanent and unlimited capacity memory system into which information from short-term memory may pass. It includes knowledge, skills, and experiences.

11. **Working memory** is the newer way of conceptualizing short-term memory as a work site for the active processing of incoming auditory and visual-spatial information, and of information retrieved from long-term memory.

12. **Explicit memories** are memories of facts and experiences that one can consciously know and "declare." They are also called *declarative memories*.

13. **Effortful processing** is encoding that requires attention and conscious effort.

14. **Automatic processing** refers to our unconscious encoding of incidental information, such as space, time, and frequency, and of well-learned information.

15. **Implicit memories** are procedural memories for automatic skills and classically conditioned associations among stimuli. These memories are evidently processed, not by the hippocampus, but by the cerebellum and basal ganglia. They are also called *nondeclarative memories*.

16. **Iconic memory** is the visual sensory memory consisting of a perfect photographic memory, which lasts no more than a few tenths of a second.
    Memory aid: Icon means "image" or "representation." **Iconic memory** consists of brief visual images.

17. **Echoic memory** is the momentary sensory memory of auditory stimuli, lasting about 3 or 4 seconds.

18. **Chunking** is the memory technique of organizing material into familiar, manageable units; often occurs automatically.

19. **Mnemonics** are memory aids (acronyms, pegwords, etc.), which often use vivid imagery and organizational devices.

20. The **spacing effect** is the tendency for distributed study or practice to yield better long-term retention than is achieved through massed study or practice.

21. The **testing effect** is the phenomenon in which memory is enhanced more by retrieval of the information than simply rereading it.

22. **Shallow processing** is encoding words on a basic level based on their appearance or some other superficial characteristic.

23. **Deep processing** is encoding words based on their meaning (semantic encoding); tends to yield the best retention.

24. The **hippocampus** is a temporal lobe neural center located in the limbic system that is important in the processing of explicit memories for storage.

25. A **flashbulb memory** is an unusually vivid memory of an emotionally important moment or event.

26. **Long-term potentiation (LTP)** is an increase in a cell's firing potential following brief, rapid stimulation. LTP is believed to be the neural basis for learning and memory.

27. **Priming** is the activation, often unconsciously, of a web of associations in memory in order to retrieve a specific memory.

28. **Mood-congruent memory** is the tendency to recall experiences that are consistent with our current mood.

29. The **serial position effect** is the tendency for items at the beginning (a primacy effect) and end (a recency effect) of a list to be more easily retained than those in the middle.

30. **Anterograde amnesia** is an inability to form new memories.

31. **Retrograde amnesia** is an inability to retrieve old memories.

32. **Proactive interference** is the disruptive effect of something you already have learned on your efforts to learn or recall new information.

33. **Retroactive interference** is the disruptive effect of new learning on the recall of old knowledge.

    Memory aid: Retro means "backward." **Retroactive interference** is "backward-acting" interference.

34. **Repression** is an example of motivated forgetting in that anxiety-arousing thoughts, feelings, and memories are prevented from entering consciousness. In psychoanalytic theory, it is the basic defense mechanism.

35. The **misinformation effect** is the tendency of eyewitnesses to an event to incorporate misleading information into their memories of the event.

36. At the heart of many false memories (along with the misinformation effect), **source amnesia** refers to attributing an event to the wrong source. (Also called *source misattribution*.)

37. **Déjà vu** is the false sense that you have already experienced a current situation.

Cross-Check

ACROSS
1. repression
4. echoic
6. semantic
7. priming
10. imagery
13. LTP
14. iconic
17. chunking
18. flashbulb
19. déjà vu
20. rehearsal

DOWN
1. recognition
2. sensory
3. misinformation
4. effortful
5. hippocampus
8. implicit
9. mnemonics
11. automatic
12. proactive
15. long-term
16. visual

Thinking, Language, and Intelligence

Chapter Overview

The first part of Chapter 9 deals with thinking, with emphasis on how people logically—or at times illogically—use tools such as algorithms and heuristics when making decisions and solving problems. Also discussed are several common obstacles to problem solving, including fixations that prevent us from taking a fresh perspective on a problem and our bias to search for information that confirms rather than challenges existing hypotheses. The section also discusses the power and perils of intuition and the meaning and development of creativity. It concludes with an exploration of animal cognitive skills.

The next section is concerned with language, including its structure, development in children, relationship to thinking, and use by animals. The section introduces Skinner's view that language develops through association, imitation, and reinforcements, as well as Chomsky's theory that humans have a biological predisposition to acquire language. The section also describes the brain's role in language processing and speech.

An ongoing controversy in psychology involves attempts to define and measure intelligence. The chapter discusses whether intelligence is a single general ability or several specific ones. It also describes the historical origins of intelligence tests and discusses several important issues concerning their use. These include the methods by which intelligence tests are constructed and whether such tests are valid, reliable, and free of bias. The chapter also explores extremes of intelligence, how aging affects (or doesn't affect) intelligence, and the extent of genetic and environmental influences on intelligence.

NOTE: Answer guidelines for all Chapter 9 questions begin on page 226.

Chapter Review

First, skim each section, noting headings and boldface items. After you have read the section, review each objective by answering the fill-in and essay-type questions that follow it. Study Tips explain how best to learn a difficult concept and Applications help you to know how well you understand the material. As you proceed, evaluate your performance by consulting the answers beginning on page 226. Do not continue with the next section until you understand each answer. If you need to, review or reread the section in the textbook before continuing.

Thinking

Objective 9-1: Define *cognition*, and describe the functions of concepts.

1. Cognition, or _____ , can be defined as _____
   _____ .

2. People tend to organize specific items into mental groupings called_____ .

3. Concepts are typically formed through the development of a best example, or
   _____ , of a category. People more easily detect _____
   (male/female) prejudice against
   _____ (males/females) than vice versa.

APPLICATION:

4. Complete the following analogy: Rose is to flower as
   a. concept is to prototype.
   b. prototype is to concept.
   c. concept is to cognition.
   d. cognition is to concept.

Objective 9-2: Describe the cognitive strategies that assist our problem solving, and identify the obstacles that hinder it.

5. Humans are especially capable of using their reasoning powers for coping with new situations, and thus for _____

   _____ .

6. When we try each possible solution to a problem, we are using _____

   _____ _____ .

7. Logical, methodical, step-by-step procedures for solving problems are called

   _____ .

8. Simple thinking strategies that provide us with problem-solving shortcuts are referred to as

   _____ .

9. When you suddenly realize a problem's solution, _____ has occurred. Research studies show that such moments are preceded by _____

   _____ activity involved in focusing attention and accompanied by a burst of activity in the _____

   _____ _____ .

10. The tendency of people to look for information that supports their preconceptions is called

    _____ _____ .

11. It is human nature to seek evidence that _____ our ideas more eagerly than to seek evidence that might _____ them.

12. Not being able to take a new perspective when attempting to solve a problem is referred to as _____ . One example of this obstacle to problem solving is the tendency to repeat solutions that have worked previously; this phenomenon is known as the development of a

    _____ _____ .

STUDY TIP/APPLICATION: We all use any of four techniques for solving problems: trial and error, algorithms, heuristics, and insight. To test your understanding of these approaches, apply them to a problem you might actually face, such as finding a misplaced set of car keys. Using the chart below, see if you can come up with an example of how you could find your keys using each of the four problem-solving approaches.

13. Problem-Solving Approach	How You Would Find Car Keys Using Each Method
a. Trial and error	
b. Algorithm	
c. Heuristics	
d. Insight	

APPLICATIONS:

14. A dessert recipe that gives you the ingredients, their amounts, and the steps to follow is an example of a(n)

    a. prototype.   **c.** heuristic.
    b. algorithm.   **d.** mental set.

15. Boris the chess master selects his next move by considering moves that would threaten his opponent's queen. His opponent, a chess-playing computer, selects its next move by considering *all* possible moves. Boris is using a(n) _____ and the computer is using a(n) _____ .

    a. algorithm; heuristic

b. prototype; mental set
c. mental set; prototype
d. heuristic; algorithm

16. Experts in a field prefer heuristics to algorithms because heuristics

    a. guarantee solutions to problems.
    b. prevent mental sets.
    c. often save time.
    d. prevent fixation.

Objective 9-3: Explain what is meant by intuition, and describe how the availability heuristic, overconfidence, belief perseverance, and framing influence our decisions and judgments.

17. Effortless, immediate, and automatic feelings or thoughts characterize our _____ .

18. When we judge the likelihood of something occurring in terms of how readily it comes to mind, we are using the _____

_____ .

Explain how this heuristic may lead us to make judgmental errors.

19. (Thinking Critically) Many people fear

_____ more than _____ ,

despite the fact that these fears are not supported by death and injury statistics. This type of faulty thinking occurs because we fear

    a. _____
    b. _____
    c. _____
    d. _____

20. The tendency of people to overestimate the accuracy of their knowledge results in

_____ .

21. Overconfidence has _____ value because self-confident people tend to live _____ (more/less) happily, find it _____ (easier/harder) to make

tough decisions, and seem _____ (more/less) credible.

22. When research participants are given feedback on the accuracy of their judgments, such feedback generally _____ (helps/does not help) them become more realistic about how much they know.

23. Research has shown that once we form a belief or a concept, it may take more convincing evidence for us to change the concept than it did to create it; this is because of _____

_____ .

24. A cure for this is to _____

_____ _____ .

25. The way an issue is posed is called _____ . This effect influences political and business decisions, suggesting that our judgments _____ (may/may not) always be well reasoned.

APPLICATIONS:

26. During a televised political debate, the Republican and Democratic candidates each argued that the results of a recent public opinion poll supported their party's platform regarding sexual harassment. Because both candidates saw the information as supporting their belief, it is clear that both were victims of

    a. fixation.
    b. mental set.
    c. belief perseverance.
    d. confirmation bias.

27. In relation to ground beef, consumers respond more positively to an ad describing it as "75 percent lean" than to one referring to its "25 percent fat" content. This is an example of

    a. the framing effect.   **c.** mental set.
    b. confirmation bias.   **d.** overconfidence.

28. Most people tend to

    a. accurately estimate the accuracy of their knowledge and judgments.
    b. underestimate the accuracy of their knowledge and judgments.
    c. overestimate the accuracy of their knowledge and judgments.
    d. lack confidence in their decision-making strategies.

29. Dominic is certain that he will be able to finish reading the assigned text chapter over the weekend even though he also has to write a five-page essay on the U.S. political process and will be going to a party on Saturday night. If he's like most people, Dominic
    a. is accurate in knowing how much he can do over the weekend.
    b. underestimates how much he'll get done over the weekend.
    c. overestimates how much he can get done over the weekend.

30. Which of the following illustrates belief perseverance?
    a. Your belief remains intact even in the face of evidence to the contrary.
    b. You refuse to listen to arguments counter to your beliefs.
    c. You tend to become flustered and angered when your beliefs are refuted.
    d. You tend to search for information that supports your beliefs.

31. Marilyn was asked to solve a series of five math problems. The first four problems could only be solved by a particular sequence of operations. The fifth problem could also be solved following this sequence; however, a much simpler solution was possible. Marilyn did not realize this simpler solution and solved the problem in the way she had solved the first four. Her problem-solving strategy was hampered by
    a. fixation.
    b. the overconfidence phenomenon.
    c. mental set.
    d. her lack of a prototype for the solution.

32. The number of airline reservations typically declines after a highly publicized airplane crash because people overestimate the incidence of such disasters. In such instances, their decisions are being influenced by
    a. belief perseverance.
    b. the availability heuristic.
    c. mental set.
    d. fixation.

Objective 9-4: Describe how smart thinkers use intuition.

33. Researchers have shown that in making complex decisions, we benefit from using _____ (rational/intuitive) thinking. Although critics disagree, letting a problem "_____" while we attend to other things can pay dividends.

34. Another advantage of intuition is that it enables us to react quickly, which is _____ .

35. Finally, intuition is _____ knowledge, resulting from experience.

Objective 9-5: Define *creativity*, and describe how creativity is fostered.

36. The ability to produce ideas that are both novel and valuable is called _____ .

37. Standard intelligence tests, which demand single correct answers to questions, measure _____ thinking. Tests that allow multiple possible answers to problems measure _____ thinking.

Describe five components of creativity other than aptitude (the ability to learn).

(Close-Up) Describe research findings on how to foster creativity.

APPLICATION:

38. Vanessa is a very creative sculptress. We would expect that Vanessa also
    a. scores well on aptitude tests, which require convergent thinking.
    b. tries to solve problems in ways that worked before.
    c. has a venturesome personality and is intrinsically motivated.
    d. lacks expertise in most other skills.

Objective 9-6: Describe what is known about animal thinking.

39. Animals are capable of forming _____ . Wolfgang Köhler demonstrated that chimpanzees also exhibit the "Aha!" reaction that characterizes reasoning by _____ .

40. Forest-dwelling chimpanzees learn to use different sticks as _____ . These behaviors, along with behaviors related to grooming and courtship, _____ (vary/do not vary) from one group of chimpanzees to another, suggesting the transmission of _____ customs.

41. Animals _____ (do/do not) have many other cognitive skills. For example, chimpanzees have demonstrated _____ , _____ , and group aggression.

Language

Objective 9-7: Describe the structural components of a language.

42. Language is defined as _____
_____ .

43. The smallest distinctive sound units of language are its _____ . English has approximately _____ of these units.

44. Phonemes are grouped into units of meaning called _____ .

45. The system of rules that enables us to use our language to speak to and understand others is called _____ .

APPLICATIONS:

46. The word "predates" contains _____ phonemes and _____ morphemes.
a. 7; 3   **c.** 7; 2
b. 3; 7   **d.** 3; 2

47. The sentence "Blue jeans wear false smiles" has correct _____ but incorrect _____ .
a. morphemes; phonemes
b. phonemes; morphemes
c. semantics; syntax
d. syntax; semantics

Objective 9-8: Identify the milestones in language development, and describe how we acquire language.

48. By _____ months of age, babies can read lips and discriminate speech sounds. This marks the beginning of their _____ _____ , their ability to comprehend speech. This ability begins to mature before their

_____ _____ , or ability to produce words.

49. The first stage of language development, in which children spontaneously utter different sounds, is the _____ stage. This stage typically begins at about _____ months of age. The sounds children make during this stage _____ (do/do not) include only the sounds of the language they hear.

50. Deaf infants _____ (do/do not) babble with their hands. Many natural babbling sounds are _____-_____ pairs formed by _____ .

51. By about _____ months of age, infant babbling begins to resemble the household language. At about the same time, the ability to perceive speech sounds outside their native language is _____ (lost/acquired).

52. During the second stage, called the _____-_____ stage, children convey complete thoughts using single words. This stage begins at about _____ year(s) of age.

53. During the _____-_____ stage, children speak in sentences containing mostly nouns and verbs. This type of speech is called _____ speech. It _____ (does/does not) follow the rules of syntax.

54. The theorist who believed that language development could be explained by principles of learning was_____ . These familiar learning principles include _____ , _____ , and _____ .

55. According to linguist _____ , all human languages have the same grammatical building blocks, which suggests that there is a _____ _____ .

56. Research studies of infants' knack for soaking up language suggest that babies come with a built-in readiness to learn _____ _____ .

57. Childhood seems to represent a _____ _____ for mastering certain aspects of language. Those who learn a second language as adults usually speak it with the _____ of their first language. Moreover, they typically show _____ (poorer/better) mastery of the _____ of the second language.

58. The window for learning language gradually begins to close after age _____ . When a young brain doesn't learn any language, its language-learning capacity _____ (never/may still) fully develop(s).

59. People who learn sign language as teens or adults _____ (eventually do/do not) learn to sign as fluently as those who learned sign as infants.

APPLICATIONS:

60. A listener hearing a recording of Japanese, Spanish, and North American children babbling would
    a. not be able to tell them apart.
    b. be able to tell them apart if they were older than 6 months.
    c. be able to tell them apart if they were older than 8 to 10 months.
    d. be able to tell them apart at any age.

61. The child who says "Milk gone" is engaging in _____ . This type of utterance demonstrates that children are actively experimenting with the rules of _____ .
    a. babbling; syntax
    b. telegraphic speech; syntax
    c. babbling; semantics
    d. telegraphic speech; semantics

62. In preparing her class presentation, "Updating Chomsky's Understanding of Language Development," Britney's outline includes all of the following evidence, EXCEPT that
    a. computers programmed to learn to form the past tense of irregular verbs can learn to do so, even without "inborn" linguistic rules.
    b. infants rapidly learn to detect subtle differences between simple sequences of syllables.
    c. no matter what language they learn, children start speaking it mostly in verbs and adjectives.
    d. children isolated from language during the first seven years of life never fully develop language.

Objective 9-9: Identify the brain areas involved in language processing and speech.

63. Brain injuries may produce an impairment in language use called _____ . Studies of people with such impairments have shown that
    (a) _____ _____ is involved in producing speech and (b) _____ _____ is involved in understanding speech.

(a) **Speaking words** (_____ and the motor cortex)

64. Although our conscious experience of language seems indivisible, functional MRI scans show that different _____ _____ are activated by nouns and verbs, or objects and actions, for example.

(b) **Hearing words** (auditory cortex and _____)

65. As in other forms of information processing, the brain operates by dividing its mental functions into _____ .

APPLICATION:

66. In a soccer game, Laura suffered damage to her left temporal lobe. As a result, she is unable to speak in meaningful sentences. The damage affected
    a. Wernicke's area.
    b. Broca's area.
    c. the hypothalamus.
    d. the hippoccampus.

Objective 9-10: Discuss whether other species share our capacity for language.

67. Animals definitely _____ (do/do not) communicate.

68. The Gardners attempted to communicate with the chimpanzee Washoe by teaching her _____ _____ .

69. Most now agree that humans _____ (alone/along with primates) possess language that involves complex grammar.

Summarize some of the arguments of skeptics of the "talking apes" research and some responses of believers.

Summarize the probable relationship between thinking and language.

Thinking and Language

Objective 9-11: Describe the relationship between language and thinking, and discuss the value of thinking in images.

70. According to the _____ _____ hypothesis, language shapes our thinking. The linguist who proposed this hypothesis is _____ .

71. Although this hypothesis is too extreme, many people who are bilingual report feeling a different sense of _____ , depending on which language they are using.

72. In several studies, researchers have found that using the pronoun "he" (instead of "he or she") _____ (does/does not) influence people's thoughts concerning gender.

73. Bilingual children, who learn to inhibit one language while using their other language, are better able to inhibit their _____ to irrelevant information. This has been called the _____ _____ .

74. One study of Canadian children found that English-speaking children who were _____ in French had higher _____ scores and math scores than control children.

75. It appears that thinking _____ (can/cannot) occur without the use of language. Athletes often supplement physical training with _____ practice.

76. In one study of psychology students preparing for a midterm exam, the greatest benefits were achieved by those who used _____ (outcome/process) simulation and visualized themselves _____ (receiving a high grade/studying effectively).

APPLICATION:

77. Luke is the back-up quarterback for his high school football team. The starting quarterback has been injured, so Luke will play on Saturday. In addition to physical practice, Luke should visualize throwing the ball, a process called

_____ _____ ,

rather than seeing a touchdown noted on the scoreboard, called _____

_____ .

Intelligence

Objective 9-12: Describe how psychologists define *intelligence*, and identify the arguments for *g*.

78. Psychologists _____ (do/do not) agree on a definition of intelligence.

79. Psychologists agree that intelligence is a _____ and not a "thing." It has been defined as whatever _____ _____ measure, but that _____ (does/does not) take into account the different qualities that enable success in different cultures.

80. In any context, intelligence can be defined as ____ _____ .

81. The statistical procedure used to identify clusters of items that appear to measure a common ability is called _____ _____ .

82. Charles Spearman, using this technique, believed that a factor called *g*, or _____ _____ , runs through the more specific aspects of intelligence.

Objective 9-13: Compare Gardner's and Sternberg's theories of intelligence.

83. People with _____ _____ score at the low end of intelligence tests but possess extraordinary specific skills.

84. Howard Gardner proposes that there are _____ _____ , each independent of the others.

85. Sternberg's _____ theory distinguishes three types of intelligence: _____ intelligence, _____ intelligence, and _____ intelligence.

86. Critics of theories of multiple intelligences point out that the world is not so just: Using factor analysis, recent research has _____ (confirmed/refuted) the idea that there is a general intelligence factor that predicts performance on various complex tasks and in various jobs. Even so, success requires a combination of talent and _____ .

APPLICATIONS:

87. Melvin is limited in mental ability but has an exceptional ability to play complex music on the piano after hearing it only once. He has been diagnosed as having

_____ _____ .

88. Don's intelligence scores were only average, but he has been enormously successful as a corporate manager. Psychologists Sternberg and Wagner would probably suggest that
   a. Don's verbal intelligence exceeds his performance intelligence.
   b. Don's performance intelligence exceeds his verbal intelligence.
   c. Don's academic intelligence exceeds his practical intelligence.
   d. Don's practical intelligence exceeds his academic intelligence.

Objective 9-14: Describe the four components of emotional intelligence.

89. The know-how involved in comprehending social situations and managing oneself successfully differs from _____ intelligence and is referred to as _____ intelligence.

90. A critical part of social intelligence is _____ _____ —the ability to _____ , _____ , _____ , and _____ emotions.

91. More specifically, the four components of emotional intelligence are as follows: the ability to _____ emotions in faces, the ability to _____ them and how they change and blend, the ability to _____ them correctly in varied situations, and the ability to use them to enable _____ or creative thinking.

Briefly describe emotionally intelligent people.

92. Some scholars believe that the concept of _____ intelligence stretches the idea of multiple intelligences too far.

APPLICATION:

93. Gerardeen has superb social skills, manages conflicts well, and has great empathy for her friends and co-workers. Researchers would probably say that Gerardeen possesses a high degree of

_____ _____ .

Objective 9-15: Discuss the history of intelligence testing, and explain how today's tests differ from early intelligence tests.

94. Tests designed to measure what you already have learned are called _____ tests. Tests designed to predict your ability to learn something new are called _____ tests.

95. The French psychologist who devised a test to predict the success of children in school was _____ . Predictions were made by comparing children's chronological ages with

their _____ ages, which were determined by the test. This test _____ (was/was not) designed to measure inborn intelligence. Binet's collaborator was

_____ .

96. Lewis Terman's revision of Binet's test is referred to as the _____ - _____ . From this test, _____ derived the famous _____ _____ , or _____ .

Give the original formula for computing IQ, and explain any items used in the formula.

97. Today's tests compute _____ (IQ/ an intelligence test score) by comparing the individual's performance to the average performance of people of _____ (the same/different) age(s). These tests are designed so that a score of _____ is considered average.

98. The most widely used intelligence test is the

_____ _____

_____ _____ .

Consisting of 15 subtests, it provides not only a general intelligence score but also separate scores for _____ _____ ,

_____ _____ ,

_____ _____ , and

_____ _____ .

APPLICATIONS:

99. Before becoming attorneys, law students must pass a special licensing exam, which is an _____ test. Before entering college, high school students must take the SAT Reasoning Test, which is an _____ test.

100. Benito was born in 1937. In 1947, he scored 130 on an intelligence test. Using the original IQ formula, Benito's mental age when he took the test was _____ .

101. If asked to guess the intelligence score of a stranger, your best guess would be

_____ .

Objective 9-16: Describe a normal curve, and explain what is meant when we say that a test has been standardized and is reliable and valid.

102. One requirement of a good test is the process of defining meaningful scores relative to a pretested comparison group, which is called

_____ .

103. When scores on a test are compiled, they generally result in a bell-shaped pattern called the _____ curve.

Describe this bell-shaped pattern, and explain its significance in the standardization process.

104. If a test yields consistent results, it is said to be

_____ .

105. The Stanford-Binet, WAIS, and WISC have reliabilities of about _____ .

106. The degree to which a test measures or predicts what it is supposed to is referred to as the test's

_____ .

107. The degree to which a test measures the behavior it was designed to measure, or _____ , is referred to as the test's _____ _____ .

108. The degree to which a test predicts future performance of a particular behavior is referred to as the test's _____ _____ .

Choose a specific example and use it to illustrate and explain the concept of criterion and its relationship to test validity.

109. Generally speaking, the predictive validity of general aptitude tests _____ (is/is not) as high as their reliability. The predictive validity of these tests _____ (increases/diminishes) as individuals move up the educational ladder.

APPLICATIONS:

110. If you wanted to develop a test of musical aptitude in North American children, which would be the appropriate standardization group?
   a. children all over the world
   b. North American children
   c. children of musical parents
   d. children with known musical ability

111. Jack takes the same test of mechanical reasoning on several different days and gets virtually identical scores. This suggests that the test has
   a. high content validity.
   b. high reliability.
   c. high predictive validity.
   d. been standardized.

112. You would not use a test of hearing ability as an intelligence test because it would lack
   a. content reliability.
   b. predictive reliability.
   c. predictive validity.
   d. content validity.

113. A school psychologist found that 85 percent of those who scored above 115 on an aptitude test were A students and 75 percent of those who scored below 85 on the test were D students. The psychologist concluded that the test had
   a. a high degree of standardization because scores on it correlated highly with the criterion behavior.

   b. high validity because scores on it correlated highly with the criterion behavior.
   c. high reliability because the test yielded inconsistent results.
   d. high reliability because the test yielded consistent results.

Objective 9-17: Describe the traits of those at the low and high intelligence extremes.

114. (Close-Up) Individuals whose intelligence scores fall below 70 and who have difficulty adapting to life may be labeled _____ _____ .

115. (Close-Up) An intellectual disability sometimes has a physical basis, such as _____ _____ , a genetic disorder caused by an extra chromosome.

116. (Close-Up) The current view is that people with an intellectual disability might be better able to live independently today because tests have been periodically _____ and those individuals suddenly lost 6 IQ points.

117. (Close-Up) At the high extreme, Lewis Terman's "gifted children" turned out to be _____ , well-_____ , and unusually successful _____ .

APPLICATION:

118. Twenty-two-year-old Dan has an intelligence score of 63 and the academic skills of a fourth-grader and is unable to live independently. Dan *probably*
   a. is in the middle of the normal curve for intelligence test scores.
   b. has savant syndrome.
   c. is intellectually disabled.
   d. will eventually achieve self-supporting social and vocational skills.

Objective 9-18: Describe how aging affects crystallized and fluid intelligence.

119. The accumulation of knowledge and verbal skills is referred to as _____ intelligence.

120. The ability to reason speedily and abstractly is referred to as _____ intelligence.

121. During adulthood, _____ intelligence declines beginning in the _____ and _____ , slowly until about age _____ , and then more rapidly, especially after about age _____ . To study the way intelligence and other traits change with age, developmental psychologists use _____ (cross-sectional/longitudinal) studies to restudy the same group at different times across their life span and _____ (cross-sectional/longitudinal) studies to compare members of different age groups at the same time.

122. Although _____ intelligence may decline with age, older adults' _____ _____ increases. Also, their decisions becomes less distorted by _____ _____ .

Objective 9-19: Discuss the evidence for a genetic influence on intelligence, and explain what is meant by heritability.

123. The intelligence scores of identical twins reared together are _____ (more/no more) similar than those of fraternal twins. Brain scans also reveal that identical twins have similar volume to their brain's _____ and _____ matter, and those areas associated with _____ and _____ intelligence.

124. The amount of variation in a trait within a group that is attributed to genetic factors is called its _____ . For intelligence, estimates range from _____ to _____ percent.

125. Identical twins exhibit substantial similarity (and _____) in specific talents.

126. Because intelligence is influenced by many genes, it is said to be _____ .

127. Where environments differ widely, as they do among children of _____ - _____ parents, environmental differences are _____ (more/less) predictive of intelligence scores.

128. Studies of adopted children and their adoptive and biological families demonstrate that with age, genetic influences on intelligence become _____ (more/less) apparent.

Thus, children's intelligence scores are more like those of their _____ (biological/adoptive) parents than their _____ (biological/adoptive) parents.

STUDY TIP: Heritability is a difficult concept to grasp in part because it is often confused with genetic determination, which refers to what causes a characteristic to develop. The number of toes on your feet is genetically determined because your genes cause five toes to develop on each foot. Heritability, on the other hand, is what causes differences in a characteristic. To say that the heritability of intelligence is 50 percent does not mean that half of an individual's intelligence is inherited. Rather, it means that we can attribute to heredity 50 percent of the variation of intelligence among those studied. A good way to keep the two concepts straight is to remember that while the concept of genetic determination makes sense in the case of a single person, heritability does not. Genetic determination is biological; heritability is a statistical measure. Heritability only makes sense relative to differences among groups of people. It doesn't make sense to ask, "What's the heritability of my intelligence?"

APPLICATIONS:

129. Raoul and Fidel are identical twins separated at birth. Because they have similar heredity and different environments, heritability for their intelligence is likely to be _____ (high/low). Ramona was adopted by Francesa's parents when she was 2 months old. The heritability for their intelligence is likely to be _____ (high/low).

130. If you compare the same trait in people of similar heredity who live in very different environments, heritability for that trait will be _____ ; heritability for the trait is most likely to be _____ among people of very different heredities who live in similar environments.
    a. low; high
    b. high; low
    c. environmental; genetic
    d. genetic; environmental

Objective 9-20: Discuss the evidence for environmental influences on intelligence.

131. Studies indicate that neglected children _____ (do/do not) show signs of recovery in intelligence and behavior when placed in more nurturing environments.

132. Although normal brain development can be retarded by _____ , _____ deprivation, and

_____ _____ , there is no sure environment that will transform a normal baby into a genius.

133. Two factors that interact in promoting income are _____ and

_____ .

Objective 9-21: Describe how and why the genders differ in mental ability scores.

134. Girls tend to outscore boys on _____ tests and are more _____ fluent. They also have an edge in _____ objects, in sensation, in _____-detecting ability, and in sensitivity to _____ , _____ , and _____ .

135. Although boys and girls hardly differ in math _____ , boys score higher in _____ _____ and complex _____ _____ .

136. Working from an _____ perspective, some theorists speculate that these gender differences in spatial manipulation helped our ancestors survive.

Objective 9-22: Describe how and why racial and ethnic groups differ in mental ability scores.

137. Group differences in intelligence scores _____ (do/do not) provide an accurate basis for judging individuals. Individual differences within a race are _____ (greater than/less than) between-race differences.

Explain why heredity may contribute to individual differences in intelligence but not necessarily contribute to group differences.

138. Under the skin, the races _____ (are/are not) alike. Race _____ (is/is not) a neatly defined biological category.

139. The intelligence test performance of today's population exceeds that of the 1930s population because they are better-_____ , better-_____ , and more _____-_____ .

APPLICATION:

140. The contribution of environmental factors to racial gaps in intelligence scores is indicated by
    a. evidence that individual differences within a race are much greater than differences between races.
    b. evidence that when Whites and Blacks receive pertinent information, they exhibit similar information-processing skills.
    c. the fact that Asian students outperform North American students on math achievement and aptitude tests.
    d. all of this evidence.

Objective 9-23: Discuss whether intelligence tests are inappropriately biased.

141. In the sense that they detect differences caused by cultural experiences, intelligence tests probably _____ (are/are not) biased.

142. Most psychologists agree that, in terms of predictive validity, the major aptitude tests _____ (are/are not) racially biased.

143. When women and members of ethnic minorities are led to expect that they won't do well on a test, a _____ _____ may result, and their scores may actually be lower.

APPLICATION:

144. According to the text, what can be concluded from early intelligence testing in the United States?
    a. Most European immigrants were "feeble-minded."
    b. Army recruits of other than West European heritage were intellectually deficient.
    c. The tests were biased against people who did not share the culture assumed by the test.
    d. None of these things could be concluded.

Progress Test 1

Multiple-Choice Questions

Circle your answers to the following questions and check them with the answers beginning on page 231. If your answer is incorrect, read the explanation for why it is incorrect and then consult the text.

1. The text defines *cognition* as
   a. silent speech.
   b. all mental activity.
   c. the mental activities associated with thinking, knowing, remembering, and communicating information.
   d. logical reasoning.

2. A mental grouping of similar things, events, or people is called a(n)
   a. prototype.   c. algorithm.
   b. concept.   d. heuristic.

3. When forming a concept, people often develop a best example, or _____ , of a category.
   a. denoter   c. prototype
   b. heuristic   d. algorithm

4. Confirmation bias refers to the tendency to
   a. allow preexisting beliefs to distort logical reasoning.
   b. cling to one's initial conceptions after the basis on which they were formed has been discredited.
   c. search randomly through alternative solutions when problem solving.
   d. look for information that is consistent with one's beliefs.

5. The English language has approximately _____ phonemes.
   a. 25   c. 40
   b. 30   d. 45

6. Which of the following is NOT true of babbling?
   a. It is imitation of adult speech.
   b. It is the same in all cultures.
   c. It typically occurs from about age 4 months to 1 year.
   d. Babbling increasingly comes to resemble a particular language.

7. Mental set is an example of a(n)
   a. algorithm.   c. fixation.
   b. heuristic.   d. insight.

8. Which of the following has been argued by critics of ape language research?
   a. Ape language is merely imitation of the trainer's behavior.
   b. There is little evidence that apes can equal even a 3-year-old's ability to order words with proper syntax.
   c. By seeing what they wish to see, trainers attribute greater linguistic ability to apes than actually exists.
   d. All of these are arguments by critics.

9. Whorf's linguistic determinism hypothesis states that
   a. language is primarily a learned ability.
   b. language is partially an innate ability.
   c. the size of a person's vocabulary reflects his or her intelligence.
   d. our language shapes our thinking.

10. Which of the following BEST describes Chomsky's view of language development?
    a. Language is an entirely learned ability.
    b. Language is an innate ability.
    c. Humans have a biological predisposition to acquire language.
    d. There are no cultural influences on the development of language.

11. Thoughts and feelings that are automatic, effortless, immediate, and unreasoned are examples of
    a. mental set.
    b. confirmation bias.
    c. heuristics.
    d. intuition.

12. Which of the following is an example of the use of heuristics?
    a. trying every possible letter ordering when unscrambling a word
    b. considering each possible move when playing chess
    c. using the formula "area = length × width" to find the area of a rectangle
    d. playing chess using a defensive strategy that has often been successful for you

13. The chimpanzee Sultan used a short stick to pull a longer stick that was out of reach into his cage. He then used the longer stick to reach a piece of fruit. Researchers hypothesized that Sultan's discovery of the solution to his problem was the result of
    a. trial and error.   c. fixation.
    b. heuristics.   d. insight.

14. Damage to _____ will usually cause a person to lose the ability to comprehend language.
    a. any area of the brain
    b. Broca's area
    c. Wernicke's area
    d. frontal lobe association areas

15. Researchers who are convinced that animals can think point to evidence that
    a. chimpanzees demonstrate the ability to "count" by learning to touch pictures of objects in ascending numerical order.
    b. chimpanzees regularly use sticks as tools in their natural habitats.
    c. chimps invent grooming and courtship customs and pass them on to their peers.
    d. they exhibit all of these skills.

16. Deaf children who are not exposed to sign language until they are teenagers
    a. are unable to master the basic words of sign language.
    b. learn the basic words but not how to order them.
    c. are unable to master either the basic words or syntax of sign language.
    d. never become as fluent as those who learned to sign at a younger age.

17. According to the text, language acquisition is best described as
    a. the result of conditioning and reinforcement.
    b. a biological process of maturation.
    c. an interaction between biology and experience.
    d. a mystery of which researchers have no real understanding.

18. The linguistic determinism hypothesis is challenged by the finding that
    a. chimps can learn to communicate spontaneously by using sign language.
    b. people with no word for a certain color can still perceive that color accurately.
    c. the Eskimo language contains a number of words for snow, whereas English has only one.
    d. infants' babbling contains many phonemes that do not occur in their own language and that they therefore cannot have heard.

19. Several studies have indicated that the generic *he*
    a. tends for children and adults alike to trigger images of both males and females.
    b. tends for adults to trigger images of both males and females, but for children to trigger images of males.
    c. tends for both children and adults to trigger images of males but not females.
    d. for both children and adults triggers images of females about one-fourth of the time it is used.

20. Studies of adopted children and their biological and adoptive families demonstrate that with age, genetic influences on intelligence
    a. become more apparent.
    b. become less apparent.
    c. become more difficult to disentangle from environmental influences.
    d. become easier to disentangle from environmental influences.

21. A 6-year-old child has a mental age of 9. The child's IQ is
    a. 96.   c. 125.
    b. 100.   d. 150.

22. Which of the following is NOT true?
    a. In math grades, the average girl typically equals the average boy.
    b. The gender gap in math and science scores is increasing.
    c. Women are better than men at detecting emotions.
    d. Men score higher than women on tests of spatial abilities.

23. Most psychologists believe that racial gaps in test scores
    a. have been exaggerated when they are, in fact, insignificant.
    b. indicate that intelligence is in large measure inherited.
    c. are in large measure caused by environmental factors.
    d. are increasing.

24. Standardization refers to the process of
    a. determining the accuracy with which a test measures what it is supposed to.
    b. defining meaningful scores relative to a representative pretested group.
    c. determining the consistency of test scores obtained by retesting people.
    d. measuring the success with which a test predicts the behavior it is designed to predict.

25. Down syndrome is normally caused by
    a. an extra chromosome in the person's genetic makeup.
    b. a missing chromosome in the person's genetic makeup.
    c. malnutrition during the first few months of life.
    d. prenatal exposure to an addictive drug.

26. Which of the following is NOT a requirement of a good test?
    a. reliability
    b. standardization
    c. heritability
    d. validity

27. First-time parents Geena and Brad want to give their baby's intellectual abilities a jump-start by providing a super enriched learning environment. Experts would suggest that the new parents should
    a. pipe stimulating classical music into the baby's room.
    b. hang colorful mobiles and artwork over the baby's crib.
    c. take the child to one of the new "superbaby" preschools that specialize in infant enrichment.
    d. relax, since there is no surefire environmental recipe for giving a child a superior intellect.

28. Which of the following statements is true?
    a. The predictive validity of intelligence tests is not as high as their reliability.
    b. The reliability of intelligence tests is not as high as their predictive validity.
    c. Modern intelligence tests have extremely high predictive validity and reliability.
    d. The predictive validity and reliability of most intelligence tests is very low.

29. The existence of _____ reinforces the generally accepted notion that intelligence is a multidimensional quality.
    a. adaptive skills
    b. intellectual disability
    c. general intelligence
    d. savant syndrome

30. Which of the following provides the strongest evidence of the role of heredity in determining intelligence?
    a. The IQ scores of identical twins raised separately are more similar than those of fraternal twins raised together.
    b. The intelligence scores of fraternal twins are more similar than those of ordinary siblings.
    c. The intelligence scores of identical twins raised together are more similar than those of identical twins raised apart.
    d. The intelligence scores of adopted children show relatively weak correlations with scores of adoptive as well as biological parents.

31. Reported racial gaps in average intelligence scores are most likely attributable to
    a. the use of biased tests of intelligence.
    b. the use of unreliable tests of intelligence.
    c. genetic factors.
    d. environmental factors.

32. The bell-shaped distribution of intelligence scores in the general population is called a
    a. g distribution.
    b. standardization curve.
    c. bimodal distribution.
    d. normal curve.

33. Which of the following is most likely to DECREASE with age?
    a. vocabulary
    b. accumulated knowledge
    c. speed of processing
    d. practical intelligence

34. The basic mental abilities that go into learning and understanding any subject have been classified as
    a. crystallized intelligence.
    b. plastic intelligence.
    c. fluid intelligence.
    d. rote memory.

35. Some psychologists contend that intelligence consists of fluid intelligence, which _____ during adulthood, and crystallized intelligence, which _____.
    a. remains stable; declines
    b. declines; remains stable
    c. increases; declines
    d. declines; increases

36. To say that the heritability of a trait is approximately 50 percent means

    a. that genes are responsible for 50 percent of the trait in an individual, and the environment is responsible for the rest.

    b. that the trait's appearance in a person will reflect approximately equal genetic contributions from both parents.

    c. that of the variation in the trait within a group of people, 50 percent can be attributed to heredity.

    d. all of these things.

Matching Items

Match each definition or description with the appropriate term.

Definitions or Descriptions

_____ 1. the basic units of sound in a language

_____ 2. the way an issue or question is posed

_____ 3. being unable to see a problem from a different angle

_____ 4. the basic units of meaning in a language

_____ 5. controls speech production

_____ 6. responsible for language comprehension

_____ 7. language disorder

_____ 8. the consistency with which a test measures performance

_____ 9. the degree to which a test measures what it is designed to measure

_____ 10. Terman's revision of Binet's original intelligence test

_____ 11. the behavior that a test is designed to predict

_____ 12. a very low intelligence score accompanied by one extraordinary skill

_____ 13. identifies a single solution to a problem

_____ 14. a statistical technique that identifies related items on a test

_____ 15. intellectual skills used in everyday problem solving

_____ 16. the ability to react adaptively to new situations and generate novel ideas

_____ 17. academic problem-solving

Terms

a. morphemes

b. phonemes

c. framing

d. fixation

e. aphasia

f. Broca's area

g. Wernicke's area

h. convergent thinking

i. savant syndrome

j. factor analysis

k. Stanford-Binet

l. criterion

m. content validity

n. reliability

o. analytic intelligence

p. creative intelligence

q. practical intelligence

Progress Test 2

Progress Test 2 should be completed during a final chapter review. Answer the following questions after you thoroughly understand the correct answers for the section reviews and Progress Test 1.

Multiple-Choice Questions

1. A common problem in everyday reasoning is our tendency to
   a. accept as logical those conclusions that agree with our own opinions.
   b. accept as logical those conclusions that disagree with our own opinions.
   c. underestimate the accuracy of our knowledge.
   d. accept as logical conclusions that involve unfamiliar concepts.

2. Phonemes are the basic units of ____ in language.
   a. sound
   b. meaning
   c. grammar
   d. semantics

3. Syntax refers to the
   a. sounds in a word.
   b. rules for ordering words into sentences.
   c. rules by which meaning is derived from sentences.
   d. overall rules of a language.

4. Our ability to learn a new language
   a. diminishes with age.
   b. is limited by a sharply defined critical period.
   c. remains constant throughout our lives.
   d. depends on the language.

5. Many psychologists are skeptical of claims that chimpanzees can acquire language because the chimps have not shown the ability to
   a. use symbols meaningfully.
   b. acquire speech.
   c. acquire even a limited vocabulary.
   d. use syntax in communicating.

6. Availability is an example of a(n)
   a. mental set.
   b. belief bias.
   c. algorithm.
   d. heuristic.

7. The basic units of cognition are
   a. phonemes.
   b. concepts.
   c. prototypes.
   d. morphemes.

8. Assume that Congress is considering revising its approach to welfare and to this end is hearing a range of testimony. A member of Congress who uses the availability heuristic would be most likely to
   a. want to experiment with numerous possible approaches to see which of these seems to work best.
   b. want to cling to approaches to welfare that seem to have had some success in the past.
   c. refuse to be budged from his or her beliefs despite persuasive testimony to the contrary.
   d. base his or her ideas on the most vivid, memorable testimony given, even though many of the statistics presented run counter to this testimony.

9. If you want to be absolutely certain that you will find the solution to a problem you know *is* solvable, you should use
   a. a heuristic.
   b. an algorithm.
   c. insight.
   d. trial and error.

10. Complete the following: *-ed* is to *sh* as _____ is to _____.
    a. phoneme; morpheme
    b. morpheme; phoneme
    c. grammar; syntax
    d. syntax; grammar

11. Which of the following is cited by Chomsky as evidence that humans are born with a predisposition to learn language?
    a. Children master the complicated rules of grammar with ease.
    b. Different languages do not have the same grammatical building blocks.
    c. Children make unpredictable mistakes as they acquire grammar.
    d. Children raised in isolation from language spontaneously begin speaking words.

12. Telegraphic speech is typical of the _____ stage.
    a. babbling
    b. one-word
    c. two-word
    d. three-word

13. Children first demonstrate a rudimentary understanding of syntax during the _____ stage.
    a. babbling
    b. one-word
    c. two-word
    d. three-word

14. The study in which people who immigrated to the United States at various ages were compared in terms of their ability to understand English grammar found that
    a. age of arrival had no effect on mastery of grammar.
    b. those who immigrated as children understood grammar as well as native speakers.
    c. those who immigrated as adults understood grammar as well as native speakers.
    d. whether English was spoken in the home was the most important factor in mastering the rules of grammar.

15. Researchers taught the chimpanzee Washoe to communicate by using
    a. various sounds.
    b. plastic symbols of various shapes and colors.
    c. sign language.
    d. all of these methods.

16. Regarding the relationship between thinking and language, which of the following most accurately reflects the position taken in the text?
    a. Language determines everything about our thinking.
    b. Language determines the way we think.
    c. Thinking without language is not possible.
    d. Thinking affects our language, which then affects our thought.

17. The bilingual advantage refers to the fact that people who are fluent in two languages are better at
    a. inhibiting their attention to irrelevant information.
    b. acquiring large vocabularies in both languages.
    c. thinking in images.
    d. all of these abilities.

18. Which of the following is true regarding the relationship between thinking and language?
    a. "Real" thinking requires the use of language.
    b. People sometimes think in images rather than in words.
    c. A thought that cannot be expressed in a particular language cannot occur to speakers of that language.
    d. All of these statements are true.

19. One reason an English-speaking adult may have difficulty pronouncing Russian words is that
    a. the vocal tracts of English- and Russian-speaking people develop differently in response to the demands of the two languages.
    b. although English and Russian have very similar morphemes, their phonemic inventories are very different.
    c. although English and Russian have very similar phonemes, their morphemic inventories are very different.
    d. after the babbling stage, a child who hears only English stops uttering other phonemes.

20. The test created by Alfred Binet was designed specifically to
    a. measure inborn intelligence in adults.
    b. measure inborn intelligence in children.
    c. predict school performance in children.
    d. identify intellectually disabled children so that they could be institutionalized.

21. Which of the following provides the strongest evidence of environment's role in intelligence?
    a. Adopted children's intelligence scores are more like their adoptive parents' scores than their biological parents'.
    b. Children's intelligence scores are more strongly related to their mothers' scores than to their fathers'.
    c. Children moved from a deprived environment into an intellectually enriched one show gains in intellectual development.
    d. The intelligence scores of identical twins raised separately are no more alike than those of siblings.

22. If a test designed to indicate which applicants are likely to perform the best on the job fails to do so, the test has
    a. low reliability.
    b. low content validity.
    c. low predictive validity.
    d. not been standardized.

23. The formula for the intelligence quotient was devised by
    a. Robert Sternberg.   c. Lewis Terman.
    b. Alfred Binet.   d. William Stern.

24. Current intelligence tests compute an individual's intelligence score as
    a. the ratio of mental age to chronological age multiplied by 100.

b. the ratio of chronological age to mental age multiplied by 100.

c. the amount by which the test-taker's performance deviates from the average performance of others the same age.

d. the ratio of the test-taker's verbal intelligence score to his or her nonverbal intelligence score.

25. J. McVicker Hunt found that institutionalized children given "tutored human enrichment"

a. showed no change in intelligence test performance compared with institutionalized children who did not receive such enrichment.

b. responded so negatively as a result of their impoverished early experiences that he felt it necessary to disband the program.

c. thrived intellectually and socially on the benefits of positive caregiving.

d. actually developed greater intelligence than control subjects who had lived in foster homes since birth.

26. The concept of a *g* factor implies that intelligence

a. is a single overall ability.

b. is several specific abilities.

c. cannot be defined or measured.

d. is a socially constructed concept.

27. The accumulation of knowledge that comes about with education and experience has been classified as

a. crystallized intelligence.

b. plastic intelligence.

c. fluid intelligence.

d. rote memory.

28. In his study of children with high intelligence scores, Terman found that

a. the children were more emotional and less healthy than a control group.

b. the children were ostracized by classmates.

c. the children were healthy and well-adjusted, and did well academically.

d. later, as adults, they nearly all achieved great vocational success.

29. Most experts view intelligence as a person's

a. ability to perform well on intelligence tests.

b. innate mental capacity.

c. ability to learn from experience, solve problems, and adapt to new situations.

d. diverse skills acquired throughout life.

30. From an evolutionary perspective, men's greater edge in _____ contributed to their survival.

a. verbal reasoning

b. spatial abilities

c. overall intelligence

d. all of these aspects of intelligence

31. Originally, IQ was defined as

a. mental age divided by chronological age and multiplied by 100.

b. chronological age divided by mental age and multiplied by 100.

c. mental age subtracted from chronological age and multiplied by 100.

d. chronological age subtracted from mental age and multiplied by 100.

32. Tests of _____ measure what an individual can do now, whereas tests of _____ predict what an individual will be able to do later.

a. aptitude; achievement

b. achievement; aptitude

c. reliability; validity

d. validity; reliability

33. Which of the following statements most accurately reflects the text's position regarding the relative contribution of genes and environment in determining intelligence?

a. Except in cases of a neglectful early environment, each individual's basic intelligence is largely the product of heredity.

b. Except in those with genetic disorders such as Down syndrome, intelligence results primarily from environmental experiences.

c. Both genes and life experiences significantly influence performance on intelligence tests.

d. Because intelligence tests have such low predictive validity, the question cannot be addressed until psychologists agree on a more valid test of intelligence.

34. Research indicates that during adulthood declines occur in

a. crystallized intelligence.

b. fluid intelligence.

c. both crystallized and fluid intelligence.

d. neither crystallized nor fluid intelligence.

35. In recent years, researchers are more likely than before to consider intelligence as

a. a single entity.

b. primarily determined by heredity.

c. entirely the product of learning.

d. made up of several abilities.

36. The psychologist who has proposed that intelligence is composed of analytic, creative, and practical aspects is
a. Charles Spearman.
b. Howard Gardner.
c. Robert Sternberg.
d. Sandra Scarr.

True–False Items

Indicate whether each statement is true or false by placing *T* or *F* in the blank next to the item.

_____ **1.** The order in which children acquire an understanding of various morphemes is unpredictable.

_____ **2.** According to the confirmation bias, people often interpret ambiguous evidence as support for their beliefs.

_____ **3.** Most human problem solving involves the use of heuristics rather than reasoning that systematically considers every possible solution.

_____ **4.** When asked, most people underestimate the accuracy of their judgments.

_____ **5.** Studies have shown that even animals may sometimes have insight reactions.

_____ **6.** Mental set is the tendency to repeat problem-solving solutions that have worked in the past.

_____ **7.** Although the morphemes differ from language to language, the phonemes for all languages are the same.

_____ **8.** Children of all cultures babble using the same phonemes.

_____ **9.** Thinking without using language is not possible.

_____ **10.** In the current version of the Stanford-Binet intelligence test, one's performance is compared only with the performance of others the same age.

_____ **11.** The gap in intelligence scores between Black and White children is increasing.

_____ **12.** The intelligence scores of adopted children are more similar to those of their adoptive parents than their biological parents.

_____ **13.** The Stanford-Binet test and the Wechsler scales are periodically restandardized.

_____ **14.** The variation in intelligence scores within a racial group is much larger than that between racial groups.

_____ **15.** Telling students they are unlikely to succeed often erodes their performance on aptitude tests.

_____ **16.** Today, most researchers studying cognitive abilities believe that intelligence is multidimensional.

Essay Questions

1. The lectures of your linguistics professor, who happens to be a staunch behaviorist, clearly imply that she believes language development can be explained according to principles of conditioning. What evidence should you present to convince her that she is wrong? (Use the space below to list the points you want to make, and organize them. Then write the essay on a separate piece of paper.)

2. You have been asked to devise a Psychology Achievement Test (PAT) that will be administered to freshmen who declare psychology as their major. What steps will you take to ensure that the PAT is a good intelligence test? (Use the space below to list the points you want to make, and organize them. Then write the essay on a separate sheet of paper.)

Terms and Concepts to Remember

Writing Definitions

Using your own words, on a piece of paper write a brief definition or explanation of each of the following terms.

1. cognition
2. concept
3. prototype
4. algorithm
5. heuristic
6. insight
7. confirmation bias
8. mental set
9. intuition
10. availability heuristic
11. overconfidence
12. belief perseverance
13. framing
14. creativity
15. convergent thinking
16. divergent thinking
17. language
18. phoneme
19. morpheme
20. grammar
21. babbling stage
22. one-word stage
23. two-word stage
24. telegraphic speech
25. aphasia
26. Broca's area
27. Wernicke's area
28. linguistic determinism
29. intelligence
30. general intelligence (g)
31. savant syndrome
32. emotional intelligence
33. intelligence test
34. mental age
35. Stanford-Binet
36. intelligence quotient (IQ)
37. aptitude test
38. achievement test
39. Wechsler Adult Intelligence Scale (WAIS)
40. standardization
41. normal curve
42. reliability
43. validity
44. content validity
45. predictive validity
46. intellectual disability
47. Down syndrome
48. crystallized intelligence
49. fluid intelligence
50. heritability
51. stereotype threat

Cross-Check

As you learned in Chapter 1, reviewing and overlearning of material are important to the learning process. After you have written the definitions of the key terms in this chapter, you should complete the crossword puzzle to ensure that you can reverse the process—recognize the term, given the definition.

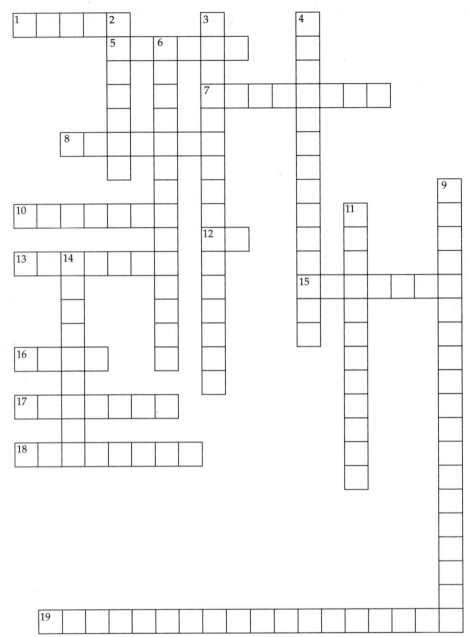

ACROSS

1. French educator who devised a test to predict children's learning potential.
5. The chimpanzee taught by Allen and Beatrice Gardner to use sign language.
7. An inability to approach a problem in a new way.
8. Theorist who argues for the existence of multiple intelligences.
10. Linguist who views language development as a process of maturation.
12. Originally defined as the ratio of mental age to chronological age.
13. The stage of language development between 1 and 2 years of age.
15. Behaviorist who explains language development with familiar learning principles.
16. The most widely used intelligence test (abbreviation).
17. A mental grouping of similar objects.
18. Degree to which a test measures what it is supposed to measure.
19. An obstacle to rational thinking that may be eliminated by considering an opposing viewpoint.

11. Heuristic in which we estimate the likelihood of events based on how readily they come to mind.
14. A critical part of social intelligence.

DOWN

2. Stage of language development characterized by the use of telegraphic speech.
3. Tendency of people to search for information that confirms their preconceptions.
4. Statistical procedure that identifies clusters of items that seem to define a common ability.
6. Condition in which a person of limited mental ability has one amazing skill.
9. Charles Spearman's concept of *g*.

Answers

Chapter Review

Thinking

1. thinking; the mental activities associated with thinking, knowing, remembering, and communicating
2. concepts
3. prototype; male; females

4. **b.** is the answer. A rose is a prototypical example of the concept *flower*.
c. & d. Cognition is the overall term for thinking. This example is more specific, dealing with a prototype of a concept.

5. problem solving

6. trial and error

7. algorithms

8. heuristics

9. insight; frontal lobe; right temporal lobe

10. confirmation bias

11. verifies; refute

12. fixation; mental set

13. **a.** Trial and error: randomly looking everywhere in the house

    b. Algorithm: methodically checking every possible location in the house as well as all the pockets in your clothes

    c. Heuristics: thinking about the most logical place for you to have left your keys

    d. Insight: suddenly realizing that you left your keys in the car when you took the groceries out

14. **b.** is the answer. Follow the directions precisely and you can't miss!
    a. A prototype is the best example of a concept.
    c. Heuristics are simple thinking strategies that help solve problems but, in contrast to a recipe that is followed precisely, do not guarantee success.
    d. A mental set is a tendency to approach a problem in a way that has been successful in the past.

15. **d.** is the answer.
    b. & c. If Boris always attacks his opponent's queen when playing chess, he is a victim of mental set; prototypes, however, have nothing to do with chess playing.

16. **c.** is the answer.
    a., b., & d. Heuristics do not guarantee solutions or prevent mental sets.

17. intuition

18. availability heuristic

The availability heuristic leads us to estimate the likelihood of events based on how readily they come to mind. Thus, we may think certain ethnic groups are more likely to be terrorists because of the vividness of the events of September 11, 2001.

19. flying; driving
    a. what our ancestral history has prepared us to fear.
    b. what we cannot control.

c. what is immediate.
    d. what is most readily available in memory.

20. overconfidence

21. adaptive; more; easier; more

22. helps

23. belief perseverance

24. consider the opposite

25. framing; may not

26. **d.** is the answer. The confirmation bias is the tendency to search for information that confirms one's preconceptions. In this example, the politicians' preconceptions are biasing their interpretation of the survey results.
    a. Fixation is the inability to see a problem from a fresh perspective
    b. Mental set is the tendency to approach a problem in a particular way. There is no problem per se in this example.
    c. Belief perseverance is the tendency to cling to one's beliefs despite evidence to the contrary.

27. **a.** is the answer. In this example, the way the issue is posed, or framed, has evidently influenced consumers' judgments.
    b. Confirmation bias is the tendency to search for information that confirms one's preconceptions.
    c. Mental set is the tendency to approach a problem in a particular way.
    d. Overconfidence is the tendency to be more confident than correct.

28. **c.** is the answer. This is referred to as overconfidence.

29. **c.** is the answer. Most people are more confident than correct in estimating their knowledge and the amount of time a task will take.

30. **a.** is the answer. Although b. and c. may be true, they do not describe belief perseverance. The d. answer is the confirmation bias.

31. **c.** is the answer. By simply following a strategy that has worked well in the past, Marilyn is hampered by the type of fixation called mental set.
    a. Fixation is too broad an answer.
    b. Overconfidence is exhibited by the person who overestimates the accuracy of his or her judgments.
    d. Prototypes are best examples of categories, not strategies for solving problems.

32. **b.** is the answer. The publicity surrounding disasters makes such events vivid and seemingly more probable than they actually are.
    a. Belief perseverance is the tendency to cling to one's beliefs despite evidence to the contrary.
    c. Mental set is a type of fixation.

d. Fixation is an inability to see a problem from a fresh perspective.

33. intuitive; incubate

34. adaptive

35. implicit

36. creativity

37. convergent; divergent

Creative people tend to have expertise, or a solid base of knowledge; imaginative thinking skills, which allow them to see things in new ways, to recognize patterns, and to make connections; intrinsic motivation, or the tendency to focus on the pleasure and challenge of their work; and a venturesome personality that tolerates ambiguity and risk and seeks new experiences. Creative people also have generally benefited from living in creative environments.

Research suggests that you can boost your creativity by developing your expertise in an area you care about and enjoy; allow time for a problem to incubate (sleep on it!); set aside time for your mind to roam freely; and experience other cultures and ways of thinking, which will expose you to multiple perspectives and facilitates flexible thinking.

38. **c.** is the answer.
    a. Creativity requires divergent thinking.
    b. Just the opposite is true of creative people.
    d. This may or may not be true, but most likely it isn't.

39. concepts; insight

40. tools; vary; cultural

41. do; altruism; cooperation

Language

42. our spoken, written, or signed words and the ways we combine them to communicate meaning.

43. phonemes; 40

44. morphemes

45. grammar

46. **a.** is the answer. Each sound of the word is a phoneme (note that the second letter "e" does not itself represent a sound); the morphemes are "pre," which means before; "date"; and "s," which indicates the plural.

47. **d.** is the answer. This sentence, although semantically meaningless, nevertheless follows the grammatical rules of English syntax for combining words into sentences.

    a. & b. The phonemes (smallest units of sound) and morphemes (smallest units of meaning) of this sentence are equally correct.

48. 4; receptive language; productive language

49. babbling; 4; do not

50. do; consonant-vowel; bunching the tongue in the front of the mouth

51. 10; lost

52. one-word; 1

53. two-word; telegraphic; does

54. B. F. Skinner; association; imitation; reinforcement

55. Noam Chomsky; universal grammar

56. grammar rules

57. critical period; accent; poorer; grammar

58. 7; never

59. do not

60. **a.** is the answer.

61. **b.** is the answer. Such utterances, characteristic of a child of about 2 years, are like telegrams, in that they consist mainly of nouns and verbs and show use of syntax.

    a. & c. Babbling consists of phonemes, not words.

    d. Semantics refers to the rules by which meaning is derived from sounds; this speech example indicates nothing in particular about the child's understanding of semantics.

62. **c.** is the answer. Children begin speaking mostly with nouns.

63. aphasia; Broca's area; Wernicke's area

64. neural networks

65. subfunctions

66. **a.** is the answer.

    b. Broca's area is involved in speech production.

    c. & d. The hypothalamus and the hippocampus have nothing to do with language.

67. do

68. sign language

69. alone

Chimps have acquired only limited vocabularies and—in contrast to children—have acquired these vocabularies only with great difficulty. Also in contrast to children, it's unclear whether chimps can use syntax to express meaning. The signing of chimps is often nothing more than imitation of the trainer's actions. People tend to interpret such ambiguous behavior in terms of what they want to see. Believers contend that although animals do not have our facility for language, they have the abilities to communicate. For example, Washoe and Loulis sign spontaneously. Also, bonobos can learn to comprehend syntax in spoken English.

Thinking and Language

70. linguistic determinism; Benjamin Whorf

71. self

72. does

73. attention; bilingual advantage

74. immersed; aptitude

75. can; mental

76. process; studying effectively

The relationship is probably a two-way one: the linguistic determinism hypothesis suggests that language helps shape thought; that words come into the language to express new ideas indicates that thought also shapes language.

77. process simulation; outcome simulation
    Imagining the procedure activates the brain areas involved in actually performing the activity, so process simulation produces better results than outcome simulation.

Intelligence

78. do not

79. concept; intelligence tests; does not

80. a mental quality consisting of the ability to learn from experience, solve problems, and use knowledge to adapt to new situations

81. factor analysis

82. general intelligence

83. savant syndrome

84. multiple intelligences

85. triarchic; analytical (academic problem-solving); practical; creative

86. confirmed; grit

87. savant syndrome

88. **d.** is the answer. Sternberg distinguishes among *academic* intelligence, as measured by intelligence tests; *practical* intelligence, which is involved in everyday life and tasks, such as managerial work; and *creative* intelligence.

    a. & b. Verbal and performance intelligence are both measured by standard intelligence tests such as the WAIS and would be included in Sternberg and Wagner's academic intelligence.

    c. Academic intelligence refers to skills assessed by intelligence tests; practical intelligence applies to skills required for everyday tasks and, often, for occupational success.

89. academic; social

90. emotional intelligence; perceive; understand; manage; use

91. recognize; predict; express; adaptive

Emotionally intelligent people are both socially aware and self-aware. They can manage their emotions and they can delay gratification. They handle others' emotions skillfully. They also exhibit modestly better job performance.

92. emotional

93. emotional intelligence

94. achievement; aptitude

95. Alfred Binet; mental; was not; Théodore Simon

96. Stanford-Binet; William Stern; intelligence quotient; IQ

In the original formula for IQ, measured mental age is divided by chronological age and multiplied by 100. "Mental age" refers to the chronological age that most typically corresponds to a given level of performance.

97. an intelligence test score; the same; 100

98. Wechsler Adult Intelligence Scale; verbal comprehension; perceptual organization; working memory; processing speed

99. achievement; aptitude

100. 13. At the time he took the test, Benito's chronological age (CA) was 10. Knowing that IQ = 130 and CA = 10, solving the equation for mental age yields a value of 13.

101. 100. Modern intelligence tests are periodically restandardized so that the average remains near 100.

102. standardization

103. normal

The normal curve (bell-shaped pattern) describes the distribution of many physical phenomena and psychological attributes (including intelligence test scores), with most scores falling near the average and fewer near the extremes. When a test is standardized on a normal curve, individual scores are assigned according to how much they deviate above or below the distribution's average.

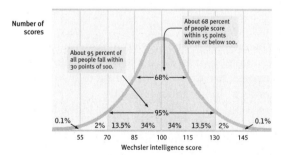

104. reliable

105. +.9

106. validity

107. criterion; content validity

108. predictive validity

The criterion is the particular behavior a test, such as an aptitude test, is intended to measure and predict. For example, performance in a relevant job situation would be the criterion for a test measuring managerial aptitude. The criterion determines whether a test has predictive validity. For example, the on-the-job success of those who do well on a job aptitude test would indicate the test has predictive validity.

109. is not; diminishes

110. **b.** is the answer. A standardization group provides a representative comparison for the trait being measured by a test. Because this test will measure musical aptitude in North American children, the standardization group should be limited to North American children but should include children of all degrees of musical aptitude.

111. **b.** is the answer.

112. **d.** is the answer. Because the hearing acuity test would in no way sample behaviors relevant to intelligence, it would not have content validity as a test of intelligence.
    a. & b. There is no such thing as content reliability or predictive reliability.
    c. There is nothing to indicate that, used to test hearing, this test would lack predictive validity.

113. **b.** is the answer.
    a. Standardization refers to the process of defining meaningful scores by comparison with a pretested standardization group.
    c. & d. Reliability is the degree to which a test yields consistent results. There is no indication in the question as to whether the test's results are consistent or inconsistent.

114. intellectually disabled

115. Down syndrome

116. restandardized

117. healthy; adjusted; academically

118. **c.** is the answer. To be labeled intellectually disabled a person must have a test score below 70 and experience difficulty adapting to the normal demands of living independently.
    a. Dan would most likely be closer to the lower end of the curve.
    b. There is no indication that Dan possesses one extraordinary skill, as do people with savant syndrome.

d. The text does not suggest that intellectually disabled people eventually become self-supporting.

119. crystallized

120. fluid

121. fluid; twenties; thirties; 75; 85; cross-sectional; longitudinal

122. fluid; social reasoning; negative emotions

123. more; gray; white; verbal; spatial

124. heritability; 50; 80

125. heritability

126. polygenetic

127. less-educated; more

128. more; biological; adoptive

129. low; high

130. **a.** is the answer. If everyone has nearly the same heredity, then heritability—the variation in a trait attributed to heredity—must be low. If individuals within a group come from very similar environments, environmental differences cannot account for variation in a trait; heritability, therefore, must be high.

131. do

132. malnutrition; sensory; social isolation

133. intelligence; schooling

134. spelling; verbally; locating; emotion; touch; taste; color

135. computation; spatial ability; math problems

136. evolutionary

137. do not; greater than

Because of the impact of environmental factors such as education and nutrition on intelligence test performance, even if the heritability of intelligence is high within a particular group, differences in intelligence among groups may be environmentally caused. One group may, for example, thrive in an enriched environment while another of the same genetic predisposition may falter in an impoverished one.

138. are; is not

139. fed; educated; test-prepared

140. **d.** is the answer. These reasons, along with other historical and cross-cultural reasons, all argue for the role of environment in creating and perpetuating the gap.

141. are

142. are not

143. stereotype threat

144. **c.** is the answer.

Progress Test 1

Multiple-Choice Questions

1. **c.** is the answer.
2. **b.** is the answer.
   a. A prototype is the best example of a particular category, or concept.
   c. & d. Algorithms and heuristics are problem-solving strategies.
3. **c.** is the answer.
   a. There is no such thing as a "denoter."
   b. & d. Heuristics and algorithms are problem-solving strategies.
4. **d.** is the answer. It is a major obstacle to problem solving.
   a. & b. These refer to belief bias and belief perseverance, respectively.
   c. This is trial-and-error problem solving.
5. **c.** is the answer.
6. **a.** is the answer. Babbling is not the imitation of adult speech since babbling infants produce phonemes from languages they have not heard and could not be imitating.
7. **c.** is the answer. Both involve failing to see a problem from a new perspective.
   a. & b. Algorithms and heuristics are problem-solving strategies.
   d. Insight is the sudden realization of a problem's solution.
8. **d.** is the answer.
9. **d.** is the answer.
   a. This is Skinner's position regarding language development.
   b. This is Chomsky's position regarding language development.
   c. The linguistic determinism hypothesis is concerned with the content of thought, not intelligence.
10. **c.** is the answer.
    a. This is Skinner's position.
    b. According to Chomsky, although the *ability* to acquire language is innate, the child can only acquire language in association with others.
    d. Cultural influences are an important example of the influence of learning on language development, an influence Chomsky fully accepts.
11. **d.** is the answer.
    a. Mental set is the tendency to approach a problem in a particular way that worked previously.
    b. Confirmation bias is the tendency to search for information that supports our preconceptions.
    c. Heuristics are simple thinking strategies that are based on past successes in similar situations.
12. **d.** is the answer. Heuristics are simple thinking strategies—such as playing chess defensively—that are based on past successes in similar situations.
    a., b., & c. These are all algorithms.
13. **d.** is the answer. Sultan suddenly arrived at a novel solution to his problem, thus displaying apparent insight.
    a. Sultan did not randomly try various strategies of reaching the fruit; he demonstrated the "light bulb" reaction that is the hallmark of insight.
    b. Heuristics are simple thinking strategies.
    c. Fixation is an impediment to problem solving. Sultan obviously solved his problem.
14. **c.** is the answer.
    b. Broca's area is involved in speech production.
    d. The association areas are involved in higher-order activities such as planning.
15. **d.** is the answer.
16. **d.** is the answer. Compared with Deaf children exposed to sign language from birth, those who learn to sign as teens have the same grammatical difficulties as do hearing adults trying to learn a second spoken language.
17. **c.** is the answer. Children are biologically prepared to learn language as they and their caregivers interact.
    a. This would be the view of a behaviorist.
    b. No psychologist, including Chomsky, believes that language is entirely a product of biological maturation.
    d. Although language acquisition is not completely understood, research has shed sufficient light on it to render it less than a complete mystery.
18. **b.** is the answer. The evidence that absence of a term for a color does not affect ability to perceive the color challenges the idea that language always shapes thought.
    a. & d. These findings are not relevant to the linguistic determinism hypothesis, which addresses the relationship between language and thought.
    c. This finding is in keeping with the linguistic determinism hypothesis.
19. **c.** is the answer. The generic pronoun *he* evidently tends, for both adults and children, to conjure up images of males.
20. **a.** is the answer.
    c. & d. Separating genetic from environmental influences is difficult *at any age*.
21. **d.** is the answer. If we divide 9, the measured mental age, by 6, the chronological age, and multiply the result by 100, we obtain 150.

22. **b.** is the answer. As social expectations have changed, the gender gap in math and science scores is narrowing.

23. **c.** is the answer.
   a. On the contrary, many *group* differences are highly significant, even though they tell us nothing about specific *individuals*.
   b. Although heredity contributes to individual differences in intelligence, it does not necessarily contribute to group differences.
   d. In fact, the difference has diminished somewhat in recent years.

24. **b.** is the answer.
   a. This answer refers to a test's content validity.
   c. This answer refers to test-retest reliability.
   d. This answer refers to predictive validity.

25. **a.** is the answer.
   b. Down syndrome is normally caused by an extra, rather than a missing, chromosome.
   c. & d. Down syndrome is a genetic disorder that is manifest during the earliest stages of prenatal development, well before malnutrition and exposure to drugs would produce their harmful effects on the developing fetus.

26. **c.** is the answer. Heritability is the proportion of variation among individuals that can be attributed to genes.

27. **d.** is the answer.

28. **a.** is the answer.
   c. & d. Most modern tests have high reliabilities of about +.9; their validity scores are much lower.

29. **d.** is the answer. That people with savant syndrome excel in one area but are intellectually disabled in others suggests that there are multiple intelligences.
   a. The ability to adapt defines the capacity we call intelligence.
   b. Intellectual disability is at the lower end of the range of human intelligence.
   c. A general intelligence factor was hypothesized by Spearman to underlie each specific factor of intelligent behavior, but its existence is controversial and remains to be proved.

30. **a.** is the answer. Identical twins who live apart have the same genetic makeup but different environments; if their scores are similar, this is evidence for the role of heredity.
   b. Because fraternal twins are no more genetically alike than ordinary siblings, this could not provide evidence for the role of heredity.
   c. That twins raised together have more similar scores than twins raised apart provides evidence for the role of the environment.

d. As both sets of correlations are weak, little evidence is provided either for or against the role of heredity.

31. **d.** is the answer. Findings from a range of studies—including studies related to the Flynn effect and adoption studies—have led experts to focus on the influence of environmental factors.
   a. Most experts believe that in terms of predictive validity, the major tests are not racially biased.
   b. The reliability of the major tests is actually very high.
   c. The bulk of the evidence on which experts base their findings points to the influence of environmental factors.

32. **d.** is the answer.
   a. *g* is Spearman's term for "general intelligence"; there is no such thing as a "*g* distribution."
   b. There is no such thing.
   c. A bimodal distribution is one having two (bi-) modes, or averages. The normal distribution has only one mode.

33. **c.** is the answer.
   a., b., & d. These often increase with age.

34. **c.** is the answer.
   a. Crystallized intelligence is the accumulation of knowledge and verbal skills that comes with education and experience.
   b. Although intelligence is characterized by plasticity, "plastic intelligence" is not discussed as a specific type of intelligence.
   d. Rote memory is memory that is based on the conscious repetition of to-be-remembered information.

35. **d.** is the answer.

36. **c.** is the answer. Heritability is a measure of the extent to which a trait's variation within a group of people can be attributed to heredity.
   a. & b. Heritability is *not* a measure of how much of an *individual's* behavior is inherited, nor of the relative contribution of genes from that person's mother and father. Further, the heritability of any trait depends on the context, or environment, in which that trait is being studied.

Matching Items

1. b	**7.** e	**13.** h
2. c	**8.** n	**14.** j
3. d	**9.** m	**15.** q
4. a	**10.** k	**16.** p
5. f	**11.** l	**17.** o
6. g	**12.** i	

Progress Test 2

Multiple-Choice Questions

1. **a.** is the answer. Reasoning in daily life is often distorted by our beliefs, which may lead us, for example, to accept conclusions that haven't been arrived at logically.
b., c., & d. These are just the opposite of what we tend to do.

2. **a.** is the answer.
b. Morphemes are the basic units of meaning.
c. & d. The text does not refer to basic units of grammar or semantics.

3. **b.** is the answer.
a. Phonemes are the sounds in a word.
c. Such rules are known as semantics.
d. Such rules are the language's grammar, which includes its syntax as well as its semantics.

4. **a.** is the answer.

5. **d.** is the answer. Syntax is one of the fundamental aspects of language, and chimps seem unable, for example, to use word order to convey differences in meaning.
a. & c. Chimps' use of sign language demonstrates both the use of symbols and the acquisition of fairly sizable vocabularies.
b. No psychologist would require the use of speech as evidence of language; significantly, all the research and arguments focus on what chimps are and are not able to do in acquiring other facets of language.

6. **d.** is the answer. This is a simple thinking strategy that allows us to make quick judgments.
a. Mental sets are obstacles to problem solving, in which the person tends to repeat solutions that have worked in the past and is unable to conceive of other possible solutions.
b. Belief perseverance is the tendency to cling to a belief even after the information that led to the formation of the belief is discredited.
c. Algorithms are methodical strategies that guarantee a solution to a particular problem.

7. **b.** is the answer.
a. & d. Phonemes and morphemes are units of sound and meaning in language, respectively.
c. Prototypes are the best examples of specific categories.

8. **d.** is the answer. If we use the availability heuristic, we base judgments on the availability of information in our memories, and more vivid information is often the most readily available.
a. This would exemplify use of the trial-and-error approach to problem solving.

b. This would exemplify a mental set.
c. This would exemplify belief perseverance.

9. **b.** is the answer. Because they involve the systematic examination of all possible solutions to a problem, algorithms guarantee that a solution will be found.
a., c., & d. None of these methods guarantees that a problem's solution will be found.

10. **b.** is the answer. The morpheme *-ed* changes the *meaning* of a regular verb to form its past tense; the phoneme *sh* is a unique *sound* in the English language.
c. & d. Syntax, which specifies rules for combining words into grammatical sentences, is one aspect of the grammar of a language.

11. **a.** is the answer.

12. **c.** is the answer.

13. **c.** is the answer. Although the child's utterances are only two words long, the words are placed in a sensible order. In English, for example, adjectives are placed before nouns.
a. & b. Syntax specifies rules for *combining* two or more units in speech.
d. There is no three-word stage.

14. **b.** is the answer.

15. **c.** is the answer.

16. **d.** is the answer.

17. **a.** is the answer.

18. **b.** is the answer.
a. Researchers do not make a distinction between "real" and other thinking, nor do they consider nonlinguistic thinking less valid than linguistic thinking.
c. As indicated by several studies cited in the text, this is not true.

19. **d.** is the answer. Following the babbling stage, the child's ability to produce all phonemes becomes in a sense shaped and limited to the ability to produce those phonemes he or she hears.
a. The vocal tract of *Homo sapiens* does not develop in specialized ways for different languages.
b. & c. English and Russian differ significantly in both their phonemes and their morphemes. Nor is there any reason why differences in morphemes would in and of themselves cause pronunciation difficulties.

20. **c.** is the answer. French compulsory education laws brought more children into the school system, and the government didn't want to rely on teachers' subjective judgments to determine which children would require special help.

a. & b. Binet's test was intended for children, and Binet specifically rejected the idea that his test measured inborn intelligence, which is an abstract capacity that cannot be quantified.
d. This was not a purpose of the test, which dealt with children in the school system.

21. **c.** is the answer.
    a., b., & d. None of these is true.

22. **c.** is the answer. Predictive validity is the extent to which tests predict what they are intended to predict.
    a. Reliability is the consistency with which a test samples the particular behavior of interest.
    b. Content validity is the degree to which a test measures what it is designed to measure.
    d. Standardization is the process of defining meaningful test scores based on the performance of a representative group.

23. **d.** is the answer.

24. **c.** is the answer.
    a. This is William Stern's original formula for the intelligence quotient.
    b. & d. Neither of these formulas is used to compute the score on current intelligence tests.

25. **c.** is the answer. Enrichment led to dramatic results and thereby testified to the importance of environmental factors.
    a. & d. The study involved neither intelligence tests nor comparisons with control groups.
    b. The children showed a dramatic positive response.

26. **a.** is the answer.

27. **a.** is the answer.
    b. Although intelligence is characterized by plasticity, "plastic intelligence" is not discussed as a specific type of intelligence.
    c. Fluid intelligence is the ability to reason speedily and abstractly.
    d. Rote memory is based on the conscious repetition of to-be-remembered information.

28. **c.** is the answer.
    a. & b. There was no evidence of either in the individuals studied by Terman.
    d. Vocational success in adulthood varied.

29. **c.** is the answer.
    a. Performance ability and intellectual ability are separate traits.
    b. This has been argued by some, but certainly not most, experts.
    d. Although many experts believe that there are multiple intelligences, this would not be the same thing as diverse acquired skills.

30. **b.** is the answer.

31. **a.** is the answer.

32. **b.** is the answer.
    c. & d. Reliability and validity are characteristics of good tests.

33. **c.** is the answer.
    a. & b. Studies of twins, family members, and adopted children point to a significant hereditary contribution to intelligence scores. These same studies, plus others comparing children reared in neglectful or enriched environments, indicate that life experiences also significantly influence test performance.
    d. Although the issue of how intelligence should be defined is controversial, intelligence tests generally have predictive validity, especially in the early years.

34. **b.** is the answer.
    a., c., & d. Crystallized intelligence typically increases during adulthood.

35. **d.** is the answer.
    a. Contemporary researchers emphasize the different aspects of intelligence.
    b. & c. Contemporary researchers see intelligence as the product of both heredity and learning.

36. **c.** is the answer.
    a. Charles Spearman proposed the existence of an underlying general intelligence, which he called *g*.
    b. Howard Gardner proposed that intelligence consists of eight autonomous abilities.
    d. Sandra Scarr believes that parents who try to turn their children into geniuses at a young age are wasting their time.

True–False Items

1.	F	9.	F
2.	T	10.	T
3.	T	11.	F
4.	F	12.	F
5.	T	13.	T
6.	T	14.	T
7.	F	15.	T
8.	T	16.	T

Essay Questions

1. You should point out that the rate at which children acquire words and grammar is too extraordinary to be explained solely according to principles of learning. Children also utter all sorts of word forms they have never heard and could not, therefore, be imitating. Furthermore, children begin using morphemes in a predictable order, which learning theorists would not expect since

each child experiences a unique linguistic environment. It therefore seems clear that children are biologically prepared to acquire language and that the behaviorist position is incorrect.

2. The first step in constructing the test is to create a valid set of questions that measure psychological knowledge and therefore give the test content validity. If your objective is to predict students' future achievement in psychology courses, the test questions should be selected to measure a criterion, such as information faculty members expect all psychology majors to master before they graduate.

   To enable meaningful comparisons, the test must be standardized. That is, the test should be administered to a representative sample of incoming freshmen at the time they declare psychology to be their major. From the scores of your pretested sample you will then be able to assign an average score and evaluate any individual score according to how much it deviates above or below the average.

   To check your test's reliability you might retest a sample of people using the same test or another version of it. If the two scores are correlated, your test is reliable. Alternatively, you might split the test in half and determine whether scores on the two halves are correlated.

Terms and Concepts to Remember

Writing Definitions

1. **Cognition** refers to all the mental activities associated with thinking, knowing, remembering, and communicating information.

2. A **concept** is a mental grouping of similar objects, events, ideas, and people.

3. A **prototype** is a mental image or best example of a category.

4. An **algorithm** is a methodical, logical rule or procedure that, while sometimes slow, guarantees success.

5. A **heuristic** is a simple thinking strategy that often allows us to make judgments and solve problems efficiently. Although heuristics are more efficient than algorithms, they do not guarantee success and sometimes even impede problem solving.

6. **Insight** is a sudden and often novel realization of the solution to a problem. Insight contrasts with trial and error and, indeed, may often follow an unsuccessful episode of trial and error.

7. The **confirmation bias** is an obstacle to problem solving in which people tend to search for information that supports their preconceptions.

8. **Mental set** refers to the tendency to continue applying a particular problem-solving strategy even when it is no longer helpful.

9. **Intuition** is an immediate, automatic, and effortless feeling or thought.

10. The **availability heuristic** is based on estimating the probability of certain events in terms of how readily they come to mind.

11. Another obstacle to problem solving, **overconfidence** refers to the tendency to overestimate the accuracy of our beliefs and judgments.

12. **Belief perseverance** is the tendency for people to cling to a particular belief even after the information that led to the formation of the belief is discredited.

13. **Framing** refers to the way an issue or question is posed. It can affect people's perception of the issue or answer to the question.

14. Most experts agree that **creativity** refers to an ability to produce novel and valuable ideas.

15. **Convergent thinking** determines the best solution to a problem.

16. **Divergent thinking** identifies multiple possible solutions to a problem.

17. **Language** refers to spoken, written, or signed words and how we combine them to communicate meaning.

18. **Phonemes** are the smallest distinctive units of sound in a language that are distinctive for speakers of the language.

19. **Morphemes** are the smallest units of language that carry meaning.

    Example: The word "dogs," which contains four phonemes, contains only two **morphemes**—"dog" and "-s." Although most morphemes are combinations of two or more phonemes, the plural "-s" conveys a distinctive meaning of "more than one."

20. **Grammar** is a system of rules that enables us to communicate with and understand others.

21. The **babbling stage** of speech development, which begins around 4 months, is characterized by the spontaneous utterance of speech sounds. During the babbling stage, children the world over sound alike.

22. Between 1 and 2 years of age, children speak mostly in single words; they are therefore in the **one-word stage** of linguistic development.

23. Beginning about age 2, children are in the **two-word stage** and speak mostly in two-word sentences.

24. **Telegraphic speech** is the economical, telegram-like speech of children in the two-word stage. Utterances consist mostly of nouns and verbs; however, words occur in the correct order, showing that the child has learned some of the language's syntactic rules.

25. **Aphasia** is an impairment of language, usually caused by left-hemisphere damage either to Broca's area or to Wernicke's area.

26. **Broca's area,** located in the left frontal lobe, is involved in controlling the motor ability to produce speech.

27. **Wernicke's area,** located in the left temporal lobe, is involved in language comprehension and expression.

28. **Linguistic determinism** is Benjamin Whorf's hypothesis that language determines the way we think.

29. Most experts define **intelligence** as a mental quality consisting of the ability to learn from experience, solve problems, and use knowledge to adapt to new situations.

30. **General intelligence (*g*),** according to Spearman and others, is a general intelligence factor that underlies each of the more specific mental abilities identified through factor analysis.

31. A person with **savant syndrome** has a very low intelligence score, yet possesses one exceptional ability, for example, in music or drawing.

32. **Emotional intelligence** is the ability to perceive, manage, understand, and use emotions.

33. **Intelligence tests** measure people's mental aptitudes and compare them with those of others, using numerical scores.

34. A concept introduced by Binet, **mental age** is the chronological age that most typically corresponds to a given level of performance.

35. The **Stanford-Binet** is Lewis Terman's widely used revision of Binet's original intelligence test.

36. The **intelligence quotient (IQ)** was defined originally as the ratio of mental age to chronological age multiplied by 100. Contemporary tests of intelligence assign a score of 100 to the average performance for a given age and define other scores as deviations from this average.

37. **Aptitude tests** are designed to predict future performance. They measure your capacity to learn new information, rather than measuring what you already know.

38. **Achievement tests** measure a person's current knowledge.

39. The **Wechsler Adult Intelligence Scale (WAIS)** is the most widely used intelligence test. It is individually administered, contains 15 subtests, and yields separate scores for verbal comprehension, perceptual organization, working memory, and processing speed, as well as an overall intelligence score.

40. **Standardization** is the process of defining meaningful scores by comparison with a pretested standardization group.

41. The **normal curve** is a bell-shaped curve that represents the distribution (frequency of occurrence) of many physical and psychological attributes. The curve is symmetrical, with most scores near the average and fewer near the extremes.

42. **Reliability** is the extent to which a test produces consistent results.

43. **Validity** is the degree to which a test measures or predicts what it is supposed to.

44. The **content validity** of a test is the extent to which it samples the behavior that is of interest.

45. **Predictive validity** is the extent to which a test predicts the behavior it is designed to predict; also called *criterion-related validity.*

46. The two criteria that designate **intellectual disability** are an IQ below 70 and difficulty adapting to the normal demands of independent living; formerly called *mental retardation.*

47. A condition of mild to severe intellectual disability and associated physical disorders, **Down syndrome** is usually the result of an extra chromosome in the person's genetic makeup.

48. **Crystallized intelligence** is the accumulated knowledge and verbal skills that comes with education and experience.

49. **Fluid intelligence** is the ability to reason speedily and abstractly.

50. **Heritability** is the proportion of variation among individuals that can be attributed to genes.

51. **Stereotype threat** is the phenomenon in which a person's concern that he or she will be evaluated based on a negative stereotype (as on an aptitude test, for example) is actually followed by lower performance.

Cross-Check

ACROSS
1. Binet
5. Washoe
7. fixation
8. Gardner
10. Chomsky
12. IQ
13. one-word
15. Skinner
16. WAIS
17. concept
18. validity
19. belief perseverance

DOWN
2. two-word
3. confirmation bias
4. factor analysis
6. savant syndrome
9. general intelligence
11. availability
14. emotional

Motivation and Emotion

Chapter Overview

Motivation is the study of forces that energize and direct our behavior. Chapter 10 discusses various motivational concepts and looks closely at three motives: hunger, the need to belong, and achievement. Research on hunger points to the fact that our biological drive to eat is strongly influenced by psychological and social-cultural factors. Research on the need to belong and social networking reveals that social networking tends to increase self-disclosure and strengthen relationships with people we already know. Research on achievement motivation underscores the importance of self-discipline and persistence in achieving one's goals.

Chapter 10 also discusses the nature of emotion. Emotions are responses of the whole individual, involving physiological arousal, expressive behaviors, and conscious experience. The chapter first discusses several theoretical controversies concerning the relationship and sequence of the components of emotion, primarily regarding whether the body's response to a stimulus causes the emotion and whether thinking is necessary to and must precede the experience of emotion. After describing the physiology of emotion, the chapter examines how we communicate emotions, as well as the differences in emotional expression among different groups.

NOTE: Answer guidelines for all Chapter 10 questions begin on page 255.

Chapter Review

First, skim each section, noting headings and boldface items. After you have read the section, review each objective by answering the fill-in and essay-type questions that follow it. Study Tips explain how best to learn a difficult concept and Applications help you to know how well you understand the material. As you proceed, evaluate your performance by consulting the answers beginning on page 255. Do not continue with the next section until you understand each answer. If you need to, review or reread the section in the textbook before continuing.

Introduction and Motivational Concepts

Objective 10-1: Define *motivation* as psychologists use the term, and identify the perspectives useful for studying motivated behavior.

1. Motivation is defined as _____ _____ _____ .

2. Four perspectives on motivation are _____ theory (which has been replaced by the _____ perspective), _____ - _____ theory, _____ theory, and the _____ of needs proposed by _____ .

3. As a result of Darwin's influence, many complex behaviors were classified as rigid, unlearned behavior patterns that are characteristic of a species, called _____ . Although early instinct theory_____ (did/ did not) explain human motives, the underlying assumption that _____ predispose species-typical behavior remains strong.

4. According to another view of motivation, organisms may experience a physiological _____ , which creates a state of arousal that _____ the organism to reduce the need.

5. The physiological aim of drive reduction is to maintain a constant internal state, called _____ .

6. Behavior is often not so much pushed by our drives as it is pulled by _____ in the environment.

7. Rather than reduce a physiological need, some motivated behaviors actually _____ arousal. This demonstrates that human motives _____ (do/do not) always satisfy some biological need.

8. Human motivation aims not to eliminate _____ but to seek _____ _____ of arousal. According to the _____-_____ law, _____ (low/moderate/high) levels of arousal lead to optimal performance.

9. Starting from the idea that _____-_____ needs such as the need for water take precedence over others, Maslow constructed a hierarchy of needs.

10. According to Maslow, the _____ needs are the most pressing, whereas the highest-order needs relate to _____ and _____ .

11. A criticism of Maslow's theory is that the sequence is _____ and not _____ fixed.

12. Surveys of life satisfaction reveal that _____ satisfaction is strongly predictive of subjective well-being in poorer nations, whereas _____-_____ satisfaction matters more in wealthy nations.

APPLICATIONS:

13. Mary loves hang-gliding. It would be most difficult to explain Mary's behavior according to
   a. incentives.
   b. drive-reduction theory.
   c. Maslow's hierarchy of needs.
   d. none of these concepts.

14. For two weeks, Orlando has been on a hunger strike to protest his country's involvement in what he perceives as an immoral war. Orlando's willingness to starve himself to make a political statement conflicts with the theory of motivation advanced by
   a. Darwin.   c. Dodson.
   b. Yerkes.   d. Maslow.

15. Which of the following is NOT an example of homeostasis?
   a. perspiring to restore normal body temperature
   b. feeling hungry and eating to restore the level of blood glucose to normal
   c. feeling hungry at the sight of an appetizing food
   d. All of these are examples of homeostasis.

Hunger

Objective 10-2: Describe the physiological factors that produce hunger.

16. Researchers observed that men became preoccupied with thoughts of food when they underwent _____ .

17. Cannon and Washburn's experiment using a balloon indicated that there is an association between hunger and _____ .

18. When rats had their stomachs removed, hunger _____ (did/did not) continue.

19. A major source of energy in the body is the blood sugar _____ . When levels of this sugar drop, _____ is triggered.

20. The brain area that plays a role in hunger and other bodily maintenance functions is the _____ . One area, called the _____ _____ , has a center that secretes appetite-stimulating hormones and another center that secretes appetite-suppressing hormones.

21. The hunger-arousing hormone secreted by an empty stomach is (a) _____ .

22. When a portion of an obese person's stomach is surgically sealed off, the remaining stomach produces _____ (more/less) of this hormone. Other appetite hormones include (b) _____ , which is secreted by the pancreas and controls blood glucose; (c) _____ , which is secreted by fat cells and decreases hunger; (d) _____ , which is secreted by the hypothalamus and triggers hunger; and (e) _____ from the digestive tract, which decreases hunger.

23. The weight level at which an individual's body is programmed to stay is referred to as the body's

_____ _____ .

A person whose weight goes beyond this level will tend to feel _____ (more/less) hungry than usual and expend _____ (more/less) energy.

24. The rate of energy expenditure in maintaining basic functions when the body is at rest is the

_____ _____

rate. When food intake is reduced, the body compensates by _____ (raising/lowering) this rate.

25. The concept of a precise body set point that drives hunger _____ (is accepted/is not accepted) by all researchers. Some researchers believe that set point can be altered by _____

_____ ,

and that _____

_____ also sometimes drive our feelings of hunger. In support of this idea is evidence that when people and other animals are given unlimited access to tasty foods, they tend to _____ and _____

_____ . For these reasons, some researchers prefer to use the term

_____ _____ as an alternative to the idea that there is a fixed set point.

APPLICATION:

26. Lucille has been sticking to a strict diet but can't seem to lose weight. What is the most likely explanation for her difficulty?
   a. Her body has a very low set point.
   b. Her prediet weight was near her body's set point.
   c. Her weight problem is actually caused by an increase in basal metabolic rate.
   d. Lucille is influenced primarily by external factors.

Objective 10-3: Discuss psychological and situational factors that influence hunger.

27. Research with amnesia patients indicates that part of knowing when to eat is our

_____ of our last meal.

28. Carbohydrates boost levels of the neurotransmitter _____ , which _____ (calms/arouses) the body.

29. Taste preferences for sweet and salty are _____ (genetic/learned). Other influences on taste include _____ and _____ .

30. We have a natural dislike of many foods that are _____ ; this _____ was probably adaptive for our ancestors, and protected them from toxic substances.

31. The phenomenon by which situations control our eating has been called the _____

_____ _____ .

Because of _____ facilitation, people tend to eat _____ (less/more) when they are with other people. The phenomenon of _____

_____ is the tendency to mindlessly eat more when portions are larger. Another factor that stimulates eating is food

_____ .

APPLICATION:

32. Randy, who has been under a lot of stress lately, has intense cravings for sugary junk foods, which tend to make him feel more relaxed. Which of the following is the most likely explanation for his craving?
    a. Randy feels that he deserves to pamper himself with sweets because of the stress he is under.
    b. The extra sugar gives Randy the energy he needs to cope with the demands of daily life.
    c. Carbohydrates boost levels of serotonin, which has a calming effect.
    d. The extra sugar tends to lower blood insulin level, which promotes relaxation.

Objective 10-4: Discuss the factors that predispose some people to become and remain obese.

33. Obesity has been associated with lower _____ well-being, especially among _____ , and increased risk of _____ . Clinical obesity is defined as a BMI of _____ or more. In the United States, _____ percent of adults are obese. Significant obesity increases the risk of _____
    _____
    _____ .

34. Obesity has also been linked in women to their risk of late-life _____ disease and brain tissue loss.

35. Fat tissue has a _____ (higher/lower) metabolic rate than lean tissue. The result is that fat tissue requires _____ (more/less) food energy to be maintained.

Explain why, metabolically, many obese people find it so difficult to become and stay thin.

36. Studies of adoptees and twins _____ (do/do not) provide evidence of a genetic influence on obesity.

37. Also contributing to the problem of obesity are _____ factors. For example, adults who suffer from _____ _____ are more vulnerable to obesity. Also, people are _____ (less/more) likely to become obese when a friend becomes obese, thus demonstrating _____ influence as a factor in obesity.

38. Two reasons for the global increase in weight are changing _____ _____ and _____ _____ .

(Close-Up) State several pieces of advice for those who want to lose weight.

APPLICATIONS:

39. Owen is on a diet. After an initial _____ (slow/rapid) weight loss, he loses weight _____ (more slowly/more rapidly). This slowdown occurs because his metabolism rate has _____ (increased/decreased).

40. Kenny and his brother have nearly identical eating and exercise habits, yet Kenny is obese and his brother is very thin. The MOST LIKELY explanation for the difference in their body weights is that they differ in
    a. their bone structure.
    b. amygdala activity.
    c. their set points and their metabolic rates.
    d. their differing exposure to carbohydrate-laden foods.

41. (Close-Up) Which of the following would be the WORST piece of advice to offer to someone trying to lose weight?
    a. "To treat yourself to one 'normal' meal each day, eat very little until the evening meal."
    b. "Reduce your consumption of saturated fats."
    c. "Boost your metabolism by exercising regularly."
    d. "Begin only if you feel motivated and self-disciplined."

The Need to Belong

Objective 10-5: Describe the evidence that points to our human need to belong.

42. The philosopher _____ referred to humans as the _____ animal. Social bonds in humans boosted our ancestors' _____ rates. As adults, those who formed _____ were more likely to _____ and co-nurture their offspring to maturity.

43. When asked what makes life meaningful, most people mention _____ _____ .

   People experience a deep sense of well-being when their need for relatedness is satisfied along with two other basic psychological needs: _____ and _____ .

44. Feelings of love activate our brain's _____ and _____ systems, including an area in the _____ _____ than dampens feelings of pain.

45. Much of our _____ behavior aims to increase our belonging. For most people, familiarity leads to _____ (liking/disliking).

46. Children who grow up without a sense of belonging to anyone may become _____ _____ and display _____ _____ attachment as they constantly crave acceptance. Others display _____ _____ attachment and feel discomfort over getting close to others.

47. After years of placing individual refugee and immigrant families in _____ communities, U.S. policies today encourage _____ _____ .

48. _____ (Throughout the world/ Only in certain cultures do) people use social exclusion, or _____ , to control social behavior. Researchers have found that social exclusion elicits increased activity in brain areas, such as the _____ _____ _____ , that also activate in response to _____ .

49. Researchers have found that people who are rejected are more likely to engage in _____ behaviors, to underperform on _____ _____ , and to act in disparaging or _____ ways against those who had excluded them.

Objective 10-6: Describe how social networking influences us.

50. History's most rapidly adopted technology is the _____ _____ .

51. Phone talking is being displaced by the greater use of _____ and _____ .

52. People who are _____ tend to spend greater-than-average time online.

53. People who are active in _____ . _____ are less likely to know their real-world neighbors.

54. Texting and e-mailing can stimulate healthy _____ but an even better predictor of life satisfaction is _____ _____ .

55. Generally speaking, social networks _____ (reveal/do not reveal) people's real personalities.

56. People who are overly self-important, self-focused, and self-promoting are said to be _____ . People who score high on this trait tend to be _____ (especially active/less active) on social networking sites.

APPLICATIONS:

57. Summarizing her report on the need to belong, Rolanda states that
  a. "Cooperation amongst our ancestors was uncommon."
  b. "Social bonding is not in our nature; it is a learned human trait."
  c. "Because bonding with others increased our ancestors' success at reproduction and survival, it became part of our biological nature."
  d. "Our male ancestors were more likely to bond than were females."

58. Right after dinner, Dennis goes to his room, turns on his computer, and begins chatting with friends on Facebook. Which of the following is true, according to the most recent research?
  a. His connections with friends have been strengthened.
  b. He is more willing to disclose personal thoughts and feelings, which deepens his friendships.
  c. He reveals his true personality to friends and others online.
  d. All of these statements are true.

Achievement Motivation

Objective 10-7: Define *achievement motivation.*

59. Psychologists refer to the desire for significant accomplishments, for mastering skills or ideas, for control, and for attaining a high standard as _____ _____ .

60. Research has shown that _____ is a better predictor of school performance than _____ _____ have been. Extremely successful individuals differ from equally talented peers in their _____ , their passionate dedication to a long-term goal.

STUDY TIP: Research studies have shown that people who possess a low need for achievement tend to prefer situations and tasks that are either very easy or impossibly hard. Conversely, people with a high need for achievement tend to prefer tasks that are moderately difficult. Why do you think this might be? Which types of tasks (e.g., college courses) do you prefer?

APPLICATIONS:

61. During a meeting with the parents of a struggling high school student, the guidance counselor notes which of the following as the best predictor of school performance?
  a. attendance
  b. intelligence scores
  c. talent
  d. self-discipline

62. The golfer Phil Mickelson has enough money to live well for the rest of his life and has won most of golf's major championships. However, he continues to want to win tournaments. He would be considered a high achiever because
  a. he has the talent to continue golfing.
  b. his self-discipline and grit lead him to continue reaching for higher and higher goals.
  c. he is a strategic golfer and will be able to win many more tournaments.
  d. he needs to accumulate more money to enable his children to live well.

Emotion: Arousal, Behavior, and Cognition

Objective 10-8: Describe how arousal, cognition, and expressive behaviors interact in emotion.

63. Emotions have three components: _____ _____ , _____ _____ , and _____ _____ .

Identify two major questions in understanding emotions.

64. According to the James-Lange theory, emotional states _____ (precede/follow) bodily responses.

Describe two problems that Walter Cannon identified with the James-Lange theory.

65. Cannon proposed that emotional stimuli in the environment are routed simultaneously to the _____ , which results in awareness of the emotion, and to the _____ nervous system, which causes the body's reaction. Because another scientist concurrently proposed similar ideas, this theory has come to be known as the _____-_____ theory.

66. The two-factor theory of emotion proposes that emotion has two components: _____ arousal and a _____ label. This theory was proposed by _____ and _____ .

67. The *spillover effect* refers to occasions when our _____ response to one event carries over into our response to another event.

68. Schachter and Singer found that physically aroused college men told that an injection would cause arousal _____ (did/did not) become emotional in response to an accomplice's aroused behavior. Physically aroused volunteers not expecting arousal _____ (did/did not) become emotional in response to an accomplice's behavior.

69. Arousal _____ emotion; cognition _____ emotion.

70. Robert Zajonc believes that the feeling of emotion _____ (can/cannot) precede our cognitive labeling of that emotion.

Cite two pieces of evidence that support Zajonc's position.

71. Sometimes emotions take what LeDoux has called the " _____ _____ ": A pathway from the _____ via the (a) _____ to the (b) _____ enables us to experience emotion before _____ . For more complex emotions, sensory input is routed through the (c) _____ for interpretation.

72. The researcher who disagrees with Zajonc and argues that most emotions require cognitive processing, whether or not it is _____ , is _____ . According to this view, emotions arise when we _____ an event as beneficial or harmful to our well-being.

73. Complex emotions are affected by our _____ , _____ , and _____ .

Express some general conclusions that can be drawn about cognition and emotion.

STUDY TIP/APPLICATION: The theories of emotion discussed in this chapter seem so similar that it's often hard to tell them apart. As you think about the theories, remember: The theories differ in the order of importance they assign to the three components of emotions: physical arousal (increased heart rate, for example), the expression of the emotion (feeling angry, for example), and the importance of cognitive appraisal of the situation in which the emotion has occurred. To help ensure your understanding of the theories, see if you can fill in the missing information in the chart below for a common emotional experience: Hearing the screeching of a car's tires. For example, the first response might be a physical reaction such as increased heart beat or an emotional expression of fear, or it might be the opposite.

74. Theory	Stimulus Event	First Response	Second Response	Third Response
James-Lange	Screeching tires			
Cannon-Bard	Screeching tires			
Schachter-Singer	Screeching tires			

APPLICATIONS:

75. You are on your way to school to take a big exam. Suddenly, you feel nervous and you notice that your pulse is racing and you are sweating. This fits with the _____-_____ theory of emotion.

76. Two years ago, Maria was in an automobile accident in which her spinal cord was severed, leaving her paralyzed from the neck down. Today, Maria finds that she experiences emotions less intensely than she did before her accident. This tends to support the _____-_____ theory of emotion.

77. After hitting a grand-slam home run, Mike noticed that his heart was pounding. Later that evening, after nearly having a collision while driving on the freeway, Mike again noticed that his heart was pounding. That he interpreted this reaction as fear, rather than as ecstasy, can best be explained by the _____-_____ theory of emotion.

Embodied Emotion

Objective 10-9: Name some basic emotions.

78. Carroll Izard believes that there are _____ basic emotions, most of which _____ (are/are not) present in infancy. Although others claim that emotions such as pride and love should be added to the list, Izard contends that they are _____ of the basic emotions.

Objective 10-10: Describe the link between emotional arousal and the autonomic nervous system.

79. Describe the major physiological changes that each of the following undergoes during emotional arousal

   a. heart: _____
   b. liver: _____
   c. respiration: _____
   d. digestion: _____
   e. salivation: _____
   f. pupils: _____
   g. blood: _____
   h. skin: _____
   i. immune system: _____

80. The responses of arousal are activated by the _____ nervous system. In response to its signal, the _____ glands release the stress hormones _____ and _____ .

81. When the need for arousal has passed, the body is calmed through activation of the _____ nervous system.

Objective 10-11: Discuss whether different emotions activate different physiological and brain-pattern responses.

82. The various emotions are associated with _____ (similar/different) forms of physiological arousal. In particular, the emotions of _____ , _____ , and _____ _____ are difficult to distinguish physiologically.

83. A neural center in the brain called the _____ is activated when we experience lust, pride, and _____ .

84. The emotions _____ and _____ are sometimes accompanied by differing _____ temperatures and _____ secretions.

85. The emotions _____ and _____ stimulate different facial muscles.

86. The brain circuits underlying different emotions _____ (are/are not) different. For example, seeing a fearful face elicits greater activity in the _____ than seeing a(n) _____ face. People who have generally negative personalities, and those who are prone to _____ , show more _____ _____ lobe activity.

87. When people experience positive moods, brain scans reveal more activity in the _____ _____ _____ .

88. Individuals with more active _____ (right/left) _____ lobes tend to be more cheerful than those in whom this pattern of brain activity is reversed.

Objective 10-12: Discuss the effectiveness of polygraphs in using body states to detect lies.

89. (Thinking Critically) The technical name for the "lie detector" is the _____ .

(Thinking Critically) Explain how lie detectors supposedly indicate whether a person is lying.

90. (Thinking Critically) How well the lie detector works depends on whether a person exhibits _____ while lying.

91. (Thinking Critically) Those who criticize lie detectors feel that the tests are particularly likely to err in the case of the _____ (innocent/guilty), because different _____ all register as _____ .

92. (Thinking Critically) By and large, experts _____ (agree/do not agree) that lie detector tests are highly accurate.

93. (Thinking Critically) A test that assesses a suspect's knowledge of details of a crime that only the guilty person should know is the _____ _____ _____ .

APPLICATIONS:

94. A student participating in an experiment concerned with physical responses that indicate emotions reports that her mouth is dry, her heart is racing, and she feels flushed. Can the emotion she is experiencing be determined?
   a. Yes, it is anger.
   b. Yes, it is fear.
   c. Yes, it is ecstasy.
   d. No, it cannot be determined from the information given.

95. Julio was extremely angry when he came in for a routine EEG of his brain activity. When he later told this to the doctor, she was no longer concerned about the
   a. increased electrical activity in Julio's right hemisphere.
   b. increased electrical activity in Julio's left hemisphere.
   c. decreased electrical activity in Julio's amygdala.
   d. increased electrical activity in Julio's amygdala.

96. As part of her job interview, Jan is asked to take a lie-detector test. Jan politely refuses and points out the problems with the test, which are that

a. _____

b. _____

97. Nine-month-old Nicole's left frontal lobe is more active than her right frontal lobe. We can expect that, all other things being equal, Nicole

a. may suffer from mild depression for most of her life.
b. may have trouble "turning off" upsetting feelings later in her life.
c. may be more cheerful than those with more active right frontal lobes.
d. may have trouble expressing feelings later in her life.

Expressed and Experienced Emotion

Objective 10-13: Describe our ability to communicate nonverbally.

98. Most people are especially good at interpreting nonverbal _____ . Although we are good at detecting emotions, we find it difficult to detect _____ expressions.

99. Introverts are _____ (better/ worse) at reading others' emotions, whereas extraverts are themselves _____ (easier/harder) to read.

100. The absence of nonverbal cues to emotion is one reason that _____ _____ are easy to misread.

Objective 10-14: Discuss how men and women differ in their emotional expressions and experiences.

101. Women are generally _____ (better/worse) than men at detecting nonverbal signs of emotion. Women possess greater emotional _____ than men, as revealed by the tendency of men to describe their emotions in _____ terms. This gender difference may contribute to women's greater emotional _____ . Although women are _____ (more/less) likely than men to describe themselves as empathic, physiological measures reveal a _____ (smaller/larger) gender difference. Women are _____ (more/less) likely than men to express empathy.

102. Pat is very accurate at reading others' non-verbal behavior and is more likely to express empathy. Based on body responses, Alex seems to feel almost as much empathy. Pat is _____ (male/female); Alex is _____ (male/female).

Objective 10-15: Discuss whether gestures and facial expressions mean the same thing in all cultures.

103. Gestures have _____ (the same/ different) meanings in different cultures.

104. Studies of adults indicate that in different cultures facial expressions have _____ (the same/different) meanings. Studies of children indicate that the meaning of their facial expressions _____ (varies/ does not vary) across cultures. The emotional facial expressions of blind children _____ (are/are not) the same as those of sighted children.

105. According to _____ , human emotional expressions evolved because they helped our ancestors communicate before language developed. It has also been adaptive for us to _____ faces in particular _____ .

106. Cultures that encourage _____ display mostly visible emotions. In cultures such as that of Japan people _____ emotions from the surrounding context. This points to the importance of realizing that emotions are not only biological and psychological but also _____-_____ .

107. Who is the LEAST likely to display personal emotions openly?
a. Paul, a game warden in Australia
b. Niles, a stockbroker in Belgium
c. Deborah, a physicist in Toronto
d. Yoko, a dentist in Japan

Objective 10-16: Describe how facial expressions influence our feelings.

108. Darwin believed that when an emotion is accompanied by an outward facial expression, the emotion is _____ (intensified/diminished).

109. In one study, students who were induced to _____ reported feeling a little angry.

110. The _____ _____ effect occurs when expressions amplify our emotions by activating muscles associated with specific states.

111. Studies have found that imitating another person's facial expressions _____ (leads/does not lead) to greater empathy with that person's feelings.

112. Similarly, moving our body as we would when experiencing a particular emotion causes us to feel that emotion. This is the _____ _____ effect.

APPLICATIONS:

113. The candidate stepped before the hostile audience, panic written all over his face. It is likely that the candidate's facial expression caused him to experience
    a. a lessening of his fear.
    b. an intensification of his fear.
    c. a surge of digestive enzymes in his body.
    d. increased body temperature.

114. Children in New York, Nigeria, and New Zealand smile when they are happy and frown when they are sad. This suggests that
    a. the Cannon-Bard theory is correct.
    b. some emotional expressions are learned at a very early age.
    c. the two-factor theory is correct.
    d. facial expressions of emotion are universal and biologically determined.

Progress Test 1

Multiple-Choice Questions

Circle your answers to the following questions and check them with the answers beginning on page 259. If your answer is incorrect, read the explanation for why it is incorrect and then consult the text.

1. Motivation is best understood as a state that
    a. reduces a drive.
    b. aims at satisfying a biological need.
    c. energizes an organism to act.
    d. energizes and directs behavior.

2. Which of the following is a difference between a drive and a need?
    a. Needs are learned; drives are inherited.
    b. Needs are physiological states; drives are psychological states.
    c. Drives are generally stronger than needs.
    d. Needs are generally stronger than drives.

3. One problem with the idea of motivation as drive reduction is that
    a. because some motivated behaviors do not seem to be based on physiological needs, they cannot be explained in terms of drive reduction.
    b. it fails to explain any human motivation.
    c. it cannot account for homeostasis.
    d. it does not explain the hunger drive.

4. One shortcoming of the instinct theory of motivation is that it
    a. places too much emphasis on environmental factors.
    b. focuses on cognitive aspects of motivation.
    c. applies only to animal behavior.
    d. does not explain human behaviors; it simply names them.

5. The text suggests that a *neophobia* for unfamiliar tastes
    a. is more common in children than in adults.
    b. protected our ancestors from potentially toxic substances.
    c. may be an early warning sign of obesity.
    d. only grows stronger with repeated exposure to those tastes.

6. The brain area known as the arcuate nucleus is notable in the study of motivation because it
    a. secretes hormones that affect appetite.
    b. secretes hormones that affect achievement motivation.
    c. is enlarged in adults.
    d. is enlarged in children.

7. Instinct theory and drive-reduction theory both emphasize _____ factors in motivation.
    a. environmental   c. psychological
    b. cognitive   d. biological

8. Few human behaviors are rigidly patterned enough to qualify as
    a. needs.   c. instincts.
    b. drives.   d. incentives.

9. In their study of men on a semistarvation diet, researchers found that
   a. the metabolic rate of the men increased.
   b. the men eventually lost interest in food.
   c. the men became obsessed with food.
   d. the men's behavior directly contradicted predictions made by Maslow's hierarchy of needs.

10. When asked what makes life meaningful, most people first mention
    a. good health.
    b. challenging work.
    c. satisfying relationships.
    d. serving others.

11. Research on genetic influences on obesity reveals that
    a. the body weights of adoptees correlate with that of their biological parents.
    b. the body weights of adoptees correlate with that of their adoptive parents.
    c. identical twins usually have very different body weights.
    d. the body weights of identical twin women are more similar than those of identical twin men.

12. Research on obesity indicates that
    a. pound for pound, fat tissue requires more calories to maintain than lean tissue.
    b. given an obese parent, boys are more likely than girls to be obese.
    c. dieters lose weight slowly at first, then more rapidly.
    d. when weight drops below the set point, hunger increases.

13. Which division of the nervous system is especially involved in bringing about emotional arousal?
    a. somatic nervous system
    b. peripheral nervous system
    c. sympathetic nervous system
    d. parasympathetic nervous system

14. Concerning emotions and their accompanying bodily responses, which of the following appears to be true?
    a. Each emotion has its own bodily response and underlying brain circuit.
    b. All emotions involve the same bodily response as a result of the same underlying brain circuit.
    c. Many emotions involve similar bodily responses but have different underlying brain circuits.

d. All emotions have the same underlying brain circuits but different bodily responses.

15. The Cannon-Bard theory of emotion states that
    a. emotions have two ingredients: physical arousal and a cognitive label.
    b. the conscious experience of an emotion occurs at the same time as the body's physical reaction.
    c. emotional experiences are based on an awareness of the body's responses to an emotion-arousing stimulus.
    d. emotional ups and downs tend to balance in the long run.

16. Which of the following was NOT raised as a criticism of the James-Lange theory of emotion?
    a. The body's responses are too similar to trigger the various emotions.
    b. Emotional reactions occur before the body's responses can take place.
    c. The cognitive activity of the cortex plays a role in the emotions we experience.
    d. People with spinal cord injuries at the neck typically experience less emotion.

17. (Thinking Critically) Current estimates are that an innocent person taking a polygraph test would have been declared guilty approximately
    _____ of the time.
    a. three-fourths   c. one-third
    b. one-half   d. one-fourth

18. In the Schachter-Singer experiment, which college men reported feeling an emotional change in the presence of the experimenter's highly emotional confederate?
    a. those receiving epinephrine and expecting to feel physical arousal
    b. those receiving a placebo and expecting to feel physical arousal
    c. those receiving epinephrine but not expecting to feel physical arousal
    d. those receiving a placebo and not expecting to feel physical arousal

19. Emotions consist of which of the following components?
    a. physiological reactions
    b. behavioral expressions
    c. conscious feelings
    d. all of these components

20. (Thinking Critically) Law enforcement officials sometimes use a lie detector to assess a suspect's responses to details of the crime believed to be known only to the perpetrator. This is known as the

    a. inductive approach.
    b. deductive approach.
    c. guilty knowledge test.
    d. screening examination.

21. Research on nonverbal communication has revealed that

    a. it is easy to hide your emotions by controlling your facial expressions.
    b. facial expressions tend to be the same the world over, while gestures vary from culture to culture.
    c. most authentic expressions last between 7 and 10 seconds.
    d. most gestures have universal meanings; facial expressions vary from culture to culture.

Matching Items

Match each definition or description with its term.

Definitions or Descritpions

    1. the body's weight-maintenance setting
    2. the body's tendency to maintain a balanced internal state
    3. moderate levels of motivation produce optimal performance
    4. emotions consist of physical arousal and a cognitive label
    5. an emotion-arousing stimulus triggers cognitive and body responses simultaneously
    6. the division of the nervous system that calms the body following arousal
    7. the division of the nervous system that activates arousal
    8. a device that measures the physiological correlates of emotion
    9. environmental stimulus that motivates behavior
    10. we are sad because we cry

Terms

    a. set point
    b. two-factor theory
    c. incentive
    d. sympathetic nervous system
    e. James-Lange theory
    f. polygraph
    g. Cannon-Bard theory
    h. parasympathetic nervous system
    i. homeostasis
    j. Yerkes-Dodson law

Progress Test 2

Progress Test 2 should be completed during a final chapter review. Answer the following questions after you thoroughly understand the correct answers for the section reviews and Progress Test 1.

Multiple-Choice Questions

1. Which of the following influences on hunger motivation does NOT belong with the others?

    a. set/settling point
    b. attraction to sweet and salty tastes
    c. reduced production of ghrelin after stomach bypass surgery
    d. memory of time elapsed since your last meal

2. Homeostasis refers to

    a. the tendency to maintain a steady internal state.
    b. the tendency to seek external incentives for behavior.
    c. the setting of the body's "weight thermostat."
    d. the second level of Maslow's hierarchy of needs.

3. The tendency to overeat when food is plentiful
   a. is a recent phenomenon that is associated with the luxury of having ample food.
   b. emerged in our prehistoric ancestors as an adaptive response to periods when food was scarce.
   c. is greater in developed, than in developing, societies.
   d. is stronger in women than in men.

4. Unit bias refers to the research finding that people tend to
   a. eat more when a portion of food is supersized.
   b. avoid unfamiliar tasting foods.
   c. overeat during celebrations with other people.
   d. do all of these things.

5. According to Maslow's theory
   a. the most basic motives are based on physiological needs.
   b. needs are satisfied in a specified order.
   c. the highest motives relate to self-transcendence.
   d. all of these statements are true.

6. Which of the following is INCONSISTENT with the drive-reduction theory of motivation?
   a. When body temperature drops below 98.6° Fahrenheit, blood vessels constrict to conserve warmth.
   b. A person is driven to seek a drink when his or her cellular water level drops below its optimum point.
   c. Monkeys will work puzzles even if not given a food reward.
   d. A person becomes hungry when body weight falls below its biological set point.

7. Which of the following is NOT an aspect of Murray's definition of achievement motivation?
   a. the desire to master skills
   b. the desire for control
   c. the desire to gain approval
   d. the desire to attain a high standard

8. Which of the following is NOT necessarily a reason that obese people have trouble losing weight?
   a. Fat tissue has a lower metabolic rate than lean tissue.
   b. Once a person has lost weight, it takes fewer calories to maintain his or her current weight.
   c. The tendency toward obesity may be genetically based.
   d. Obese people are weak-willed gluttons.

9. Beginning with the most basic needs, which of the following represents the correct sequence of needs in the hierarchy described by Maslow?
   a. safety; physiological; esteem; belongingness and love; self-fulfillment
   b. safety; physiological; belongingness and love; esteem; self-fulfillment
   c. physiological; safety; esteem; belongingness and love; self-fulfillment
   d. physiological; safety; belongingness and love; esteem; self-fulfillment

10. Which of the following most accurately describes emotional arousal?
    a. Emotions prepare the body to fight or flee.
    b. Emotions are voluntary reactions to emotion-arousing stimuli.
    c. Because all emotions have the same physiological basis, emotions are primarily psychological events.
    d. Emotional arousal is always accompanied by cognition.

11. Schachter's and Singer's two-factor theory emphasizes that emotion involves both
    a. the sympathetic and parasympathetic divisions of the nervous system.
    b. verbal and nonverbal expression.
    c. physical arousal and a cognitive label.
    d. universal and culture-specific aspects.

12. Which theory of emotion emphasizes the simultaneous experience of the body's response and emotional feeling?
    a. James-Lange theory
    b. Cannon-Bard theory
    c. two-factor theory
    d. Yerkes-Dodson law

13. Izard believes that there are _____ basic emotions.
    a. 3   c. 7
    b. 5   d. 10

14. (Thinking Critically) The polygraph measures
    a. lying.
    b. brain rhythms.
    c. chemical changes in the body.
    d. physiological indexes of arousal.

15. Which of the following is true regarding gestures and facial expressions?
    a. Gestures are universal; facial expressions, culture-specific.
    b. Facial expressions are universal; gestures, culture-specific.

c. Both gestures and facial expressions are universal.

d. Both gestures and facial expressions are culture-specific.

16. Which theory of emotion implies that every emotion is associated with a unique physiological reaction?

a. James-Lange theory

b. Cannon-Bard theory

c. two-factor theory

d. Yerkes-Dodson law

17. Which of the following was NOT presented in the text as evidence that some emotional reactions involve no deliberate, rational thinking?

a. Some of the neural pathways involved in emotion are separate from those involved in thinking and memory.

b. Emotional reactions are sometimes quicker than our interpretations of a situation.

c. People can develop an emotional preference for visual stimuli to which they have been unknowingly exposed.

d. Arousal of the sympathetic nervous system will trigger an emotional reaction even when artificially induced by an injection of epinephrine.

18. In an emergency situation, emotional arousal will result in

a. increased rate of respiration.

b. increased blood sugar.

c. a slowing of digestion.

d. all of these events.

19. (Thinking Critically) Many psychologists are opposed to the use of lie detectors because

a. they represent an invasion of a person's privacy and could easily be used for unethical purposes.

b. there are often serious discrepancies among the various indicators such as perspiration and heart rate.

c. polygraphs cannot distinguish the various possible causes of arousal.

d. they are accurate only about 50 percent of the time.

20. Research with subliminally flashed stimuli supports Robert Zajonc's view that

a. the heart is always subject to the mind.

b. emotional reactions involve deliberate rational thinking.

c. cognition is not necessary for emotion.

d. responding to a subliminal stimulus is a learned skill.

21. With regard to emotions, Darwin believed that

a. the expression of emotions helped our ancestors to survive.

b. all humans express basic emotions using similar facial expressions.

c. human facial expressions of emotion retain elements of animals' emotional displays.

d. all of these statements are true.

True–False Items

Indicate whether each statement is true or false by placing *T* or *F* in the blank next to the item.

_____ 1. When body weight rises above set point, hunger increases.

_____ 2. All taste preferences are conditioned.

_____ 3. Obesity is often a sign of social status and affluence in developing countries.

_____ 4. Men are generally better than women at detecting nonverbal emotional expression.

_____ 5. The sympathetic nervous system triggers physiological arousal during an emotion.

_____ 6. When one imitates an emotional facial expression, the body may experience physiological changes characteristic of that emotion.

_____ 7. Physical arousal can intensify emotion.

_____ 8. All emotions involve conscious thought.

_____ 9. The two-factor theory states that emotions are given a cognitive label before physical arousal occurs.

Essay Questions

1. Differentiate the three major theories of motivation, discuss their origins, and explain why they cannot fully account for human behavior. (Use the space below to list the points you want to make, and organize them. Then write the essay on a separate sheet of paper.)

2. Discuss biological and cultural influences on emotions. (Use the space below to list the points you want to make, and organize them. Then write the essay on a separate sheet of paper.)

Terms and Concepts to Remember

Writing Definitions

Using your own words, write on a separate piece of paper a brief definition or explanation of each of the following terms.

1. motivation
2. instinct
3. drive-reduction theory
4. homeostasis
5. incentive
6. Yerkes-Dodson law
7. hierarchy of needs
8. glucose
9. set point
10. basal metabolic rate
11. achievement motivation
12. emotion
13. James-Lange theory
14. Cannon-Bard theory
15. two-factor theory
16. polygraph
17. facial feedback effect

Cross-Check

As you learned in Chapter 1, reviewing and over-learning of material are important to the learning process. After you have written the definitions of the key terms in this chapter, you should complete the crossword puzzle to ensure that you can reverse the process—recognize the term, given the definition.

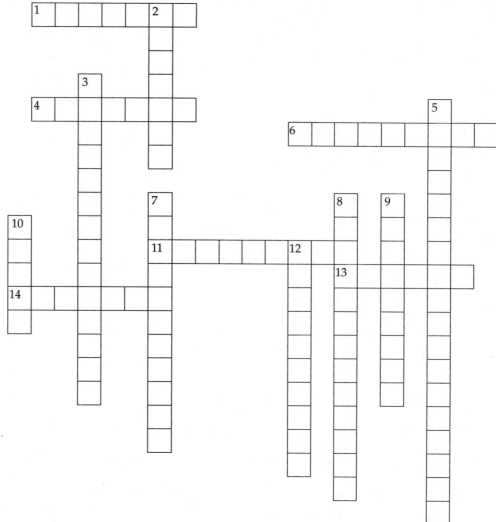

ACROSS

1. A response of the whole organism involving physical arousal, expressive behaviors, and conscious experience.
4. Hormone secreted by an empty stomach.
6. Device that measures several of the physiological responses accompanying emotion.
11. In Maslow's theory, human needs are organized into a _____ .
13. In Maslow's theory, the needs that follow physiological needs in order of priority.
14. Major energy source for the body.

DOWN

2. A BMI of 30 or more.
3. Theory that explains behavior as arising from physiological needs and the states of tension they create.
5. The body's rate of energy expenditure at rest.
7. Type of motivation that reflects the degree to which a person is motivated by a desire for significant accomplishment.
8. In Maslow's theory, the most basic types of needs.
9. Theory that emotions have two ingredients: physical arousal and a cognitive label.
10. Theory that emotional experiences are based on an awareness of the body's responses to emotion-arousing stimuli was proposed by James and _____ .

12. Theory that the subjective experience of an emotion occurs at the same time as the body's physical reaction.

Answers
Chapter Review

Introduction and *Motivational Concepts*

1. a need or desire that energizes behavior and directs it toward a goal
2. instinct; evolutionary; drive-reduction; arousal; hierarchy; Abraham Maslow
3. instincts; did not; genes
4. need; drives
5. homeostasis
6. incentives
7. increase; do not

8. arousal; optimum levels; Yerkes-Dodson; moderate

9. lower-level

10. physiological; self-actualization; self-transcendence

11. arbitrary; universally

12. financial; home-life

13. **b.** is the answer. Drive-reduction theory maintains that behavior is motivated when a biological need creates an aroused state, driving the individual to satisfy the need. It is difficult to believe that Mary's hang-gliding is satisfying a biological need.
a. & c. Mary may enjoy hang-gliding because it is a challenge that "is there" (incentive) or because it increases her self-esteem and sense of fulfillment in life (Maslow's hierarchy of needs).

14. **d.** is the answer. According to Maslow's theory, physiological needs, such as the need to satisfy hunger, must be satisfied before a person pursues loftier needs, such as making political statements.
a. Darwin focused on genetically predisposed behaviors.
b. & c. Yerkes and Dodson dealt with optimal levels of arousal, not the sequencing of needs.

15. **c.** is the answer. This is an example of salivating in response to an incentive rather than to maintain a balanced internal state.
a. & b. Both examples are behaviors that maintain a balanced internal state (homeostasis).

Hunger

16. semistarvation

17. stomach contractions

18. did

19. glucose; hunger

20. hypothalamus; arcuate nucleus

21. ghrelin

22. less; insulin; leptin; orexin; PYY

23. set point; less; more

24. basal metabolic; lowering

25. is not accepted; slow, sustained changes in body weight; psychological factors; overeat; gain weight; settling point

26. **b.** is the answer. The body acts to defend its set point, or the weight to which it is predisposed. If Lucille was already near her set point, weight loss would prove difficult.
a. If the weight level to which her body is predisposed is low, weight loss upon dieting should not be difficult.

c. An increase in basal metabolic rate would help her to lose weight.
d. People influenced by external factors might have greater problems losing weight because they tend to respond to food stimuli, but this can't be the explanation in Lucille's case because she has been sticking to her diet.

27. memory

28. serotonin; calms

29. genetic; conditioning; culture

30. unfamiliar; neophobia

31. ecology of eating; social; more; unit bias; variety

32. **c.** is the answer. Serotonin is a neurotransmitter that is elevated by the consumption of carbohydrates and has a calming effect.
a. & b. These answers do not explain the feelings of relaxation that Randy associates with eating junk food.
d. The consumption of sugar tends to elevate insulin level rather than lower it.

33. psychological; women; depression; 30; 34; diabetes, high blood pressure, heart disease, gallstones, arthritis, and certain types of cancer

34. Alzheimer's

35. lower; less

Obese persons have higher set-point weights than nonobese persons. During a diet, metabolic rate drops to defend the set-point (or settling-point) weight. The dieter therefore finds it hard to progress beyond an initial weight loss. When the diet is concluded, the lowered metabolic rate continues, so that relatively small amounts of food may prove fattening. Also, some people have lower metabolic rates than others.

36. do

37. environmental; sleep loss; more; social

38. food consumption; activity levels

Begin only if you are motivated and self-disciplined. Minimize exposure to tempting food cues. Limit variety and eat healthy foods. Don't starve all day and eat one big meal at night. Beware of binge eating. Be realistic and moderate. Boost your metabolism through exercise. Get enough sleep. Reduce portion sizes. Connect to a support group.

39. rapid; more slowly; decreased

40. **c.** is the answer. Individual differences in metabolism and set point explain why it is possible for two people to have very different weights despite similar patterns of eating and exercise.

41. **a.** is the answer. Dieting, including fasting, lowers the body's metabolic rate and reduces the amount of food energy needed to maintain body weight.

b., c., & d. Each of these strategies would be a good piece of advice to a dieter.

The Need to Belong

42. Aristotle; social; survival; attachments; reproduce

43. close, satisfying relationships with family, friends, or romantic partners; autonomy; competence

44. reward; safety; prefrontal cortex

45. social; liking

46. withdrawn, frightened, or speechless; insecure anxious; insecure avoidant

47. isolated; chain migration

48. Throughout the world; ostracism; anterior cingulate cortex; pain

49. self-defeating; aptitude tests; aggressive

50. cell phone

51. e-mail; texting

52. lonely

53. social networking

54. self-disclosure; eye-to-eye conversation

55. reveal

56. narcissistic; especially active

57. **c.** is the answer.

58. **d.** is the answer.

Achievement Motivation

59. achievement motivation

60. self-discipline; intelligence scores; grit

61. **d.** is the answer.

62. **b.** is the answer.

Emotion: Arousal, Behavior, and Cognition

63. bodily arousal; expressive behaviors; conscious experience

Does bodily arousal come before or after emotional feelings? How do thinking and feeling interact?

64. follow

Cannon argued that the body's responses were not sufficiently distinct to trigger the different emotions and, furthermore, that bodily changes occur too slowly to trigger sudden emotion.

65. cortex; sympathetic; Cannon-Bard

66. physical; cognitive; Stanley Schachter; Jerome Singer

67. arousal

68. did not; did

69. fuels; channels

70. can

First, experiments on subliminal perception indicate that although stimuli are not consciously perceived, people later prefer those stimuli to others they have never been exposed to. Second, there is some separation of the neural pathways involved in emotion and cognition.

71. low road; eye or ear; thalamus; amygdala; cognition; cortex

72. conscious; Richard Lazarus; appraise

73. interpretations; expectations; memories

It seems that some emotional responses—especially simple likes, dislikes, and fears—involve no conscious thinking. Other emotions are greatly affected by our interpretations, expectations, and memories.

74. Answers are given in order: first response, second response, third response.

    James-Lange theory: physical arousal, expressed emotion, cognitive appraisal is unimportant

    Cannon-Bard theory: physical arousal and cognitive appraisal occur simultaneously, expressed emotion

    Two-factor theory: physical arousal, cognitive appraisal, expressed emotion

75. James-Lange. The James-Lange theory proposes that the experienced emotion is an awareness of a prior body response: Your pulse races, and so you feel nervous.

76. James-Lange. According to the James-Lange theory, Maria's emotions should be greatly diminished because her brain is unable to sense physical arousal.

77. two-factor. According to the two-factor theory, it is cognitive interpretation of the same general physiological arousal that distinguishes the two emotions.

Embodied Emotion

78. 10; are; combinations

79. **a.** Heart rate increases.

    b. The liver pours extra sugar into the bloodstream.

    c. Respiration rate increases.

    d. Digestion slows.

    e. Salivation decreases.

    f. Pupils dilate.

    g. If wounded, blood tends to clot more rapidly.

    h. Skin perspires.

    i. Immune system functioning decreases.

80. sympathetic; adrenal; epinephrine (adrenaline); norepinephrine (noradrenaline)

81. parasympathetic

82. similar; fear; anger; sexual arousal

83. insula; disgust

84. fear; rage; finger; hormone

85. fear; joy

86. are; amygdala; angry; depression; right frontal

87. left frontal lobe

88. left; frontal

89. polygraph

The polygraph measures several of the physiological responses that accompany emotion, such as changes in breathing, cardiovascular activity, and perspiration. The assumption is that lying is stressful, so a person who is lying will become physiologically aroused.

90. anxiety

91. innocent; emotions; arousal

92. do not agree

93. guilty knowledge test

94. d. is the answer.

95. a. is the answer. As people experience negative emotions, such as anger, the right hemisphere becomes more electrically active.
    c. & d. The EEG measures electrical activity on the surface of the cortex, not at the level of structures deep within the brain, such as the amygdala.

96. a. Our physiological arousal is much the same from one emotion to another.
    b. Many innocent people respond with heightened tension to the accusations implied by the critical questions.

97. c. is the answer.
    a. Individuals with more active right frontal lobes tend to be less cheerful and are more likely to be depressed.
    b. In fact, just the opposite is true: people with greater left frontal activity tend to be better able to turn off upsetting feelings.
    d. The text does not suggest that greater left or right frontal activity influences a person's ability to express his or her feelings.

Expressed and Experienced Emotion

98. threats; deceiving

99. better; easier

100. electronic communications

101. better; literacy; simpler; responsiveness; more; smaller; more

102. female; male

103. different

104. the same; does not vary; are

105. Charles Darwin; interpret; contexts

106. individuality; infer; social-cultural

107. d. is the answer. In Japan and China, cultures that encourage people to adjust to others, personal emotional displays are less visible.
    a., b., & c. In cultures that encourage individuality, as in Western Europe, Australia, and North America, personal emotions are displayed openly.

108. intensified

109. frown

110. facial feedback

111. leads

112. behavior feedback

113. b. is the answer. Expressions may amplify the associated emotions.
    a. Laboratory studies have shown that facial expressions intensify emotions.
    c. Arousal of the sympathetic nervous system, such as occurs when one is afraid, slows digestive function.
    d. Increased body temperature accompanies anger but not fear.

114. d. is the answer.
    a. & c. The Cannon-Bard and two-factor theories of emotion do not address the universality of emotional expressions.
    b. Even if it is true that emotional expressions are acquired at an early age, this would not necessarily account for the common facial expressions of children from around the world. If anything, the different cultural experiences of the children might lead them to express their feelings in very *different* ways.

Progress Test 1

Multiple-Choice Questions

1. **d.** is the answer.
   a. & b. Although motivation is often aimed at reducing drives and satisfying biological needs, this is by no means always the case, as achievement motivation illustrates.
   c. Motivated behavior not only is energized but also is directed at a goal.

2. **b.** is the answer. A drive is the psychological consequence of a physiological need.
   a. Needs are unlearned states of deprivation.
   c. & d. Because needs are physical and drives psychological, their strengths cannot be compared directly.

3. **a.** is the answer. The curiosity of a child or a scientist is an example of behavior apparently motivated by something other than a physiological need.
   b. & d. Some behaviors, such as thirst and hunger, are partially explained by drive reduction.
   c. Drive reduction is directly based on the principle of homeostasis.

4. **d.** is the answer.
   a. & b. Instinct theory emphasizes biological factors rather than environmental or cognitive factors.
   c. Instinct theory applies to both humans and other animals.

5. **b.** is the answer.
   a. Neophobia for taste is typical of all age groups.
   c. Neophobia for taste is *not* an indicator of obesity.
   d. With repeated exposure, our appreciation for a new taste typically *increases*.

6. **a.** is the answer.

7. **d.** is the answer.

8. **c.** is the answer.
   a. & b. Needs and drives are biologically based states that stimulate behaviors but are not themselves behaviors.
   d. Incentives are the external stimuli that motivate behavior.

9. **c.** is the answer. The deprived men focused on food almost to the exclusion of anything else.
   a. To conserve energy, the men's metabolic rate actually *decreased*.
   b. & d. Far from losing interest in food, the men came to care only about food—a finding consistent with Maslow's hierarchy, in which physiological needs are at the base.

10. **c.** is the answer.

11. **a.** is the answer.

12. **d.** is the answer.

13. **c.** is the answer.
    a. The somatic division of the peripheral nervous system carries sensory and motor signals to and from the central nervous system.
    b. The peripheral nervous system is too general an answer, since it includes the sympathetic and parasympathetic divisions, as well as the somatic division.
    d. The parasympathetic nervous system restores the body to its unaroused state.

14. **c.** is the answer. Although many emotions have the same general body arousal, resulting from activation of the sympathetic nervous system, they appear to be associated with different brain circuits.

15. **b.** is the answer.
    a. This expresses the two-factor theory.
    c. This expresses the James-Lange theory.
    d. This theory was not discussed.

16. **d.** is the answer. The finding that people whose brains can't sense the body's responses experience considerably less emotion in fact supports the James-Lange theory, which claims that experienced emotion follows from the body's responses.
    a., b., & c. All these statements go counter to the theory's claim that experienced emotion is essentially just an awareness of the body's response.

17. **c.** is the answer.

18. **c.** is the answer. The men who received epinephrine without an explanation felt arousal and experienced this arousal as whatever emotion the experimental confederate in the room with them was displaying.
    a. Epinephrine recipients who expected arousal attributed their arousal to the drug and reported no emotional change in reaction to the confederate's behavior.
    b. & d. In addition to the two groups discussed in the text, the experiment involved placebo recipients; these subjects were not physically aroused and did not experience an emotional change.

19. **d.** is the answer. These are the three components of emotions identified in the text.

20. **c.** is the answer. If the suspect becomes physically aroused while answering questions about details only the perpetrator of the crime could know, it is presumed that he or she committed the crime.

21. **b.** is the answer.

Matching Items

1.	a	**6.**	h
2.	i	**7.**	d
3.	j	**8.**	f
4.	b	**9.**	c
5.	g	**10.**	e

Progress Test 2

Multiple-Choice Questions

1. **d.** is the answer. Memory of the time of the last meal is an example of a psychological influence on hunger motivation.
   a., b., & c. Each of these is a biological influence on hunger motivation.

2. **a.** is the answer.
   b. This describes extrinsic motivation.
   c. This describes set point.
   d. Homeostasis has nothing to do with Maslow's hierarchy.

3. **b.** is the answer.
   c. If anything, just the opposite is true.
   d. Men and women do not differ in the tendency to overeat.

4. **a.** is the answer.
   b. This is an example of neophobia.
   c. This is an example of social facilitation.

5. **d.** is the answer.

6. **c.** is the answer. Such behavior, presumably motivated by curiosity rather than any biological need, is inconsistent with a drive-reduction theory of motivation.
   a., b., & d. Each of these examples is consistent with a drive-reduction theory of motivation.

7. **c.** is the answer.

8. **d.** is the answer. Most researchers today discount the idea that people are obese because they lack willpower.

9. **d.** is the answer.

10. **a.** is the answer. Emotional arousal activates the sympathetic nervous system, causing the release of sugar into the blood for energy, pupil dilation, and the diverting of blood from the internal organs to the muscles, all of which help prepare the body to meet an emergency.
    b. Being autonomic responses, most emotions are *involuntary* reactions.
    c. All emotions do *not* have the same physiological basis.
    d. Some emotions occur without cognitive awareness.

11. **c.** is the answer. According to Schachter and Singer, the two factors in emotion are (1) physical arousal and (2) conscious interpretation of the arousal.

12. **b.** is the answer.
    a. The James-Lange theory states that the experience of an emotion is an awareness of one's physical response to an emotion-arousing stimulus.
    c. The two-factor theory states that to experience emotion one must be physically aroused and attribute the arousal to an emotional cause.
    d. The Yerkes-Dodson law states that moderate arousal leads to optimal performance. It has nothing to do with emotional experience.

13. **d.** is the answer.

14. **d.** is the answer. No device can literally measure lying. The polygraph measures breathing, cardiovascular activity, and perspiration for changes indicative of physiological arousal.

15. **b.** is the answer. Whereas the meanings of gestures vary from culture to culture, facial expressions seem to have the same meanings around the world.

16. **a.** is the answer. If, as the theory claims, emotions are triggered by physiological reactions, then each emotion must be associated with a unique physiological reaction.
    b. According to the Cannon-Bard theory, the same general body response accompanies many emotions.
    c. The two-factor theory states that the cognitive interpretation of a general state of physical arousal determines different emotions.
    d. The Yerkes-Dodson law states that moderate arousal leads to optimal performance. It has nothing to do with emotional experience.

17. **d.** is the answer. As the Schachter-Singer study indicated, physical arousal is not always accompanied by an emotional reaction. Only when arousal was attributed to an emotion was it experienced as such. The results of this experiment, therefore, support the viewpoint that conscious interpretation of arousal must precede emotion.
    a., b., & c. Each of these was presented as a supporting argument in the text.

18. **d.** is the answer.

19. **c.** is the answer. As heightened arousal may reflect feelings of anxiety or irritation rather than of guilt, the polygraph, which simply measures arousal, may easily err.
    a. Misuse and invasion of privacy are valid issues, but researchers primarily object to the use of lie detectors because of their inaccuracy.

b. Although there are discrepancies among the various measures of arousal, this was not what researchers objected to.

d. The lie detector declares an innocent person guilty about one-third of the time and about one-fourth of the guilty innocent.

20. **c.** is the answer.

a. & b. These answers imply that cognition *always* precedes emotion.

d. These responses are unconscious and automatic and so are not learned.

21. **d.** is the answer.

True–False Items

1.	F	6.	T
2.	F	7.	T
3.	T	8.	F
4.	F	9.	F
5.	T		

Essay Questions

1. Under the influence of Darwin's evolutionary theory, it became fashionable to classify all sorts of behaviors as instincts. Instinct theory fell into disfavor for several reasons. First, instincts do not explain behaviors, they merely name them. Second, to qualify as an instinct, a behavior must have a fixed and automatic pattern and occur in all people, regardless of differing cultures and experiences. Apart from a few simple reflexes, however, human behavior is not sufficiently automatic and universal to meet these criteria. Although instinct theory failed to explain human motives, the underlying assumption that genes predispose many behaviors is as strongly believed as ever.

   Instinct theory was replaced by drive-reduction theory and the idea that biological needs create aroused drive states that motivate the individual to satisfy these needs and preserve homeostasis. Drive-reduction theory failed as a complete account of human motivation because many human motives do not satisfy any obvious biological need. Instead, such behaviors are motivated by environmental incentives.

   Arousal theory emerged in response to evidence that some motivated behaviors *increase*, rather than decrease, arousal.

2. All emotions involve some degree of physiological arousal of the sympathetic nervous system. Although the arousal that occurs with different emotions is in most ways undifferentiated, there may be subtle differences in the brain pathways and hormones associated with different emotions.

Other examples of the influence of biological factors on emotion are the universality of facial expressions of emotion.

   Unlike facial expressions of emotion, the meaning of many gestures is culturally determined. Culture also influences how people express their feelings. In cultures that encourage individuality, for example, personal emotions are displayed openly. In cultures that emphasize human interdependence, the display of personal emotions is discouraged.

Terms and Concepts to Remember

Writing Definitions

1. **Motivation** is a need or desire that energizes and directs behavior.

2. An **instinct** is a complex behavior that is rigidly patterned throughout a species and is unlearned.

3. **Drive-reduction theory** attempts to explain behavior as arising from a physiological need that creates an aroused tension state (drive) that motivates an organism to satisfy the need.

4. **Homeostasis** refers to the body's tendency to maintain a balanced or constant internal state.

5. An **incentive** is a positive or negative environmental stimulus that motivates behavior.

6. The **Yerkes-Dodson law** states that performance improves with arousal only up to a certain point, after which it decreases.

7. Maslow's **hierarchy of needs** proposes that human motives may be ranked from the basic, physiological level through higher-level needs for safety, love, esteem, self-actualization, and self-transcendence; until they are satisfied, the more basic needs are more compelling than the higher-level ones.

8. **Glucose**, or blood sugar, is the major source of energy for body tissues. Elevating the level of glucose in the body will reduce hunger.

9. **Set point** is an individual's regulated weight level, which is maintained by adjusting food intake and energy output.

10. **Basal metabolic rate** is the body's base rate of energy expenditure when resting.

11. **Achievement motivation** is a desire for significant accomplishment, for mastery of skills or ideas, for control, and for rapidly attaining a high standard.

12. **Emotion** is a response of the whole organism involving three components: (1) bodily arousal, (2) expressive behaviors, and (3) conscious experience.

13. The **James-Lange theory** states that emotional experiences are based on an awareness of the body's responses to emotion-arousing stimuli: a stimulus triggers the body's responses that in turn trigger the experienced emotion.

14. The **Cannon-Bard theory** states that the subjective experience of an emotion occurs at the same time as the body's physical reaction.

15. Schachter and Singer's **two-factor theory** of emotion proposes that emotions have two ingredients: physical arousal and a cognitive label. Thus, physical arousal is a necessary, but not a sufficient, component of emotional change. For an emotion to be experienced, arousal must be attributed to an emotional cause.

16. The **polygraph** is a machine, commonly used to detect lies, that measures several of the physiological responses accompanying emotion.

17. The **facial feedback effect** is the tendency of the muscles in the face to trigger corresponding emotional feelings.

Cross-Check

ACROSS
1. emotion
4. ghrelin
6. polygraph
11. hierarchy
13. safety
14. glucose

DOWN
2. obesity
3. drive-reduction
5. basal metabolic rate
7. achievement
8. physiological
9. two-factor
10. Lange
12. Cannon-Bard

CHAPTER 1

Stress, Health, and Human Flourishing

Chapter Overview

Behavioral factors play a major role in maintaining health and causing illness. The effort to understand this role more fully has led to the emergence of the interdisciplinary field of behavioral medicine. The subfield of health psychology focuses on questions such as: How do our perceptions of a situation determine the stress we feel? How do our emotions and personality influence our risk of disease? How can psychology contribute to the prevention of illness?

Chapter 11 addresses key topics in health psychology. First and foremost is stress—its nature, its effects on the body, psychological factors that determine how it affects us, and how stress contributes to infectious diseases, cancer, and heart disease. The chapter looks at physical and psychological factors that promote good health, including exercise and social support.

The last section is a discussion of happiness, the goal of all people everywhere. It begins with an explanation of positive psychology, the study of subjective well-being. The chapter then concludes with an examination of the factors that affect our well-being.

NOTE: Answer guidelines for all Chapter 11 questions begin on page 277.

Chapter Review

First, skim each section, noting headings and bold-face items. After you have read the section, review each objective by answering the fill-in and essay-type questions that follow it. Study Tips explain how best to learn a difficult concept and Applications help you to know how well you understand the material. As you proceed, evaluate your performance by consulting the answers beginning on page 277. Do not continue with the next section until you understand each answer. If you need to, review or reread the section in the textbook before continuing.

Stress and Health

Objective 11-1: Identify events that provoke stress responses, and describe how we respond and adapt to stress.

1. Stress is not merely a _____ or a _____ . Rather, it is the _____ by which we perceive and respond to environmental threats and challenges.

2. This definition highlights the fact that stress arises less from the events than from how we _____ them and that stressors can have _____ (only negative/both positive and negative) effects, depending on how they are perceived.

STUDY TIP/APPLICATION: The words *stress* and *stressor* are so similar it's easy to think that they mean the same thing. To understand the difference, remember that *stress* is the process by which we appraise and cope with challenging environmental events (the *stressors*). But they are different concepts describing different aspects of a behavior. It may help you to see the difference between these concepts if you realize that stressors can be external events, such as having your flight cancelled, or internal events, such as worrying about an upcoming term paper assignment, and that stress includes those events plus your response to them. To make sure you understand the differences between stress and stressors, see if you can come up with examples of each as you complete the chart on the following page. The first example has already been filled in.

| Appraisal | Response | | | |
3. Stressor (Stressful Event)	Threat	Challenge	Threat	Challenge
Getting cut off by a driver on the freeway	"I'm going to be in an accident"	"I need to watch more carefully"	Heart races; hit the brakes hard	Heart races; swerve out of the way

4. Catastrophic events, such as floods, hurricanes, and fires, usually result in significant damage to _____ and _____ health.

5. Another source of stress is significant life changes. _____ (Negative/Positive/Both negative and positive) events can cause stress.

6. Research studies have found that people who have recently been widowed, fired, or divorced are _____ (more/no more) vulnerable to illness than other people.

7. Another source of stress comes from _____ _____ , such as rush-hour traffic and family frustration.

8. Daily economic pressures, often compounded by anti-gay prejudice or racism, can have both _____ and _____ consequences. For example, when prolonged, stress may drive up _____ _____ levels for many African-Americans.

9. In the 1920s, physiologist _____ began studying the effect of stress on the body. He discovered that the hormones _____ and _____ are released into the bloodstream in response to stress. This and other bodily changes due to stress are mediated by the _____ nervous system, thus preparing the body for _____ _____ _____ .

10. In studying animals' reactions to stressors, Hans Selye referred to the bodily response to stress as the _____ _____ _____ .

11. During the first phase of the GAS—the _____ reaction—the person is in a state of shock due to the sudden arousal of the _____ nervous system. Your heart rate zooms and blood is diverted to your _____ _____ .

12. This is followed by the stage of _____ , in which the body's resources are mobilized to cope with the stressor.

13. If stress continues, the person enters the stage of _____ . During this stage, a person is _____ (more/less) vulnerable to disease.

14. A common response to stress among women has been called "_____ _____ _____ ," which refers to the increased tendency to _____ . This tendency in women may in part due to _____ , a stress-moderating hormone.

APPLICATIONS:

15. Each semester, Bob does not start studying until just before midterms. Then he is forced to work around the clock until after final exams, which makes him sick, probably because he is in the _____ phase of the _____ .
   a. alarm; general adaptation syndrome
   b. resistance; general adaptation syndrome
   c. exhaustion; general adaptation syndrome
   d. depletion; general adaptation syndrome

16. Connie complains to the campus psychologist that she has too much stress in her life. The psychologist tells her that the level of stress people experience depends primarily on

    a. how many activities they are trying to do at the same time.

    b. how they appraise the events of life.

    c. their physical hardiness.

    d. how predictable stressful events are.

Objective 11-2: Describe how stress makes us more vulnerable to disease.

17. The field that integrates behavioral and medical knowledge relevant to health and disease is _____ _____ . The subfield of psychology that contributes to behavioral medicine is called _____ psychology.

18. The new field of _____ investigates how psychological, neural, and endocrine systems together affect the immune system and health.

19. The body's system of fighting disease is the _____ system. This system includes two types of white blood cells, called _____ : the _____ _____ , which fight bacterial infections, and the _____ _____ , which mature in the _____ and attack viruses, cancer cells, and foreign substances.

20. Two other immune agents are the _____ , which pursues and ingests foreign substances, and _____ _____ cells, which pursue diseased cells.

21. Responding too strongly, the immune system may attack the body's tissues and cause some form of _____ or an _____ reaction, for example. Or it may _____ , allowing a dormant herpes virus to erupt or _____ cells to multiply.

22. Stress can suppress the lymphocyte cells, resulting in a(n) _____ (increase/

decrease) in disease resistance. Stress diverts energy from the _____ _____ to the _____ and _____ , mobilizing the body for action and making us more vulnerable to disease.

23. Worldwide, the fourth leading cause of death is _____ , caused by the _____ _____ , which is spread primarily through the exchange of _____ and _____ .

24. Stressful life circumstances _____ (have/have not) been shown to accelerate the progression of this chronic disease.

25. Educational initiatives, support groups, and other efforts to control stress _____ (have/have not) been shown to have positive consequences on HIV-positive individuals.

26. Stress _____ (does/does not) create cancer cells. However, some studies find that people are at increased risk for cancer within a year after experiencing _____ , _____ , or _____ .

27. When rodents were inoculated with _____ cells or given _____ , tumors developed sooner in those that were also exposed to _____ stress.

APPLICATIONS:

28. A white blood cell that matures in the thymus and that attacks cancer cells is

    a. a macrophage.   **c.** a T lymphocyte.

    b. a B lymphocyte.   **d.** any of these cells.

29. When would you expect that your immune responses would be WEAKEST?

    a. during summer vacation

    b. during exam weeks

    c. just after receiving good news

    d. Immune activity would probably remain constant during these times.

Objective 11-3: Explain why some of us are more prone than others to coronary heart disease.

30. The leading cause of death in North America is

    _____ _____

    _____ . List several risk factors for

    developing this condition: _____

    _____

    _____ .

31. Friedman, Rosenman, and their colleagues discovered that tax accountants experience an increase in blood _____ level and blood-_____ speed during tax season. This showed there was a link between coronary warning indicators and

    _____ .

Friedman and Rosenman, in a subsequent study, grouped people into Type A and Type B personalities. Characterize these types, and indicate the difference that emerged between them over the course of this nine-year study.

32. The Type A characteristic that is most strongly linked with coronary heart disease is

    _____ _____ ,

    especially _____

    _____ .

33. When a _____ (Type A/Type B) person is angered, bloodflow is diverted away from the internal organs, including the liver, which is responsible for removing _____ and fat from the blood. Thus, such people have elevated levels of these substances in the blood.

34. Another toxic emotion is _____ ; researchers have found that _____ are more than twice as likely to develop heart disease as _____ .

35. Depression _____ (increases/has no effect on) one's risk of having a heart attack or developing other heart problems.

36. Heart disease and depression may both result when chronic _____ triggers persistent _____ .

APPLICATION:

37. Jill is an easygoing, noncompetitive person who is happy in her job and enjoys her leisure time. She would PROBABLY be classified as
    a. Type A.
    b. Type B.
    c. Type C.
    d. There is too little information to tell.

Objective 11-4: Describe some healthful ways to cope with anger.

38. (Close-Up) The belief that expressing pent-up emotion is adaptive is most commonly found in cultures that emphasize _____ . This presumes that we can achieve emotional release, or _____ , through aggressive action or fantasy. In cultures that emphasize _____ , such as those of _____ or _____ , expressions of anger are less common.

(Close-Up) Identify some potential problems with expressing anger.

39. (Close-Up) List two suggestions offered by experts for handling anger.
    a. _____
    b. _____

40. (Close-Up) Researchers have found that students who mentally rehearsed the times they _____ someone who had hurt them had lower bodily arousal than when they thought of times when they did not.

APPLICATIONS:

41. Who will probably be angrier after getting a parking ticket?
    a. Bob, who has just awakened from a nap
    b. Veronica, who has just finished eating a big lunch

c. Dan, who has just completed a tennis match
d. Alicia, who has been reading a romantic novel

42. Marysol was so mad at her brother that she exploded at him when he entered her room. That she felt less angry afterward is best explained by _____ .

43. Expressing anger can be adaptive when you
   a. retaliate immediately.
   b. have mentally rehearsed all the reasons for your anger.
   c. count to 10, then blow off steam.
   d. first wait until the anger subsides, then deal with the situation in a civil manner.

Coping With Stress

Objective 11-5: Identify two ways that people cope with stress.

44. When we cope directly with a stressor, we are using _____-_____ coping.

45. When we attempt to alleviate stress by avoiding it and attending to emotional needs, we are using _____-_____ coping.

46. People tend to use _____-_____ coping when they feel a sense of _____ over a situation. They turn to _____-_____ coping when they cannot or believe they cannot _____ a situation.

STUDY TIP/APPLICATION: Two basic strategies for coping with stressors are problem-focused coping and emotion-focused coping. *Problem-focused coping* is an action-oriented strategy in which we attempt to reduce stress by changing the stressor or the way we interact with that stressor. In contrast, with *emotion-focused coping* we focus on our feelings and try to change how we think about stressors. Think about how you typically cope with stress. Do you more often rely on problem-focused coping or emotion-focused coping? Now complete the chart below. For each stressor, write down one example of a problem-focused strategy and one example of an emotion-focused strategy.

47. Stressor	Emotion-Focused Strategy	Problem-Focused Strategy
You are worried about the amount of reading needed to prepare for an exam.	To take your mind off things, you go to a movie.	You divide the reading into manageable, daily sessions, and get started!
a. You get into an argument with your roommate.		
b. Your car muffler falls off.		
c. You develop a cold sore on your lip the day of an important dance.		

APPLICATIONS:

48. Ricardo has been unable to resolve a stressful relationship with a family member. To cope, he turns to a close friend for social support. Ricardo's coping strategy is an example of
   a. problem-focused coping.
   b. emotion-focused coping.
   c. managing rather than coping.
   d. general adaptation.

49. To help him deal with a stressful schedule of classes, work, and studying, Randy turns to a regular program of exercise and relaxation training. Randy's strategy is an example of
   a. problem-focused coping.
   b. emotion-focused coping.
   c. managing rather than coping.
   d. general adaptation.

Objective 11-6: Describe how a perceived lack of control can affect health.

50. Negative situations are especially stressful when they are appraised as _____ .

51. Seligman found that exposure to inescapable punishment produced a passive resignation in behavior called _____

    _____ .

52. People become happier and show improved health and morale when they are given _____ (more/less) control over what happens to them.

53. With higher economic status comes lower risks of infant _____ , a low

    _____ _____ ,

    smoking, and _____ .

54. In animals and humans, sudden lack of control is followed by a drop in immune responses, a(n) _____ (increase/decrease) in blood pressure, and a rise in the levels of

    _____ _____ .

55. Individuals who believe that they control their own destinies are said to perceive an

    _____ _____

    _____ _____ .

    Individuals who believe that their fate is determined by outside forces are said to perceive an

    _____ _____

    _____ _____ .

56. More Americans today perceive an _____ (internal/external) locus of control. This shift may help explain the increased rates of _____ and other _____ _____.

57. Self-control, which is the ability to control _____ and _____ short-term gratification, predicts good _____ , better _____ , and _____ success. However, it requires attention and energy and so depletes the _____ _____ and _____ _____ associated with mental focus.

APPLICATION:

58. Karen and Kyumi attend different universities, but both have rooms in on-campus dorms. Karen's dorm is large, roomy, with only two students to a suite. Kyumi attends a city school, where the dorms are small, overcrowded, and noisy, with five students to a room, which makes study very difficult. Which student is probably under more stress?
    a. Karen
    b. Kyumi
    c. There should be no difference in their levels of stress.
    d. It is impossible to predict stress levels in this situation.

Objective 11-7: Discuss the links among basic outlook on life, social support, stress, and health.

59. People who have an optimistic outlook on life expect to have more _____ , to _____ better with stressful events, and to enjoy better _____ .

60. Another buffer against the effects of stress is _____ support.

61. People whose marriages are characterized by low levels of _____ live longer, healthier lives than people who are

    _____ .

62. Longitudinal research reveals that a

    _____ _____ at age 50 predicts healthy aging better than

    _____ _____ at the same age.

State some possible reasons for the link between health and social support.

63. (Close-Up) Some research studies suggest that the presence of _____ may help some people handle stress.

64. James Pennebaker has found that emotional _____ can adversely affect our physical health.

65. Health can be improved by _____ about personal traumas in a diary. Another way to reduce stress is to talk about it. In another study by Pennebaker, Holocaust survivors who were the most _____ had the most improved health.

APPLICATIONS:

66. You have just transferred to a new campus and find yourself in a potentially stressful environment. According to the text, which of the following would help you cope with the stress?
   a. believing that you have some control over your environment
   b. having a friend to confide in
   c. feeling optimistic that you will eventually adjust to your new surroundings
   d. All of these behaviors would help.

67. Which of the following would be the best piece of advice to offer a person who is trying to minimize the adverse effects of stress on his or her health?
   a. "Avoid challenging situations that may prove stressful."
   b. "Learn to play as hard as you work."
   c. "Maintain a sense of control and a positive approach to life."
   d. "Keep your emotional responses in check by keeping your feelings to yourself."

Reducing Stress

Objective 11-8: Discuss the advantages of aerobic exercise as a way to manage stress and improve well-being.

68. Sustained exercise that increases heart and lung fitness is known as _____ exercise.

69. Regular exercise in later life also predicts better _____ functioning and reduced risk of _____ _____ and Alzheimer's disease.

By one estimate, moderate exercise adds _____ (how many?) years to one's life expectancy.

70. Experiments _____ (have/have not) been able to demonstrate conclusively that such exercise reduces anxiety, depression, and stress.

71. Exercise increases the body's production of mood-boosting neurotransmitters such as _____ , _____ , and the _____ . It also may foster _____ .

Objective 11-9: Describe how relaxation and meditation might influence stress and health.

72. A system for recording a physiological response and providing information concerning it is called _____ . The instruments used in this system _____ (provide/do not provide) the individual with a means of monitoring physiological responses. Most recently, researchers have found that this system works best on _____ .

73. Simple relaxation procedures have been shown to help alleviate _____ , _____ , _____ , and _____ . Lowered blood pressure, heart rate, and oxygen consumption have been found to be characteristic of people who regularly practice _____ . The _____ response is a state of calm resulting from sitting quietly, with closed eyes, while breathing deeply.

74. Brain scans of experienced meditators reveal decreased activity in the _____ lobe and increased activity in the _____ lobe.

APPLICATION:

75. Philip's physician prescribes a stress management program to help Philip control his headaches, based on research by Herbert Benson. The core of this program involves the _____ _____ .

Objective 11-10: Describe what is meant by the faith factor, and offer some possible explanations for the link between faith and health.

76. Several recent studies demonstrate that religious involvement _____ (predicts/ does not predict) health and longevity.

State possible intervening variables that might account for the faith factor in health.

APPLICATIONS:

77. Concluding her presentation on spirituality and health, Maja notes that
    a. faith is a communal experience.
    b. religious involvement predicts health and longevity.
    c. people who attend religious services weekly have healthier lifestyles.
    d. all of these statements are true.

Happiness

Objective 11-11: Describe the main effects of being happy.

78. Happy people tend to perceive the world as _____ and live _____ and more energized and satisfied lives.

79. Happy people are also _____ (more/less) willing to help others. This is called the _____-_____ , _____-_____ phenomenon.

Objective 11-12: Define *subjective well-being*, and describe the topics explored by positive psychology researchers, noting the three "pillars" of the movement.

80. The _____ _____ were interested in human fulfillment. _____ _____ is using scientific methods to study human flourish-

ing. These psychologists explore _____ _____, _____, _____ , and _____ . The three pillars of this movement are
    a. _____
    b. _____
    c. _____

81. An individual's self-perceived happiness or satisfaction with life is called his or her _____ _____ .

Objective 11-13: Discuss how our happiness levels are affected by time, wealth, adaptation, and comparison.

82. Using web science, social psychologists have found that the most positive moods days of the week are _____ and _____ .

83. Positive emotions _____ (rise/fall) in the early to middle part of most days. The gloom of stressful events usually _____ (is gone by/continues into) the next day.

84. After experiencing tragedy or dramatically positive events, people generally _____ (regain/do not regain) their previous degree of happiness.

85. Most people tend to _____ (underestimate/overestimate) the duration of emotions and _____ (underestimate/overestimate) their resiliency and capacity to adapt.

86. Researchers have found that, after people achieve a certain level of income, money _____ (does/does not) increase their feelings of happiness.

87. During the last half-century, buying power in the United States has almost tripled; personal happiness has _____ (increased/ decreased/remained almost unchanged).

88. Research has demonstrated that people generally experience a higher quality of life and greater well-being when they strive for _____ _____ than when they strive for _____ .

89. The idea that happiness is relative to one's recent experience is stated by the _____-_____ phenomenon.

Explain how this principle accounts for the fact that, for some people, material desires can never be satisfied.

90. The principle that one feels worse off than others is known as _____ _____ . This helps to explain why the middle- and upper-income people who compare themselves with the relatively poor are _____ (more/less/equally) satisfied with life.

Objective 11-14: Identify some predictors of happiness, and discuss how we can be happier.

91. List six factors that have been shown to be positively correlated with feelings of happiness.

_____

_____

_____

_____

_____

_____

92. List four factors that are evidently unrelated to happiness.

_____

_____

_____

_____

93. Research studies of identical and fraternal twins have led to the estimate that _____ percent of the variation in people's happiness ratings is heritable. Personal history and _____ also matter. Westerners value _____ and _____ , while communal cultures value _____ _____ and _____ .

(Close-Up) State several research-based suggestions for increasing your satisfaction with life.

APPLICATIONS:

94. As elderly Mr. Hooper crosses the busy intersection, he stumbles and drops the packages he is carrying. Which passerby is most likely to help Mr. Hooper?
   a. Drew, who has been laid off from work for three months
   b. Leon, who is on his way to work
   c. Bonnie, who earned her doctoral degree the day before
   d. Nancy, whose father recently passed away

95. Cindy was happy with her promotion until she found out that Janice, who has the same amount of experience, receives a higher salary. Cindy's feelings are BEST explained according to the
   a. adaptation-level phenomenon.
   b. two-factor theory.
   c. catharsis hypothesis.
   d. principle of relative deprivation.

96. When Professor Simon acquired a spacious new office, he was overjoyed. Six months later, however, he was taking the office for granted. His behavior illustrates the
   a. relative deprivation principle.
   b. adaptation-level phenomenon.
   c. two-factor theory.
   d. optimum arousal principle.

Progress Test 1

Multiple-Choice Questions

Circle your answers to the following questions and check them with the answers beginning on page 280. If your answer is incorrect, read the explanation for why it is incorrect and then consult the text.

1. Researchers Friedman and Rosenman refer to individuals who are very time-conscious, supermotivated, verbally aggressive, and easily angered as _____ personalities.
   a. ulcer-prone   **c.** Type A
   b. cancer-prone   **d.** Type B

2. During which stage of the general adaptation syndrome is a person especially vulnerable to disease?
   a. alarm reaction
   b. stage of resistance
   c. stage of exhaustion
   d. stage of adaptation

3. The leading cause of death in North America is
   a. lung cancer.
   b. AIDS.
   c. coronary heart disease.
   d. alcohol-related accidents.

4. Which of the following is true regarding happiness?
   a. People with less education tend to be happier.
   b. Beautiful people tend to be happier than plain people.
   c. Women tend to be happier than men.
   d. People who are socially outgoing or who exercise regularly tend to be happier.

5. Research suggests that people generally experience the greatest well-being when they strive for
   a. wealth.
   b. modest income increases from year to year.
   c. slightly higher status than their friends, neighbors, and co-workers.
   d. intimacy and personal growth.

6. Research indicates that a person is most likely to be helpful to others if he or she
   a. is feeling guilty about something.
   b. is happy.
   c. recently received help from another person.
   d. recently offered help to another person.

7. A graph depicting the course of positive emotions over the hours of the day since waking would
   a. start low and rise steadily until bedtime.
   b. start high and decrease steadily until bedtime.
   c. remain at a stable, moderate level throughout the day.
   d. rise over the early hours and fall during the day's last several hours.

8. Stress has been demonstrated to place a person at increased risk of
   a. cancer.
   b. progressing from HIV infection to AIDS.
   c. bacterial infections.
   d. all of these conditions.

9. *Stress* is defined as
   a. unpleasant or aversive events that cannot be controlled.
   b. situations that threaten health.
   c. the process by which we perceive and respond to challenging or threatening events.
   d. anything that decreases immune responses.

10. Attempting to alleviate stress directly by changing a stressor or how we interact with it is an example of
    a. problem-focused coping.
    b. emotion-focused coping.
    c. managing rather than coping with stress.
    d. catharsis.

11. A study in which Holocaust survivors spent time recalling their experiences found that
    a. most did not truthfully report feelings and events.
    b. all survivors experienced a sustained increase in blood pressure until they finished talking about their experiences.
    c. those who were most self-disclosing later had the most improved health.
    d. all the survivors denied undergoing concentration camp horrors.

12. Which of the following was NOT mentioned in the text as a potential health benefit of exercise?
    a. Exercise can increase ability to cope with stress.
    b. Exercise can lower blood pressure.
    c. Exercise can reduce stress, depression, and anxiety.
    d. Exercise improves functioning of the immune system.

13. Social support _____ our ability to cope with stressful events.
    a. has no effect on
    b. usually increases
    c. usually decreases
    d. has an unpredictable effect on

14. Research has demonstrated that as a predictor of health and longevity, religious involvement
    a. has a small, insignificant effect.
    b. is more accurate for women than men.
    c. is more accurate for men than women.
    d. equals nonsmoking and exercise.

15. Behavioral and medical knowledge about factors influencing health form the basis of the field of
    a. health psychology.
    b. holistic medicine.
    c. behavioral medicine.
    d. osteopathic medicine.

16. The stress hormones epinephrine and norepi-nephrine are released by the _____ gland(s) in response to stimulation by the _____ branch of the nervous system.
    a. pituitary; sympathetic
    b. pituitary; parasympathetic
    c. adrenal; sympathetic
    d. adrenal; parasympathetic

17. Research on locus of control indicates that internals are _____ than externals.
    a. more dependent
    b. more intelligent
    c. better able to cope with stress
    d. more sociable

18. Seligman has found that humans and animals who are exposed to aversive events they cannot escape may develop
    a. an internal locus of control.
    b. relative deprivation.
    c. learned helplessness.
    d. neurotic anxiety.

19. During a class discussion, Trevor argues that positive psychology is sure to wane in popularity because it suffers from the same criticisms as humanistic psychology. You counter his argument by pointing out that, unlike humanistic psychology, positive psychology
    a. focuses on advancing human fulfillment.
    b. is rooted in science.
    c. is not based on the study of individual characteristics.
    d. has all of these characteristics.

20. James attributes his failing grade in chemistry to an unfair final exam. His attitude exemplifies
    a. internal locus of control.
    b. external locus of control.
    c. relative deprivation.
    d. emotion-focused coping.

Matching Items

Match each definition or description with the appropriate term.

Definitions or Descriptions

_____ 1. the tendency to react to changes on the basis of recent experience
_____ 2. an individual's self-perceived happiness
_____ 3. emotional release
_____ 4. the tendency to evaluate our situation negatively against that of other people
_____ 5. the scientific study of optimal human functioning
_____ 6. the process by which we perceive and respond to threatening events
_____ 7. the coronary-prone behavior pattern
_____ 8. the coronary-resistant behavior pattern
_____ 9. attempting to alleviate stress by avoiding a stressor
_____ 10. the tendency of people to be helpful when they are in a good mood
_____ 11. attempting to alleviate stress by managing how we interact with the stressor

Terms

a. adaptation-level phenomenon
b. positive psychology
c. catharsis
d. Type A
e. Type B
f. problem-focused
g. emotion-focused
h. stress
i. relative deprivation principle
j. feel-good, do-good phenomenon
k. subjective well-being

Progress Test 2

Progress Test 2 should be completed during a final chapter review. Answer the following questions after you thoroughly understand the correct answers for the section reviews and Progress Test 1.

Multiple-Choice Questions

1. When students studied others who were worse off than themselves, they felt greater satisfaction with their own lives. This is an example of the principle of
   a. relative deprivation.
   b. adaptation level.
   c. behavioral contrast.
   d. opponent processes.

2. During which stage of the general adaptation syndrome is a person's ability to physically cope with a stressor strongest?
   a. alarm
   b. resistance
   c. exhaustion
   d. mobilization

3. In order, the sequence of stages in the general adaptation syndrome is
   a. alarm reaction, stage of resistance, stage of exhaustion.
   b. stage of resistance, alarm reaction, stage of exhaustion.
   c. stage of exhaustion, stage of resistance, alarm reaction.
   d. alarm reaction, stage of exhaustion, stage of resistance.

4. Concerning the concept of catharsis, which of the following is true?
   a. Expressing anger can be temporarily calming if it does not leave one feeling guilty or anxious.
   b. The arousal that accompanies unexpressed anger never dissipates.
   c. Expressing one's anger always calms one down.
   d. Psychologists agree that under no circumstances is catharsis beneficial.

5. AIDS is a disorder that causes a breakdown in the body's
   a. endocrine system.
   b. circulatory system.
   c. immune system.
   d. respiratory system.

6. *Tend and befriend* refers to
   a. the final stage of the general adaptation syndrome.
   b. the health-promoting impact of having a strong system of social support.
   c. an alternative to the fight-or-flight response that may be more common in women.
   d. the fact that spiritual people typically are not socially isolated.

7. Research studies in Scotland and elsewhere have demonstrated that high economic status predicts
   a. higher levels of happiness.
   b. weaker immune functioning.
   c. lower risk of heart and respiratory diseases.
   d. increased prevalence of autoimmune disorders.

8. Which of these factors have researchers NOT found to correlate with happiness?
   a. age
   b. high self-esteem
   c. religious faith
   d. optimism

9. Which of the following statements concerning Type A and Type B persons is true?
   a. Even when relaxed, Type A persons have higher blood pressure than Type B persons.
   b. When stressed, Type A persons redistribute bloodflow to the muscles and away from internal organs.
   c. Type B persons tend to suppress anger more than Type A persons.
   d. Type A persons tend to be more outgoing than Type B persons.

10. The disease- and infection-fighting cells of the immune system are
    a. B lymphocytes.
    b. T lymphocytes.
    c. macrophages.
    d. all of these types of cells.

11. One effect of stress on the body is to
    a. suppress the immune system.
    b. facilitate the immune system response.
    c. increase disease resistance.
    d. increase the growth of B and T lymphocytes.

12. Allergic reactions and arthritis are caused by
    a. an overreactive immune system.
    b. an underreactive immune system.
    c. the presence of B lymphocytes.
    d. the presence of T lymphocytes.

13. Research on cancer patients reveals that
    a. stress affects the growth of cancer cells by weakening the body's natural resources.
    b. patients' attitudes can influence their rate of recovery.
    c. cancer occurs slightly more often than usual among those widowed, divorced, or separated.
    d. all of these statements are true.

14. The component of Type A behavior that is the most predictive of coronary disease is
    a. time urgency.   c. high motivation.
    b. competitiveness.   d. anger.

15. Which of the following is true of biofeedback training?
    a. A person is given sensory feedback for a subtle body response.
    b. Biological functions controlled by the autonomic nervous system may come under conscious control.
    c. The accompanying relaxation is much the same as that produced by other, simpler methods of relaxation.
    d. All of these statements are true.

16. Which of the following was NOT suggested as a possible explanation of the faith factor in health?
    a. Having a coherent worldview is a buffer against stress.
    b. Religious people tend to have healthier lifestyles.
    c. Those who are religious have stronger networks of social support.
    d. Because they are more affluent, religiously active people receive better health care.

17. The field of health psychology is concerned with
    a. the prevention of illness.
    b. the promotion of health.
    c. the treatment of illness.
    d. all of these things.

18. The belief that your fate is determined by chance or luck reflects
    a. internal locus of control.
    b. external locus of control.
    c. emotion-focused coping.
    d. learned helplessness.

19. Which of the following is most likely to strengthen the functioning of your immune system?
    a. high levels of stress
    b. Type A behavior
    c. social support
    d. reduced macrophage activity

20. Positive psychology focuses on
    a. positive well-being.
    b. positive character.
    c. positive groups.
    d. all of these factors.

True–False Items

Indicate whether each statement is true or false by placing *T* or *F* in the blank next to the item.

_____ 1. Stressors tend to increase activity in the immune system and in this way make people more vulnerable to illness.
_____ 2. Our satisfaction with life generally is not influenced by factors under our control.
_____ 3. Optimism tends to run in families.
_____ 4. Events are most stressful when perceived as both negative and controllable.
_____ 5. People who experience tragedy generally recover near-normal levels of happiness.
_____ 6. Optimists cope more successfully with stressful events than do pessimists.
_____ 7. Wealthy people tend to be much happier than middle-income people.
_____ 8. Religiously active people tend to live longer than those who are not religiously active.
_____ 9. Aerobic exercise can reduce stress, depression, and anxiety.
_____ 10. Type A persons are more physiologically reactive to stress than are Type B persons.
_____ 11. People with few social and community ties are more likely to die prematurely than are those with many social ties.

Essay Question

Discuss several factors that enhance a person's ability to cope with stress. (Use the space below to list the points you want to make, and organize them. Then write the essay on a separate sheet of paper.)

Terms and Concepts to Remember

Writing Definitions

Using your own words, on a separate piece of paper write a brief definition or explanation of each of the following terms.

1. stress
2. general adaptation syndrome (GAS)
3. tend and befriend
4. health psychology
5. psychoneuroimmunology
6. coronary heart disease
7. Type A
8. Type B
9. catharsis
10. coping
11. problem-focused coping
12. emotion-focused coping
13. learned helplessness
14. external locus of control
15. internal locus of control
16. self-control
17. aerobic exercise
18. feel-good, do-good phenomenon
19. positive psychology
20. subjective well-being
21. adaptation-level phenomenon
22. relative deprivation

Cross-Check

As you learned in Chapter 1, reviewing and overlearning of material are important to the learning process. After you have written the definitions of the key terms in this chapter, you should complete the crossword puzzle to ensure that you can reverse the process—recognize the term, given the definition.

ACROSS

4. Emotional release.
5. Coronary-prone behavior pattern.
7. Phenomenon in which people tend to be helpful when they are in a good mood.
8. During the _____ stage of the stress reaction, the body's sympathetic nervous system is suddenly activated.
9. The process by which people appraise and react to events they perceive as threatening.
11. White blood cells of the immune system that fight bacterial infections and viruses, cancer cells, and foreign substances in the body.

DOWN

1. Principle that we are worse off relative to those with whom we compare ourselves.
2. The "big eater" of the immune system.
3. Friedman and Rosenman's term for easygoing, relaxed people.
6. Type of exercise that may help alleviate anxiety.
8. Phenomenon referring to our tendency to judge things relative to our prior experience.
10. Psychologist who first described the general adaptation syndrome.

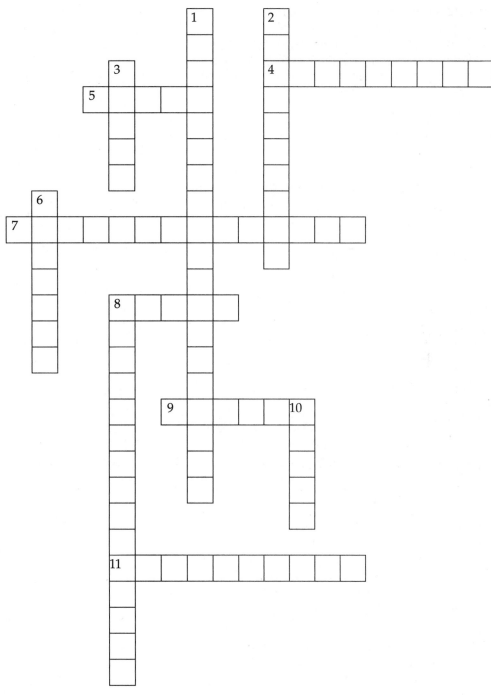

Answers
Chapter Review

Stress and Health

1. stimulus; response; process
2. appraise; both positive and negative
3. Many answers will complete the table. Just think about stressful events in your life—an upcoming exam, a first date, a job interview. For each one, consider how you would appraise it (as a subject

beyond your ability or as a task to be completed with extra work), then ask yourself how you would respond (if beyond your ability, you might go out with friends the night before the exam; as a challenge, you would stay home and study hard).

4. emotional; physical
5. Both negative and positive
6. more
7. daily hassles
8. psychological; physical; blood pressure
9. Walter Cannon; epinephrine (adrenaline); norepinephrine (noradrenaline); sympathetic; fight or flight
10. general adaptation syndrome
11. alarm; sympathetic; skeletal muscles
12. resistance
13. exhaustion; more
14. tend and befriend; seek and give support; oxytocin
15. **c.** is the answer. According to Selye's general adaptation syndrome, diseases are most likely to occur in this final stage.
    a. & b. Resistance to disease is greater during the alarm and resistance phases because the body's mobilized resources are not yet depleted.
    d. There is no such thing as the "depletion phase." Moreover, the posttraumatic stress syndrome refers to the haunting nightmares and anxiety of those who have suffered extreme stress, such as that associated with combat.
16. **b.** is the answer.
    a., c., & d. Each of these is a factor in coping with stress, but it is how an event is perceived that determines whether it is stressful.
17. behavioral medicine; health
18. psychoneuroimmunology
19. immune; lymphocytes; B lymphocytes; T lymphocytes; thymus
20. macrophage; natural killer (NK)
21. arthritis; allergic; underreact; cancer
22. decrease; immune system; brain; muscles
23. AIDS; human immunodeficiency virus (HIV); blood; semen
24. have
25. have
26. does not; depression; helplessness; bereavement
27. tumor; carcinogens; uncontrollable
28. **c.** is the answer.
    a. Macrophages are immune agents that search for and ingest harmful invaders.

    b. B lymphocytes form in the bone marrow and release antibodies that fight bacterial infections.
29. **b.** is the answer. Stressful situations, such as exam weeks, decrease immune responses.
30. coronary heart disease; smoking, obesity, high-fat diet, physical inactivity, elevated cholesterol level, stress responses, personality traits
31. cholesterol; clotting; stress

Type A people are reactive, competitive, hard-driving, supermotivated, impatient, time-conscious, verbally aggressive, and easily angered. Type B people are more relaxed and easygoing. In the Friedman and Rosenman study, heart attack victims came overwhelmingly from the Type A group.

32. negative emotions; the anger associated with an aggressively reactive temperament
33. Type A; cholesterol
34. pessimism; pessimists; optimists
35. increases
36. stress; inflammation
37. **b.** is the answer.
    a. Type A persons are hard-driving and competitive.
    c. There is no such thing as a "Type C" person.
38. individuality; catharsis; interdependence; Tahiti; Japan

One problem with expressing anger is that it breeds more anger, in part because it may trigger retaliation. Expressing anger can also magnify anger and reinforce its occurrence.

39. **a.**   Wait to calm down.
    b.   Deal with anger in a way that involves neither chronic anger nor sulking and rehearsing your grievances.
40. forgave
41. **c.** is the answer. Because physical arousal tends to intensify emotions, Dan (who is likely to be physically aroused after playing tennis) will probably be angrier than Alicia, Bob, or Veronica, who are in more relaxed states.
42. catharsis
43. **d.** is the answer.
    a. Venting anger immediately may lead you to say things you later regret and/or may lead to retaliation by the other person.
    b. Going over the reasons for your anger merely prolongs the emotion.
    c. Counting to 10 may give you a chance to calm down, but "blowing off steam" may rekindle your anger.

Coping With Stress

44. problem-focused

45. emotion-focused

46. problem-focused; control; emotion-focused; change

47. **a.** Emotion-focused: You go next door to be comforted by another close friend.

Problem-focused: You talk with your roommate about resolving your disagreement.

b. Emotion-focused: You call a friend but keep driving, leaving the muffler where it is and listening to the loud noises of the car.

Problem-focused: You immediately drive to the nearest muffler shop to have a new muffler put on.

c. Emotion-focused: You start crying, saying you can't possibly go to the dance.

Problem-focused: You go to the local drug store to find out what kind of cream you can buy to get rid of the cold sore.

48. **b.** is the answer. Ricardo is attempting to address his emotional needs, since he has been unable to alleviate stress directly.

49. **c.** is the answer.

50. uncontrollable

51. learned helplessness

52. more

53. mortality; birth weight; violence

54. increase; stress hormones

55. internal locus of control; external locus of control

56. external; depression; psychological disorders

57. impulses; delay; adjustment; grades; social; blood sugar; neural activity

58. **b.** is the answer. Living under crowded conditions contributes to feeling a lack of control, which is the situation in Kyumi's case.

59. control; cope; health

60. social

61. conflict; unmarried

62. good marriage; low cholesterol

Close relationships provide the opportunity to confide painful feelings, which may mitigate physical reactions to stressful events. Environments that foster our need to belong also foster stronger immune functioning. Social support calms us and reduces blood pressure and stress hormones.

63. pets

64. suppression

65. writing; self-disclosing

66. **d.** is the answer.

67. **c.** is the answer.
a. This is not realistic.
b. & d. These might actually increase the health consequences of potential stressors.

Reducing Stress

68. aerobic

69. cognitive; neurocognitive disorder; two

70. have

71. norepinephrine; serotonin; endorphins; neurogenesis

72. biofeedback; provide; tension headaches

73. headaches; hypertension; anxiety; insomnia; meditation; relaxation

74. parietal; frontal

75. relaxation response

76. predicts

Religiously active people have healthier lifestyles. They also tend to have stronger networks of social support and are more likely to be married. Finally, they may benefit from a stable, coherent worldview and a sense of hope for the long-term future.

77. **d.** is the answer.

Happiness

78. safer; healthier

79. more; feel-good, do-good

80. humanistic psychologists; Positive psychology; positive emotions; health; neuroscience; education
a. positive well-being
b. positive character
c. positive groups, communities, and cultures

81. subjective well-being

82. Friday; Saturday

83. rise; is gone by

84. regain

85. overestimate; underestimate

86. does not

87. remained almost unchanged

88. intimacy, personal growth, and contribution to the community; wealth

89. adaptation-level

If we acquire new possessions, we feel an initial surge of pleasure. But we then adapt to having these new possessions, come to see them as normal, and require other things to give us another surge of happiness.

90. relative deprivation; more

91. high self-esteem; satisfying marriage or close friendships; active religious faith; optimistic, outgoing, and agreeable; good sleeping habits and regular exercise; having work and leisure that engage our skills

92. age; gender; parenthood; physical attractiveness

93. 50; culture; self-esteem; achievement; social acceptance; harmony

Realize that happiness doesn't come from financial success. Take control of your time. Act happy. Seek work and leisure that engage your skills. Engage in regular aerobic exercise. Get plenty of sleep. Give priority to close relationships. Focus beyond self. Be grateful. Nurture your spiritual self.

94. **c.** is the answer. People who are in a good mood are more likely to help others. Bonnie, who is probably pleased with herself for earning a Ph.D., is likely to be in a better mood than Drew, Leon, or Nancy.

95. **d.** is the answer. Cindy is unhappy with her promotion because she feels deprived relative to Janice.
    a. The adaptation-level phenomenon would predict that Cindy's raise would cause an increase in her happiness, since her most recent experience was to earn a lower salary.
    b. The two-factor theory has to do with the cognitive labeling of physical arousal.
    c. The catharsis hypothesis maintains that venting one's anger may relieve aggressive urges.

96. **b.** is the answer. Professor Simon's judgment of his office is affected by his recent experience: When that experience was of a smaller office, his new office seemed terrific; now, however, it is commonplace.
    a. Relative deprivation is the sense that one is worse off than those with whom one compares oneself.
    c. The two-factor theory has to do with the cognitive labeling of physical arousal.
    d. This is the idea that there is an inverse relationship between the difficulty of a task and the optimum level of arousal. It is not discussed in this chapter.

Progress Test 1

Multiple-Choice Questions

1. **c.** is the answer.
   a. & b. Researchers have not identified such personality types.
   d. Individuals who are more easygoing are labeled Type B.

2. **c.** is the answer.
   a. & b. During these stages, the body's defensive mechanisms are at peak function.
   d. This is not a stage of the GAS.

3. **c.** is the answer.

4. **d.** is the answer. Education level, parenthood, gender, and physical attractiveness seem unrelated to happiness.

5. **d.** is the answer.

6. **b.** is the answer.
   a., c., & d. Research studies have not found these factors to be related to altruistic behavior.

7. **d.** is the answer.

8. **d.** is the answer. Because stress depresses the immune system, stressed individuals are prone to all of these conditions.

9. **c.** is the answer.
   a., b., & d. Whether an event is stressful depends on how it is appraised.

10. **a.** is the answer.
    b. In emotion-focused coping, we attempt to alleviate stress by avoiding or ignoring it.
    c. This is an example of coping rather than managing stress because it involves an attempt to actually alleviate a stressor.
    d. Catharsis refers to the release of emotion.

11. **c.** is the answer. The finding that talking about grief leads to better health makes a lot of sense in light of this physiological finding.
    a., b., & d. The study by Pennebaker did not find these to be true.

12. **d.** is the answer. Regular aerobic exercise has been shown to increase ability to cope with stress, lower blood pressure, and reduce depression and anxiety. The text does not cite evidence that exercise enhances immune function.

13. **b.** is the answer.

14. **d.** is the answer.
    b. & c. The text does not indicate that a gender difference exists in the faith factor in health.

15. **c.** is the answer.
    a. Health psychology is a subfield of behavioral medicine.
    b. Holistic medicine is an older term that refers to medical practitioners who take more of an interdisciplinary approach to treating disorders.
    d. Osteopathy is a medical therapy that emphasizes manipulative techniques for correcting physical problems.

16. **c.** is the answer.
    a., b., & d. The pituitary does not produce stress hormones nor is the parasympathetic division involved in arousal.

17. **c.** is the answer.
    a. & d. In fact, just the opposite is true.
    b. Locus of control is not related to intelligence.

18. **c.** is the answer. In such situations, passive resignation, called learned helplessness, develops.
    a. This refers to the belief that one controls one's fate; the circumstances described lead to precisely the opposite belief.
    b. Relative deprivation refers to the perception that we are worse off relative to those with whom we compare ourselves.
    d. Seligman did not specify that neurotic anxiety occurs.
19. **b.** is the answer.
20. **b.** is the answer.

Matching Items

1. a	5. b	9. g
2. k	6. h	10. j
3. c	7. d	11. f
4. i	8. e	

Progress Test 2

Multiple-Choice Questions

1. **a.** is the answer. The principle of relative deprivation states that happiness is relative to others' attainments. This helps explain why those who are relatively well off tend to be slightly more satisfied than the relatively poor, with whom the better-off can compare themselves.
   b. Adaptation level is the tendency for our judgments to be relative to our prior experience.
   c. This phenomenon has nothing to do with the interpretation of emotion.
   d. Opponent processes are not discussed in the text in relation to emotion.

2. **b.** is the answer.
   a. During the alarm stage a person's coping resources are just being activated.
   c. During the exhaustion stage a person's coping ability is the weakest.
   d. This is not a stage of the general adaptation syndrome.

3. **a.** is the answer.

4. **a.** is the answer.
   b. The opposite is true. Any emotional arousal will simmer down if you wait long enough.
   c. Catharsis often magnifies anger, escalates arguments, and leads to retaliation.
   d. When counterattack is justified and can be directed at the offender, catharsis may be helpful.

5. **c.** is the answer.

6. **c.** is the answer.
   a. The final stage of the general adaptation syndrome is exhaustion.

b. & d. Although both of these are true, neither has anything to do with "tend and befriend."

7. **c.** is the answer.

8. **a.** is the answer.

9. **b.** is the answer. The result is that their blood may contain excess cholesterol and fat.
   a. Under relaxed situations, there is no difference in blood pressure.
   c. Anger, both expressed and suppressed, is more characteristic of Type A people.
   d. The text doesn't indicate that Type A persons are more outgoing than Type B persons.

10. **d.** is the answer. B lymphocytes fight bacterial infections; T lymphocytes attack cancer cells, viruses, and foreign substances; and macrophages ingest harmful invaders.

11. **a.** is the answer. A variety of studies have shown that stress depresses the immune system, increasing the risk and potential severity of many diseases.

12. **a.** is the answer.
    b. An *under*reactive immune system would make an individual more susceptible to infectious diseases or the proliferation of cancer cells.
    c. & d. Lymphocytes are disease- and infection-fighting white blood cells in the immune system.

13. **d.** is the answer.

14. **d.** is the answer. The crucial characteristic of Type A behavior seems to be a tendency to react with negative emotions, especially anger; other aspects of Type A behavior appear not to predict heart disease, and some appear to be helpful to the individual.

15. **d.** is the answer. In biofeedback training, people are given sensory feedback about autonomic responses. Although biofeedback may promote relaxation, its benefits may be no greater than those produced by simpler, and less expensive, methods.

16. **d.** is the answer. As a group, religiously active people are no more affluent than other people.

17. **d.** is the answer. This chapter deals with the topics of health psychology, namely, preventing illness, by developing better ways to cope with stress; treating illness, by improving the ways in which people notice and explain symptoms; and promoting health, for example, through nutrition and weight control.

18. **b.** is the answer.
    a. People with an internal locus of control would believe that they are in control of their fate.

c. Emotion-focused coping refers to the tendency to alleviate stress by avoiding or ignoring a stressor.

d. Learned helplessness is the passive resignation of a person or animal previsously subjected to unavoidable aversive events.

19. c. is the answer.

20. d. is the answer.

True–False Items

1.	F	5.	T	9.	T
2.	F	6.	T	10.	T
3.	T	7.	F	11.	T
4.	F	8.	T		

Essay Question

When potentially stressful events occur, a person's appraisal is a major determinant of their impact. Catastrophes, significant life events, and daily hassles are especially stressful when appraised as negative and uncontrollable and when the person has a pessimistic outlook on life. Under these circumstances, stressful events may suppress immune responses and make the person more vulnerable to disease. If stressors cannot be eliminated, aerobic exercise, relaxation, meditation, and spirituality can help the person cope. Aerobic exercise can reduce stress, depression, and anxiety, perhaps by increasing production of mood-boosting neurotransmitters. Research demonstrates that people who regularly practice relaxation or meditation techniques enjoy a greater sense of tranquility and have lower blood pressure and stronger immune responses. People with strong social ties eat better, exercise more, and smoke and drink less. Social support may also help people evaluate and overcome stressful events. In addition, confiding painful feelings to others has been demonstrated to reduce the physiological responses linked to stress.

Terms and Concepts to Remember

Writing Definitions

1. **Stress** refers to the process by which we perceive and respond to certain events, called *stressors,* that we perceive as threatening or challenging.

2. The **general adaptation syndrome (GAS)** is the three-stage sequence of the body's adaptive reaction to stress outlined by Hans Selye.

3. **Tend and befriend** refers to the tendency of some people (especially women) to provide support (tend) and bond with and seek support from others (befriend) when under stress.

4. **Health psychology** is a subfield of psychology that provides psychology's contribution to behavioral medicine.

5. **Psychoneuroimmunology** is the study of how psychological, neural, and endocrine processes together affect the immune system and resulting health.

6. The leading cause of death in North America today, **coronary heart disease** results from the clogging of the vessels that nourish the heart muscle.

7. **Type A** is Friedman and Rosenman's term for the coronary-prone behavior pattern of competitive, hard-driving, impatient, verbally aggressive, and anger-prone people.

8. **Type B** is Friedman and Rosenman's term for the coronary-resistant behavior pattern of easygoing, relaxed people.

9. **Catharsis** is emotional release; in psychology, the idea that "releasing" aggressive energy (through action or fantasy) relieves aggressive urges.

9. **Coping** refers to any effort to alleviate stress using emotional, cognitive, or behavioral methods.

10. **Problem-focused coping** involves attempting to alleviate stress directly by changing a stressor or how we interact with it.

11. **Emotion-focused coping** involves attempting to alleviate stress by avoiding or ignoring a stressor and attending to emotional needs related to one's stress reaction.

12. **Learned helplessness** is the passive resignation and hopelessness that a person or animal learns from repeated exposure to inescapable aversive events.

13. **External locus of control** is the perception that your fate is determined by chance or outside forces not under personal control.

14. **Internal locus of control** is the perception that you control your own destiny.

15. **Self-control** is the ability to control impulses and delay short-term gratification for greater long-term rewards.

16. **Aerobic exercise** is any sustained activity such as running, swimming, or cycling that promotes heart and lung fitness and may help alleviate depression and anxiety.

17. The **feel-good, do-good phenomenon** is the tendency of people to be helpful when they are in a good mood.

18. Focusing on positive emotions, positive character traits, and enabling institutions, **positive psychology** is the scientific study of optimal human functioning.

19. **Subjective well-being** refers to self-perceived happiness or satisfaction with life.

20. The **adaptation-level phenomenon** refers to our tendency to judge things relative to a neutral level defined by our prior experience.

21. The principle of **relative deprivation** is the perception that we are worse off relative to those with whom we compare ourselves.

Cross-Check

ACROSS
4. catharsis
5. Type A
7. feel-good, do-good
8. alarm
9. stress
11. lymphocyte

DOWN
1. relative deprivation
2. macrophage
3. Type B
6. aerobic
8. adaptation level
10. Selye

Personality

Chapter Overview

Personality refers to each individual's characteristic pattern of thinking, feeling, and acting. Chapter 12 examines four perspectives on personality. Psycho-dynamic theories emphasize the unconscious and irrational aspects of personality. Humanistic theories draw attention to the concept of self and to the human potential for healthy growth. Trait theory led to advances in techniques for evaluating and describing personality. The social-cognitive perspective emphasizes the effects of our interactions with the environment. The text first describes and then evaluates the contributions, shortcomings, and historical significance of the psychoanalytic and humanistic perspectives. Next, the text turns to contemporary research on personality, focusing on how the trait and social-cognitive perspectives explore and assess traits and the focus of many of today's researchers on the concept of self.

NOTE: Answer guidelines for all Chapter 12 questions begin on page 301.

Chapter Review

First, skim each section, noting headings and bold-face items. After you have read the section, review each objective by answering the fill-in and essay-type questions that follow it. Study Tips explain how best to learn a difficult concept and Applications help you to know how well you understand the material. As you proceed, evaluate your performance by consulting the answers beginning on page 301. Do not continue with the next section until you understand each answer. If you need to, review or reread the section in the textbook before continuing.

Introducing Personality

1. Personality is defined as an individual's characteristic pattern of _____ , _____ , and _____ .

2. The psychoanalytic perspective on personality was proposed by _____ . A second, historically significant perspective was the _____ approach, which focused on people's capacities for _____ and _____ .

Psychodynamic Theories

Objective 12-1: Explain how Freud's treatment of psychological disorders led to his view of the unconscious mind.

3. Freud's perspective is an example of a _____ theory in that it views human behavior as an interaction between the _____ and _____ minds.

4. Sigmund Freud was a medical doctor who specialized in _____ disorders.

5. Freud developed his theory in response to his observation that many patients had disorders that did not make _____ sense.

6. At first, Freud tried using _____ to uncover his patients' thoughts, wishes, feelings, and memories.

7. The technique later used by Freud, in which the patient relaxes and says whatever comes to mind, is called _____ _____ .

8. Freud called his theory and associated techniques, whereby painful unconscious memories are exposed, _____ .

9. According to this theory, many of a person's thoughts, wishes, and feelings are hidden in a large _____ region. Some of the thoughts in this region can be retrieved at will into consciousness; these thoughts are said to be _____ . Many of the memories of this region, however, are blocked, or _____ , from consciousness.

Objective 12-2: Describe Freud's view of personality.

10. Freud believed that all facets of personality arise from conflict between our _____ internalized urges and the _____ controls over them.

11. According to Freud, personality consists of three interacting structures: the
(a) _____ ,
the (b) _____ ,
and the
(c) _____ .

12. The id is a reservoir of psychic energy that is primarily _____ (conscious/ unconscious) and operates according to the _____ principle.

13. The ego develops _____ (before/after) the id and consists of perceptions,

thoughts, and memories that are mostly _____ (conscious/unconscious). The ego operates according to the _____ principle.

14. The personality structure that reflects moral values is the _____ , which Freud believed began emerging at about age _____ .

Explain why the ego is considered the "executive" of personality.

15. A person with a _____ (strong/ weak) superego may be self-indulgent; one with an unusually _____ (strong/ weak) superego may be virtuous but guilt-ridden.

STUDY TIP/APPLICATION: Each of Freud's three interacting systems—the id, the ego, and the super-ego—has a different role in our conscious and unconscious thought processes. To help you understand the systems and how they differ, try completing the table on the next page. It includes three real-life conflicts and asks you to explain how each system would respond in each situation.

16. Conflict	The Id's Response	The Ego's Response	The Superego's Response
a. The driver ahead of you is driving 10 miles/hour below the speed limit.			
b. You have pledged a charitable donation but now need money to buy a new sweater.			
c. You've procrastinated about completing a term paper and a friend suggests buying one online.			

17. A psychoanalyst would characterize a person who is impulsive and self-indulgent as possessing

    a strong _____ and a weak _____ .

    a. id and ego; superego   **c.** ego; superego
    b. id; ego and superego   **d.** id; superego

18. According to the psychoanalytic perspective, a child who frequently "slips" and calls her teacher "Mom" PROBABLY

    a. has some unresolved conflicts concerning her mother.
    b. is fixated in the oral stage of development.
    c. is ruled by the pleasure principle.
    d. has a superego that overrides her id.

Objective 12-3: Identify the developmental stages proposed by Freud.

19. According to Freud, personality is formed as the child passes through a series of

    _____ stages, each of which is focused on a distinct body area called an

    _____ _____ .

20. The first stage is the _____ stage, which takes place during the first 18 months of life. During this stage, the id's energies are focused on behaviors such as

    _____ .

21. The second stage is the _____ stage, which lasts from about age

    _____ months to

    _____ months.

22. The third stage is the _____ stage, which lasts roughly from ages

    _____ to _____

    years. During this stage, the id's energies are

    focused on the _____ . Freud

    also believed that during this stage children

    develop sexual desires for the _____

    (same/opposite)-sex parent. Freud referred to

    these feelings as the _____

    _____ in boys. Some psychoana-

    lysts in Freud's era believed that girls experience

    a parallel _____

    _____ .

23. Freud believed that _____ with

    the same-sex parent is the basis for what psychol-

    ogists now call _____

    _____ .

Explain how this complex of feelings is resolved through the process of identification.

24. During the next stage, sexual feelings are repressed: this phase is called the

    _____ stage and lasts until puberty.

25. The final stage of development is called the
_____ stage.

26. According to Freud, it is possible for a person's development to become blocked in any of the stages; in such an instance, the person is said to be _____ .

APPLICATIONS:

27. Jill has a biting, sarcastic manner. According to Freud, she is
   a. projecting her anxiety onto others.
   b. fixated in the oral stage of development.
   c. fixated in the anal stage of development.
   d. identifying with her mother.

28. Song Yi works in a smoke-free office. So, she frequently has to leave work and go outside to smoke a cigarette. Freud would probably say that Song Yi is _____
   at the _____ stage of development.

Objective 12-4: Describe Freud's views on how people defended themselves against anxiety.

29. The ego attempts to protect itself against anxiety through the use of _____
_____ . The process underlying each of these mechanisms is _____ .

30. All defense mechanisms function
_____ and _____ .

APPLICATIONS:

38. Match each defense mechanism in the following list with the proper example of how it could show itself.

Defense Mechanisms

_____ 1. displacement
_____ 2. projection
_____ 3. reaction formation
_____ 4. rationalization
_____ 5. regression
_____ 6. denial

31. Freud believed that a person's
_____ wishes are often reflected in his or her _____ of the tongue, jokes, and dreams. Freud called the remembered content of dreams the _____
_____ , which he believed to be a censored version of the dream's true

_____ _____ .

32. Dealing with anxiety by returning to an earlier stage of development is called
_____ .

33. When a person reacts in a manner opposite that of his or her true feelings, _____
_____ is said to have occurred.

34. When a person attributes his or her own feelings to another person, _____ has occurred.

35. When a person offers a false, self-justifying explanation for his or her actions, _____ has occurred.

36. When impulses are directed toward an object other than the one that caused arousal,
_____ has occurred.

37. When a person refuses to believe or even perceive a painful reality, he or she is experiencing
_____ .

Example

a. nail biting or thumb sucking in an anxiety-producing situation
b. overzealous crusaders against "immoral behaviors" who don't want to admit to their own sexual desires
c. saying you drink "just to be sociable" when in reality you have a drinking problem
d. a parent will not admit that his child could cheat on a test
e. thinking someone hates you when in reality you hate that person
f. a child who is angry at his parents and vents this anger on the family pet, a less threatening target

39. Suzy bought a used, high-mileage automobile because it was all she could afford. Attempting to justify her purchase, she raves to her friends about the car's attractiveness, good acceleration, and stereo. According to Freud, Suzy is using the defense mechanism of

   a. displacement.   **c.** rationalization.
   b. reaction formation.   **d.** projection.

Objective 12-5: Identify which of Freud's ideas were accepted or rejected by his followers.

40. The theorists who established their own, modified versions of psychoanalytic theory are called

   _____-_____ .

   These theorists typically place _____ (more/less) emphasis on the conscious mind than Freud did and _____ (more/less) emphasis on sex and aggression.

Briefly summarize how each of the following theorists departed from Freud.

   a. Adler _____

   _____

   b. Horney _____

   _____

   c. Jung _____

   _____

41. Today's psychologists _____ (accept/reject) the idea of inherited experiences, which _____ (which theorist?) called a _____ _____ , a reservoir of images, or _____ .

42. More recently, some of Freud's ideas have been incorporated into _____ theory. Unlike Freud, the theorists advocating this perspective do not believe that _____ is the basis of personality. They do agree, however, that much of mental life is _____ , that _____ shapes personality, and that we often struggle with _____ _____ .

Objective 12-6: Describe projective tests and how they are used, and discuss some criticisms of them.

43. Tests that provide test-takers with ambiguous stimuli for interpretation are called

   _____ tests.

44. The most widely used projective test is the _____ , in which people are shown a series of _____ . Critics contend that these tests have _____ (little/significant) validity and reliability.

APPLICATION:

45. Teresa is taking a personality test that asks her to describe random patterns of dots. This is a _____ test.

Objective 12-7: Discuss how contemporary psychologists view Freud's psychoanalysis.

46. Contrary to Freud's theory, research indicates that human development is _____ (fixed in childhood/lifelong), children gain their gender identity at a(n) _____ (earlier/later) age, and the presence of a same-sex parent _____ (is/is not) necessary for the child to become strongly masculine or feminine.

47. Research also disputes Freud's belief that dreams disguise and fulfill _____ and that defense mechanisms disguise _____ and _____ impulses. Another Freudian idea that is no longer widely accepted is that psychological disorders are caused by

   _____ _____ .

48. Criticism of psychoanalysis as a scientific theory centers on the fact that it provides

   _____-_____-_____ explanations and does not offer _____ _____ .

49. Psychoanalytic theory rests on the assumption that the human mind often _____ painful experiences. Many of today's researchers

think that this process is much _____ (more common/rarer) than Freud believed. They also believe that when it does occur, it is a reaction to terrible _____ .

State several of Freud's ideas that have endured.

Objective 12-8: Explain how modern research developed our understanding of the unconscious.

50. Today's psychologists agree with Freud that we have limited access to all that goes on in our minds. However, they believe that the unconscious involves the _____ that control our perceptions and interpretations, the _____ of stimuli not consciously attended, and our _____ memories, for example.

51. An example of the defense mechanism that Freud called _____ is what researchers today call the _____ _____ effect. This refers to our tendency to _____ the extent to which others share our beliefs and behaviors.

52. Another Freudian idea that has received support is that people have unconscious mechanisms that defend _____ , such as

_____ _____ .

Humanistic Theories

Objective 12-9: Describe how humanistic psychologists view personality, and explain their goal in studying personality.

53. Two influential theories of humanistic psychology were proposed by _____ and _____ . These theorists offered a _____-_____

perspective that emphasized human

_____ .

54. According to Maslow, humans are motivated by needs that are organized into a _____ . Maslow refers to the process of fulfilling one's potential as _____ and the process of finding meaning, purpose, and communion beyond the self as _____ . Many people who fulfill their potential have been moved by

_____ _____ that surpass ordinary consciousness.

List some of the characteristics Maslow associated with those who fulfilled their potential.

55. According to Rogers, a person nurtures growth in a relationship by being _____ , _____ , and _____ .

56. People who are accepting of others offer them

_____ _____ _____ . By so doing, they enable others to be _____ without fearing the loss of their esteem.

57. For both Maslow and Rogers, an important feature of personality is how an individual perceives himself or herself; this is the person's

_____ .

Objective 12-10: Explain how humanistic psychologists assessed a person's sense of self.

58. Humanistic psychologists sometimes use _____ to assess personality, that is, to evaluate the _____ .

59. One questionnaire, inspired by Carl Rogers, asked people to describe themselves both as they would _____ like to be and as they _____ are. When these two selves are alike, the self-concept is

_____ .

60. Some humanistic psychologists feel that question-naires are _____ and prefer to use _____ to assess personality.

Objective 12-11: Describe how humanistic theories have influenced psychology, and discuss the criticisms they have faced.

61. Humanistic psychologists have influenced such diverse areas as _____ , _____ , _____ , _____ , and _____ . They laid the groundwork for today's scientific _____ _____ . They have also had a major impact on today's _____ psychology.

62. Critics contend that the concepts of humanistic theory are _____ and _____ .

63. Another criticism of humanistic theory is that it encourages _____ , which can lead to _____ _____ .

64. A third criticism of humanistic theory is that it is _____ and fails to appreciate the human capacity for _____ .

APPLICATIONS:

65. Professor Minton believes that people are basically good and are endowed with self-actualizing tendencies. Evidently, Professor Minton is a proponent of
    a. psychoanalysis.
    b. psychodynamic theory.
    c. the humanistic perspective.
    d. self theory.

66. Andrew's grandfather, who has lived a rich and productive life, is a spontaneous, loving, and self-accepting person. Maslow might say that he
    a. is fixated at the latency stage.
    b. has a collective unconscious.
    c. has resolved all the conflicts of the psycho-sexual stages.
    d. is a self-actualizing person.

67. The school psychologist believes that having a positive self-concept is necessary before students can achieve their potential. Evidently, the school psychologist is working within the _____ perspective.
    a. psychoanalytic   c. humanistic
    b. psychodynamic   d. neo-Freudian

68. Wanda wishes to instill in her children an accepting attitude toward other people. Maslow and Rogers would probably recommend that she
    a. teach her children first to accept themselves.
    b. use discipline sparingly.
    c. be affectionate with her children only when they behave as she wishes.
    d. exhibit all of these behaviors.

Trait Theories

Objective 12-12: Explain how psychologists use traits to describe personality.

69. Gordon Allport developed trait theory, which defines personality in terms of people's characteristic _____ and conscious _____ . Unlike Freud, he was generally less interested in _____ individual traits than in _____ them.

70. To reduce the number of traits to a few basic ones, psychologists use the statistical procedure of _____ _____ .

71. The Eysencks think that two or three personality dimensions are sufficient; these include (a) _____ – _____ and (b) emotional _____ – _____ .

72. Some researchers believe that extraverts seek stimulation because their level of _____ _____ is relatively low. PET scans reveal an area of the brain's _____ lobe that is less active in _____ (extraverts/introverts) than in _____ (extraverts/introverts). Dopamine and dopamine-related neural activity tend to be higher in _____ (extraverts/introverts).

73. Research increasingly reveals that our _____ play an important role in defining our _____ and _____ style.

74. Children's _____ and _____ may differ as an aspect of autonomic nervous system reactivity.

75. Personality differences among dogs, birds, and other animals _____ (are/are not) stable.

APPLICATIONS:

76. Isaiah is sober and reserved; Rashid is fun-loving and affectionate. The Eysencks would say that Isaiah _____ and Rashid
_____ .
   a. has an overactive id; has an overactive super-ego
   b. has a negative self-concept; has a positive self-concept
   c. is an extravert; is an introvert
   d. is an introvert; is an extravert

77. Because you have a relatively low level of brain arousal, a trait theorist would suggest that you are an _____ who would natu-rally seek _____ .
   a. introvert; stimulation
   b. introvert; isolation
   c. extravert; stimulation
   d. extravert; isolation

78. Nadine has a relatively high level of brain arousal. Trait theorists would probably predict that she is an _____ .

Objective 12-13: Describe personality inventories, and discuss their strengths and weaknesses as trait-assessment tools.

79. Questionnaires that categorize personality traits are called _____
   _____ .

80. The most widely used of all such personality tests is the _____ _____
   _____ _____ ;
   its questions are grouped into _____
   (how many?) clinical scales.

81. This test was developed by testing a large pool of items and selecting those that differentiated par-ticular individuals; in other words, the test was _____ derived.

(Thinking Critically) Explain several techniques used by astrologers to persuade people to accept their advice.

APPLICATION:

82. A psychologist at the campus mental health center administered an empirically derived per-sonality test to diagnose an emotionally troubled student. Which test did the psychologist MOST LIKELY administer?
   a. the MMPI
   b. the Narcissism Index
   c. the Rorschach
   d. the Eysenck Personality Questionnaire

Objective 12-14: Identify the traits that seem to pro-vide the most useful information about personality variation.

83. Researchers have arrived at a cluster of five fac-tors that seem to describe the major features of personality. List and briefly describe the Big Five.
   a. _____
   b. _____
   c. _____
   d. _____
   e. _____

84. While some traits wane a bit during early and middle adulthood, others increase. For example, as young adults mature and learn to manage their commitments, _____ increases. From the thirties through the sixties, _____ increases.

85. In adulthood, the Big Five are quite _____ (stable/variable), with heritability estimated at _____ percent or more for each dimension. Moreover, these traits _____ (do/do not) predict other attributes.

APPLICATION:

86. For his class presentation, Bruce plans to discuss the Big Five personality factors used by people throughout the world to describe others or themselves. Which of the following is NOT a factor that Bruce will discuss?
    a. extraversion   c. independence
    b. openness   d. conscientiousness

Objective 12-15: Discuss whether research supports the consistency of personality traits over time and across situations.

87. Human behavior is influenced both by our inner _____ and by the external _____ . The issue of which of these is the more important influence on personality is called the _____- _____ controversy.

88. To be considered a personality trait, a characteristic must persist over _____ and across _____ . Research studies reveal that personality trait scores _____ (correlate/do not correlate) with scores obtained seven years later. The consistency of specific behaviors from one situation to the next is _____ (predictably consistent/not predictably consistent).

89. An individual's score on a personality test _____ (is/is not) very predictive of his or her behavior in any given situation.

Explain the apparent contradiction between behavior in specific situations and average behavior patterns.

90. People's expressive styles, which include their _____ , manner of _____ , and _____ , are quite _____ (consistent/inconsistent), which _____ (does/does not) reveal distinct personality traits.

Social-Cognitive Theories

Objective 12-16: Describe how social-cognitive theorists view personality development, and explain how they explore behavior.

91. Social-cognitive theory, which focuses on how the individual and the _____ interact, was proposed by _____ .

92. Social-cognitive theorists propose that personality is shaped by the mutual influence of our internal _____ , our _____ , and _____ factors, as reflected in the _____ approach to personality. This is the principle of _____ _____ .

Describe three different ways in which the environment and personality interact.

93. It follows from the social-cognitive perspective that the best means of predicting people's future behavior is their _____ _____ .

Objective 12-17: State the criticism social-cognitive theorists have faced.

94. The major criticism of the social-cognitive perspective is that it fails to appreciate a person's _____ _____ .

APPLICATIONS:

95. Ramona identifies with her politically conservative parents. At college, most of her friends also held conservative views. After four years in this environment Ramona's politics have become even more conservative. According to the social-cognitive perspective, in this case Ramona's parents (_____ factor) helped shape her political beliefs (_____ factor), which influenced her choice of college (also a _____ factor) and created an _____ that fostered her already formed political attitudes.

96. In high school, Chella and Nari were best friends. They thought they were a lot alike, as did everyone else who knew them. After high school, they went on to very different colleges, careers, and life courses. Now, at their twenty-fifth reunion, they are shocked at how little they have in common. Bandura would suggest that their differences reflect the interactive effects of environment, personality, and behavior, which he refers to as _____

_____ .

97. Dayna is not very consistent in showing up for class and turning in assignments when they are due. Research studies would suggest that Dayna's inconsistent behavior
   a. indicates that she is troubled and may need professional counseling.
   b. is a sign of emotional instability.
   c. is not necessarily unusual.
   d. probably reflects a temporary problem in another area of her life.

Exploring the Self

Objective 12-18: Explain why psychology has generated so much research on the self, and discuss the importance of self-esteem to psychology and to our well-being.

98. One of Western psychology's most vigorously researched topics today is the _____ .

99. Hazel Markus and colleagues introduced the concept of an individual's _____ _____ to emphasize how our aspirations motivate us through specific goals.

100. Our tendency to overestimate the extent to which others are noticing and evaluating us is called the _____ _____ .

101. According to self theorists, personality development hinges on our feelings of self-worth, or _____ . People who feel good about themselves are relatively _____ (dependent on/independent of) outside pressures.

102. Also important to personality development is our sense of competence on a task, or our _____ .

103. In a series of experiments, researchers found that people who were made to feel insecure were _____ (more/less) critical of other persons or tended to express heightened _____

_____ .

APPLICATION:

104. The behavior of many people has been described in terms of a *spotlight effect*. This means that they
   a. tend to see themselves as being above average in ability.
   b. have a sense of competence about their ability to complete a task.
   c. overestimate the extent to which other people are noticing them.
   d. do all of these things.

Objective 12-19: Discuss some evidence for self-serving bias, and contrast defensive and secure self-esteem.

105. Research has shown that most people tend to have _____ (low/high) self-esteem.

106. The tendency of people to judge themselves favorably is called the _____ bias.

107. Responsibility for success is generally accepted _____ (more/less) readily than responsibility for failure.

108. Most people perceive their own behavior and traits as being _____ (above/below) average.

109. Bushman and Baumeister found that students with unrealistically _____ (low/high) self-esteem were most likely to become exceptionally aggressive after criticism. Some psychologists believe that today's new generation expresses more _____ than earlier generations.

Identify some of the attitudes and behaviors that seem to be on the rise in *Generation Me*.

110. Some researchers distinguish _____ self-esteem, which is fragile and sensitive to _____ , from _____ self-esteem, which is less focused on _____ evaluations.

APPLICATION:

111. James attributes his failing grade in chemistry to an unfair final exam. His attitude exemplifies
    a. repression.
    b. unconditional positive regard.
    c. self-serving bias.
    d. reciprocal determinism.

Objective 12-20: Discuss how individualist and collectivist cultures influence people.

112. Cultures based on _____ value personal _____ and individual _____ . Examples of such cultures occur in _____

    _____ , _____

    _____ , _____ ,

    and _____ _____ .

113. In contrast, cultures based on _____ value _____ ,

    _____ , and _____ .

    Examples of such cultures occur in

    _____ , _____ ,

    and _____ .

114. Whereas people in _____ cultures value freedom, they suffer more

    _____ , divorce,

    _____ , and

    _____ -related disease.

APPLICATION:

115. Chad, who grew up in the United States, is more likely to encourage _____ in his future children than Asian-born Hidiyaki, who is more likely to encourage _____ in his future children.
    a. obedience; independence
    b. independence; emotional closeness
    c. emotional closeness; obedience
    d. loyalty; emotional closeness

Progress Test 1

Multiple-Choice Questions

Circle your answers to the following questions and check them with the answers beginning on page 304. If your answer is incorrect, read the explanation for why it is incorrect and then consult the text.

1. The text defines *personality* as
    a. the set of personal attitudes that characterizes a person.
    b. an individual's characteristic pattern of thinking, feeling, and acting.
    c. a predictable set of responses to environmental stimuli.
    d. an unpredictable set of responses to environmental stimuli.

2. Which of the following places the greatest emphasis on the unconscious mind?
    a. the humanistic perspective
    b. the social-cognitive perspective
    c. the trait perspective
    d. the psychoanalytic perspective

3. Which of the following is the correct order of psychosexual stages proposed by Freud?
    a. oral; anal; phallic; latency; genital
    b. anal; oral; phallic; latency; genital
    c. oral; anal; genital; latency; phallic
    d. anal; oral; genital; latency; phallic

4. According to Freud, defense mechanisms are methods of reducing
    a. anger.   c. anxiety.
    b. fear.   d. lust.

5. Neo-Freudians such as Adler and Horney believed that
    a. Freud placed too great an emphasis on the conscious mind.
    b. Freud placed too great an emphasis on sexual and aggressive instincts.
    c. the years of childhood were more important in the formation of personality than Freud had indicated.
    d. Freud's ideas about the id, ego, and superego as personality structures were incorrect.

6. Collectivist cultures
    a. give priority to the goals of their groups.
    b. value the maintenance of social harmony.
    c. foster social interdependence.
    d. have all of these characteristics.

7. Which two dimensions of personality have the Eysencks emphasized?
   a. extraversion–introversion and emotional stability–instability
   b. conscientiousness and agreeableness
   c. neuroticism and openness
   d. aggressiveness and hostility

8. With regard to personality, it appears that
   a. there is little consistency of behavior from one situation to the next and little consistency of traits over the life span.
   b. there is little consistency of behavior from one situation to the next but significant consistency of traits over the life span.
   c. there is significant consistency of behavior from one situation to the next but little consistency of traits over the life span.
   d. there is significant consistency of behavior from one situation to the next and significant consistency of traits over the life span.

9. Humanistic theories of personality
   a. emphasize the driving force of unconscious motivations in personality.
   b. emphasize the growth potential of "healthy" individuals.
   c. emphasize the importance of interaction with the environment in shaping personality.
   d. describe personality in terms of scores on various personality scales.

10. According to Rogers, three conditions are necessary to promote growth in personality. These are
    a. honesty, sincerity, and empathy.
    b. high self-esteem, honesty, and empathy.
    c. high self-esteem, genuineness, and acceptance.
    d. genuineness, acceptance, and empathy.

11. Regarding high self-esteem, psychologists who study the self have found that self-affirming thinking
    a. is generally maladaptive to the individual because it distorts reality by overinflating self-esteem.
    b. is generally adaptive to the individual because it reduces shyness, anxiety, and loneliness.
    c. tends to prevent the individual from viewing others with compassion and understanding.
    d. tends *not* to characterize people who have experienced unconditional positive regard.

12. Which of Freud's ideas would NOT be accepted by most contemporary psychologists?
    a. Development is essentially fixed in childhood.
    b. Sexuality is a potent drive in humans.

c. The mind is an iceberg with consciousness being only the tip.
d. Repression can be the cause of forgetting.

13. Projective tests such as the Rorschach inkblot test have been criticized because
    a. their scoring system is too rigid and leads to unfair labeling.
    b. they were standardized with unrepresentative samples.
    c. they have low reliability and low validity.
    d. it is easy for people to fake answers in order to appear healthy.

14. A major criticism of trait theory is that it
    a. places too great an emphasis on early childhood experiences.
    b. overestimates the consistency of behavior in different situations.
    c. underestimates the importance of heredity in personality development.
    d. places too great an emphasis on positive traits.

15. For humanistic psychologists, many of our behaviors and perceptions are ultimately shaped by whether our _____ is _____ or _____ .
    a. ego; strong; weak
    b. personality; inherited; learned
    c. personality structure; introverted; extraverted
    d. self-concept; positive; negative

16. In studying personality, a trait theorist would MOST LIKELY
    a. use a projective test.
    b. observe a person in a variety of situations.
    c. use a personality inventory.
    d. use the method of free association.

17. Id is to ego as _____ is to _____ .
    a. reality principle; pleasure principle
    b. pleasure principle; reality principle
    c. conscious forces; unconscious forces
    d. conscience; "personality executive"

18. Which of the following is the major criticism of the social-cognitive perspective?
    a. It focuses too much on early childhood experiences.
    b. It focuses too little on the inner traits of a person.
    c. It provides descriptions but not explanations.
    d. It lacks appropriate assessment techniques.

19. Recent research has provided more support for defense mechanisms such as _____ than for defense mechanisms such as _____ .

    a. displacement; reaction formation
    b. reaction formation; displacement
    c. displacement; regression
    d. displacement; projection

20. Free association is a key technique in

    a. self-actualization.
    b. humanistic theory.
    c. psychoanalysis.
    d. projective testing.

Matching Items

Match each definition or description with the appropriate term.

Definitions or Descriptions

    _____ **1.** redirecting impulses to a less threatening object
    _____ **2.** test consisting of a series of inkblots
    _____ **3.** the conscious executive of personality
    _____ **4.** personality inventory
    _____ **5.** disguising an impulse by imputing it to another person
    _____ **6.** switching an unacceptable impulse into its opposite
    _____ **7.** the unconscious repository of instinctual drives
    _____ **8.** a statistical technique that identifies clusters of personality traits
    _____ **9.** personality structure that corresponds to a person's conscience
    _____ **10.** providing self-justifying explanations for an action
    _____ **11.** excessive self-love

Terms

    a. id
    b. ego
    c. superego
    d. reaction formation
    e. rationalization
    f. displacement
    g. factor analysis
    h. projection
    i. narcissism
    j. Rorschach
    k. MMPI

Progress Test 2

Progress Test 2 should be completed during a final chapter review. Answer the following questions after you thoroughly understand the correct answers for the section reviews and Progress Test 1.

Multiple-Choice Questions

1. Which personality theory emphasizes the interaction between the individual and the environment in shaping personality?

    a. psychoanalytic   **c.** humanistic
    b. trait   **d.** social-cognitive

2. According to Freud's theory, personality arises in response to conflicts between

    a. our unacceptable urges and our tendency to become self-actualized.
    b. the process of identification and the ego's defense mechanisms.
    c. the collective unconscious and our individual desires.
    d. our biological impulses and the social restraints against them.

3. The concept of a collective unconscious is most closely associated with

    a. Freud.
    b. Rogers.
    c. Adler.
    d. Jung.

4. Compared with people in communal societies, people in individualist societies

    a. have a stronger sense of family.
    b. exhibit greater shyness toward strangers.
    c. exhibit greater concern for loyalty and social harmony.
    d. have a stronger sense of self.

5. Research has shown that individuals who are made to feel insecure are subsequently
   a. more critical of others.
   b. less critical of others.
   c. more likely to display self-serving bias.
   d. less likely to display self-serving bias.

6. An example of self-serving bias described in the text is the tendency of people to
   a. see themselves as average on nearly any desirable dimension.
   b. accept more responsibility for successes than failures.
   c. be overly critical of other people.
   d. exhibit heightened racial prejudice.

7. The Minnesota Multiphasic Personality Inventory (MMPI) is a(n)
   a. projective personality test.
   b. empirically derived and objective personality test.
   c. personality test developed mainly to assess job applicants.
   d. personality test used primarily to assess the self-concept.

8. Trait theory attempts to
   a. show how development of personality is a lifelong process.
   b. describe and classify people in terms of their predispositions to behave in certain ways.
   c. determine which traits are most conducive to individual self-actualization.
   d. explain how behavior is shaped by the interaction between traits, behavior, and the environment.

9. The spotlight effect refers to
   a. the tendency of people to overestimate the extent to which others are evaluating them.
   b. an individual's feeling of self-worth.
   c. excessive self-love and self-absorption.
   d. a person's sense of competence on a task.

10. Which of the following statements about self-esteem is NOT correct?
    a. People with low self-esteem tend to be negative about others.
    b. People with high self-esteem are less prone to drug addiction.
    c. People with low self-esteem tend to be non-conformists.
    d. People with high self-esteem suffer less from insomnia.

11. The Oedipus and Electra complexes have their roots in the
    a. anal stage.   c. latency stage.
    b. oral stage.   d. phallic stage.

12. Which of the following is a common criticism of the humanistic perspective?
    a. Its concepts are vague and subjective.
    b. The emphasis on the self encourages selfishness in individuals.
    c. Humanism fails to appreciate the reality of evil in human behavior.
    d. All of these are common criticisms.

13. In studying personality, a social-cognitive theorist would MOST LIKELY make use of
    a. personality inventories.
    b. projective tests.
    c. observing behavior in different situations.
    d. factor analyses.

14. A major difference between the psychoanalytic and trait perspectives is that
    a. trait theory defines personality in terms of behavior; psychoanalytic theory, in terms of its underlying dynamics.
    b. trait theory describes behavior but does not attempt to explain it.
    c. psychoanalytic theory emphasizes the origins of personality in childhood sexuality.
    d. all of these are differences.

15. The Big Five personality factors are
    a. emotional stability, openness, introversion, sociability, locus of control.
    b. neuroticism, extraversion, openness, emotional stability, sensitivity.
    c. neuroticism, gregariousness, extraversion, impulsiveness, conscientiousness.
    d. emotional stability, extraversion, openness, agreeableness, conscientiousness.

16. Which of the following was NOT mentioned in the text as a criticism of Freud's theory?
    a. The theory is sexist.
    b. It offers few testable hypotheses.
    c. There is no evidence of anything like an "unconscious."
    d. The theory ignores the fact that human development is lifelong.

17. According to Freud, _____ is the process by which children incorporate their parents' values into their _____ .
    a. reaction formation; superegos
    b. reaction formation; egos

c. identification; superegos
d. identification; egos

18. Which of the following refers to the tendency to overestimate the extent to which others share our beliefs?
a. the spotlight effect
b. projection
c. rationalization
d. the false consensus effect

19. In promoting personality growth, the person-centered perspective emphasizes all but
a. empathy.
b. acceptance.
c. genuineness.
d. altruism.

20. Research on the Big Five personality factors provides evidence that
a. some tendencies decrease during adulthood, while others increase.
b. these traits only describe personality in Western, individualist cultures.
c. the heritability of individual differences in these traits generally runs about 25 percent or less.
d. all of these statements are true.

Matching Items

Match each term with the appropriate definition or description.

Terms

_____ 1. projective test
_____ 2. identification
_____ 3. collective unconscious
_____ 4. reality principle
_____ 5. psychosexual stages
_____ 6. pleasure principle
_____ 7. empirically derived test
_____ 8. reciprocal determinism
_____ 9. personality inventory
_____ 10. Oedipus complex
_____ 11. preconscious
_____ 12. collectivism
_____ 13. individualism

Definitions or Descriptions

a. the id's demand for immediate gratification
b. a boy's sexual desires toward his mother
c. information that is retrievable but currently not in conscious awareness
d. giving priority to one's own goals
e. stages of development proposed by Freud
f. questionnaire used to assess personality traits
g. the two-way interactions of behavior with personal and environmental factors
h. giving priority to group goals
i. personality test that provides ambiguous stimuli
j. the repository of universal memories proposed by Jung
k. the process by which children incorporate their parents' values into their developing superegos
l. the process by which the ego seeks to gratify impulses of the id in nondestructive ways
m. developed by testing a pool of items and then selecting those that discriminate the group of interest

Essay Question

You are an honest, open, and responsible person. Discuss how these characteristics would be explained according to the major perspectives on personality. (Use the space below and to the right to list points you want to make, and organize them. Then write the essay on a separate piece of paper.)

Terms and Concepts to Remember

Writing Definitions

Using your own words, on a separate piece of paper write a brief definition or explanation of each of the following terms.

1. personality
2. psychodynamic theories
3. psychoanalysis
4. unconscious
5. free association
6. id
7. ego
8. superego
9. psychosexual stages
10. Oedipus complex
11. identification
12. fixation
13. defense mechanisms
14. repression
15. collective unconscious
16. projective tests
17. Rorschach inkblot test
18. humanistic theories
19. self-actualization
20. unconditional positive regard
21. self-concept
22. trait
23. personality inventory
24. Minnesota Multiphasic Personality Inventory (MMPI)
25. empirically derived test
26. social-cognitive perspective
27. reciprocal determinism
28. self
29. spotlight effect
30. self-esteem
31. self-efficacy
32. self-serving bias
33. narcissism
34. individualisml
35. collectivism

Cross-Check

As you learned in Chapter 1, reviewing and overlearning of material are important to the learning process. After you have written the definitions of the key terms in this chapter, you should complete the crossword puzzle to ensure that you can reverse the process—recognize the term, given the definition.

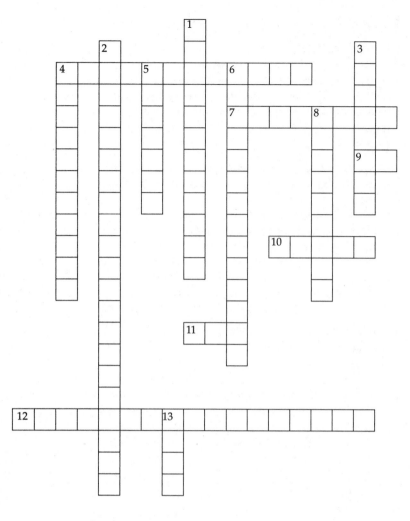

ACROSS

4. In Freud's theory, the area of the unconscious containing material that is retrievable into conscious awareness.
7. Locus of control that reflects the belief that one's fate is determined by forces not under personal control.
9. In Freud's theory, the personality system consisting of basic sexual and aggressive drives.
10. A person's characteristic pattern of behavior.
11. In Freud's theory, the conscious division of personality.
12. The ego's methods of unconsciously protecting itself against anxiety.

DOWN

1. Defense mechanism in which an impulse is shifted to an object other than the one that originally aroused the impulse.
2. The social-cognitive concept that behavior is the result of interactions between people's traits (including their thinking) and their social context.
3. According to Freud, _____ occurs when development becomes arrested in an immature psychosexual stage.
4. An individual's characteristic pattern of thinking, feeling, and acting.
5. In Freud's theory, the complex developed by boys in which they are sexually attracted to their mother and resent their father.
6. In Freud's theory, the process by which the child's superego develops and incorporates the parents' values.
8. A widely used test in which people are asked to interpret 10 inkblots.
13. The most widely used personality inventory.

Answers

Chapter Review

Introducing Personality

1. thinking; feeling; acting
2. Sigmund Freud; humanistic; growth; self-fulfillment

Psychodynamic Theories

3. psychodynamic; conscious; unconscious
4. nervous
5. neurological
6. hypnosis
7. free association
8. psychoanalysis
9. unconscious; preconscious; repressed
10. biological; social
11. id; ego; superego
12. unconscious; pleasure

13. after; conscious; reality

14. superego; 4 or 5

The ego is considered the executive of personality because it directs our actions as it intervenes among the impulsive demands of the id, the reality of the external world, and the restraining demands of the superego.

15. weak; strong

16. There are no right or wrong answers. Here's a sample answer to a. Complete b. and c. on your own.
   a. The id's response: "I'm so angry; the driver is extremely thoughtless. I think I'll speed up and tailgate."
   The ego's response: "I'll relieve my frustration by mentioning the other driver to my friend in the car, then wait for a safe opportunity to pass."
   The superego's response: "The driver may be going way below the speed limit because he or she is an elderly person or is sick or having car trouble."

17. **d.** is the answer. Impulsiveness is the mark of a strong id; self-indulgence is the mark of a weak superego. Because the ego serves to mediate the demands of the id, the superego, and the outside world, its strength or weakness is judged by its decision-making ability, not by the character of the decision—so the ego is not relevant to the question asked.

18. **a.** is the answer. Freud believed that dreams and such slips of the tongue reveal unconscious conflicts.

19. psychosexual; erogenous zone

20. oral; sucking (also biting, chewing)

21. anal; 18; 36

22. phallic; 3; 6; genitals; opposite; Oedipus complex; Electra complex

23. identification; gender identity

Children eventually cope with their feelings for the opposite-sex parent by repressing them and by identifying with the rival (same-sex) parent. Through this process children incorporate many of their parents' values, thereby strengthening the superego.

24. latency

25. genital

26. fixated

27. **b.** is the answer. Sarcasm is said to be an attempt to deny the passive dependence characteristic of the oral stage.
   a. A person who is projecting attributes his or her own feelings to others.

   c. Such a person might be either messy and disorganized or highly controlled and compulsively neat.
   d. Identification involves incorporating the parent's values into one's superego.

28. fixated; oral. Song Yi was probably orally deprived (weaned too early) as an infant, so she is fixated at the oral stage. Smoking satisfies her id's needs.

29. defense mechanisms; repression

30. indirectly; unconsciously

31. unconscious; slips; manifest content; latent content

32. regression

33. reaction formation

34. projection

35. rationalization

36. displacement

37. denial

Matching Items

38. **1.** f   **4.** c
    2. e   **5.** a
    3. b   **6.** d

39. **c.** is the answer. Suzy is trying to justify her purchase by generating (inaccurate) explanations for her behavior.
   a. Displacement is the redirecting of impulses toward an object other than the one responsible for them.
   b. Reaction formation is the transformation of unacceptable impulses into their opposites.
   d. Projection is the attribution of one's own unacceptable thoughts and feelings to others.

40. neo-Freudians; more; less
   a. Adler emphasized the social, rather than the sexual, tensions of childhood and said that much of behavior is driven by the need to overcome feelings of inferiority.
   b. Horney questioned the male bias in Freud's theory, such as the assumptions that women have weak egos and suffer "penis envy." Like Adler, she emphasized social tensions.
   c. Jung emphasized an inherited collective unconscious.

41. reject; Jung; collective unconscious; archetypes

42. psychodynamic; sex; unconscious; childhood; inner conflicts

43. projective

44. Rorschach; inkblots; little

45. projective
46. lifelong; earlier; is not
47. wishes; sexual; aggressive; sexual suppression
48. after-the-fact; testable predictions
49. represses; rarer; trauma

Freud drew attention to the unconscious and the irrational, to human defenses against anxiety, to the importance of human sexuality, and to the tension between our biological impulses and our social well-being.

50. schemas; priming; implicit
51. projection; false consensus; overestimate
52. self-esteem; reaction formation

Humanistic Theories

53. Abraham Maslow; Carl Rogers; third-force; potential
54. hierarchy; self-actualization; self-transcendence; peak experiences

For Maslow, such people were self-aware, self-accepting and open, spontaneous, loving and caring, not paralyzed by others' opinions, secure, and problem-centered rather than self-centered.

55. genuine; accepting; empathic
56. unconditional positive regard; spontaneous
57. self-concept
58. questionnaires; self-concept
59. ideally; actually; positive
60. depersonalizing; interviews
61. counseling; education; child rearing; management; positive psychology; popular
62. vague; subjective
63. individualism; self-indulgence, selfishness, and an erosion of moral restraints
64. naive; evil
65. **c.** is the answer.
    b., c., & d. None of these theories or perspectives offers any particular explanation of these tendencies.
66. **d.** is the answer.
    a. & c. These are concepts used by Freud rather than humanistic theorists such as Maslow.
    b. This reflects Jung's viewpoint.
67. **c.** is the answer.
    a., b., & d. The self-concept is not relevant to psychodynamic theories.
68. **a.** is the answer.
    b. The text does not discuss the impact of discipline on personality.
    c. This would constitute conditional, rather than

unconditional, positive regard and would likely cause the children to be less accepting of themselves and others.

Trait Theories

69. behaviors; motives; explaining; describing
70. factor analysis
71. extraversion–introversion; stability–instability
72. brain arousal; frontal; extraverts; introverts; extraverts
73. genes; temperament; behavioral
74. shyness; inhibition
75. are
76. **d.** is the answer.
    a. This refers to psychoanalytic concepts.
    b. This refers to humanistic concepts.
77. **c.** is the answer.
    a. & b. According to this theory, introverts have relatively high levels of arousal, causing them to crave solitude.
    d. Isolation might lower arousal level even further.
78. introvert
79. personality inventories
80. Minnesota Multiphasic Personality Inventory; 10
81. empirically

Astrologers use a "stock spiel" that includes information that is generally true of almost everyone. The willingness of people to accept this type of phony information is called the "Barnum effect." A second technique used by astrologers is to "read" a person's clothing, features, reactions, and so on and build their advice from these observations.

82. **a.** is the answer.
    b. There is no such test.
    c. The Rorschach is a projective test that was not empirically derived.
    d. A personality test that measures personality traits would not be helpful in identifying troubled behaviors.
83. **a.** Conscientiousness: from disciplined to impulsive
    b. Agreeableness: from soft-hearted to ruthless
    c. Neuroticism (emotional stability or instability): on a continuum from calm to anxious; secure to insecure
    d. Openness: from preference for variety to routine
    e. Extraversion: from sociable to retiring
84. conscientiousness; agreeableness
85. stable; 50; do

86. **c.** is the answer.

87. traits (or dispositions); situation (or environment); person-situation

88. time; situations; correlate; not predictably consistent

89. is not

At any given moment a person's behavior is powerfully influenced by the immediate situation, so that it may appear that the person does not have a consistent personality. But averaged over many situations a person's outgoingness, happiness, and carelessness, for instance, are more predictable.

90. animation; speaking; gestures; consistent; does

Social-Cognitive Theories

91. environment; Albert Bandura

92. cognition; behaviors; environmental; biopsychosocial; reciprocal determinism

Different people choose different environments partly on the basis of their dispositions. Our personality shapes how we interpret and react to events. It also helps create the situations to which we react.

93. past behavior in similar situations

94. inner traits

95. situational; internal; situational; environment. This shows the interaction of internal and situational factors, using the social-cognitive view of how personality develops.

96. reciprocal determinism. This shows how the interaction of behavior, internal personal factors, and environment can change behavior.

97. **c.** is the answer.

Exploring the Self

98. self

99. possible selves

100. spotlight effect

101. self-esteem; independent of

102. self-efficacy

103. more; racial prejudice

104. **c.** is the answer.
    a. This describes self-serving bias.
    b. This describes self-efficacy.

105. high

106. self-serving

107. more

108. above

109. high; narcissism

Narcissism correlates with materialism, the desire to be famous, inflated expectations, more hookups with fewer committed relationships, more gambling, and more cheating, all of which have been on the rise.

110. defensive; criticism; secure; external

111. **c.** is the answer.
    a. There is no indication that his reaction results from the repression of unconscious wishes.
    b. Unconditional positive regard is an attitude of total acceptance directed toward others.
    d. Reciprocal determinism refers to the mutual influences among personality, environment, and behavior.

112. individualism; independence (or control); achievement; North America; Western Europe; Australia; New Zealand

113. collectivism; interdependence; tradition; harmony; Korea; Japan; China

114. individualist; loneliness; homicide; stress

115. **b.** is the answer. Westerners value independence and achievement, and so they would want their children to think for themselves, while people from Asia and Africa place greater value on emotional closeness.
    a. Both of these values are more typical of Western than Asian cultures.
    c. & d. These values are more typical of Asian than Western cultures.

Progress Test 1

Multiple-Choice Questions

1. **b.** is the answer. Personality is defined as patterns of response—of thinking, feeling, and acting—that are relatively consistent across a variety of situations.

2. **d.** is the answer.
   a. & b. Conscious processes are the focus of these perspectives.
   c. The trait perspective focuses on the description of behaviors.

3. **a.** is the answer.

4. **c.** is the answer. According to Freud, defense mechanisms reduce anxiety unconsciously, by disguising one's threatening impulses.
   a., b., & d. Unlike these specific emotions, anxiety need not be focused. Defense mechanisms help us cope when we are unsettled but are not sure why.

5. **b.** is the answer.
   a. According to most neo-Freudians, Freud placed too great an emphasis on the *unconscious* mind.
   c. Freud placed great emphasis on early childhood, and the neo-Freudians basically agreed with him.

d. The neo-Freudians accepted Freud's ideas about the basic personality structures.

6. **d.** is the answer.

7. **a.** is the answer.
b. & c. These are among of the "Big Five" personality factors.
d. These are not traits in any trait theory discussed.

8. **b.** is the answer. Studies have shown that people do not act with predictable consistency from one situation to the next. But, over a number of situations, consistent patterns emerge, and this basic consistency of traits persists over the life span.

9. **b.** is the answer.
a. This is true of the psychodynamic perspective.
c. This is true of the social-cognitive perspective.
d. This is true of the trait perspective.

10. **d.** is the answer.

11. **b.** is the answer. Psychologists who study the self emphasize that for the individual, self-affirming thinking is generally adaptive. People with high self-esteem have fewer sleepless nights, succumb less easily to pressures to conform, and are just plain happier.

12. **a.** is the answer. Developmental research indicates that development is lifelong.
b., c., & d. To varying degrees, research has partially supported these Freudian ideas.

13. **c.** is the answer. As scoring is largely subjective and the tests have not been very successful in predicting behavior, their reliability and validity have been called into question.
a. This is untrue.
b. Unlike empirically derived personality tests, projective tests are not standardized.
d. Although this may be true, it was not mentioned as a criticism of projective tests.

14. **b.** is the answer. In doing so, it underestimates the influence of the environment.
a. The trait perspective does not emphasize early childhood experiences.
c. This criticism is unlikely because trait theory does not seek to explain personality development.
d. Trait theory does not look on traits as being "positive" or "negative."

15. **d.** is the answer.
a. & c. Personality structure is a concern of the psychoanalytic perspective.
b. Humanistic psychologists don't concern themselves with the source of personality.

16. **c.** is the answer.
a. & d. A psychodynamic theorist would be most likely to use a projective test or free association.
b. This would most likely be the approach taken by a social-cognitive theorist.

17. **b.** is the answer. In Freud's theory, the id operates according to the pleasure principle; the ego operates according to the reality principle.
c. The id is presumed to be unconscious.
d. The superego is, according to Freud, the equivalent of a conscience; the ego is the "personality executive."

18. **b.** is the answer. The social-cognitive theory has been accused of putting so much emphasis on the situation that inner traits are neglected.
a. Such a criticism has been made of the psychodynamic perspective but is not relevant to the social-cognitive perspective.
c. Such a criticism might be more relevant to the trait perspective; the social-cognitive perspective offers an explanation in the form of reciprocal determinism.
d. There are assessment techniques appropriate to the theory, namely, questionnaires and observations of behavior in situations.

19. **b.** is the answer.
a., c., & d. The evidence supports defenses that defend self-esteem, rather than those that are tied to instinctual energy.

20. **c.** is the answer.

Matching Items

1. f	5. h	9. c
2. j	6. d	10. e
3. b	7. a	11. i
4. k	8. g	

Progress Test 2

Multiple-Choice Questions

1. **d.** is the answer.
a. This perspective emphasizes unconscious dynamics in personality.
b. This perspective is more concerned with *describing* than *explaining* personality.
c. This perspective emphasizes the healthy, self-actualizing tendencies of personality.

2. **d.** is the answer.
a. Self-actualization is a concept of the humanistic perspective.
b. Through identification, children *reduce* conflicting feelings as they incorporate their parents' values.

c. Jung, rather than Freud, proposed the concept of the collective unconscious.

3. **d.** is the answer.

4. **d.** is the answer.
a., b., & c. These are characteristic of people in communal societies.

5. **a.** is the answer. Feelings of insecurity reduce self-esteem, and those who feel negative about themselves tend to feel negative about others.

6. **b.** is the answer.

7. **b.** is the answer. The MMPI was developed by selecting from many items those that differentiated between the groups of interest; hence, it was empirically derived. That it is an objective test is shown by the fact that it can be scored by computer.
a. Projective tests present ambiguous stimuli for people to interpret; the MMPI is a questionnaire.
c. Although sometimes used to assess job applicants, the MMPI was developed to assess emotionally troubled people.
d. The MMPI does not focus on self-concept but, rather, measures various aspects of personality.

8. **b.** is the answer. Trait theory attempts to describe behavior and not to develop explanations or applications. The emphasis is more on consistency than on change.

9. **a.** is the answer.
b. This is self-esteem.
c. This is narcissism.
d. This is self-efficacy.

10. **c.** is the answer. In actuality, people with *high* self-esteem are generally more independent of pressures to conform.

11. **d.** is the answer.

12. **d.** is the answer.

13. **c.** is the answer. In keeping with their emphasis on interactions between people and situations, social-cognitive theorists would most likely make use of observations of behavior in relevant situations.
a. & d. Personality inventories and factor analyses would more likely be used by a trait theorist.
b. Projective tests would more likely be used by a psychologist working within the psychodynamic perspective.

14. **d.** is the answer. Trait theory defines personality in terms of behavior and is therefore interested in describing behavior; psychoanalytic theory defines personality as dynamics underlying behavior and therefore is interested in explaining behavior in terms of these dynamics.

15. **d.** is the answer.

16. **c.** is the answer. Although many researchers think of the unconscious as information processing without awareness rather than as a reservoir of repressed information, they agree with Freud that we do indeed have limited access to all that goes on in our minds.

17. **c.** is the answer.
a. & b. Reaction formation is the defense mechanism by which people transform unacceptable impulses into their opposites.
d. It is the superego, rather than the ego, that represents parental values.

18. **d.** is the answer.

19. **d.** is the answer.

20. **a.** is the answer. Neuroticism, extraversion, and openness tend to decrease, while agreeableness and conscientiousness tend to increase.
b. The Big Five dimensions describe personality in various cultures reasonably well.
c. Heritability generally runs 50 percent or more for each dimension.

Matching Items

1. i	6. a	11. c
2. k	7. m	12. h
3. j	8. g	13. d
4. l	9. f	
5. e	10. b	

Essay Question

Since you are apparently in good psychological health, according to the psychodynamic perspective you must have experienced a healthy childhood and successfully passed Freud's stages of psychosexual development. Freud would also say that your ego is functioning well in balancing the demands of your id with the restraining demands of your superego and reality. Freud might also say that your honest nature reflects a well-developed superego, while Jung might say it derives from a universal value found in our collective unconscious.

According to the humanistic perspective, your open and honest nature indicates that your basic needs have been met and you are in the process of self-actualization or even self-transcendence (Maslow). Furthermore, your openness indicates that you have a healthy self-concept and were likely nurtured by genuine, accepting, and empathic caregivers (Rogers). More recently, researchers who emphasize the self would also focus on the importance of a positive self-concept.

Trait theorists would be less concerned with explaining these specific characteristics than with describing them, determining their consistency, and classifying your personality type. Some trait theorists, such as Allport and Eysenck, attribute certain trait differences to biological factors such as heredity.

According to the social-cognitive perspective, your personal factors, behavior, and environmental influences interacted in shaping your personality and behaviors. The fact that you are a responsible person indicates that you perceive yourself as controlling, rather than as controlled by, your environment.

Terms and Concepts to Remember

Writing Definitions

1. **Personality** is an individual's characteristic pattern of thinking, feeling, and acting.

2. **Psychodynamic theories** view human behavior as a dynamic interaction between the conscious and unconscious minds. They stress the importance of childhood experiences.

3. **Psychoanalysis** is Freud's theory of personality that attributes thoughts and actions to unconscious motives and conflicts; also, the techniques used in treating psychological disorders by seeking to expose and interpret the tensions within a patient's unconscious.

4. In Freud's theory, the **unconscious** is the reservoir of mostly unacceptable thoughts, wishes, feelings, and memories. According to contemporary psychologists, it is a level of information processing of which we are unaware.

5. **Free association** is the Freudian technique in which the person is encouraged to say whatever comes to mind as a means of exploring the unconscious.

6. In Freud's theory, the **id** is the unconscious system of personality, consisting of basic sexual and aggressive drives, that supplies psychic energy to personality. It operates on the *pleasure principle*.

7. In psychoanalytic theory, the **ego** is the largely conscious, "executive" division of personality that attempts to mediate among the demands of the id, the superego, and reality. It operates on the *reality principle*.

8. In Freud's theory, the **superego** is the division of personality that represents internalized ideals and provides standards for judgment (the conscience) and for future aspirations.

9. Freud's **psychosexual stages** are developmental periods children pass through during which the id's pleasure-seeking energies are focused on different erogenous zones.

10. According to Freud, boys in the phallic stage develop a collection of feelings, known as the **Oedipus complex**, that center on sexual attraction to the mother and resentment of the father. Some psychoanalysts in Freud's era believed girls have a parallel *Electra complex*.

11. In Freud's theory, **identification** is the process by which the child's superego develops and incorporates the parents' values. Freud saw identification as crucial, not only to resolution of the Oedipus complex, but also to the development of what psychologists now call *gender identity*.

12. In Freud's theory, **fixation** occurs when development becomes arrested, due to unresolved conflicts, in an earlier psychosexual stage.

13. In psychoanalytic theory, **defense mechanisms** are the ego's methods of unconsciously protecting itself against anxiety by distorting reality.

14. The basis of all defense mechanisms, **repression** is the unconscious exclusion of anxiety-arousing thoughts, feelings, and memories from consciousness.

15. The **collective unconscious** is Jung's concept of an inherited unconscious shared by all people and deriving from our species' history.

16. **Projective tests**, such as the Rorschach, present ambiguous stimuli onto which people supposedly *project* their own inner feelings.

17. The **Rorschach inkblot test**, the most widely used projective test, consists of 10 inkblots that people are asked to interpret; it seeks to identify people's inner feelings by analyzing their interpretations of the blots.

18. **Humanistic theories** of personality focus on our potential for healthy personal growth.

19. In Maslow's theory, **self-actualization** describes the process of fulfilling one's potential and becoming spontaneous, loving, self-accepting, and not paralyzed by others' opinions. Self-actualization becomes active only after the more basic physical and psychological needs have been met.

20. According to Rogers, **unconditional positive regard** is an attitude of total acceptance toward another person.

21. **Self-concept** refers to one's personal awareness of "who I am." In the humanistic perspective, the self-concept is a central feature of personality; life happiness is significantly affected by whether the self-concept is positive or negative.

22. A **trait** is a characteristic pattern of behavior or a disposition to feel and act, as assessed by self-report inventories and peer reports.

23. **Personality inventories**, associated with the trait perspective, are questionnaires used to assess selected personality traits.

24. Consisting of 10 clinical scales, the **Minnesota Multiphasic Personality Inventory (MMPI)** is the most widely researched and clinically used personality inventory.

25. An **empirically derived test** is one developed by testing many items to see which best distinguish between groups of interest.

26. According to the **social-cognitive perspective,** behavior is the result of interactions between people's traits (including their thinking) and their social context.

27. According to the social-cognitive perspective, personality is shaped through **reciprocal determinism,** or the interacting influences of behavior, internal cognition, and environment.

28. In contemporary psychology, the **self** is the organizer of our thoughts, feelings, and actions.

29. The **spotlight effect** is the tendency of people to overestimate the extent to which other people are noticing and evaluating their appearance, performance, and blunders.

30. **Self-esteem** refers to an individual's feeling of self-worth.

31. **Self-efficacy** is our sense of competence on a task.

32. **Self-serving bias** is the tendency to perceive oneself favorably.

33. **Narcissism** is excessive self-love and self-absorption.

34. **Individualism** is giving priority to personal goals over group goals and defining one's identity in terms of personal attributes rather than group identification.

35. **Collectivism** is giving priority to the goals of one's group and defining one's identity accordingly.

Cross-Check

ACROSS
 4. preconscious
 7. external
 9. id
10. trait
11. ego
12. defense mechanisms

DOWN
 1. displacement
 2. reciprocal determinism
 3. fixation
 4. personality
 5. Oedipus
 6. identification
 8. Rorschach
13. MMPI

Social Psychology

Chapter Overview

Chapter 13 demonstrates the powerful influences of social situations on the behavior of individuals. Central to this topic are research studies on attitudes and actions, conformity, obedience, and group and cultural influences. The social principles that emerge help us to understand how individuals are influenced by advertising, political candidates, and the various groups to which they belong. Although social influences are powerful, it is important to remember the significant role of individuals in choosing and creating the social situations that influence them.

The chapter also discusses how people relate to one another, from the negative—developing prejudice and behaving aggressively—to the positive—being attracted to people who are nearby and/or similar and behaving altruistically.

The chapter concludes with a discussion of situations that provoke conflict and techniques that have been shown to promote conflict resolution.

Although there is some terminology for you to learn in this chapter, your primary task is to absorb the findings of the many research studies discussed. The chapter headings, which organize the findings, should prove especially useful to you here. In addition, you might, for each main topic (conformity, group influence, aggression, etc.), ask yourself the question, "What situational factors promote this phenomenon?" The research findings can then form the basis for your answers.

NOTE: Answer guidelines for all Chapter 13 questions begin on page 325.

Chapter Review

First, skim each section, noting headings and bold-face items. After you have read the section, review each objective by answering the fill-in and essay-type questions that follow it. As you proceed, evaluate your performance by consulting the answers beginning on page 325. Do not continue with the next section until you understand each answer. If you need to, review or reread the section in the textbook before continuing.

Social Thinking

Objective 13-1: Identify what social psychologists study, and discuss how we tend to explain others' behavior and our own.

1. Psychologists who study how we think about, influence, and relate to one another are called

   _____ _____ .

2. Fritz Heider's theory of how we explain others' behavior is the _____ theory. According to this theory, we attribute behavior either to an internal cause, which is called a

   _____ _____ ,

   or to an external cause, which is called a

   _____ _____ .

3. Most people tend to_____ (overestimate/underestimate) the extent to which people's actions are influenced by social situations because their _____ is focused on the person. This tendency is called the

   _____ _____

   _____ . When explaining our own behavior, or that of someone we know well, this tendency is _____ (stronger/weaker). When observers view the world from others' perspectives, attributions are _____ (the same/reversed).

Give an example of the practical consequences of attributions.

When are attitudes especially likely to affect behavior?

STUDY TIP: To drive home the concept of the fundamental attribution error, think about a recent embarrassing moment. Perhaps you made an unkind remark that you later regretted. In explaining your behavior, you likely would say, "I was caught up in the moment," or "It was the people I was with." These are *external* (situational) attributions. Now think about how you would explain the same type of behavior in another person, especially someone you have just met. If you committed the fundamental attribution error, you would be less likely to "forgive" the person by making an external attribution. Instead, you would attribute it to personality and expect the person to behave similarly in the future.

APPLICATION:

4. Professor Washington's students did very poorly on the last exam. The tendency to make the fundamental attribution error might lead her to conclude that the class did poorly because
   a. the test was unfair.
   b. not enough time was given for students to complete the test.
   c. students were distracted by some social function on campus.
   d. students were unmotivated.

Objective 13-2: Describe how attitudes and actions interact.

5. Feelings, often based on our beliefs, that predispose our responses are called

   _____ . When people focus on an issue and respond favorably to an argument,

   _____ _____

   _____ has occurred.
   Persuasion may also occur through the

   _____ (slower/faster)

   _____ _____ as

   people respond to incidental cues such as a speaker's appearance.

6. Many research studies demonstrate that our attitudes are strongly influenced by our

   _____ . One example of this is the tendency for people who agree to a small request to comply later with a larger one. This is the _____-_____-

   _____-_____

   phenomenon.

7. When you follow the social prescriptions for how you should act as, say, a college student, you are adopting a _____ .

8. Taking on a set of behaviors, or acting in a certain way, generally _____ (changes/does not change) people's attitudes.

9. According to _____

   _____ theory, thoughts and feelings change because people are motivated to justify actions that would otherwise seem hypocritical. This theory was proposed by

   _____ .

10. Dissonance theory predicts that people induced (without coercion) to behave contrary to their true attitudes will be motivated to reduce the resulting _____ by changing their _____ .

STUDY TIP/APPLICATION: Cognitive dissonance theory and the foot-in-the-door phenomenon are two powerful examples of our attitudes following our actions. Think about these examples as you complete the following exercises.

11. a. Using the foot-in-the-door technique, how might you persuade a friend to take on an important, time-consuming task such as becoming treasurer of a ski club?

b. Suppose your roommate thinks climate change is nothing more than a hoax foisted by politicians on a gullible public. Using cognitive dissonance theory, how might you go about changing your roommate's attitude?

APPLICATIONS:

12. Which of the following is an example of the foot-in-the-door phenomenon?
   a. To persuade a customer to buy a product, a store owner offers a small gift.
   b. After agreeing to wear a small "Enforce Recycling" lapel pin, a woman agrees to collect signatures on a petition to make recycling required by law.
   c. After offering to sell a car at a ridiculously low price, a car salesperson is forced to tell the customer the car will cost $1000 more.
   d. All of these are examples.

13. Which of the following situations should produce the GREATEST cognitive dissonance?
   a. A soldier is forced to carry out orders he finds disagreeable.
   b. A student who loves animals has to dissect a cat in order to pass biology.
   c. As part of an experiment, a subject is directed to deliver electric shocks to another person.
   d. A student volunteers to debate an issue, taking the side he personally disagrees with.

14. Before she gave a class presentation favoring gun control legislation, Wanda opposed it. Her present attitude favoring such legislation can best be explained by
   a. attribution theory.
   b. cognitive dissonance theory.
   c. reward theory.
   d. evolutionary psychology.

Social Influence

Objective 13-3: Describe how cultural norms affect our behavior.

15. The enduring behaviors, ideas, attitudes, values, and traditions of a group of people and transmitted from one generation to the next defines the group's _____ .

16. One landmark of human culture is the preservation of _____ , which is derived from our mastery of _____ , so that we can pass it on to future generations. Culture also enables an efficient division of _____ .

17. All cultural groups evolve their own rules for accepted and expected behavior, called _____ .

18. The speed at which culture changes is much _____ (faster/slower) than the pace of evolutionary changes in the human _____ _____ .

Objective 13-4: Describe automatic mimicry, and explain how conformity experiments reveal the power of social influence.

19. People take on the _____ tones of others around them. This natural tendency is called _____ _____ . The *chameleon effect* refers to our natural tendency to unconsciously _____ others' expressions, postures, and voice tones. This helps us to feel what they are feeling, referred to as _____ . It also helps explain why studies of British nurses and accountants have revealed _____ _____ — sharing up and down moods.

20. The term that refers to the tendency to adjust one's behavior to coincide with an assumed group standard is _____ .

21. The psychologist who first studied the effects of group pressure on conformity is _____ .

22. In this study, when the opinion of other group members was contradicted by objective evidence about the lengths of the lines (see below), research participants _____ (were/were not) willing to conform to the group opinion.

1   2   3

List the conditions under which we are more likely to conform.

List the conditions under which obedience was highest in Milgram's studies.

23. One reason that people comply with social pressure is to gain approval or avoid rejection; this is called _____

_____ _____ .

24. Another reason people comply is that they have genuinely been influenced by what they have learned from others; this type of influence is called _____

_____ _____ .

25. Cultures based on _____ tend to focus on an independent self. Conformity rates tend to be _____ (lower/higher) in cultures that place a higher value on group standards.

APPLICATION:

26. Maria recently heard a speech calling for a ban on aerosol sprays that endanger the earth's ozone layer. Maria's subsequent decision to stop using aerosol sprays is an example of
    a. informational social influence.
    b. normative social influence.
    c. the foot-in-the-door phenomenon.
    d. cognitive dissonance.

Objective 13-5: Describe what we learned about the power of social influence from Milgram's obedience experiments.

27. The classic social psychology studies of obedience were conducted by _____ .
    When ordered by the experimenter to electrically shock the "learner," the majority of participants (the "teachers") in these studies _____ (complied/refused). In 10 later studies, women obeyed at rates that were _____ (higher than/lower than/similar to) men's.

28. In getting people to administer increasingly larger shocks, Milgram was in effect applying the

    _____-_____-

    _____-_____

    technique.

29. The Asch and Milgram studies demonstrate that strong _____ influences can make _____ people _____ to falsehoods and commit cruel acts.

APPLICATIONS:

30. José is the one student member on his school's board of trustees. At the board's first meeting, José wants to disagree with the others on several issues but in each case decides to say nothing. Studies on conformity suggest all except one of the following are factors in José's not speaking up. Which one is NOT a factor?
    a. The board is a large group.
    b. The board is prestigious and most of its members are well known.
    c. The board members are already aware that José and the student body disagree with them on these issues.
    d. Because this is the first meeting José has attended, he feels insecure and not fully competent.

31. Twenty-year-old Marge belonged to a sorority. During pledge week, she was ordered to force potential members to strip in front of their friends. Although Marge disapproved of asking fellow students to embarrass themselves, she did it anyway. She respected the sorority officers, and all her fellow sisters were also hazing the pledges. How would Milgram explain Marge's behavior?

Objective 13-6: Describe how our behavior is affected by the presence of others.

32. The tendency to perform a task better when other people are present is called _____ _____ . In general, people become aroused in the presence of others, and arousal enhances the correct response on a(n) _____ (easy/difficult) task. Later research revealed that arousal strengthens the response that is most _____ in a given situation.

33. Researchers have found that the reactions of people in crowded situations are often _____ (lessened/amplified).

34. Researchers found that people worked _____ (harder/less hard) in a team tug-of-war than they had in an individual contest. This phenomenon has been called

_____ _____ .

35. The feeling of anonymity and loss of self-restraint that an individual may develop when in a group is called _____ .

STUDY TIP: To help solidify the idea of social facilitation in your mind, think about sports you play—or don't play (because you do not do well). Think about your friends in similar situations, your children if you are a parent. Then think about professional athletes. Does the same hold true for the performing arts (acting, playing a musical instrument, dancing)? What about your everyday activities?

APPLICATIONS:

36. Which of the following would most likely be subject to social facilitation?
    a. proofreading a page for spelling errors
    b. typing a letter with accuracy
    c. playing a difficult piece on a musical instrument
    d. running quickly around a track

37. Concluding her presentation on deindividuation, Renée notes that deindividuation is less likely in situations that promote
    a. anonymity.
    b. decreased self-awareness.
    c. increased self-awareness.
    d. the fundamental attribution error.

Objective 13-7: Explain group polarization and groupthink, and discuss the power of the individual.

38. Over time, the initial differences between groups usually _____ (increase/decrease).

39. The enhancement of each group's prevailing tendency over time is called _____ _____ . Electronic discussions in _____ groups provide a medium for this tendency.

40. When the desire for group harmony overrides realistic thinking in individuals, the phenomenon known as _____ has occurred.

41. In considering the power of social influence, we cannot overlook the interaction of

_____ _____

(the power of the situation) and

_____ _____

(the power of the individual).

42. The power of one or two individuals to sway the opinion of the majority is called

_____ _____ .

43. A minority opinion will have the most success in swaying the majority if it takes a stance that is _____ (unswerving/flexible).

APPLICATION:

44. Jane and Sandy were best friends in their first year of university. Jane joined a sorority; Sandy didn't. By the end of their last year, they found that they had less in common with each other than with the other members of their respective circles of friends. Which of the following phenomena most likely explains their feelings?
    a. group polarization   c. deindividuation
    b. groupthink   d. social facilitation

Social Relations

Objective 13-8: Define *prejudice*, and identify its social and emotional roots.

45. Prejudice is an _____ (and usually _____) attitude toward a group that involves overgeneralized beliefs known as _____ .

46. Like all attitudes, prejudice is a mixture of
_____ , _____ ,
and predispositions to _____ .

47. Prejudice is a negative _____ ,
and _____ is a negative
_____ .

48. Americans today express _____
(less/the same/more) racial and gender prejudice
than they did in the last half-century.

49. (text and Close-Up) Blatant forms of prejudice
_____ (have/have not) dimin-
ished. However, even people who deny holding
prejudiced attitudes may carry negative
_____ about race.

50. (Close-Up) Studies of prejudice indicate that it is
often an unconscious, or _____ ,
action. Research has shown that _____
people with a flashed Black rather than White
face makes them _____ (more/
less) likely to perceive a flashed tool as a gun.

51. (Close-Up) Today's biopsychosocial approach has
stimulated neuroscience studies that have detected implicit prejudice in people's
_____ -muscle responses and in
the activation of their brain's
_____ .

52. Worldwide, _____
(women/men) are more likely to live in poverty.

53. The belief that people get what they deserve—
that the good are rewarded and the bad punished—is expressed in the
_____ - _____
phenomenon.

54. For those with money, power, and prestige, prejudice often serves as a means of
_____ social inequalities. People
tend to perceive women as being more
_____ and _____
and less _____ than men, and so
better suited for caretaking tasks.

55. Discrimination increases prejudice through the
tendency of people to _____
victims for their plight.

56. Through our _____
_____ , we associate ourselves
with certain groups and contrast ourselves with
others.

57. Prejudice is also fostered by the
_____ _____ , a
tendency to favor groups to which one belongs—
called the _____ —while exclud-
ing others, or the _____ .

58. That prejudice derives from attempts to blame
others for one's frustration is proposed by the
_____ theory.

59. People who feel loved and supported become
more _____ to and
_____ of those who differ from
them.

60. Prejudice is also nourished by _____
emotions.

Objective 13-9: Identify the cognitive roots of
prejudice.

61. Research suggests that prejudice may also derive
from _____ , the process by
which we attempt to simplify our world by
classifying people into groups. One by-product
of this process is that people tend to
_____ the similarity of those
within a group. One manifestation of this is the
_____ - _____
_____ , the tendency to recall
faces of one's own race more accurately than
those of other races.

62. Another factor that fosters the formation of group
stereotypes and prejudice is the tendency to
_____ from vivid or memorable
cases.

63. The belief that people get what they deserve is
based in part on _____
_____ , the tendency to believe
that one would have foreseen how something
turned out.

APPLICATIONS:

64. Students at State University are convinced that their school is better than any other; this most directly illustrates
    a. an ingroup bias.
    b. prejudice and discrimination.
    c. the scapegoat effect.
    d. the just-world phenomenon.

65. Alexis believes that all male athletes are self-centered and sexist. Her beliefs are an example of
    a. ingroup bias.
    b. groupthink.
    c. stereotypes.
    d. the fundamental attribution error.

66. Ever since their cabin lost the camp softball competition, the campers have become increasingly hostile toward one camper in their cabin, blaming her for every problem in the cabin. This behavior is best explained in terms of
    a. the ingroup bias.
    b. prejudice.
    c. the scapegoat theory.
    d. attribution theory.

67. Given the tendency of people to categorize information according to preformed schemas, which of the following stereotypes would Juan, a 65-year-old political liberal and fitness enthusiast, be most likely to have?
    a. "People who exercise regularly are very extraverted."
    b. "All political liberals are advocates of a reduced defense budget."
    c. "Young people today have no sense of responsibility."
    d. "Older people are lazy."

Objective 13-10: Explain how psychology's definition of *aggression* differs from everyday usage, and identify the biological factors that make us more prone to hurt one another.

68. Aggressive behavior is defined by psychologists as _____

    _____ .

    Thus, psychologists _____ (do/do not) consider assertive salespeople to be aggressive.

69. Like other behaviors, aggression emerges from the interaction of _____ and

    _____ .

70. Today, most psychologists _____ (do/do not) consider human aggression to be instinctive.

71. In humans, aggressiveness _____ (varies/does not vary) greatly from culture to culture, era to era, and person to person.

72. That there are genetic influences on aggression can be shown by the fact that many species of animals have been _____ for aggressiveness.

73. Twin studies suggest that genes _____ (do/do not) influence human aggression. One genetic marker of those who commit the most violence is the _____ chromosome. Another marker is the _____

    _____ _____ gene, which helps break down neurotransmitters such as dopamine and serotonin.

74. In humans and animals, aggression is facilitated by _____ systems, which are in turn influenced by _____ , alcohol, and other substances in the blood. Studies of violent criminals reveal diminished activity in the brain's _____ _____ , which play an important role in controlling

    _____ .

75. The aggressive behavior of animals can be manipulated by altering the levels of the hormone _____ . When this level is _____ (increased/decreased), aggressive tendencies are reduced.

76. High levels of testosterone correlate with _____ , low tolerance for _____ , _____ , and _____ . Among teenage boys and adult men, high testosterone also correlates with _____ , hard _____ _____ , and aggressive-bullying responses to _____ .

77. One drug that unleashes aggressive responses to provocation is _____ .

Objective 13-11: Outline psychological and social-cultural triggers of aggressive behavior.

78. According to the _____-
_____ principle, inability to achieve a goal leads to anger, which may generate aggression.

79. Other aversive stimuli can provoke hostility, including _____
_____ .

80. Aggressive behavior can be learned through _____ , as shown by the fact that people use aggression where they've found it pays, and through _____ of others.

81. Parent-training programs often advise parents to avoid _____ violence by screaming and hitting. _____ curbs aggressive and criminal behavior. One _____-_____ program with juvenile offenders and gang members and their parents has been successful in bringing down the youths' re-arrest rates.

82. Crime rates are higher in countries in which there is a large disparity between those who are _____ and those who are _____ . High violence rates also are typical of cultures and families in which there is minimal _____
_____ .

83. Repeatedly viewing on-screen violence may create _____
_____ to which people respond when they are in new situations or are uncertain how to act.

84. The "rape myth" is the mistaken idea that _____ .
Most rapists _____ (accept/do not accept) this myth.

Comment on the impression of women that pornography frequently conveys and the effects this impression has on attitudes and behavior.

Summarize the findings of the study in which undergraduates viewed either sexually explicit films or nonerotic films.

85. Experiments have shown that, among other factors, depictions by the media of _____
_____ most directly affect men's acceptance and performance of aggression against women.

86. Violence on television tends to _____ people to cruelty and _____ them to respond aggressively when they are provoked.

87. Kids who play a lot of violent video games see the world as more _____ , get into more _____ and _____ , and get worse _____ .

88. Many factors contribute to aggression, including _____ factors, such as an increase in testosterone; _____ factors, such as frustration; and _____-_____ factors, such as deindividuation.

APPLICATIONS:

89. Summarizing his report on the biology of aggression, Sam notes that
   a. biology does not significantly influence aggression.
   b. when one identical twin has a violent temperament, the other member of the twin pair rarely does.
   c. hormones and alcohol influence the neural systems that control aggression.
   d. testosterone reduces dominance behaviors in animals.

90. After waiting in line for an hour to buy concert tickets, Teresa is told that the concert is sold out. In her anger she pounds her fist on the ticket counter, frightening the clerk. Teresa's behavior is best explained by
   a. evolutionary psychology.
   b. deindividuation.
   c. reward theory.
   d. the frustration-aggression principle.

Objective 13-12: Explain why we befriend or fall in love with some people but not with others.

91. A prerequisite for, and perhaps the most powerful predictor of, attraction is _____ .

92. (Close-up) Compared with relationships formed in person, Internet-formed relationships are _____ (more/less) likely to last beyond two years. Studies of people who engage in _____ dating reveal that observers can read a _____ (woman's/man's) level of romantic interest more accurately than a _____ (woman's/man's).

93. When people are repeatedly exposed to unfamiliar stimuli, their liking of the stimuli _____ (increases/decreases). This phenomenon is the _____ _____ effect.

94. Our first impression of another person is most influenced by the person's _____ .

95. In a sentence, list several of the characteristics that physically attractive people are judged to possess: _____ _____ .

96. A person's attractiveness _____ (is/is not) strongly related to his or her self-esteem or happiness.

97. Cross-cultural research reveals that men judge women as more attractive if they have a _____ appearance, whereas women judge men who appear _____ , _____ , _____ , and _____ as more attractive.

98. Compared with strangers, friends and couples are more likely to be similar in terms of _____ _____ .

Explain what a reward theory of attraction is and how it can account for the three predictors of liking—proximity, attractiveness, and similarity.

APPLICATIONS:

99. Ahmed and Monique are on a blind date. Which of the following will probably be MOST influential in determining whether they like each other?
    a. their personalities
    b. their beliefs
    c. their social skills
    d. their physical attractiveness

100. Having read the chapter, which of the following is best borne out by research on attraction?
    a. Birds of a feather flock together.
    b. Opposites attract.
    c. Familiarity breeds contempt.
    d. Absence makes the heart grow fonder.

Objective 13-13: Describe how romantic love typically changes as time passes.

101. Hatfield has distinguished two types of love: _____ love and _____ love.

102. According to the two-factor theory, emotions have two components: physical _____ and a _____ label.

103. When college men were placed in an aroused state, their feelings toward an attractive woman _____ (were/were not) more positive than those of men who had not been aroused.

104. Companionate love is promoted by _____—mutual sharing and giving by both partners.

105. Another key ingredient of loving relationships is the revealing of intimate aspects of ourselves through _____ . A third key to enduring love is _____ _____ .

APPLICATION:

106. Opening her mail, Joan discovers a romantic greeting card from her boyfriend. According to the two-factor theory, she is likely to feel the most intense romantic feelings if, prior to reading the card, she has just
    a. completed her daily run.
    b. finished reading a chapter in her psychology textbook.
    c. awakened from a nap.
    d. finished eating lunch.

Objective 13-14: Identify the times when people are most—and least—likely to help.

107. An unselfish regard for the welfare of others is called _____ .

Give an example of altruism.

108. According to Darley and Latané, people will help only if a three-stage decision-making process is completed: Bystanders must first _____ the incident, then _____ it as an emergency, and finally _____ _____ for helping.

109. When people who overheard a seizure victim calling for help thought others were hearing the same plea, they were _____ (more/less) likely to go to his aid than when they thought no one else was aware of the emergency.

110. In a series of staged accidents, Latané and Darley found that a bystander was _____ (more/less) likely to help when more people shared responsibility for helping, that is, when there was a _____ _____ . This phenomenon has been called the _____ .

Identify the circumstances in which a person is most likely to offer help during an emergency.

STUDY TIP: As with other concepts, altruism is best understood by relating it to your own experiences. Can you think of instances of altruism in your home town? At school? Have you personally stopped to help a person who seemed to be in need—for example, an older woman struggling to carry groceries to her car? What are some other examples of truly altruistic behavior?

Objective 13-15: Discuss how social exchange theory and social norms explain helping behavior.

111. The idea that social behavior aims to maximize rewards and minimize costs is proposed by the _____ _____ theory.

112. One rule of social behavior tells us to return help to those who have helped us; this is the _____ norm.

113. Another rule tells us to help those who need our help; this is the _____ - _____ norm.

Objective 13-16: Explain how social traps and mirror-image perceptions fuel social conflict.

114. A perceived incompatibility of actions, goals, or ideas is called _____ . This perception can take place between _____ at war, _____ groups feuding within a society, or _____ sparring in a relationship.

115. Situations in which conflicting parties become caught in mutually destructive behavior by pursuing their own self-interests are called _____ _____ .

116. The distorted images people in conflict form of each other are called _____-_____ perceptions.

117. When contact is _____ and between parties of _____ _____ , it typically helps. But in most situations, establishing contact between two conflicting groups _____ (is/is not) sufficient to resolve conflict.

118. In Muzafer Sherif's study, two conflicting groups of campers were able to resolve their conflicts by working together on projects in which they shared _____ goals. Shared _____ breed solidarity, as demonstrated by a surge in the use of the word _____ in the weeks after 9/11.

Objective 13-17: Discuss how we can transform feelings of prejudice, aggression, and conflict into attitudes that promote peace.

119. When conflicts arise, a third-party _____ may facilitate communication and promote understanding.

120. Charles Osgood has advanced a strategy of conciliation called GRIT, which stands for _____ and _____ _____ in _____-_____ . The key to this method is each side's offering of a small _____ gesture in order to increase mutual trust and cooperation.

APPLICATIONS:

121. Mr. and Mrs. Samuels are constantly fighting, and each perceives the other as hard-headed and insensitive. Their conflict is being fueled by
a. self-disclosure.
b. stereotypes.
c. a social norm.
d. mirror-image perceptions.

122. Which of the following strategies would be MOST likely to foster positive feelings between two conflicting groups?
a. Take steps to reduce the likelihood of mirror-image perceptions.
b. Separate the groups so that tensions diminish.
c. Increase the amount of contact between the two conflicting groups.
d. Have the groups work on a superordinate goal.

Progress Test 1

Multiple-Choice Questions

Circle your answers to the following questions and check them with the answers beginning on page 329. If your answer is incorrect, read the explanation for why it is incorrect and then consult the text.

1. In his study of obedience, Stanley Milgram found that the majority of participants
   a. refused to shock the learner even once.
   b. complied with the experiment until the "learner" first indicated pain.
   c. complied with the experiment until the "learner" began screaming in agony.
   d. complied with all the demands of the experiment.

2. According to cognitive dissonance theory, dissonance is most likely to occur when
   a. a person's behavior is not based on strongly held attitudes.
   b. two people have conflicting attitudes and find themselves in disagreement.
   c. an individual does something that is personally disagreeable.
   d. an individual is coerced into doing something that he or she does not want to do.

3. Which of the following statements is true?
   a. Groups are almost never swayed by minority opinions.
   b. Group polarization is most likely to occur when group members frequently disagree with one another.
   c. Groupthink provides the consensus needed for effective decision making.
   d. A group that is like-minded will probably not change its opinions through discussion.

4. Conformity increased under which of the following conditions in Asch's studies of conformity?
   a. The group had three or more people.
   b. The group had high status.
   c. Individuals were made to feel insecure.
   d. All of these conditions increased conformity.

5. Violent criminals often have diminished activity in the _____ of the brain, which play(s) an important role in _____ .
   a. occipital lobes; aggression
   b. hypothalamus; hostility
   c. frontal lobes; controlling impulses
   d. temporal lobes; patience

6. The phenomenon in which individuals lose their identity and relinquish normal restraints when they are part of a group is called
   a. groupthink.
   b. cognitive dissonance.
   c. empathy.
   d. deindividuation.

7. Subjects in Asch's line-judgment experiment conformed to the group standard when their judgments were observed by others but not when they were made in private. This tendency to conform in public demonstrates
   a. social facilitation.
   b. overjustification.
   c. informational social influence.
   d. normative social influence.

8. Based on findings from Milgram's obedience studies, participants would be LESS likely to follow the experimenter's orders when
   a. they hear the "learner" cry out in pain.
   b. they merely administer the test while someone else delivers the shocks.
   c. the "learner" is an older person or mentions having some physical problem.
   d. they see another person disobey instructions.

9. *Aggression* is defined as behavior that
   a. hurts another person.
   b. is intended to hurt another person.
   c. is hostile, passionate, and produces physical injury.
   d. has all of these characteristics.

10. Which of the following is true about aggression?
   a. It varies too much to be instinctive in humans.
   b. It is just one instinct among many.
   c. It is instinctive but shaped by learning.
   d. It is the most important human instinct.

11. Which of the following is NOT true regarding cultural diversity?
   a. Culture influences how we raise our children.
   b. Culture influences how punctual we are.
   c. Culture does not have a strong influence on how strictly social roles are defined.
   d. All cultures evolve their own norms..

12. Research studies have indicated that the tendency of viewers to trivialize rape is
   a. increased by exposure to pornography.
   b. not changed after exposure to pornography.
   c. decreased in men by exposure to pornography.
   d. decreased in both men and women by exposure to pornography.

13. Increasing the number of people present during an emergency tends to
   a. increase the likelihood that people will cooperate in rendering assistance.
   b. decrease the empathy that people feel for the victim.
   c. increase the role that social norms governing helping will play.
   d. decrease the likelihood that anyone will help.

14. Which of the following was NOT mentioned in the text discussion of the roots of prejudice?
   a. people's tendency to overestimate the similarity of people within groups
   b. people's tendency to assume that exceptional, or especially memorable, individuals are unlike the majority of members of a group
   c. people's tendency to assume that the world is just and that people get what they deserve
   d. people's tendency to discriminate against those they view as "outsiders"

15. The mere exposure effect demonstrates that
   a. familiarity breeds contempt.
   b. opposites attract.
   c. birds of a feather flock together.
   d. familiarity breeds fondness.

16. In one experiment, college men were physically aroused and then introduced to an attractive woman. Compared with men who had not been aroused, these men
   a. reported more positive feelings toward the woman.
   b. reported more negative feelings toward the woman.
   c. were ambiguous about their feelings toward the woman.
   d. were more likely to feel that the woman was "out of their league" in terms of attractiveness.

17. The deep affection that is felt in long-lasting relationships is called _____ love; this feeling is fostered in relationships in which _____ .
   a. passionate; there is equity between the partners
   b. passionate; traditional roles are maintained
   c. companionate; there is equity between the partners
   d. companionate; traditional roles are maintained

18. Which of the following is associated with an increased tendency on the part of a bystander to offer help in an emergency situation?
    a. being in a good mood
    b. having recently needed help and not received it
    c. observing someone as he or she refuses to offer help
    d. being a female

19. The belief that those who suffer deserve their fate is expressed in the
    a. just-world phenomenon.
    b. phenomenon of ingroup bias.

    c. fundamental attribution error.
    d. mirror-image perception principle.

20. Which of the following phenomena is best explained by cognitive dissonance theory?
    a. group polarization
    b. the foot-in-the-door phenomenon
    c. normative social influence
    d. informational social influence

Matching Items

Match each term with the appropriate definition or description.

Terms

_____ 1. social facilitation
_____ 2. social loafing
_____ 3. bystander effect
_____ 4. conformity
_____ 5. ingroup bias
_____ 6. normative social influence
_____ 7. informational social influence
_____ 8. group polarization
_____ 9. stereotype
_____ 10. attribution
_____ 11. altruism
_____ 12. mere exposure effect
_____ 13. central route persuasion
_____ 14. social script
_____ 15. norm

Definitions or Descriptions

a. a causal explanation for someone's behavior
b. a generalized belief about a group of people
c. people work less hard in a group
d. performance is improved by an audience
e. a set of expected behaviors in a culture
f. the effect of social approval or disapproval
g. adjusting one's behavior to coincide with a group standard
h. group discussion enhances prevailing tendencies
i. the effect of accepting others' opinions about something
j. unselfish regard for others
k. the tendency that a person is less likely to help someone in need when others are present
l. the increased liking of a stimulus that results from repeated exposure to it
m. responding favorably to arguments as a result of systematic thinking about an issue
n. a culturally specific model of how to act in a given situation
o. the tendency to favor one's own group

Progress Test 2

Progress Test 2 should be completed during a final chapter review. Answer the following questions after you thoroughly understand the correct answers for the section reviews and Progress Test 1.

Multiple-Choice Questions

1. (Close-Up) Which of the following is an example of implicit prejudice?
   a. Jake, who is White, gives higher evaluations to essays he believes to be written by Blacks than to White-authored essays.
   b. Carol believes that White people are arrogant.
   c. Brad earns more than Jane, despite having the same job skills, performance level, and seniority.
   d. In certain countries, women are not allowed to drive.

2. We tend to perceive the members of an ingroup as _____ and the members of an outgroup as _____ .
   a. similar to one another; different from one another
   b. different from one another; similar to one another
   c. above average in ability; below average in ability
   d. below average in ability; above average in ability

3. Regarding the influence of alcohol and testosterone on aggressive behavior, which of the following is true?
   a. Consumption of alcohol increases aggressive behavior; injections of testosterone reduce aggressive behavior.
   b. Consumption of alcohol reduces aggressive behavior; injections of testosterone increase aggressive behavior.
   c. Consumption of alcohol and injections of testosterone both promote aggressive behavior.
   d. Consumption of alcohol and injections of testosterone both reduce aggressive behavior.

4. Most people prefer mirror-image photographs of their faces. This is best explained by
   a. the principle of equity.
   b. the principle of self-disclosure.
   c. the mere exposure effect.
   d. mirror-image perceptions.

5. Research studies have shown that frequent exposure to sexually explicit films
   a. provides an outlet for bottled-up impulses.
   b. diminishes the attitude that rape is a serious crime.
   c. decreases punitive behavior toward women.
   d. may produce all of these effects.

6. Research studies indicate that in an emergency situation, the presence of others often
   a. prevents people from even noticing the situation.
   b. prevents people from interpreting an unusual event as an emergency.
   c. prevents people from assuming responsibility for assisting.
   d. leads to all of these behaviors.

7. Two neighboring nations are each stockpiling weapons. Each sees its neighbor's actions as an act of aggression and its own actions as self-defense. Evidently, these nations are victims of
   a. prejudice.
   b. groupthink.
   c. self-serving bias.
   d. the fundamental attribution error.

8. Which of the following factors is the MOST powerful predictor of friendship?
   a. similarity in age
   b. common racial and religious background
   c. similarity in physical attractiveness
   d. physical proximity

9. Most researchers agree that
   a. media violence is a factor in aggression.
   b. there is a negative correlation between media violence and aggressiveness.
   c. paradoxically, watching excessive pornography ultimately diminishes an individual's aggressive tendencies.
   d. media violence is too unreal to promote aggression in viewers.

10. When male students in an experiment were told that a woman to whom they would be speaking had been instructed to act in a friendly or unfriendly way, most of them subsequently attributed her behavior to
    a. the situation.
    b. the situation *and* her personal disposition.
    c. her personal disposition.
    d. their own skill or lack of skill in a social situation.

11. Research studies have found a positive correlation between aggressive tendencies in animals and levels of the hormone
    a. estrogen.
    b. adrenaline.
    c. noradrenaline.
    d. testosterone.

12. People with power and status may become prejudiced because
    a. they tend to justify the social inequalities between themselves and others.
    b. those with less status and power tend to resent them.
    c. those with less status and power appear less capable.
    d. they feel proud and are boastful of their achievements.

13. Which of the following most accurately states the effects of crowding on behavior?
    a. Crowding makes people irritable.
    b. Crowding sometimes intensifies people's reactions.
    c. Crowding promotes altruistic behavior.
    d. Crowding usually weakens the intensity of people's reactions.

14. Research has found that for a minority to succeed in swaying a majority, the minority must
    a. make up a sizable portion of the group.
    b. express its position as consistently as possible.
    c. express its position in the most extreme terms possible.
    d. be able to convince a key majority leader.

15. Which of the following conclusions did Milgram derive from his studies of obedience?
    a. Even ordinary people, without any particular hostility, can become agents in a destructive process.
    b. Under the proper circumstances, most people can suppress their natural aggressiveness.
    c. The need to be accepted by others is a powerful motivating force.
    d. He reached all of these conclusions.

16. Which of the following best summarizes the relative importance of personal control and social control of our behavior?
    a. Situational influences on behavior generally are much greater than personal influences.
    b. Situational influences on behavior generally are slightly greater than personal influences.
    c. Personal influences on behavior generally are much greater than situational influences.

    d. Situational and personal influences interact in determining our behavior.

17. Which of the following BEST describes how GRIT works?
    a. The fact that two sides in a conflict have great respect for the other's strengths prevents further escalation of the problem.
    b. The two sides engage in a series of reciprocated conciliatory acts.
    c. The two sides agree to have their differences settled by a neutral, third-party mediator.
    d. The two sides engage in cooperation in those areas in which shared goals are possible.

18. Which of the following is important in promoting conformity in individuals?
    a. whether an individual's behavior will be observed by others in the group
    b. whether the individual is male or female
    c. the size of the group's meeting room
    d. whether the individual is of a higher status than other group members

19. Which theory describes how we explain others' behavior as being due to internal dispositions or external situations?
    a. cognitive dissonance theory
    b. reward theory
    c. two-factor theory
    d. attribution theory

20. Which of the following is most likely to promote groupthink?
    a. The group's leader fails to take a firm stance on an issue.
    b. A minority faction holds to its position.
    c. The group consults with various experts.
    d. Group polarization is evident.

True–False Items

Indicate whether each statement is true or false by placing *T* or *F* in the blank next to the item.

_____ 1. When explaining another's behavior, we tend to underestimate situational influences.

_____ 2. When explaining our own behavior, we tend to underestimate situational influences.

_____ 3. An individual is more likely to conform when the rest of the group is unanimous.

_____ 4. The tendency of people to conform is influenced by their culture.

_____ 5. A bystander is more likely to offer help in an emergency if other bystanders are present.

_____ 6. Counterattitudinal behavior (acting contrary to our beliefs) often leads to attitude change.

_____ 7. Human aggression is instinctual.

_____ 8. Group polarization tends to prevent groupthink from occurring.

_____ 9. Crowded conditions usually subdue people's reactions.

_____ 10. When individuals lose their sense of identity in a group, they often become more uninhibited.

_____ 11. Peripheral route persuasion allows for fast responding to an issue.

_____ 12. In our relations with others of similar status, we tend to give more than we receive.

Essay Question

The Panhellenic Council on your campus has asked you to make a presentation on the topic "Social Psychology" to all freshmen who have signed up to "rush" a fraternity or sorority. In a fit of cynicism following your rejection last year by a prestigious fraternity or sorority, you decide to speak on the negative influences of groups on the behavior of individuals. What will you discuss? (Use the space below to list the points you want to make, and organize them. Then write the essay on a separate sheet of paper.)

Terms and Concepts to Remember

Writing Definitions

Using your own words, on a separate piece of paper write a brief definition or explanation of each of the following terms.

1. social psychology

2. attribution theory

3. fundamental attribution error

4. attitude

5. peripheral route persuasion

6. central route persuasion

7. foot-in-the-door phenomenon

8. role

9. cognitive dissonance theory

10. culture

11. norm

12. conformity

13. normative social influence

14. informational social influence

15. social facilitation

16. social loafing

17. deindividuation

18. group polarization

19. groupthink

20. prejudice

21. stereotype

22. discrimination

23. just-world phenomenon

24. ingroup

25. outgroup

26. ingroup bias

27. scapegoat theory

28. other-race effect

29. aggression

30. frustration-aggression principle

31. social script

32. mere exposure effect

33. passionate love

34. companionate love

35. equity

36. self-disclosure

37. altruism

38. bystander effect

39. social exchange theory

40. reciprocity norm

41. social-responsibility norm

42. conflict

43. social trap

44. mirror-image perceptions

45. superordinate goals

46. GRIT

Cross-Check

As you learned in Chapter 1, reviewing and overlearning of material are important to the learning process. After you have written the definitions of the key terms in this chapter, you should complete the cross-word puzzle to ensure that you can reverse the process—recognize the term, given the definition.

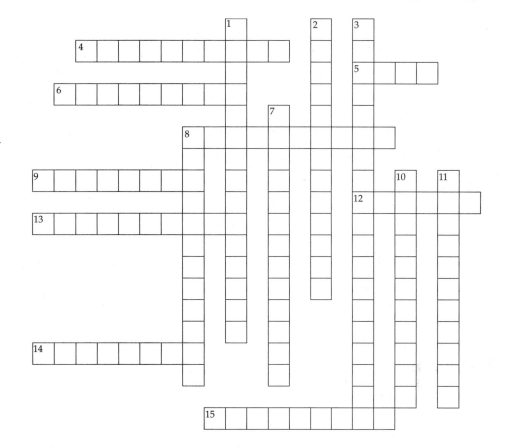

ACROSS

4. A generalized belief about a group of people.
5. A strategy of conflict resolution in which both groups make conciliatory gestures. (abbrev.)
6. Theory that proposes that prejudice provides an outlet for anger by finding someone to blame.
8. The tendency to change one's attitudes to coincide with those held by a group.
9. An unselfish regard for the welfare of others.
12. Mutual giving and receiving in a relationship.
13. Type of love that refers to an aroused state of intense positive absorption in another person.
14. Perceived incompatibility between individuals or groups.
15. Personal beliefs and feelings that influence our behavior.

DOWN

1. A person's tendency not to offer help to someone if others are present.
2. Type of social influence that results when one goes along with a group when one is unsure of what to do.
3. Psychological discomfort we experience when two of our thoughts conflict.
7. Phenomenon whereby people who agree to a small request are more likely to comply later with a larger request.
8. Type of love in which there is a deep, enduring attachment.
10. Our tendency to underestimate situational influences and overestimate dispositional influences upon the behavior of others is the _____ attribution error.
11. A causal explanation of a given behavior.

Answers

Chapter Review

Social Thinking

1. social psychologists
2. attribution; dispositional attribution; situational attribution
3. underestimate; attention; fundamental attribution error; weaker; reversed

Our attributions—to individuals' dispositions or to situations—have important practical consequences. A hurtful remark from an acquaintance, for example, is more likely to be forgiven if it is attributed to a temporary situation than to a mean disposition.

4. **d.** is the answer. The fundamental attribution error refers to the tendency to underestimate situational influences in favor of this type of dispositional attribution when explaining the behavior of other people.
   a., b., & c. These are situational attributions.
5. attitudes; central route persuasion; faster; peripheral route

Attitudes are especially likely to affect behavior when external influences are minimal and when the attitude is stable, specific to the behavior, and easily recalled.

6. actions (or behavior); foot-in-the-door

7. role

8. changes

9. cognitive dissonance; Leon Festinger

10. dissonance; attitudes

11. No single answer is correct. A possible answer for a. is to ask the friend to check some figures from the monthly expenses. For b., you might get your roommate to debate the issue and have him or her argue that climate change is a major concern.

12. **b.** is the answer. In the foot-in-the-door phenomenon, compliance with a small initial request, such as wearing a lapel pin, later is followed by compliance with a much larger request, such as collecting petition signatures.

13. **d.** is the answer. In this situation, the counterattitudinal behavior is performed voluntarily and cannot be attributed to the demands of the situation.
    a., b., & c. In all of these situations, the counterattitudinal behaviors should not arouse much dissonance because they can be attributed to the demands of the situation.

14. **b.** is the answer. Dissonance theory focuses on what happens when our actions contradict our attitudes.
    a. Attribution theory holds that we give causal explanations for others' behavior, often by crediting either the situation or people's dispositions.
    c. Reward theory maintains that we continue relationships that maximize benefits and minimize costs. This has nothing to do with relationships.
    d. This is not a theory of social thinking.

Social Influence

15. culture
16. innovation; language; labor
17. norms
18. faster; gene pool
19. emotional; automatic mimicry; mimic; empathy; mood linkage
20. conformity
21. Solomon Asch
22. were

We are more likely to conform when we are made to feel incompetent or insecure, when the group has at least three people, when everyone else in the group agrees, when we admire the group's status and attractiveness, when we have not made a prior commitment to any response, when others will observe our behavior, and when our culture encourages respect for social standards.

23. normative social influence

24. informational social influence

25. individualism; higher

26. **a.** is the answer. As illustrated by Maria's decision to stop buying aerosol products, informational social influence occurs when people have genuinely been influenced by what they have learned from others.
    b. Had Maria's behavior been motivated by the desire to avoid rejection or to gain social approval (which we have no reason to suspect is the case), it would have been an example of normative social influence.
    c. The foot-in-the-door phenomenon is the tendency for people who agree to a small request to comply later with a larger request.
    d. Cognitive dissonance is the psychological discomfort we experience when our behavior conflicts with what we think and feel.

27. Stanley Milgram; complied; similar to

Obedience was highest when the person giving the orders was close at hand and perceived to be a legitimate authority figure, the authority figure was supported by a prestigious institution, the victim was depersonalized, and when there were no role models for defiance.

28. foot-in-the-door

29. social; ordinary; conform

30. **c.** is the answer. Prior commitment to an opposing view generally tends to work against conformity. In contrast, large group size, prestigiousness of a group, and an individual's feelings of incompetence and insecurity all strengthen the tendency to conform.

31. Milgram would say that Marge's behavior was a product of the situation, not her personal traits. She respected the officers of the sorority and everyone else was participating in the hazing.

32. social facilitation; easy; likely

33. amplified

34. less hard; social loafing

35. deindividuation

36. **d.** is the answer. Social facilitation, or better performance in the presence of others, occurs for easy tasks but not for more difficult ones. For tasks such as proofreading, typing, or playing an instrument, the arousal resulting from the presence of others can lead to mistakes.

37. **c.** is the answer. Deindividuation involves the loss of self-awareness and self-restraint in group situations that involve arousal and anonymity, so (a.) and (b.) cannot be right.

38. increase

39. group polarization; Internet

40. groupthink

41. social control; personal control

42. minority influence

43. unswerving

44. **a.** is the answer. Group polarization means that the tendencies within a group—and therefore the differences among groups—grow stronger over time. Thus, because the differences between the sorority and nonsorority students have increased, Jane and Sandy are likely to have little in common.
    b. Groupthink is the tendency for realistic decision making to disintegrate when the desire for group harmony is strong.
    c. Deindividuation is the loss of self-restraint and self-awareness that sometimes occurs when one is part of a group.
    d. Social facilitation refers to improved performance of a task in the presence of others.

Social Relations

45. unjustifiable; negative; stereotypes

46. beliefs; emotions; action

47. attitude; discrimination; behavior

48. less

49. have; associations

50. implicit; priming; more

51. facial; amygdala

52. women

53. just-world

54. justifying; nurturant; sensitive; assertive

55. blame

56. social identities

57. ingroup bias; ingroup; outgroup

58. scapegoat

59. open; accepting

60. negative

61. categorization; overestimate; other-race effect

62. overgeneralize

63. hindsight bias

64. **a.** is the answer.

b. Prejudices are unjustifiable and usually negative attitudes toward other groups. They may result from an ingroup bias, but they are probably not why students favor their own university.
c. Scapegoats are individuals or groups toward which prejudice is directed as an outlet for the anger of frustrated individuals or groups.
d. The just-world phenomenon is the tendency for people to believe that others "get what they deserve."

65. **c.** is the answer.
    a. The ingroup bias is the tendency to favor one's own group.
    b. Groupthink refers to the unrealistic thought processes and decision making that occur within groups when the desire for group harmony becomes paramount.
    d. The fundamental attribution error is our tendency to underestimate the impact of situations and to overestimate the impact of personal dispositions on the behavior of others.

66. **c.** is the answer. According to the scapegoat theory, when things go wrong, people look for someone on whom to take out their anger and frustration.
    a. These campers are venting their frustration on a member of their *own* cabin group (although this is not always the case with scapegoats).
    b. Prejudice refers to an unjustifiable and usually negative attitude toward another group.
    d. Attribution theory refers to whether we attribute a person's behavior to an internal disposition or to the situation.

67. **c.** is the answer. People tend to overestimate the similarity of people within groups other than their own. Thus, Juan is not likely to form stereotypes of fitness enthusiasts (a.), political liberals (b.), or older adults (d.), because these are groups to which he belongs.

68. any physical or verbal behavior intended to hurt or destroy; do not

69. biology; experience

70. do not

71. varies

72. bred

73. do; Y; monoamine oxidase A (MAOA)

74. neural; hormones; frontal lobes; impulses

75. testosterone; decreased

76. irritability; frustration; assertiveness; impulsiveness; delinquency; drug use; frustration

77. alcohol

78. frustration-aggression
79. physical pain, personal insults, foul odors, hot temperatures, cigarette smoke, crowding
80. rewards; observation (or imitation)
81. modeling; Self-control; aggression-replacement
82. rich; poor; father care
83. social scripts
84. some women invite or enjoy rape; accept

Pornography tends to portray women as enjoying being the victims of sexual aggression, and this perception increases the acceptance of coercion in sexual relationships. Repeatedly watching X-rated films and Internet pornography also makes sexual aggression seem less serious.

The study found that after viewing sexually explicit films for several weeks, undergraduates were more likely to recommend a lighter prison sentence for a convicted rapist than were those who viewed nonerotic films.

85. sexual violence
86. desensitize; prime
87. hostile; arguments; fights; grades
88. biological; psychological; social-cultural
89. **c.** is the answer.
    a. & b. Biology is an important factor in aggressive behavior. This includes genetics, which means identical twins would have similar temperaments.
    d. Just the opposite is true.
90. **d.** is the answer. According to the frustration-aggression principle, the blocking of an attempt to achieve some goal—in Teresa's case, buying concert tickets—creates anger and can generate aggression.
    a. Evolutionary psychology maintains that aggressive behavior is a genetically based drive. Teresa's behavior clearly was a reaction to a specific situation.
    b. Deindividuation refers to loss of self-restraint in group situations that foster arousal. Teresa's action has only to do with her frustration.
    c. Reward theory views behavior as an exchange process in which people try to maximize the benefits of their behavior by minimizing the costs. Teresa's behavior likely brought her few benefits while exacting some costs, including potential injury, embarrassment, and retaliation by the clerk.
91. proximity
92. more; speed; man's; woman's
93. increases; mere exposure
94. appearance

95. Attractive people are perceived as healthier, happier, more sensitive, more successful, and more socially skilled.
96. is not
97. youthful; mature; dominant; masculine; affluent
98. attitudes, beliefs, interests, religion, race, education, intelligence, smoking behavior, economic status, and age

A reward theory of attraction says that we are attracted to, and continue relationships with, those people whose behavior provides us with more benefits than costs. Proximity makes it easy to enjoy the benefits of friendship at little cost, attractiveness is pleasing, and similarity is reinforcing to us.

99. **d.** is the answer. Hundreds of experiments indicate that first impressions are most influenced by physical appearance.
100. **a.** is the answer. Friends and couples are much more likely than randomly paired people to be similar in views, interests, and a range of other factors.
    b. The opposite is true.
    c. The mere exposure effect demonstrates that familiarity tends to breed fondness.
    d. This is unlikely, given the positive effects of proximity and intimacy.
101. passionate; companionate
102. arousal; cognitive
103. were
104. equity
105. self-disclosure; positive support
106. **a.** is the answer. According to the two-factor theory, physical arousal can intensify whatever emotion is currently felt. Only in the situation described in (a.) is Joan likely to be physically aroused.
107. altruism

An example of altruism is giving food and shelter to people displaced by a hurricane or other major disaster without expectation of reward.

108. notice; interpret; assume responsibility
109. less
110. less; diffusion of responsibility; bystander effect

People are most likely to help someone when they have just observed someone else being helpful; when they are not in a hurry; when the victim appears to need and deserve help; when they are in some way similar to the victim; when the person is a woman; when in a small town or rural area; when feeling guilty; when not preoccupied; and when in a good mood.

111. social exchange

112. reciprocity
113. social-responsibility
114. conflict; nations; cultural; partners
115. social traps
116. mirror-image
117. noncompetitive; equal status; is not
118. superordinate; predicaments; "we"
119. mediator
120. Graduated; Reciprocated Initiatives; Tension-Reduction; conciliatory
121. **d.** is the answer. The couple's similar, and presumably distorted, feelings toward each other fuel their conflict.
    a. Self-disclosure, or the sharing of intimate feelings, fosters love.
    b. Stereotypes are overgeneralized ideas about groups.
    c. A social norm is an understood rule for expected and accepted behavior.
122. **d.** is the answer. Sherif found that hostility between two groups could be dispelled by giving the groups superordinate, or shared, goals.
    a. Although reducing the likelihood of mirror-image perceptions might reduce mutually destructive behavior, it would not lead to positive feelings between the groups.
    b. Such segregation would likely increase ingroup bias and group polarization, resulting in further group conflict.
    c. Contact by itself is not likely to reduce conflict.

Progress Test 1

Multiple-Choice Questions

1. **d.** is the answer. In Milgram's initial experiments, 63 percent of the subjects complied fully with the experiment.
2. **c.** is the answer. Cognitive dissonance is the tension we feel when we are aware of a discrepancy between our thoughts and actions, as would occur when we do something we find distasteful.
    a. Dissonance requires strongly held attitudes, which must be perceived as not fitting behavior.
    b. Dissonance is a personal cognitive process.
    d. In such a situation the person is less likely to experience dissonance, since the action can be attributed to "having no choice."
3. **d.** is the answer. In such groups, discussion usually strengthens prevailing opinion; this phenomenon is known as group polarization.

    a. Minority opinions, especially if consistently and firmly stated, can sway the majority in a group.
    b. Group polarization, or the strengthening of a group's prevailing tendencies, is most likely in groups where members agree.
    c. When groupthink occurs, there is so much consensus that decision making becomes less effective.
4. **d.** is the answer.
5. **c.** is the answer.
6. **d.** is the answer.
    a. Groupthink refers to the mode of thinking that occurs when the desire for group harmony overrides realistic and critical thinking.
    b. Cognitive dissonance refers to the discomfort we feel when two thoughts (which include the knowledge of our *behavior*) are inconsistent.
    c. Empathy is feeling what another person feels.
7. **d.** is the answer. Normative social influence refers to influence on behavior that comes from a desire to look good to others. Subjects who were observed conformed because they didn't want to look like oddballs.
    a. Social facilitation involves performing tasks better or faster in the presence of others.
    b. Overjustification occurs when a person is rewarded for doing something that is already enjoyable.
    c. Informational social influence is the tendency of individuals to accept the opinions of others, especially in situations where they themselves are unsure.
8. **d.** is the answer. Role models for defiance reduce levels of obedience.
    a. & c. These did not result in diminished obedience.
    b. This "depersonalization" of the victim resulted in increased obedience.
9. **b.** is the answer. Aggression is any behavior, physical or verbal, that is intended to hurt or destroy.
    a. A person may accidentally be hurt in a nonaggressive incident; aggression does not necessarily prove hurtful.
    c. Verbal behavior, which does not result in physical injury, may also be aggressive. Moreover, acts of aggression may be cool and calculated, rather than hostile and passionate.
10. **a.** is the answer. The very wide variations in aggressiveness from culture to culture indicate that aggression cannot be considered an unlearned instinct.

11. **c.** is the answer.

12. **a.** is the answer.

13. **d.** is the answer. This phenomenon is known as the bystander effect.
    a. This answer is incorrect because individuals are less likely to render assistance at all if others are present.
    b. Although people are less likely to assume responsibility for helping, this does not mean that they are less empathic.
    c. This answer is incorrect because norms such as the social responsibility norm encourage helping others, yet people are less likely to help with others around.

14. **b.** is the answer. In fact, people tend to overgeneralize from vivid cases, rather than assume that they are unusual.
    a., c., & d. Each of these is an example of a cognitive (a. & c.) or a social (d.) root of prejudice.

15. **d.** is the answer. Being repeatedly exposed to novel stimuli increases our liking for them.
    a. For the most part, the opposite is true.
    b. & c. The mere exposure effect concerns our tendency to develop likings on the basis, not of similarities or differences, but simply of familiarity, or repeated exposure.

16. **a.** is the answer. This result supports the two-factor theory of emotion and passionate attraction, according to which arousal from any source can facilitate an emotion, depending on how we label the arousal.

17. **c.** is the answer. Deep affection is typical of companionate love, rather than passionate love, and is promoted by equity, whereas traditional roles may be characterized by the dominance of one sex.

18. **a.** is the answer.
    b. & c. These factors would most likely decrease a person's altruistic tendencies.
    d. There is no evidence that one sex is more altruistic than the other.

19. **a.** is the answer.
    b. Ingroup bias is the tendency of people to favor their own group.
    c. The fundamental attribution error is the tendency of people to underestimate situational influences when observing the behavior of other people.
    d. The mirror-image perception principle is the tendency of conflicting parties to form similar, diabolical images of each other.

20. **b.** is the answer.
    a. Group polarization involves group opinions.

c. & d. Normative and informational social influence have to do with reasons for influence.

Matching Items

1. d	6. f	11. j
2. c	7. i	12. l
3. k	8. h	13. m
4. g	9. b	14. n
5. o	10. a	15. e

Progress Test 2

Multiple-Choice Questions

1. **a.** is the answer.
   b. This is an example of overt prejudice.
   c. & d. These are examples of discrimination.

2. **b.** is the answer.
   a. We are keenly sensitive to differences within our group, less so to differences within other groups.
   c. & d. Although we tend to look more favorably on members of the ingroup, the text does not suggest that ingroup bias extends to evaluations of abilities.

3. **c.** is the answer.

4. **c.** is the answer. The mere exposure effect refers to our tendency to like what we're used to, and we're used to seeing mirror images of ourselves.
   a. Equity refers to equality in giving and taking between the partners in a relationship.
   b. Self-disclosure is the sharing of intimate feelings with a partner in a loving relationship.
   d. Although people prefer mirror images of their faces, mirror-image perceptions are often held by parties in conflict. Each party views itself favorably and the other negatively.

5. **b.** is the answer.

6. **d.** is the answer.

7. **d.** is the answer. In this case, each nation has mistakenly attributed the other's action to a *dispositional* trait, whereas its own action is viewed as a *situational* response.

8. **d.** is the answer. Because it provides people with an opportunity to meet, proximity is the most powerful predictor of friendship, even though, once a friendship is established, the other factors mentioned become more important.

9. **a.** is the answer.

10. **c.** is the answer. In this example of the fundamental attribution error, even when given the situational explanation for the woman's behavior,

students ignored it and attributed her behavior to her personal disposition.

11. d. is the answer.

12. a. is the answer. Such justifications arise as a way to preserve inequalities. The just-world phenomenon presumes that people get what they deserve. According to this view, someone who has less must deserve less.

13. b. is the answer.
a. & c. Crowding may amplify irritability or altruistic tendencies that are already present. Crowding does not, however, produce these reactions as a general effect.
d. In fact, just the opposite is true. Crowding often intensifies people's reactions.

14. b. is the answer.
a. Even if they made up a sizable portion of the group, although still a minority, their numbers would not be as important as their consistency.
c. & d. These aspects of minority influence were not discussed in the text; however, they are not likely to help a minority sway a majority.

15. a. is the answer.

16. d. is the answer. The text emphasizes the ways in which personal and social controls interact in influencing behavior. It does not suggest that one factor is more influential than the other.

17. b. is the answer.
a. GRIT is a technique for reducing conflict through a series of conciliatory gestures, not for maintaining the status quo.
c. & d. These measures may help reduce conflict but they are not aspects of GRIT.

18. a. is the answer. As Solomon Asch's experiments demonstrated, individuals are more likely to conform when they are being observed by others in the group. The other factors were not discussed in the text and probably would not promote conformity.

19. d. is the answer.

20. d. is the answer. Group polarization, or the enhancement of a group's prevailing attitudes, promotes groupthink, which leads to the disintegration of critical thinking.
a. Groupthink is more likely when a leader highly favors an idea, which may make members reluctant to disagree.
b. A strong minority faction would probably have the opposite effect: It would diminish group harmony while promoting critical thinking.
c. Consulting experts would discourage groupthink by exposing the group to other opinions.

True–False Items

1. T	6. T	11. T
2. F	7. F	12. F
3. T	8. F	
4. T	9. F	
5. F	10. T	

Essay Question

Your discussion might focus on some of the following topics: normative social influence; conformity, which includes suggestibility; obedience; group polarization; and groupthink.

As a member of any group with established social norms, individuals will often act in ways that enable them to avoid rejection or gain social approval. Thus, a fraternity or sorority pledge would probably be very suggestible and likely to eventually conform to the attitudes and norms projected by the group—or be rejected socially. In extreme cases of pledge hazing, acute social pressures may lead to atypical and antisocial individual behaviors—for example, on the part of pledges complying with the demands of senior members of the fraternity or sorority. Over time, meetings and discussions will probably enhance the group's prevailing attitudes (group polarization). This may lead to the unrealistic and irrational decision making that is groupthink. The potentially negative consequences of groupthink depend on the issues being discussed, but may include a variety of socially destructive behaviors.

Terms and Concepts to Remember

Writing Definitions

1. **Social psychology** is the scientific study of how we think about, influence, and relate to one another.

2. **Attribution theory** deals with our causal explanations of behavior. We attribute behavior to the individual's disposition or to the situation.

3. The **fundamental attribution error** is our tendency to underestimate the impact of situations and to overestimate the impact of personal dispositions on the behavior of others.

4. **Attitudes** are feelings, often influenced by our beliefs, that may predispose us to respond in particular ways to objects, people, and events.

5. **Peripheral route persuasion** occurs when people are influenced by more superficial and incidental cues, such as a speaker's appearance.

6. **Central route persuasion** occurs when people respond favorably to arguments as a result of engaging in systematic thinking about an issue.

7. The **foot-in-the-door phenomenon** is the tendency for people who agree to a small request to comply later with a larger request.

8. A **role** is a set of explanations (norms) about how people in a specific social position ought to behave.

9. **Cognitive dissonance theory** refers to the theory that we act to reduce the psychological discomfort we experience when our behavior conflicts with what we think and feel, or more generally, when two of our thoughts are inconsistent. This is frequently accomplished by changing our attitude rather than our behavior.

   Memory aid: *Dissonance* means "lack of harmony." **Cognitive dissonance** occurs when two thoughts, or cognitions, are at variance with one another.

10. A **culture** is the enduring behaviors, ideas, attitudes, values, and traditions shared by a group of people and transmitted from one generation to the next.

11. **Norms** are understood rules for accepted and expected behavior.

12. **Conformity** is the tendency to change our thinking or behavior to coincide with a group standard.

13. **Normative social influence** refers to the pressure on individuals to conform to avoid rejection or gain social approval.

    Memory aid: *Normative* means "based on a norm, or pattern, regarded as typical for a specific group." **Normative social influence** is the pressure groups exert on the individual to behave in ways acceptable to the group standard.

14. **Informational social influence** results when one is willing to accept others' opinions about reality.

15. **Social facilitation** is stronger performance of simple or well-learned tasks that occurs when other people are present.

16. **Social loafing** is the tendency for individual effort to be diminished when one is part of a group working toward a common goal.

17. **Deindividuation** refers to the loss of self-restraint and self-awareness that sometimes occurs in group situations that foster arousal and anonymity.

    Memory aid: As a prefix, *de-* indicates reversal or undoing. To **deindividuate** is to undo one's individuality.

18. **Group polarization** refers to the enhancement of a group's prevailing tendencies through discussion, which often has the effect of accentuating the group's differences from other groups.

    Memory aid: To *polarize* is to "cause thinking to concentrate about two poles, or contrasting positions."

19. **Groupthink** refers to the unrealistic thought processes and decision making that occur within groups when the desire for group harmony overrides a realistic appraisal of alternatives.

    Example: The psychological tendencies of self-justification, conformity, and group polarization foster the development of the "team spirit" mentality known as **groupthink**.

20. **Prejudice** is an unjustifiable (and usually negative) attitude toward a group and its members.

21. A **stereotype** is a generalized (sometimes accurate but often overgeneralized) belief about a group of people.

22. **Discrimination** is unjustifiable negative behavior toward a group and its members.

23. The **just-world phenomenon** is the tendency for people to believe that the world is just and that people therefore get what they deserve and deserve what they get. It is a manifestation of the commonly held belief that good is rewarded and evil is punished. The logic is indisputable: "If I am rewarded, I must be good."

24. The **ingroup** refers to the people and groups with whom we share a common identity.

25. The **outgroup** refers to the people and groups that are excluded from our ingroup.

26. The **ingroup bias** is the tendency to favor our own group.

27. The **scapegoat theory** proposes that prejudice provides an outlet for anger by finding someone to blame.

28. The **other-race effect** is our tendency to recall the faces of our own race more accurately than those of other races.

29. **Aggression** is any physical or verbal behavior intended to hurt or destroy.

30. The **frustration-aggression principle** states that aggression is triggered when people become angry because their efforts to achieve a goal have been blocked.

31. A **social script** is a culturally specific modeled guide for how to behave in various situations.

32. The **mere exposure effect** refers to the fact that repeated exposure to unfamiliar stimuli increases our liking of them.

33. **Passionate love** refers to an aroused state of intense positive absorption in another person, usually present at the beginning of a relationship.

34. **Companionate love** refers to a deep, enduring, affectionate attachment to those with whom we share our lives.

35. **Equity** refers to the condition in which there is mutual giving and receiving between the partners in a relationship.

36. **Self-disclosure** refers to revealing intimate aspects of oneself to others.

37. **Altruism** is unselfish regard for the welfare of others.

38. The **bystander effect** is the tendency for a person to be less likely to offer help to someone if there are other people present.

39. **Social exchange theory** states that our social behavior revolves around exchanges, in which we try to minimize our costs and maximize our benefits.

40. The **reciprocity norm** is the expectation that people will help, not hurt, those who have helped them.

41. The **social-responsibility norm** is the expectation that people will help those who depend on them.

42. **Conflict** is a perceived incompatibility of actions, goals, or ideas between individuals or groups.

43. A **social trap** is a situation in which conflicting parties become caught in mutually destructive behaviors because each persists in pursuing its own self-interest.

44. **Mirror-image perceptions** are the negative, mutual views that conflicting people often hold about one another.

45. **Superordinate goals** are shared goals that override differences among people and require their cooperation.

46. **GRIT** (Graduated and Reciprocated Initiatives in Tension-Reduction) is a strategy of conflict resolution based on the defusing effect that conciliatory gestures can have on parties in conflict.

Cross-Check

ACROSS	DOWN
4. stereotype	1. bystander effect
5. GRIT	2. informational
6. scapegoat	3. cognitive dissonance
8. conformity	7. foot-in-the-door
9. altruism	8. companionate
12. equity	10. fundamental
13. passionate	11. attribution
14. conflict	
15. attitudes	

Psychological Disorders

Chapter Overview

Although there is no clear-cut line between normal and abnormal behavior, we can characterize as abnormal those behaviors that represent a clinically significant disturbance in a person's cognition, emotion regulation, or behavior. Chapter 14 discusses anxiety disorders, obsessive-compulsive disorder, post-traumatic stress disorder, mood disorders, schizophrenia, dissociative disorders, eating disorders, and personality disorders, as classified by the *Diagnostic and Statistical Manual of Mental Disorders* (DSM-5). Although this classification system follows a medical model, in which disorders are viewed as illnesses, the chapter discusses psychological as well as physiological factors, as advocated by the current biopsychosocial approach. Thus, psychoanalytic theory, learning theory, social-cognitive theory, and other psychological perspectives are drawn on when relevant. The chapter concludes with a discussion of the incidence of serious psychological disorders in society today.

Your major task in this chapter is to learn about psychological disorders, their various subtypes and characteristics, and their possible causes. Since the material to be learned is extensive, it may be helpful to rehearse it by mentally completing the Chapter Review several times.

NOTE: Answer guidelines for all Chapter 14 questions begin on page 353.

Chapter Review

First, skim each section, noting headings and bold-face items. After you have read the section, review each objective by answering the fill-in and essay-type questions that follow it. Study Tips explain how best to learn a difficult concept and Applications help you to know how well you understand the material. As you proceed, evaluate your performance by consult-ing the answers beginning on page 353. Do not continue with the next section until you understand each answer. If you need to, review or reread the section in the textbook before continuing.

What Is a Psychological Disorder?

Objective 14-1: Discuss how we draw the line between normal behavior and psychological disorder.

1. A psychological disorder is defined as a

   _____

   _____ .

2. Disturbed, or _____ , behaviors are _____ , and they _____ (have/have not) varied over time.

STUDY TIP: To be said to have a psychological disorder, a person must exhibit a clinically significant disturbance in cognition, emotion regulation, or behavior. Most people sometimes behave in ways that seem disturbed yet fall short of being clinically significant; the behaviors don't interfere with the person's daily life. For example, a fear of horses may be abnormal, but if you have no contact with horses, your fear doesn't affect your life and so is not disordered. Think about your own behavior patterns and see if you can think of examples that fit the criteria that characterize psychological disorders.

APPLICATION:

3. Kitty has agreed to appear on the TV show *Fear Factor.* Her test involves eating roaches, a practice that disgusts most North Americans, including Kitty. Although Kitty's task is disgusting, it does not interfere with her _____-

   _____-_____

   _____ and so is not

   disordered.

Objective 14-2: Discuss the controversy over the diagnosis of attention-deficit/hyperactivity disorder.

4. (Thinking Critically) ADHD, or

_____-_____/

_____ _____ ,

plagues children who display its three key symptoms: extreme _____ ,

_____ , and _____ .

5. (Thinking Critically) ADHD is diagnosed more often in _____ (boys/girls). In the decades after 1987, the proportion of American children being treated for this disorder _____ (increased/decreased) dramatically. Experts _____ (agree/do not agree) that ADHD is a real disorder.

6. (Thinking Critically) ADHD _____ (is/is not) thought by some to be heritable, and it _____ (is/is not) caused by eating too much sugar or poor schools. ADHD is often accompanied by a _____ disorder or with behavior that is _____ or temper-prone.

APPLICATION:

7. (Thinking Critically) Thirteen-year-old Ronald constantly fidgets in his seat at school, frequently blurts out answers without being called, and is extremely distractible. A psychiatrist might diagnose Ronald with _____-

_____

_____ .

Objective 14-3: Discuss how our understanding of disorders is affected by whether we use a medical model or a biopsychosocial approach.

8. The view that psychological disorders are sicknesses is the basis of the _____ model. According to this view, psychological disorders are viewed as mental _____ , or _____ , diagnosed on the basis of _____ and, in most cases, cured through _____ .

9. One of the first reformers to advocate this position and call for providing more humane living conditions for the mentally ill was _____ .

10. All behavior arises from the interaction of _____ and _____ . To presume that a person is "mentally ill" attributes the condition solely to a "_____" that must be identified and cured.

11. Major psychological disorders such as _____ and _____ are universal; others, such as _____ _____ and _____ _____ , are culture-bound. These culture-bound disorders may share an underlying _____ , such as _____ , yet differ in their _____ .

12. The _____ approach assumes that disorders are influenced by

_____ _____ and _____ _____ , inner _____ _____ , and _____ and _____ circumstances.

_____ influences:
• evolution
• individual genes
• brain structure and chemistry

_____ influences:
• stress
• trauma
• learned helplessness
• mood-related perceptions and memories

Psychological disorder

_____-_____ influences:
• roles
• expectations
• definitions of *normality* and *disorder*

STUDY TIP: Think about the implications of the medical model and the biopsychosocial approach to psychological disorders. If a behavior pattern that represents a clinically significant disturbance in a person's cognition is caused by a brain abnormality, for example, how would you answer the following questions?

1. How should this behavior be diagnosed?
2. How should this behavior be treated in efforts to cure it?
3. How will people view people who are diagnosed with this disorder? For example, are they to blame for their plight?

Now think about a disordered behavior that is caused by a person's environment, thinking patterns, and habits. Would your answers to these questions change for this type of behavior? Why or why not?

APPLICATION:

13. Haya, who suffers from *taijin-kyofusho*, is afraid of direct eye contact with another person. A therapist who believes in the medical model would say that her problem has a _____ basis. A biopsychosocial therapist would want to look into the interaction of her _____ , _____ , and _____-_____ environment.

Objective 14-4: Describe how and why clinicians classify psychological disorders, and explain why some psychologists criticize the use of diagnostic labels.

14. The most widely used system for classifying psychological disorders is the American Psychiatric Association manual, commonly known by its abbreviation, _____ . This manual aims to _____ a disorder and to _____ its future course, which implies appropriate _____ and stimulates research into its _____ .

15. Some new or altered diagnoses _____ (are/are not) controversial. Critics fear that the new DSM will extend the _____ of everyday life.

16. The more fundamental complaint of critics of the DSM is that these labels are at best _____ and at worst _____ _____

17. Studies have shown that labeling has _____ (little/a significant) effect on our interpretation of individuals and their behavior.

Outline the pros and cons of labeling psychological disorders.

18. (Thinking Critically) Most people with psychological disorders _____ (are/are not) violent. Most people whose _____ defense is accepted are nonetheless institutionalized, often for as long as those convicted of crimes.

Anxiety Disorders, OCD, and PTSD

Objective 14-5: Identify the main anxiety disorders, and describe how they differ from the ordinary worries and fears we all experience.

19. Anxiety disorders are psychological disorders characterized by _____ _____ .

20. Four anxiety disorders discussed in the text are _____ _____ _____ , _____ _____ , _____ , and _____ _____ _____ .

21. When a person is continually tense, apprehensive, and physiologically aroused for no apparent reason, he or she is diagnosed as suffering from a _____ _____ disorder. In Freud's term, the anxiety is _____-_____ .

22. Generalized anxiety disorder can lead to physical problems, such as _____ _____ _____ .

    In some instances, anxiety may intensify dramatically and unpredictably and be accompanied by heart palpitations or choking, for example; people with these symptoms are said to have _____ _____ . This anxiety may escalate into a minutes-long episode of intense fear, or a _____ _____ .

23. People who _____ have at least a doubled risk of a first-time _____ _____ because _____ is a stimulant.

24. When a person has an irrational fear and avoidance of a specific object, activity, or situation, the diagnosis is a _____ . Although in many situations, the person can live with the problem, some _____ _____ , such as a fear of thunderstorms, are incapacitating.

25. When a person has an intense fear of being scrutinized by others, the diagnosis is a

_____ _____

_____ . People who fear situations in which escape or help might not be possible when panic strikes suffer

from _____ .

Objective 14-6: Describe OCD.

26. When a person cannot control repetitive thoughts and actions, an _____-_____ disorder is diagnosed. Older people are _____ (more/less) likely than teens and young adults to suffer from this disorder.

Objective 14-7: Describe PTSD.

27. Traumatic stress, such as that associated with witnessing atrocities or combat, can produce

_____ _____

disorder. The symptoms of this disorder include recurring _____

_____ and _____ ,

_____ _____ ,

_____ _____ ,

and _____ .

28. People who have a sensitive _____

_____ are more vulnerable to this disorder. The odds of getting this disorder after a traumatic event are higher for

_____ (women/men) than for

_____ (women/men).

29. Researchers who believe this disorder may be overdiagnosed point to the _____

_____ of most people who suffer trauma. Some also experience

_____-_____

_____ .

APPLICATIONS:

30. Irene occasionally experiences unpredictable episodes of intense dread accompanied by heart palpitations and a sensation of smothering. Since her symptoms have no apparent cause, they would probably be classified as indicative of
   a. obsessive-compulsive disorder.
   b. generalized anxiety disorder.
   c. posttraumatic stress disorder.
   d. panic attack.

31. Han has an intense, irrational fear of snakes. He is suffering from
   a. generalized anxiety disorder.
   b. obsessive-compulsive disorder.
   c. a phobia.
   d. a panic attack.

32. Isabella is continually tense, jittery, and apprehensive for no specific reason. She would probably be diagnosed as suffering from
   a. a phobia.
   b. posttraumatic stress disorder.
   c. obsessive-compulsive disorder.
   d. generalized anxiety disorder.

33. Jason is so preoccupied with staying clean that he showers as many as 10 times each day. Jason would be diagnosed as suffering from
   a. specific phobia.
   b. generalized anxiety disorder.
   c. agoraphobia.
   d. obsessive-compulsive disorder.

34. Although she escaped from war-torn Bosnia two years ago, Zheina still has haunting memories and nightmares. Because she is also severely depressed, her therapist diagnoses her condition as
   a. panic disorder.
   b. obsessive-compulsive disorder.
   c. generalized anxiety disorder.
   d. posttraumatic stress disorder.

Objective 14-8: Describe how conditioning, cognition, and biology contribute to the feelings and thoughts that mark anxiety disorders, OCD, and PTSD.

35. Freud assumed that anxiety is a symptom of submerged mental energy that derives from intolerable impulses that were _____ during childhood.

36. Learning theorists, drawing on research in which rats are given unpredictable electric shocks, link general anxiety with _____ conditioning of _____ and

_____ .

37. Some fears arise from _____ _____ , such as when a person who fears heights after a fall also comes to fear airplanes. Phobias and compulsive behaviors reduce anxiety and thereby are

_____ .

38. Through _____ learning, someone might also learn fear by seeing others display their own fears. Another cognitive influence on anxiety is that our _____ and _____ shape our reactions.

39. The anxiety response probably _____ (is/is not) genetically influenced. There may be anxiety _____ that affect brain levels of the neurotransmitter _____ , which influences mood, as well as the neurotransmitter _____ , which regulates the brain's alarm centers.

40. Brain scans of persons with obsessive-compulsive disorder reveal excessive activity in a brain region called the _____ _____ cortex. Some antidepressant drugs dampen fear-circuit activity in the _____ , thus reducing this behavior.

41. Humans probably _____ (are/ are not) biologically prepared to develop certain fears. Compulsive acts typically are exaggerations of behaviors that contributed to our species' _____ .

STUDY TIP: Phobias are persistent fears of certain objects, activities, or situations. They are irrational because they are much stronger than the actual danger. Also, many *specific phobias* may be unrelated to a direct, negative experience with the feared object. Are there any specific objects, activities, or situations that you find particularly frightening? How do you think you acquired these fears? Can you remember a bad experience? Did you see someone else have a problem? Does your fear ever interfere with your daily life?

APPLICATIONS:

42. Julia's psychologist believes that Julia's fear of heights can be traced to a conditioned fear she developed after falling from a ladder. This explanation reflects a _____ perspective.
   a. medical   c. social-cognitive
   b. psychoanalytic   d. learning

43. Before he can study, Rashid must arrange his books, pencils, paper, and other items on his desk so that they are "just so." The campus counselor suggests that Rashid's compulsive behavior may help alleviate his feelings of anxiety about failing in school, which reinforces the compulsive actions. This explanation of obsessive-compulsive behavior is most consistent with which perspective?
   a. learning   c. humanistic
   b. psychoanalytic   d. social-cognitive

44. After falling from a ladder, Joseph is afraid of airplanes, although he has never flown. This demonstrates that some fears arise from

_____ _____ .

45. To which of the following is a person MOST likely to acquire a phobia?
   a. heights
   b. being in public
   c. being dirty
   d. All of these are equally likely.

Mood Disorders

Objective 14-9: Define *mood disorders,* and contrast major depressive disorder and bipolar disorder.

46. Mood disorders are psychological disorders characterized by _____ _____ . They come in two forms: The experience of prolonged depression with no discernible cause is called _____ _____ disorder. When a person's mood alternates between depression and the hyperactive state of _____ , a _____ disorder is diagnosed.

47. For those suffering a mood disorder, symptoms may have a _____ _____ , with depression during the fall or winter and mania (or reprieve from depression) during the spring.

48. The possible symptoms of depression include

_____

_____ .

49. Although _____ are more common, _____ is the number-one reason that people seek mental health services. It is also the leading cause of disability worldwide.

50. Major depression occurs when its signs last _____ _____ or more with no apparent cause. A milder form of depression that lasts for at least two years is called persistent depressive disorder, or _____ .

51. Symptoms of mania include _____ _____ .

52. Bipolar disorder is less common among professionals who rely on _____ and _____ than among those who rely on _____ expression and vivid _____ . With the DSM-5, bipolar diagnoses among children and adolescents may decrease because of the new classification of _____ _____ _____ _____ in those with emotional volatility.

APPLICATIONS:

53. For the past six months, Haeji has complained of feeling isolated from others, dissatisfied with life, and discouraged about the future. Haeji could be diagnosed as suffering from
    a. bipolar disorder.
    b. major depressive disorder.
    c. generalized anxiety disorder.
    d. panic disorder.

54. On Monday, Delon felt optimistic, energetic, and on top of the world. On Tuesday, he felt hopeless and lethargic, and thought that the future looked very grim. Delon would MOST likely be diagnosed as having
    a. bipolar disorder.
    b. major depressive disorder.
    c. posttraumatic stress disorder.
    d. panic disorder.

Objective 14-10: Describe how the biological and social-cognitive perspectives explain mood disorders.

55. The commonality of depression suggests that its _____ must also be common.

56. Compared with men, women are _____ (more/less) vulnerable to major depression. In general, women are most vulnerable to disorders involving _____ states, such as _____ _____ .

57. Men's disorders tend to be more _____ and include _____ _____ .

58. Most people suffering major depression _____ (do/do not) eventually return to normal even without professional help. It usually _____ (is/is not) the case that a depressive episode has been triggered by a stressful event. An individual's vulnerability to depression also increases following, for example, _____ .

59. With each new generation, the rate of depression is _____ (increasing/decreasing) and the disorder is striking _____ (earlier/later). In North America, today's young adults are _____ (how many?) times more likely than their grandparents to suffer depression.

60. Mood disorders _____ (tend/do not tend) to run in families. Studies of _____ also reveal that genetic influences on mood disorders are _____ (weak/strong).

61. To determine which genes are involved in depression, researchers use _____ _____ , in which they examine the _____ of both affected and unaffected family members.

62. The brains of depressed people tend to be _____ (more/less) active, especially in an area of the _____ _____ lobe and an adjacent brain _____ _____ . In severely depressed patients, this brain area may also be _____ (smaller/larger) in size. The brain's _____ , which is

important in processing _____ , is vulnerable to stress-related damage.

63. Depression may also be caused by _____ (high/low) levels of two neurotransmitters, _____ and _____ . Most people with a history of depression also were habitual _____ .

64. Drugs that alleviate mania reduce _____ ; drugs that relieve depression increase _____ or _____ supplies by blocking either their _____ or their chemical _____ .

65. According to the social-cognitive perspective, depression may be linked with _____ beliefs and a _____ _____ style. Such beliefs may arise from _____ _____ , the feeling that can arise when the individual repeatedly experiences uncontrollable, painful events.

66. Gender differences in responding to _____ help explain why women have been twice as vulnerable to depression. According to Susan Nolen-Hoeksema, when trouble strikes, women tend to _____ .

Describe how depressed people differ from others in their explanations of failure and how such explanations tend to feed depression.

67. According to Martin Seligman, depression is more common in Western cultures that emphasize _____ and that have shown a decline in commitment to _____ and family.

68. Depression-prone people respond to bad events in an especially _____ way.

69. Being withdrawn, self-focused, and complaining tends to elicit social _____ (empathy/rejection).

Outline the vicious cycle of depression.

APPLICATIONS:

70. Connie's therapist has suggested that her depression stems from unresolved anger toward her parents. Evidently, Connie's therapist is working within the _____ perspective.
    a. learning
    b. social-cognitive
    c. biological
    d. psychoanalytic

71. Ken's therapist suggested that his depression is a result of his self-defeating thoughts and negative assumptions about himself, his situation, and his future. Evidently, Ken's therapist is working within the _____ perspective.
    a. learning
    b. social-cognitive
    c. biological
    d. psychoanalytic

72. Alicia's doctor, who thinks that Alicia's depression has a biochemical cause, prescribes a drug that
    a. reduces norepinephrine.
    b. increases norepinephrine.
    c. reduces serotonin.
    d. increases acetylcholine.

73. Complete the following flow chart comparing how a depressed person and a person who is not depressed would deal with this situation.

Receiving failing grade on psychology exam

| Stable | Temporary |
| _____ | _____ |

| Global | Specific |
| _____ | _____ |

| Internal | External |
| _____ | _____ |

Depression   Successful coping

Objective 14-11: Discuss the factors that affect suicide and self-injuring, and identify important warning signs to watch for in suicide prevention efforts.

(Close-Up) Identify several group differences in suicide rates.

74. (Close-Up) Factors that affect suicide are _____ use disorder and social _____ . For the elderly, it may be an alternative to current or future _____ . People who engage in nonsuicidal self-injury do so to gain relief from int ense _____ _____ , to ask for help and gain _____ , to relieve _____ , or to get others to change their negative behavior.

75. (Close-Up) Important warning signs to watch for in suicide prevention efforts include _____ _____ , giving _____ _____ , or _____ and _____ .

Schizophrenia

Objective 14-12: Describe the patterns of thinking, perceiving, and feeling that characterize schizophrenia.

76. Schizophrenia, or "split mind," refers not to a split personality but rather to a split from _____ . This disorder is an example of a _____ because it is marked by _____ and _____ .

77. Four characteristics of schizophrenia are _____ , _____ , disorganized _____ , and/or diminished, inappropriate _____ .

78. People with schizophrenia who display inappropriate behavior are said to have _____ .

79. People with schizophrenia who exhibit toneless voices and expressionless faces are said to have _____ .

80. The distorted, false beliefs of schizophrenia patients are called _____ . Disorganized thinking may appear as _____ _____ , jumbled ideas that make no sense to others.

81. Many psychologists attribute the disorganized thinking of schizophrenia to a breakdown in the capacity for _____

_____ .

82. The disturbed perceptions of people suffering from schizophrenia may take the form of _____ , which usually are _____ (images/sounds).

83. Some victims of schizophrenia lapse into a zombielike state of apparent apathy, or

_____ _____ ;

others, who exhibit _____ , may remain motionless for hours and then become agitated.

APPLICATION:

84. Claiming that she heard a voice commanding her to warn other people that eating is harmful, Sandy attempts to convince others in a restaurant not to eat. The psychiatrist to whom she is referred finds that Sandy's thinking and speech are often fragmented and incoherent. In addition, Sandy has an unreasonable fear that someone is "out to get her" and consequently trusts no one. Her condition is most indicative of _____ symptoms of schizophrenia.

Objective 14-13: Contrast chronic and acute schizophrenia.

85. When schizophrenia develops slowly (called _____ schizophrenia), recovery is _____ (more/less) likely than when it develops rapidly in reaction to particular life stresses (called _____ schizophrenia).

Objective 14-14: Describe the brain abnormalities associated with schizophrenia.

86. The brain tissue of schizophrenia patients has been found to have an excess of receptors for the neurotransmitter _____ . Drugs that block these receptors have been found to _____ (increase/decrease) schizophrenia symptoms.

87. Brain scans have shown that many people suffering from schizophrenia have abnormally _____ (high/low) brain activity in the _____ lobes.

88. Enlarged, _____-filled areas and a corresponding _____ of cerebral tissue is also characteristic of schizophrenia. Schizophrenia patients also have a smaller-than-normal _____ , which may account for their difficulty in filtering

_____ _____

and focusing _____ .

Objective 14-15: Identify prenatal events that are associated with increased risk of developing schizophrenia.

89. Some scientists contend that the brain abnormalities of schizophrenia may be caused by a prenatal problem, such as _____

_____ _____ ,

maternal _____ , older

_____ age, and

_____ _____

during delivery. Another possible culprit is a mid-pregnancy _____

_____ .

List several pieces of evidence for the fetal-virus idea.

Objective 14-16: Discuss how genes influence schizophrenia.

90. Twin studies _____ (support/do not support) the contention that heredity plays a role in schizophrenia.

91. The role of the prenatal environment in schizophrenia is demonstrated by the fact that identical twins who share the same _____ , and are therefore more likely to experience the same prenatal _____ , are more likely to share the disorder.

92. Adoption studies _____ (confirm/do not confirm) a genetic link in the development of schizophrenia.

93. It appears that for schizophrenia to develop there must be both a _____ predisposition and the _____ factors such as those listed earlier that "_____" the _____ that predispose this disease.

APPLICATIONS:

94. Wayne has been diagnosed with schizophrenia. His doctor attempts to help Wayne by prescribing a drug that blocks receptors for

_____ .

95. Janet, whose class presentation is titled "Current Views on the Causes of Schizophrenia," concludes her talk with the statement
    a. "Schizophrenia is caused by intolerable stress."
    b. "Schizophrenia is inherited."
    c. "Genes may predispose some people to react to particular experiences by developing schizophrenia."
    d. "As of this date, schizophrenia is completely unpredictable and its causes are unknown."

Other Disorders

Objective 14-17: Describe the dissociative disorders, and discuss why they are controversial.

96. In _____ disorders, a person experiences a sudden loss of _____ or change in _____ .

97. Dissociation means to become _____ from painful memories, thoughts, and feelings.

98. Dissociation itself _____ (is/is not so) rare.

99. A person who develops two or more distinct personalities is suffering from _____ _____ disorder.

100. Nicholas Spanos has argued that such people may merely be playing different

_____ .

101. Those who accept this as a genuine disorder point to evidence that differing personalities may be associated with distinct _____ and _____ states.

Identify two pieces of evidence brought forth by those who do not accept dissociative identity disorder as a genuine disorder.

102. The psychoanalytic and learning perspectives view dissociative disorders as ways of dealing with _____ . Others view them as a protective response to histories of

_____ _____ ,

a kind of _____-

_____ _____

disorder. Skeptics claim these disorders are sometimes contrived by _____-

_____ people and sometimes constructed out of the _____-

_____ interaction.

APPLICATIONS:

103. Multiple personalities have long been a popular subject of films and novels. For example, Dr. Jekyll, whose second personality was Mr. Hyde, had _____ _____ disorder.

104. As a child, Monica was criticized severely by her mother for not living up to her expectations. This criticism was always followed by a beating with a whip. As an adult, Monica is generally introverted and extremely shy. Sometimes, however, she acts more like a young child, throwing tantrums if she doesn't get her way. At other times, she is a flirting, happy-go-lucky young lady. Most likely, Monica is suffering from
    a. a phobia.
    b. dissociative schizophrenia.
    c. dissociative identity disorder.
    d. bipolar disorder.

Objective 14-18: Identify the three main eating disorders, and discuss how biological, psychological, and social-cultural influences make people more vulnerable to these disorders.

105. The disorder in which a person becomes significantly underweight and yet feels fat is known as _____ .

106. A more common disorder is _____ _____ , which is characterized by repeated _____-_____ episodes and by feelings of depression or anxiety. When bouts of excessive eating followed by remorse are not accompanied by purging or fasting, the _____-_____ disorder may be diagnosed.

107. The families of bulimia patients have a high incidence of childhood _____ and _____ self-evaluation. The families of anorexia patients tend to be _____ , _____-_____ , and _____ .

108. Genetic factors _____ (do/do not) influence susceptibility to eating disorders.

109. Vulnerability to eating disorders _____ (increases/does not increase) with greater body dissatisfaction.

110. In impoverished areas of the world, where thinness can signal poverty, _____ is better. In _____ cultures, however, the rise in eating disorders has coincided with an increasing number of women having a poor _____ .

111. When young women were shown pictures of unnaturally thin models, they felt more _____ , _____ , and _____ with their own bodies.

APPLICATION:

112. Of the following individuals, who might be most prone to developing an eating disorder?
    a. Jason, an adolescent boy who is somewhat overweight and is unpopular with his peers
    b. Jennifer, a teenage girl who has a poor self-image and a fear of not being able to live up to her parents' high standards
    c. Susan, a 35-year-old woman who is a "workaholic" and devotes most of her energies to her high-pressured career
    d. Bill, a 40-year-old man who has had problems with alcohol misuse and is seriously depressed after losing his job of 20 years

Objective 14-19: Identify the three clusters of personality disorders, and describe the behaviors and brain activity that characterize the antisocial personality.

113. Personality disorders exist when an individual has character traits that are enduring and impair _____ _____ .

114. A fearful sensitivity to rejection may predispose the _____ personality disorder. Eccentric behaviors, such as emotionless disengagement, are characteristic of the _____ personality disorder. The third cluster exhibits dramatic or _____ behaviors, such as the _____ or _____ personality disorders.

115. An individual who seems to have no conscience, lies, steals, is generally irresponsible, and may be criminal is said to have an _____ personality. Previously, this person was labeled a _____ .

116. Studies of biological relatives of those with anti-social and unemotional tendencies suggest that there _____ (is/is not) a bio-logical predisposition to such traits.

117. Antisocial adolescents tended to have been

_____ , _____ ,

unconcerned with _____

_____ , and low in

_____ .

118. PET scans of murderers' brains reveal reduced activity in the _____ _____ , an area of the cortex that helps control _____ .

119. As in other disorders, in antisocial personality, genetics _____ (is/is not) the whole story. Rather, genes

some children to be more sensitive to

_____ influences such as

_____ .

APPLICATION:

120. Ming has never been able to keep a job. He's been in and out of jail for charges such as theft, sexual assault, and spousal abuse. Ming would most likely be diagnosed as having
   a. a dissociative identity disorder.
   b. major depressive disorder.
   c. schizophrenia.
   d. an antisocial personality.

SUMMARY STUDY TIP: This chapter discusses eight categories of psychological disorders. To help orga-nize your study of this material, complete the fol-lowing table. For each category, list the specific disorders discussed. Then, for each disorder, give a description and a brief explanation of possible causes of the disorders. To get you started, portions of the first category of disorders, plus some random information, has been provided.

Category	Specific Disorders	Description of the Disorder	Possible Explanations of Causes
Anxiety disorders	Generalized anxiety disorder Panic disorder Phobias	Distressing, persistent anxiety or maladaptive behaviors that reduce anxiety	Conditioning and reinforcement of fears. For example, stimulus generalization. Also, observational learning. Pairing of a traumatic event with a genetic predisposition.
Obsessive-compulsive disorder			
Posttraumatic stress disorder			
Mood disorders	Major depressive disorder Bipolar disorder		
Schizophrenia			
Dissociative disorders			
Eating disorders			
Personality disorders			

Rates of Psychological Disorders

Objective 14-20: State how many people suffer, or have suffered, from a psychological disorder, and discuss whether poverty is a risk factor.

121. Research reveals that approximately _____ percent of adult Americans suffered a diagnosable mental disorder during the prior year.

122. The incidence of serious psychological disorders is _____ (higher/lower) among those below the poverty line.

123. In terms of age of onset, most psychological disorders appear by _____ (early/middle/late) adulthood. Some, such as the _____ _____ and _____ , appear during childhood.

Progress Test 1

Multiple-Choice Questions

Circle your answers to the following questions and check them with the answers on page 356. If your answer is incorrect, read the explanation for why it is incorrect and then consult the text.

1. Gender differences in the prevalence of depression may partly result from the fact that when stressful experiences occur
   a. women tend to act, while men tend to think.
   b. women tend to think, while men tend to act.
   c. women tend to distract themselves by drinking, while men tend to delve into their work.
   d. women tend to delve into their work, while men tend to distract themselves by drinking.

2. When schizophrenia is slow to develop, called _____ schizophrenia, recovery is _____ .
   a. reactive; unlikely
   b. process; likely
   c. process; unlikely
   d. reactive; likely

3. Most mental health workers today take the view that disordered behaviors
   a. are usually genetically triggered.
   b. are organic diseases.
   c. arise from the interaction of nature and nurture.
   d. are the product of learning.

4. The view that all behavior arises from the interaction of heredity and environment is referred to as the _____ approach.
   a. biopsychosocial
   b. psychodynamic
   c. medical
   d. conditioning

5. Which of the following is the most pervasive of the psychological disorders?
   a. depression
   b. schizophrenia
   c. bipolar disorder
   d. generalized anxiety disorder

6. Which of the following is NOT true concerning depression?
   a. Depression is more common in women than in men.
   b. Most depressive episodes appear not to be preceded by any particular factor or event.
   c. With each new generation, depression is striking earlier.
   d. Most people recover from depression without professional therapy.

7. Which of the following is NOT true regarding schizophrenia?
   a. It occurs more frequently in people born in winter and spring months.
   b. It occurs less frequently as infectious disease rates have declined.
   c. It occurs more frequently in lightly populated areas.
   d. It usually appears during adolescence or early adulthood.

8. Evidence of environmental effects on psychological disorders is seen in the fact that certain disorders, such as _____ , are universal, whereas others, such as _____ , are culture-bound.
   a. schizophrenia; depression
   b. depression; schizophrenia
   c. antisocial personality; neurosis
   d. depression; anorexia nervosa

9. The effect of drugs that block receptors for dopamine is to
   a. alleviate schizophrenia symptoms.
   b. alleviate depression.
   c. increase schizophrenia symptoms.
   d. increase depression.

10. Mental health workers use the DSM-5's "diagnostic criteria and codes" to
    a. guide medical diagnoses.
    b. define who is eligible for treatments.
    c. define who can receive medication.
    d. do all of these things.

11. Because of some troubling thoughts, Carl recently had a PET scan of his brain that revealed excessive activity in the anterior cingulate area. Carl's psychiatrist believes that Carl suffers from
    a. schizophrenia.
    b. a mood disorder.
    c. a personality disorder.
    d. obsessive-compulsive disorder.

12. (Thinking Critically) The term *insanity* refers to
    a. legal definitions.
    b. psychotic disorders only.
    c. personality disorders only.
    d. both psychotic disorders and personality disorders.

13. Phobias and panic disorders are classified as
    a. anxiety disorders.
    b. mood disorders.
    c. dissociative disorders.
    d. personality disorders.

14. According to the social-cognitive perspective, a person who experiences unexpected aversive events may develop helplessness and manifest a(n)
    a. obsessive-compulsive disorder.
    b. dissociative disorder.
    c. personality disorder.
    d. mood disorder.

15. Which of the following was presented in the text as evidence of biological influences on anxiety disorders, OCD, and PTSD?
    a. Identical twins often develop similar phobias.
    b. Brain scans of persons with obsessive-compulsive disorder reveal unusually high activity in the anterior cingulate cortex.

c. Drugs that dampen fear-circuit activity in the amygdala also alleviate OCD.
    d. All of these findings were presented.

16. Most of the hallucinations of schizophrenia patients involve the sense of
    a. smell.   c. hearing.
    b. vision.   d. touch.

17. When expecting to be electrically shocked, people with an antisocial personality disorder, as compared with normal people, show
    a. less fear and greater arousal of the autonomic nervous system.
    b. less fear and less autonomic arousal.
    c. greater fear and greater autonomic arousal.
    d. greater fear and less autonomic arousal.

18. Hearing voices would be a(n) _____ ; believing that you are Napoleon would be a(n) _____ .
    a. obsession; compulsion
    b. compulsion; obsession
    c. delusion; hallucination
    d. hallucination; delusion

19. Which of the following is true concerning eating disorders?
    a. Genetic factors may influence susceptibility.
    b. Cultural pressures for thinness strongly influence teenage girls.
    c. Family background is a significant factor.
    d. All of these statements are true.

20. In treating depression, a psychiatrist would probably prescribe a drug that would
    a. increase levels of acetylcholine.
    b. decrease levels of dopamine.
    c. increase levels of norepinephrine.
    d. decrease levels of serotonin.

Matching Items

Match each term with the appropriate definition or description.

Terms

_____ 1. dissociative disorder
_____ 2. medical model
_____ 3. mood disorders
_____ 4. social anxiety disorder
_____ 5. biopsychosocial approach
_____ 6. mania
_____ 7. obsessive-compulsive disorder
_____ 8. schizophrenia
_____ 9. hallucination
_____ 10. panic attack

Definitions or Descriptions

a. psychological disorders marked by emotional extremes
b. an extremely elevated mood
c. a false sensory experience
d. approach that considers behavior disorders as illnesses that can be diagnosed, treated, and, in most cases, cured
e. a sudden escalation of anxiety often accompanied by a sensation of choking or other physical symptoms
f. a disorder in which conscious awareness becomes separated from previous memories, feelings, and thoughts
g. approach that considers behavior disorders to be the result of biological, psychological, and social-cultural influences
h. intense fear of being scrutinized by others
i. a psychological disorder characterized by delusions, hallucinations, disorganized speech, and/or diminished, inappropriate emotional expression
j. a disorder characterized by repetitive thoughts and actions

Progress Test 2

Progress Test 2 should be completed during a final chapter review. Answer the following questions after you thoroughly understand the correct answers for the Chapter Review and Progress Test 1.

Multiple-Choice Questions

1. Which of the following is true concerning a "clinically significant disturbance"?
   a. It has had the same meaning since behavior was first studied.
   b. It interferes with normal day-to-day life.
   c. It involves an intense emotion but does not affect normal activities.
   d. It does not involve feelings of distress.

2. The psychodynamic perspective would most likely view phobias as
   a. conditioned fears.
   b. displaced responses to incompletely repressed impulses.
   c. biological predispositions.
   d. manifestations of self-defeating thoughts.

3. Many psychologists believe the disorganized thoughts of people with schizophrenia result from a breakdown in
   a. selective attention.   c. motivation.
   b. memory storage.   d. memory retrieval.

4. Research evidence links the brain abnormalities of schizophrenia to _____ during prenatal development.
   a. maternal stress
   b. a viral infection contracted
   c. abnormal levels of certain hormones
   d. the weight of the unborn child

5. The fact that disorders such as schizophrenia are universal and influenced by heredity, whereas other disorders such as anorexia nervosa are culture-bound provides evidence for the _____ model of psychological disorders.
   a. medical   c. social-cultural
   b. biopsychosocial   d. psychodynamic

6. In earlier times, people attributed disordered behavior to
   a. "bad blood."
   b. evil spirits.
   c. brain injury.
   d. laziness.

7. In general, women are more vulnerable than men to
   a. external disorders such as anxiety.
   b. internal disorders such as depression.
   c. external disorders such as antisocial conduct.
   d. internal disorders such as alcohol use disorder.

8. Which of the following statements concerning the labeling of disordered behaviors is NOT true?
   a. Labels interfere with effective treatment of psychological disorders.
   b. Labels promote research studies of psychological disorders.
   c. Labels may create preconceptions that bias people's perceptions.
   d. Labels may influence behavior by creating self-fulfilling prophecies.

9. (Thinking Critically) Nicholas Spanos considers dissociative identity disorder to be
   a. a genuine disorder.
   b. merely role playing.
   c. a disorder that cannot be explained according to the learning perspective.
   d. a biological phenomenon.

10. Which neurotransmitter is present in overabundant amounts during the manic phase of bipolar disorder?
    a. dopamine
    b. serotonin
    c. epinephrine
    d. norepinephrine

11. Although the cause of eating disorders is still unknown, proposed explanations focus on all of the following, EXCEPT
    a. metabolic factors.
    b. genetic factors.
    c. family background factors.
    d. cultural factors.

12. Which of the following provides evidence that human fears have been subjected to the evolutionary process?
    a. Compulsive acts typically exaggerate behaviors that contributed to our species' survival.
    b. Most phobias focus on objects that our ancestors also feared.
    c. It is easier to condition some fears than others.
    d. All of these provide evidence.

13. Which of the following is true of the medical model?
    a. In recent years, it has been in large part discredited.
    b. It views psychological disorders as sicknesses that are diagnosable and treatable.
    c. It emphasizes the role of psychological factors in disorders over that of physiological factors.
    d. It focuses on cognitive factors.

14. Psychodynamic and learning theorists both agree that dissociative disorders, anxiety disorders, OCD, and PTSD are symptoms that represent the person's attempt to deal with
    a. unconscious conflicts.
    b. anxiety.
    c. unfulfilled wishes.
    d. unpleasant responsibilities.

15. Women in _____ consider "bigger" to be the ideal body shape.
    a. Western cultures
    b. countries such as Africa, where thinness can signal poverty,
    c. the United States
    d. Australia, New Zealand, and England

16. The DSM-5's new diagnosis of disruptive mood dysregulation disorder
    a. will clearly help parents who struggle with unstable children.
    b. will turn temper tantrums into a mental disorder.
    c. will lead to overmedication.
    d. is controversial because its effect is as yet unknown.

17. Which of the following is NOT a symptom of schizophrenia?
    a. diminished, inappropriate emotional expression
    b. disturbed perceptions
    c. panic attacks
    d. disorganized thinking

18. Social-cognitive theorists contend that depression is linked with
    a. negative moods.
    b. maladaptive explanations of failure.
    c. self-defeating beliefs.
    d. all of these characteristics.

19. Which of the following is NOT true of mood disorders, according to the biological perspective?
    a. Activity in the left frontal lobe is increased during a depressed state.

b. Norepinephrine is scarce during depression.

c. Brain reward centers are less active during a depressed state.

d. The hippocampus, which is linked with the brain's emotion circuitry, is vulnerable to stress-related damage.

20. Among the following, which is generally accepted as a possible cause of schizophrenia?

    a. an excess of endorphins in the brain

    b. being a twin

    c. extensive learned helplessness

    d. a genetic predisposition

Matching Items

Match each term with the appropriate definition or description.

Terms

_____ 1. dissociative identity disorder
_____ 2. phobia
_____ 3. dopamine
_____ 4. panic disorder
_____ 5. antisocial personality
_____ 6. norepinephrine
_____ 7. serotonin
_____ 8. bipolar disorder
_____ 9. delusions
_____ 10. agoraphobia
_____ 11. psychosis
_____ 12. anorexia nervosa

Definitions or Descriptions

a. a neurotransmitter for which there are excess receptors in some schizophrenia patients

b. a neurotransmitter that is overabundant during mania and scarce during depression

c. an individual who seems to have no conscience

d. false beliefs that may accompany psychological disorders

e. an anxiety disorder marked by a persistent, irrational fear of a specific object, activity, or situation

f. a disorder formerly called multiple personality disorder

g. a neurotransmitter possibly linked to anxiety disorders

h. a type of mood disorder

i. an anxiety disorder marked by episodes of intense dread

j. a fear of situations in which help might not be available during a panic attack

k. marked by irrationality and loss of contact with reality

l. a type of eating disorder

Essay Question

Clinical psychologists label people disordered if their behavior is dysfunctional. Demonstrate your understanding of the classification process by giving examples of behaviors that might be considered dysfunctional but, because they do not interfere with everyday life, would not necessarily be labeled disordered. (Use the space below to list the points you want to make, and organize them. Then write the essay on a separate piece of paper.)

Terms and Concepts to Remember

Writing Definitions

Using your own words, on a separate piece of paper write a brief definition or explanation of each of the following terms.

1. psychological disorder

2. attention-deficit/hyperactivity disorder (ADHD)

3. medical model

4. DSM-5

5. anxiety disorders

6. generalized anxiety disorder

7. panic disorder

8. phobia

9. obsessive-compulsive disorder (OCD)

10. posttraumatic stress disorder (PTSD)

11. mood disorders

12. major depressive disorder

13. bipolar disorder

14. mania

15. schizophrenia

16. psychosis

17. delusions

18. dissociative disorders

19. dissociative identity disorder (DID)

20. anorexia nervosa

21. bulimia nervosa

22. binge-eating disorder

23. personality disorders

24. antisocial personality disorder

Cross-Check

As you learned in Chapter 1, reviewing and overlearning of material are important to the learning process. After you have written the definitions of the key terms in this chapter, you should complete the crossword puzzle to ensure that you can reverse the process—recognize the term, given the definition.

ACROSS

3. The "common cold" of psychological disorders.
16. A euphoric, hyperactive state.
17. Category of disorders that includes major depression and bipolar disorder.
18. Mood disorder in which a person alternates between depression and mania.
19. Category of disorders that includes phobias and panic disorder.

DOWN

1. When schizophrenia is a slow-developing process, it is said to be _____ .
2. A widely used system of classifying psychological disorders.
4. A psychological disorder characterized by extreme inattention, for example.

5. Disorders that involve a separation of conscious awareness from one's previous memories, thoughts, and feelings.

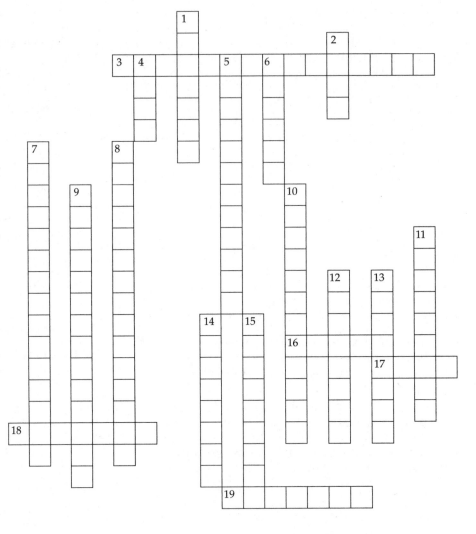

6. A persistent, irrational fear of a specific object or situation.
7. Biomedical research technique used to determine which genes are involved in a specific psychological disorder.
8. Approach that assumes that genes, psychological factors, and social and cultural circumstances combine and interact to produce psychological disorders.
9. False sensory experiences.
10. The viewpoint that psychological disorders are illnesses.
11. False beliefs that often are symptoms of schizophrenia.
12. A possible cause of schizophrenia is a _____ mishap, such as oxygen deprivation.
13. Neurotransmitter for which there are excess receptors in the brains of schizophrenia patients.
14. Category of schizophrenia symptoms that includes having a toneless voice, expressionless face, and a mute or rigid body.
15. Neurotransmitter that influences sleep and mood and that therefore may be a factor in anxiety disorders.

Answers

Chapter Review

What Is a Psychological Disorder?

1. syndrome marked by a clinically significant disturbance in a person's cognition, emotion regulation, or behavior.
2. maladaptive; have
3. day-to-day life
4. attention-deficit/hyperactivity disorder; inattention; hyperactivity; impulsivity
5. boys; increased; do not agree
6. is; is not; learning; defiant
7. attention-deficit/hyperactivity disorder
8. medical; sickness; psychopathology; symptoms; therapy
9. Philippe Pinel
10. nature; nurture; sickness
11. depression; schizophrenia; anorexia nervosa; bulimia nervosa; dynamic; anxiety; symptoms
12. biopsychosocial; genetic predispositions; physiological states; psychological dynamics; social; cultural
13. biological; biology; psychology; social-cultural. Haya's behavior is directed by a specific situation.
14. DSM-5; describe; predict; treatment; causes

15. are; pathologizing
16. increased; increased
17. arbitrary; value judgments

Psychological labels may be arbitrary. They can create preconceptions that bias our perceptions and interpretations and they can affect people's self-images. Moreover, labels can change reality, by serving as self-fulfilling prophecies. Despite these drawbacks, labels are useful for communicating about disorders, researching the causes of psychological disorders, and sharing information about effective treatments.

18. are not; insanity

Anxiety Disorders, OCD, and PTSD

19. distressing, persistent anxiety or maladaptive behaviors that reduce anxiety
20. generalized anxiety disorder; panic disorder; phobias; social anxiety disorder
21. generalized anxiety; free-floating
22. high blood pressure; panic disorder; panic attack
23. smoke; panic attack; nicotine
24. phobia; specific phobias
25. social anxiety disorder; agoraphobia
26. obsessive-compulsive; less
27. posttraumatic stress; haunting memories; nightmares; social withdrawal; jumpy anxiety; numbness of feeling; insomnia
28. limbic system; women; men
29. survivor resiliency; posttraumatic growth
30. **d.** is the answer.
    a. Obsessive-compulsive disorder involves repetitive thoughts and actions.
    b. Generalized anxiety disorder involves a continually tense, apprehensive state.
    c. There is no indication that she suffered a trauma.
31. **c.** is the answer. An intense fear of a specific object is a phobia.
    a. His fear is focused on a specific object, not generalized.
    b. In this disorder a person is troubled by repetitive thoughts and actions.
    d. A panic attack does not involve a specific object, such as a snake.
32. **d.** is the answer.
    a. In phobias, anxiety is focused on a specific object.
    b. Posttraumatic stress disorder is tied to a specific traumatic experience.
    c. The obsessive-compulsive disorder is characterized by repetitive and unwanted thoughts and/or actions.

33. **d.** is the answer. Jason is obsessed with cleanliness; as a result, he has developed a compulsion to shower.
    a. A specific phobia is an irrational fear of a specific object or situation.
    b. Generalized anxiety disorder does not have a specific focus.
    c. Agoraphobia is fear or avoidance of situations in which escape might not be possible.

34. **d.** is the answer.
    a. There is no evidence that Zheina is having panic attacks.
    b. Zheina shows no signs of being obsessed with certain thoughts or behaviors.
    c. There is no evidence that Zheina has a general (free-floating) fear or anxiety; she has suffered a definite trauma.

35. repressed

36. classical; fear; anxiety

37. stimulus generalization; reinforced

38. observational; expectations; interpretations

39. is; genes; serotonin; glutamate

40. anterior cingulate; amygdala

41. are; survival

42. **d.** is the answer. In the learning perspective, a phobia, such as Julia's, is seen as a conditioned fear.
    a. Because the fear is focused on a specific stimulus, the medical model does not easily account for the phobia. In any event, it would presumably offer an internal, biological explanation.
    b. The psychoanalytic view of phobias would be that they represent incompletely repressed anxieties that are displaced onto the feared object.
    c. The social-cognitive perspective would emphasize a person's conscious, cognitive processes, not reflexive conditioned responses.

43. **a.** is the answer. According to the learning view, compulsive behaviors are reinforced because they reduce the anxiety created by obsessive thoughts. Rashid's obsession concerns failing, and his desk-arranging compulsive behaviors apparently help him control these thoughts.
    b. The psychoanalytic perspective would view obsessive thoughts as a symbolic representation of forbidden impulses. These thoughts may prompt the person to perform compulsive acts that counter these impulses.
    c. & d. The text does not offer explanations of obsessive-compulsive behavior based on the humanistic or social-cognitive perspectives. Presumably, however, these explanations would emphasize growth-blocking difficulties in the person's environment (humanistic perspective)

and the reciprocal influences of personality and environment (social-cognitive perspective), rather than symbolic expressions of forbidden impulses.

44. stimulus generalization. Joseph's fear has generalized from ladders to airplanes.

45. **a.** is the answer. Humans seem biologically prepared to develop a fear of heights and other dangers that our ancestors faced.

Mood Disorders

46. emotional extremes; major depressive; mania; bipolar

47. seasonal pattern

48. lethargy, feelings of worthlessness, and markedly diminished interest or pleasure in activities most of the day (these and other symptoms must cause near-daily distress or impairment)

49. phobias; depression

50. two weeks; dysthymia

51. intensely happy, hyperactive, and wildly optimistic states

52. precision; logic; emotional; imagery; disruptive mood dysregulation disorder

53. **b.** is the answer. The fact that this woman has had these symptoms for more than two weeks indicates that she is suffering from major depressive disorder.

54. **a.** is the answer. Matt's alternating states of the hopelessness and lethargy of depression and the energetic, optimistic state of mania are characteristic of bipolar disorder.
    b. Although he was depressed on Tuesday, Matt's manic state on Monday indicates that he is not suffering from major depressive disorder.
    c. Matt was depressed, not suffering from a trauma, as in posttraumatic stress disorder.
    d. That Matt is not exhibiting episodes of intense dread indicates that he is not suffering from panic disorder.

55. causes

56. more; internal; depression, anxiety, and inhibited sexual desire

57. external; alcohol use disorder, antisocial conduct, and lack of impulse control

58. do; is; a family member's death, loss of a job, a marital crisis, or a physical assault

59. increasing; earlier; three

60. tend; twins; strong

61. linkage analysis; DNA

62. less; left frontal; reward center; smaller; hippocampus; memories

63. low; norepinephrine; serotonin; smokers

64. norepinephrine; norepinephrine; serotonin; reuptake; breakdown

65. self-defeating; negative explanatory; learned helplessness

66. stress; overthink (ruminate)

Depressed people are more likely than others to explain failures or bad events in terms that are stable (it's going to last forever), global (it will affect everything), and internal (it's my fault). Such explanations lead to feelings of hopelessness, which in turn feed depression.

67. individualism; religion

68. self-blaming

69. rejection

Depression is often brought on by negative, stressful experiences. Depressed people brood over such experiences with maladaptive explanations that produce self-blame and amplify their depression, which in turn triggers other symptoms of depression. In addition, being withdrawn and complaining tends to elicit social rejection and other negative experiences.

70. **d.** is the answer. Freud believed that the anger once felt toward parents was internalized and would produce depression.
    a. & b. The learning and social-cognitive perspectives focus on environmental experiences, conditioning, and self-defeating attitudes in explaining depression.
    c. The biological perspective focuses on genetic predispositions and biochemical imbalances in explaining depression.

71. **b.** is the answer.

72. **b.** is the answer. Norepinephrine, which increases arousal and boosts mood, is scarce during depression. Drugs that relieve depression tend to increase norepinephrine.
    c. Increasing serotonin, which is sometimes scarce during depression, might relieve depression.
    d. This neurotransmitter is involved in motor responses but has not been linked to psychological disorders.

73. There are no right or wrong answers to this. Possible responses of a depressed person might be "I'll never be able to pass this course (stable)," "I'm never going to do well in any college courses (global)," and "It's my fault; I didn't study hard enough (internal)."

Suicide rates are higher among White and Native Americans, the rich, older people, the nonreligious, and those who are single, widowed, or divorced. Although women more often attempt suicide, men are more likely to succeed. Suicide rates also vary widely around the world.

74. alcohol; suggestion; suffering; negative thoughts; attention; guilt

75. verbal hints; possessions away, withdrawal; preoccupation with death

Schizophrenia

76. reality; psychosis; irrationality; lost contact with reality

77. delusions; hallucinations; speech; emotional expression

78. positive symptoms

79. negative symptoms

80. delusions; word salad

81. selective attention

82. hallucinations; sounds

83. flat affect; catatonia

84. positive

85. chronic (or process); less; acute (or reactive)

86. dopamine; decrease

87. low; frontal

88. fluid; shrinkage; thalamus; sensory input; attention

89. low birth weight; diabetes; paternal; oxygen deprivation; viral infection

Risk of schizophrenia increases for those who undergo fetal development during a flu epidemic, or simply during the flu season. People born in densely populated areas and those born during winter and spring months are at increased risk. The months of excess schizophrenia births are reversed in the Southern Hemisphere, where the seasons are the reverse of the Northern Hemisphere's. Mothers who were sick with influenza during their pregnancy may be more likely to have children who develop schizophrenia. Blood drawn from pregnant women whose children develop schizophrenia have higher-than-normal levels of viral infection antibodies.

90. support

91. placenta; viruses

92. confirm

93. genetic; epigenetic; turn on; genes

94. dopamine

95. **c.** is the answer.

Other Disorders

96. dissociative; memory; identity

97. separated

98. is not so

99. dissociative identity

100. roles

101. brain; body

Skeptics point out that the recent increase in the number of reported cases of dissociative identity disorder indicates that it has become a fad. The fact that the disorder is much less prevalent outside North America also causes skeptics to doubt the disorder's genuineness.

102. anxiety; childhood trauma; posttraumatic stress; fantasy-prone; therapist-patient

103. dissociative identity

104. **c.** is the answer.
a. Phobias focus anxiety on a specific object, activity, or situation.
b. There is no such disorder.
d. In this mood disorder, a person alternates between feelings of hopeless depression and overexcited mania.

105. anorexia nervosa

106. bulimia nervosa; binge-purge; binge-eating

107. obesity; negative; competitive; high-achieving; protective

108. do

109. increases

110. bigger; Western; body image

111. ashamed; depressed; dissatisfied

112. **b.** is the answer. Adolescent females with low self-esteem and high-achieving families seem especially prone to eating disorders such as anorexia nervosa.
a. & d. Eating disorders occur much more frequently in women than in men.
c. Eating disorders usually develop during adolescence, rather than during adulthood.

113. social functioning

114. avoidant; schizoid; impulsive; histrionic; narcissistic

115. antisocial; psychopath (or sociopath)

116. is

117. impulsive; uninhibited; social rewards; anxiety

118. frontal lobe; impulses

119. is not; predispose; environmental; maltreatment

120. **d.** is the answer. Repeated wrongdoing and aggressive behavior are part of the pattern associated with the antisocial personality disorder, which may also include marital problems and an inability to keep a job.
a. Although dissociative identity disorder may involve an aggressive personality, there is noth-

ing in the example to indicate a dissociation.
b. Nothing in the question indicates that Ming is passive and resigned and having the self-defeating thoughts characteristic of depression.
c. Ming's behavior does not include the disorganized thinking and disturbed perceptions typical of schizophrenia.

Summary Study Tip: Using the text discussion and tables to complete this chart will enhance your understanding of the material in this chapter.

Rates of Psychological Disorders

121. 26

122. higher

123. early; antisocial personality; phobias

Progress Test 1

Multiple-Choice Questions

1. **b.** is the answer.
c. & d. Men are more likely than women to cope with stress in these ways.

2. **c.** is the answer.

3. **c.** is the answer. Most clinicians agree that psychological disorders may be caused by both psychological (d.) and physical (a. and b.) factors.

4. **a.** is the answer.

5. **a.** is the answer.

6. **b.** is the answer. Depression is often preceded by a stressful event related to work, marriage, or a close relationship.

7. **c.** is the answer.

8. **d.** is the answer. Although depression is universal, anorexia nervosa and bulimia are rare outside of Western culture.
a. & b. Schizophrenia and depression are both universal.
c. The text mentions only schizophrenia and depression as universal disorders. Furthermore, neurosis is no longer a category of diagnosis.

9. **a.** is the answer.
b. & d. Thus far, only norepinephrine and serotonin have been implicated in depression and bipolar disorder.
c. Schizophrenia has been associated with an excess of dopamine receptors. Blocking them alleviates schizophrenia symptoms.

10. **d.** is the answer.

11. **d.** is the answer. These areas show increased activity during compulsive behaviors.

12. **a.** is the answer.

13. **a.** is the answer.
    b. The mood disorders include major depressive disorder and bipolar disorder.
    c. Dissociative identity disorder is the only dissociative disorder discussed in the text.
    d. The personality disorders include the antisocial, avoidant, histrionic, narcissistic, and schizoid personalities.

14. **d.** is the answer. Learned helplessness may lead to self-defeating beliefs, which in turn are linked with depression, a mood disorder.

15. **d.** is the answer.

16. **c.** is the answer.

17. **b.** is the answer. Those with an antisocial personality disorder show less autonomic arousal in such situations, and emotions, such as fear, are tied to arousal.

18. **d.** is the answer. Hallucinations are false sensory experiences; delusions are false beliefs.
    a. & b. Obsessions are repetitive and unwanted thoughts. Compulsions are repetitive behaviors.

19. **d.** is the answer.

20. **c.** is the answer. Drugs that relieve depression tend to increase levels of norepinephrine.
    a. Acetylcholine is a neurotransmitter involved in muscle contractions.
    b. It is in certain types of schizophrenia that decreasing dopamine levels is helpful.
    d. On the contrary, it appears that a particular type of depression may be related to *low* levels of serotonin.

Matching Items

1. f
2. d
3. a
4. h
5. g
6. b
7. j
8. i
9. c
10. e

Progress Test 2

Multiple-Choice Questions

1. **b.** is the answer.
   a. The meaning of a clinically significant disturbance has varied over time.
   c. & d. By definition, a clinically significant disturbance interferes with daily life and involves distress in the person suffering from a psychological disorder.

2. **b.** is the answer.
   a. This answer reflects the learning perspective.
   c. Although certain phobias are biologically predisposed, this could not fully explain phobias, nor

is it the explanation offered by psychodynamic theory.
   d. Social-cognitive theorists propose self-defeating thoughts as a cause of depression.

3. **a.** is the answer. Schizophrenia sufferers are easily distracted by irrelevant stimuli, evidently because of a breakdown in the capacity for selective attention.

4. **b.** is the answer.

5. **b.** is the answer. The fact that some disorders are universal and at least partly genetic in origin implicates biological factors in their origin. The fact that other disorders appear only in certain parts of the world implicates sociocultural and psychological factors in their origin.

6. **b.** is the answer.

7. **b.** is the answer.
   a. Anxiety is an internal disorder.
   d. Alcohol use disorder is an external disorder.

8. **a.** is the answer. In fact, just the opposite is true. Labels are useful in promoting effective treatment of psychological disorders.

9. **b.** is the answer.
   c. Playing a role is most definitely a learned skill.
   d. Role playing, being completely learned, is not biologically based.

10. **d.** is the answer. In bipolar disorder, norepinephrine appears to be overabundant during mania and in short supply during depression.
    a. There is an overabundance of dopamine receptors in some schizophrenia patients.
    b. Serotonin sometimes appears to be scarce during depression.
    c. Epinephrine has not been implicated in psychological disorders.

11. **a.** is the answer. The text does not indicate whether their metabolism is higher or lower than most.
    b., c., & d. Genes, family background, and cultural influence have all been proposed as factors in eating disorders.

12. **d.** is the answer.

13. **b.** is the answer.
    a. This isn't the case; in fact, the medical model has gained credibility from recent discoveries of genetic and biochemical links to some disorders.
    c. & d. The medical perspective tends to place more emphasis on physiological factors.

14. **b.** is the answer. The psychodynamic explanation is that these disorders are a manifestation of incompletely repressed impulses over which the person is anxious. According to the learning

perspective, the troubled behaviors that result from these disorders have been reinforced by anxiety reduction.

a. & c. These are true of the psychodynamic, but not the learning, perspective.

15. **b.** is the answer.

16. **d.** is the answer. All of the other answers reflect various opinions about the effect of creating this category. With time, we will know the true effect.

17. **c.** is the answer. Panic attacks are characteristic of certain anxiety disorders, not of schizophrenia.

18. **d.** is the answer.

19. **a.** is the answer. Just the opposite is true.

20. **d.** is the answer. Risk for schizophrenia increases for individuals who are related to a schizophrenia victim, and the greater the genetic relatedness, the greater the risk.

a. Schizophrenia victims have an overabundance of the neurotransmitter dopamine, not endorphins.

b. Being a twin is, in itself, irrelevant to developing schizophrenia.

c. Although learned helplessness has been suggested by social-cognitive theorists as a cause of self-defeating depressive behaviors, it has not been suggested as a cause of schizophrenia.

Matching Items

1. f	5. c	9. d
2. e	6. b	10. j
3. a	7. g	11. k
4. i	8. h	12. l

Essay Question

There is more to a psychological disorder than being different from other people. Gifted artists, athletes, and scientists have abnormal capabilities, yet are not considered psychologically disordered. Also, what is abnormal in one culture may not be in another, or at another time. Homosexuality, for example, was once classified as a psychological disorder, but it is no longer. Similarly, nudity is common in some cultures and disturbing in others. Maladaptive behaviors are more likely to be considered disordered when judged as dysfunctional to the individual. Prolonged feelings of depression or the use of drugs to avoid dealing with problems are examples of abnormal behaviors that may signal a psychological disorder if the person is unable to function, to perform routine behaviors (becomes dysfunctional).

Terms and Concepts to Remember

Writing Definitions

1. A **psychological disorder** is a syndrome marked by a "clinically significant disturbance in an individual's cognition, emotion regulation, or behavior."

2. **Attention-deficit/hyperactivity disorder (ADHD)** is a psychological disorder characterized by the appearance by age 7 of one or more of three symptoms: extreme inattention, hyperactivity, and impulsivity.

3. The **medical model** holds that psychological disorders are illnesses that can be diagnosed, treated, and, in most cases, cured, often through treatment in a hospital.

4. **DSM-5** is a short name for the American Psychiatric Association's *Diagnostic and Statistical Manual of Mental Disorders,* Fifth Edition, which provides a system of classifying psychological disorders.

5. **Anxiety disorders** involve distressing, persistent anxiety or maladaptive behaviors that reduce anxiety.

6. In the **generalized anxiety disorder**, the person is continually tense, apprehensive, and in a state of autonomic nervous system arousal for no apparent reason.

7. A **panic disorder** is an episode of intense dread accompanied by chest pain, choking, or other frightening sensations. It is essentially an escalation of the anxiety associated with generalized anxiety disorder.

8. A **phobia** is an anxiety disorder in which a person has a persistent, irrational fear and avoidance of a specific object, activity, or situation.

9. **Obsessive-compulsive disorder (OCD)** is a disorder in which the person experiences uncontrollable and repetitive thoughts (obsessions), actions (compulsions), or both.

10. **Posttraumatic stress disorder (PTSD)** is a disorder characterized by haunting memories and nightmares, social withdrawal, jumpy anxiety, and/or insomnia lasting four weeks or more following a traumatic experience.

11. **Mood disorders** are psychological disorders characterized by emotional extremes.

12. **Major depressive disorder** is the mood disorder that occurs when a person experiences significantly depressed moods or diminished interest or pleasure in most activities, along with at least three other symptoms, for two or more weeks and for no discernible reason.

13. **Bipolar disorder** is the mood disorder in which a person alternates between the hopelessness and lethargy of depression and the overexcited state of mania.

    Memory aid: *Bipolar* means having two poles, that is, two opposite qualities. In **bipolar disorder,** the opposing states are mania and depression.

14. **Mania** is the wildly optimistic, hyperactive state that alternates with depression in the bipolar disorder; dangerously poor judgment is common in this state.

15. **Schizophrenia** is a psychological disorder characterized by delusions, hallucinations, disorganized speech, and/or diminished, inappropriate emotional expression.

16. **Psychosis** refers to a psychological disorder in which a person loses contact with reality, experiencing irrational ideas and distorted perceptions.

17. **Delusions** are false beliefs that often are symptoms of psychotic disorders.

18. **Dissociative disorders** involve a separation of conscious awareness from previous memories, thoughts, and feelings.

    Memory aid: To *dissociate* is to separate or pull apart. In the **dissociative disorders** a person becomes dissociated from his or her memories and identity.

19. The **dissociative identity disorder (DID)** is a rare dissociative disorder in which a person exhibits two or more distinct and alternating personalities; formerly called *multiple personality disorder.*

20. **Anorexia nervosa** is an eating disorder, most common in adolescent females, in which a person restricts food intake to become significantly underweight and yet still feels fat.

21. **Bulimia nervosa** is an eating disorder characterized by episodes of overeating followed by purging (by vomiting or laxative use) or fasting.

22. **Binge-eating disorder** is characterized by episodes of overeating, followed by distress, but without the purging or fasting that marks bulimia nervosa.

23. **Personality disorders** are psychological disorders characterized by inflexible and enduring maladaptive character traits that impair social functioning.

24. The **antisocial personality disorder** is a personality disorder in which the person is aggressive, ruthless, and shows no sign of a conscience that would inhibit wrongdoing.

Cross-Check

ACROSS
 3. major depressive
16. mania
17. mood
18. bipolar
19. anxiety

DOWN
 1. chronic
 2. DSM-5
 4. ADHD
 5. dissociative
 6. phobia
 7. linkage analysis
 8. biopsychosocial
 9. hallucinations
10. medical model
11. delusions
12. prenatal
13. dopamine
14. negative
15. serotonin

Therapy

Chapter Overview

Chapter 15 discusses the major psychotherapies and biomedical therapies for maladaptive behaviors. The various psychotherapies all derive from the personality theories discussed earlier, namely, the psychodynamic, humanistic, behavioral, and cognitive theories. The chapter groups the therapies by perspective but also emphasizes the common threads that run through them. In evaluating the therapies, the chapter points out that, although people who are untreated often improve, those receiving psychotherapy tend to improve somewhat more, regardless of the type of therapy they receive. This section includes a discussion of several popular alternative therapies.

The biomedical therapies discussed are drug therapies, electroconvulsive therapy and other forms of brain stimulation, and psychosurgery, which is seldom used. By far the most important of these, drug therapies are being used in the treatment of psychotic, anxiety, obsessive-compulsive, posttraumatic, and mood disorders.

Because the origins of problems often lie beyond the individual, the chapter concludes with approaches that aim at preventing psychological disorders by focusing on the family or on the larger social environment as possible contributors to psychological disorders.

NOTE: Answer guidelines for all Chapter 15 questions begin on page 377.

Chapter Review

First, skim each section, noting headings and boldface items. After you have read the section, review each objective by answering the fill-in and essay-type questions that follow it. Study Tips explain how best to learn a difficult concept and Applications help you to know how well you understand the material. As you proceed, evaluate your performance by consulting the answers beginning on page 377. Do not continue with the next section until you understand each answer. If you need to, review or reread the section in the textbook before continuing.

Treating Psychological Disorders

Objective 15-1: Discuss how *psychotherapy, biomedical therapy,* and an *eclectic approach* to therapy differ.

1. Mental health therapies are classified as either _____ therapies or _____ therapies.

2. Some therapists blend several psychotherapy techniques and so are said to take an _____ approach.

The Psychological Therapies

Objective 15-2: Discuss the goals and techniques of psychoanalysis, and describe how they have been adapted in psychodynamic therapy.

3. The goal of Freud's psychoanalysis, which is based on his personality theory, is to help the patient gain _____ .

4. Freud's theory aimed to bring _____ feelings into _____ awareness where they can be dealt with.

5. Psychoanalytic theory emphasizes the formative power of _____ _____ and their ability to mold the adult.

6. Freud's technique in which a patient says whatever comes to mind is called _____ _____ .

7. When, in the course of therapy, a person omits shameful or embarrassing material, _____ is occurring. Insight is facilitated by the analyst's _____ of the meaning of such omissions, of dreams, and of other information revealed during therapy.

8. When strong feelings, similar to those experienced in other important relationships, are developed toward the therapist, _____ has occurred.

9. Today, psychoanalysis _____ (is/is not) commonly practiced in the United States. Critics point out that psychoanalysts' interpretations are hard to _____

_____ _____ and that therapy takes a long time and is very _____ .

10. Therapists who are influenced by Freud's psychoanalysis but who talk to the patient face to face are _____ therapists. In addition, they work with patients only _____ (how often?) and for only a few weeks or months.

11. These therapists focus on _____ across important relationships.

12. Without embracing all aspects of Freud's theory, these therapists aim to help people gain _____ into the their childhood experiences and _____ dynamics.

APPLICATIONS:

13. During a session with his psychoanalyst, Jamal hesitates while describing a highly embarrassing thought. In the psychoanalytic framework, this is an example of
   a. transference.   c. mental repression.
   b. insight.   d. resistance.

14. During psychoanalysis, Jane has developed strong feelings of hatred for her therapist. The analyst interprets Jane's behavior in terms of a _____ of her feelings toward her father.

15. Ernesto is seeing a psychodynamic therapist. Unlike a psychoanalyst, his therapist does not talk about _____ , _____ , and _____ , but rather about themes across important _____ .

16. Isadora's psychoanalyst would be most likely to interpret her fear of intimate relationships in terms of _____ _____ .

Objective 15-3: Identify the basic themes of humanistic therapy, and describe the specific goals and techniques of Rogers' client-centered approach.

17. Humanistic therapies attempt to help people meet their potential for _____ . Like psychodynamic therapies, humanistic therapies attempt to reduce inner conflicts by providing clients with new _____ .

List several ways that humanistic therapy differs from psychodynamic therapy.

18. The humanistic therapy based on Rogers' theory is called _____-_____ therapy, which is described as _____ therapy because the therapist _____ (interprets/does not interpret) the person's problems.

19. To promote growth in clients, Rogerian therapists exhibit _____ , _____ , and _____ .

20. Rogers' technique of echoing, restating, and clarifying what a person is saying is called

_____ _____ .

Given a nonjudgmental environment that provides _____ _____ _____ , patients are better able to accept themselves as they are and to feel valued and whole.

21. Three tips for listening more actively in your own relationships are to _____ ,

_____ _____ ,

and _____ _____ .

Objective 15-4: Explain how the basic assumption of behavior therapy differs from the assumptions of psychodynamic and humanistic therapies, and describe the techniques used in exposure therapies and aversive conditioning.

22. Behavior therapy applies principles of _____ to eliminate troubling behaviors.

Contrast the assumptions of the behavior therapies with those of psychodynamic and humanistic therapies.

23. One cluster of behavior therapies is based on the principles of _____ _____ , as developed in Pavlov's experiments. This technique, in which a new, incompatible response is substituted for a maladaptive one, is called _____ . Two examples of this technique are

_____ _____

and _____ _____ .

24. Mary Cover Jones' procedures were refined by _____ as the _____ _____ . One form of this therapy, systematic desensitization, assumes that one cannot simultaneously be _____ and relaxed.

25. The first step in systematic desensitization is the construction of a _____ of anxiety-arousing stimuli. The second step involves training in _____ _____ . In the final step, the person is trained to associate the _____ state with the _____-arousing stimuli.

26. For those who are unable to visually imagine an anxiety-arousing situation, or too afraid or embarrassed to do so, _____ _____ _____ therapy offers a promising alternative.

27. In aversive conditioning, the therapist attempts to substitute a _____ (positive/negative) response for one that is currently _____ (positive/negative) to a harmful stimulus. In this technique, a person's unwanted behaviors become associated with _____ feelings. In the long run, aversive conditioning _____ (does/does not) work.

APPLICATIONS:

28. To help Sam quit smoking, his therapist blew a blast of smoke into Sam's face each time Sam inhaled. Which technique is the therapist using?
    a. exposure therapy
    b. psychodynamic therapy
    c. systematic desensitization
    d. aversive conditioning

29. To help him overcome his fear of flying, Duane's therapist has him construct a hierarchy of anxiety-triggering stimuli and then learn to associate each with a state of deep relaxation. Duane's therapist is using the technique called
    a. systematic desensitization.
    b. aversive conditioning.
    c. transference.
    d. free association.

Objective 15-5: State the basic idea of operant conditioning therapy, and discuss the arguments that have been used for and against it.

30. Reinforcing desired behaviors and withholding reinforcement for undesired behaviors are key aspects of _____ _____ .

31. Therapies that influence behavior by controlling its consequences are based on principles of _____ conditioning.

32. One application of this form of therapy to institutional settings is the _____ _____ , in which desired behaviors are rewarded.

State two criticisms of behavior modification.

State some responses of proponents of behavior modification.

STUDY TIP/APPLICATION: Each type of behavior therapy discussed is derived from principles of either classical conditioning or operant conditioning. Recall from Chapter 7 that classical conditioning is based on the formation of a learned association between two stimulus situations or events. Operant conditioning is based on the use of reinforcement and punishment to modify the future likelihood of behaviors.

Several problem behaviors are described in the chart below. Test your understanding of behavior therapy by completing the chart and explaining how you would treat the problem behavior using one of the behavior therapies. Be sure to identify any reinforcers, conditioned stimuli, and unconditioned stimuli that you would use. The first example is completed for you.

33. Situation	Type of Conditioning	Procedure
A friend is trying to quit smoking	Aversive conditioning, a type of counterconditioning (classical conditioning)	Each time your friend puffs the cigarette, the taste of the cigarette (conditioned stimulus) is paired with a blast of hot air delivered to his/her face (unconditioned stimulus).
a. A relative has a fear of flying (Hint: use imagined situations)		
b. The parents of a sloppy teenager want to get him to clean up his room		
c. A child is terrified of dogs (Hint: use real situations)		

Objective 15-6: Discuss the goals and techniques of cognitive therapy and of cognitive-behavioral therapy.

34. Therapists who teach people new, more constructive ways of thinking are using _____ therapy.

35. One variety of cognitive therapy attempts to reverse clients' _____ beliefs about themselves, their situations, and their futures, which is often associated with _____ , by helping them see their irrationalities. This therapy was developed by _____ .

36. Psychologists call the relentless, overgeneralized, self-blaming behavior of depressed people _____ .

37. An integrative therapy that combines an attack on negative thinking with efforts to modify behavior is known as _____-_____ therapy. This type of therapy is an effective treatment program for anxiety and mood disorders, because they share a common problem: _____ . _____ . It is also useful for _____-_____ _____ ; people are taught to relabel their problem behaviors.

APPLICATIONS (review of all psychotherapies):

38. Given that Don Carlo's therapist attempts to help him by offering genuineness, acceptance, and empathy, she is probably practicing _____ therapy.

39. To help Sam lose weight by eating fewer sweets, his therapist laced a batch of cookies with a

nausea-producing drug. Which technique is the therapist using?

_____

40. B.J.'s therapist interprets her psychological problems in terms of repressed impulses. Which type(s) of therapy is she using? _____

41. Leota is startled when her therapist says that she needs to focus on eliminating her problem behavior rather than gaining insight into its underlying cause. Most likely, Leota has consulted a _____ therapist.

   a. behavior   **c.** cognitive
   b. humanistic   **d.** psychoanalytic

42. Ben is a cognitive-behavioral therapist. Compared with Rachel, who is a behavior therapist, Ben is more likely to

   a. base his therapy on principles of operant conditioning.
   b. base his therapy on principles of classical conditioning.
   c. address clients' attitudes as well as behaviors.
   d. focus on clients' unconscious urges.

43. A patient in a hospital receives poker chips for making her bed, being punctual at meal times, and maintaining her physical appearance. The poker chips can be exchanged for privileges, such as television viewing, snacks, and magazines. This is an example of the

   a. psychodynamic therapy technique called systematic desensitization.
   b. behavior therapy technique called token economy.
   c. cognitive therapy technique called token economy.
   d. humanistic therapy technique called systematic desensitization.

44. After Darnel dropped a pass in an important football game, he became depressed and vowed to quit the team because of his athletic incompetence. The campus psychologist used gentle questioning to reveal to Darnel that his thinking was irrational: his "incompetence" had earned him an athletic scholarship. The psychologist's response was most typical of a _____ therapist.

   a. behavior   **c.** client-centered
   b. psychodynamic   **d.** cognitive

Objective 15-7: Discuss the aims and benefits of group and family therapy.

List several advantages of group therapy.

45. Although _____ therapy does not provide the same degree of therapist involvement with each client, it does save time and money and permits therapeutic benefits from _____ interaction.

46. The type of group interaction that focuses on the fact that we live and grow in relation to others is _____ _____ .

47. In this type of group, therapists focus on improving _____ within the family.

48. Many people also participate in _____ -_____ and _____ groups. One such group is _____ _____ .

═══════════════════════════════════════

STUDY TIP/APPLICATION: To organize your thinking about the modern psychological therapies discussed in this chapter, complete the chart on the next page. For each category of therapy, state the assumed underlying cause of psychological disorders, the overall goal of therapy, and the role of the therapist. To help you get started, the first example is already filled in.

49. Type of Psychotherapy	Assumed Cause of Psychological Disorder	Goal of Therapy	Role of Therapist
Psychodynamic therapies	Unconscious conflicts from childhood	Self-insight	Interpreting patients' memories and feelings
Humanistic therapies			
Behavior therapies			
Cognitive therapies			
Cognitive-behavioral therapy			
Group and family therapies			

Evaluating Psychotherapies

Objective 15-8: Explain whether psychotherapy works, and discuss who decides.

50. A majority of psychotherapy clients express _____ (satisfaction/dissatisfaction) with their therapy.

Give three reasons that client testimonials are not persuasive evidence for psychotherapy's effectiveness.

51. Clinicians tend to _____ (overestimate/underestimate) the effectiveness of psychotherapy.

52. One reason clinicians' perceptions of the effectiveness of psychotherapy are inaccurate is that clients justify entering therapy by emphasizing their _____ and justify leaving therapy by emphasizing their _____ .

53. In hopes of better assessing psychotherapy's effectiveness, psychologists have turned to _____ research studies.

54. The debate over the effectiveness of psychotherapy began with a study by _____ ; it showed that the rate of improvement for those who received therapy _____ (was/was not) higher than the rate for those who did not.

55. In the best studies of the effectiveness of therapy, researchers randomly assign people on a waiting list to therapy or no therapy and later evaluate everyone. These are _____ _____ trials.

56. A statistical digest of the results of many studies is called _____ . Overall, the results of such analyses indicate that psychotherapy is, on average, _____ (somewhat effective/ineffective).

57. Studies show that when people seek psychological treatment, their search for other medical treatment _____ (does/does not) decrease. Thus, psychotherapy is _____ -effective.

Objective 15-9: Describe which psychotherapies are more effective than others for specific disorders.

58. Comparisons of the effectiveness of different forms of therapy reveal _____ (clear/no clear) differences, that the type of therapy provider _____ (matters greatly/does not matter), and that whether therapy is provided by an individual therapist or within a group _____ (makes a difference/does not make a difference).

59. Some forms of therapy are best for particular problems. With phobias, compulsions, and other specific behavior problems, _____ _____ therapies have been the most effective. Other studies have demonstrated that anxiety, posttraumatic stress disorder, and depression may be effectively treated with _____ or _____- _____ therapy.

60. As a rule, psychotherapy is most effective with problems that are _____ (specific/nonspecific).

61. Clinical decision making that integrates research with clinical expertise and with patient preferences and characteristics is called _____-_____ _____ .

APPLICATION:

62. Your best friend Armand wants to know which type of therapy works best. You should tell him that
    a. psychotherapy does not work.
    b. behavior therapy is the most effective.
    c. cognitive therapy is the most effective.
    d. no one type of therapy is consistently the most successful.

Objective 15-10: Discuss how alternative therapies fare under scientific scrutiny.

63. Today, many forms of _____ _____ are touted as effective treatments for a variety of complaints.

64. Aside from testimonials, there is very little evidence based on _____ research for such therapies.

65. In one popular alternative therapy, a therapist triggers eye movements in patients while they imagine _____ _____ . This therapy, called _____ _____ _____ _____ _____ , has proven _____ (completely ineffective/ somewhat effective) as a treatment for nonmilitary _____- _____ _____ . However, skeptics point to evidence that _____ _____ is just as effective as triggered eye movements in producing beneficial results. The key seems to be in the person's _____ traumatic memories and in a _____ effect.

66. For people with a _____ _____ of depression symptoms, timed _____ _____ therapy may be beneficial.

APPLICATION:

67. A close friend who for years has suffered from wintertime depression is seeking your advice regarding the effectiveness of light exposure therapy. What should you tell your friend?
    a. "Don't waste your time and money. It doesn't work."
    b. "A more effective treatment for a seasonal pattern of depression symptoms is eye movement desensitization and reprocessing."
    c. "You'd be better off with a prescription for lithium."
    d. "It might be worth a try. There is some evidence that morning light exposure produces relief."

Objective 15-11: Describe the three elements shared by all forms of psychotherapy.

68. All forms of psychotherapy offer three benefits: _____ for demoralized people; a new _____ on oneself; and a relationship that is _____ , _____ , and _____ .

69. The emotional bond between therapist and client—the _____ _____—is a key aspect of effective therapy. In one study of depression treatment, the most effective therapists were those who were perceived as most _____ and _____ .

Objective 15-12: Discuss how culture and values influence the therapist-client relationship.

70. Generally speaking, psychotherapists' personal values _____ (do/do not) influence their therapy. This is particularly significant when the therapist and client are from different _____ . Another area of potential value conflict is _____ .

71. In North America, Europe, and Australia, most therapists reflect their culture's _____ .

72. Differences in values may help explain the reluctance of some _____ populations to use mental health services.

Objective 15-13: Identify some guidelines for selecting a therapist.

73. The American Psychological Association suggests that a person should seek help when he or she has feelings of _____ , a deep and lasting _____ , _____ behavior, disruptive _____ , sudden _____ shifts, and _____ rituals, for example.

APPLICATION:

74. Seth enters therapy to talk about some issues that have been upsetting him. The therapist prescribes some medication to help him. The therapist is most likely a
    a. clinical psychologist.
    b. psychiatrist.
    c. psychiatric social worker.
    d. clinical social worker.

The Biomedical Therapies

Objective 15-14: Identify and describe the drug therapies, and explain how double-blind studies help researchers evaluate a drug's effectiveness.

75. As noted earlier, therapy involving changing the brain's functioning is referred to as _____ therapy. The most widely used biomedical treatments are the _____ therapies. Thanks to these therapies, the number of residents in mental hospitals has _____ (increased/ decreased) sharply.

76. The field that studies the effects of drugs on the mind and behavior is _____ .

77. To guard against the _____ effect and normal _____ , neither the patients nor the staff involved in a study may be aware of which condition a given individual is in; this is called a _____- _____ procedure.

78. One effect of _____ drugs such as _____ is to help those experiencing _____ (positive/ negative) symptoms of schizophrenia by decreasing their responsiveness to irrelevant stimuli.

79. The antipsychotic drugs work by blocking the receptor sites for the neurotransmitter _____ .

80. Long-term use of antipsychotic drugs can produce _____ , which involves involuntary movements of the muscles of the _____ , _____ , and _____ .

81. Xanax and Ativan are classified as _____ drugs.

82. These drugs depress activity in the _____ _____ .

83. When used in combination with _____ _____ , these drugs can help people relieve the symptoms of posttraumatic stress disorder and obsessive-compulsive disorder.

84. Antianxiety drugs have been criticized for merely reducing _____ , rather than resolving underlying _____ .

These drugs can also create a _____ _____ .

85. Drugs that are prescribed to alleviate depression are called _____ drugs. Because the most commonly prescribed drugs in this group are increasingly being used to treat strokes and other disorders, including _____ disorders, _____-_____ disorder, and _____ _____ _____ , they are more commonly called _____ _____ inhibitors.

86. One example of this type of drug is _____ , which works by blocking the reabsorption and removal of _____ from synapses. Increased

serotonin promotes _____ , the development of new brain cells. Drugs that work by blocking the reabsorption or breakdown of norepinephrine and serotonin are called _____-_____ drugs. These drugs have _____ (more/fewer) side effects.

87. Also effective in calming anxious people and energizing depressed people is _____ _____ , which has positive side effects. Even better is to use antidepressant drugs, which work _____ (bottom-up/top-down), in conjunction with _____-_____ therapy, which works _____ (bottom-up/top-down).

88. Although people with depression often improve after one month on antidepressants, studies demonstrate that a large percentage of the effectiveness is due to natural recovery or a _____ _____ .

89. To treat the emotional highs and lows of _____ disorder, a _____-_____ drug such as the simple salt _____ is often prescribed.

90. Another effective drug in the control of mania was originally used to treat epilepsy; it is _____ .

APPLICATIONS:

91. In an experiment testing the effects of a new antipsychotic drug, neither Dr. Cunningham nor her patients know whether the patients are in the experimental or the control group. This is an example of
a. outcome research.
b. within-subjects research.
c. the double-blind procedure.
d. the single-blind procedure.

92. Linda's doctor prescribes medication that blocks the activity of dopamine in her nervous system. Evidently, Linda is being treated with an _____ drug.
a. antipsychotic   c. antidepressant
b. antianxiety   d. anticonvulsive

93. Abraham's doctor prescribes medication that increases the availability of norepinephrine or serotonin in his nervous system. Evidently, Abraham is being treated with a(n) _____ drug.
a. antipsychotic
b. mood-stabilizing
c. antidepressant
d. anticonvulsive

94. A psychiatrist has diagnosed a patient as having bipolar disorder. It is likely that she will prescribe
a. an antipsychotic drug.
b. lithium.
c. an antianxiety drug.
d. a drug that blocks receptor sites for serotonin.

Objective 15-15: Describe the use of brain stimulation techniques and psychosurgery in treating specific disorders.

95. The therapeutic technique in which the patient receives an electric shock to the brain is referred to as _____ therapy, abbreviated as _____ .

96. ECT is most often used with patients suffering from severe _____ . Research evidence _____ (confirms/does not confirm) ECT's effectiveness with such patients. The mechanism by which ECT works is

_____ .

97. An electrical device implanted in the chest stimulates a nerve deep in the neck; the device periodically sends signals to the limbic system. This is called _____ _____

_____ .

98. Another treatment being investigated for treatment of patients with depression is

_____-_____

stimulation of a neural hub that bridges the frontal lobes to the limbic system.

99. A painless procedure called _____

_____ _____

_____ aims to treat depression by presenting pulses through a magnetic coil held close to a person's skull above the right eyebrow. Unlike ECT, this procedure produces no

_____ , _____

loss, or other side effects. Although how it works is unclear, one explanation is that it energizes the brain's left _____

_____ , which is relatively inactive in depressed patients.

100. The biomedical therapy in which a portion of brain tissue is removed or destroyed is called

_____ .

101. In the 1930s, Moniz developed an operation called the _____ . In this procedure, the _____ lobe of the brain is disconnected from the rest of the brain.

102. Today, most psychosurgery has been replaced by the use of _____ or some other form of treatment.

APPLICATION:

103. In concluding her talk titled "Psychosurgery Today," Ashley states that
   a. "Psychosurgery is still widely used throughout the world."
   b. "Electroconvulsive therapy is the only remaining psychosurgical technique that is widely practiced."
   c. "With advances in psychopharmacology, psychosurgery has largely been abandoned."

   d. "Although lobotomies remain popular, other psychosurgical techniques have been abandoned."

Objective 15-16: Describe how, by taking care of themselves with a healthy lifestyle, people might find some relief from depression, and explain how this reflects our being biopsychosocial systems.

104. A recent approach to therapy promotes

_____ _____

change, which includes regular aerobic exercise, adequate sleep, light exposure, social connection, anti-rumination, and nutritional supplementation.

105. The relative success of this _____ approach seems to confirm that everything psychological is also biological and that we are all social creatures.

Preventing Psychological Disorders

Objective 15-17: Explain the rationale of preventive mental health programs.

106. Lifestyle changes may also help prevent some disorders by building an individual's _____ . Struggling with challenging crises can also lead to

_____ _____ .

107. Psychotherapies and biomedical therapies locate the cause of psychological disorders within the _____ . An alternative viewpoint is that many psychological disorders are responses to _____

_____ .

108. According to this viewpoint, it is not just the _____ who needs treatment but also the person's _____

_____ .

109. One advocate of _____ mental health, George Albee, believes that many social stresses undermine people's sense of

_____ , _____

_____ , and _____ .

These stresses include _____ , work that is _____ , constant

_____ , _____ ,

_____ , _____ ,

and _____ .

110. Albee's views remind us that disorders are not just biological and not just environmental or psychological because we are all an _____ _____ system.

Progress Test 1

Multiple-Choice Questions

Circle your answers to the following questions and check them with the answers beginning on page 380. If your answer is incorrect, read the explanation for why it is incorrect and then consult the text.

1. Electroconvulsive therapy is most useful in the treatment of
   a. schizophrenia.
   b. depression.
   c. personality disorders.
   d. anxiety disorders.

2. The technique in which a person is asked to report everything that comes to his or her mind is called _____ ; it is favored by_____ therapists.
   a. active listening; cognitive
   b. unconditional positive regard; humanistic
   c. free association; psychoanalytic
   d. systematic desensitization; behavior

3. Of the following categories of psychotherapy, which is known for its nondirective nature?
   a. psychoanalysis   c. behavior therapy
   b. humanistic therapy   d. cognitive therapy

4. Which of the following is NOT a common criticism of psychoanalysis?
   a. It emphasizes the existence of repressed memories.
   b. It provides interpretations that are hard to disprove.
   c. It is generally a very expensive process.
   d. It gives therapists too much control over patients.

5. Which of the following types of therapy does NOT belong with the others?
   a. cognitive therapy
   b. family therapy
   c. behavior therapy
   d. psychosurgery

6. Which of the following is NOT necessarily an advantage of group therapies over individual therapies?
   a. They tend to take less time for the therapist.
   b. They tend to cost less money for the client.
   c. They are more effective.
   d. They allow the client to test new behaviors in a social context.

7. Which biomedical therapy is MOST likely to be practiced today?
   a. psychosurgery
   b. electroconvulsive therapy
   c. drug therapy
   d. counterconditioning

8. The effectiveness of psychotherapy has been assessed both through clients' perspectives and through controlled research studies. What have such assessments found?
   a. Clients' perceptions and controlled studies alike strongly affirm the effectiveness of psychotherapy.
   b. Whereas clients' perceptions strongly affirm the effectiveness of psychotherapy, studies point to more modest results.
   c. Whereas studies strongly affirm the effectiveness of psychotherapy, many clients feel dissatisfied with their progress.
   d. Clients' perceptions and controlled studies alike paint a very mixed picture of the effectiveness of psychotherapy.

9. Cognitive-behavioral therapy aims to
   a. alter the way people act.
   b. make people more aware of their irrational negative thinking.
   c. alter the way people think and act.
   d. countercondition anxiety-provoking stimuli.

10. The results of outcome research on the effectiveness of different psychotherapies reveal that
    a. no single type of therapy is consistently superior.
    b. behavior therapies are most effective in treating specific problems, such as phobias.
    c. cognitive therapies are most effective in treating depressed emotions.
    d. all of these statements are true.

11. The antipsychotic drugs appear to produce their effects by blocking the receptor sites for
    a. dopamine.   c. norepinephrine.
    b. epinephrine.   d. serotonin.

12. Psychologists who advocate a _____ approach to mental health contend that many psychological disorders could be prevented by changing the disturbed individual's _____ .
    a. biomedical; diet
    b. family; behavior
    c. humanistic; feelings
    d. preventive; environment

13. An eclectic psychotherapist is one who
    a. takes a nondirective approach in helping clients solve their problems.
    b. views psychological disorders as usually stemming from one cause, such as a biological abnormality.
    c. uses one particular technique, such as psychoanalysis or counterconditioning, in treating disorders.
    d. uses a variety of techniques, depending on the client and the problem.

14. The technique in which a therapist echoes and restates what a person says in a nondirective manner is called
    a. active listening.
    b. free association.
    c. systematic desensitization.
    d. transference.

15. A new approach to therapy promotes regular exercise, adequate sleep, social connection, and other aspects of
    a. cognitive therapy.
    b. behavior therapy.
    c. free association.
    d. therapeutic lifestyle change.

16. The technique of systematic desensitization is based on the premise that maladaptive symptoms are
    a. a reflection of irrational thinking.
    b. conditioned responses.
    c. expressions of unfulfilled wishes.
    d. all of these things.

17. The operant conditioning technique in which desired behaviors are rewarded with points or poker chips that can later be exchanged for various rewards is called
    a. counterconditioning.
    b. systematic desensitization.
    c. a token economy.
    d. exposure therapy.

18. One variety of _____ therapy is based on the finding that depressed people often attribute their failures to _____ .
    a. humanistic; themselves
    b. behavior; external circumstances
    c. cognitive; external circumstances
    d. cognitive; themselves

19. A person can derive benefits from psychotherapy simply by believing in it. This illustrates the importance of
    a. natural recovery.
    b. the placebo effect.
    c. the transference effect.
    d. interpretation.

20. Before 1950, the main mental health providers were
    a. psychologists.   c. psychiatrists.
    b. paraprofessionals.   d. the clergy.

Matching Items

Match each term with the appropriate definition or description.

Terms

_____ 1. cognitive therapy
_____ 2. behavior therapy
_____ 3. systematic desensitization
_____ 4. cognitive-behavioral therapy
_____ 5. client-centered therapy
_____ 6. exposure therapy
_____ 7. aversive conditioning
_____ 8. psychoanalysis
_____ 9. preventive mental health
_____ 10. biomedical therapy
_____ 11. counterconditioning
_____ 12. insight therapy

Definitions or Descriptions

a. associates unwanted behavior with unpleasant experiences
b. associates a relaxed state with anxiety-arousing stimuli
c. emphasizes the social context of psychological disorders
d. integrative therapy that focuses on changing self-defeating thinking and unwanted behavior
e. category of therapies that teach people more adaptive ways of thinking
f. behavior therapies in which people are confronted by things they fear or avoid
g. therapy developed by Carl Rogers
h. therapy based on Freud's theory of personality
i. treatment with psychosurgery, electroconvulsive therapy, or drugs
j. classical conditioning procedure in which new responses are conditioned to stimuli that trigger unwanted behaviors
k. category of therapies based on learning principles derived from classical and operant conditioning
l. therapies that aim to increase the client's awareness of underlying motives and defenses

Progress Test 2

Progress Test 2 should be completed during a final chapter review. Answer the following questions after you thoroughly understand the correct answers for the section reviews and Progress Test 1.

Multiple-Choice Questions

1. Carl Rogers was a _____ therapist who was the creator of _____ .

   a. behavior; systematic desensitization
   b. psychoanalytic; insight therapy
   c. humanistic; client-centered therapy
   d. cognitive; cognitive therapy for depression

2. Using techniques of classical conditioning to develop an association between unwanted behavior and an unpleasant experience is known as

   a. aversive conditioning.
   b. systematic desensitization.
   c. transference.
   d. electroconvulsive therapy.

3. Which type of psychotherapy emphasizes the individual's inherent potential for self-fulfillment?

   a. behavior therapy
   b. psychodynamic therapy
   c. humanistic therapy
   d. biomedical therapy

4. Light exposure therapy has proven useful as a form of treatment for people suffering from

   a. bulimia.
   b. a seasonal pattern of depression symptoms.
   c. schizophrenia.
   d. dissociative identity disorder.

5. Which type of psychotherapy focuses on changing unwanted behaviors rather than on discovering their underlying causes?

   a. behavior therapy
   b. cognitive therapy
   c. humanistic therapy
   d. psychodynamic therapy

6. The techniques of counterconditioning are based on principles of
   a. observational learning.
   b. classical conditioning.
   c. operant conditioning.
   d. behavior modification.

7. In which of the following does the client learn to associate a relaxed state with a hierarchy of anxiety-arousing situations?
   a. cognitive therapy
   b. aversive conditioning
   c. counterconditioning
   d. systematic desensitization

8. Principles of operant conditioning underlie which of the following techniques?
   a. counterconditioning
   b. systematic desensitization
   c. aversive conditioning
   d. the token economy

9. Which of the following is NOT a common criticism of behavior therapy?
   a. Clients may rely too much on extrinsic rewards for their new behaviors.
   b. Behavior control is unethical.
   c. Outside the therapeutic setting, the new behavior may disappear.
   d. All of these are criticisms of behavior therapy.

10. Which type of therapy focuses on eliminating irrational thinking?
    a. EMDR
    b. client-centered therapy
    c. cognitive therapy
    d. behavior therapy

11. Antidepressant drugs are believed to work by affecting serotonin or
    a. dopamine.   c. norepinephrine.
    b. lithium.   d. acetylcholine.

12. After many years of taking antipsychotic drugs, Greg's facial muscles sometimes twitch involuntarily. This behavior is called
    a. tardive dyskinesia.   c.   rTMS.
    b. natural recovery.   d.   EMDR.

13. The mood-stabilizing drug most commonly used to treat bipolar disorder is
    a. Ativan.   c. Xanax.
    b. chlorpromazine.   d. lithium.

14. The type of drugs criticized for reducing symptoms without resolving underlying problems are the _____ drugs.
    a. antianxiety   c. antidepressant
    b. antipsychotic   d. amphetamine

15. Which form of therapy is MOST likely to be successful in treating depression?
    a. behavior modification c. cognitive therapy
    b. psychoanalysis   d. humanistic therapy

16. The lobotomy procedure is not widely used today because
    a. it produces a lethargic, immature personality.
    b. it is irreversible.
    c. calming drugs became available in the 1950s.
    d. of all of these reasons.

17. A psychotherapist who believes that the best way to treat psychological disorders is to prevent them from developing would be MOST likely to view disordered behavior as
    a. maladaptive thoughts and actions.
    b. expressions of unconscious conflicts.
    c. conditioned responses.
    d. an understandable response to stressful social conditions.

18. Among the common ingredients of the psychotherapies is
    a. the offer of a therapeutic relationship.
    b. the expectation among clients that the therapy will prove helpful.
    c. the chance to develop a fresh perspective on oneself and the world.
    d. all of these are common ingredients.

19. Family therapy differs from other forms of psychotherapy because it focuses on
    a. using a variety of treatment techniques.
    b. conscious rather than unconscious processes.
    c. the present instead of the past.
    d. how family tensions may cause individual problems.

20. One reason that aversive conditioning may only be temporarily effective is that
    a. for ethical reasons, therapists cannot use sufficiently intense unconditioned stimuli to sustain classical conditioning.
    b. patients are often unable to become sufficiently relaxed for conditioning to take place.
    c. patients know that outside the therapist's office they can engage in the undesirable behavior without fear of aversive consequences.
    d. most conditioned responses are elicited by many nonspecific stimuli and it is impossible to countercondition them all.

Matching Items

Match each term with the appropriate definition or description.

Terms

_____ 1. active listening
_____ 2. token economy
_____ 3. placebo effect
_____ 4. lobotomy
_____ 5. lithium
_____ 6. psychopharmacology
_____ 7. double-blind technique
_____ 8. Xanax
_____ 9. free association
_____ 10. evidence-based practice

Definitions or Descriptions

a. type of psychosurgery
b. mood-stabilizing drug
c. clinical decision making that integrates research, clinical expertise, and patient characteristics
d. empathic technique used in person-centered therapy
e. the beneficial effect of a person's expecting that treatment will be effective
f. antianxiety drug
g. technique of psychoanalytic therapy
h. an operant conditioning procedure
i. the study of the effects of drugs on the mind and behavior
j. experimental procedure in which both the patient and staff are unaware of a patient's treatment condition

Essay Question

Willie has been diagnosed as suffering from major depressive disorder. Describe the treatment he might receive from a psychodynamic therapist, a cognitive therapist, and a biomedical therapist. (Use the space below to list points you want to make, and organize them. Then write the essay on a separate sheet of paper.)

Terms and Concepts to Remember

Writing Definitions

Using your own words, on a separate piece of paper write a brief definition or explanation of each of the following terms.

1. psychotherapy
2. biomedical therapy
3. eclectic approach
4. psychoanalysis
5. resistance
6. interpretation
7. transference
8. psychodynamic therapy
9. insight therapies
10. client-centered therapy
11. active listening
12. unconditional positive regard
13. behavior therapy
14. counterconditioning
15. exposure therapies
16. systematic desensitization

17. virtual reality exposure therapy

18. aversive conditioning

19. token economy

20. cognitive therapy

21. cognitive-behavioral therapy (CBT)

22. group therapy

23. family therapy

24. evidence-based practice

25. psychopharmacology

26. antipsychotic drugs

27. antianxiety drugs

28. antidepressant drugs

29. electroconvulsive therapy (ECT)

30. repetitive transcranial magnetic stimulation (rTMS)

31. psychosurgery

32. lobotomy

33. resilience

Cross-Check

As you learned in Chapter 1, reviewing and overlearning of material are important to the learning process. After you have written the definitions of the key terms in this chapter, you should complete the crossword puzzle to ensure that you can reverse the process—recognize the term, given the definition.

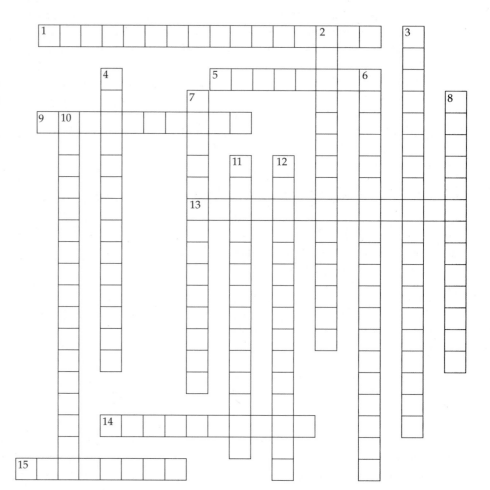

ACROSS

1. Therapy that teaches people new and more adaptive ways of thinking.

5. Approach that draws on a variety of forms of therapy to best suit clients' needs.

9. Blocking anxiety-provoking memories from consciousness.

13. Therapy that attempts to change behavior by removing or destroying brain tissue.

14. Therapy that uses prescribed medications or medical procedures to treat psychological disorders.

15. Conditioning in which an unpleasant state is associated with an unwanted behavior.

DOWN

2. Nondirective technique in which the listener echoes and restates, but does not interpret, clients' remarks.

3. Integrative therapy that focuses on changing self-defeating thinking and unwanted behaviors.

4. Humanistic therapy developed by Carl Rogers.

6. Behavior therapy in which new responses are classically conditioned to stimuli that trigger unwanted behaviors.

7. Psychoanalytic term for the analyst's helping a client to gain deeper insights into unwanted thoughts and behaviors.

8. Therapy that views problem behaviors as partially engendered by the client's environment.

10. Biomedical therapy often used to treat severe depression.

11. Therapy developed by Sigmund Freud.
12. Therapy that applies principles of operant or classical conditioning to eliminate problem behaviors.

Answers

Chapter Review

Treating Psychological Disorders

1. psychological; biomedical
2. eclectic

The Psychological Therapies

3. insight
4. repressed; conscious
5. childhood experiences
6. free association
7. resistance; interpretation
8. transference
9. is not; prove or disprove; expensive
10. psychodynamic; once or twice a week
11. themes
12. insight; unconscious
13. **d.** is the answer. Resistances are blocks in the flow of free association that hint at underlying anxiety.
    a. In transference, a patient redirects feelings from other relationships to his or her analyst.
    b. The goal of psychoanalysis is for patients to gain insight into their feelings.
    c. Although such hesitation may well involve material that has been repressed, the hesitation itself is a resistance.
14. transference
15. id; ego; superego; relationships
16. repressed impulses
17. self-fulfillment; insights

Unlike psychodynamic therapy, humanistic therapy is focused on the present and future instead of the past, on conscious rather than unconscious processes, on promoting growth and self-fulfillment instead of curing illness, and on helping clients take immediate responsibility for their feelings and actions rather than on uncovering the obstacles to doing so.

18. client-centered; nondirective; does not interpret
19. genuineness; acceptance; empathy
20. active listening; unconditional positive regard
21. paraphrase; invite clarification; reflect feelings

22. learning

Whereas psychodynamic and humanistic therapies assume that problems diminish as self-awareness grows, behavior therapists doubt that self-awareness is the key. Instead of looking for the inner cause of unwanted behavior, behavior therapy applies learning principles to directly attack the unwanted behavior itself.

23. classical conditioning; counterconditioning; exposure therapy; aversive conditioning
24. Joseph Wolpe; exposure therapies; anxious
25. hierarchy; progressive relaxation; relaxed; anxiety
26. virtual reality exposure
27. negative; positive; unpleasant; does not
28. **d.** is the answer. Aversive conditioning is the classical conditioning technique in which a positive response is replaced by a negative response. (In this example, the US is the blast of smoke, the CS is the taste of the cigarette as it is inhaled, and the intended CR is aversion to cigarettes.)
    a. Exposure therapy exposes someone, in imagination (virtual reality exposure therapy) or actuality, to a feared situation.
    b. Psychodynamic therapy focuses on insight and unconscious processes.
    c. Systematic desensitization is used to help people overcome specific anxieties.
29. **a.** is the answer.
    b. Aversive conditioning associates unpleasant states with unwanted behaviors.
    c. In psychoanalytic therapy, transference is the patient's redirecting to the analyst emotions from other relationships.
    d. Free association is a psychoanalytic technique in which a patient says whatever comes to mind.
30. behavior modification
31. operant
32. token economy

Behavior modification is criticized because the desired behavior may stop when the rewards are stopped. Also, critics contend that one person should not be allowed to control another.

Proponents of behavior modification contend that some clients request this therapy and that the behaviors will persist if patients are properly weaned from the tokens. Also, control already exists.

33. **a.** Virtual reality exposure therapy, a type of counterconditioning (classical conditioning).
    b. Token economy, based on operant conditioning principles.
    c. Systematic desensitization, an exposure therapy, which is a form of counterconditioning.

Specific procedures may vary. Refer to the text for general descriptions.

34. cognitive

35. negative; depression; Aaron Beck

36. catastrophizing

37. cognitive-behavioral; emotion regulation; obsessive-compulsive disorder

38. humanistic

39. aversive conditioning

40. psychoanalysis

41. **a.** is the answer.
b. & c. These types of therapists are more concerned with promoting self-fulfillment (humanistic) and healthy patterns of thinking (cognitive) than with correcting specific problem behaviors.
d. Psychoanalysts see the behavior merely as a symptom and focus their treatment on its presumed underlying cause.

42. **c.** is the answer.
a. & b. Behavior therapists make extensive use of techniques based on both operant and classical conditioning.
d. Neither behavior therapists nor cognitive behavioral therapists focus on clients' unconscious urges.

43. **b.** is the answer.

44. **d.** is the answer. Because the psychologist is focusing on Darnel's irrational thinking, this response is most typical of Beck's cognitive therapy for depression.
a. Behavior therapists treat behaviors rather than thoughts.
b. Psychoanalysts focus on helping patients gain insight into previously repressed feelings.
c. Client-centered therapists attempt to facilitate clients' growth by offering a genuine, accepting, empathic environment.

Group therapy saves therapists time and clients money. It offers a social laboratory for exploring social behaviors and developing social skills. It enables people to see that others share their problem. It provides feedback as clients try out new ways of behaving.

45. group; social

46. family therapy

47. communication

48. self-help; support; Alcoholics Anonymous

49. Humanistic therapies focus on the present and future, conscious thoughts, and having the person take responsibility for his or her feelings and actions. The goal is self-fulfillment. The therapist is genuine, accepting, and empathic and uses active listening in this nondirective therapy.

Behavior therapies focus on the problem behavior. The goal is to change undesirable behaviors to desirable behaviors. They use techniques based on classical and operant conditioning principles—for example, exposure therapies, aversive conditioning, and token economies.

Cognitive therapies focus on the person's way of thinking about himself or herself. Self-blaming and overgeneralized explanations of bad events cause the problem. The goal is to change the person's negative thinking. They use gentle questioning to reveal the patient's irrational thinking and persuade a depressed person, for example, to adopt a more positive attitude.

Cognitive-behavioral therapy is an integrative therapy that focuses on training people to change their self-harmful thoughts and behaviors. Its goal is to make people aware of their irrational negative thinking, to replace it with new ways of thinking, and to apply that to their everyday behavior.

Group and family therapies assume that problems arise from social interactions. They help people to see that others have similar problems and that communication can resolve most problems. During sessions, for example, they try to guide family members toward positive relationships and improved communication.

Evaluating Psychotherapies

50. satisfaction

People often enter therapy in crisis. When the crisis passes, they may attribute their improvement to the therapy. Clients, who may need to believe the therapy was worth the effort, may overestimate its effectiveness. Clients generally find positive things to say about their therapists, even if their problems remain.

51. overestimate

52. unhappiness; well-being

53. controlled

54. Hans Eysenck; was not

55. randomized clinical

56. meta-analysis; somewhat effective

57. does; cost

58. no clear; does not matter; does not make a difference

59. behavioral conditioning; cognitive; cognitive-behavioral

60. specific

61. evidence-based practice
62. **d.** is the answer.
    a. Psychotherapy has proven "somewhat effective" and more cost-effective than physician care for psychological disorders.
    b. & c. Behavior and cognitive therapies are both effective in treating depression, and behavior therapy is effective in treating specific problems such as phobias.
63. alternative therapy
64. controlled
65. traumatic events; eye movement desensitization and reprocessing (EMDR); somewhat effective; posttraumatic stress disorder; finger tapping; reliving; placebo
66. seasonal pattern; light exposure
67. **d.** is the answer.
    a. In fact, there is evidence that light exposure therapy can be effective in treating SAD.
    b. There is no evidence that EMDR is effective as a treatment for SAD.
    c. Lithium is a mood-stabilizing drug that is often used to treat bipolar disorder.
68. hope; perspective; caring; trusting; empathic
69. therapeutic alliance; empathic; caring
70. do; cultures; religion
71. individualism
72. minority
73. hopelessness; depression; self-destructive; fears; mood; compulsive
74. **b.** is the answer. Psychiatrists are physicians who specialize in treating psychological disorders. As doctors they can prescribe medications.
    a., c., & d. These professionals cannot prescribe drugs.

The Biomedical Therapies

75. biomedical; drug; decreased
76. psychopharmacology
77. placebo; recovery; double-blind
78. antipsychotic; chlorpromazine (Thorazine); positive
79. dopamine
80. tardive dyskinesia; face; tongue; limbs
81. antianxiety
82. central nervous system
83. exposure therapy

84. symptoms; problems; learned response
85. antidepressant; anxiety; obsessive-compulsive; posttraumatic stress disorder; selective serotonin reuptake
86. fluoxetine (Prozac); serotonin; neurogenesis; dual-action; more
87. aerobic exercise; bottom-up; cognitive-behavioral; top-down
88. placebo effect
89. bipolar; mood-stabilizing; lithium
90. Depakote
91. **c.** is the answer.
    a. This is a statistical digest that combines the results of many different research studies.
    b. In this design, which is not mentioned in the text, there is only a single research group.
    d. This answer would be correct if the experimenter, but not the research participants, knew which condition was in effect.
92. **a.** is the answer.
93. **c.** is the answer.
94. **b.** is the answer.
95. electroconvulsive; ECT
96. depression; confirms; unknown
97. vagus nerve stimulation
98. deep-brain
99. repetitive transcranial magnetic stimulation (rTMS); seizures; memory; frontal lobe
100. psychosurgery
101. lobotomy; frontal
102. drugs
103. **c.** is the answer.
    b. Although still practiced, electroconvulsive therapy is not a form of psychosurgery.
104. therapeutic lifestyle
105. biopsychosocial

Preventing Psychological Disorders

106. resilience; posttraumatic growth
107. person; a disturbing and stressful society
108. person; social context
109. preventive; competence; personal control; self-esteem; poverty; meaningless; criticism; unemployment; racism; sexism; heterosexism
110. integrated biopsychosocial

Progress Test 1

Multiple-Choice Questions

1. **b.** is the answer. Although no one is sure how ECT works, one possible explanation is that it increases release of norepinephrine, the neurotransmitter that elevates mood.

2. **c.** is the answer.
   a. Active listening is a Rogerian technique in which the therapist echoes, restates, and seeks clarification of the client's statements.
   b. Unconditional positive regard refers to an open, caring attitude toward a client.
   d. Systematic desensitization is a process in which a person is conditioned to associate a relaxed state with anxiety-triggering stimuli.

3. **b.** is the answer.

4. **d.** is the answer. This is not among the criticisms commonly made of psychoanalysis. (It would more likely be made of behavior therapies.)

5. **d.** is the answer.
   a., b., & c. Each of these is a type of psychological therapy.

6. **c.** is the answer. Outcome research on the relative effectiveness of different therapies reveals no clear winner; the other factors mentioned are advantages of group therapies.

7. **c.** is the answer.
   a. The fact that its effects are irreversible makes psychosurgery a drastic procedure, and with advances in psychopharmacology, psychosurgery was largely abandoned.
   b. ECT is still widely used as a treatment of severe depression, but in general it is not used as frequently as drug therapy.
   d. Counterconditioning is not a biomedical therapy.

8. **b.** is the answer. Clients' testimonials regarding psychotherapy are generally very positive. The research, in contrast, seems to show that therapy is only *somewhat* effective.

9. **c.** is the answer.

10. **d.** is the answer.

11. **a.** is the answer. By occupying receptor sites for dopamine, these drugs block its activity and reduce its production.

12. **d.** is the answer.

13. **d.** is the answer. Today, half of all psychotherapists describe themselves as eclectic—as using a blend of therapies.
    a. An eclectic therapist may use a nondirective approach with certain behaviors; however, a more directive approach might be chosen for other clients and problems.
    b. In fact, just the opposite is true. Eclectic therapists generally view disorders as stemming from many influences.
    c. Eclectic therapists, in contrast to this example, use a combination of treatments.

14. **a.** is the answer.

15. **d.** is the answer.
    a. Cognitive therapy focuses on teaching people more adaptive ways of thinking.
    b. Behavior therapy uses principles of learning theory to eliminate unwanted behaviors.
    c. Free association is a tool of psychoanalysis in which a person is encourage to say aloud whatever comes to mind.

16. **b.** is the answer.
    a. This reflects a cognitive perspective.
    c. This reflects a psychodynamic perspective.

17. **c.** is the answer.
    a. & b. Counterconditioning involves the replacement of an undesired response with a desired one by means of aversive conditioning or systematic desensitization.
    d. Exposure therapy exposes a person, in imagination or in actuality, to a feared situation.

18. **d.** is the answer.

19. **b.** is the answer.
    a. Natural recovery refers to improvement without any treatment.
    c. Transference is the psychoanalytic phenomenon in which a client transfers feelings from other relationships onto his or her analyst.
    d. Interpretation is the psychoanalytic procedure through which the analyst helps the client become aware of resistances and understand their meaning.

20. **c.** is the answer.

Matching Items

1. e	5. g	9. c
2. k	6. f	10. i
3. b	7. a	11. j
4. d	8. h	12. l

Progress Test 2

Multiple-Choice Questions

1. **c.** is the answer.
   a. This answer would be a correct description of Joseph Wolpe.
   b. There is no such thing as insight therapy.
   d. This answer would be a correct description of Aaron Beck.

2. **a.** is the answer.
b. In systematic desensitization, a hierarchy of anxiety-provoking stimuli is gradually associated with a relaxed state.
c. Transference refers to a patient's transferring of feelings from other relationships onto his or her psychoanalyst.
d. Electroconvulsive therapy is a biomedical shock treatment.

3. **c.** is the answer.
a. Behavior therapy focuses on behavior, not self-awareness.
b. Psychodynamic therapy focuses on bringing unconscious feelings into awareness.
d. Biomedical therapy focuses on physical treatment through drugs, ECT, or psychosurgery.

4. **b.** is the answer.

5. **a.** is the answer. For behavior therapy, the problem behaviors *are* the problems.
b. Cognitive therapy teaches people to think and act in more adaptive ways.
c. Humanistic therapy promotes growth and self-fulfillment by providing an empathic, genuine, and accepting environment.
d. Psychodynamic therapy focuses on uncovering and interpreting unconscious feelings.

6. **b.** is the answer. Counterconditioning techniques involve taking an established stimulus, which triggers an undesirable response, and pairing it with a new stimulus in order to condition a new, and more adaptive, response.
a. As indicated by the name, counterconditioning techniques are a form of conditioning; they do not involve learning by observation.
c. & d. The principles of operant conditioning are the basis of behavior modification, which, in contrast to counterconditioning techniques, involves use of reinforcement.

7. **d.** is the answer.
a. This is a confrontational therapy, which is aimed at teaching people to think and act in more adaptive ways.
b. Aversive conditioning is a form of counterconditioning in which unwanted behavior is associated with unpleasant feelings.
c. Counterconditioning is a general term, including not only systematic desensitization, in which a hierarchy of fears is desensitized, but also other techniques, such as aversive conditioning.

8. **d.** is the answer.
a., b., & c. These techniques are based on classical conditioning.

9. **d.** is the answer.

10. **c.** is the answer.
a. This is an alternative therapy in which the practitioner triggers eye movements in patients who are imagining traumatic events.
b. In this humanistic therapy, the therapist facilitates the client's growth by offering a genuine, accepting, and empathic environment.
d. Behavior therapy concentrates on modifying the actual symptoms of psychological problems.

11. **c.** is the answer.

12. **a.** is the answer.

13. **d.** is the answer. Lithium works as a mood stabilizer.
a. & c. Ativan and Xanax are antianxiety drugs.
b. Chlorpromazine is an antipsychotic drug.

14. **a.** is the answer.

15. **c.** is the answer.
a. Behavior modification is most likely to be successful in treating specific behavior problems, such as bed wetting.
b. & d. The text does not single out particular disorders for which these therapies tend to be most effective.

16. **d.** is the answer.

17. **d.** is the answer.
a. This would be the perspective of a cognitive-behavioral therapist.
b. This would be the perspective of a psychoanalyst.
c. This would be the perspective of a behavior therapist.

18. **d.** is the answer.

19. **d.** is the answer.
a. This is true of most forms of psychotherapy.
b. & c. This is true of humanistic, cognitive, and behavior therapies.

20. **c.** is the answer. Although aversive conditioning may work in the short run, the person's ability to discriminate between the situation in which the aversive conditioning occurs and other situations can limit the treatment's effectiveness.
a., b., & d. These are not limitations of the effectiveness of aversive conditioning.

Matching Items

1. d	**5.** b	**9.** g
2. h	**6.** i	**10.** c
3. e	**7.** j	
4. a	**8.** f	

Essay Question

Psychodynamic therapists assume that psychological problems such as depression are caused by unconscious conflicts from childhood experiences. A psychodynamic therapist would probably attempt to bring these feelings into Willie's conscious awareness and interpret those memories and feelings in order to help him gain insight into his depression.

Cognitive therapists assume that a person's emotional reactions are influenced by the person's thoughts in response to the event in question. A cognitive therapist would probably try to teach Willie new and more constructive ways of thinking in order to reverse his catastrophizing beliefs about himself, his situation, and his future.

Biomedical therapists attempt to treat disorders by altering the functioning of the patient's brain. A biomedical therapist would probably prescribe an antidepressant drug such as fluoxetine to increase the availability of norepinephrine and serotonin in Willie's nervous system. If Willie's depression is especially severe, a *psychiatrist* might treat it with several sessions of electroconvulsive therapy.

Terms and Concepts to Remember

Writing Definitions

1. **Psychotherapy** is an interaction between a trained therapist and someone who suffers from psychological difficulties or wants to achieve personal growth.

2. **Biomedical therapy** is the use of prescribed medications or medical procedures that act on a person's physiology to treat psychological disorders.

3. With an **eclectic approach**, therapists are not locked into one form of psychotherapy, but draw on whatever combination seems best suited to a client's problems.

4. **Psychoanalysis**, the therapy developed by Sigmund Freud, attempts to give clients self-insight by bringing into awareness and interpreting previously repressed feelings.

   Example: The tools of the **psychoanalyst** include free association, the analysis of dreams and transferences, and the interpretation of repressed impulses.

5. **Resistance** is the psychoanalytic term for the blocking from consciousness of anxiety-laden memories. Hesitation during free association may reflect resistance.

6. **Interpretation** is the psychoanalytic term for the analyst's helping the patient to understand resistances and other aspects of behavior, so that the patient may gain deeper insights.

7. **Transference** is the psychoanalytic term for a patient's redirecting to the analyst emotions from other relationships.

8. Derived from the psychoanalytic tradition, **psychodynamic therapy** seeks to enhance patients' self-insight into their symptoms by focusing on childhood experiences and important relationships in addition to unconscious forces.

9. **Insight therapies** such as psychodynamic and humanistic therapies aim to improve psychological functioning by increasing the person's awareness of underlying motives and defenses.

10. **Client-centered therapy** is a humanistic nondirective therapy developed by Carl Rogers, in which growth and self-awareness are facilitated in an environment that offers genuineness, acceptance, and empathy.

11. **Active listening** is a nondirective technique of Rogers' client-centered therapy, in which the listener echoes, restates, and clarifies clients' remarks.

12. **Unconditional positive regard** refers to the caring, accepting, nonjudgmental attitude that is the basis of client-centered therapy. Rogers believed it would help clients develop self-awareness and self-acceptance.

13. **Behavior therapy** is therapy that applies learning principles to the elimination of unwanted behaviors.

14. **Counterconditioning** refers to behavior therapy procedures in which new responses are classically conditioned to stimuli that trigger unwanted behaviors.

15. **Exposure therapies** treat anxiety by exposing people (in imagination or actual situations) to things they normally fear and avoid. Among these therapies are systematic desensitization and virtual reality exposure therapy.

16. **Systematic desensitization** is a type of exposure therapy in which a state of relaxation is classically conditioned to a hierarchy of gradually increasing anxiety-provoking stimuli.

   Memory aid: This is a form of **counterconditioning** in which sensitive, anxiety-triggering stimuli are *desensitized* in a progressive, or **systematic**, fashion.

17. **Virtual reality exposure therapy** progressively exposes people to electronic simulations of feared situations to treat their anxiety.

18. **Aversive conditioning** is a form of counterconditioning in which an unpleasant state is associated with an unwanted behavior.

19. A **token economy** is an operant conditioning procedure in which desirable behaviors are promoted in people by rewarding them with tokens, or positive reinforcers, which can be exchanged for privileges or treats. For the most part, token economies are used in hospitals, schools, and other institutional settings.

20. **Cognitive therapy** focuses on teaching people new and more adaptive ways of thinking. The therapy is based on the idea that our feelings and responses to events are strongly influenced by our thinking, or cognition.

21. **Cognitive-behavioral therapy (CBT)** is an integrative therapy that focuses on changing self-defeating thinking (cognitive therapy) and unwanted behaviors (behavior therapy).

22. **Group therapy** is therapy conducted with groups rather than individuals.

23. **Family therapy** views problem behavior as influenced by, or directed at, other members of the individual's family. Therapy therefore focuses on relationships and problems among the various members of the family.

24. **Evidence-based practice** is clinical decision making that integrates the best available research with clinical expertise and with patient characteristics and preferences.

25. **Psychopharmacology** is the study of the effects of drugs on mind and behavior.

    Memory aid: Pharmacology is the science of the uses and effects of drugs. *Psychopharmacology* is the science that studies the psychological effects of drugs.

26. **Antipsychotic drugs** are used to treat schizophrenia and other severe thought disorders.

27. **Antianxiety drugs** help control anxiety and agitation by depressing activity in the central nervous system.

28. **Antidepressant drugs** treat depression, anxiety disorders, obsessive-compulsive disorder, and posttraumatic stress disorder. (Several widely used antidepressant drugs are selective serotonin reuptake inhibitors—SSRIs.)

29. In **electroconvulsive therapy (ECT)**, a biomedical therapy often used to treat severe depression, a brief electric shock is passed through the brain of an anesthetized patient.

30. **Repetitive transcranial magnetic stimulation (rTMS)** is the delivery of repeated pulses of magnetic energy to stimulate or suppress brain activity.

31. **Psychosurgery** is a biomedical therapy that attempts to change behavior by removing or destroying brain tissue. Since drug therapy became widely available in the 1950s, psychosurgery has been infrequently used.

32. Once used to control violent patients, the **lobotomy** is a form of psychosurgery in which the nerves linking the emotion centers of the brain to the frontal lobes are severed.

33. **Resilience** is the personal strength that helps most people to cope with stress and recover from adversity and even trauma.

Cross-Check

ACROSS
1. cognitive therapy
5. eclectic
9. resistance
13. psychosurgery
14. biomedical
15. aversive

DOWN
2. active listening
3. cognitive-behavioral
4. client-centered
6. counterconditioning
7. interpretation
8. family therapy
10. electroconvulsive
11. psychoanalysis
12. behavior therapy

Statistical Reasoning in Everyday Life

Appendix Overview

A basic understanding of statistical reasoning has become a necessity in everyday life. Statistics are tools that help the psychologist and layperson to interpret the vast quantities of information they are confronted with on a daily basis. Appendix A discusses how statistics are used to describe data and to generalize from instances.

In studying this appendix, you must concentrate on learning a number of procedures and understanding some underlying principles in the science of statistics. The graphic and computational procedures in the section called "Describing Data" include how data are distributed in a sample; measures of central tendency such as the mean, median, and mode; variation measures such as the range and standard deviation; and correlation, or the degree to which two variables are related. Most of the conceptual material is then covered in the section titled "Signficant Differences." You should be able to discuss three important principles concerning populations and samples, as well as the concept of significance in testing differences. The ultimate goal is to make yourself a better consumer of statistical research by improving your critical thinking skills.

NOTE: Answer guidelines for all questions in Appendix A begin on page 392.

Appendix Review

First, skim each section, noting headings and bold-face items. After you have read the section, review each objective by answering the fill-in and essay-type questions that follow it. Applications help you to know how well you understand the material. As you proceed, evaluate your performance by consulting the answers on page 392. Do not continue with the next section until you understand each answer. If you need to, review or reread the section in the textbook before continuing.

Introduction and Describing Data

Objective A-1: Discuss how we can describe data with measures of central tendency and variation.

1. We should be skeptical when presented with numbers that are _____ , _____ , and _____ .

2. The first step in describing data is to _____ it in some meaningful way, such as by displaying it as a _____ _____ .

3. The three measures of central tendency are the _____ , the _____ , and the _____ .

4. The most frequently occurring score in a distribution is called the _____ .

5. The mean is computed as the _____ of all the scores divided by the _____ of scores.

6. The median is the score at the _____ percentile.

7. When a distribution is lopsided, or _____ , the _____ (mean/median/mode) can be biased by a few extreme scores.

8. Averages derived from scores with _____ (high/low) variability are more reliable than those with _____ (high/low) variability.

385

9. The measures of variation include the
_____ and the

_____ _____ .

10. The range is computed as the _____

_____ .

11. The range provides a(n) _____
(crude/accurate) estimate of variation because it
_____ (is/is not) influenced by
extreme scores.

12. The standard deviation is a _____
(more accurate/less accurate) measure of variation than the range. Unlike the range, the standard deviation _____ (uses/does
not use) information from each score in the distribution. The standard deviation is calculated as
the square root of the sum of _____
squared divided by the _____

_____ _____ .

13. The bell-shaped distribution that often describes
large amounts of data is called the

_____ _____ .

14. In this distribution, approximately
_____ percent of the individual
scores fall within 1 standard deviation on either
side of the mean. Within 2 standard deviations on
either side of the mean fall _____
percent of the individual scores.

Explain what it means to score 116 on the normally
distributed Wechsler IQ test. (Recall that the mean is
100; the standard deviation is ±15 points. Hint: You
might find it helpful to draw the normal curve first.)

APPLICATIONS:

15. The football team's punter wants to determine
how consistent his punting distances have been
during the past season. He should compute the
   a. mean.   **c.** mode.
   b. median.   **d.** standard deviation.

16. Esteban refuses to be persuaded by an adver-
tiser's claim that people using their brand of gas-
oline average 50 miles per gallon. His decision
probably is based on
   a. the possibility that the average is the mean,
   which could be artificially inflated by a few
   extreme scores.
   b. the absence of information about the size of
   the sample studied.
   c. the absence of information about the variation
   in sample scores.
   d. all of these statements.

17. Bob scored 43 out of 70 points on his psychology exam. He was worried until he discovered that
most of the class earned the same score. Bob's
score was equal to the
   a. mean.   **c.** mode.
   b. median.   **d.** range.

18. The four families on your block all have annual
household incomes of $25,000. If a new fam-
ily with an annual income of $75,000 moved in,
which measure of central tendency would be
most affected?
   a. mean   **c.** mode
   b. median   **d.** standard deviation

Objective A-2: Explain what it means when we say
two things are correlated.

19. A measure of the direction and extent of relationship between two sets of scores is called the

_____ _____ .

Numerically, this measure can range from
_____ to _____ .

20. To depict a correlation, researchers create a graph
called a _____ , which uses dots to
represent the values of the two variables.

21. When there is no relationship at all between two
sets of scores, the correlation coefficient is
_____ . The strongest possible correlation between two sets of scores is either

_____ or _____ .

When the correlation between two sets of scores
is negative, as one increases, the other

_____ .

Cite an example of a positive correlation and a negative correlation. Your examples can be drawn from previous chapters of the text or can be based on observations from daily life.

An example of a positive correlation is

An example of a negative correlation is

22. The correlation coefficient _____ (gives/does not give) information about cause-effect relationships. It does, however, tell how well one factor _____ the other related factor.

APPLICATIONS:

23. Meagan has found a positive correlation between the height and body weight of students at her school. Which of the following is true?
    a. There is a cause-effect relationship between height and weight.
    b. As height increases, weight decreases.
    c. Knowing a person's height, one can predict his or her weight.
    d. All of these statements are true.

24. Given the positive correlation found by Meagan, how should she depict the relationship on a scatterplot?
    a. All the points should fall on a straight line.
    b. The points should be spread randomly about the plot.
    c. All the points should fall on a curved line.
    d. It is impossible to determine from the information given.

Objective A-3: Define *regression toward the mean*.

25. A correlation that is perceived but doesn't really exist is called an _____ _____ .

26. When we believe that a relationship exists between two things, we are most likely to recall instances that _____ (confirm/disconfirm) our belief.

27. This type of correlation feeds the illusion of _____—that we can control events that actually are due to _____ .

It is also fed by a statistical phenomenon called _____ _____ _____ _____ , the idea that average results are more typical than extreme results.

APPLICATIONS:

28. Which of the following exemplifies regression toward the mean?
    a. In his second season of varsity basketball, Edward averaged 5 points more per game than in his first season.
    b. A gambler rolls 5 consecutive "sevens" using her favorite dice.
    c. After earning an unusually low score on the first exam in a class, a "B student" scores much higher on the second exam.
    d. A student who usually gets Bs earns grades of A, C, C, and A on four exams, thus maintaining a B average overall for the class.

29. Joe believes that his basketball game is always best when he wears his old gray athletic socks. Joe is a victim of the phenomenon called
    a. regression toward the mean.
    b. the availability heuristic.
    c. illusory correlation.
    d. skewed scoring.

Significant Differences

Objective A-4: Explain how we know whether an observed difference can be generalized to other populations.

30. The best basis for generalizing is not from _____ cases but from a _____ sample of cases.

31. Observations are more reliable when they are based on scores with _____ (high/low) variability.

32. Averages based on a large number of cases are _____ (more/less) reliable than those based on a few cases.

33. Tests of statistical _____ are used to estimate whether observed differences are real, that is, to make sure they are not simply the result of _____ variation. The differences are probably real if the sample averages are _____ and the difference between them is _____ .

APPLICATION:

34. Dr. Salazar recently completed an experiment in which she compared reasoning ability in a sample of women and a sample of men. The means of the female and male samples equaled 21 and 19, respectively, on a 25-point scale. A statistical test revealed that her results were not statistically significant. What can Dr. Salazar conclude?

    a. Women have superior reasoning ability.
    b. The difference in the means of the two samples is probably due to chance variation.
    c. The difference in the means of the two samples is reliable.
    d. She cannot reach any of these conclusions.

Objective A-5: Define *cross-sectional studies* and *longitudinal studies,* and discuss why it is important to know which method was used.

35. (Close-Up) Researchers use _____-_____ studies to investigate a randomly sampled group of people of _____ (the same/different) age(s). This type of study generally extends over a very _____ (long/short) period of time.

36. (Close-Up) Researchers use _____ studies to study, test, and re-test _____ (the same/different) group(s) over a _____ (long/short) period of time.

37. (Close-Up) The first kind of study found evidence of intellectual _____ (stability/decline) during adulthood; the second found evidence of intellectual _____ (stability/decline).

(Close-Up) Explain why the conflicting results of these two types of studies point to the importance of knowing how researchers reached their conclusions.

Progress Test 1

Multiple-Choice Questions

Circle your answers to the following questions and check them with the answers beginning on page 393. If your answer is incorrect, read the explanation for why it is incorrect and then consult the appropriate pages of the text (in parentheses following the correct answer). Use the page margins if you need extra space for your computations.

1. What is the mean of the following distribution of scores: 2, 3, 7, 6, 1, 4, 9, 5, 8, 2?
    a. 5   c. 4.7
    b. 4   d. 3.7

2. What is the median of the following distribution of scores: 1, 3, 7, 7, 2, 8, 4?
    a. 1   c. 3
    b. 2   d. 4

3. What is the mode of the following distribution: 8, 2, 1, 1, 3, 7, 6, 2, 0, 2?
    a. 1   c. 3
    b. 2   d. 7

4. Compute the range of the following distribution: 9, 14, 2, 8, 1, 6, 8, 9, 1, 3.
    a. 10   c. 8
    b. 9   d. 13

5. Which of the following is true of the longitudinal method?
    a. It compares people of different ages.
    b. It studies the same people at different times.
    c. It usually involves a larger sample than do cross-sectional tests.
    d. It usually involves a smaller sample than do cross-sectional tests.

6. If two sets of scores are negatively correlated, it means that
    a. as one set of scores increases, the other decreases.
    b. as one set of scores increases, the other increases.
    c. there is only a weak relationship between the sets of scores.
    d. there is no relationship at all between the sets of scores.

7. Regression toward the mean is the
    a. tendency for unusual scores to fall back toward a distribution's average.
    b. basis for all tests of statistical significance.
    c. reason the range is a more accurate measure of variation than the standard deviation.
    d. reason the standard deviation is a more accurate measure of variation than the range.

8. In a normal distribution, what percentage of scores fall between +2 and −2 standard deviations of the mean?

   a. 50 percent   c. 95 percent
   b. 68 percent   d. 99.7 percent

9. Which of the following statistics must fall on or between −1.00 and +1.00?

   a. the mean
   b. the standard deviation
   c. the correlation coefficient
   d. none of these statistics

10. In generalizing from a sample to the population, it is important that

    a. the sample is representative of the population.
    b. the sample is large.
    c. the scores in the sample have low variability.
    d. all of these conditions are observed.

11. When a difference between two groups is "statistically significant," this means that

    a. the difference is statistically real but of little practical significance.
    b. the difference is probably the result of sampling variation.
    c. the difference is not likely to be due to chance variation.
    d. all of these differences exist.

12. A lopsided set of scores that includes a number of extreme or unusual values is said to be

    a. symmetrical.   c. skewed.
    b. normal.   d. dispersed.

13. Which of the following is NOT a measure of central tendency?

    a. mean   c. median
    b. range   d. mode

14. Which of the following is the measure of central tendency that would be most affected by a few extreme scores?

    a. mean   c. median
    b. range   d. mode

15. The symmetrical, bell-shaped distribution in which most scores are near the mean and fewer near the extremes forms a

    a. skewed curve.   c. normal curve.
    b. bimodal curve.   d. bar graph.

16. A homogeneous sample with little variation in scores will have a(n) _____ standard deviation.

    a. small
    b. moderate
    c. large
    d. unknown (It is impossible to determine.)

17. If there is no relationship between two sets of scores, the correlation coefficient equals

    a. 0.00   c. +1.00
    b. −1.00   d. 0.50

18. Illusory correlation refers to

    a. the perception that two negatively correlated variables are positively correlated.
    b. the perception of a relationship between two unrelated variables.
    c. an insignificant correlation coefficient.
    d. a correlation coefficient that equals −1.00.

19. Gamblers who blow on their dice "for luck" are victims of

    a. regression toward the mean.
    b. the illusion of control.
    c. hindsight bias.
    d. the fundamental attribution error.

Matching Items

Match each term with the appropriate definition or description.

Terms

_____ 1. bar graph
_____ 2. median
_____ 3. normal curve
_____ 4. regression toward the mean
_____ 5. mode
_____ 6. range
_____ 7. standard deviation
_____ 8. skewed
_____ 9. mean
_____ 10. measures of central tendency
_____ 11. measures of variation

Definitions or Descriptions

a. the mean, median, and mode
b. the difference between the highest and lowest scores
c. the arithmetic average of a distribution
d. the range and standard deviation
e. a symmetrical, bell-shaped distribution
f. the most frequently occurring score
g. the tendency for extremes of unusual scores to fall back toward the average
h. a graph depicting a table of data
i. the middle score in a distribution
j. an asymmetrical distribution
k. the square root of the average squared deviation of scores from the mean

Progress Test 2

Progress Test 2 should be completed during a final chapter review. Answer the following questions after you thoroughly understand the correct answers for the Chapter Review and Progress Test 1.

Multiple-Choice Questions

1. What is the mode of the following distribution of scores: 2, 2, 4, 4, 4, 14?
   a. 2   c. 5
   b. 4   d. 6

2. What is the mean of the following distribution of scores: 2, 5, 8, 10, 11, 4, 6, 9, 1, 4?
   a. 2   c. 6
   b. 10   d. 15

3. What is the median of the following distribution: 10, 7, 5, 11, 8, 6, 9?
   a. 6   c. 8
   b. 7   d. 9

4. Which statistic is the average amount by which the scores in a distribution vary from the average?
   a. standard deviation   c. median
   b. range   d. mode

5. The most frequently occurring score in a distribution is the
   a. mean.   c. mode.
   b. median.   d. range.

6. In the following distribution, the mean is _____ the mode and _____ the median: 4, 6, 1, 4, 5.
   a. less than; less than
   b. less than; greater than
   c. equal to; equal to
   d. greater than; equal to

7. In which type of study are the same people tested and retested over a period of years?
   a. cross-sectional   c. longitudinal
   b. correlational   d. scatterplot

8. Which of the following is true of the cross-sectional method?
   a. It compares people of different ages with one another.
   b. It studies the same group of people at different times.
   c. It tends to paint too favorable a picture of the effects of aging on intelligence.
   d. It is more appropriate than the longitudinal method for studying intellectual change over the life span.

9. Which of the following sets of scores would likely be most representative of the population from which it was drawn?
   a. a sample with a relatively large standard deviation
   b. a sample with a relatively small standard deviation
   c. a sample with a relatively large range

d. a sample with a relatively small range

10. The *value* of the correlation coefficient indicates the _____ of relationship between two variables, and the *sign* (positive or negative) indicates the _____ of the relationship.
a. direction; strength
b. strength; direction
c. direction; reliability
d. reliability; strength

11. If a difference between two samples is NOT statistically significant, which of the following can be concluded?
a. The difference is probably not a true one.
b. The difference is probably not reliable.
c. The difference could be due to sampling variation.
d. All of these statements are true.

12. The first step in constructing a bar graph is to
a. measure the standard deviation.
b. organize the data.
c. calculate a correlation coefficient.
d. determine the range.

13. Why is the median at times a better measure of central tendency than the mean?
a. It is more sensitive to extreme scores.
b. It is less sensitive to extreme scores.
c. It is based on more of the scores in the distribution than the mean.
d. Both a. and c. explain why.

14. Standard deviation is to mode as _____ is to _____ .
a. mean; median
b. variation; central tendency
c. median; mean
d. central tendency; variation

15. In a normal distribution, what percentage of scores fall between −1 and +1 standard deviation units of the mean?
a. 50 percent
b. 68 percent
c. 95 percent
d. 99.7 percent

16. The precision with which sample statistics reflect population parameters is greater when the sample is
a. large.
b. characterized by high variability.
c. small in number but consists of vivid cases.
d. statistically significant.

17. The following scatterplot depicts a correlation coefficient that would be close to

a. +1.0.
b. −1.0.
c. 0.00.
d. 0.50.

18. Which of the following correlation coefficients indicates the strongest relationship between two variables?
a. −.73
b. +.66
c. 0.00
d. −.50

19. A correlation coefficient
a. indicates the direction of relationship between two variables.
b. indicates the strength of relationship between two variables.
c. does *not* indicate whether there is a cause-effect relationship between two variables.
d. does all of these things.

True–False Items

Indicate whether each statement is true or false by placing a *T* or *F* in the blank next to the item.

_____ 1. The first step in describing raw data is to organize it.

_____ 2. In almost all distributions, the mean, the median, and the mode will be the same.

_____ 3. When a distribution has a few extreme scores, the range is more misleading than the standard deviation.

_____ 4. If increases in the value of variable *x* are accompanied by decreases in the value of variable *y*, the two variables are negatively correlated.

_____ 5. Over time, extreme results tend to fall back toward the average.

_____ 6. If a sample has low variability, it cannot be representative of the population from which it was drawn.

_____ 7. The mean is always the most precise measure of central tendency.

_____ 8. Averages that have been derived from scores with low variability are more reliable than those derived from scores that are more variable.

_____ 9. A relationship between two variables is depicted on a scatterplot.

_____ 10. Small samples are less reliable than large samples for generalizing to the population.

Essay Question

Discuss several ways in which statistical reasoning can improve your own everyday thinking. (Use the space below to list the points you want to make, and organize them. Then write the essay on a separate sheet of paper.)

Terms and Concepts to Remember

Using your own words, on a separate piece of paper write a brief definition or explanation of each of the following terms.

1. mode

2. mean

3. median

4. range

5. standard deviation

6. normal curve

7. correlation coefficient

8. scatterplot

9. regression toward the mean

10. cross-sectional study

11. longitudinal study

12. statistical significance

Answers

Chapter Review

Introduction and *Describing Data*

1. big; round; undocumented

2. organize; bar graph

3. mean; median; mode

4. mode

5. sum; number

6. 50th

7. skewed; mean

8. low; high

9. range; standard deviation

10. difference between the lowest and highest scores in a distribution

11. crude; is

12. more accurate; uses; deviations; number of scores

13. normal curve

14. 68; 95

Because the mean equals 100 and the standard deviation is 15 points, a score of 116 is just over one standard deviation unit above the mean. Because 68 percent of the population's scores fall within one standard deviation on either side of the mean, 34 percent fall between 0 and +1 standard deviation unit. By definition, 50 percent of the scores fall below the mean. Therefore, a score at or above 115 is higher than that obtained by 84 percent of the population (50 percent + 34 percent = 84 percent).

15. **d.** is the answer. A small or large standard deviation indicates whether a distribution is homogeneous or variable.
    a., b., & c. These statistics would not give any information regarding the consistency of performance.

16. **d.** is the answer.

17. **c.** is the answer.
    a. The mean is computed as the sum of the scores divided by the number of scores.
    b. The median is the midmost score in a distribution.
    d. The range is the difference between the highest and lowest scores in a distribution.

18. **a.** is the answer. The mean is strongly influenced by extreme scores. In this example, the mean would change from $25,000 to (75,000 + 25,000 + 25,000 + 25,000 + 25,000)/5 = $35,000.
    b. & c. Both the median and the mode would remain $25,000, even with the addition of the fifth family's income.

d. The standard deviation is a measure of variation, not central tendency.

19. correlation coefficient; +1.00; –1.00

20. scatterplot

21. 0.00; +1.00; –1.00; decreases

An example of a positive correlation is the relationship between air temperature and ice cream sales: As one increases so does the other.

An example of a negative correlation is the relationship between good health and the amount of stress a person is under: As stress increases, the odds of good health decrease.

22. does not give; predicts

23. **c.** is the answer. If height and weight are positively correlated, increased height is associated with increased weight. Thus, one can predict a person's weight from his or her height.
    a. Correlation does not imply causality.
    b. This situation depicts a negative correlation between height and weight.

24. **a.** is the answer. Because the two variables—height and weight—correlate perfectly, they would vary together perfectly and form a straight line.

25. illusory correlation

26. confirm

27. control; chance; regression toward the mean

28. **c.** is the answer. Regression toward the mean is the phenomenon that average results are more typical than extreme results. Thus, after an unusual event (the low exam score in this example) things tend to return toward their average level (in this case, the higher score on the second exam).
    a. Edward's improved average indicates only that, perhaps as a result of an additional season's experience, he is a better player.
    b. Because the probability of rolling 5 consecutive "sevens" is very low, the gambler's "luck" will probably prove on subsequent rolls to be atypical and things will return toward their average level. This answer is incorrect, however, because it states only that 5 consecutive "sevens" were rolled.
    d. In this example, although the average of the student's exam grades is her usual grade of B, they are all extreme grades and do not regress toward the mean.

29. **c.** is the answer. A correlation that is perceived but doesn't actually exist, as in the example, is known as an illusory correlation.
    a. Regression toward the mean is the tendency for extreme scores to fall back toward the average.

b. The availability heuristic is the tendency of people to estimate the likelihood of something in terms of how readily it comes to mind (see Chapter 9).
d. There is no such thing as skewed scoring.

Significant Differences

30. exceptional (memorable); representative

31. low

32. more

33. significance; chance; reliable; large

34. **b.** is the answer.
    a. If the difference between the sample means is not significant, then the groups probably do not differ in the measured ability.
    c. When a result is not significant it means that the observed difference is unreliable.

35. cross-sectional; different; short

36. longitudinal; the same; long

37. decline; stability

Because cross-sectional studies compare people not only of different ages but also of different eras, education levels, family size, and affluence, it is not surprising that such studies reveal cognitive decline with age. In contrast, longitudinal studies test one group over a span of years. However, because those who survive to the end of longitudinal studies may be the brightest and healthiest, these studies may underestimate the average decline in intelligence. It is therefore important to know what type of methodology was used and whether the sample was truly representative of the population being studied.

Progress Test 1

Multiple-Choice Questions

1. **c.** is the answer. The mean is the sum of scores divided by the number of scores. [(2 + 3 + 7 + 6 + 1 + 4 + 9 + 5 + 8 + 2)/10 = 4.7.]

2. **d.** is the answer. When the scores are put in order (1, 2, 3, 4, 7, 7, 8), 4 is at the 50th percentile, splitting the distribution in half.

3. **b.** is the answer. The mode is the most frequently occurring score. Since there are more "twos" than any other number in the distribution, 2 is the mode.

4. **d.** is the answer. The range is the gap between the highest and lowest scores in a distribution. (14 – 1 = 13.)

5. **b.** is the answer.
    a. This answer describes cross-sectional research.

c. & d. Sample size does not distinguish cross-sectional from longitudinal research.

6. **a.** is the answer.
   b. This situation indicates that the two sets of scores are positively correlated.
   c. Whether a correlation is positive or negative does not indicate the strength of the relationship, only its direction.
   d. In negative correlations, there *is* a relationship; the correlation is negative because the relationship is an inverse one.

7. **a.** is the answer.
   b. Regression toward the mean has nothing to do with tests of statistical significance.
   c. In fact, just the opposite is true.
   d. This is true, but not because of regression toward the mean.

8. **c.** is the answer.
   a. 50 percent of the normal curve falls on either side of its mean.
   b. 68 percent of the scores fall between –1 and +1 standard deviation units.
   d. 99.7 percent fall between –3 and +3 standard deviations.

9. **c.** is the answer.

10. **d.** is the answer.

11. **c.** is the answer.
    a. A statistically significant difference may or may not be of practical importance.
    b. This is often the case when a difference is *not* statistically significant.

12. **c.** is the answer.

13. **b.** is the answer.

14. **a.** is the answer. As an average, calculated by adding all scores and dividing by the number of scores, the mean could easily be affected by the inclusion of a few extreme scores.
    b. The range is not a measure of central tendency.
    c. & d. The median and mode give equal weight to all scores; each counts only once and its numerical value is unimportant.

15. **c.** is the answer.
    a. A skewed curve is formed from an asymmetrical distribution.
    b. A bimodal curve has two modes; a normal curve has only one.
    d. A bar graph depicts a distribution of scores.

16. **a.** is the answer. The standard deviation is the average deviation in a distribution; therefore, if variation (deviation) is small, the standard deviation will also be small.

17. **a.** is the answer.

b. & c. These are "perfect" correlations of equal strength.
d. This indicates a much stronger relationship between two sets of scores than does a coefficient of 0.00.

18. **b.** is the answer.

19. **b.** is the answer.

Matching Items

1. h	5. f	9. c
2. i	6. b	10. a
3. e	7. k	11. d
4. g	8. j	

Progress Test 2

Multiple-Choice Questions

1. **b.** is the answer.

2. **c.** is the answer. The mean is the sum of the scores divided by the number of scores. (60/10 = 6.)

3. **c.** is the answer. When the scores are put in order (5, 6, 7, 8, 9, 10, 11), 8 is at the 50th percentile, splitting the distribution in half.

4. **a.** is the answer.
   b. The range is the difference between the highest and lowest scores in a distribution.
   c. The median is the score that falls at the 50th percentile.
   d. The mode is the most frequently occurring score.

5. **c.** is the answer.
   a. The mean is the arithmetic average.
   b. The median is the score that splits the distribution in half.
   d. The range is the difference between the highest and lowest scores.

6. **c.** is the answer. The mean, median, and mode are equal to 4.

7. **c.** is the answer.
   a. In a cross-sectional study, people of different ages are compared with one another.
   b. Correlational studies deal with the relationship between two variables.
   d. A scatterplot is a type of graph.

8. **a.** is the answer.
   b. This answer describes the longitudinal research method.
   c. & d. Cross-sectional studies have tended to exaggerate the negative effects of aging on intellectual functioning; for this reason they may not be the most appropriate method for studying life-span development.

9. **b.** is the answer. Averages derived from scores with low variability tend to be more reliable estimates of the populations from which they are drawn. Thus, a. and c. are incorrect. Because the standard deviation is a more accurate estimate of variability than the range, d. is incorrect.

10. **b.** is the answer.

11. **d.** is the answer. A difference that is statistically significant is a true difference, rather than an apparent difference due to factors such as sampling variation, and it is reliable.

12. **b.** is the answer. A bar graph is based on a data distribution.

13. **b.** is the answer.
    a. In fact, just the opposite is true.
    c. Both the mean and the median are based on all the scores in a distribution. The median is based on the number of scores, while the mean is based on the average of their sum.
    d. The mean is the arithmetic average.

14. **b.** is the answer. Just as the standard deviation is a measure of variation, so the mode is a measure of central tendency.

15. **b.** is the answer.
    a. 50 percent of the scores in a normal distribution fall on one side of the mean.
    c. 95 percent fall between –2 and +2 standard deviations.
    d. 99.7 percent fall between –3 and +3 standard deviations.

16. **a.** is the answer. Figures based on larger samples are more reliable.
    b. & c. These sample characteristics would tend to lower precision.
    d. A test of significance is a determination of the likelihood that an obtained result is real.

17. **c.** is the answer.

18. **a.** is the answer. The closer the correlation coefficient is to either +1 or –1, the stronger the relationship between the variables.

19. **d.** is the answer.

True–False Items

1.	T	**6.**	F
2.	F	**7.**	F
3.	T	**8.**	T
4.	T	**9.**	T
5.	T	**10.**	T

Essay Question

The use of tables and bar graphs is helpful in accurately organizing, describing, and interpreting events, especially when there is too much information to remember and one wishes to avoid conclusions based on general impressions. Computing an appropriate measure of central tendency provides an index of the overall average of a set of scores. Knowing that the mean is the most common measure of central tendency, but that it is very sensitive to unusually high or low scores, can help one avoid being misled by claims based on misleading averages. Being able to compute the range or standard deviation of a set of scores allows one to determine how homogeneous the scores in a distribution are and provides a basis for realistically generalizing from samples to populations. Understanding the correlation coefficient can help us to see the world more clearly by revealing the extent to which two things relate. Being aware that unusual results tend to return to more typical results (regression toward the mean) helps us to avoid the practical pitfalls associated with illusory correlation. Finally, understanding the basis for tests of statistical significance can make us more discerning consumers of research reported in the media.

Terms and Concepts to Remember

1. The **mode** is the most frequently occurring score in a distribution; it is the simplest measure of central tendency to determine.

2. The **mean** is the arithmetic average, the measure of central tendency computed by adding together the scores in a distribution and dividing by the number of scores.

3. The **median**, another measure of central tendency, is the score that falls at the 50th percentile, cutting a distribution in half.
   Example: When the *mean* of a distribution is affected by a few extreme scores, the **median** is the more appropriate measure of central tendency.

4. The **range** is a measure of variation computed as the difference between the highest and lowest scores in a distribution.

5. The **standard deviation** is the average amount by which the scores in a distribution deviate from the mean. Because it is based on every score in the distribution, it is a more precise measure of variation than the range.

6. The **normal curve** is the symmetrical, bell-shaped curve that describes many types of data, with most scores centering around the mean and progressively fewer scores occurring toward the extremes.

7. The **correlation coefficient** is a statistical index of the relationship between two variables, and thus measures how well either predicts the other.

Example: When the **correlation coefficient** is positive, the two sets of scores increase together. When it is negative, increases in one set are accompanied by decreases in the other.

8. A **scatterplot** is a graph consisting of dots, each of which represents the value of two variables.

9. **Regression toward the mean** is the tendency for extreme or unusual scores to return back, or regress, toward the average.

10. In a **cross-sectional study,** people of different ages are compared with one another.

11. In a **longitudinal study,** the same people are tested and retested over a period of years.

12. **Statistical significance** means that an obtained result, such as the difference between the averages for two samples, very likely reflects a real difference rather than sampling variation or chance factors. Tests of statistical significance help researchers decide when they can justifiably generalize from an observed instance.

Psychology at Work

Appendix Overview

Appendix B discusses work motivation. People who view their work as a meaningful calling, those working in jobs that optimize their skills, and those who become absorbed in activities that result in flow find work satisfying and enriching. Effective leaders recognize this and develop management styles that focus on workers' strengths and adapt their leadership style to the situation. Research on achievement motivation underscores the importance of self-discipline and persistence in achieving one's goals. Human factors psychologists focus on developing ways of making machines and work settings user-friendly.

NOTE: Answer guidelines for all Appendix B questions begin on page 402.

Appendix Review

First, skim each section, noting headings and bold-face items. After you have read the section, review each objective by answering the fill-in and essay-type questions that follow it. Study Tips explain how best to learn a difficult concept and Applications help you to know how well you understand the material. As you proceed, evaluate your performance by consulting the answers beginning on page 402. Do not continue with the next section until you understand each answer. If you need to, review or reread the section in the textbook before continuing.

Introduction

Objective B-1: Define *flow*, and identify the three sub-fields of industrial-organizational psychology.

1. People who view their work as an unfulfilling but necessary way to make money see it as a _____ . Those who see it as an opportunity to advance from one position to a better one view work as a _____ . People who view their work as a _____ report the greatest satisfaction.

2. Psychologist Mihaly Csikszentmihalyi formulated the concept of _____ , which is defined as a focused state of _____ and diminished awareness of _____ and time. People who experience this state also experience increased feelings of _____ , _____ , and _____ .

3. In many nations, the nature of work has changed, from _____ to _____ to _____ .

4. The sense of mutual obligations between workers and employers is called the _____ _____ .

5. The field of _____ - _____ psychology applies psychology's principles to the workplace. The subfield of _____ psychology focuses on employee recruitment, training, appraisal, and development. Another subfield, _____ psychology, examines how work environments and _____ styles influence worker motivation, satisfaction, and productivity. A third subfield, _____ _____ psychology, focuses on the design of appliances, machines, and work environments.

APPLICATION:

6. Which of the following individuals would be characterized as experiencing flow?
   a. Sheila, who, despite viewing her work as merely a job, performs her work conscientiously
   b. Larry, who sees his work as an artist as a calling
   c. Arnie, who views his present job as merely a stepping stone in his career
   d. Montel, who often becomes so immersed in his writing that he loses all sense of self and time

Personnel Psychology

Objective B-2: Describe how personnel psychologists help organizations with employee selection, work placement, and performance appraisal.

7. Researchers note that the first step to a stronger organization is to institute a

   _____-_____

   selection system, which matches strengths to work.

8. (Close-Up) Satisfied and successful people devote less time to _____

   _____ than to

   _____ _____ .

9. Interviewers tend to _____ (feel confident/lack confidence) in their ability to predict job performance from unstructured interviews. These impressions tend to be highly _____ (accurate/error prone).

10. The best predictor of long-term job performance for most jobs is _____

    _____ _____ .

    Interviewers tend to _____ (over/under)estimate their interviewing skills and intuition—a phenomenon labeled the

    _____ _____ .

State four effects that fuel this phenomenon.

11. A more disciplined method of collecting information from job applicants is the

    _____ _____ ,

    which asks the same questions of all applicants. This method enhances the _____ accuracy and _____ of the interview process.

12. Performance appraisal has several purposes, including helping organizations decide

    _____ ,

    how to appropriately _____

    _____ ,

    and how to better harness employees'

    _____ . Performance appraisal methods include _____ ,

    _____ _____ scales, and _____ _____ scales.

13. Some organizations practice _____-_____ feedback, in which employees not only rate themselves but also their supervisors and other colleagues, and vice versa.

14. Performance appraisal is subject to bias. When the overall evaluation of an employee biases ratings of work-related behaviors, a

    _____ _____

    has occurred. The tendency to be too easy or too harsh results in _____ and _____ errors, respectively. When raters focus on easily remembered recent behavior, they are committing the _____ error.

Organizational Psychology

Objective B-3: State the role of organizational psychologists.

15. Positive moods at work contribute to worker _____ , _____ , and _____ .

16. Researchers have also found a positive correlation between measures of organizational success and employee _____ , or the extent of workers' involvement, satisfaction, and enthusiasm.

APPLICATION:

17. Darren, a sales clerk at a tire store, enjoys his job, not so much for the money as for its challenge and the opportunity to interact with a variety of people. The store manager asks you to recommend a strategy for increasing Darren's motivation. Which of the following is most likely to be effective?
    a. Create a competition among the salespeople so that whoever has the highest sales each week receives a bonus.
    b. Put Darren on a week-by-week employment contract, promising him continued employment only if his sales increase each week.
    c. Leave Darren alone unless his sales drop and then threaten to fire him if his performance doesn't improve.
    d. Involve Darren as much as possible in company decision making and use rewards to inform him of his successful performance.

Objective B-4: Describe some effective leadership techniques.

18. The best managers help people to _____ , match tasks to _____ , care how their people feel about their work, and _____ positive behaviors.

19. Higher worker achievement is motivated by a leader who sets _____ , _____ goals. When people state goals together with _____ and _____ _____ , they become more focused in their work.

20. Managers who are directive, set clear standards, organize work, and focus attention on specific goals are said to employ _____ _____ . More democratic managers who aim to build teamwork and mediate conflicts in the work force employ _____ _____ .

21. Effective leaders tend to exude a self-confident _____ that is a mix of a _____ of some goal, an ability to _____ the goal clearly, and enough optimism to _____ others to follow. Leadership that inspires others to

transcend their own self-interests for the sake of the group is called _____ leadership.

22. The most effective style of leadership _____ (varies/does not vary) with the situation and/or the person.

23. Effective managers _____ (rarely/often) exhibit a high degree of both task and social leadership. The _____ effect occurs when people respond more positively to managerial decisions on which they have voiced an opinion.

STUDY TIP: Think about several leaders you know. These might be group leaders, employers, teachers, and relatives. Of these people, whose leadership skills do you admire the most? Why? What type of leadership style (e.g., social leadership, task leadership) best characterizes this person? What specific aspects of this leadership style does the person exhibit?

The Human Factor

Objective B-5: Describe how human factors psychologists work to create user-friendly machines and work settings.

24. Human factors psychologists help to design machines and work settings that fit our natural _____ and _____ . They also work to devise ways to reduce the _____ , _____ , and _____ that contribute to traffic accidents.

25. One example of good design is the use of _____ _____ that broadcast sound directly through a person's own hearing aid. This is an example of an effective _____ _____ technology.

26. Safe, easy, and effective machine designs have not been more common because developes sometimes assume that others share their expertise, called the _____ _____ _____ .

Progress Test

Multiple-Choice Questions

Circle your answers to the following questions and check them with the answers beginning on page 403. If your answer is incorrect, read the explanation for why it is incorrect and then consult the text.

1. People who view work as a calling see it as
   a. an unfulfilling but necessary way to make money.
   b. an opportunity to advance to a better position.
   c. a fulfilling and socially useful activity.
   d. all of these things.

2. Workers who report the highest satisfaction with their work and their lives tend to view their work as
   a. a calling.
   b. a career.
   c. a job.
   d. a hobby.

3. Who first described the concept of flow?
   a. Maslow
   b. Csikszentmihalyi
   c. Owen
   d. Norman

4. *Flow* is best described as
   a. a completely involved, focused state of consciousness on a task.
   b. goal-oriented leadership.
   c. group-oriented leadership.
   d. a state of heightened awareness of self and time.

5. In many nations, work has shifted from
   a. knowledge work to farming.
   b. knowledge work to manufacturing.
   c. manufacturing to knowledge work.
   d. knowledge work to skill work.

6. Industrial-organizational psychologists include
   a. personnel psychologists.
   b. organizational psychologists.
   c. human factors psychologists.
   d. all of these psychologists.

7. Who is most likely to focus on selecting employees and performance appraisal?
   a. personnel psychologist
   b. organizational psychologist

   c. human factors psychologist
   d. engineering psychologist

8. Who is most likely to focus on maximizing worker satisfaction and productivity?
   a. personnel psychologist
   b. organizational psychologist
   c. human factors psychologist
   d. engineering psychologist

9. Who is most likely to focus on the design of optimal work environments?
   a. personnel psychologist
   b. organizational psychologist
   c. human factors psychologist
   d. engineering psychologist

10. The sense of mutual obligations between workers and employers is known as
    a. flow.
    b. task leadership.
    c. social leadership.
    d. the psychological contract.

11. The first step in establishing workplace effectiveness is
    a. identifying people's strengths and matching those to work.
    b. hiring a boss who focuses on task leadership.
    c. establishing a fair system of worker compensation.
    d. hiring a boss who focuses on group leadership.

12. The best predictor of on-the-job performance for all but less-skilled jobs is
    a. age.
    b. general mental ability.
    c. motivation.
    d. stated intentions.

13. To increase employee productivity, industrial-organizational psychologists advise managers to
    a. adopt a directive leadership style.
    b. adopt a democratic leadership style.
    c. instill competitiveness in each employee.
    d. deal with employees according to their individual motives.

14. For as long as she has been the plant manager, Juanita has welcomed input from employees and has delegated authority. Bill, in managing his department, takes a more authoritarian, iron-fisted approach. Juanita's style is one of _____ leadership, whereas Bill's is one of _____ leadership.

  a. task; social
  b. social; task
  c. directive; democratic
  d. democratic; participative

15. Dr. Iverson conducts research focusing on how management styles influence worker motivation. Dr. Iverson would most accurately be described as a(n)

  a. motivation psychologist.
  b. personnel psychologist.
  c. organizational psychologist.
  d. human factors psychologist.

16. Which of the following was NOT identified as a contributing factor in the interviewer illusion?

  a. The fact that interviews reveal applicants' intentions but not necessarily their habitual behaviors.
  b. The tendency of interviewers to think that interview behavior only reflects applicants' enduring traits.
  c. The tendency of interviewers to more often follow the successful careers of applicants they hired rather than those who were not hired.
  d. The tendency of most interviewers to rely on unstructured rather than structured interviews.

17. Munson is conducting his annual appraisal of employees' performance. Which of the following is NOT a type of appraisal method?

  a. graphic rating
  b. behavior rating
  c. checklist
  d. unstructured interview

18. Because Brent believes that his employees are intrinsically motivated to work for reasons beyond money, Brent would be described as a(n) _____ manager.

  a. directive   c. task-oriented
  b. social-oriented   d. charismatic

19. Jack works for a company that requires employees to periodically rate their own performance and to be rated by their managers, other colleagues, and customers. This type of assessment is called

  a. 360-degree feedback.
  b. multifactorial evaluation.
  c. analytical performance review.
  d. human resource management.

20. Thanks to _____ , TiVo and DVR have solved the TV recording problem caused by the complexity of VCRs.

  a. parapsychologists
  b. human factors psychologists
  c. psychokineticists
  d. Gestalt psychologists

Matching Items

Match each term with its definition or description.

Terms

_____ 1. human factors psychology
_____ 2. personnel psychology
_____ 3. organizational psychology
_____ 4. flow
_____ 5. task leadership
_____ 6. social leadership
_____ 7. structured interview
_____ 8. industrial-organizational psychology

Definitions or Descriptions

a. state of focused consciousness
b. applies psychological concepts and methods to optimizing human behavior in workplaces.
c. seeks to optimize person-machine interactions
d. applies psychological methods and principles to the selection and evaluation of workers
e. goal-oriented leadership that sets standards, organizes work, and focuses attention on goals
f. seeks to maximize worker satisfaction and productivity
g. group-oriented leadership that builds teamwork, mediates conflict, and offers support
h. technique in which all job applicants are asked the same questions

Essay Question

Your aunt, who is the Chief Executive Officer of a large company that manufactures electronic circuits, wonders whether an industrial-organizational psychologist could benefit her employees and business. What should you tell her?

3. personnel psychology

4. organizational psychology

5. human factors psychology

6. structured interviews

7. task leadership

8. social leadership

Answers
Apendix Review

Motivation at Work

1. job; career; calling
2. flow; consciousness; self; self-esteem, competence, well-being
3. farming; manufacturing; knowledge work
4. psychological contract
5. industrial-organizational; personnel; organizational; management; human factors
6. d. is the answer.
7. strengths-based
8. correcting deficiencies; accentuating strengths
9. feel confident; error-prone
10. general mental ability; over; interviewer illusion

TERMS AND CONCEPTS TO REMEMBER

Writing Definitions

Using your own words, write on a separate piece of paper a brief definition or explanation of each of the following terms.

1. flow

2. industrial-organizational (I/O) psychology

Four effects that fuel the interviewer illusion are

    a. Interviews disclose the interviewee's good intentions, which are less revealing than their typical behaviors.

    b. Interviewers tend to follow the successful careers of people they hired and lose track of those they did not hire.

    c. Interviewers mistakenly presume that *how* interviewees present themselves reflects only their enduring traits.

    d. Interviewers' preconceptions and moods influence their perceptions of job applicants.

11. structured interview; predictive; reliability

12. who to retain; reward and pay workers; strengths; checklists; graphic rating; behavior rating

13. 360-degree

14. halo error; leniency; severity; recency

15. creativity; persistence; helpfulness

16. engagement

17. **d.** is the answer. Because Darren appears to resonate with the principle that people are intrinsically motivated to work for reasons beyond money, giving him feedback about his work and involving him in decision making are probably all he needs to be very satisfied with his situation.

    a., b., & c. Creating competitions and using controlling, rather than informing, rewards may have the opposite effect and actually undermine Darren's motivation.

18. identify and measure their talents; talent; reinforce

19. specific; challenging; subgoals; implementation intentions

20. task leadership; social leadership

21. charisma; vision; communicate; inspire; transformational

22. varies

23. often; voice

24. perceptions; inclinations; distractions; fatigue; inattention

25. loop systems; assistive listening

26. curse of knowledge

Progress Test

Multiple-Choice Questions

1. **c.** is the answer.

    a. This is characteristic of those who view work as merely a job.

    b. This is true of those who view work as a career.

2. **a.** is the answer.

3. **b.** is the answer.

4. **a.** is the answer.

    b. & c. Goal- and task-orientations are two styles of leadership .

    d. Flow is a stated of *reduced* awareness of self and time.

5. **c.** is the answer.

6. **d.** is the answer.

7. **a.** is the answer.

    b. Organizational psychologists focus on maximizing worker satisfaction and productivity.

    c. & d. Human factors psychologists (also called engineering psychologists) focus on the design of optimal work environments.

8. **b.** is the answer.

    a. Personnel psychologists focus on selecting employees and performance appraisal.

    c. & d. Human factors psychologists (also called engineering psychologists) focus on the design of optimal work environments.

9. **d.** is the answer.

    a. Personnel psychologists focus on selecting employees and performance appraisal.

    b. Organizational psychologists focus on maximizing worker satisfaction and productivity.

    c. This answer is too general. I/O psychologists include personnel psychologists, organizational psychologists, and human factors psychologists.

10. **d.** is the answer.

    a. Flow is a completely involved, focused state of consciousness on a task.

    b. Task leadership is goal-oriented leadership that sets standards, organizes work, and focuses attention on goals.

    c. Social leadership is group-oriented leadership that builds teamwork, mediates conflict, and offers support.

11. **a.** is the answer.

12. **b.** is the answer.

13. **d.** is the answer. As different people are motivated by different things, to increase motivation and thus productivity, managers are advised to learn what motivates individual employees and to challenge and reward them accordingly.

    a. & b. The most effective management style will depend on the situation.

c. This might be an effective strategy with some, but not all, employees.

14. **b.** is the answer.
   a. Bill's style is one of task leadership, whereas Juanita's is one of social leadership.
   c. Juanita's style is democratic, whereas Bill's is directive.
   d. Participative is another term used to refer to the social or group-oriented style of leadership.

15. **c.** is the answer.

16. **d.** is the answer. Although unstructured interviews *are* more prone to bias than structured interviews, the text does not suggest that they are used more often.

17. **d.** is the answer.
   a., b., & c. These are all performance appraisal methods used by supervisors.

18. **b.** is the answer.
   a. & c. Directive, or task-oriented, managers are likely to assume that worker motivation is low.
   d. The most effective leaders are generally charismatic, which has nothing to do with whether they are directive or democratic leaders.

19. **a.** is the answer.

20. **b.** is the answer.
   a. Parapsychologists study claims of ESP.
   c. Psychokineticists are people who claim ESP has the power of "mind over matter."
   d. Gestalt psychologists emphasize the organization of sensations into meaningful perceptions.

Matching Items

1. c		**5.** e	
2. d		**6.** g	
3. f		**7.** h	
4. a		**8.** b	

Essay Question
You should tell your aunt that industrial-organizational psychologists work in varied areas as research scientists, consultants, and management professionals. A personnel psychologist could assist her in selecting, placing, and training employees, as well as in developing criteria to measure their performance and that of the overall organization. An organizational psychologist could assist in facilitating organizational changes to maximize the satisfaction and productivity of her employees. Finally, a human factors psychologist could assist in designing an optimum work environment for employees.

Terms and Concepts to Remember

1. **Flow** is a completely involved, focused state of consciousness on a task that optimally engages a person's skills, accompanied by a diminished awareness of self and time.

2. **Industrial-organizational (I/O) psychology** is a profession that applies psychological concepts and methods to optimizing human behavior in workplaces.

3. **Personnel psychology** is a subfield of I/O psychology that applies psychological methods and principles to the selection and evaluation of workers.

4. **Organizational psychology** is a subfield of I/O psychology that explores how work environments and management styles affect worker motivation, satisfaction, and productivity.

5. **Human factors psychology** is a branch of psychology that explores how people and machines interact and how physical environments can be made safer and easier to use.

6. A **structured interview** is one in which an interviewer asks the same job-relevant questions of all interviewees, who are then rated on established evaluation scales.

7. **Task leadership** is goal-oriented leadership that sets standards, organizes work, and focuses attention on goals.

8. **Social leadership** is group-oriented leadership that builds teamwork, mediates conflict, and offers support.